INTO THE
UNKNOWN

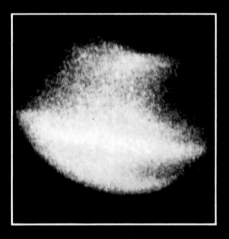

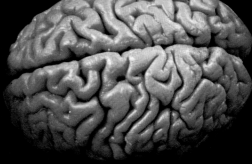

READER'S DIGEST

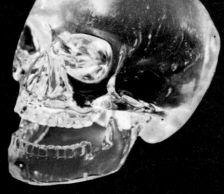

INTO THE
UNKNOWN

THE READER'S DIGEST ASSOCIATION, INC.
Pleasantville, New York / Montreal

CONTENTS

INTO THE UNKNOWN

Editor - Will Bradbury
Art Director - Vincent L. Perry
Associate Editor - Susan Brackett
Research Editors - Tanya Strage (chief), Muriel Clarke, Laurel Gilbride
Picture Researcher - Marion Bodine
Assistant Artist - Marlene Rimsky
Editorial Assistant - Carol Davis

Contributing Editor - Eve Wengler Kirk

Contributing Writers - Ron Bailey, Martin Ebon, Martha Fay, Donald Dale Jackson, David Maxey, Valerie Moolman, John Neary, Mark Strage, John von Hartz

Contributing Copy Editor - Kendra K. Ho

Contributing Researchers - Margaret D. Brawley, Martha Goolrick, Lea Guyer Gordon, Mary Jane Hodges, Marjorie B. Runnion

Contributing Picture Researchers - Natalie Goldstein, Tobi Zausner

Consultant - Dr. Marcello Truzzi, Professor of Sociology, Eastern Michigan University

SPECIAL FEATURES

Exploration of the unknown is a constant, often frustrating human preoccupation. And yet on occasion, mysteries of long standing are resolved, at least in part, in dramatic fashion. Taken by *Voyager I* from a distance of 11 million miles, the remarkable pictorial mosaic above shows the exquisite face of Saturn and the delicate tracery of the hundreds of rings that encircle it.

INTRODUCTION

The strange and bizarre, the revolutionary and outrageous, the factual and fraudulent, the ancient and modern—all catch and hold interest, however briefly, in the great and sprawling storehouse of the unknown. Yet there exists in this remarkable repository, so rich in odd occurrences, unusual claims and provocative theories, a constant presence. That presence is the human mind. For nearly all that is embraced by the unknown, no matter how fantastic, is in some way related to the perceptions of man and to his awareness of his individual consciousness and mortality.

Thus if some of the material that follows seems to demand instant acceptance—or rejection—be tolerant in passing judgment. The unknown is a tricky, beguiling realm, and in many cases productive passage may best be achieved by focusing on ideas rather than proof, on questions rather than answers. Though answers are often lacking and proof is frequently unconvincing, ideas and questions abound; and when taken together, they form a remarkably rich portrait of the human predicament.

It is not surprising, therefore, that many of man's attempts to fathom the inexplicable have been largely egocentric. The intricate permutations of astrology, for example, suggest that the heavens are interested in individual destiny, and divination in its many forms postulates an acute correspondence between man and nature. In the same manner, belief in reincarnation expresses an insistence on man's immortality, just as spiritualism in its way is a protest against the finality of death. That unidentified flying objects might be spaceships from other worlds seems to many only fitting; is it not, after all, worth traveling across the universe to catch a glimpse of man?

Early preliterate man was less egocentric in his speculations, making relatively little distinction between himself and the universe or between natural and spiritual phenomena. Even as civilizations developed, the many routes toward knowledge were often entangled. And they remained so almost until modern times; answers to questions about man's place in the universe or the reasons for his brief stay on earth were sought simultaneously in science, philosophy, religion and magic. Magicians of the Middle Ages, in fact, were scientists in active pursuit of explanations of the physical world. That they hoped to find answers in cabalistic formulas or that they sought an understanding of the life force through alchemy—and modern man does not—is but one measure of the change in outlook man has undergone.

In modern times man has become far more definite about which paths to knowledge are appropriate and which are not, and he has, as in ages past, created his own new certainties. His is a technological society, and today's certainties are overwhelmingly practical ones: what is real for the most part is what can be proved in the laboratory, read out on the computer or derived by mathematical calculation. Phenomena that do not fit or seem to challenge existing laws and principles are often banished to the occult or anomalistic category. The field of parapsychology, examined at length on these pages, has been so exiled—chided by some, ignored by many and often criticized for a lack of convincing theory and reproducible experimentation.

Few would argue for a return to ignorance or seriously abjure the scientific approach, but neither is necessary to regret the passing of that more intimate relationship between man and his environment. Proof, even what might be called scientific proof, is frequently relative: theories once buttressed by the best evidence available have collapsed; seemingly impossible hypotheses have evolved into dependable dogma.

Yet in recent times some men and women, especially in matters of health and personal philosophy, have come to look beyond existing proofs and accepted realities in their search for answers to seemingly insoluble issues. How might the reader use this book in making such a search? First, he should read carefully and patiently, keeping an eye on ideas and questions, because they form the essence of the unknown. Second, he must take note of such words and phrases as "alleged," "reportedly" and "so the story goes." These terms are important qualifiers, and they appear in this book because they are vital to a fair and balanced presentation of complex and controversial subject matter. When they appear, no matter how imposing the material they qualify, they mean that the stories and accounts have not been totally verified. Third, the reader should consider the evidence on both sides. The great mass of UFO cases is striking; the fact that investigators can offer explanations for nearly every case is also impressive. Fourth, whatever the evidence pro and con, the reader must decide for himself. Because human perceptions and experiences vary enormously, every traveler makes a uniquely personal journey through the unknown.

No matter what route the reader chooses, he will be in good company. Curiosity about an afterlife, delight in unexplained forms in the sky, the instinct to ask why—and why not—have characterized the best minds in history. Progress owes much to the willingness of such brave men and women as Newton, Darwin, Mme. Curie and Einstein to pursue unthinkable thoughts down seemingly non-existent avenues. The unknown did not send them scurrying for cover but drew them onward. In fact, one of the most reasonable approaches to the unexplained may have been that suggested more than 150 years ago by a French mathematician and astronomer, Marquis Pierre Simon de Laplace. Wrote Laplace: "We are so far from knowing all the forces of nature and their various modes of action that it would be unworthy of the philosopher to deny phenomena simply because they are inexplicable at the present state of our knowledge. The more difficult it is to acknowledge their existence, the greater care with which we must study these phenomena." In this spirit the book is offered to the reader as he journeys into the unknown.

The Editors

From earliest times man has used
magic and ritual in his attempts to
conquer the unexplained.

ANCIENT UNKNOWNS

A mid the great cave paintings of western Europe they appear regularly, sometimes in silhouette, sometimes fully colored, occasionally showing signs of mutilation—prints of the hands of early man. Yet for all their simplicity and familiarity, they speak as eloquently as the magnificent ocher beasts around them of the existence and exquisitely human preoccupations of men and women 15,000 years ago. Artist's prideful signature? Magic symbol? Sign of sacrifice? No one can answer with certainty today. But in fullness of palm and spread of finger they seem to reach toward ancient unknowns that even now, despite awesome technological advances and endless refinements in every aspect of life, continue to haunt and fascinate people everywhere.

What is life? What awaits us after death? What are the connections between mankind and the universe? What influence do the sun and moon, the planets and stars have over human affairs?

Rooted in mankind's fervent desire to understand and control his fate, these ancient—and modern—questions probe fundamental realities of nature, time and destiny, of life and of death. They remind us, too, of another human constant, the all but irresistible urge to believe that certain natural phenomena are linked with

A startling ocher-edged palm print is the enigmatic mark of a paleolithic cave artist.

human life and behavior and that the course of events may depend, in strange and mysterious ways, on the manner in which we choose to think about them.

These paired ambitions—to make sense of the vast and unpredictable world in which we live and to wrest from it a degree of control over our fate—have been driving forces throughout human history. And for thousands of years the dominant means by which man attempted to satisfy his curiosity and exert his own power was through the use of magic, an ancient art, certainly, but one that continues to wield its influence over many people today.

Perhaps more than 50,000 years ago, even before cave artists painted their heroic beasts on the rough walls of hidden chambers, Neanderthal man began the journey into the unknown. Armed with a growing awareness of self and the passage of time, he made his first rudimentary attempts to come to terms with life's inevitable terminus—death. In early Middle Eastern graves, Neanderthal bodies have been found carefully interred in carved cave-floor trenches, food and weapons arrayed about their flanks. At sites in central Asia, varieties of pollen have been detected and analyzed, suggesting that early men and women not only buried their dead with care but sought to embellish their remains with flowers and food plants. In an early Czechoslovakian grave, 14 skeletons, shrouded beneath a protective layer of stones, have been discovered together, their remains joined, perhaps to ensure continued communion in an afterlife. In another Moravian site, the

In an effort to master their prey through magical means, paleolithic hunters, many scholars feel, created animal likenesses deep inside caves in France and Spain.

body of a woman was found buried beneath the giant shoulder blades of a mammoth and a dusting of red ocher. Possibly a symbol of life-giving blood, red ocher was used again and again in European graves, spread over bodies that were sometimes bound in crouching or fetal positions, perhaps in an attempt to imitate familiar living postures or to enhance a kind of rebirth.

Yet even as early man sought to temper his fear of death and possibly redirect life's end, he was working with his hands, in bone and soft stone, painstakingly shaping likenesses of fertile women and of reindeer, horses and bison, recurring symbols of life that would later reach their artistic peak on the walls of caves in France and northern Spain.

That these lithe and beautifully hued paintings—and the earlier hands and later stick-like human figures that appear sometimes among them—had magical significance there can be little doubt. The delicacy of their design and shading, the suggestion of movement and life in their form, the sophistication of the instruments used to create them—color sticks of red and yellow ocher and black manganese oxide, powdered and liquid paints, brushes of fur and moss—all attest to the special nature of their creation. And in cave sites at Altamira in Spain and Pech-Merle, Lascaux and Les Trois Frères in France this special nature is instantly apparent, joining modern viewer and paleolithic cave artist across 15,000 years of human existence. As C. A. Burland wrote of the caves at Lascaux in his book *The Magical Arts:* "The experience of such an unlit cave is in itself magical. One is not in the outer world of light and

motion any more: but in a dark place, where the walls are peopled here and there by animals. They are mostly food animals, wild oxen, little fat horses, bison and deer. The modern man in that dark loneliness must pause to think of the other time when no man had yet grown an ear of grain, or planted a garden. But these ancient hunters were men like ourselves, with ability as artists, and technical skills in flaking flint and carving ivory which many of us might envy."

Yet one of the paradoxes of early cave art is that the painted figures themselves may have been less significant than the location of the wall space on which they were painted, and the actual positioning of the figures on the walls. For much paleolithic cave art is found not in surface living areas but in hidden stone chambers that must have been frightening to locate, dangerous to enter and difficult to leave. "When it is remembered that the artists had first to explore these perilous, eerie galleries," wrote archeologists Jacquetta Hawkes and Sir Leonard Woolley in their *History of Mankind,* "the haunt of the cave lion and huge cave bear, and then to set out to execute their works with no more light than was given by torches and fat or blubber lamps, and probably no more sure means of rekindling it than a piece of flint or a lump of iron pyrites, it is obvious how determined they were to reproduce their animal images far into the depths of the earth . . . far removed from the familiar outdoor world and the domestic life of the cave entry."

Other riddles that surround the figures are as haunting as the assumption that they were created for magical purposes. Many of the images were painted at heights that could only have been reached with the aid of earthen, or possibly wooden, supports, materials that would have to have been dragged down into the cave depths. Furthermore, modern analysis has shown that certain paintings, while close together, were executed at different times—some were done a decade or more apart—and were painted directly over earlier creations, as if the first ones were no longer significant. Equally intriguing is the discovery by some researchers that images of dangerous animals, like bison and rhinoceroses, were drawn more frequently (perhaps in an effort to limit or restrict their powers) than food animals, like reindeer, whose bones are most often found in living areas. And there are baffling indications that when hand prints were made, some showing signs of finger mutilation, left hands were most often silhouetted while right hands were printed in a solid color.

Despite the profusion of clues and theories, basic questions concerning the purpose of these magnificent primitive paintings remain. Contemporary scholars offer two interpretations, both staples of the study of primitive magic, and a beguiling body of related speculations. The animal figures depicted in the paintings might have been totems, perhaps drawn during some form of

Some 25,000 years ago, the hunters of Europe began a remarkable tradition, the decoration of spear-throwing tools (below, right) and pieces of ivory (bottom). Their bulging fertility figures (below, left) were not simply ornamental; as expressions of an inner ideal, they may have heralded the dawn of religion.

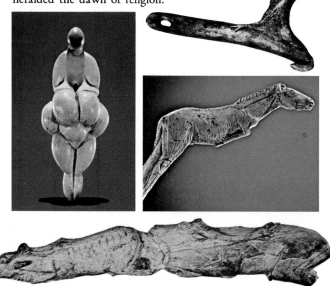

The search for magical power, many scholars believe, has motivated artists throughout the ages. At left, a Bronze Age Swedish rock etching (about 1500 B.C.) shows warriors. Above is a petroglyph created (about A.D. 1000) by Indians in Utah.

initiation ceremony for groups or clans who identified with the powers and properties the figures represented. The pictures might also have been magical symbols meant to ensure the hunters' success in the kill or to make the animals depicted more plentiful. Neither hypothesis can be proved conclusively, and it may be, as can be said of preliterate societies today, that both theories are valid. Prof. François Bordes, of the University of Bordeaux, has linked the two in an interpretation of a Lascaux painting that depicts a rhinoceros, a charging bison with arrows and spears in its flanks, and a man in a bird mask tumbling backward before the bison's charge. "Let me tell you my story of this painting," Bordes says, "a science-fiction story. Once upon a time a hunter who belonged to the bird totem was killed by a bison. One of his companions, a member of the rhinoceros totem, came into the cave and drew the scene of his friend's death—and of his revenge. The bison has spears or arrows in it and is disemboweled, probably by the horn of the rhinoceros."

If cave drawings were indeed used in such fashion, two inferences seem to follow: that ceremonial cave rituals may have been performed while the drawings were being prepared or completed and that the artists who executed the paintings may have been thought of as special, magical people, the first shamans, or priests. In the cave of Les Trois Frères in the French Pyrenees a man-animal composite appears that may represent such a shaman. With large eyes, antlers, bear paws and a horse's tail, this quasi-human creation floats high on a wall in a narrow niche—some 12 feet off the ground—and seems even now to survey scenes of ancient rite and ceremony. "In the depths of the caves," Burland wrote, "we first find pictures of that archetypal being, the Wizard, Man-Animal, Joker of the Tarot pack, at once frightening, creative, and unrestrainedly gay."

What can be said clearly amid such speculation is that early men and women lived in a world that they believed was filled with spirits—*animistic* is the mod-

ern word used to describe such a world—and that by symbol and ritual they sought to control their spirit-filled environment, in order to better survive the many perils of their day-to-day existence.

Modern scholars have attempted to understand and define the concepts that for preliterate people must have been relatively simple and obvious. It seems likely that such a body of rudimentary ideas must have included the concepts that all natural phenomena were under the control of unseen spirits, that such spirits made use of magical powers, and that humans, relying on appropriate forms of magic themselves, might sometimes control natural occurrences by influencing the spirits that existed behind them.

But what sorts of magic would work most effectively? The most famous interpretation, and also one of the simplest, is that offered by the Scottish anthropologist Sir James Frazer in his classic work *The Golden Bough*. "If we analyse the principles of thought on which magic is based," Frazer wrote, "they will probably be found to resolve themselves into two: first, that like produces like, or that an effect resembles its cause; and, second, that things which have once been in contact with each other continue to act on each other at a distance after the physical contact has been severed." The first kind of magic Frazer called imitative—a cave drawing of a speared reindeer that might result in its kill; and the second, contagious—the claw of a cave lion that might carry with it the power and ferocity of the beast that once possessed it.

Like produces like and things once in contact continue to interact—these were among the magical tenets that developed as agricultural societies sprang to life east of the Mediterranean. Farmers were more settled than hunters and thus more dependent on the shift of the seasons, the ebb and flow of natural phenomena. And in Egypt, Greece and Rome as the centuries passed, such was the profusion of ritual, the zealous dependence on astrology and divination that, in the 1st century A.D., Pliny the Elder lamented of magic that, having "taken captive the feelings of man by a triple chain [fear of illness, the gods and the future], it has reached such a pitch that it rules over all the world and in the East, governs the King of Kings."

Long before, perhaps as early as the 4th millennium B.C., in the general area of present-day Iraq, the rule of magic grew with the ancient Sumerians and the people who followed them, the Assyrians and Babylonians. For the Sumerians were creators of writing and builders of cities, but they also saw, or believed they saw, ghosts and demons in every corner and doorway, at every crossroads, and in every graveyard. They packed the skies with gods of every kind, from Anum, the sky god, to Inanna, queen of Heaven and earth and one of a very few important Sumerian goddesses. Yet these celestial figures were primarily distant deities who did not affect the daily lives of Mesopotamians. Ghosts and demons did. Because they, like the spirit forces in neolithic man's animistic world, were believed to be everywhere and included both roaming predatory ghosts of those dead by violence or tragedy and terrifying non-human monsters such as the "Croucher" and the "Seizer." Nor could they be barred, as these ancient words warn:

A door cannot exclude them,
A bolt cannot turn them back,
They slither through the door like a snake,
They blow in by the hinge like the wind;
They bear off the wife from a man's embrace,
They snatch the son from a man's knee.

Little wonder that rites and magical incantations flourished, many expressly designed to exorcise marauding spirits. One rite, created to keep dead men away, required the use of a potion made of vinegar, river water, well water and ditch water, mixed and drunk from the horn of an ox while holding a torch and offering appropriate entreaties to the gods. The Sumerians and Babylonians also probably initiated another staple of magic—the diminishing-word spell, in which "words of force" were repeated over and over, with a final letter omitted in each reprise, until only one letter remained. Found on an ancient Sumerian tablet was this diminishing spell: "Abrada Ke Dabra," meaning "perish like the word." In Roman times the spell appeared, as it does even today, as *abracadabra*. Gradually, however, rituals and magic words were refashioned to be malicious instead of protective, and black, or harmful, magic came into being. On one anti-witch cylinder seal, this imprecation appeared: "O witch, like the twirling of this seal, may your face spin and turn green." By about 2000 B.C., occult procedures of this kind were outlawed by the laws of Hammurabi.

Did such magical practices work? They almost certainly did, at least in one sense, and for good reason. Since the demons and ghosts the Mesopotamians sought to exorcise were largely creations of the mind, they would almost certainly have been affected by properly executed chants and rituals, because the Mesopotamians *believed* they would be. Even in modern times what seems real depends largely upon the perceptions of the beholder; thus if a man believes he has seen an apparition, it may not prove that such things exist, but neither can it be assumed that the man has not "seen" and been influenced by something.

Although the Mesopotamians lived in a world of ghosts and demons, they also looked to the future with great interest. Among the very earliest kinds of divinatory practice were those involving dream interpretation. They appear in what is known as the epic of Gilgamesh, the story of an animal-human god that dates back, in oral tradition, to about 4000 B.C. In one of the chronicle's tales, Gilgamesh fights and kills a great

Through oracles and dream interpretation, a Sumerian ruler named Gudea sought detailed instructions for building a temple to Ningirsu, who then ensured his city's prosperity.

With this clay model of a liver, Babylonian diviners taught students to read the future.

When the entrail-lined face of Humbaba was found in a sheep's intestines, diviners predicted that evil would follow.

With the help of favorable Sumerian gods, Gilgamesh, part man, part god, fought fierce beasts, monsters and a king, ruled a powerful city, and revived a dead friend's spirit.

beast, a dragon-like creature that may have been the precursor of the dragons in the Arthurian legends; in another he prepares for a final struggle against his enemy, Enkidu. Before the battle, Gilgamesh dreams of his enemy's advance; he tells his mother, and she, in the oldest known dream interpretation, prophesies that their struggle will end in friendship. It does, and Gilgamesh amulets, occasionally showing the opponents wrestling, were worn for thousands of years thereafter.

Other forms of divination were more popular among the early Mesopotamians, the most common being also one of the strangest—hepatoscopy, or liver reading. The Babylonians believed the liver to be the seat of the soul, and using the liver of the sheep (perhaps because the organ was easy to locate and remove), they based endless predictions on its shape, number of lobes and blood vessels. These divinatory techniques continued for nearly 3,000 years. The practice of another gory predictive art, that of entrail divining, entailed ruminations about the kind of intestines an animal might possess. Thus one ancient text suggested that sheep with thick necks and red eyes had intestines with 14 turns and that large, squinting animals had no intestines at all. The Assyrians even honored a giant named Humbaba, whose face was formed of twisting, turning entrails.

Such assumptions and techniques seem preposterous, of course, in modern times. Yet the Babylonians and Assyrians did practice one form of divination that millions of people are devoted to today even as scientists feud over its legitimacy. This is the art of reading the future in the movement of planets and stars: astrology. It is also a form of divination that echoes one of the oldest of magical principles, a variation on the primitive theme of like produces like—the principle of "as above, so below." That the Babylonians and Assyrians should have been stargazers is hardly surprising; the skies over the region are exquisitely clear, the nights awesome in their celestial splendor. And the early Mesopotamians were an agricultural society, growers and harvesters, dependent upon the stars for the timing of their planting. Nonetheless, the effort to link the steady, orderly progression of the night stars from east to west with human affairs was an extraordinary one, a step that also produced early and important scientific developments. Included among them was the creation of the 360° circle, based on Sumerian concepts of a 360-day year, in which the stars moved a single degree each night. The move also gave rise to the creation by the Babylonians of the zodiac and its 12 houses, and the development of a special class of star-priests, the astrologers, who were as canny in their predictive techniques as those who read livers and entrails. Individual horoscopes as they are known today were not widely used; in all of Mesopotamia no more than 20 have been found. Rather, the movements of the stars were studied for royal purposes. One astrological prediction offered wisdom of this sort: "During the night Saturn came near the moon. Saturn is the 'star' of the sun. This is the solution: it is favorable to the king, [because] the sun is the king's star." Another, offered by an early

Scarab, sign of sun god Ra, adorns a chest ornament from Tutankhamen's tomb.

astrologer who could probably predict exactly when the moon would appear, said: "If the moon appeareth on the fifteenth day, Akkad will prosper and Subartu fare ill; if the moon appeareth on the sixteenth day, Akkad and Ammuru will fare ill and Subartu will prosper; if the moon appeareth on the seventeenth day, Akkad and Ammuru will prosper and Subartu fare ill."

It was not until sometime around 200 B.C. that individual horoscopes became popular, produced by Macedonian Greeks living in Alexandria. And it was another 300 years before first Cicero and then Pliny the Elder in Rome pointed out certain fundamental flaws in astrological reasoning, flaws that are still pertinent and inadequately explained today. The classic writers argued, for example, that twins born under the same star ought to have identical fates but seldom do, that astrologers were often robbed and even killed without having foreknowledge of their unfortunate fates, and that it was indeed strange that the stars first exerted their heavenly influence at the very moment of birth rather than at the instant of conception.

"It is difficult for the modern mind to understand how completely the belief in magic penetrated the whole substance of life," a famous Egyptian scholar wrote more than 50 years ago, "dominating popular custom and constantly appearing in the simplest acts of the daily household routine, as much a matter of course as sleep or the preparation of food." Lying to the southwest of Mesopotamia, less than 1,000 miles distant, blessed by the sun and the flooding of the Nile, Egypt turned magic into an art of great and ubiquitous splendor. For while the Mesopotamians often employed rites and rituals to defend against—and exorcise—monsters and the marauding spirits of the dead, the Egyptians used the magical arts for nearly opposite purposes: to ensure, in a nation obsessed with death, safe passage to a joyful afterlife in the Lands of the Sunset.

At the heart of Egyptian magical procedure was a belief that survives even today; it is that certain special words or groups of words, arranged correctly and uttered properly, have a unique force. These are known as words of power, and as employed by Egyptian magicians, they were believed capable of unleashing extraordinary occurrences. One ancient manuscript provides this account of the magician Teta at work: "Then someone brought to him a goose, and having cut off its head, he laid the body on the west side of the colonnade, and the head on the east side. Teta then stood up and spake certain words of magical power, whereupon the body began to move and the head likewise, and each time they moved, the one came nearer to the other, until at length the head moved to its right place on the bird, which straightaway cackled." Today's finest surgeons would be unable to match Teta's accomplish-

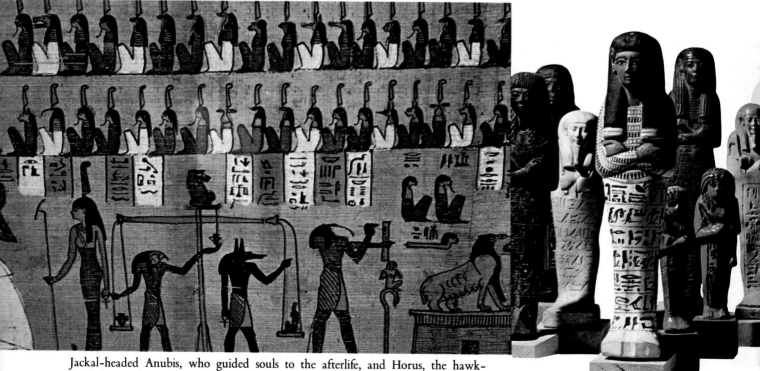

Jackal-headed Anubis, who guided souls to the afterlife, and Horus, the hawk-headed son of an underworld god, weigh an Egyptian heart in final judgment.

ment, of course, and yet, probably as a result of some form of trickery enhanced by excessive credulity, Egyptians did believe that such things could happen.

The magic of words of power, the Egyptians felt, could be transferred to objects such as amulets, which were used in much the way early man must have employed fertility and animal carvings—as power symbols. It has been estimated that every person in Egypt, every man, woman and child, wore at least one amulet or charm. Some charms took the form of exquisite jewelry, others were written out and attached to garments. There were even magic drinks, made by washing inks from charms on which words of power had been transcribed. In the mummy wrappings of Tutankhamen some 150 amulets were found.

The Eye of Horus and the Buckle of Isis were both famous amulets. But the most famous—and powerful— was the scarab, the symbol of life, dedicated to Ra, the sun god, and modeled after the lowly dung beetle. In burial rites the scarab was used to replace the heart and usually had a magical spell carved into its back, often a request to a god for immortality. Eventually the dung beetle itself became associated with the scarab's power, and infertile women dried and powdered the insect, in hopes that a drink made from the powder would help them bear children. The ankh, a cross with a ringed head, appeared perhaps as frequently as the scarab and it, too, represented life and immortality.

The Egyptians believed that human images as well as symbols might be animated by words of power, and thus, during burials, stone and wood representations of

the deceased, known as ushabti, were often placed in tombs, ready to work in the next world. The tomb of Seti I reportedly contained some 700 such laborers-to-be. The Egyptians also introduced a magical technique that has often been repeated and is used even now for destructive purposes—the waxen figure. One ancient story tells of King Nectanebo II, who fought battles with waxen sailors and fleets of waxen ships in a bowl of water. As the king downed his waxen opponents, so did the king's real enemies fall, he believed, until the gods, angered by Nectanebo's manipulative techniques, intervened and made the waxen figures victors. Nectanebo fled to Greece, according to the story, and set up shop there as a doctor and magician.

Belief in the power of magic words reached extraordinary expression in Egypt's funerary texts. The oldest of these, called the Pyramid Texts because they were written in hieroglyphic form on the inside of pyramids at Sakkara about 2500 B.C., form a book of charms, hymns, incantations, spells and special formulas, all fashioned to help a dead Pharaoh gain the afterworld. Later collections, painted on the sides of wooden coffins and known as Coffin Texts, dealt with the deceased's need for food and drink and a ready supply of fresh air. The most famous text, the Book of the Dead, was written on papyrus and included pictures and

The Egyptians believed that words of power transformed statues, or ushabti (left), into helpful servants in the afterlife (above).

15

Cheops Pyramid—Tomb of Mystery

It sits, inanimate and immutable, a fascination and a challenge to rational and mystical man alike. It invites fabulous speculation and has been the subject of rigorous, imaginative investigation. Yet in the end, the Great Pyramid of Cheops, completed around 2570 B.C., retains its essential air of mystery.

Tradition, and a fair amount of evidence, define the pyramid as the intended resting place of the Egyptian king Cheops, or Khufu, whose rule of about 22 years ended some 12 centuries before that of Tutankhamen. Deep within the pyramid's nearly solid stone mass are chambers probably meant to harbor the bodies—and the treasure—of Cheops and his queen. Writings on the great stone blocks within the pyramid note the king's name. Yet the first recorded entry into the pyramid, in A.D. 820, unearthed neither treasure nor mummies nor signs that any ruler had ever been buried there.

This riddle, as well as the Great Pyramid's immense size, intricate construction and archetypal shape, has inspired a profusion of alternative theories of the pyramid's purpose, and power, over the centuries. It has been variously suggested that the Great Pyramid, and other lesser pyramids as well, were ancient astronomical observatories; that they contain a library of ancient knowledge, including the secret to Atlantis; that they are the key to a lost source of energy; and that they are the generous, if baffling, legacy of visitors from outer space. The notion that the pyramid shape has magical effects on organic matter and that it can gather psychic energy has been widely entertained in recent years.

The Great Pyramid at Giza contains about 2.3 million blocks of rectangular limestone, weighing an average of 2½ tons. It is taller than a 40-story building and, according to one estimate, could swallow St. Paul's Cathedral and Westminster Abbey in London, St. Peter's of Rome and the cathedrals of Florence and Milan and still leave undisturbed those smooth sides that rise from the plateau at a uniform angle of 51°. The pyramid took about 20 years to build, and in the estimate of the Greek historian Herodotus, who visited Egypt in the 5th century B.C., it consumed the labor of 100,000 men a year. The individual blocks are so well fitted together that it would be difficult to insert the blade of a knife into their mortarless seams.

Because the ancient Egyptian religion held that the enjoyment of an afterlife depended largely on the corpse's remaining undisturbed, tombs were designed to last forever, with mazes of secret passages to thwart grave robbers. In anticipation of the long journey of the deceased to the land of the spirits, the tombs were equipped with food and drink, jewelry, weapons, a sacred boat and statues that might come to life.

In A.D. 820, in search of such treasures and of the valuable scientific materials he believed buried there as well, young Abdullah Al Mamun hired a band of men to break into the Pharaoh's tomb through the north wall. Some 30 yards into the pyramid, Al Mamun's tunnel intersected a descending passageway that eventually turned and led up to the crypts where Cheops and his queen were thought to repose. But both chambers were treasureless—and bodiless—and there were no signs that the seals had been broken by previous illicit entry.

With no bodies to substantiate the pyramid's purpose as a tomb, speculators went on manufacturing new reasons for the Great Pyramid's existence. A French mathematician brought out by Napoleon in 1798, Edme-François Jomard, studied the pyramid carefully and concluded that the monument was itself a record of an ancient system of measures. In 1859, John Taylor, an Englishman, determined that the architect of Cheops had used as a unit of measure the same biblical cubit employed in the construction of Noah's ark (which by his reckoning had been completed 300 years before Cheops). The sacred cubit was about 25 inches in length and was in turn based on the earth's axis: if the axis is divided by 400,000, the result is a biblical cubit.

Another avid measurer, the Royal Astronomer of Scotland, Charles Piazzi Smyth, discovered in 1865 that the base of the pyramid divided by the width of a casing stone equaled 365, the number of days in a year; he further calculated that a pyramid inch, one twenty-fifth of a paving stone, was also one ten-millionth of

The Great Pyramid of Cheops (opposite page), built of some 2.3 million blocks of stone and housing a colossal 28-foot-high Grand Gallery (left), has long been a source of wonder and mystery.

The pyramid's three empty chambers (below) are linked by passages, including an escape route for workers who sealed the tomb by pushing stone blocks from the Grand Gallery into the ascending passageway.

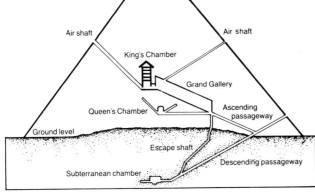

Air shaft

Air shaft

King's Chamber

Grand Gallery

Queen's Chamber

Ascending passageway

Ground level

Escape shaft

Descending passageway

Subterranean chamber

ory is that the descending and ascending passageways within the structure have been shown to be precisely angled to point one's gaze toward key constellations. The fact that the passageways were open to the heavens only for a short time during the monument's construction has never been explained away by those who believe in a pyramid observatory.

The most popular contemporary pyramid theory concerns the supposed powers inherent in the pyramid shape, and one of the concept's most devoted proponents was Czech radio engineer Karel Drbal. In the 1940s, Drbal read about a Frenchman named Antoine Bovis, who had built a model of the Cheops pyramid and used it to counteract decomposition and encourage mummification of food and dead animals placed beneath it. Drbal believed that energy inside the pyramid form could cause a used razor blade, placed east-west, to become a living entity and recover its sharp edge. After "successfully" testing his theory, he patented a cardboard model of the blade sharpener. Few, if any, researchers have been able to duplicate his findings.

Another pyramidologist, Dr. Carl Schleicher, of Mankind Research Unlimited in Washington, D.C., asserts that pyramids promote the growth of vegetables. To test his theory, Schleicher placed samples of black-eyed peas and lima beans under a pyramid, under a cube and out in the open; he reported that the legumes under the pyramid grew 1.5 times as fast as those in open air and 1.129 times as fast as those under the cube. However, similar experiments conducted by the horticultural department of the University of Guelph in Canada indicated that pyramids have no effect whatsoever on the growth of plants. Inevitably, such negative results have failed to dissuade true believers, and many people continue to invest pyramids with powers and purposes that are impossible to substantiate. Amid all the speculation, scholars of ancient Egypt are quite definite about why and how the approximately 35 traditional pyramids were built: they were tombs built by men and nothing more.

In the expectation that such certainty would sooner or later be applicable to the Great Pyramid at Giza, scientists have measured, probed, X-rayed and surveyed the stone giant through the years, with no result. In 1954, however, they were surprised by the discovery beneath the sands *outside* the pyramid of a cedar boat 142 feet long, its cabin and fittings designed to be gilded, and very likely the "sun boat" built to carry the Pharaoh on his long journey to the afterlife. Even now, the splendid boat remains the only artifact attributable to Cheops's treasure, and fundamental questions about the king and his pyramid remain unanswered. Where does King Cheops lie, and why was he not entombed in his fabulous monument? At the heart of the Great Pyramid, then, there remain an echoing, empty tomb and a continuing human mystery.

the earth's polar radius. He applied the pyramid inch to every dimension of the Great Pyramid and then made a spectacular supposition, claiming that by counting each inch as one year, he could calculate all the principal dates in the earth's past—and future. Smyth's careful measurements were a major accomplishment. His manipulations of figures had enormous appeal and his books were read by thousands, but his conclusions were debunked by scholars, who called him a "pyramidiot."

The possibilities for prophecy suggested by Taylor's and Smyth's findings were not overlooked by the apocalyptic-minded, who used their theories to predict the second coming of Christ (either 1881 or 1936, depending on the source) and the end of the world, which was to have occurred in 1953.

Considerably less preposterous in view of what we now know about the Egyptians' skill in astronomy is the theory that the Great Pyramid was a celestial observatory. The primary evidence in support of this the-charms for the use of the deceased in the afterlife, prayers to guard against demons, and special words to enhance the power of amulets designed to ward off worms, tomb robbers and even mildew.

How strongly did the Egyptians believe in the power of their words and amulets, and the reality of the afterlife they sustained with such artistry? Their belief had to be great, obviously, and the most powerful testimony to its intensity may be found in what Egyptologists call "Letters to the Dead." These were special messages often inscribed on the pottery vessels used to provide food for the departed. Some letters urged the dead to aid the living; others were defensive and even fearful, worrying that the dead might return for vengeance. One highly unusual inscription, dated 71 B.C., supposedly bears a message from an Egyptian woman who had died to her husband, who was still living. It is a remarkably poignant message, one that suggests that even words of power could not totally eradicate the death fears of those who were still alive. The inscription reads: "I no longer know where I am, now that I have arrived in this valley of the dead. Would that I had water to drink from a running stream. . . . O that my face were turned toward the north wind . . . that the coolness thereof might quiet the anguish of my heart."

What will happen next? Of all the questions men and women have asked in their pursuit of the unknown, this is perhaps the most constant and compelling. And in ancient Greece a divinatory concept first

Set on Mount Parnassus, the Delphic oracle was the most powerful in ancient Greece. For some 1,000 years, it attempted to serve the basic human need to know the future.

The Golden Spiral

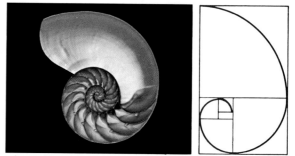

The Golden Spiral, often seen in nature, as in a nautilus shell, derives from subdivisions of a Golden Rectangle.

At the heart of ancient Greek culture was a reverence for the harmony of the universe. Greek art, science and philosophy all reflected the attempt to replicate in human endeavors the symmetry and balance of nature. A guiding aesthetic principle of this desire was a mathematical proportion called the Golden Section. For the Greeks this proportion represented perfection, and it was sought in everything from the human figure to the relationship of individuals to society.

The Golden Section is a way of dividing a line—or anything else—into two parts, so that the smaller part bears the same relationship to the larger as the larger does to the whole. Occurring in architecture (whether intended or not) at least since the ancient Egyptians, and fascinating to mathematicians even today, the proportion, or one of its derivate shapes, is displayed in a remarkable array of living things and has even been adapted to musical composition, in which time, instead of space, is subdivided.

The Golden Section determined the proportions of the human body in classic Greek sculpture; for example, the navel divides the upper and lower parts of the body into two Golden Segments. In the form of the Golden Rectangle—a rectangle whose short side is to the long side as the long side is to the two sides combined—the magical proportion dictated the dimensions of Greek architecture. The Golden Rectangle remains a constant in Western art and to many people is one of the most pleasing forms in the modern world.

A unique feature of the Golden Rectangle is that it can be divided by a single line into two parts, one a square, the other a smaller Golden Rectangle. If successively smaller rectangles are marked off within one another, and a curving line is drawn from the end of one dividing line to the next (as shown above), a Golden Spiral is formed. Did the Greeks derive this graceful curl from their calculations—or did they or even earlier peoples first perceive it in the shape and form of living things? No one can answer with certainty. And yet the Golden Spiral is a motif frequently repeated in nature by leaves around a stem, seeds inside a flower, seashells, and even the unfurling branches of the Milky Way.

tested in Mesopotamia and Egypt found powerful expression. This is the belief that although conscious man cannot foresee the future, he may, when asleep or in some other altered state of consciousness, be capable of divining events yet to come.

Set on the southern slopes of Mount Parnassus, built over a yawning volcanic chasm, shrouded in sulfurous fumes, the oracle of Apollo at Delphi was the most famous in Greece. The oracle's chief priestess, the Pythia, sat on a tripod amid the fumes, and when she spoke, her mouth foamed and her words tumbled out in disarray. What better proof that she had entered a trance and had become the medium through which Apollo might be heard. Further proof was provided by the altered tone of her voice and the fact that when the Pythia regained normal consciousness, she remembered nothing of her prophetic words. So confused and ambiguous were her messages that priests were required to intercede and interpret, often in verse. In instances of special sensitivity, such priests undoubtedly fashioned answers favorable to their own interests.

The Delphic oracle was expensive and, despite the use of three Pythias at times of great activity, not always available to petitioners without special influence. Another oracle, situated at Dodona, in the western sector of Greece, and dedicated to Zeus, seems to have been more at the service of the common man. At Dodona petitioners received strips of lead on which they wrote their queries in such fashion that they might be answered by a *yes* or *no*. Each strip was folded to mask the question. The strips were then placed in a jar and a priestess removed them in turn while indicating whether the god's answer was yes or no. The technique is certainly recognizable, and so are many of the questions, even though they are thousands of years old. "Lysanias asks Zeus whether the child is not from him with which Annyla is pregnant," one inquired. Said another: "Leontios consults concerning his son Leon whether there will be recovery from the disease on his breast which seizes him."

One of the most extraordinary figures in ancient Greece was neither a priest nor a medium, but a philosopher named Pythagoras, a man who is today most famous for the theorem named after him that is used to calculate the length of the hypotenuse, or longest side, of a right-angled triangle. Yet Pythagoras was also a mystic and a magician and as such linked science and magic in remarkable and still intriguing fashion. Born on the Greek island of Samos during the 6th century B.C., Pythagoras, it is believed, traveled widely, certainly to Egypt and perhaps to the Orient. Finally settling in Crotona, a Greek colony in southern Italy, about 530 B.C., he established a secret society for the purpose of expounding his own philosophies. According to the legends that surround his existence, Pythagoras possessed extraordinary powers: he could make himself invisible and could walk on water and had the power to cause objects to appear and disappear as he wished. He also believed in the healing arts, using tunes and rituals for such purposes, and claimed to remember previous incarnate forms, a belief similar to Oriental concepts of reincarnation.

Yet it was with numbers that Pythagoras sought to explain the chaos of human existence, offering an order even more comprehensive than that envisioned by early astrologers. In his *Metaphysics,* Aristotle, who opposed the Pythagoreans, nonetheless tried to explain their philosophy. They believed that all things are numbers, Aristotle reported, with "such a modification of numbers being justice, another being soul and reason, another being opportunity—and similarly almost all other things being numerically expressible." One story suggests that Pythagoras's interest in numbers stemmed from his discovery that the four principal notes in the Greek musical scale were interrelated. According to the story, he was passing a blacksmith's shop as four smithies were striking four anvils of different size. Weighing the anvils, Pythagoras found their weights to be in the proportion of the numbers 6, 8, 9, and 12. As a result, he came to believe that all creation existed with similar numerical interrelatedness. Thus, according to Aristotle, "they supposed the elements of numbers to be the elements of all things, and the whole heaven to be a musical scale and a number."

Such beliefs may sound naive today, and yet at the time, Pythagoras, familiar with magic and astrology,

In this detail from a painting by Raphael, Pythagoras, one of the greatest of Greek mystical figures, writes while a student holds a slate bearing the tetraktys, a sacred-number pyramid.

As if to taunt its users, this tabletop mosaic from Pompeii bore fateful symbols, a skull and wheel of fortune.

Rome, all that had gone before—from the ghosts and monsters of the Mesopotamians to Egyptian words of power and Grecian numerical schemes—seemed to intertwine ever more intensely. Ghosts were a constant worry in Rome. One famous story recounted by Pliny the Younger, at the end of the 1st century A.D., concerned a philosopher named Athenodorus. He had rented a house at a low price, only to be disturbed at night by the clanking of chains. Soon the ghost of an old man, "emaciated and filthy, with a long, flowing beard and hair standing on end," appeared, wearing chains on his legs and wrists. He led Athenodorus to the courtyard and there vanished. The next morning Athenodorus and officials dug at the spot and uncovered a skeleton, chained at the hands and ankles, which they properly buried. The ghost was never seen again. Nor was this an isolated incident, for throughout the Roman Empire the dead had to be constantly appeased. Ovid tells what happened when a feast of the dead was not celebrated: "The townsfolk heard their grandsires complaining in the quiet hours of the night, and told each other how the unsubstantial troop of monstrous specters rising from their tombs, shrieked along the city streets and up and down the fields."

Spirits as well as ghosts were believed to be everywhere, and every daily act seemed to have its corresponding spirit and name: Ednea for eating, Potina for drinking, Pecunia for money, Cloacina for the sewers and Mephitis for bad smells. Portents and signs were perceived constantly—in the appearance of the sun, in bolts of lightning, in the sound of unearthly voices. Divination of every sort was practiced; Roman priests known as haruspices consulted not only the liver but also the spleen, the kidneys, the lungs and the heart. Even such a writer as Plutarch believed in divination. He wrote that the human soul had a natural faculty for predicting the future, one that might become dominant at particular times. Dreams were considered especially important and were thought to involve the souls of humans visiting people who were asleep and the souls of the dead returned to earth. Astrology, too, occupied a position of great importance in Rome, where astrologers lived in the houses of the rich and powerful. Roman astrologers taught that the sky was constructed of layers of perfect crystal spheres, each revolving around the earth and each containing on its surface the sun or moon or one of the planets. Beyond these lay a sphere filled with unmoving stars.

Witches and their rites were another fixture of Roman belief. Horace described the machinations of a pair of witches as they crawled beneath a new moon searching for herbs, then served a banquet of black lamb, and melted waxen images of their victims.

Little wonder that Pliny the Elder would write again of magic, saying that "its authority has been very great, since alone of the arts it has embraced and united

mathematics and music, offered a system that provided order and divinatory power. At the heart of this system was the belief that all things have numbers and that the number of a thing, like its name, had special or magical significance. For instance, the base number of a person's name could be determined and then used to describe character and predict future events. To do this, under various systems, each letter of the alphabet is assigned a number and the numbers are added up. If the result is a two-digit number (16, for example), the numbers are added and the result, seven, is the base number. On various numerological scales seven has different values, but according to one scale, it is the number of people who are reclusive, introspective and able to maintain great self-control; it is the number of scholars and mystics. Five, on the other hand, characterizes people who are nervous and high-strung, while two, according to some systems, is the number of women and also of evil.

As the center of the civilized world shifted to

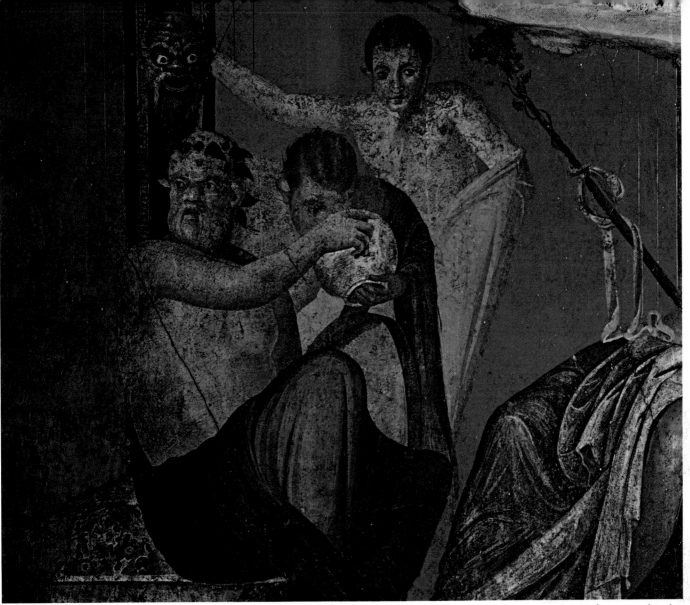

Youthful satyrs and a rotund woodland spirit—all legendary followers of the god of pleasure, Dionysus—use a mask and a vessel of wine to contemplate the uncertain future in this detail from a fresco in the Villa of Mysteries at Pompeii.

with itself the three other subjects which make the greatest appeal to the human mind." By these he meant medicine, religion and the arts of divination.

And yet it was a Greek philosopher living in Egypt in the 4th century A.D., as the Roman Empire faced division and ultimate collapse, who is credited with one of the most intriguing stories concerning magic and its practitioners. The philosopher's name was Iamblichus, and he offered an account of the special ceremonies used to initiate new members into the Magi, the famous secret society of Persian magicians who gave their name to the art. According to Iamblichus's account, which may be entirely fictitious, the process began with the initiate's being led through a massive doorway set between the forelegs of the Sphinx and then on through a nerve-racking series of tests and trials. These included facing a monstrous mechanical specter, crawling through an ever-narrowing tunnel, wading across a pool that appeared to be bottomless,

hanging from a brass ring, facing possible death by poisoning, and resisting the seductions of dancing girls. Finally, if successful, the initiate was instructed in the duties of a Zealot, the rank he had earned. He then received a demonstration of what might happen to those who broke the Magi's oath of secrecy: "At the foot of the altar a brazen trapdoor was now lowered over a pit whence came the noise of rattling chains and struggle, followed by the roars of a beast and the cry of a human voice in dreadful agony, then . . . nothing: only the cold stillness of a sepulcher."

Did the Magi possess special knowledge worth confronting torture and death to possess? Does such knowledge actually exist? Scientists and historians today would undoubtedly say no. And yet believers might reply that man's journey through the unknown has always involved a search for magical power, and if such secrets have not yet been revealed to modern man, it may be because the time to do so is not yet at hand.

21

Modern Shamans' Ancient Powers

Much of what we know today about ancient magic comes not from archeologists' studies, but from research conducted by anthropologists among modern-day tribes. In spite of variations among different cultures, the magic practiced by such contemporary groups throughout the world appears to be based on concepts that have not changed significantly in more than 25,000 years. Such classic themes as animism, fear of the dead, and the principles of imitative and contagious magic seem to exercise as powerful a hold on African tribesmen today as they did on Cro-Magnon hunters and gatherers.

At the heart of such beliefs lies the conviction that within everything, living or inanimate, there lives a spirit—unseen, but conscious, and often very powerful. Thus when a Brazilian Indian kills a jaguar, he has not finished with the beast; the potentially vengeful spirit of the animal must still be appeased. For the same reason, an Ashanti in Ghana will not cut down a tree without first performing a ritual to placate the tree spirit.

One nearly universal method of coping with the multitudes of unseen spirits is to build shrines for them. If a spirit can be persuaded to take up residence in a shrine, its power can be more easily contained. With luck, the enshrined spirit may even come to take a benign interest in the affairs of the shrine builders. Thus mountain tribesmen on New Guinea regularly build small shrines, or "spirit houses," with food inside, adjacent to the family pigpen. If the shrine can attract a *nakondisi* (forest spirit), the nakondisi will probably end up helping the tribesman watch over his pigs.

Of the many spirits that roam the world of tribal imagination, none are more prevalent or potentially troublesome than the spirits of the dead (which may also be, thanks to the widespread belief in reincarnation, spirits of the as-yet unborn). To many people, the state of death seems not very far removed from the state of life. Their villages are populated by generations of ghosts, all of them thought to be just as concerned with community affairs as they ever were. In fact, the only really important differences perceived between the dead and the living are that the dead are disembodied and, in some cultures, have more magical power. Anyone who doubts the immanence of the dead, say the Congolese, is a fool: you need only press your ear to the ground to hear the mournful throbbing of their drums.

Not surprisingly, any person believed to have suf-

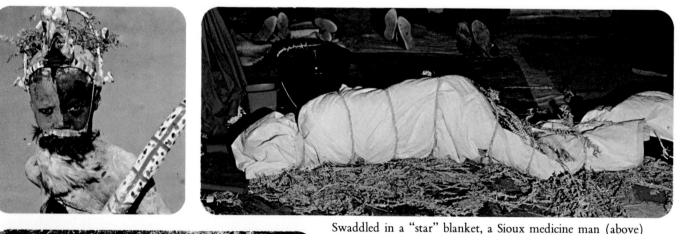

Swaddled in a "star" blanket, a Sioux medicine man (above) lies on the floor of a darkened room and listens for the whispering voices of the spirits that guide him.

The ocher face markings worn by a young initiate of the Kissi people of Liberia (upper left) protect him against evil.

Wearing eerie mud masks, New Guinea's Mandefehufo villagers (right) dance a re-enactment of a battle their ancestors supposedly won by masquerading as fierce ghosts.

Australian aborigines, in ceremonial paint, perform one of their highly elaborate ritual dances during a corroboree.

ficient power to deal with the spirit world on behalf of the community is a valuable—perhaps vital—asset to the society in which he lives. Every tribe has such a person, whether called witch doctor, priest, *nganga,* "clever person," medicine man, *houngan* or shaman, a word used by the Tungus people of eastern Siberia and adopted by modern scientists to describe such tribal priests. A tribe's shaman is its master magician, rainmaker, healer, forecaster, protector and principal link to the spirit world. Without him, the tribe would be lost.

Much of the shaman's practice falls into one of two categories: imitative magic, such as squirting water into the air in order to make rain, and contagious magic, such as placing a curse on an enemy's hair or other personal effects in order to bring evil upon him. Only a few years ago, fear of contagious magic led supporters of the exiled African king of Buganda to decline a suggestion that a pillow stuffed with the shaved-off hair of their beards be dedicated to the monarch. The danger that such a pillow might fall into the wrong shamanistic hands was too great.

Whether a person becomes a shaman through heredity, training or by giving spontaneous evidence of his vocation, his power derives primarily from his apparent ability to communicate with the spirits, usually through the medium of a trance, during which his body seems to be possessed by a spirit magically summoned for the occasion. An impressive number of anthropologists who have seen such magic in operation have testified to its power.

Some of these powers are explicable in scientific terms. For instance, many of the traditional curative herbs used by shamans over the centuries have been demonstrated by medical researchers to be extremely effective drugs. One such plant, the *Aloe vera,* is kept in the kitchen by modern-day herbalists, who use it in case of a burn accident; pharmaceutical firms use *Aloe vera* in the manufacture of sunburn ointment.

Less easily measured, and ultimately more intriguing, is the relationship between mind and body, a relationship that shamans seem always to have understood instinctively and that modern scientists continue to explore. As many psychiatrists can testify, the mind has an uncanny ability to influence physical ailments. In the closed society of shaman and tribe—a society in which nearly everyone shares a belief in the shaman's power—such unseen mental forces contribute mightily to the effectiveness of the shaman's "magic."

Voodoo: The Dark Side of Magic

Voodoo—the very word conjures up lurid images of walking dead men, lethal wax dolls riddled with pins and bizarre midnight rituals in the depths of the Haitian jungle. But there is more to voodoo than simple black, or evil, magic. Its original form was brought by African slaves to the Caribbean island of Haiti in the 16th century. There it came into contact with the Roman Catholic religion of the French colonial slave owners. The result was that voodoo absorbed many of the complexities of Catholicism without ever losing its essentially pagan nature. Thus, for example, many modern-day Haitians believe that at least one aspect of the voodoo snake god Damballah is faithfully represented by a conventional portrait of Ireland's Saint Patrick.

As with many magically oriented religions, the essential idea of voodoo is that all reality is a kind of façade, behind which work much more important spiritual forces. Trees may be the dwelling places of powerful spirits; illness and death are never fortuitous but always a sign of divine or magical retribution; crossroads are places where man and spirits may meet.

This voodoo spirit world is headed by Legba, mediator between man and the spirits. Other high gods, or loa, include the snake god Damballah, a source of virility and power; Erzulie, goddess of love, jealousy and vengeance; and Guede, who, along with such sinister helpers as the notorious Baron Samedi, presides over the mysteries of death and evil sorcery. Beneath the high gods are lesser divinities, sometimes called petro gods, and beneath them, countless spirits, including many that were formerly human.

In the elaborate rituals of voodoo, worshipers invoke these loa and spirits, hoping to become possessed by one who will bring good fortune, effect a cure, appease the soul of a dead person, ward off evil, consecrate a priest or perform some other magical service.

A typical voodoo ceremony will take place on a Saturday night at a *houmfor,* a temple in the Haitian forest. The houmfor usually consists of a small building where sacred relics are kept, an attached open-sided room, and a courtyard or clearing where the worshipers gather. A high priest called a *houngan* (or, if a woman, *mambo*) begins the ceremonies in the outer room with prayers, incantations and propitiatory libations. He draws on the ground magical symbols, or *veves,* special to the loa he wishes to summon that night. The worshipers begin to sing and dance, and as their frenzy grows, sacrifices—usually chickens or goats—are offered to the gods. At some point, if all has gone well, the bodies of at least some of the worshipers will become possessed by the loa. The possessed people will writhe uncontrollably, speak in strange voices and sometimes unintelligible tongues, and, finally, collapse on the ground. This will be taken as a sign that the loa have favored the worshipers' petition.

It is, however, the darker side of voodoo that has most captured the world's imagination. And voodoo—a system of belief rooted in fear—has a very dark side indeed. Ascribed to certain voodoo secret societies known collectively as red sects are such practices as ritual murder, cannibalism and black magic. Sorcerers known as *bokos* will, for a fee, invoke the aid of Baron Samedi in placing lethal curses on the living—and perhaps even more frightful curses on the newly dead, for it is these who can be turned into zombies, reanimated corpses condemned to serve their masters forever as mindless slaves. It is said that François ("Papa Doc") Duvalier, the late Haitian dictator, consciously invoked this darker side of voodoo as a means of maintaining control over his superstitious subjects. Popularly understood to be a houngan in his own right, Duvalier called his bloodthirsty secret police *tonton macoutes,* a Haitian title for itinerant magicians. Masked by the dark glasses that they always wore in public, their faces did indeed take on a skull-like anonymity.

While the beliefs and magical practices of voodoo are most concentrated on the island of Haiti, they did spread easily to the United States via the slave trade, gaining their first and most powerful foothold in Louisiana in the 18th century. By the mid-19th century voodoo's local influence was great enough to permit a self-promoting mambo, Marie Laveau, to become a New Orleans celebrity, patronized by white and black alike. From Louisiana, Georgia and South Carolina, voodoo spread north into the ghettos and barrios of the big industrial cities. As recently as 1978, police officer Hugh J. B. Cassidy, former commander of New York's 77th Precinct, estimated that in the Bedford-Stuyvesant section of Brooklyn there were 30 secret houmfors and perhaps 100 practicing houngans and mambos.

Does voodoo magic work? In one sense, at least, the answer must be yes. In a well-known study entitled *Voodoo Death,* Harvard physiologist Dr. Walter B. Cannon described the process whereby a believer in voodoo can, if he thinks he has been cursed, cause himself to die of fright. Self-induced shock, leading to circulation failure and a breakdown of oxygen-starved vital organs, can be precipitated, said Dr. Cannon, purely by the "fatal power of the imagination working through unmitigated terror."

Worshipers like this young Haitian engage in voodoo to ensure that their souls are possessed by a compatible loa, or spirit, rather than by the power of an evil magician.

Essential to the voodoo ceremony (right) are water, considered a magnet for spirits, and a magical, bead-wrapped rattle, with which a priest may control primitive forces.

By passing her arms through flame without harm—an important part of the voodoo initiation rite—a dancer shows that she is protected by a favorable loa.

In earth and stone early man
created awesome structures to honor
the dead and explore the skies.

EARTH SHRINES

Effigy of Antiochus I, carved
2,000 years ago, lies in Turkey.

They whisper of myth and legend, of a time before recorded history when men sought to address the unknown and exalted by means of the familiar and crude. They are to be found everywhere on earth, the ancient, awesome products of disparate cultures. Their grandeur takes magnificently varied form, repeating and reinterpreting the geometry of nature itself: the looming pillars of Stonehenge, set in a great circle on the flat Salisbury Plain; a "regiment of stones," seemingly frozen in neolithic march across Brittany; vast contoured mounds of earth that rise like the pyramids of Egypt from the floor of the Mississippi Valley; the great lines of Nazca, stretching without interruption across miles of desert and hill country in southern Peru.

What ancient peoples constructed these "earth shrines," and for what purpose? Did they hope to transcend with their labors the short span of life allotted prehistoric man, or did they hope to order the world they perceived around them? Most of the elaborate earthworks seem to have served as burial and ceremonial centers, with succeeding generations modifying existing structures to meet their needs. Yet there are also hints that these awesome shrines served other, more bizarre purposes, a concept that has fascinated observers for centuries.

Modern researchers, having more precisely dated most earthworks, have also generated new theories about their origins, possible purposes and creators. Studies in this century have demonstrated with reasonable persuasiveness that many of the great stone rings in the British Isles, of which Stonehenge is but the most famous, were, among other things, primitive celestial observatories. Similar assertions have been made concerning the grid-like alignments, made up of 3,000 stones, at Carnac, France, and the Indian medicine wheels of North America. Aerial observations of immense pictographic earthworks—observations that were all but impossible before this century—raise yet another tantalizing question: For whom did early man create such wondrous earth and stone images, visible in totality only from the skies?

Of all the different varieties of earthworks, megalithic structures, the most familiar and up to now the most studied, are probably the oldest as well. Megaliths, the word comes from the Greek and means "big stones," are found in Japan, India and Sardinia. Yet their greatest concentration—a remarkable 50,000 separate constructions in all—lies in a broad swath that stretches from Scandinavia to Italy and includes the British Isles. Some of these megaliths date to nearly 5,000 years before the birth of Christ and more than 2,000 years before the construction of the Great Pyra-

The alignment of several of its great stones with the sunrise at summer solstice hints at one of the uses of Stonehenge, built by neolithic farmers more than 4,000 years ago.

Geometric patterns (right) remarkably like the cup marks of neolithic Britain cover the walls of a passageway in a prehistoric burial mound situated on an island off Brittany.

Ranked in rows that stretch for half a mile between the remains of two ancient stone circles, Carnac's 3,000 menhirs (below) gradually diminish in height from 20 to 2 feet.

mid at Giza. Yet they were planned and erected by neolithic men, seemingly simple farmers who built and plowed without the wheel and whose life span was so short—no more than 36 years for men, 30 for women—that no major construction project begun in one man's lifetime could be completed by his son or grandson.

For research purposes these stone monuments are divided into two categories: dolmens and menhirs (or standing stones). Dolmens are rude collages of great stones stacked together like card houses and sometimes buried beneath dirt mounds. Such primal chambers vary in size from small, single enclosures with three slab sides and a capstone to enormous vaults fashioned of a great number of stones, like the Bagneux dolmen in western France. Sixty-one feet long and 20 feet wide, this great chamber is made of 13 upright slabs and four connecting capstones, the biggest of which weighs 86 tons, or about as much as an average-sized blue whale. A British admiral once calculated that it would take at least 3,000 men to wrestle such a slab into position.

Most dolmens appear to have served as collective graves, much as the barrows that dot the British countryside once served as tribal or family cemeteries for the Windmill Hill people, an earlier neolithic group. As many as 300 bodies have been found packed inside a single dolmen, the chaos of the remains indicating that the tomb was probably opened periodically to receive new corpses. "One tomb in Denmark was so stuffed," a modern writer has noted, "it gave the impression of having been filled to the brim with the capstone off and closed like an overloaded suitcase."

Not all dolmens contain human remains, however, and some scholars suspect that certain chambers were used as temples for the dead rather than as tombs. Evidence from disrupted tomb-dolmens and the discovery of bone shards at a number of sites have given rise to grisly speculations about sacrificial rites and cannibalism. Yet there are other, more succinct explanations, for prehistoric man probably believed that the body's spirit lived in the head. Thus any form of ceremonial skull breaking might have been in fact respectful and intended only to free the spirits of the dead.

The second type of stone monument, the menhir, a single free-standing stone, is less often associated with mass graves, though it, too, probably served as a life-cycle totem. Sometimes menhirs stand in forlorn isola-

This dolmen, or stone chamber, at Essay is one of more than 4,000 found in France. In typical dolmen style, heavy megaliths support the weight of more massive lintels.

The cup-and-ring stone-carving patterns found in Britain and France are repeated on a larger scale in a turf-and-stone maze (below, left) on the island of Gotland, Sweden.

tion or lie in shattered disarray, like the Grand Menhir Brisé in Locmariaquer, France. Intact, this awesome 340-ton slab would have towered 60 feet above the ground. Some historians have theorized that the stone was broken accidentally before it was erected, while others have suggested that it was toppled by a natural disaster, such as an earthquake. Most often, menhirs are grouped in circles or rings (called henges), as at Stonehenge or Avebury, 18 miles to the northeast. The British Isles contain a profusion of such stone circles, more than 900 in all, and all of varying dimension.

The mysteries of these joined rings have tantalized the human imagination for centuries. During the Middle Ages, when the stones must have seemed more imposing and dominant on the land, they were variously considered to possess the power to harm or heal or to enhance fertility. Covens of witches reportedly gathered round them to practice the occult arts. Young maidens seeking fecundity slid down the stones on their naked buttocks. (In Brittany, such stones were coated with honey or oil to smooth the ride.)

In violent reaction to the ubiquity of such pagan customs, Christian authorities attempted to demystify the menhirs. Rooting them up, they incorporated the stones in their churches; in a number of cases, earth and stone rings were occupied by Christian structures and dwellings. And in an especially bizarre application of the Inquisitor's art, the Church encouraged ritual flagellation and mutilation of the stones. In the 18th century, destructive ceremonies at Avebury were led by a farmer known as Stone-Killer Robinson. Such wanton pilgrimages were witnessed by Dr. William Stukeley, a clergyman and amateur historian, who called them "as terrible a sight as a Spanish auto-da-fé."

Yet it was Dr. Stukeley who popularized the most persistent of the menhir myths. The stone circles, he wrote, had been erected as temples by the druids, the high priests of the Celtic peoples, who inhabited Britain and western Europe during the centuries before Christ. Another stubbornly persistent theory about megaliths was propounded in modern times by Alfred Watkins, a successful English beer salesman and enthusiastic amateur student of antiquity. One summer in 1921, Watkins was riding through his native Herefordshire when he was seized by a sudden insight: "The barrier of time melted and, spread across the country," one of Wat-

The cup-and-ring markings on the entrance stone at New-grange, in Ireland, rework a motif found on many British megaliths. Deep within the tomb, a second pattern is seen once a year when the midwinter sun touches it at dawn.

kins's disciples has written, "he [Watkins] saw a web of lines linking the holy places and sites of antiquity. Mounds, old stones, crosses and old crossroads, churches placed on pre-Christian sites, legendary trees, moats and holy wells stood in exact alignments."

Watkins dubbed the prehistoric patterns he envisioned old straight tracks, or leys—the latter because the word *ley* is found in many ancient place names. It was in 1925 that Watkins, then 70, published his theory in a book, *The Old Straight Track,* and soon thousands of enthusiasts were swarming over the megaliths and other ancient sites, searching for leys.

As absurd as some of these theories may seem today, it is not surprising that each enjoyed currency, for available archeological evidence was meager, and most scholars felt that the prehistoric people of Britain and western Europe were but primitive farmers. Thus they believed that the genius necessary to produce the megaliths had to have come from the more advanced civilizations of the Mediterranean world.

There the matter stood until well into this century, not much changed from the time two centuries earlier when Daniel Defoe wrote of the megaliths, "All that can be learn'd of them is, that *there they are.*" Yet, in the past three decades, researchers have begun to extract the secrets of these stone shrines, stunning amateur theoreticians and archeologists alike.

Much of the new research focused on Stonehenge, and beginning in 1950 a decade of digging, the first full-scale excavation of the site, established that Stonehenge had been assembled over 1,000 or more years and in three distinct phases, each involving extraordinary engineering efforts.

After the excavation of Stonehenge, refinements in radiocarbon-dating techniques led to an even more startling discovery: construction of Stonehenge had been started in roughly 2700 B.C. Similar revisions dated European megaliths as far back as 5000 B.C. The conclusion: The megaliths had come *before* the fabled pyramids and other Mediterranean monuments, and the local peoples of western Europe, those primitive farmers dismissed by earlier archeologists, had indeed built them without the assistance of Egyptian or Greek advisers.

In addition, they had performed an even more astonishing engineering feat at Avebury, just 18 miles to the northeast. There, the world's largest stone circle, in the words of John Aubrey, the English antiquarian who came upon it in the middle of a fox hunt in 1649, "did as much excell Stoneheng as a Cathedral does an ordinary Parish church."

As such, Avebury blends mounds and menhirs in an unarguably fabulous structure. Yet its single most impressive feature—best seen from the air—is the vast circling ditch and bank, which marks it as a place of importance in the landscape. Within this enormous perimeter, some 1,200 feet in diameter, stand the surviving stones of two smaller circles (inside either of which Stonehenge might be placed with ease) and the northern half of a rural village that has grown up over the last three centuries.

A mile to the south of the circle looms a related and even more enigmatic structure called Silbury Hill. Its mammoth size (it is more than 500 feet in diameter and 130 feet high) suggests that it might have been a burial site for a high chieftain, a function that would relate it to the great conical burial mounds of the North American Indians, although excavations of the English mound have failed to produce skeletal remains.

Historians have been luckier with the main earthworks at Avebury. The site is rich with archeological evidences that clearly indicate its protracted use as a major religious and civic center. In his book on Avebury, English historian Aubrey Burl sounds the words that reverberate in all serious explorations of ancient earth shrines: "Death and regeneration are the themes of Avebury," Burl writes. "The Neolithic world was a place of spirits and symbols, in which a pot deliberately broken took on a new existence just as real as the one it had left. It was a world in which the dead were needed and in which life and death were not separate but were reflections of each other."

Avebury's construction stretched over a period of 500 years, perhaps 20 neolithic generations, a time when the region's population was growing, the site was becoming an important center for religious worship and

The vast earthwork called Avebury is the largest of Britain's great stone circles and predates the first erected at Stonehenge by 500 years. Within Avebury's 28½ acres, delineated by an encircling moat more than 20 feet deep and 70 feet wide, the remains of two Stonehenge-sized rings exist alongside a small village. The moat and its mysterious satellite, Silbury Hill (at upper right in photograph), a 130-foot-high earthen mound, were made by prehistoric farmers using bone tools.

trade, and its people were prospering. The impulse among the people of Stonehenge to build a center of their own must have been strong, for they produced a distinctively different shrine, at even greater cost of time and lives. The most compelling secret to emerge from studies of Stonehenge also may explain why local farmers struggled so magnificently to hew and assemble its rings of stone. A clue had been offered as far back as 1740 by Dr. William Stukeley, the clergyman who popularized the myth of the druids. Stukeley saw that the axis of the structure was aligned precisely toward the northeast sky, where the sun rose at summer solstice, June 21, the longest day of the year. Later investigators found evidence of other celestial alignments, but it remained for an American astronomer born in England, Gerald S. Hawkins, to formulate a full-scale theory of Stonehenge's astronomical meaning. In *Stonehenge Decoded*, published in 1965, Hawkins argued that practically every stone was placed to provide sightlines for the rising and setting of the sun on key dates, such as the summer and winter solstices. Hawkins, using a computer, concluded that Stonehenge was nothing less than a prehistoric observatory and that it had its own crude computational mechanism—the 56 mysterious holes just inside the perimeter of the outer bank (called Aubrey holes, after John Aubrey, the Englishman who discovered them in the 17th century). By moving stone or wooden markers from hole to hole, Hawkins theorized, ancient astronomers might have

been able to track the moon and predict lunar eclipses.

Hawkins's book greatly annoyed archeologists. Yet support for his thesis, if not for all of its details, began appearing. England's most renowned astronomer, Fred Hoyle, performed his own calculations without a computer and agreed that Stonehenge was indeed a true observatory. He even seconded the notion that the Aubrey holes were a kind of lunar-eclipse predictor, though not a computer. The holes, Hoyle contended, represented the path of the sun, while markers placed inside them were meant to represent the sun, the moon and certain junctures of lunar orbit. "A veritable Newton or Einstein must have been at work," wrote Hoyle, "but then why not?"

Stonehenge was by no means the only monument to be investigated by astro-theoreticians. In the early 1930s a practical and tireless Scotsman, Alexander Thom, professor emeritus of engineering science at Oxford, began his own meticulous on-site survey of British megaliths—with more startling results. Over 40 years' time, he surveyed more than 600 stone circles and alignments throughout Britain and western Europe in an attempt to demonstrate that *all* were aligned to facilitate study of the sun, moon and stars. A typical menhir, Thom found, formed a kind of stone sight that when lined up with natural features on the horizon such as a peak or notch pointed to a significant celestial event. In the puzzling case of the 3,000 stones at Carnac, France, Thom discovered alignments that suggested that they formed a kind of graph paper on which prehistoric astronomers might have plotted the positions of heavenly bodies, although this theory is given less credence than most by other scholars. Thom also postulated the use by megalithic engineers of a standard unit of measure of 2.72 feet, which he labeled the "megalithic yard." The shape of stone rings—some true circles, others ellipses—suggested to Thom that the builders also knew rudimentary geometry. Some circles are laid out with such precision that Thom suspected the builders had worked out the Pythagorean theorem of right triangles hundreds of years before the Egyptians, who are generally given credit for the discovery.

The work of Thom, Hawkins and others has laid the foundations for a new science, astro-archeology, which explores the celestial interests of the ancients. The evidence of these interests is now so compelling that it is accepted by a growing number of scholars, even Richard Atkinson, the Stonehenge specialist who

no longer considers it "moonshine" and is himself an enthusiastic convert to astro-archeology. The megaliths, the astronomer E. C. Krupp has written, "are wordless but emphatic evidence of our ancestors' energetic pursuit of the sky and stars. They mark the same kind of commitment that transported us to the moon and our spacecraft to the surface of Mars."

Other writers point out, however, that we have merely swapped old mysteries for new ones. How did the megalith builders acquire their knowledge of astronomy and mathematics? How did they pass their learning on without any form of writing? What force, or faith, ensured the continuity necessary to see the completion of such monumental enterprises through so many dark centuries? And why did this fire of learning, which would not be matched in Europe for another 3,000 years, blaze so brightly only to die out?

Nor were the spectacular creations of the Atlantic neolithic people confined to stones and mounds. The

Most famous of all megalithic circles, Stonehenge is the product of 1,000 years of effort. It began as an immense circular ditch and at least three monoliths, one of which, the Heel Stone, approximately aligns the center with midsummer sunrise. The existing monument—of carefully fluted and fitted stones—superseded an even earlier double circle of megaliths.

amazing 360-foot-long White Horse of Uffington gallops across a hillside in western England, its gleaming lines formed some 2,000 years ago by painstaking removal of topsoil to bare the underlying chalk surface. Why a white horse, one of a number of effigies studding the British landscape? Is it a symbol, a shrine, or merely magnificent art?

Tantalizingly enough, virtually all questions, both archeological and philosophical, raised in connection with the earth shrines of the Old World are appropriate to those of the Americas. What was strikingly different about American mounds, however, was their enormous size and their remarkable shapes. Some were softly rounded, others took precise geometric forms—circles, squares and even octagons—while others were sculpted to represent birds, reptiles and other beasts. Yet as was true in the early investigations of the European megaliths, the origins of North American mounds were long obscured by the tendency of historians to underestimate the capabilities of the people who built them.

Modern archeologists believe that the mounds were built by a succession of Indian cultures, beginning about 3,000 years ago. The first culture, the Adena, was centered in southern Ohio. Artifacts from their mounds, and the mounds themselves, suggest a people whose religious customs, like those of their European counterparts, were dominated by the theme of death. The second mound-building culture, the Hopewell, began in Illinois and spread rapidly, supplanting the Adena perhaps 200 years after the birth of Christ. The Hopewell carried the obsession with death to great extremes. In the manner of the ancient Egyptians, the Hopewell sent off their departed in the company of finely crafted treasures, generally of copper and mica, sometimes of gold and silver, and like the Egyptians, they developed a

The Enigmatic Druids

The secret rites of the druids, carefully shielded from foreigners, have intrigued students of the unknown for centuries. Yet were it not for the curiosity of their Greek and Roman contemporaries, the druids' exotic ministrations might have passed permanently into obscurity. In the 3rd century B.C., Julius Caesar was one of the first to report on the white-robed druids and their sinister activities in remote caves and hidden oak groves. He did not mention Stonehenge, but the druids might have worshiped there, for its construction had already been completed.

As priests of the ancient Celts, who populated much of France and Britain, the druids often functioned as arbiters and judges, settling disputes, passing judgments and assigning penalties. In addition, they were sometimes charged with honoring the gods by sacrifice—mostly animal, but occasionally human—and with controlling the mysterious workings of spirits and souls. The Celts considered the human head the home of the soul; they also believed that the head continued to live even after separation from the body and that it might assist whoever possessed it. A Roman writer, Diodorus, reported that the Celts kept trophy heads in cedar chests and would not part with them even in exchange for their weight in gold. After battles, the heads of heroes and prisoners were spiked on poles for decoration. Heads carved in stone and dried human heads have been found wherever the Celts settled.

Another important druid duty was to appease the spirits of the dead. In particular, the eve of Samain on the final day of October was considered a time of great danger because, as the power of the sun weakened, spirits roamed the earth. Today, Samain's druidic mood of fear and witchery survives as Halloween.

The great horse of Uffington, 360 feet long and 130 feet high, has been visible in Britain's countryside since the time of Christ. Formed by scraping away earth to reveal a layer of chalk beneath, it has been maintained by local villagers who gather every seven years—usually on Whitsuntide—to cut back the overgrowth and scrub the chalk clean.

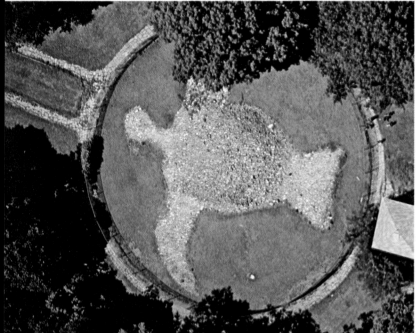

Thousands of piled rocks shape the figure of an eagle, its wingspread measuring 120 feet, on top of this 1,500-year-old mound in Georgia. The mound's purpose remains a mystery.

high tradition of art and trade in connection with their beliefs. Apparently solely for the acquisition of ceremonial grave pieces, the Hopewell operated an extensive trading network. From their mounds have come alligator teeth from Florida, obsidian from as far west as Yellowstone, and ornaments made from copper that was mined around Lake Superior. Their burial mounds were bigger than those of the Adena, and some of their more elaborate earthworks probably served as huge ceremonial centers. At Newark, Ohio, earthen embankments once outlined a ceremonial complex of giant circles, squares, and an octagon joined by avenues and covering four square miles, about three times the size of New York's Central Park.

A later society, the Mississippian, gained dominance to the south about A.D. 700 and erected monumental earthworks whose artifacts and truncated pyramidal shape suggest strong influence from the Olmecs of Mexico. Like the Olmecs, the Mississippians were fascinated by the sun, fire and human sacrifice. A principal Mississippian outpost was at Cahokia, Illinois, near St. Louis. Cahokia, which dates from about A.D. 1000, was the site of hundreds of mounds, the largest of which covered 16 acres and was more than 100 feet high. This enormous flat-topped mound, on top of which could be laid a half-dozen football fields, probably served as a temple for religious ceremonies. Recent finds suggest that the people of Cahokia, like those in western Europe, may have been astute students of the skies. Archeologists have discovered a "woodhenge," a

American Indians built wheels such as this one in the Bighorn

410-foot-diameter circle of holes where wooden posts may have once protruded, providing sightlines for an observatory. A more likely theory is that the holes were foundation work for a great public building—a "wooden cathedral." Such structures have been identified in several Indian cultures, including the Cherokee, as well as among those of the stone builders of Britain.

Interestingly enough, both "observatory" and "cathedral" theories have been proposed to help explain one of the principal anomalies among earth shrines: the Big Horn Medicine Wheel. Set on top of a remote mountain peak in the Bighorn Mountains of Wyoming, the wheel is as remote structurally from burial and ceremonial mounds as it is geographically. Attributed to various people of the West—the Crows, the Cheyennes, the Shoshones or the Arapahos—the wheel is an uneven circular tracery of simple stones, measuring

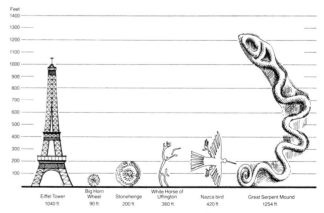

Enormous size as well as meticulous craftsmanship marks the earth monuments compared here with the Eiffel Tower.

Mountains, perhaps to predict solstices.

Unlike most Indian effigy mounds, the Great Serpent Mound in Adams County, Ohio, was not associated with burials. It thus remains an enigma to modern researchers.

some 80 feet in diameter. Six small piles, or cairns, of rocks are placed at irregular intervals around the circle, and 28 stone "spokes" crisscross through its center. One student of the wheel points out that similar stone circles have been found in other Indian districts and that the Big Horn Wheel may have been a symbolic, one-dimensional re-creation of the wooden cathedrals of the Eastern tribes, built by a people who had little wood.

Except for the mounds, most traces of the Mississippian civilization had vanished by the time white explorers arrived in the 17th and 18th centuries. Why is still a mystery, as is the sudden decline of the two earlier cultures, the Adena and the Hopewell. Other questions unanswered by archeologists involve American earthworks that do not fit neatly into the sequence of the mound-building cultures.

Such a mystery surrounds a spectacular series of six long mounds at Poverty Point, Louisiana, a series that is thought to predate even the early Adena works in Ohio. Aerial surveys suggest that before the eastern part of the Louisiana complex was washed away by a shift in the Arkansas River, it apparently consisted of six concentric octagons. Altogether, the ridges of earth may have been more than 11 miles long, containing 530,000 cubic yards of dirt, or 35 times the volume of the Great Pyramid of Cheops. The enormousness of the effort required to build the Poverty mounds may be better understood in terms of 50-pound baskets of soil—an estimated 20 million were carried to the site. Scholars believe that Poverty Point must have been a sacred ceremonial city. But for whom? And how did the builders gain the knowledge of geometry that enabled them to lay out octagons?

Similar questions haunt the beautiful and mysterious contours of the so-called effigy mounds, which must be viewed from the air to be fully appreciated. Southern Wisconsin alone has an estimated 5,000 of these earthen reliefs, variously modeled on human and animal forms. There is a panther 575 feet long and a great bird with a wingspan of 624 feet. In many of the effigies, human remains have been discovered cached at critical anatomical points—the heart, the hip or the knee. With no clues as to the cultures that spawned these earth figures, researchers can only guess at their meaning. Did each extended family or tribe build its own mound in the image of its particular totem? Was a tribesman's burial place in the anatomy of the effigy a reflection of importance and accomplishment or of the life form he expected to take in the future?

The largest and most perplexing of the effigies, the Great Serpent Mound in southern Ohio, offers no evidence at all of burials. About 20 feet wide and 5 feet high, this great soil snake uncoils for nearly a quarter of a mile through a wooded area. Its jaws gape open, seemingly to grasp a single conical mound, per-

This glinting mica figure was probably fashioned by the Hopewell serpent-cult.

haps representing an egg or a frog. The origins of the serpent mound have eluded scholars. And since it has yielded no artifacts, it cannot be dated, though a conical burial mound nearby may link it to the Adena culture. An Ohio Baptist minister once argued that God himself had created the Great Serpent Mound to commemorate the site of the temptation of Adam and Eve. A modern investigator has theorized that it is not a serpent effigy but a representation of the Little Dipper. In any case, it was a monument best viewed from the heavens. If the mound did serve as a religious symbol, as many scholars today suspect, the distant heavens may have been the realm the ancient builders were attempting to placate or influence.

This mystifying characteristic—that many earthworks constructed by earthbound people can be best seen from above—is one of a number of factors that join ancient monuments around the world. Nowhere is the importance of aerial sighting more dramatically evident than in viewing the curious markings that decorate the Nazca desert on the southern coast of Peru. These markings, straight lines, geometric patterns and huge drawings, were made by meticulously scraping away small dark stones to reveal bands, only a few inches wide in many cases, of the yellowish-white soil. The patterns formed by the naked earth, and the ridges of stones piled a few inches high alongside, may be easily overlooked by travelers on the ground, even though the markings cover an area 30 miles long and up to 10 miles wide. It was only shortly before World War II that bush pilots spotted the patterns and scholars eventually became aware of them.

Archeologists think the patterns were created about 2,000 years ago by the Nazca Indians, a pre-Inca culture that adorned its pottery with similar markings. The speculations of some scholars focus on the remarkable ground drawings that extend hundreds of feet and depict a giant stylized flower and assorted other plants, a lizard, a condor, a spider and a monkey. These drawings, it has been suggested, may be astrological symbols of heavenly bodies or totems of Indian kinship groups.

Other scholars, including Maria Reiche, a German mathematician who has studied the markings for nearly 40 years, suspect the lines may have astronomical significance. A number of lines seem to point in the direction of sunrise and sunset on crucial days of the year, such as the summer solstice. If so, then the hundreds of small mounds of rocks that Reiche found near the lines might have served as counting devices for marking off days of the year. Some years ago, however, Gerald S. Hawkins, the American astronomer who calculated alignments at Stonehenge, undertook an extensive aerial photographic survey of Nazca. But when he fed his results into a computer, he could find no evidence that the markings had celestial significance.

Just as provocative, certainly, as their design and

orientation is the precision with which the Nazca markings were laid down. The drawings of plants and animals are accurately proportioned, and the straight lines dart like arrows for many miles over hills and through gullies with an accuracy greater than could be pinpointed by Hawkins's aerial-survey techniques.

Although the Nazca people might have attained such precision by sighting from nearby hilltops and using wooden markers, more intriguing theories have been advanced. One theory is wildly speculative and suggests that extraterrestrial visitors were responsible for transmitting the idea of the lines to the Indians. According to this theory, suggested by Erich von Däniken, a Swiss innkeeper turned prehistorian and best-selling author, these alien invaders made tracks with their spaceships, and these marks triggered imitation by the natives. The first pathways may have been produced, Von Däniken says, by the landing of a single extraterrestrial vehicle, possibly one cushioned by pressurized air, which caused sand and stones to be blown away. Other tracks were created whenever the vehicle flew off. As a result, the Indians saw both patterns, the landing and the takeoff tracks, and in deference to the "fiery gods" from the heavens began building their own long, straight tracks and protecting and revering all such markings. Another theory, devised by Bill Spohrer, an American explorer residing in Peru, also sounds farfetched, but has a particular appeal for a world that has nearly forgotten how recently modern man took to the heavens. Spohrer made the tantalizing speculation that the Indians were able to engineer their markings by soaring aloft in hot-air balloons.

Spohrer was aware, of course, that the first recorded balloon flight did not occur until 1709, in Lis-

Marvelously precise figures such as this one—an enormous bird with a 420-foot wingspan—enhance the Nazca legend.

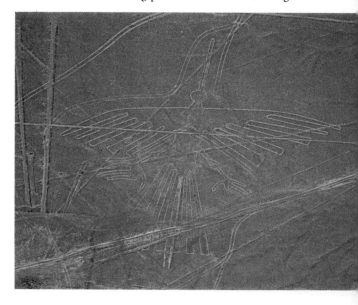

bon, some 17 centuries after the creation of the Nazca markings. Yet he based his theory on several clues and a daring experiment. One clue was the frequent depiction on ancient Nazca pottery of what appeared to be balloons or kites, flying high in the air, with tails streaming in the wind. A second clue was the exceptionally fine weave of the Nazca-crafted fabrics that had been uncovered at tombs near the markings. The fabric was even lighter than the synthetic material used to manufacture modern hot-air balloons; when tested, it proved to be more densely woven than that used to make parachutes. A third clue was to be found in the ancient and continuing ceremonial practice common among many Indian tribes of Central and South America of releasing small hot-air balloons at the conclusion of religious festivals. When Spohrer learned of an Inca battle legend that told of heroic reconnaissance flights over enemy lines by a young Inca boy, his theory seemed ever more plausible. The last bit of circumstan-

tial evidence taken into account by Spohrer was the blackened rocks found in large circular formations at the end of many Nazca lines. Tests showed that the blackening might have been produced by fires kindled to heat air in preparation for launching great balloons.

In 1975 Spohrer and some colleagues tested his theory. They built a balloon, dubbed *Condor I*, using only materials and techniques thought to have been available to the Nazca Indians. Then, with two pilots crouched inside a gondola fashioned from reeds, the crude craft soared high above the Nazca desert.

Yet *Condor I*'s remarkable flight, while providing evidence that the markings may have been engineered by balloon, leaves obscure their purpose. Perhaps, as old legends suggest, Nazca chiefs were sent to the heavens after death, rising ever higher, the sun warming the balloons that bore their bodies. If so, the markings may have provided symbolic guidance or a farewell message.

Is there any link between the Nazca pictures and the effigies of North America, perhaps hinting at the existence of an invisible network that bound Peruvian Indians with North American and possibly even European effigy artists? Certainly not, most scholars would agree, rejecting such speculations as wild and unfounded. And yet it seems fair to suggest that if not in actual communication, early men were nonetheless linked by two basic, yet conflicting, impulses: the need to cling fast to the solid and certain earth even as they reached out in hope toward the distant, mysterious heavens.

The intricate markings at Nazca cover more than 200 square miles of desert and are fully visible only from the skies.

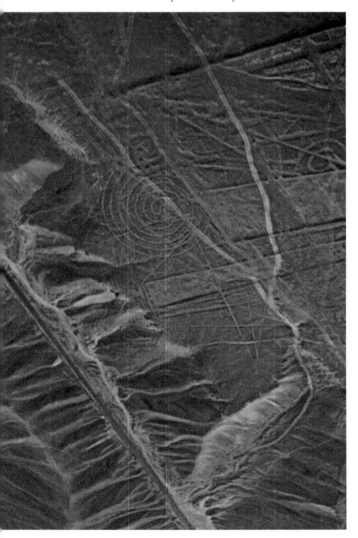

Passing 575 miles above Peru, a NASA camera picked out the faint crisscross of the Nazca lines, circled in white.

Great Heads of Stone and Mystery

The ancient urge to create crude monuments from stone and earth sometimes expressed itself in sculptured heads of colossal size and weight—and comparable mystery.

In Corsica some 3,500 years ago, for reasons that are still not clear, simple menhirs—or standing stones—long used to mark graves, were gradually replaced by distinctively sculptured warrior figures. The island's coast is dotted with some 60 of these giant statues, preserved only because they were toppled—probably by the very invaders that the statues are thought to represent—and used to build the fortification walls in which they have remained undisturbed for centuries. Even earlier in Guatemala, prehistoric craftsmen carved colossi of such rotundity that they are now known to the local people as *Muchachos Gordos* in Spanish, or "Fat Boys." In addition, researchers have recently determined that certain parts of the Fat Boys' anatomy—the temple and navel—are magnetized. They believe pre-Olmec sculptors somehow determined that certain rocks contained areas of naturally magnetized stone. The sculptors then carved at least a dozen figures so that the navel or temple (possibly as sites of life-giving force or energy) was made of the magnetized rock. And they did so at least 2,000 years before the first evidences of Chinese experiments with magnetism.

Yet in size, number and brooding configuration of face and torso, no colossi can match the stone giants scattered over the grasslands and volcanoes of Easter Island. Some 600 statues, ranging from 3 feet to more than 70 feet in height, dominate this 45-square-mile eastern outpost of the Polynesian islands, now a dependency of Chile, 2,300 miles to the east.

When in 1722 the first Europeans, Dutchmen, paid a daylong visit to the island on Easter Sunday, giving it its name, nearly half the strange statues, known to the natives as *moai*, stood erect on volcanic slopes, staring skyward or out to sea. Most of the rest faced inland, mounted on stone platforms and topped with cylindrical red stone crowns in the shape of a topknot—or *pukao*—the hairstyle favored by the natives. Yet 52 years later, when the English navigator James Cook tied up at Easter Island, the statues facing inland had been rudely toppled from their platforms, possibly as the result of bitter civil war among the volcanic island's inhabitants.

The nature of this conflict is but one of many puzzles that shroud the statues. Why, for example, do some 80 of the moai lie in rough, unfinished form in the crater of yellowish-gray volcanic rock from which they were being hacked, the stone picks of their sculptors scattered about as if suddenly abandoned in mid stroke? Why were these particular statues—some up to 70 feet in length—started, then abandoned, and by whom? And what is the significance of the white coral and red lava eyes, found only recently, that were designed to fill the statues' eye sockets?

Scholars generally believe that Easter Island was settled by Polynesians paddling eastward in outrigger canoes about the 12th century. According to island folklore, there were two different waves of immigration. The "Long-ears," people who deformed their earlobes with heavy ornamental discs, came first and began carving and erecting the first statues, the moai, to honor their dead. The "Short-ears" arrived later and were impressed into helping with the scraping and carving of the statues. One legend tells of a successful Short-ear rebellion during which the Long-ears were destroyed by a wall of flame built in a broad ditch. Yet charred materials found in the ditch have been radiocarbon dated to 1680, nearly a century before the actual toppling of the giant statues.

Thor Heyerdahl, the Norwegian anthropologist and adventurer who mounted an archeological expedition to Easter Island during the 1950s, has his own controversial ideas about the statue builders and the fate of their creations. He theorizes that the first settlers, the Long-ears, came not from Polynesia but from Peru, perhaps as early as A.D. 300. One bit of evidence he offers is that the Easter Island colossi bear some resemblance to ancient statues found in South America. A second clue is the profusion of wood-carved ideograms on the island, all still undeciphered, and all inscribed on hardwood tablets known to Easter Islanders as *Rongo-Rongo*. The people of ancient Polynesia, Heyerdahl points out, unlike the Peruvians, had no such written language. Heyerdahl's most important argument for Peruvian derivation, however, comes from his own maverick thesis—demonstrated in his famous voyage on the raft *Kon Tiki* in 1947—that Polynesia was originally settled by Indians sailing westward from South America rather than eastward from Asian lands.

Whatever the origin of the moai builders, the task they set for themselves must have required the painstakingly coordinated efforts of the island's entire population. An experiment staged by Heyerdahl showed that 180 men were needed just to move a single statue. Why was such exertion necessary, and what motivated it? Modern-day psychologists have suggested a possible motive to account for the shaping of the moai. Easter Island was so barren, they theorize, that there were few animals to hunt and so remote that there were no neighboring tribes to fight. As a result, the Long-ears might have begun building their awesome statues just to pass the time away.

This basalt head, weighing approximately 18 tons, sits in Veracruz, Mexico.

Warrior figure (below) at San Agustín, in Colombia, wears the image of a protective god on its head.

Easter Island's famous lava colossi (above) overlook inland villages from the top of a huge burial platform.

Old and toothless, the god below sits among ruins at Copán, Honduras, once an important Mayan religious and astronomical center.

Farmers on Corsica carved this seven-foot-tall, 3,000-year-old figure of a victorious enemy warrior.

The pre-Inca colossus above, right, is one of many that tower—up to 24 feet—in Tiahuanaco, Bolivia.

One of Guatemala's 4,000-year-old, six-foot-tall Fat Boys (right) was found to have magnetized stone at the temple and navel.

39

Quicksteps in Creation—Anomalies

A sacred shroud bearing a haunting negative image, an exquisitely polished crystal skull, a seemingly ancient battery, what may be a 2,000-year-old analog computer—all raise tantalizing questions about the most elemental of unknowns: the power of the human mind. Challenging both the skills of modern researchers and traditional concepts of history, such bizarre and anomalous objects provide dramatic—if often controversial—evidence that man's brain from earliest times has been capable of astonishing achievement.

The remarkable 14-foot-long strip of linen shown in part below, bearing the image of a bearded Christ-like figure, may reflect unusual human achievement or an unknown phenomenon, or it may be a hoax. Known as the Shroud of Turin, the cloth first intrigued modern investigators in 1898, when it was photographed and its strange image turned out to be a negative one, an unlikely accomplishment for ancient forgers. Modern supporters of the shroud's biblical origins theorize that the relic traveled through Asia Minor and then to Constantinople on its way to Europe, where it first appeared in the 14th century. Investigation in this century has produced intriguing evidence to support such claims. Biochemical analysis has identified traces of pollen in the shroud from both Palestine and Asia Minor. Computerized enhancement of the image has shown that it was not created by painting or the application of herbs. Further study may determine whether the shroud dates from the early Christian Era. Although such tests cannot prove the shroud was Christ's, they might provide evidence that the shroud, like some other biblical artifacts, rests on a solid historical foundation.

In many ways the crystal skull at right is even more difficult to explain or accept. Shortly after its discovery in Lubaantun, British Honduras, in 1927, it became known as the Skull of Doom, and news accounts linked it with a number of unexplained deaths.

For scientific observers, the skull's essential unknown is logistic: how did it get into the 1,000-year-old Mayan temple where it was found? Carved from a single piece of rare quartz crystal, the head (it is five inches high and weighs more than 11½ pounds) seems an impossible achievement for the vanished Mayas. Hidden prisms in the base and hand-ground lenses in the eyes combine to produce a dazzling luminescence.

Yet investigators have found no trace of the use of modern-day tools. In fact, the skull's crystalline structure was disregarded in its creation, something modern lapidaries would never do. Is the skull a fraud, or proof that Mayan technology was far more advanced than generally believed? Like many anomalies, the skull raises more questions than it answers.

The Shroud of Turin (above and at right) bears a Christ-like negative image. Both front (above) and back images appear on the shroud, as if half had been spread beneath a body, as in Gerard David's Renaissance painting at left, and half had been draped over the top.

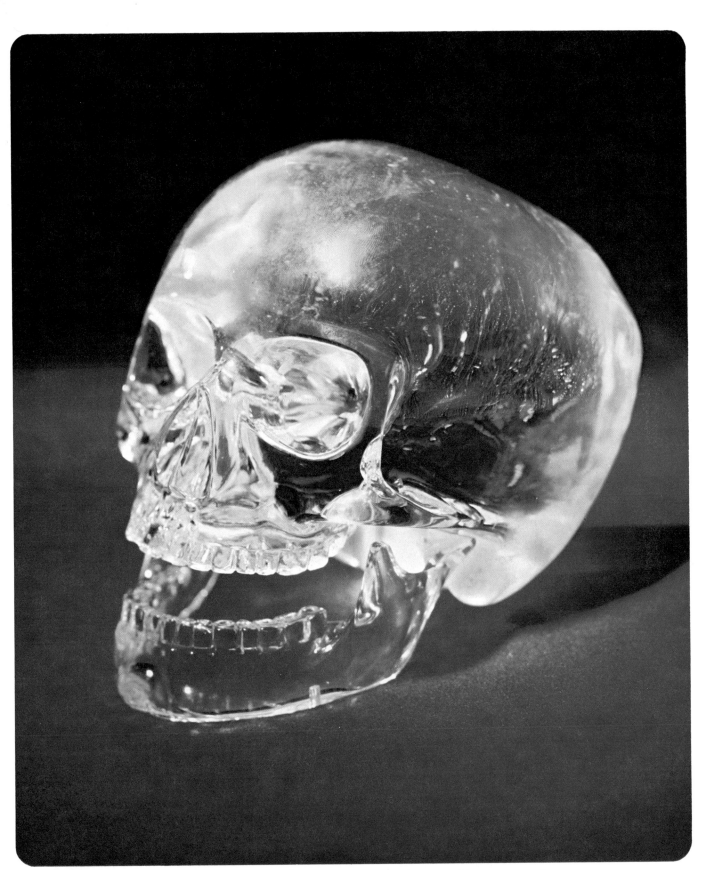

Life-size, female in configuration and rumored to possess supernatural powers, this quartz-crystal skull may have served as a divine oracle in Mayan culture more than 1,000 years ago. Although investigation of the skull's surface and internal structure tends to confirm its ancient origin, the artifact's design suggests a remarkably advanced knowledge of optics and incredible lapidary skill.

Ancient Marvels: A Computer, Compass and Battery

The discovery of a single artifact—the mechanical calculator shown in replica below—in the remains of a sunken 2,000-year-old Greek ship may revolutionize modern conceptions of Hellenic technology: the ancient Greeks, it now appears, were capable of constructing and operating intricate computational devices. When American scholar Derek de Solla Price examined X-rays of chunks of the device (like the encrusted metallic blob at left), he made an exciting discovery—the number and relationship of more than 30 gears made it seem likely that the device was used to "work out and exhibit the motions of the sun and moon and probably also the planets."

If made to float, this naturally magnetic metal fragment—found in a 3,000-year-old Olmec mound in Veracruz, Mexico—points 35.5° west of magnetic north. The Olmecs might have used such a bar as a compass by placing it on a mat in water or floating it in mercury, made by heating the mineral cinnabar. If the bar was used as a compass, perhaps to orient the Olmecs' northward-turned temples, then it predates by 1,000 years Chinese compasses, long thought to be the world's first.

While exploring a 2,000-year-old Parthian town in present-day Iraq, German archeologist Wilhelm König discovered an earthenware vase containing an iron rod set inside a copper cylinder (a replica is shown above). The arrangement reminded him of a dry-cell battery, a notion supported by the discovery of rods apparently corroded by acid (possibly vinegar or wine). König's conclusion: the Parthians had generated electricity 1,600 years before 1800, the date of the first battery.

Analysis of ore from the uranium mine at right, located in the African republic of Gabon, produced evidence of an extraordinary and completely spontaneous kind of anomaly: a natural nuclear reaction. Because ore samples show an unusually small amount of U-235 (the isotope that divides during nuclear fission) and an abundance of fission products, it seems likely that 2 billion years ago, when uranium rich in U-235 existed in concentrated amounts, enough was drawn together to touch off a chain reaction. Prehistoric rivers may have gathered the uranium and then damped it to permit years of fission.

In his Dialogues, Plato launched
an endless adventure of paradise lost to
catastrophe and reason to romance.

ATLANTIS

The Greek philosopher Plato
created the first known written accounts of Atlantis.

Of all the mysteries that glitter in the realm of the unknown, just beyond the grasp of scientific proof, few can claim the enduring fascination of lost lands and vanished civilizations, especially those that are said to have slipped beneath the dark waters of the sea. To this day men still speculate on the existence of fabulous sunken cities off the coast of England or in French waters beyond Brittany. And the story of Atlantis, the all-time champion of drowned-world mysteries, has never been more provocative. First recounted by the Greek philosopher Plato, the chronicle of Atlantis is now more than 2,000 years old. Yet new Atlantis books appear every year (adding to the total of more than 2,000 already in print), and teams of contemporary archeologists claim to have discovered evidence of its existence on both sides of the Atlantic Ocean as well as in the Mediterranean Sea.

What special hold do such legends have on the human imagination? Why have people persisted in believing in the reality of these drowned worlds, undaunted by lack of proof or even very persuasive evidence? Skeptics are quick to speak of the capacity of even the most learned of men to believe in nonsense. Thus, Henri Martin, a noted 19th-century French au-

thority on Plato, dismissed with a sneer those scholars who set "sail in quest of Atlantis with a more or less heavy cargo of erudition, but without any compass except their imagination and caprice." Yet belief in lands vanished beneath the sea is too ancient and too widespread to be attributed solely to the foolishness of a handful of errant pedants. For such beliefs are and always have been an essential thread in the web of human existence, and if they seem more a creation of emotion and yearning than of fact and tangible discovery, they have nonetheless generated over the centuries a rich and revealing trove of human invention and investigation.

Celtic mythology is rife with stories of sunken lands. According to one tradition, the narrow strip of the Atlantic Ocean that lies between the coast of Cornwall, England, and the Scilly Islands was once the dry-land kingdom of Lyonnesse and was covered with prosperous towns and handsome churches. The story has it that at some time in the 5th century A.D. the ocean abruptly engulfed Lyonnesse, and only one man, named Trevilian, escaped to tell of its destruction. To this day, his descendants' family coat of arms bears a picture of the white horse on which the ancestral Trevilian reportedly rode to safety.

Similar stories are told of drowned kingdoms off the Welsh coast and of the lost French city of Ys, off the coast of Brittany. Although it is highly unlikely that any of these places, if they ever existed, could have been suddenly engulfed, it is remotely possible that the

Volcanic forces like those depicted at left could have destroyed the island of Atlantis, legendary site of an empire older, richer and more powerful than any other.

45

old traditions refer to lands that gradually subsided beneath the level of the sea over the course of centuries. In any event, no clear proof of their existence has ever been discovered.

For the existence of Atland, a prehistoric island-kingdom that supposedly sank beneath the North Sea, there is not even an old tradition, let alone archeological evidence. The sole source for the Atland story is a manuscript written in ancient Frisian, an early Germanic language, and said to have been discovered in Holland in 1871. The manuscript tells of a highly civilized society that inhabited a large semi-circular land mass located northeast of the British Isles. According to the manuscript, an unexplained cosmic catastrophe totally destroyed Atland in 2193 B.C. With its heavy-handed Atlantean allusions, its sheer outlandishness and its doubtful pedigree, the Atland story has all the earmarks of a hoax, though its author remains unknown.

Few people have ever heard of Atland and even fewer believe in it. But with little more factual information to go on, many people apparently still believe in the reality of two fabulous vanished islands, Lemuria and Mu. The origins of these phantom lands lie in the jumbled convergence of several different trains of thought. For example, some 19th-century supporters of Charles Darwin's evolutionary theories speculated that because of similarities in fossil records in Africa and Brazil, there must have been dry-land links between these lands. Several biologists and paleontologists of the same period explained such similarities in terms of "land bridges," which had sunk without a trace. One such link, a presumed third continent that vanished in the Indian Ocean, was named Lemuria, after the lemurs, small furry animals common to Madagascar but at the time thought to be prevalent in both Africa and Asia. Ernst Haeckel, a German botanist-zoologist, used the idea of an Indian Ocean Lemuria not only to explain the dissemination of plants and animals but also to locate paradise, the "primeval home of man."

Lost lands have also been targets of opportunity for occult theorizing and claims of special knowledge. For example, Mme. Helena Blavatsky, the bizarre founder of Theosophy, is supposed to have learned about creation, evolution and the truth concerning Lemuria from a work that survived the destruction of Atlantis, *The Book of Dzyan*. According to Mme. Blavatsky, the inhabitants of Lemuria, large red, egg-laying creatures who had four arms, three eyes, no intellect, and well-developed psychic powers, were the forebears of both the Atlantean and human races. Another occultist, James Churchward, claimed that he had learned about Lemuria, or, as he called it, Mu, from some Naacal Tablets found in a monastery in India.

In incidental fashion these speculations, some well meaning, some clearly preposterous, became intertwined, and people began applying the name Lemuria to a hypothetical lost continent in the Pacific. Lewis Spence, an early-20th-century Atlantologist, used such arguments to support the existence of several Pacific land masses. Spence even claimed that Quetzalcoatl, the white-skinned civilizing god of Central American legend, resembled a Buddhist priest who had come to the New World to proselytize the Indians.

This medieval map succeeds where Atlantologists failed. It places paradise—the Garden of Eden—at the top of the world.

For the most part, the stories of Lemuria and Mu hardly require refutation. They are at best lingering vestiges of garbled theorizing now more than 100 years old. Atlantis is different in almost every way. Its antecedents, history and the profusion of locations assigned to it over the centuries are impressive and intriguing. If Atlantis is still more a creation of imagination than fact, and likely to remain so, it is at least the best of its breed, a truly awesome will-o'-the-wisp empire that has been variously situated in Mongolia, Brazil, Greenland and Ceylon. And despite evidence that suggests that Atlantis is little more than a dream, the story is sustained by a compelling possibility: like Troy and the Minoan ruins on Crete, Atlantis might one day be found!

What, then, are the Atlantis facts as they exist today? Impressively enough, the first recorded mention of Atlantis appears in one of the greatest works of Western philosophy, Plato's *Dialogues*. Specifically, the story is told in two of the later dialogues, both composed around 350 B.C. The first, the *Timaeus*, is the record of a conversation that supposedly took place in Athens in 421 B.C. between the philosopher Socrates and three of his disciples. In the course of the discussion, one of the disciples, Critias, tells the others a tale that had been told to his grandfather by Solon, a famous Athenian poet, statesman and lawgiver. Apparently Solon, during a visit to Egypt, had met a priest in the city of Saïs. The priest told Solon that Egyptian historical records contained an account of a great war that had been fought in very ancient times, around 9600 B.C., between Athens and "a mighty host which, starting from a distant point in the Atlantic Ocean, was insolently advancing to attack the whole of Europe, and Asia to boot." The invaders, the priest said, came from an island called Atlantis, which lay outside the Pillars of Hercules (Strait of Gibraltar). This island, bigger than North Africa and Asia Minor combined, was the center of a powerful empire that included not only many neighboring Atlantic islands but large parts of the mainland as well ("Libya as far as Egypt" and "Europe as far as Tuscany"). Greece, however, "was pre-eminent in courage and military skill, and was the leader of the Hellenes. And when the rest fell off from her, being compelled to stand alone . . . she defeated and triumphed over the invaders, and preserved from slavery those who were not yet subjugated, and generously liberated all the rest . . . who dwell within the Pillars. But afterward there occurred violent earthquakes and floods, and in a single day and night of misfortune all . . . warlike men in a body sank into the earth, and the island of Atlantis in like manner disappeared in the depths of the sea. For which reason the sea in those parts is impassable and impenetrable, because there is a shoal of mud in the way, and this was caused by the subsidence of the island."

Plato tells us no more about Atlantis in the *Timaeus,* but in a subsequent, unfinished dialogue, the *Critias,* he has Critias take up the subject once again. This time Critias is more descriptive and factual. The island of Atlantis, he reports, was mountainous at its coast, but descended to a broad, fertile plain in the center. It was rich in minerals of all sorts and abounded in game (including elephants), timber and edible plants. The ancient metropolis was a marvel of wealth and advanced engineering. In its center were the royal palace and a temple dedicated to the sea god Poseidon, patron of Atlantis. His temple was heavily decorated with gold, silver, ivory and a mysterious bronze-like metal called orichalch, which, according to Critias, "gleamed like fire." The central island was entirely enclosed by a circular canal 600 feet wide. This canal was surrounded by a circle of land 1,200 feet wide, which in turn was ringed by a 1,200-foot canal, then by another 1,800-foot ring of land, and finally by an 1,800-foot canal, which could easily accommodate large ships. On one side this multi-ring complex was cut by a canal that ran from the center out to the sea.

Critias describes at length Atlantis's administrative system, its 1,200-ship maritime establishment, some of its ceremonials, and the many splendors of its architecture. But these were of minor importance. Atlantis and its people, he sums up, scorned "all things save virtue and counted their present prosperity a little thing."

Unfortunately, this did not last. Instead, says Critias, "when the god's part in them began to wax faint by constant crossing with much mortality, and the human temper to predominate, then they could no longer carry their fortunes, but began to behave themselves unseemly. To the seeing eye they now began to seem foul, for they were losing the fairest bloom from their most precious treasure . . . now that they were taking the infection of wicked coveting and pride of power."

Eventually Zeus, king of the gods, resolved to inflict punishment on Atlantis that would temper its worldly ambitions and restore it to piety. Accordingly, he "gathered all the gods in his most honorable residence, even that that stands at the world's center and overlooks all that has part in becoming, and when he had gathered them there, he said—" And there Plato's dialogue breaks off.

How is this vivid story, at once so detailed and so

Writers have speculated that the 1513 Piri Reis map, showing portions of the Americas and Africa, must have been made with the help of an advanced culture like Atlantis.

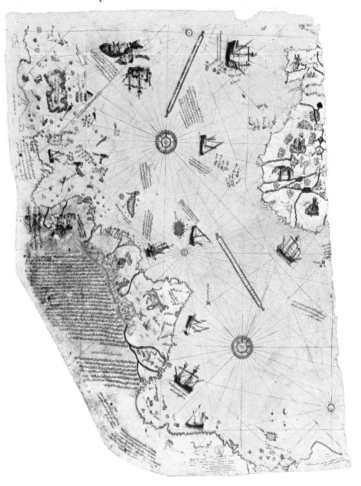

unlikely, to be interpreted? Did Plato fabricate the whole thing? Or was it a fanciful tale woven by Critias, or Solon, or the priest of Saïs? Why in existing historical and mythological records written prior to Plato's time is there no direct reference to Atlantis? Is it possible that an Athenian state of any consequence could have actually existed in 9600 B.C., or that Egyptian records included that distant epoch, nearly 10 millenniums before the birth of Christ? And why did Aristotle, Plato's most eminent pupil, simply dismiss the whole subject of Atlantis with the pithy comment, "He who created it also destroyed it"?

These or similar questions must have occurred to Plato's contemporaries and immediate successors, and yet, aside from Aristotle, there is almost no record of what conclusions they might have drawn. For the next existing reference to Atlantis appeared 300 years later in the work of a geographer and historian, Strabo, a contemporary of Christ's, who doubted the story's authenticity. Influential scholars of the early Christian Era took varying positions on Atlantis: Philo of Alexandria believed in it; Pliny the Elder was skeptical; Plutarch was evasive. But with one exception, none cited any authority for the story save Plato. That exception was a 5th-century A.D. philosopher named Proclus, who referred to a manuscript by a historian and geographer, Marcellus. In the manuscript it was claimed that the traditions of Atlantis were collected by travelers to a remote island and that the subject of Atlantis had long been a topic of lively discussion in the academy at Alexandria in Egypt. Unfortunately, the manuscript has been lost, and there is today no way to corroborate the assertions made by Marcellus.

Speculation about Atlantis waxed and waned during the tumultuous millennium that followed the fall of Rome, and for nearly six centuries thereafter no significant new evidence or ideas were added to the controversy. With the dawning of the Age of Exploration, however, interest in the fabulous lost continent rekindled. As men set off across the oceans, some suggested that Atlantis might not have sunk beneath the waves and that the lands newly discovered by Christopher Columbus were in fact Atlantis. Others, taking a more traditional view, were content to see in the West Indies, the Azores, the Canaries or other Atlantic islands the remnants of Plato's sea-swallowed land of

In 1803, Bory de Saint-Vincent, a French naturalist and traveler, published this map to illustrate his theory that Atlantis had existed just west of Africa. All that remained of the great empire, he claimed, was the Canary Islands, Madeira and the Azores.

German geographer Sebastian Munster, working in 1540, thought that South America might be Atlantis.

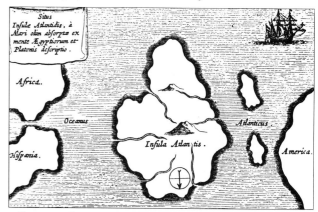

Following Plato, Father Athanasius Kircher situated Atlantis in the mid Atlantic in his 1678 map. For inexplicable reasons he reversed north and south, putting the North Pole at the bottom of the map.

burnished orichalch, circular islands, harbors and canals.

Throughout the 16th, 17th, 18th and 19th centuries, Atlantean speculation proliferated. Citing such sources as the Bible, classical literature, ancient myths and a smattering of amateur archeology, theorists were able to find reasons for spotting Atlantis not only in the Atlantic but also in Sweden, the North Sea, the Mediterranean and even the Sahara.

Today Atlantologists may smile at such fanciful hypotheses—even in their own time they were not taken very seriously—but the ideas of at least one man were not to be dismissed so lightly.

Ignatius Donnelly was neither a professional scientist, explorer nor historian. He was, in fact, a politician, a U.S. congressman and former lieutenant governor of Minnesota. He was also an intelligent, indefatigably curious person (he was reputed to be the best-read man in Congress) who happened to read Plato with absolute seriousness. His book *Atlantis: The Antediluvian World*, published in 1882, quickly became an international best seller, is still widely read today and remains a model for most contemporary Atlantean theorizing.

Donnelly did not present new evidence for the existence of Atlantis. Rather, he created a brilliantly persuasive synthesis of existing evidence, including seemingly unconnected bits of information garnered from such diverse fields as archeology, oceanography, philology, geology, history, mythology, ethnology, zoology and botany. These he fashioned into a complex sequence of arguments that not only seemed to support Plato's story in nearly every respect but added many new and intriguing details as well.

According to Donnelly, an overwhelming mass of diverse and circumstantial evidence pointed to the fact that in prehistoric times there must have existed in the Atlantic Ocean a great and highly civilized empire. Its center, Donnelly reasoned, was a large island-continent located to the west of the Strait of Gibraltar. Chains of lesser islands and ridges, like steppingstones, linked it geographically to both the Old and New Worlds. The empire's outlying colonies extended as far west as Peru and the Mississippi Valley, as far east as the Mediterranean, including Egypt, and as far north as Ireland. Its economic and cultural contacts supposedly reached all the way to India and China.

The inhabitants of this empire, said Donnelly, in-

In the 2,000 years since Plato first described the wonders of Atlantis, hundreds of scholars and well-meaning amateurs have searched for them and, in the process, have dotted the globe with possible sites. Some 45 are shown on the map above.

Labels on the illustration:

Palace Temple to Poseidon
Grove of Poseidon Temples
Gymnasiums Gardens
Barracks Orichalch-covered wall
SMALLER RING ISLAND
Tin wall
Copper wall LARGER RING ISLAND Race course
Barracks
Bridge Dockyards Shipping basins
Entry to subterranean canal for triremes
Canal to sea
Stone wall
Trireme
SEA

According to Plato, the capital of Atlantis was a 14-mile-wide complex of canals, walls, gardens, barracks and a public race track, arranged in circles around a royal palace and temple to the sea god Poseidon, the city's patron.

the middle of the Atlantic to serve as a bridge and that it was not merely a bridge but the source of Bronze Age culture as well.

Atlantis, he proposed provocatively, if incorrectly, was in fact all legendary worlds—the Bible's Garden of Eden, Homer's Elysian fields, the Asgard of Norse mythology. And the pantheons of ancient gods in such scattered locations as Greece, Scandinavia, Phoenicia and India were in fact mythical re-creations of the kings and queens who had once lived in Atlantis.

We now know that much of the information on which Donnelly relied was not accurate, although this was due less to any fault of Donnelly's than to defects in the state of scientific knowledge at the time he was writing. Nonetheless, Donnelly overstated and misinterpreted much of the information that he did have. As Atlantologist L. Sprague de Camp wrote some 70 years later: "Since Donnelly's formidable learning is likely to stun the average reader into taking his statements at face value, a close look at his book is needed to show how careless, tendentious, and generally worthless it is." A more basic challenge to Donnelly's reasoning today is that many anthropologists now reject such a sweeping diffusionist theory, arguing that evidence shows that cultures *do* frequently tend to evolve in similar ways (according to this, the convergence theory), regardless of whether they have contact with one another or not.

Another problem concerns the nature of the catastrophe that allegedly destroyed Atlantis. Donnelly was

cluded three racial groups. The most civilized was composed of small-boned and brown-reddish people somewhat similar to present-day Central American Indians, Berbers or Egyptians. The second group was the sons of Shem, possibly the yellow or Turanian race. The third group, largest and white-skinned, resembled modern Greeks, Scandinavians or Celts. Despite some struggles among the different peoples for supremacy, the groups worked together to create an exceptionally sophisticated Bronze Age culture and had advanced well into Iron Age technology by the time the great catastrophe overtook them.

What was the evidence that led Donnelly to these conclusions? For the most part he relied on what anthropologists now call the diffusionist theory, a theory that suggests that if similar cultures arise in widely separated geographic locations, they probably have not done so independently but must somehow have been linked to one another, either by direct contact or through some intermediary. Thus when Donnelly found what he considered to be striking similarities in temples and pyramids in Yucatan, Mexico; Egypt and the Middle East, he immediately assumed that such architecture must have come from a common source. In the same way, any similarities Donnelly could find between Bronze Age agricultural implements in Switzerland and Africa, or between words used by American Indians and Chinese, became grist for his diffusionist mill. And because Bronze Age culture could not easily have spread between Europe and the Americas across 3,000 miles of empty ocean, Donnelly made two fabulous assumptions: that Atlantis must have been in

Many parallels exist between Plato's mythical Atlantis and the Minoan culture on Crete. Both netted bulls, as shown on the Minoan cup at left; both worshiped Poseidon, the sea god who appears on the Greek coin at right.

content to ascribe Atlantis's end to a combination of earthquakes, volcanic eruptions and floods, but modern geophysicists say that it is unimaginable that any such convulsion could destroy an entire continent, and certainly not in the space of 48 hours. Some modern writers have tried to meet this objection by hypothesizing other forms of catastrophe. Immanuel Velikovsky, for example, suggested in his book *Worlds in Collision* that the legend of Atlantis's destruction might have been related to a global disaster caused when a giant comet—now the planet Venus—brushed close to Earth. In a similar vein, the German physicist Otto Muck assembled evidence to indicate that Atlantis must have been demolished by a massive asteroid. But all such suppositions are unproven and have found little, if any, support where they need it most: in the scientific community. And in the end, no matter how ingenious and elaborate the explanations, only the actual physical discovery of Atlantis in incontrovertible form is going to convince the skeptics, scientific or otherwise.

What has the search for tangible proof produced at three likely sites—the mid Atlantic, the western Atlantic and the Mediterranean?

Atlantis was famed for its powerful fleet, as were the Minoans, whose ships, like the trireme depicted on this bas-relief, regularly sailed to Egypt, Asia Minor and Sicily.

Plato's Paradise

Plato's accounts of Atlantis included lush descriptions, such as this one from the Critias:

Though their empire brought them a great external revenue, it was the island itself which furnished the main provision for all purposes of life. In the first place it yielded all products of the miner's industry, solid and fusible alike, including one which is now only a name but was then something more, orichalch, which was excavated in various parts of the island, and had then a higher value than any metal except gold. It also bore in its forests a generous supply of all timbers serviceable to the carpenter and builder and maintained a sufficiency of animals wild and domesticated; even elephants were plentiful. There was ample pasture for this the largest and most voracious of brutes, no less than for all the other creatures of marsh, lake and river, mountain and plain. Besides all this, the soil bore all aromatic substances still to be found on earth, roots, stalks, canes, gums exuded by flowers and fruits, and they throve on it. Then, as for cultivated fruits, the dry sort which is meant to be our food supply . . . as well as the woodland kind which gives us meat and drink and oil together, the fruit of trees that ministers to our pleasure and merriment and is so hard to preserve, and that we serve as welcome dessert to a jaded man to charm away his satiety—all these were produced by that sacred island, which then lay open to the sun, in marvelous beauty and inexhaustible profusion. So the kings employed all these gifts of the soil to construct and beautify their temples, royal residences, harbors, docks, and domain.

The mid Atlantic, opposite the Strait of Gibraltar, seems to be the area where Plato said Atlantis existed and is, therefore, where most traditional Atlantologists suppose it may be found. Donnelly, like many others before and since, argued that the Azores must be the last above-water traces of the lost continent, the tips of mountains that encircled the island of the royal city. But thus far, neither archeological investigations of the Azores nor oceanographic explorations of the neighboring seabed have produced any evidence of either a lost civilization or a large, submerged island. In fact, contemporary geologic thinking makes it seem extremely unlikely that any such evidence will ever be found.

According to the scenario most favored today by geologists and oceanographers, North and South America were once joined with Europe, Asia and Africa, and for the past 180 to 200 million years have been drifting apart. More accurately stated, they have been separated by the pull of gravity and the push of igneous materials bubbling out of a gigantic crack in the earth's crust. Up through this fracture in the ocean floor, which separates the Eastern and Western hemispheres, molten rock has forced its way from the earth's searing core. Cooled rock, constantly shouldered aside to make room for new molten material, has spread to the east and west to form oceanic plains. And it is the constant, mushrooming growth of these igneous shoals, along with the pull of gravity, that has moved the initially joined continents ever farther apart.

If this dramatic scenario is correct, and most scientists believe it is, the Atlantic Ocean contains no sunken land masses at all. The Azores, for example, would almost certainly have been formed not when continental mountains sank *beneath* the waves, but when volcanoes associated with the mid-Atlantic fracture thrust *upward* from the seabed. And even if other volcanic islands near the fracture might once have risen above sea level, only to sink back, their size could never have approached that of the magnificent complex of island rings described by Plato.

Curiously, the kind of evidence traditional Atlantologists have vainly sought in the mid Atlantic may have turned up along the western edge of the Atlantic on the continental shelf. Whatever the meaning of this evidence may be—and it may have nothing to do with Atlantis at all—the story of its discovery is one of the most bizarre in the annals of modern archeology.

Underwater blocks of stone that look like parts of roads and walls have led some to speculate that Atlantis lies near Bimini's coast. Most researchers feel, however, that the blocks are natural formations.

The Azores (the volcanic lake of São Miguel is shown above) have often been linked with Atlantis. The theory of continental drift makes this an unlikely possibility.

Through an awesome ocean-bottom crack in the Mid-Atlantic Ridge (right, center), molten rock boils up and helps move continents apart. No Atlantean continent could have disappeared in the area because (according to the theory of plate tectonics) continents have moved sideways while the ocean bottom has been formed of new igneous rock.

In 1933 the popular American seer and alleged clairvoyant Edgar Cayce, while in a self-induced trance, made this prediction: "In the sunken portion of Atlantis, or Poseidia, . . . a portion of the temples may yet be discovered under the slime of ages of sea water—near what is known as Bimini, off the coast of Florida." Strangely enough, in 1968 a team of underwater explorers discovered what appeared to be a 1,900-foot-long J-shaped structure made of huge rectangular stones lying on the sea floor, a half-mile off Paradise Point, North Bimini, in the Bahamas.

Although many geologists were quick to dismiss these stones as an unusual natural rock formation, others, abetted by numerous amateur archeologists and Atlantologists, were equally sure the arrangement was man-made. In recent years the site's most persistent investigator has been Dr. David Zink, who became interested in the Bimini find while teaching English at the U.S. Air Force Academy. Since 1974, Zink has conducted repeated underwater explorations in the ocean off North Bimini and has located several more sites. Among his reported findings are a shaped stone with tongue-and-groove edges, a piece of eroded marble that might once have been a sculptured head, and geometric patterns in the placement of the stones that suggest, according to Zink, astronomical references to the seven-starred constellation Pleiades, some 400 light-years away. The stones, says Zink, are enormously old and are not native to the area. Although they cannot be related to any known culture on lands even remotely adjacent to the site, the Bimini stones, insists Zink, must nonetheless have been carved and set in place by human hands.

But even if this were so, would the stones relate in any way to Atlantis? That they now lie underwater does not necessarily indicate a past catastrophe. The seabed on which the mysterious stones rest is not part of the Atlantic Ocean abyss but lies along the comparatively shallow North American continental shelf. The steady rise of the sea level since the last ice age is sufficient to account for the depth at which the stones are found, even if they *had* been on dry land as recently as 6,000 years ago. Nor do the Bimini stones—even supposing they were fashioned by man, a tenuous speculation at best—show any of the architectural sophistication that

Plate Tectonics: No Room for Atlantis

The strongest challenge to the possibility that the ruins of Atlantis lie somewhere in the depths of the Atlantic Ocean comes from a complicated geophysical theory known as plate tectonics.

Yet for all the intricacy of its arguments and evidence, the theory—sometimes referred to as the theory of continental drift—derives from a commonplace observation that schoolchildren have been making for years. It is that the edges of some opposing continents look as if they might fit together in jigsaw-puzzle fashion. For geologists, however, the corollary of this observation, that all the continents must at one time have been joined, was for centuries both unacceptable and annoying, because they knew of no explanation that would account for any type of continental movement. In fact, when German meteorologist Alfred Wegener produced in 1915 a coherent picture of how the prehistoric earth might have looked (right) with its land masses joined, he was ridiculed by some of his peers and thought a wild man. Today Wegener, now considered to be the father of continental drift, is so highly regarded that it has been suggested that a crater on the moon be named for him.

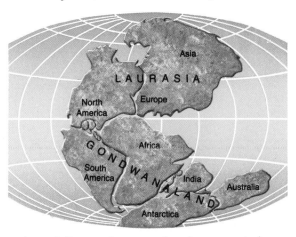

Geologists believe continents may have begun as a single mass, named Pangaea by meteorologist Alfred Wegener in 1915.

It was not until the 1960s that geologists began to find evidence that would support Wegener's hypotheses. The result, based on modern topographic and core-sampling techniques, is a different, more dynamic picture of the earth's crust. According to the old view, a cross section of our planet would reveal a solid core encased by molten lead and layers of rock in gradually lessening degrees of liquefaction, the whole being wrapped in a thin, rigid crust. The crucial variation in the new view is that the crust, though composed of rigid elements, is itself mobile. Thus, upper crust chunks, such as continents and large islands, are thought to ride on top of plate-like slabs of lower crust. These plate-like slabs, known collectively as the lithosphere, float in turn on a semi-molten sea of crystal slush called the asthenosphere. As a result, when molten rock from the asthenosphere boils into a crack separating two plates, it helps force the plates and continents apart. When the lava cools, it hardens and becomes part of the lithosphere.

Since asthenospheric rock is constantly forcing its way up through cracks between plates, why don't the plates run out of room and jam? The answer is that there are also "swallowing" cracks, called subduction zones. Here, gravity is at work, drawing plate edges downward, and it may be as active a force in moving continents as the upward thrust of molten rock. Subduction zones develop where two plates collide with such force that one buckles and its edge slides under the edge of the other, more resistant plate.

According to this new concept, the Atlantic Ocean sprawls east and west of a crack known as the Mid-Atlantic Ridge. This means that the Atlantic basin on either side is, in effect, a gradually expanding field of cooled rock. Three giant plates are constantly being shifted by the slow expansion of this massive field— the North American Plate, the South American Plate and the African Plate.

The irresistible—and for Atlantologists damaging—conclusion of this concept is that a continent-sized land mass could never have existed in the Atlantic basin. Because the only subduction zone in the entire area is a small one in the vicinity of the Caribbean, and its function seems to be to adjust tension between the great North and South American plates. If a continent-sized Atlantis existed, did it ride on its own plate? And if so, where did that plate go? Thus, on the basis of modern plate tectonics, a theory accepted by the vast majority of geophysicists and oceanographers, Atlantis cannot have been where it was supposed to have been—in the Atlantic.

Plato attributed to Atlantis. If they are indeed the primitive remains of some unknown megalithic culture, it must have been a far cry from the fabled empire that could launch a fleet of 1,200 ships and threaten the civilizations that dotted the Mediterranean world.

This problem of trying to find evidence commensurate with Plato's description of Atlantis has inevitably drawn investigators back to the Mediterranean Sea, the cradle of classical civilization. As early as 1909, Prof. K. T. Frost of The Queen's University, Belfast, advanced the theory that Plato's legend may actually have referred to the Minoan civilization that flourished on Crete until about 1400 B.C. Crete, argued Frost, was an imperial island that dominated the ancient Mediterranean through trade and force of arms. In addition, its royal city, Knossos, apparently bore some resemblance to the city described by Plato, and several Cretan ceremonies, especially bullfighting, are similar to those mentioned in the *Critias*. But there are many difficulties with Frost's hypothesis, not the least of which is that Crete quite obviously did not sink beneath the sea as the result of a devastating calamity.

In 1939 the Greek archeologist Spyridos Marinatos attempted to circumvent this objection by suggesting

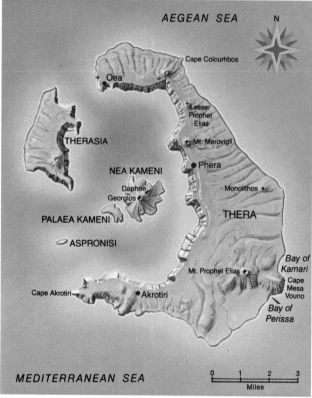

The spectacular volcanic eruption of Santorini in 1470 B.C. buried the Minoan outpost there. When the volcano's cone collapsed, it created jagged cliffs and an island-dotted harbor (above). Some Atlantologists have made the point that the cliffs' reds and blacks (left) match the hues of certain buildings described by Plato in his *Dialogues*.

that a gigantic volcanic eruption, which in 1470 B.C. partially destroyed the Aegean island of Thera, 62 miles north of Crete, may have been the cause of the Minoan civilization's collapse. The sequence: a deadly spate of ash, then a monstrous volcanic eruption, followed by tidal waves and earthquakes. In recent years Marinatos's idea has received considerable support with the discovery of extensive Minoan artifacts on what today remains of the shattered volcano Santorini. These discoveries, in turn, have prompted some scholars and archeologists to support what is currently the most fashionable theory about Atlantis.

Santorini, they argue, must itself have been Atlantis, the ancient metropolis of the Minoan empire. And, indeed, some of the facts seem to fit. The Minoan civilization at Santorini was probably advanced enough to meet Platonic precepts of Atlantean sophistication. Santorini's circular form would seem to conform to the size and plan Plato attributed to Atlantis's ancient capital city. And most gratifying of all for Atlantologists, Santorini's violent eruption provides a believable catastrophe to end the civilization.

All this is persuasive as far as it goes. But does it go far enough? If we believe that Santorini was Atlantis, we must also believe that Plato was wildly wrong not only about the location of Atlantis, but also about its size and the date of its destruction. Some researchers have theorized that the story, since it first appeared in Egyptian accounts, may have been naturally enhanced in its retellings before it reached Plato's ears. Others have suggested that because of a mix-up in translation, a factor of 10 was added both to the size of Atlantis and the date of its destruction. Yet because Plato is the sole known authority for Atlantis, it seems opportunistic to believe the facts that fit and rework those that seem not to apply; for example, by suggesting that when Plato said "Pillars of Hercules," he meant not the Atlantic beyond Gibraltar but the Aegean instead. Moreover, since we know little of Minoan history, we cannot be absolutely sure that the relationship between the Minoan and Atlantean empires is as direct as it might appear. Some scholars doubt that there ever really was a Minoan empire in the modern sense of the word. Others insist that there is good reason to believe that Minoan civilization continued to flourish after Santorini exploded. The ongoing archeological investigation of Thera and Crete may help solve some of these mysteries. Nonetheless, one of the most compelling unknowns involving the Atlantean apocrypha lies beyond the facts, raising questions about the mind and man's past that are as provocative as those engendered by the Atlantis legend itself.

Why does the captivating story of Atlantis live on today with such vigor, two millenniums after its first telling? Could it be a kind of perfect myth, one that plucked ancient and modern strings so attuned to hu-

Houses on the island of Thera were lavishly decorated with enormous frescoes, like that of the children fighting above. The picture may be the first to show a kind of boxing glove.

man need that it could not be resisted? Could it reflect in some elemental biological manner a desire to return to our watery beginnings, and could such ancient influences now be inherent in the myriad connections that bind the 10 billion cells in our brains?

No one can say with certainty, of course; and yet the very heft of human industry and conjecture that surround Atlantis has led to endless and sometimes professional speculation. In simplest terms, it may be that we really need such stories to transport us beyond everyday cares. "Just as there may be a fear of the unknown," says Dr. Gertrude Williams, a St. Louis psychologist, "there is embedded in the human psyche a wish for the unknown, a desire to explore the offbeat."

Specialists in mythology make a different point, emphasizing that most cultures have legends about earthly paradises. As the noted mythologist Mircea Eliade has suggested, there is a nearly universal myth about "the perfection of the beginning of things," about the earthly paradise or golden age that once existed when God and man were in harmony. But, as Eliade

The expulsion from the Garden of Eden, above, painted by 15th-century Italian artist Giovanni di Paolo, parallels paradise-lost myths found in many cultures.

puts it, "When Heaven was rudely 'separated' from Earth, when it became 'distant,' as it is today, . . . the paradisial stage was over and humanity arrived at its present state."

A second theme, apocalypse, is often connected with the first. Heaven, offended by some human transgression, ends the golden age in a holocaust of fire or flood. Subsequent ages of man may, for similar reasons, be terminated in a similar way. Does this mean, as some people have inferred, that all or most of the drowned-world legends must be mythologized versions of real events that occurred before the dawn of written history? Most modern mythologists would say no. Myths, they say, are primarily concerned with explaining the nature of man's relationship to the natural and supernatural world around him. Even though myths may appear to describe *what* happened, their real purpose is to reveal the *hows* and *whys* of happenings. For this reason, myths tend to cluster around certain basic themes, and one that has recurred with surprising frequency is the theme of drowned worlds.

Some scholars suggest that the whole idea of Atlantis, for example, can be traced not to any historical reality, but to the golden age and apocalypse myths that flourished in the Middle East long before Plato's time and from which some Greek myths were borrowed. Plato, they argue, merely took these myths, combined them with then-fashionable Greek philosophic ideas about alternate cycles of growth and decay, and fabricated for his readers a moral fable of what can happen when a virtuous and prosperous society displeases the gods. If this is true, Plato may have had a more sophisticated understanding of the function of myth than a good many of his Atlantologist successors.

Men have sailed to mist-covered islands like these near South America, tracked through jungles and probed the depths of the

Even now the mythical elements of the Atlantis story, paradise destroyed by catastrophe, remain inescapable. Certainly, it is possible to speculate that in a world of remarkable accomplishment—a world nonetheless threatened by nuclear disaster—interest in Atlantis is particularly relevant. Nor is it surprising that other stories of disaster, in whatever guise, remain popular. Science-fiction tales of invasion by interplanetary armies, near-mythic accounts of war, and even the oft-told story of the sinking of the lavish and impregnable *Titanic* clearly embody the essentials of the Atlantis chronicle and, by implication, the course of human life itself.

According to other modern theorists, myths may be able to influence us even though we have never heard them. The psychiatrist and philosopher Carl G. Jung argued that we are born with certain archetypical mythical ideas embedded in our minds just as surely as we are born with fingers and toes. This brain-bound reservoir of inherited mythical knowledge was called by Jung "the collective unconscious." Jung's assertions may be unprovable, but a number of contemporary researchers—notably in the fields of ethnology and linguistics—have produced enough evidence to suggest that Jung may not have been altogether wrong.

To such psychic speculation, modern geologic theory now adds a tantalizing footnote. Scientists today believe that an extraordinary period of flooding may have caused the filling in of the Mediterranean some 5.5 million years ago, just about the time early man was struggling to walk on the African plains. That such human prototypes could have formed any memories of the event, or even been aware of it, seems highly unlikely, even preposterous. And yet the flooding of the then-empty Mediterranean basin at the end of the

Bizarre tales of creatures on Mount Shasta in California have led to fanciful speculation that they might be Lemurians, ancient inhabitants of a mythical Pacific continent.

Miocene epoch must have been a truly extraordinary event, one that launched a deluge that lasted 1,000 years and roared with a thunder hundreds of times greater than that unleashed by any of today's great cascades.

Does the myth of Atlantis echo such realities, or is it a tale oft told primarily to enliven the tedium of human existence? The fairest answer probably is that it reflects both elements, and as such will be forever lost and forever found again in the human mind.

ocean in their efforts to find a lost paradise on earth, a near-universal myth of which Atlantis is but one example.

Velikovsky: Theories in Collision

*I*n the lifetime of Yao, the sun did not set for ten full days and the entire land was flooded . . . [by an immense wave] that reached the sky.

—Canons of the [Chinese] emperor Yao, c. 2400 B.C.

At the same time that the seas were heaped up in immense tides, a pageant went on in the sky which presented itself to the horrified onlookers on earth as a gigantic battle.

—Immanuel Velikovsky, *Worlds in Collision*, 1950

Until relatively recent times many people believed that the history of our planet might best be understood in terms of a series of global catastrophes. How else to explain such mysteries as lost cities beneath the sea, evidence of cultivation in the midst of deserts or the bones of extinct animals? Prehistoric mythmakers and sophisticated 18th-century natural philosophers may have differed in their various interpretations of the agencies that produced such cosmic paroxysms, but they did agree on one essential point: some catastrophic event must have occurred.

In the mid-19th century, however, existing catastrophic wisdom underwent revision. In the 1600s Sir Isaac Newton (1642–1727) had provided the scientific world with a model of celestial mechanics that was as serene and orderly as clockwork. Now, evolutionist Charles Darwin (1809–82) and geologist Sir Charles Lyell (1797–1875) did much the same for the history of the earth. All the forces that have acted on our planet, they said, are operating right now, albeit so slowly that we have difficulty recognizing them. Living species are incessantly mutating, increasing, decreasing, even becoming extinct. Mountains, oceans and deserts are constantly in the process of either forming or disappearing. Change is everywhere, but it is uniform and slow, not cataclysmic. By the mid-20th century, this uniformitarianism had become an orthodox scientific principle.

Then in 1950 with the publication of his book *Worlds in Collision,* Immanuel Velikovsky (1895–1979) introduced what was perhaps the most astonishing and provocative catastrophe theory ever propounded: that, contrary to popular belief, the planet Venus is a recent addition to our solar system and twice precipitated vast upheavals on Earth. The Establishment reacted, in the words of journalist Russell Lynes, as if it "had been stung by a hornet from outer space." Efforts were made to suppress Velikovsky's book even before publication, and subsequently such pressure was applied to the book's publisher, Macmillan, that it gave Velikovsky's contract to another house. Meanwhile, to the fury of Velikovsky's opponents, *Worlds in Collision* rapidly became an international best seller.

Why did the scientific world react so violently to the ideas of a 55-year-old Russian immigrant? Possibly because, unlike most other recent catastrophists, Velikovsky was far from being an obvious crank. An accomplished linguist, well trained in law, medicine and ancient history, he had pursued a career as a psychoanalyst in Israel and Europe before going to the United States in 1939. It was while preparing a treatise on Freud's heroes that Velikovsky became interested in

A runaway Venus, far left, careening past Earth about 3,500 years ago accounted for such legendary catastrophes as the parting of the Red Sea, Immanuel Velikovsky claimed. His fiercely disputed theories proposed that Venus, then a fragment of Jupiter, wreaked planetary havoc before settling into its present orbit.

like a gigantic comet, according to Velikovsky, Venus then passed close enough to Earth around 1500 B.C. to cause global devastation—hurricanes, earthquakes, meteor showers, tidal waves, the destruction of whole continents (including, perhaps, Atlantis), even a violent tilting of the earth's rotational axis. Subsequently, near the beginning of the 8th century B.C., Venus spun so close to Mars that it threw that planet out of its orbit and thus brought about a series of near collisions between Earth and Mars, ending in 687 B.C. Eventually, Venus settled into its own stable planetary orbit, though it retains to this day many unusual features—such as anomalous rotation, high surface temperature and a dense atmosphere—all of which, Velikovsky believed, testify to its violent origins and bizarre history.

Briefly summarized, this theory may sound fantastic, but in fact its author buttressed his arguments with massive documentation, drawing on many disciplines, from astronomy to archeology. Indeed, he proposed enough circumstantial "evidence" to keep certain scientists arguing for decades, which is precisely what they have done since 1950.

Recent space probes have not only confirmed several of Velikovsky's astrophysical predictions, but have also overturned some of the shibboleths of conventional science in the process. Scientists have found that Venus is hot and does have an anomalous rotation. And electromagnetism does appear to be, like gravity, an essential element in celestial mechanics. Jupiter does emit radio noise. The moon's rocks are magnetic. Yet many of Velikovsky's other predictions remain unproven, and a few, for example that Mars's polar caps are composed of frozen carbohydrates, appear to have been disproved.

During his controversy-ridden lifetime, Velikovsky was at times able to defend himself successfully against specific criticisms from such world-renowned astronomers as Carl Sagan and the late Donald Menzel. Yet the essential question remains: Was Velikovsky's theory of global catastrophe correct? Most scientists refuse to believe it. But, thanks to Velikovsky, many of them are almost certainly less adamantly uniformitarian than they once were. As Robert Jastrow, famed director of NASA's Institute for Space Studies, grudgingly conceded shortly after Velikovsky's death, "It may have been Dr. Velikovsky's special genius that he was able to divine the truth although he could not support it with convincing evidence."

both the universality and the similarity of ancient catastrophe legends. Like Ignatius Donnelly and others before him, Velikovsky began to wonder if these legends might not be reflections of historical truth. Yet unlike Donnelly, Velikovsky was able to bring to these speculations a formidable array of academic talents.

The fruit of Velikovsky's researches, the theory introduced in *Worlds in Collision* and elaborated on in *Earth in Upheaval*, *Ages in Chaos* and other works, was startling. It argued that the planet Venus was ejected from Jupiter thousands of years before the birth of Christ. Wandering erratically through the solar system

For centuries men and women have believed
in the existence and power of secret knowledge
and the elitism of occult societies.

ART OF MAGIC

Union of opposites illustrated
a German text on alchemy.

*M*agic has power to experience and fathom
things which are inaccessible to human
reason. For magic is a great secret wisdom, just
as reason is a great public folly.

—Paracelsus (1493–1541)

*Magic is the traditional science of the secrets of
Nature which has been transmitted to us from
the magi. By means of this science the adept
becomes invested with a species of relative om-
nipotence and can operate superhumanly—that
is, after a manner which transcends the normal
possibility of man.*

—Eliphas Lévi (1810-75)

Mankind's drive to comprehend and con-
trol unseen forces in the universe is one of the great
themes in human history. Over the centuries men and
women have created remarkable systems of thought
and belief, each with the potential to explain and interpret the world to willing listeners, each extending the
promise of order and control.

In modern times three such systems—religion, science, philosophy—continue to flourish, buoyed by the
heft of historical respectability and nurtured by their
ability to adapt as man has penetrated the mysteries of
the natural world and struggled to refine his social and
cerebral powers. Only the art of magic, once as worthy

The promises of magic range from conjuring a demon—
shown as "a king, bearded, riding on a dragon" in Francis
Barrett's 1801 text *The Magus*—to finding eternal truth.

and binding a discipline as the others, has
dropped from intellectual favor: as conjur-
ers' stage art, it is tolerated; as a system of
belief, it is scorned.

Yet there was a time when the art of
magic and the painstaking and often covert
pursuit of its lore and ritual, its paraphernalia and fundamental principles, occupied
the minds of great scholars across Europe.
And if the tenets of their belief—that man
is but a tiny model of the greater natural
world, that all existence is linked either in
opposite or corresponding terms, that intuitive thought may have far greater potency
than rational pursuits, that in every age there have been
certain men possessed of secret knowledge capable of
unleashing supernatural power—seem unwieldy today,
they nonetheless continue to provoke considerable
interest in a world ever more intrigued by parapsychological exploration.

Even before the rise of scholar-magicians and the
pursuit of ritual magic in Renaissance Europe, men
with special powers had appeared in lands along the
eastern end of the Mediterranean, their pursuits often
in conflict with developing systems of religious belief.

"But there was a man named Simon who had
previously practiced magic in the city and amazed the
nation of Samaria, saying that he himself was somebody
great. They all gave heed to him, from the least to the
greatest, saying, 'This man is that power of God which
is called Great.'" So reads the New Testament Book of

The Acts of the Apostles. According to other early Christian writings, the magician Simon could make himself invisible, assume the form of other people and animals, walk through stone walls, pass unharmed through fire, and fly through the air. One story describes how, after having been condemned to death by the emperor Nero, he supposedly survived decapitation and became an imperial court wizard. Perhaps the most famous of all stories about Simon relates the circumstances of his final downfall: he had challenged the Apostle Peter to a magical duel and was about to fly through a window when Peter, using the power of prayer, sent him crashing to his doom.

Little is known about the actual life of Simon the magician, or Simon Magus. Some scholars have identified him as Simon the Gnostic, leader of an early heretical Christian sect that believed that the way to salvation was through the use of secret knowledge. Because early Church fathers were assiduous in obliterating heretical texts, the truth will probably never be known.

Yet whatever the connection between Simon Magus and the Gnostics, neither Peter's triumph nor the suppression of Gnostic texts succeeded in wiping out certain Gnostic tenets. And just as early Christianity was indebted to Judaism, so did Gnosticism probably draw on earlier Oriental and pagan beliefs, in which magical systems were accepted practice and charms and numerology, or number mysticism, common. In addition, when Judaism became uprooted, it sought spiritual refuge in its own body of secret knowledge, the cabala, which promised, if properly studied, to reveal the secrets of life. The cabala, which surely owes much to the principles of the Gnostics, is regarded as one of the world's most ancient systems of mystical thought. One of its essential doctrines is that the human being possesses a "spirit body," one that can detach itself from the mortal body and ascend to a higher plane.

Moving to the north across barbarian lands, various forms of secret knowledge penetrated the Celtic fastness of Britain and Ireland, where druidism, with its practice of magic, was already flourishing. Most villages had their practitioners of simple magic, "canny folk," as they were known, and as late as 1638 a British document spoke of "Mother Nottingham, who for her time was prettily well skilled in casting of waters . . . and one Hatfield in Pepper Alley, he doeth pretty well for a thing that's lost. There's another in Coleharbour that's skilled in the planets."

Alongside this spell-casting magic, however, there developed, inspired by the printed word and infusions of foreign systems of occult knowledge, a group of special scholarly men, men for whom magic seemed to be the means to extraordinary ends: the discovery and harnessing of the supernatural forces of nature. Some were scholars whose searches led them deeply into the poorly understood realm of the mind, and, indeed, the words *scholar* and *magician* often carried the same meaning. Others were engaging charlatans. One was a Catholic saint whose magical demonstrations were called miracles by the Church. Yet despite their many differences, they were all in some manner fluent in that elusive tongue we call magic.

Simon Magus was defeated, according to legend, when the Apostle Peter's prayers overwhelmed the evil forces holding him up during a display of levitation. The sorcerer fell to the earth, shattered both his legs and eventually died.

With the possible exception of the legendary Merlin, believed by some to be a 6th-century Welsh bard whose exploits at King Arthur's court were entirely literary invention, no figure so embodies the popular concept of the magician as does Faust, whose name is synonymous with the selling of one's soul to the devil in exchange for great knowledge and power. The legend has grown in its lengthy retellings, but a self-proclaimed magician named Faust, whose given name was either Johann or Georg, was born in the late 15th century and was infamous by general report. On August 20, 1507, the learned physicist Johannes Tritheim wrote to his colleague Johannes Virdung, a professor of astrology at the University of Heidelberg, about Faust: "The man of whom you wrote me, who has presumed to call himself the prince of necromancers, is a vagabond, a babbler and a rogue." The official municipal records of the city of Ingolstadt for June 17, 1528, also contained a short reference to the unsavory character: "A certain man who called himself Dr. Georg Faust of Heidelberg was told to spend his penny elsewhere, and he pledged himself not to take vengeance on or to make fools of the authorities for this order."

Neither writer explained how Faust had earned scorn through his "magical" acts, but later reports suggested reasons for concern. It was told that Faust had once threatened a churchman by vowing that he could cause all the pots in the kitchen to fly up through the chimney. According to another account—he apparently performed much of his magic in taverns—he was able to treat his cronies to endless rounds of drinks by boring numerous holes through a tabletop and causing them to gush forth a variety of fine wines.

The sulfurous odor of the devil hung over many of the Faustian stories. It was said that Faust owed his knowledge and power to a pact he had made with the devil. Martin Luther, a contemporary, believed this was true. Faust never denied it. But there are certain indications that he may have started the story himself, in the hope of reaping some personal gain.

Faust may have been a shoddy character, but there was something admirable about his quest for knowledge. As Colin Wilson writes in the introduction to his book *The Occult*, "Faust can be seen to be the greatest symbolic drama of the West, since it is the drama of the rationalist suffocating in the dusty room of his personal consciousness, caught in the vicious circle of futility. . . . Faust's longing for the 'occult' is the instinctive desire to believe in the unseen forces, the wider significances that can break the circuit."

It may well be that the blurred record of the historical Faust is precisely what made him so appealing. Less malleable are the histories of two figures who were roughly contemporary with Faust and who must be termed proper and pious scholar-magicians of the Renaissance: Cornelius Agrippa, who like Faust was

"Hidden Wisdom" of the Cabala

The word means nothing less than "the words received" or "hidden wisdom" in Hebrew, and it defines a body of esoteric Jewish tradition that purports to offer a path to an understanding of God and the many mysteries of the universe. The cabala's origins cannot be precisely dated, but as a form of Jewish mysticism, the cabala is believed to date back at least to the time of Christ. An oral tradition for centuries, the cabala, in written form, is not a single, comprehensive text but a collection of writings, generally complementary but occasionally contradictory. The most important are the Book of Creation, written sometime between the 2nd and 6th centuries A.D., and the Book of Splendor, by the 13th-century Spaniard Moses de Leon.

The cabala's chief belief deals with a hidden reality accessible only through mystical approaches and ritualistic study. Specifically, the cabala attempts to reconcile the apparent contradictions between an unknowable God and a God who makes himself known; between a God who is good and the creator of all things and a world in which evil thrives; between a God who is infinite and eternal and a world—his creation—that is so obviously finite and doomed. The linchpin of the cabala is a diagram called the tree of life, consisting of 10 "emanations" of God and the many relationships that exist among them. The cabala also includes a number science called gematria, through which all manner of arcane interpretations of Scripture can be made. A major contributor to the revival of Jewish and Christian mysticism in the Renaissance, the cabala survives today in Judaism and, in distorted form, within occult tradition itself.

A scholar ponders the meaning of the tree of life in a 1516 edition of a 13th-century cabalistic work.

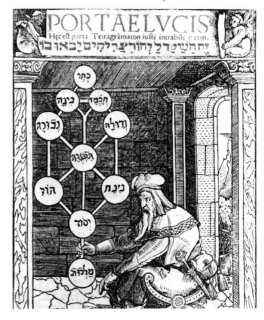

German and was born in Cologne in 1486, and Dr. John Dee, an Englishman who was born in 1527.

Agrippa, whose real name was Heinrich Cornelis, was a hard-luck genius of more than contemporary celebrity. As a young man he attended the University of Cologne, where he studied the Neoplatonists, especially the work of Proclus, and discovered the cabala. From these two sources Agrippa forged the theme that would shape his lifework: the possibility of the union of human consciousness with the One, or Godhead, that is at the center of all things.

By the age of 20, Agrippa was a court secretary to Maximilian, the Holy Roman emperor, who apparently dispatched the young man to Paris as a spy. While there, Agrippa continued his studies at the university but soon became entangled in an Italian intrigue that ended badly. After a meandering tour of Europe, Agrippa settled for a time at the University of Dôle, in France. There he became a popular lecturer on the cabala and received the degree of doctor of divinity. His quite public interest in the cabala, particularly in the number science known as gematria, eventually drew the wrath of the orthodox, and pressure from the clergy caused his patron, Maximilian's daughter, Margaret of Ghent, to withdraw her favor.

Although the book would not be published for another 20 years, it was at Dôle, when he was 24, that Agrippa wrote the masterwork of magic for which he is best remembered. *Of the Occult Philosophy* is a three-volume treatise that even now is considered to be one of the major texts on the subject. In it Agrippa declared his belief that magic had not to do with the devil or sorcery but with the obscure abilities of the mind. He postulated the supremacy of the mind over the body and indirectly anticipated modern psychiatric theory with his assertion that "the fantasy, or imagina-tive power, has a ruling power over the passions of the soul, when these are bound to sensual apprehen-sions. . . . For imagination does, of its own accord, according to the diversity of the passions, first of all change the physical body with a sensible transmutation, by changing the accidents in the body, and by moving the spirit upward or downward, inward or outward."

It is difficult to assess the extent to which Agrippa might have made use of these insights—to know, in short, whether he practiced a form of psychic magic based on his understanding of the mind's workings. The stories that come down of his "magic" are all but comic-Faustian. The most famous concerns an unfortu-nate student who sneaked into his master's study while Agrippa was out. The student was in the act of reading Agrippa's book of spells when he was confronted by a demon he had unwittingly summoned. Angrily de-manding to know why he had been called, the demon seized the young man and strangled him. When Agrip-pa returned, he commanded the demon to revive the victim long enough to escort him to the village mar-ketplace, where a sudden collapse might explain his death. The demon complied with Agrippa's order, but a scandal ensued nevertheless.

Late in life, Agrippa turned away from magic and toward the study of theology. In 1530 he published *Of the Vanity of Sciences and Arts,* a despairing work that argued that the quest for knowledge was futile. With terrifically bad timing Agrippa chose to publish his ear-ly, jubilant writings on magic at about the same time (1531), and the contradictions between the two resulted in the earlier work's being viewed as insincere. Agrippa spent the last few years of his life as a transient, and he died before he reached the age of 50, prematurely worn out and discredited by his peers.

The spark of his early interest in magic and the

In one story, Faust used magic to ride and win a wine keg; its owner had offered it to anyone able to raise it from the cellar.

As protection against demons, the scholar-magician Agrippa devised a magic circle using the three traditional conjurer's rings and the six-pointed Seal of Solomon.

workings of the mind survived, however, in *Occult Philosophy,* which would greatly influence later generations of scholars. Among them was the pre-eminent magus of England, Dr. John Dee. In contrast to the speculation surrounding Faust and Agrippa, the facts of Dee's life are well documented by his own hand and by many in his circle of acquaintances, a circle that included at least five English monarchs.

Born in 1527, the son of a minor official at the court of Henry VIII, Dee was accepted at Cambridge at the age of 15. By limiting his sleep to some four hours a night, he managed to absorb an incredible amount of knowledge, and at 19, he became an assistant professor at the newly founded Trinity College, where he developed a particular fascination for mathematics. He went on to pursue his own studies at the great universities of Louvain and Paris. He had already acquired a knowledge of alchemy and probably had studied the magical contents of the cabala.

When Dee returned to England at the age of 24, already reputed to be exceedingly wise, he was arrested, charged with treason and thrown into prison. It was the common belief of the day that the position and movement of celestial bodies had an effect on people and events on earth. Dee's mistake had been to call upon his knowledge of astrology to satisfy the request of Queen Mary to "calculate her nativity." Unfortunately the queen, also known as Bloody Mary, did not like Dee's horoscope. He was finally cleared of the treason charges and released in 1555.

Elizabeth, Mary's younger sister and successor, was more kindly disposed toward Dee and turned to him to choose the most favorable day for her coronation. Later, when the court was shaken by the discovery in Lincoln's Inn Fields of a wax effigy of the queen with a needle through its breast, Dee was consulted. After examining the effigy, he persuaded the queen that it was an insignificant practical joke.

Dee eventually retired to the country, where he assembled a library of some 4,000 volumes—a staggering achievement, considering that the university library at Cambridge then consisted of 451 books and manuscripts. He wrote widely on mathematics, astrology and geography; in 1583 he formulated a plan for the colonization of America. But always the deepest knowledge he sought eluded him. "All my lifetime," he wrote, "I had spent in learning. . . . And I found (at length) that neither any man, nor any Book . . . was able to teach me those truths I desired, and longed for."

Whereas Faust had turned to the devil, the devout Dee tried to communicate with angels. Seeking a scryer, a person with occult powers, to help him in his pursuit of the occult, he chose a disreputable young Irishman named Edward Kelley, whose prior occupation as a forger had cost him both ears. Despite his handicap, Kelley was persuasive about his ability to talk with spirits. In his first attempt with Dee, Kelley said he saw an angel, which Dee identified from his cabalistic knowledge as Uriel. Dee soon became fascinated by Kelley's angels and constructed a show stone, a special table painted in brilliant colors and inscribed with appropriate mottoes. It included the names of the seven most powerful governing angels—Zabathiel, Zedekiel, Madimiel, Semeliel, Nogabel, Corabiel, Lavaniel. With the show stone, Kelley was supposedly able to communicate with spirits, and Dee carefully recorded the conversations. Much of the contents was unintelligible, but parts were provocative. On one occasion Dee set down in detail a description of the beheading of a tall, beautiful woman. On another there was a warning of an

(continued on page 68)

Alchemy's Murky Search for Perfection

Among the familiar figures in the history of magic and magicians is that of the bearded, wizened old man in a tattered cloak who mumbles strange incantations to himself while he stirs a noxious, bubbling concoction, hoping to turn it to gold. He is the alchemist, at best a comical, deluded simpleton; at worst, a charlatan perpetrating fraud on the gullible.

If this unflattering and inaccurate portrait is what has survived of an intellectual quest that occupied some of the world's best minds during 20 centuries, it is largely the alchemists' own fault. Because both the State and the Church looked on them with suspicion and because they wished to keep their activities a mystery to the uninitiated, they devised an extremely complex and obscure language to describe what they were doing. Only as scholars unraveled this language and its symbolism did alchemy's accomplishments begin to emerge.

"Alchemy," wrote Prof. Lynn Thorndike in his monumental eight-volume *History of Magic and Experimental Science*, ". . . perhaps originated on the one hand from the practices of Egyptian goldsmiths . . . who experimented with alloys, and on the other hand from the theories of the Greek philosophers concerning world grounds, first matter, and the elements."

One of the greatest of these philosophers, Aristotle, had taught—and it would be some 2,000 years before anyone disagreed with him—that all matter was composed of four elements—earth, air, water, fire—which together possessed the four basic properties of heat, cold, wetness and dryness. Different combinations of these elements, it was thought, accounted for all known forms of matter. Furthermore, the proportion of elements could be rearranged to transmute matter from one form to another. That this not only could be done but, in fact, happened all the time was evident to anyone who was appropriately observant. For did not water when heated sufficiently turn to air? And was nature not able, seemingly at whim, to add water to grass and turn it into flowers and fruits?

The transmutation of base metals into gold was, of course, an abiding goal of alchemists, though financial gain was, for most, only a secondary concern. The production of gold was a steppingstone to a higher ambition—spiritual and physical immortality. If a substance or process could be found capable of turning ordinary matter into the noblest of metals, could it not be used to ensure man's perfection as well? It was this elusive prize, sometimes called the philosophers' stone, sometimes called the elixir of life, that was the true object of the alchemists' quest. Thus alchemy was, in the words of one historian, "a system of philosophy which claimed to penetrate the mystery of life, as well as the formation of inanimate substances."

Saint Albertus Magnus, Roger Bacon and Sir Isaac Newton were among the great and learned men who studied alchemy. Although Newton is justly known as the culminating figure of the scientific revolution, hermetic tradition influenced him in the early years of his career, and he continued to devote himself to alchemy as part of his inquiries into the structure and philosophy of nature. In a major work, *Opticks,* Newton observed that "Nature . . . seems delighted with Transmutations." That transmutation should extend to all of nature's elements was a reasonable assumption made by the great rationalist investigator.

But the fruitless quest inevitably attracted its share of frauds and confidence men. One of them, a German chemist named Johann Rudolf Glauber, was able to persuade a number of his 17th-century contemporaries that he had discovered the vital constituent of the elixir of life in the waters of a certain mineral spring. Those who believed him may not have achieved spiritual perfection, but at least they did themselves no harm, and possibly even some good. The mineral in the spring

Paracelsus, shown lecturing on the elixir of life, helped steer medieval alchemy toward modern chemistry. He devised new processes

water has since been identified as sodium sulfate and, under the name of Glauber's salt, still finds use today as a laxative, if not as the elixir of life.

Sometimes the consequences of alchemy were tragic, as in the case of the English chemist James Price, who, as late as 1782, claimed to have turned mercury into gold. So convincing was his story that King George III himself examined Price's sample of newly created gold and, finding it genuine, naturally asked for more. Price pleaded that he had exhausted his supply of the powders necessary for the transmutation, but the Royal Society pestered him into agreeing to a new demonstration. On the appointed day, Price showed the learned gentlemen around his laboratory, excused himself for a moment, swallowed a beakerful of poison, then returned to die at their feet.

But the most famous and, by his own account, the most accomplished practitioner of alchemy was Philippus Aureolus Theophrastus Bombastus von Hohenheim, better known as Paracelsus.

Born in Switzerland in 1493, he taught himself all there was to learn about medicine, astrology and the related sciences, then set off to practice and teach throughout Europe and the Middle East. Modesty was not one of his virtues. "Let me tell you this," he once said to an audience of distinguished physicians, "every little hair on my neck knows more than you and all your scribes, and my shoebuckles are more learned than your Galen and Avicenna, and my beard has more experience than all your high colleges." He also alienated his peers by lecturing in his native Swiss German rather than Latin, the language of scholars. Despite these problems, which made it difficult for him to settle in any one place, Paracelsus wrote extensively, frequently with great perception. Among his contributions was a proposal that venereal disease, then making its first appearance in Europe, could be treated with a mild form of mercury, a technique that was eventually adapted and used until the advent of antibiotics. He also worked among miners for a year and later composed the first medical treatise to describe occupational disease.

By the 19th century, however, the assumptions upon which alchemy was founded were shattered by proof that there were many more than four basic elements. The notion that someone might tinker with these elements and change one into another thus became little more than medieval superstition—until the dawn of the atomic age in the 20th century.

rather than relying on those mentioned in ancient texts, then used them to concoct medicines instead of trying to fabricate gold.

Alchemists pursued both material and spiritual goals, a duality reflected in their procedures. The harnessing of spiritual forces was attempted with specific scientific techniques, as shown in this 1589 illumination in which the master studies alchemic texts as he carefully tends his fire.

attack by sea from a foreign power. Mary Queen of Scots was executed in 1587 in the manner Dee described; the Spanish Armada sailed against England in 1588. Dee's notebook entries were made in 1583.

After his partner Kelley died, apparently in jail, Dee continued his search alone until his own death in 1608 at the age of 81. Although he failed to achieve his life's goal, Dee helped pave the way toward rationalism. He was, a biographer noted, "the founder of modern psychical research, two hundred years before his time."

In terms of temperament, intellect and achievement, it would be hard to imagine anyone more unlike Dr. John Dee than Joseph Desa, born five years before Dee's death, in the village of Copertino in the heel of Italy's boot. Yet if the measure of a magician is his reputation for performing uncanny, unexplainable acts, this poor Italian cleric, the antithesis of a scholar, deserves to be included among the great names in the history of the supernatural.

At the village school that he attended briefly, Desa's inattention and lack of comprehension, which were later interpreted as signs of mystic communication, earned him the nickname of Open Mouth. By the time Desa was 17, he decided that religion was the only refuge for him. He offered himself to the Capuchin order, where he was put to work in the refectory but was dismissed because he had broken too much crockery. He then joined the Order of Conventuals, working there as a stable boy.

Eventually, in recognition of his piety, he was received into the Order of Saint Francis as a cleric in 1625. In 1628, Brother Joseph was elevated to the priesthood and, after taking his vows, was known as Father Joseph.

Father Joseph's bizarre conduct, his ecstasies that disrupted Mass, drew the attention of the Holy Office in Naples, and he was summoned for examination. The charges against him were dropped, and he was allowed to say Mass at St. Gregory of Armenia. It was in this church in Naples that the first of his remarkable acts of ecstasy was reported to have taken place. Father Joseph, who had been praying in a corner of the church, suddenly stood

Scryer Edward Kelley duped a wealthy patron, possibly through ventriloquism, by making a freshly exhumed corpse seem to predict the future in a British churchyard.

up, floated off the ground and landed on the altar. He was unmarked by the flaming candles and flew back to his original place of prayer. When the astonished church superiors took him to the Vatican, he repeated his remarkable performance for Pope Urban VIII and remained suspended in the air until ordered down by the Father-General of the Order.

Such happenings could have slipped into unexceptional legend had not a number of unusually distinguished people reported that they had been witnesses to the flights of the Italian priest. One of them was the Duke of Brunswick, a serious scholar and the patron of the philosopher G. W. Leibniz. Others included Frederic Maurice de la Tour d'Auvergne, a distinguished French aristocrat, and the Infant Maria, daughter of the Duke of Savoy. If it is difficult to believe in the feats of "the flying friar," it is also hard to understand why these people should conspire to perpetrate a fraud. It

enhances speculation to note that several of the eyewitness accounts, given over a period of time, carried the same detail: during his flights Father Joseph's vestments did not become disarranged, as though an invisible hand were assuring his modesty.

Father Joseph died on September 18, 1663. "This time," his biographer commented, "the spirit had flown, leaving the body behind." A century later, in 1767, after exhaustive examination by the Congregation of Rites, the remarkable cleric was canonized as Saint Joseph of Copertino.

For all their fragility and the lack of proof surrounding them, the exploits of Agrippa, Dee and Father Joseph have about them a sense of sincerity. If their accomplishments seem unlikely today, these men at least appear to have pursued them in a manner devoid of trickery. As the 18th century began, men striving to be magicians seemed to lose such inhibitions. With this transformation, the popularity of the grimoires, magic's how-to books, increased along with a growing reliance on the symbols, incantations and rituals that were used, most often, to summon demons.

Of many conjuring symbols, the magic circle, a carefully placed and designed protective perimeter, was essential, serving not only to guard the magician from the forces being summoned but also to focus his own powers. According to one edition of the *Key of Solomon,* one of the most influential grimoires, the circle was normally traced with a magic knife at the end of a rope nine feet long. A second circle was often drawn within the first, and in the area between the two, objects of special significance were placed: plants that demons sought to avoid, bowls of holy water, names of power, crosses and other symbols. No break was permitted in the circle, and once the magician entered the ring, it had to be carefully sealed.

Before entering the magic circle, however, the magician was required to prepare himself and his equipment. A wand, specially cut from hazelwood, a sword, knife and robe were among the crucial items. Agrippa's *Occult Philosophy* recommended a robe of white linen covering the body from neck to feet and closely tied by a girdle. Fastenings of all kinds—buttons, buckles, knots—were avoided, as they might restrict the gathering of the magician's powers. Prayers, fasting, sexual abstinence and washing were also thought to be important. As one early grimoire instructed: "The operator should be clean and purified for the space of nine days before beginning the work; he should be confessed also, and should receive the Holy Communion."

When all was ready, the summoning began with the chanting of various incantations. Gradually the pace quickened as the magician concentrated the power of

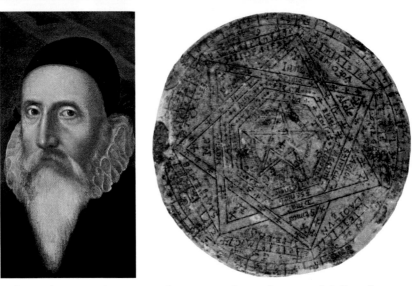

When John Dee, above, turned to magic, he used a crystal ball and a brilliantly painted table that stood on four round, magically inscribed seals, including the one above. The inscriptions, Dee said, were revealed in visions.

his mind and sought to find an incantation that would work. Over and over, various words were repeated, threatening, cajoling, ordering, as in this refrain from the *Lemegeton,* a 16th-century grimoire: "By the dreadful Day of Judgement, by the Sea of Glass which is before the face of the Divine Majesty, by the four beasts before the Throne, having eyes before and behind . . . by the Seal of Basdathea, by the name Primematum which Moses uttered and the earth opened and swallowed up Corah, Dathan and Abriam, answer all my demands and perform all that I desire. Come peaceably, visibly and without delay."

A fascinating example of a character who made a reputation and a living out of the trappings of magic without ever doing anything overtly "magical" is the mysterious Count Saint-Germain. He appeared precipitously in the middle of the 18th century and became a fixture at the court of Louis XV. Claiming intimate, firsthand knowledge of the court of Babylon and the Queen of Sheba, Saint-Germain implied that he possessed Methuselah's life span and a limitless future. The count's notoriety seems largely the result of his own publicity, since, except for his claim to have transmuted a piece of silver into gold, there are no recorded acts of magic attached to his name. Nevertheless, his contemporaries reported him alive for many years after his death, and today, almost 200 years later, wishful followers say he is thriving in Tibet.

If Saint-Germain achieved occult fame through the force of his personality, one of his near contemporaries, known as Count Alessandro di Cagliostro, achieved it by sheer industry. Cagliostro, whose real name was Joseph Balsamo, was born in Palermo, Sicily, in 1743. A botched gold swindle caused him to flee at an early age to Medina, in Arabia, where he met a Greek named Althotas, an accomplished "alchemist" and experienced hustler. The two spent several years

The Elusive Rosicrucians

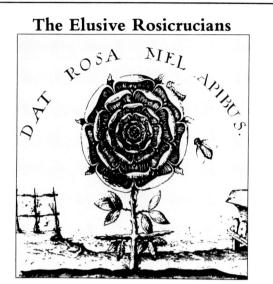

The rose and cross, symbol of the Rosicrucians, appeared in a 17th-century work by Robert Fludd, a believer in the society.

Secret societies have long been an essential ingredient in mankind's fascination with the art and power of magic. One of the most elusive yet oft mentioned is the Fraternity of the Rosy Cross, the order of Rosicrucians, which was heralded in a small pamphlet published in Kassel, Germany, probably in 1614. Entitled *Fama fraternitatis,* the anonymous tract told the story of Christian Rosenkreuz, a pious and learned young man who had traveled for years in the Near East and returned to Germany a master of mathematics and the natural sciences as well as the possessor of certain occult knowledge. Gathering seven disciples around him, the story goes, Rosenkreuz directed the compilation of a vast library, after which five of the brotherhood went into the world to perform good works, pledging to reunite annually, to seek out worthy successors and to maintain secrecy for 100 years.

The *Fama* went on to describe the discovery—120 years after Christian Rosenkreuz's death at the age of 106—of his perfectly preserved corpse. A second pamphlet, *Confessio fraternitatis,* appeared in 1615 and explained the purpose of the brotherhood. A third pamphlet, dated 1616, recounted a mysterious allegory with occult overtones about a seemingly different Christian Rosenkreuz. Recent scholars have attributed this third and final pamphlet to a well-known German theologian of the period, Johann Valentin Andreä. It is thought that Andreä might also have written the *Fama* and the *Confessio,* but whether his motives were chiding or sincere is unknown. In any case, the effect of his invention on 17th-century Europe was electric. People became desperate to join such an elitist society, though no one could actually find it. Would-be members advertised; more creative minds announced that they belonged. The phenomenon passed by about 1620, in Germany at least, though the appeal of the Rosy Cross lingers even today.

traveling together through the Near East and Africa. In Egypt, according to his own account, Cagliostro became "acquainted with the priests of the various temples, who had the complacence to introduce me into such places as no ordinary traveler had even entered before."

Returning to Italy in his mid-twenties, Cagliostro married the beautiful 14-year-old Lorenza Feliciana, daughter of a penniless noble family, and the Count and Countess di Cagliostro set out to earn their living as itinerant magicians. It was a bumpy life for the pair until the count launched what he called Egyptian Freemasonry. Claiming to have learned of this exotic branch of the Masonic brotherhood by reading a manuscript discovered in a London bookstall, Cagliostro became the sole authority on its precepts and promises. The content of Egyptian Freemasonry remains somewhat obscure. Its rites were supposedly secret, but numerous stories about scandalous goings-on succeeded in drumming up business. In a stroke of promotional genius Cagliostro expanded membership to include women and people of all religions.

During one elaborate ritual, the Grand Copt (Cagliostro) was lowered into a room on a gold sphere, naked and holding a snake in his hand. He reportedly urged his female disciples to "dispense with the profanity of clothing, for if they would receive the truth, they must be as naked as life itself." Cagliostro promised even more: Egyptian Freemasonry would lead its adherents to physical and moral perfection through regeneration; it would restore them to a state of grace lost through original sin. To achieve these goals, he proposed a regimen of 40 days of mortification and fasting, at the end of which the successful devotee would be guaranteed at least a 5,557-year-long life.

This complicated racket proved a great success in Paris, and Cagliostro and Lorenza (who headed the women's section) lived handsomely off the initiation fees. Then a scandal involving a diamond necklace and Marie Antoinette landed the couple in the Bastille. The count and countess were acquitted. But arriving in Rome, they had the bad judgment to try to open a branch of Egyptian Freemasonry in the shadow of St. Peter's. Cagliostro was tried by the Inquisition and found guilty of heresy and sorcery. He was sentenced to death (later commuted to life imprisonment), and Lorenza was arrested and then sent to a convent. Like Saint-Germain, Cagliostro was to some degree the focus of others' need to believe in something or someone. Yet he remains a favorite of latter-day occultists, and, indeed, the flamboyant 20th-century magician Aleister Crowley claimed to be his reincarnation.

The last burst of magical scholarship in the tradition of Agrippa and John Dee was generated by the blunt personage of Eliphas Lévi, born Alphonse Louis Constant in Paris in 1810. Lévi, the son of a poor shoemaker, exhibited a sincere interest in religion from boyhood and was accordingly enrolled in the seminary of Saint Sulpice. But the young man, although devout, was also unusual and independent and was eventually expelled for espousing "strange doctrines" (whose contents were never disclosed).

After leaving the seminary, Lévi was briefly entangled with a minor sect devoted to the restoration of the monarchy and supported himself by writing on Catholic subjects. This seeming contradiction, in view of his expulsion, would recur throughout his life and reflected not hypocrisy but a sincere effort to reconcile his devout Christian belief with magical theory.

In his thirties Lévi married a girl of 16, but the union was short-lived and she left him. For the next 10 years, Lévi applied himself to a study of the occult, and in the early 1850s he published *The Dogma and Ritual of High Magic*, a florid synthesis of a great many existing magical and occult doctrines. In comparison with the serious inquiries of Agrippa and Dee, Lévi's efforts seem pinched and derivative, and his interest appears to focus more on the mechanics than the precepts of magic. His books—several more followed *Dogma and Ritual*—earned little in his lifetime. In fact, he is known to have tried his hand at magic only once, and his account of his attempt to raise the ghost of Apollonius of Tyana suggests considerable ambivalence about the event. It seems as if this stocky, lonely man could not believe his own success, and although he reported the appearance of a man "wrapped from head to foot in a species of shroud which seemed more gray than white; he was lean, melancholy and beardless," Lévi also admitted being so scared that he could not ask the apparition the two questions he had planned to.

"I do not explain the physical laws by which I saw and touched," Lévi later wrote, "I affirm solely that I did see and that I did touch, that I saw clearly and distinctly, apart from dreaming, and this is sufficient to establish the real efficacy of magical ceremonies. . . . I command the greatest caution to those who propose devoting themselves to similar experiences; their result is intense exhaustion, and frequently a shock sufficient to occasion illness."

The details of Lévi's life suggest a fertile, puerile imagination that must have isolated him in the Paris of the mid-19th century. Yet his written works grew in popularity after his death, endearing their author to followers of stylized magic.

Eliphas Lévi died in 1875, roughly 400 years after Faust's birth. In that time, Europe had been transformed not once, but several times over, and the marvelous body of knowledge that had once seemed to await a single, great unlocking had been split into many parts, each sufficiently rich and complex to occupy a scholar for a lifetime. As a result, belief in magic as the path to great wisdom and understanding was no longer a possibility for rational man.

The Golden Dawn

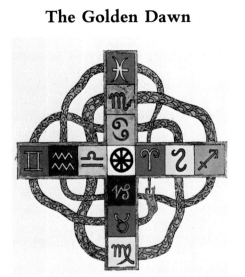

The Golden Dawn drew on such sources as the cabala, Book of the Dead and astrology, whose signs adorn this insignia.

If the Fraternity of the Rosy Cross was in all probability more Utopian fantasy than anything else, the pre-eminent occult organization of the late 19th century possessed a real, identifiable membership and a tangible history. The Hermetic Order of the Golden Dawn was founded in 1887 by three British Freemasons—Dr. William Wynn Westcott, a coroner; S. L. MacGregor Mathers, a translator of occult texts; and Dr. William Robert Woodman, a physician—who were also members of the Rosicrucian Society of England. Inevitably, the Golden Dawn owed much to Masonic and Rosicrucian tradition, but its founders claimed that it was based primarily on a cipher manuscript discovered, according to one account, in a London bookstall. The manuscript, clearly the work of someone familiar with the cabala, alchemy, astrology and the magical theories of Eliphas Lévi, supplied the rude outlines of the Golden Dawn. The society's three founders, assisted by the long-distance communiqués of a mysterious, probably fictitious, German woman named Fräulein Anna Sprengel, did the rest.

The Golden Dawn was a stylish, high-minded haven for sophisticated occultists interested in what was called "rejected knowledge"—or knowledge that was disdained by the Establishment because it was based on magic or superstition. The society offered marvelously ornate rituals and an orderly rise through a hierarchy of ranks (10) and orders (three). It also claimed a noble purpose: "to obtain control of the nature and power of my own being." Its many prominent members included the young William Butler Yeats and the actress Florence Farr. At first the order prospered sufficiently to open several outposts, including a branch in Paris, headed by the now-expatriate Mathers. But despite such arrangements, the Golden Dawn quickly foundered and after less than 15 years was torn asunder by internal disputes and power struggles.

Perverse Tricks of the "Great Beast"

The man who became perhaps the 20th century's most famous occult magician faced a typically 20th-century problem—how best to advertise himself. Few magicians in history have solved this problem more spectacularly than Aleister Crowley, the self-styled Great Beast. He determined early to shock the public into paying attention and eventually succeeded to such a degree that he was thrown out of three countries and, at the height of his career, was characterized in newspapers as "the king of depravity" and "the wickedest man in the world." All this he accomplished under a serious handicap: in the millions of words written by or about him, there is no instance where he performed what might be considered an undeniable feat of magic.

Crowley's father, a prosperous brewer from Leamington, near Stratford-on-Avon, discovered religion late in life and became a lay evangelist. His mother was, in Crowley's own words, a "brainless bigot." The magician himself, after a not-very-happy childhood, entered Cambridge in 1895 and threw himself into writing incomprehensible, mildly erotic poetry. "A strange coincidence," he later remarked, "that one small county should have given England her two greatest poets—for one must not forget Shakespeare."

Since this view was not shared by his tutors, Crowley left Cambridge and settled in London. There he began to dabble in the occult; he joined one of the period's fashionable secret societies, the Hermetic Order of the Golden Dawn. When, in the early years of the 20th century, he attempted to take control of the organization, he failed and was expelled. He then formed his own secret society, the notorious Astrum Argentinum, or Silver Star.

The distinguishing feature of the newly formed group was that it practiced what Crowley called "sexual magic." Although ancient magicians had stressed the connection between human sexuality and fertility of field and flock, abundant harvests were far from Crowley's purpose. For him, sex, like drugs, was a means of temporarily destroying the conscious moral self and of laying open the psyche to possession by primitive and powerful supernatural entities.

Crowley had always been attracted to women—in his autobiography, he ruefully conceded having contracted gonorrhea at the age of 19. He had chosen his working name, the Great Beast, from the biblical Book of Revelation: "And I saw a beast rising out of the sea, with ten horns and seven heads . . . and a blasphemous name upon its heads." Readers of the Book of Revelation will recall that sitting upon the beast was "the

woman . . . arrayed in purple and scarlet . . . holding in her hand a golden cup." There was no shortage of scarlet women at the rituals of the Silver Star, in spite of Crowley's scathing comment that they should be "brought round to the back door like the milk."

As his career progressed, Crowley made extended trips to Egypt, India, Mexico and the United States, where he sat out World War I writing spiteful anti-British propaganda. It was during his stay in New York that he performed a remarkable feat, one that might have had magical overtones. A friend, writer William Seabrook, agreed to witness a display of his powers. Crowley led him to Fifth Avenue and fell in step with a man ahead of him. "Their footfalls began to synchronize," Seabrook wrote, "and then I observed that Crowley . . . had dropped his shoulders, thrust his head forward a little, like the man's in front, and had begun to swing his arms in perfect synchronization—like a moving shadow or astral ghost of the other." Suddenly, Crowley buckled at the knees, squatted for a split second and rose again. The man in front "fell as if his legs had been shot out from under him." Seabrook, who knew a good deal about stage magic, considered the rational explanations. Perhaps the man was a

By his late thirties Aleister Crowley had begun to taste success as a poet and as a magician, and his "do what thou wilt" creed was becoming a dominant force in his life.

Crowley elevates the lamp of arcane knowledge in one of his seven rites of Eleusis, rites in which he attempted to solve the riddles of existence in front of a paying audience.

stooge. Perhaps Crowley was using some trick based on physical or psychic resonance. Perhaps . . . but Seabrook concluded the story by saying, "I think I know all the answers—but I'm not satisfied with any of them."

In the course of his travels, Crowley produced *The Book of the Law*, which, he claimed, was dictated to him by his holy guardian angel, Aiwass, minister of the Egyptian god Hoor-Paar-Kraat. The book was difficult to read, but its central message, "Do what thou wilt shall be the whole of the Law," was a clear reference to Crowley's basic belief that the way to enlightenment lay through orgiastic abandon.

Crowley took the idea from the French writer François Rabelais, who had made it the motto of his mythical Abbey of Theleme in *Gargantua and Pantagruel.* In 1920, Crowley founded his own Abbey of Thelema. Actually, it was a crumbling villa on the outskirts of the dusty town of Cefalù, on the northern coast of Sicily. It did not, like Rabelais' abbey, become a center of learning, but it did attract the interest of newspapermen, one of whom reported in the London *Sunday Express* that the curriculum consisted of "unspeakable orgies, impossible of description . . . suffice it to say that they are horrible beyond the misgivings of decent people." Rumors—mostly of doubtful provenance—hinted at blood sacrifices, bestiality and even infanticide. When reports of this gruesome activity reached the freshly installed Benito Mussolini, Crowley and his disciples were ordered to leave the country, which they did in 1923.

Crowley next moved to France but was asked to leave because he was dealing in heroin. Earlier, in 1914, he had joined the Order of the Templars of the Orient (OTO), a German group that promised prospective converts that "our Order possesses the KEY which opens up all Masonic and Hermetic secrets, namely the teaching of sexual magic, and this teaching explains, without exception, all the secrets of Nature, all the symbolism of Freemasonry and all systems of religion." Now declared *persona non grata* in Italy and France, Crowley took refuge in Germany as the leader of OTO. In the end the Great Beast returned to England. He was for a time reduced to peddling a cure-all elixir of his own invention; he finally retired to a rooming house in Hastings, on the English Channel. There he died peacefully in bed on December 1, 1947.

The modern-day occult historian Colin Wilson, one of the few people who can still find something good to say of Crowley, insists: "What Crowley realized instinctively was that magic is somehow connected with the human will, with man's *true will,* the deep instinctive will. Man is a passive creature because he lives too much in rational consciousness and the trivial worries of every day. Crowley, with his animal instinct and his powerful sexual urge, glimpsed the truth expressed in Nietzsche's phrase 'There is so much that has not yet been said or thought.'"

Be that as it may, Crowley can hardly be said to have done the cause of magic much service. If it is possible to see him as a celebrant of the dark powers of the irrational, it is even easier to perceive of him as a self-aggrandizing charlatan.

Even today tantalizing questions
remain concerning the power and
persecutions of early witches.

WITCHCRAFT

A compact with the devil distinguished a witch from a magician or sorcerer.

Early in March 1620, in the quaint Belgian village of Warêt-la-Chausée, a woman named Anne de Chantraine was arrested and charged with witchcraft.

Although she readily admitted her evil acts, which included such extraordinary and impossible occurrences as night flights and intimacies with the devil, the examining magistrate wished to gather more information and so ordered that she be questioned. Three times in all, Anne was subjected to the most brutal and torturous interrogations before the court, satisfied at last, sentenced her to death for her alleged misdeeds. Yet the sentence was not immediately carried out, and Anne languished in prison for more than a year. During that time questions arose concerning her sanity, and her jailer testified that "the prisoner was stupid, and did not understand what she said, though sometimes she seemed quite right in her mind." Finally, on October 18, 1622, Anne was burned at the stake.

Today, thanks in part to the passage of time, the currency of fanciful tales such as those spun by the brothers Grimm, and the malevolent-looking creations of cartoon artists, we may think of a witch as a cackling crone with, as Archbishop Samuel Harsnett wrote in 1603, "chin and her knees meeting for age, walking

like a bow, leaning on a staff; hollow-eyed, untoothed, furrowed on her face, having her limbs trembling with palsy, going mumbling in the streets." And among the thousands of women who were tortured and burned as witches, many were indeed old and isolated, mentally unstable and physically unattractive. Yet Anne de Chantraine, at the time of her arrest, was a girl of 17 years, and, according to the records, she was a lively, intelligent and unusually pretty girl.

"To understand witchcraft," wrote Jeffrey Burton Russell in his scholarly *Witchcraft in the Middle Ages*, "we must descend into the darkness of the deepest oceans of the mind." It is a descent that probes a bizarre and barbarous chapter in human history and provides a discomfiting examination of forces that even now, despite constant reappraisal, cannot be adequately explained by modern scholars. For during the 15th, 16th and 17th centuries, a time of glorious human achievement throughout Europe, belief in witchcraft led to the vicious depopulation of entire towns and the agonizing deaths of, by one widely accepted estimate, 200,000 human beings, most of them women.

Who were these pathetic, yet feared, victims? What, if anything, could and did they do in terms of magic, sorcery or other occult pursuits to merit such murderous treatment? Why were they killed in such numbers? And why did their excruciating plight engage the age's great minds and command the uneasy attention of the highest rulers of Church and State?

Walpurgis Night (May Day eve) is one of the nights on which witches were thought to fly to nocturnal sabbats where they frolicked and worshiped the devil.

Even now, despite all the advantages of modern scholarship, there are no complete answers, for the witchcraft horrors derived from a mosaic of causes, a patchwork of ancient beliefs and evolving Christian concepts of the devil, of changing laws and intolerant inquisitorial procedures, of traditional folk magic and the intricate rituals of scholar-magicians, of natural catastrophe and human preoccupation with wealth, sexuality and power. Yet there are constants in the pattern, and two of the most significant are also among the oldest. For from earliest times most societies have believed, first, that certain women possessed special powers and appetites, and, second, that witch women could perform what are known as maleficia, damaging acts against others effected by occult means.

If only in myth or fiction, there have always been women like Homer's Circe, who seduced men and turned them into swine; Medea, who brewed such things as herbs, owl wings and bowels of a werewolf to cast spells; the *strigae* of Latin writers such as Ovid and Apuleius, who flew through the night on their amorous, murderous errands; the lamias, whose lust for love and human flesh were immortalized by the poet John Keats; the Valkyrie, who could change at will as they went on their wild rides; and, before all of them, the archetypal Lilith, whose loveliness was more than human but whose true nature was revealed by a single flaw—her feet were great, sharp claws.

There was Diana as well, virginal Roman goddess of the hunt, but also goddess of the moon and instigator of all manner of strange happenings. The Bible describes how "when Saul saw the army of the Philistines, he was afraid, and his heart trembled greatly." So he betook himself for counsel to the medium of Endor. As Julio Caro Baroja, one of the great modern scholars on the subject, wrote in *The World of the Witches,* "In conclusion, there is documentary evidence of the existence over a period of *centuries* of the belief that certain women (not necessarily always old ones) could change

themselves and others at will into animals in classical times; that they could fly through the air by night and enter the most secret and hidden places by leaving their body behind; that they could make spells and potions to further their own love affairs or to inspire hatred for others; that they could bring about storms, illness both in men and animals, and strike fear into their enemies or play terrifying jokes on them."

Maleficia were acts that expressed the malevolent power of such supernatural women. "Misfortunes, injuries and calamities suffered by persons, animals or property, for which no immediate explanation could be found," wrote Rossell Hope Robbins in *The Encyclopedia of Witchcraft and Demonology,* "were called maleficia. These mishaps were attributed to the vindictive malice of witches." As such, maleficia date back to antiquity. Possibly first used with occult overtones in the 4th century, the term by the end of the Middle Ages was employed to explain everything from curdled milk to stillborn calves. In some cases the means by which such seemingly spontaneous destruction might occur was not explained; in others, traditional magical preparations, potions and waxen figures, knotted cords and nail and hair clippings provided occult causes for unexplained effects. In one 16th-century example a harvest disaster was said to be the result of a potion made from the ashes of a burned child, "mixed with dew, shaken from the ears of corn and the heads of grasses, into a mass that could be easily crumbled, and with this they dusted the vines and crops and trees, causing their flowers to fade and preventing them from bearing fruit." In another instance, invisibility seemed to be all that was needed to permit a witch to strike: "When the master was bringing his horses home from pasture and was carelessly riding upon one of them, she and her familiar came invisible and so bore upon the horse's neck that the rider fell to the ground and broke his leg; and he was still lame and crippled by that fall when he appeared as a witness against the witch."

Witches of myth were evildoers, such as Circe (above), who turned Odysseus' crew into swine. Some accused of witchcraft in the Middle Ages may have been followers of a wood god (right).

Belief in the doing of harm by occult means and the supernatural power of special women existed for centuries before the explosion of barbarism in the 15th, 16th and 17th centuries. Other elements were required to fuel the disaster. Yet from about A.D. 800 on, Europe's view of witchcraft was often surprisingly benign. In about 800, for example, the Irish synod merely advised that night flights were incompatible with Christian belief; and a

Sorceress Morgan le Fay, sister of legendary King Arthur, learned her art from Merlin, the magician at Arthur's court.

number of early medieval writers labeled them, rightly enough, a delusion. The earliest Christian document to examine witchcraft was the Canon Episcopi, which appeared around 906, though it may have been composed centuries earlier. The canon was intended as a guide for the use of bishops in carrying out their duties, and, as such, it warned that "certain abandoned women, perverted by the Devil, seduced by illusions and phantasms of demons, believe and openly profess that, in the dead of night, they ride upon certain beasts with Diana . . . and in the silence of the dead of night fly over vast tracts of the country, and obey her commands." The text went on to note that many people believed such stories to be true, and enjoined that "wherefore the priests throughout their churches should preach with all insistence to the people that they may know this to be in every way false."

Thus Christianity's first official mention of witchcraft denied its existence. In 1154 a learned English cleric named John of Salisbury reiterated the Church's position. He repeated some of the stories about witches' doings and asked, "Who could be so blind as not to see in all this a pure manifestation of wickedness created by sporting demons? Indeed, it is obvious from this

that it is only poor old women and the simple-minded kinds of men who enter into these credences."

One hundred and seventy years later in Ireland, in one of the most bizarre cases in the history of witchcraft, this fragile verbal barrier collapsed as sorcery and rising religious concepts of the devil became inextricably entwined. The victim in the proceedings, Ireland's first major witch, was neither helpless nor an aging crone, and desire for her property and power was certainly an essential motivation behind her trial. For Lady Alice Kyteler was the wealthiest woman in Kilkenny when she was accused in 1324 of being a witch; and her accuser, Bishop Richard de Ledrede, a Franciscan trained in France, was at the time probably less powerful than Lady Alice. Among the charges brought against the woman were that she denied Church allegiances, sacrificed animals, parodied religious ceremonies, using the words "Fi, fi, fi, amen," created powders and ointments containing "horrible worms," herbs, parts of dead men and unborn babies, and engaged in intimacies with a man who appeared as a cat and a black shaggy dog.

Though she undoubtedly *was* involved in the practice of some sort of ritual magic, Lady Alice fought the charges—and the bishop—repeatedly before finally seeking refuge in England. Unfortunately, she left her maid Petronilla behind, and Petronilla was tortured until she admitted that her mistress was a sorceress of extraordinary talents and a participant in lavish nocturnal orgies. As a result, on November 3, 1324, Petronilla was burned alive, one of the first victims of the insanity that would reach devastating proportions in Europe some 200 years later.

Crucial to the Kyteler trial was a third element in the witchcraft mosaic: the seductive man in animal guise. The appearance of this satanic figure heralded a dramatic change in medieval concepts about demons and demonology. As Alan Kors and Edward Peters wrote in their introduction to *Witchcraft in Europe, 1100-1700,* "Before the work of the scholastic philosophers and systematic theologians the role of the demons in the affairs of man was part of a variegated folklore, and their activities ranged from the horrific and utterly diabolical to a mere impishness and mischievousness often betraying a whimsical humor. In Aquinas and his contemporaries this folklore became complex and rigorous Church doctrine. The demons were evil angels . . . a hierarchically organized army in the service of Satan working for the perdition of the faithful. Satan and his hosts could tempt human beings into their service, and these humans became the witches of the theologians, the visible agents of diabolic power."

A pact with the devil and confession under torture were also essential ingredients in another early witchcraft trial, one that occurred at the end of the 14th century in Switzerland, this time under the jurisdiction of a secular judge. The accused was a man

(continued on page 80)

Among the devil's many guises was Belphegor, patron of "ingenious discoveries and inventions."

The enormous human form Michelangelo gave such figures as Charon, boatman to Hell, in his apocalyptic *Last Judgment* reflected a remarkable break with the artistic traditions of the Middle Ages.

In Luca Signorelli's *Last Judgment*, painted around 1500, a winged demon carries off a young woman.

A wizened, wraith-like devil drags a lost soul to Hell in a 15th-century German illustration.

The Devil: Master of Witchcraft

To medieval Christians, the devil was a real and active enemy, to whose powers and malevolence every mishap, whether full-blown disaster or minor inconvenience, might be traced. Floods were the work of water devils, storms were brewed by sky devils; one monk reported that devils made him itch, grow sleepy and feel ill when he had overeaten. Like the God he opposed, the devil was interested in all men, proud or humble, and like the gods of ancient myth, he or one of his legion was constantly interfering in human affairs.

The vivid image Christians had of this ubiquitous meddler—the horned and hoofed ruler of the world—was drawn in part from the Bible and Church teaching. Yet it also owed much to displaced pagan figures, such as the half-goat god Pan and Loki, the Teutonic god of fire and father of Hel, guardian of the underworld.

Belief in a literal devil was not confined to the untutored: Saint Augustine said he had heard of a possible physical union between devils and humans. Martin Luther's writings are filled with tales of his painful battles with supernatural fiends who tried to distract him from his godly work. Yet for Luther and his contemporaries, living at the height of the witchcraft persecutions, the devil's greatest threat was his relentless determination to capture human souls.

Late medieval Flemish artist Hieronymus Bosch pictured this scrawny devil watching over a deathbed scene.

Pan-like devils and witch accomplices dance around a fairy ring in this 17th-century scene.

The legendary pact between Mephistopheles and Faust guaranteed the German doctor wealth, knowledge, power and love, but cost him his soul for all eternity.

The proud and brooding fallen angel Lucifer was the hero of Milton's 17th-century tragedy *Paradise Lost*.

In his insatiable campaign for souls, the devil tries to tip the scales of judgment in his favor.

named Stedelen, and after repeated torture he admitted that he and members of his secret sect could indeed unleash maleficia—by burying a lizard under a threshold to produce infertility; by sacrificing a black cock to the prince of demons at a crossroads in order to decimate crops with hailstorms.

By the end of this trial, all the evil powers attributed to witches had been delineated. As Norman Cohn, a major analyst in the modern study of witchcraft, noted in *Europe's Inner Demons,* "A witch was imagined as (1) an individual who practiced maleficium, i.e. who did harm by occult means; (2) an individual who was bound to the Devil as his servant; (3) an uncanny being who flew through the air at night for evil purposes, such as devouring babies, and who was associated with wild and desolate places; (4) a member of a society or sect which held periodical meetings or sabbats."

As inquisitors, clerics and secular officials began to torture and burn in France and Switzerland during the first half of the 15th century, it was this last, impossibly inflated belief—in the size, frequency, power and inherent obscenity of the sabbat—that grew to monstrous

proportions. Various derivations have been proposed for the word, including its French origin as *s'ébattre* (to fling oneself about). More likely, it is taken directly from the Hebrew *Shabbat*—a plausible link, since the ceremony had earlier been called a "synagogue"—and, as such, carried implications of heathenism and heresy.

Although witches might meet informally in covens, there were, according to the torture-engendered lore of witchcraft, four "grand" sabbats a year, and the order of occult and nefarious business was strict. First, there was the assembly itself, which the witchcraft expert Pierre de Lancre has described as "a fair of merchants, mingling together, angry and half crazed, arriving from all quarters, a surging crowd of some one hundred thousand devotees of Satan." Certainly an enormous assemblage in medieval times, especially since the largest attendance sworn to by a participant was 10,000, and most accounts, if they are to be believed, place it nearer 50 or 100.

Next came homage to the devil, who might appear in a variety of guises. While he sat on a throne, the witches would approach him in various ways: "sometimes they bend their knees as suppliants," one account explained, "and sometimes they stand with their back turned, and sometimes they kick their legs high up so that their heads are bent back and their chins point to the sky." But whatever the approach, the form of homage was the *osculum infame,* the infamous kiss. Jean Bodin, a witch hunter, described it as being administered "in that place which modesty forbids writing or mentioning."

Next came the banquet. "There are tables placed and drawn up," an account read, "and they sit and start to eat of the food which the demon has provided, or which they have themselves brought." The menu consisted of such dishes as "the flesh of young children which they cook and make ready in the synagogue," as well as "feasts all foul in appearance and smell, so that they would easily nauseate the most hungry stomach."

Early stories of sabbats had an additional inflammatory effect, one that would help ignite the persecutions to come. For in 1484, Pope Innocent VIII spoke out: "It has recently come to our attention," he wrote in his *Summis Desiderantes Affectibus,* "not without bitter sorrow, that . . . many persons of both sexes, unmindful of their own salvation and deviating from the Catholic Faith, have abused themselves with devils male, and female, and by their incantations, spells and conjurations, and other horrid charms, enormities and offenses, destroy the fruit of the womb in women." As a result, the pope announced, "our beloved sons Henrich Institor and Jakob Sprenger, Professors of Theology of the Order of Friars Preachers, have been delegated as inquisitors of these heretical depravities."

What the two did was create a book, the *Malleus Maleficarum* (Hammer of Witches), which George Lin-

Familiars: Impish Minions

Cats might be familiars.

According to lore, witches were often served by familiars—imps or minor demons in the form of such small animals as cats, dogs, ferrets, rats and toads—which helped in spell-casting and ran all manner of errands. In one of the earliest English witch trials, Elizabeth Francis, tried at Chelmsford in 1566, confessed that the devil had given her a familiar "in the lykenesse of a whyte spotted Catte . . . by the name of Sathan." Every time Sathan did something for Elizabeth, it was said, "he required a drop of bloude, which she gave him by prycking herselfe."

The idea that a witch nourished her familiar with her own blood or milk was a central element of proof in British witch trials. The point on the witch's body from which the familiar drew sustenance was thought to be marked by some sort of protuberance—a "witch's mark"—that was insensitive. Any accused witch who could be prodded on a witch's mark without registering pain was assumed to be guilty. Matthew Hopkins, England's Witch-Finder General, notorious for detecting witch's marks, kept track of the familiars he discovered and recorded such names as Pynewacket, Vinegar Tom, Sack and Sugar, Greedigut and Peckin the Crow. Since these were names "which no mortal could invent," said Hopkins, they clearly indicated diabolic origin.

The Tools of Witchcraft

Whether German, French, Italian, Spanish, English or Scottish, witches all seemed to use similar paraphernalia to do similar things. Perhaps more than anything else, it is this commonality, based for the most part on myth, clerical stereotypes and confessions extracted under torture, that has served to imprint the image of the witch so vividly on the Western imagination.

The lore of witches, for example, is rife with stories of witches riding on broomsticks. This tradition appears to be ancient—perhaps even pre-Christian—and the transcripts of the 16th- and 17th-century witch trials are filled with references to it. Thus the late-16th-century French witch hunter Henri Boguet recorded that "Françoise Secretain avowed that in order to go to the sabbat she placed a white stick between her legs and then uttered certain words and then was borne through the air to the sorcerers' assembly." The Scottish witch Isobel Gowdie went so far in her confession as to give her formula for making a broom, beanstalk or straw fly: "Horse and Hattock, horse and goe,/ Horse and pellattis, ho! ho!" A confessed witch in the Savoy region of France told inquisitors that she simply instructed her broomstick to "Go! In the devil's name, go!"

"Flying ointment" contained belladonna.

Equally familiar accessories were the long black hooded cloak and the bubbling caldron. The cloak, though of ancient origin, seems to have had no special function apart from helping to preserve the witch's anonymity, but the caldron was a commonplace of magic-making. From unsavory caldron brews the witch might manufacture lethal poisons and enchanted potions and ointments. Anne Marie de Georgel, a 14th-century French witch from Toulouse, admitted making a stew composed of poisonous herbs, parts of the dead bodies of men and animals, and shreds of clothing taken from a hanged man. The record of her trial does not state the purpose of this concoction, but it can hardly have been benign.

The herbs that went into such wicked stews were probably gathered when the moon had waned. When the moon was full, herbs were picked to produce wholesome effects. For example, the green and silver leaves of mugwort, plucked at full moon, were carefully brewed and drunk in the hope of improving clairvoyant powers.

For their sabbats, or meetings, witches needed such items as candles. At his trial in 1616 accused witch Barthélemy Minguet of Brécy, France, described a ceremony: "[When] the worshipers go to the offering, they hold in their hands black pitch candles which are given to them by the devil." Also part of sabbat ritual was a magic circle that had been traced on the ground by the tip of a magical knife. Such circles were created to gather the witches' powers.

Medieval witches may have felt they could fly.

To hold spell-casting concoctions a witch might use a household bottle or bellarmine jug. In post–World War II London several such jugs were found buried in the foundations of old houses. They contained human hair entangled with metal nails, fingernail parings and pieces of heart-shaped cloth pierced with pins.

Another bit of witches' paraphernalia was found in 1886. According to a folklore journal, builders in Somerset, England, discovered in a secret room a five-foot length of rope into which goose, crow or rook feathers had been inserted. When questioned, an elderly villager hinted that the object was a witch's garland, a device used for placing curses.

Broomstick and magic sword are part of the sabbat, as shown in David Teniers the Younger's view of such an assembly.

coln Burr, one of the deans of American witchcraft scholarship, described as "the terrible book which has been said, and perhaps truly, to have caused more suffering than any other written by human pen." It is a massive work, some 250,000 words in length, so closely reasoned that it makes the selection of sections for quotation difficult. The first part describes the conditions necessary for witchcraft and systematically refutes the arguments against its reality. The second part treats "the methods by which the Works of Witchcraft are Wrought and Directed, and how they may be Successfully Annulled and Dissolved." The third, "relating to the Judicial Proceedings . . . against Witches," recounts in detail how these unfortunates were to be identified, arraigned, tried, tortured, convicted and sentenced.

Invention as well as design added to the book's malevolent impact. As Russell observed in *Witchcraft in the Middle Ages,* "It was an unfortunate coincidence that printing should have been invented just as the fervor of the witch hunters was mounting." The first printed work on witchcraft, the *Fortalicium Fidei,* appeared in 1464, eight years after Gutenberg's first Bible. The *Malleus Maleficarum* appeared in 1486 and enjoyed a success that any modern author would envy: 16 successive German editions, 11 in French, 2 in Italian and 6 in English. Nor was its appeal limited to Catholic readers. Martin Luther made that clear when, in his *Commentary on Saint Paul's Epistle to the Galatians,* he wrote that "witchcraft and sorcery therefore are the works of the devil; whereby he doth not only hurt men, but also, by the permission of God, he sometimes destroyeth them."

The witchcraft persecutions were at hand. Who were the victims?

As the international success of the *Malleus* indicates, the witch-hunt craze spread indiscriminately across European boundaries. Even within countries, the attacks were inconsistent, and a region that had never convicted and burned a witch might suddenly erupt to kill hundreds, while an area infamous for its persecutions might just as abruptly become quiescent. There were, however, distinct national characteristics to the grisly torments the accused were forced to endure.

In Spain, where the Inquisition assumed its most extreme form, there were relatively few witch trials. In England the first witch was not executed until 1566— and then by hanging, not burning; and in all, less than 1,000 were tried and convicted. Because they were not goaded into making the elaborate satanic confessions that the French inquisitors specialized in inventing, English witches, by comparison, seemed to lead relatively ordinary lives.

Germany was different. A shocked traveler in 1600 reported that the country "is almost entirely occupied with building fires for the witches," and the chancellor of the prince-bishop of Würzburg recounted with alarm in 1629: "A third of the city is surely implicated. . . . A week ago a girl of nineteen was burned of whom it was said everywhere that she was

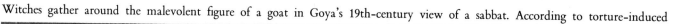

Witches gather around the malevolent figure of a goat in Goya's 19th-century view of a sabbat. According to torture-induced

the fairest and of exceptional modesty and purity."

In the city of Bamberg, witch hunting became a local industry. A special prison, the Hexenhaus, was built in 1627 for suspected witches. Drawings of the period show it to be a handsome stone building with a decorative facade. Inside, it contained two chapels, a torture chamber and accommodations for 40 witches—all laid out with such efficiency that, in a four-year period, some 400 accused passed through it. As industries went, witch hunting was profitable. It was customary to confiscate the property of convicted witches and, after deducting the cost of their trial and execution, turn it over to the authorities.

As the torture mounted, the "naming of names," the implicating of others, became commonplace. One study, examining the cases of some 300 witches, found that each named an average of 20 others, thus producing a list of 6,000 victims in a single local court in but six to seven years. One of the most poignant examples of the tragedy of implication by torture is expressed in these pathetic words, spoken by a German victim upon confronting a burgher's wife, a woman totally removed from all occult activities: "I have never seen you at a sabbat, but to end the torture I had to accuse someone. You came into my mind because, as I was being led to prison, you met me and said you would never have believed it of me. I beg forgiveness, but were I tortured again, again I would accuse you."

Yet brave men did begin to speak out, even at the risk of their own lives. Johann Wier, sometimes known as the father of psychiatry, was one. Wier argued, in a book published in 1563, that delusion and superstition turned lawyers and theologians into murderers, that the accused required humane treatment and examination by a physician, and that mental illness played a crucial role in some witchcraft cases. The Catholics listed Wier on the Index; Protestants set fire to his books. Between 1626 and 1628 the Jesuit Father Friedrich Spee accompanied nearly 200 victims to the stake at Paderborn. In 1631, Father Spee published, anonymously, *Precautions for Persecutors,* indicating that he knew exactly how to find witches. All that was required, he wrote, was torture, for if applied to Jesuits, bishops or members of *any* religious order, confessions would result. Spee explained why innocent victims refused to recant their confessions at the stake. If they did so, they would be burned alive. If they did not recant, they were first strangled, a merciful death before the fire. Gradually, as more men and women spoke up, doubts began to appear among the witch hunters, secular and clerical, and the killing and torture decreased. England abolished witch persecutions in 1684, France in 1745, Germany in 1775, Spain in 1781, Switzerland in 1782, and Poland, where the last witch was executed, in 1793.

Who had suffered and died during the witch-hunt centuries? Even now, after numerous retrospective studies, it is hard to provide specifics, despite the fact that victims numbered an estimated 200,000. Because

testimony given at witch trials, such gatherings included ceremonies honoring Satan, dancing, feasting and orgies.

records were kept by witch hunters, such information is rigidly biased. In many instances, of course, it didn't matter who one was if torture and persecutory proceedings were already under way. In other cases, more subtle mechanisms were at work. In a fascinating study, Alan MacFarlane, a British historian, reviewed some 1,200 witchcraft cases taken from court records and pamphlets in the county of Essex during the 120 years following 1560. What MacFarlane found was that the most common kind of accusation involved a local person who refused the request of a neighbor, sometimes an older woman or a person living alone, then discovered some act of maleficia. The refuser then blamed the maleficia on the person he had rejected. As MacFarlane wrote, "It was the victim who had made an open breach in neighborly conduct, rather than the witch. It was the victim who had reason to feel guilty and anxious at having turned away a neighbor, while the suspect might become hated as the agent causing such a feeling." MacFarlane's broader theory was that such rejection-accusation exchanges were a common means of severing relationships that had become a burden, perhaps as a result of fundamental changes in the tightknit structure of rural village life.

In another major study, conducted by H. C. Erik Midelfort and involving trials in southwestern Germany from 1562 to 1684, other factors emerged. "Two attributes of women did obviously increase the likelihood that they would be suspected of witchcraft," the author wrote. "One was melancholy, a depressed state charac-

terized occasionally by obscure or threatening statements and odd behavior. . . . The other dangerous attribute was isolation." Prof. Richard A. Horsley of the University of Massachusetts, in a paper called "Who Were the Witches: The Social Role of the Accused in the European Witch Trials," made a third point, drawing on evidence from Austria, Lucerne, Lorraine and England. It was that sorcerers were usually not the same as diviner-healers in rural communities and, of the two, it was the diviner-healers (including midwives), almost exclusively women, who were most often singled out. Why? Because of their outcast role in society. "In some areas of Europe," Horsley wrote, "judging from available evidence, these diviners and healers would probably account for nearly half the victims."

Were there really covens of witches? Did the obscene fantasy of the sabbat have any basis in fact? Believable accounts are difficult to find; yet there is an incident that deserves consideration. It involves the town of Bernau in southwestern Germany in the year 1588. Wine, according to the story, was disappearing for unaccountable reasons in a local tavern. In an effort to explain the mystery, the innkeeper hid in the cellar. That night he watched as 17 old women "poured wine for themselves and drank joyously with one another according to their established custom." When charges were filed, the women reportedly admitted that they had done such things for years. They were burned to death; their relatives retaliated by fire, causing the destruction of some 120 buildings in the town. An active, organized coven of witches or merely a simple folk tale expressing country-village tensions in the Black Forest? Possibly both.

Another account, set in Italy in the area around Venice and based on an examination of records by Carlo Ginzberg, indicates something quite different. About the middle of the 16th century, the *benandanti*, the records suggest, were a group of men and women who performed a number of symbolic yearly battles against the forces of evil, demons, spirits and such, usually to protect crops. Often they would go out at night in defense of the fertility of their fields. The Inquisition, however, began to question how true Christians might go out when they were supposed to be asleep, and how they might fight witches without, in turn, resorting to witchcraft. The result, according to Ginzberg, was that the benandanti, between 1620 and 1650, began to wonder, too, and came to see themselves as a witch cult rather than a protective fertility order.

Perhaps the safest approach to an understanding of the identities of the witchcraft victims is that offered by Lucy Mair in her book *Witchcraft*. In it she suggested the existence of six broad categories of victims: the socially disadvantaged, the physically disadvantaged, the successful, those who would profit, personal enemies and outsiders. All certainly supplied victims to the

---

A Day's Torture

The following is a report on the torturing of a woman accused of witchcraft in Germany in 1629:

1. The hangman bound her hands, cut her hair and placed her on the ladder. He threw alcohol over her head and set fire to it so as to burn her hair.

2. He tied her hands behind her back and pulled her up to the ceiling.

3. He left her hanging there from three to four hours, while the torturer went to breakfast.

4. On his return he attached very heavy weights on her body and drew her up again to the ceiling.

5. Then he squeezed her thumbs and big toes in the vise, and he trussed her arms with a stick, and in this position kept her hanging about a quarter of an hour.

6. Then he whipped her with a rawhide whip.

7. Once again he placed her thumbs and big toes in the vise and left her in this agony on the torture stool from 10:00 a.m. to 1:00 p.m., while the hangman and the court officials went out to get a bite to eat.

In the afternoon a functionary came who disapproved this pitiless procedure. But then they whipped her again in a frightful manner. This concluded the first day of torture.

Cruelest of Executioners: The Witch Hunters

The witch-hunting mania that convulsed western Europe during the 15th, 16th and 17th centuries may not have revealed the existence of supernatural demons, but it did generate an extraordinary array of human monsters: the witch hunters, a pathologically righteous brotherhood that devoted itself to ferreting out suspected handmaidens of the devil. The bible of these macabre killers was the infamous *Malleus Maleficarum* (Hammer of Witches), a book written by two fanatical Dominican priests and published in 1486. For the book's authors no deceit was too devious, no torture too extreme to be used in pursuit of confessions. Nor was there any room for skepticism or moderation: "Not to believe in witchcraft," the book's motto read, "is the greatest of heresies."

One of the most famous of the disciples of the *Malleus* was the French lawyer-philosopher Jean Bodin (1529-96). Possibly the first to formulate a "legal" definition of a witch—"someone who, knowing God's laws, tries to bring about some act through an agreement with the Devil"—Bodin was hideously efficient in his prosecution of suspected witches. He personally tortured young children and invalids in the effort to extract confessions, and proclaimed that burning condemned witches brought death too quickly—in not much more than half an hour. In 1580, toward the end of his life, Bodin wrote a book of his own, *Demonomanie.* Harsher and more insidiously circumstantial even than the *Malleus,* it was well received and widely read.

Matthew Hopkins was known as England's Witch-Finder General.

The inquisitor of Lorraine, Nicholas Remy, was Bodin's contemporary and, if not his intellectual equal, certainly his persecutional peer. During 15 years of judging witchcraft cases he was responsible for the execution of approximately 900 people. When his eldest son died in 1582, Remy inevitably suspected witchcraft, later accusing and condemning a beggar whom he had turned away shortly before his son's death. As Remy explained, "Witches have a most treacherous manner of applying their poison, for having their hands smeared with it, they take hold of . . . a man's garment as it were to entreat and propitiate him." Like Bodin, Remy retired an honored man and wrote a book on his experiences. His main regret in life, he confessed, was that he had not killed more witch children.

Various tools of torture are shown in this 1508 German print.

By far the most lethal of the witch hunters was Jesuit-trained Peter Binsfeld, Suffragan Bishop of Trier, Germany, in the late 16th century. A relentless witch prosecutor who insisted that "light" torture amounted to no torture at all, Binsfeld is said to have been responsible for the deaths of about 6,500 men, women and children.

His *Treatise on Confessions by Evildoers and Witches* was considered by many of his contemporaries to be one of the great legal works of its day. Few voices were raised in opposition to the bloody business of witch hunting. When Dutch scholar Cornelius Loos, horrified at the enormity of Binsfeld's judicially sanctioned murders, attempted to protest in the name of humanity, he was condemned and made to recant publicly.

The fact that most of the witch hunters sincerely believed in the rightness of their murderous pursuits does not make their perverse logic, immoderate prejudice and inhuman methods any less horrifying today. Henri Boguet (1550-1619), a French lawyer credited with exterminating about 600 witches, was, for example, able to help condemn one pious suspect on the grounds that the crucifix she wore on her rosary had a minute flaw in it—a clear indication, said Boguet, that she was in league with the devil.

Pierre de Lancre, French King Henry IV's official witch hunter in the Basque country, was equally skilled at detecting the presence of Satanism. For reasons that are obscure but that seem to have had morbid sexual undertones, de Lancre became convinced that *all* 30,000 inhabitants (including priests) of the Labourd district were witches. When news of de Lancre's conclusions became known, thousands fled their homes, some emigrating as far as Newfoundland to escape the inevitable conflagration. In the space of four months, de Lancre burned some 600 of the people who remained, then returned to Paris in triumph to be made state counselor by a grateful King Henry.

The most notorious of the English witch hunters was a puritanical, failed lawyer named Matthew Hopkins. Unlike some of his counterparts on the Continent, Hopkins, who flourished for a relatively brief period in the 1640s, managed to kill only a few hundred people. In addition, because of a parliamentary decree, he was obliged to forgo his early method of identifying witches—throwing suspects, trussed, into a lake or river to see if they floated, in which case they were considered guilty. Yet his reputation remains particularly odious. Accompanied by a group of assistants, this self-proclaimed Witch-Finder General traveled the eastern English countryside, exacting fees from terrified local authorities for ridding their communities of witches. One of the methods he used most successfully was a form of psychological torture, in which victims were forced to walk constantly, without food or sleep, until, exhausted or delirious, they confessed to witchcraft.

witch hunters; some were probably influenced by an additional factor—the practice of magic. For magic practitioners did exist, and though their actual number might have been small among the victims, they did wield, if only through the force of suggestion, certain power. As John W. Connor wrote in an article entitled "The Social and Psychological Reality of European Witchcraft Beliefs," "To the inhabitants of that age, witchcraft and the powers of Satan were as real, as rational, and yet as mysterious as vitamins, electricity, and atomic energy are to the average person of our own time."

Yet of all the characteristics of the victims, the most obvious is also the most horrifying. The great majority were women, a factor that even now remains deeply disturbing. For the depravity of the persecutions seems to outweigh the sum of its causes. Why?

A number of writers, mindful of Freudian theory, have proposed psychological answers. The basis of such speculation is the reality that probably 85 percent of accused witches were women. In many ways, sexual activity was central to witchcraft beliefs. The devil's method in recruiting witches was seduction, and the periodic orgies at sabbats were their reward for faithful service. "The curiosity of the judges," wrote the historian Henry C. Lea, "was insatiable to learn all the possible details as to sexual intercourse, and their industry in pushing the examinations was rewarded by an abundance of foul imaginations."

Distinguished historians such as Hugh Trevor-Roper, on the other hand, have proposed that the witchcraft craze—for that, in their view, is what it was—was the result of severe social pressures. Men began discovering and punishing witches at a time when the conditions of life, as noted earlier, had reached a base point. The Four Horsemen of the Apocalypse were indeed loose in the land. The Black Death, which swept across Europe in 1348, afflicted so many, with no hope of cure, that it required nearly two centuries just to regain previous population levels. Wars were endemic. Simple survival hung in such precarious balance that a single ruined harvest could condemn whole regions to starvation—which may explain why the calling down of hailstorms was considered among the witches' most heinous crimes.

Dr. Gregory Zilboorg, a psychiatrist, made an additional point, suggesting that the great witch hunt was "a reaction against the disquieting signs of growing instability of the established order." Even in modern times disaster has caused persecution of scapegoats. In Japan, in 1923, the Kwanto earthquake was blamed by some on hundreds of Korean immigrants living in Tokyo.

Yet witchcraft, while haunted by misogyny and racked by the convulsions of a society moving through catastrophic times, was also labeled heresy, or denial of the Church, a bitter truth that, according to certain scholars, transports it out of the realm of folklore, sociology and anthropology and puts it irrevocably into theology. "This fact," George Lincoln Burr wrote, "that witchcraft was heresy, and that persecution for witchcraft was persecution for heresy, we cannot bear too carefully in mind, for it is the essence of the matter."

A compelling recent study of witchcraft in Russia helps emphasize, by comparison, the insidious effects of such religious justification. For in some ways, witchcraft in Russia was startlingly similar to European witchcraft. As early as the 12th century an Arab traveler reported, "Every twenty years the old women of this country become guilty [suspected?] of witchcraft, which causes great concern among the people. They then seize all of those [women] they find in this area and throw them feet and fists tied [together] into a big river [Dnieper?] that passes through there. Those who stay afloat are considered to be witches and are burned; those who, on the contrary, go under are declared innocent of all witchcraft and are set free again."

A remarkably accurate account of dunking in Russia, three centuries before the European persecutions. But Russell Zguta, in his paper "Witchcraft Trials in Seventeenth-Century Russia," reported on vital differences in Russian witchcraft: the frequency with which men outnumbered women in trials, the relatively high rate of acquittal in some trials, the absence of children in the persecutions and the lack of belief that witches were heretics. "Without Satan," he wrote, "and without the Sabbat, Russian witches bore little—and sometimes no—resemblance to their Continental counterparts. The Russian witch could be tried and punished, much like the English witch, for the secular crime of malign sorcery—but not for heresy."

Hecate, Greek goddess of ghosts, witches and magic, appears with her spectral followers in a painting by William Blake.

Trial by Madness: Witchcraft in Salem

After a number of Salem girls testified that the devil, in George Jacob's body, caused their fits, Jacob was hanged.

Although several isolated instances of witchcraft had been reported in the American colonies during the 17th century, none compared with the witch-hunting madness that had seized Europe—until Salem.

The troubles in Salem began in the bleak New England winter of 1692, a year of political uncertainty throughout the Massachusetts Bay Colony. Colonial leaders feared that Puritan domination was nearing an end, and with it, a once cohesive society. In the kitchen of the Salem parsonage, a West Indian slave named Tituba amused the minister's 9-year-old daughter, Elizabeth Parris, and her excitable 11-year-old cousin, Abigail, with tricks and spells and tales of the occult. Sometimes Tituba told fortunes by studying patterns of egg white in a glass, a pastime that to the 17th-century Puritan was devilry, but one that captivated the adolescent neighbor girls who visited Tituba's kitchen.

As winter wore on, the girls began to behave bizarrely: Elizabeth had frequent fits of sobbing, and Abigail would race about on all fours, barking like a dog. The other girls had seizures, and one day 12-year-old Ann Putnam told of a frantic struggle with a witch who tried to cut off her head with a knife. When the village doctor could find nothing physically wrong with the girls, he concluded that "the evil hand is on them."

In vain the Reverend Mr. Parris begged the afflicted girls to name the witches who tormented them. And when he learned of a "witch cake" concocted by Tituba's husband (of rye meal baked with urine from the children), he raised such a cry that Elizabeth blurted out the name of Tituba. The other girls quickly added the names of Sarah Good, a despised pipe-smoking beggar, and Sarah Osborne, who had scandalized the village by living openly with a man before marriage. At a hearing in early March, Tituba confessed that she was indeed a witch and that she—or rather her specter—had attacked Ann Putnam with a knife. What's more, she claimed she was one of many witches in the village and that a "tall man from Boston" had shown her a book listing all the witches in the colony.

With that, the Salem witch hunt was on. Precocious Ann Putnam and her mother accused 71-year-old Rebecca Nurse of infanticide. Susanna Martin was charged with bewitching her neighbor's oxen following a quarrel. The Reverend George Burroughs, the former village minister, was named as the witches' ringleader, and Capt. John Alden was identified as Tituba's "tall man from Boston."

In seven months' time 7 men and 13 women were executed, many on the basis of the "testimony" of ghosts and specters. The Reverend Mr. Burroughs was hanged on August 19, and 80-year-old Giles Cory, who refused to testify, was slowly pressed to death by heavy stones. Only those who would not confess were killed; Tituba was spared and then sold by the Parrises.

When the frenzied accusations reached the apex of colonial society—even the president of Harvard University was accused—public opinion turned. Within 18 months of the start of the episode, Gov. William Phips had pardoned all suspected witches who had not been executed. Ultimately, even the executed were exonerated, though the name Salem endures as a symbol of societal madness.

Fact vs. Phenomenon

Modern Witchcraft's Quest for Power

For centuries . . . the witch was both honoured and loved. Whether man or woman, the witch was consulted by all, for relief in sickness, for counsel in trouble, or for foreknowledge of coming events." In 1921 English anthropologist Margaret Murray introduced her startling theory that witchcraft, far from being a figment of medieval imagination, was a powerful, ancient pagan religion with roots stretching back to the paleolithic cave dwellers. Witches, Murray said, worshiped a god that appeared in many guises, as a man, woman or animal, and in her book *The Witch-Cult in Western Europe,* she described the elaborate sabbats (including Halloween and Candlemas) and esbats of the 13-member covens of the ancient cult.

Modern scholars discount most of Murray's theory, but her books sparked widespread fascination with the ancient practice of witchcraft. When self-proclaimed witch Gerald Gardner announced that he belonged to a coven with an oral tradition dating from pre-Christian times, devotees flocked to his headquarters.

Raymond Buckland, a high priest and author of *Witchcraft From the Inside,* is a follower of Gardner's. Buckland's coven celebrates eight annual witchcraft sabbats, and in 1969 it met in his New York State home to celebrate Halloween. To prepare for the ceremony the 13 coven members took off their clothes (clothing, they believe, inhibits their powers) and purified themselves by washing in salt water. Then "skyclad," as they call ritual nudity, they gathered inside a nine-foot-diameter circle to sing, dance and listen to the coven's high priestess read from the *Book of Shadows.* Many people consider such ceremonies to be little more than inducement to sexual licentiousness, but, according to Sybil Leek, one of the craft's most famous practitioners, they represent a "return to a nature religion" that "teaches people their place in the universe." Her forebears, she says, practiced it in the 12th century, and she has taught it to her own children.

Many witches such as Buckland say that they do not perform evil magic. They point out the difference between their white witchcraft and black witchcraft, such as that practiced by the notorious California Satanist Anton La Vey. La Vey and the church he founded worship Satan through such rituals as the one in which a nude woman serves as an altar.

Witches white and black are outspoken in their belief that witchcraft is the answer to the strictures and hypocrisies they find in modern society. They publish books, give lectures and, especially around Halloween, grant interviews and enjoy a form of celebrity.

Worlds removed from this sort of show-business witchery, however, the traditional practice of witchcraft by simple people continues as it has for centuries, so much a part of the life of its adherents as to go largely unremarked. In *Witchcraft and Sorcery* anthropologist John A. Rush examined the modern-day practice of witchcraft among the Italian immigrant community in Toronto, Canada, as well as several European and African peoples, and found that it constantly affects the lives and thinking of its subjects. When a Toronto man who had sores on his face could not be cured by his family doctor, his wife consulted a witch who told her to cover the sores with melted wax from a blessed church candle; the cure seemed to work. Newspapers reported a case in Lisbon where a boy was told by doctors that he needed an operation on his legs, but after consulting a local witch, he decided to ignore their advice and apparently suffered no ill effects. When the witch, a 54-year-old illiterate, was tried for practicing medicine, she was acquitted and proclaimed a rustic psychotherapist.

In communities where witchcraft evokes the same hope and terror that it did 600 years ago, it is not taken lightly. A 1945 murder case in the Cotswolds, in England, was never solved, primarily because investigators met a wall of silence from townspeople who had known the victim. But the ritualistic nature of the crime—the victim had been stabbed with a pitchfork, and crosses had been cut into his chest—and its timing, on Candlemas Day, convinced those familiar with witchcraft lore that the victim had been killed by people who feared he was a witch. When a young girl in Lower Saxony, Germany, became gravely ill with tuberculosis, her father, believing she had been cursed by a witch, brutally stoned the woman he suspected.

Even people not driven to such extremes may follow age-old practices to guard themselves against witchcraft. Babies in many Italian communities are hung with horn-shaped charms to distract approaching witches; at night, brooms are placed near keyholes so that a witch who might enter would become fascinated and begin to count broomstraws, then have no time left for evildoing. Disbelievers are sometimes at a disadvantage. In one case in Russia, a magazine's press broke down just as it was about to publish an exposé of a local woman who claimed that through witchcraft she could restore the love of wandering husbands. Like many a devout follower of the ancient craft, she had long considered seven to be her lucky number, and, sure enough, seven days after she was arrested, a general amnesty was declared.

Ann Stewart was suspended from her job in a Tucson, Arizona, school after she was accused in 1970 of "teaching about witchcraft." She was later reinstated.

In a highly publicized trial in Cornwall, England, in 1965, Harriet Richards was accused by her victims of practicing witchcraft. She was convicted of theft.

On England's Yorkshire moors witches who perceive their craft as a return to a pre-Christian religion perform a ceremony to "draw down the moon," a rite described by ancient Greeks and Romans.

Practitioners of black witchcraft, led by Anton La Vey, attempt to ally themselves with the devil; they may also perform rituals that mock accepted religions.

Grotesque distortions of animals and
humans have long been part of the mind's adventures and
occasionally part of the real world as well.

MONSTERS

A Russian were-beast with wings, claws and antlers dates from about 500 B.C.

"I was shocked to full wakefulness by a swishing noise to starboard," wrote Capt. John Ridgway, who had been half-asleep at the oars of a 20-foot open boat that was surging gently through the darkness of a north Atlantic night. "I looked out into the water and suddenly saw the writhing, twisting shape of a great creature. It was outlined by the phosphorescence in the sea as if a string of neon lights were hanging from it. It was an enormous size, some thirty-five or more feet long, and it came towards me quite fast. I must have watched it for some ten seconds. It headed straight at me and disappeared right beneath me."

Whatever it was vanished beneath the lightweight boat in which Ridgway and his companion, British Army Sgt. Chay Blyth, then asleep, were attempting to row across the Atlantic.

"I am not an imaginative man," Ridgway continued in his written account, "and I searched for a rational explanation. . . . Chay and I had seen whales and sharks, dolphins and porpoises, flying fish—all sorts of sea creatures but this monster in the night was none of these. I reluctantly had to believe that there was only one thing it could have been—a sea serpent."

The captain's hesitation is easy to understand.

The gaping mouth and fangs of a cat-like monster form the gates to Hell, opened wide to receive damned souls pushed in by devils, in this illumination from a 15th-century manuscript, *The Hours of Catherine of Cleves.*

Sightings of "sea monsters" have for two centuries been greeted with incredulity. When, in the 1800s, Scandinavian fishermen reported seeing a gigantic squid, they were generally thought to have conjured it up with the aid of potent liquor; any sensible layman knew that no squid measured more than eight inches or so. And when the commander and entire crew of the French sloop *Alecton,* on passage from Cádiz to Tenerife late in 1861, reported an attempt to capture a giant calamary with tentacles five or six feet long, the French Academy of Sciences concluded that the witnesses had been subject to mass hallucination.

But Capt. John Ridgway saw his sea monster in 1966—and he was not an overly imaginative man. He and Blyth were paratroopers on leave from the British Army, rowing across the Atlantic on a personal survival test, and afterward they told their story of 92 harrowing days at sea in low-key style. "I can only tell what I saw with my own eyes," Ridgway reported, "and I am no longer a disbeliever." And in one sense there is no reason to doubt his straightforward account, for even the most conservative of modern scientists concede that huge and monstrous creatures may exist in the sea, not in uncharted dimensions of the mind, but in the incredible flesh.

This is the trouble with monsters: how is someone like John Ridgway to know whether the monstrous thing he perceives is a figment of the imagination, a projection of long-repressed psychic horrors or, in fact, proof of the existence of some unknown creature? From the scaly, fire-snorting dragons and hydra-headed serpents of ancient days to the mystifying underwater creatures and man-apes of today, monsters that may or may not exist have regularly posed such questions. Usually enormous, nearly always repulsive, generally menacing and sometimes instantly lethal, otherworldly beasts have played dual roles since the earliest telling of tales. They fascinate while they repel, inspire courage as well as fear, serve as symbols for otherwise inexplicable natural forces and as targets for man's heroic spirit. And yet real or unreal, they clearly fill a need.

Child psychologist Bruno Bettelheim, who explores the psychosocial importance of fairy tales in his book *The Uses of Enchantment,* asserts that man creates monsters to give form to his fears. "Unnamed anxieties are much more threatening than something to which we can attach a name and form," Dr. Bettelheim points out. "Anything we know, or believe to know, is more comforting than the unknown." And the less attractive aspects of the human psyche are easier to deal with when projected onto some other creature, factual or fictitious. Ape monsters such as the fantastic King Kong are, says Dr. John Napier, a British primate biologist and monster buff, "convenient repositories for all that is savage, ignoble and libidinous in man."

Early man, fearing the unknown, imagined a dark and evil underworld into which the sun disappeared every night. Out of this labyrinthine pit shambled the fire-breathing dragon, man's primary and prototypical imaginary monster, a gigantic creature from a nether world alive with reptilian figures, from small lizards and venomous snakes to great pythons and boas. Characteristics of lizard and snake were merged and enlarged and overlaid with an aura of evil . . . and thus the dragon monster was born.

In different places and in different times the world's dragons grew in size, acquired wings, sprouted extra heads, exhaled noxious fumes, split ranks into land and water creatures, became variously good and evil. They turned up in Egypt and Mesopotamia about 3000 B.C. and in India only a little later. The classical mythology of ancient Greece and Rome rings with thrilling tales of contests between sorely tried heroes and hideous beasts, composed either of ill-assorted parts of monstrous creatures or of equal parts of ferocious beast and malevolent human. Well into the Middle Ages, Europeans regarded dragons as the embodiment of all evil and even blamed them for the loathsome epidemics that afflicted much of the world. Divine anger, they believed, had inspired the dragon's depredations; microorganisms were as yet unknown.

Implausible tales, born of ignorance and superstition, are easily dismissed. Harder to dismiss is Edward Topsell's *Historie of Serpents,* dated 1608, in which the English author described how a dragon would wind itself around a wild animal of considerable girth—an

elephant, for example—and relentlessly squeeze it to death. "They get and hide themselves in trees," Topsell explained, "covering their head and letting the other part hang downe like a rope. In those trees they watch untill the Elephant comes to eate and croppe of the branches; then suddainly, before he be aware, they leape into his face and digge out his eyes. Then doe they claspe themselves about his necke, and with their tayles or hinder parts, beate and vexe the Elephant, untill they have made him breathlesse, for they strangle him with theyr foreparts, as they beat him with the hinder." A remarkably complete description of how a large python, perhaps 30 feet in length, might wait for and fall upon its prey.

Few were the Europeans who were privileged to see pythons, but travelers from earliest times brought home tales of extraordinary animals that one can, even today, recognize as real: elephant, giraffe, Bengal tiger, hippopotamus and crocodile. From as early as the 5th and 4th centuries B.C., returning wanderers enthralled their listeners with plausible descriptions of human oddities perhaps even more remarkable than gargantuan reptiles or horned quadrupeds with impenetrable hides. The explorers had seen, they said, people with the heads of dogs or no heads at all; semi-human beings with a single huge foot or the feet of goats; tribes with enormously elongated ears or dangling lips or bird beaks or pig snouts or single eyes or long, hairy tails.

It is possible that tales of such races grew out of faulty observations of malformed beings, either genetic freaks or individuals subjected to tribal mutilations. Add to this the chance witnessing of tribal ceremonies requiring the wearing of masks, excited glimpses of apes

Grotesques reported by Greek travelers such as Herodotus and Ctesias appeared in *Liber Chronicarum* in 1493.

and monkeys on their hind legs, distorted views of huge, upright birds with beaks agape or heads tucked beneath folded wings, and the human-like monster is born. Indeed, the combination of genuine sightings and colorful embellishment is common to all types of monsters. "The shapes of monsters are always based, ultimately, upon observation of nature," points out Heinz Mode in *Fabulous Beasts and Demons.* "On the other hand what is characteristic is the exaggeration and mixing of shapes, the combination of the qualities, abilities and powers of various natural beings into one composite figure, a process which can only be achieved in the human imagination."

A touch of imagination, with its core of reality and layer of fantasy, may be evident in the earliest tales of sea monsters. "In Libya," wrote Aristotle in his *Historia Animalium* of the 4th century B.C., "the serpents are very large. Mariners sailing along that coast have told how they have seen the bones of many oxen which, it was apparent to them, had been devoured by the serpents. And as their ships sailed on, the serpents came to attack them, some of them throwing themselves on a trireme and capsizing it." Such sea creatures, widely described by classical writers, were further elaborated in the Middle Ages.

Olaus Magnus, Archbishop of Uppsala, reported on a terrifying sea-thing in his *History of the Northern People,* accepted by readers in 1555 as the serious study it was meant to be. The Scandinavian serpent, according to the archbishop, measured some 200 feet long by 20 feet thick and was often seen by sailors plying the coastal waters of Norway. "He hath commonly hair hanging from his neck a Cubit long, and sharp Scales,

A die used by 6th-century Scandinavians to emboss battle helmets shows a *berserker,* a warrior dressed as a wolf.

and is black, and he hath flaming shining eyes."

Something scarcely less disquieting was witnessed by a Norwegian missionary named Hans Egede while on a voyage to Greenland nearly two centuries later. "Anno 1734, July," he wrote as his vessel neared the Danish colony of Good Hope on the Davis Strait. "On the 6th appeared a very terrible sea-animal, which raised itself so high above the water, that its head reached above our maintop. It had a long, sharp snout, and blew like a whale, had broad, large flappers, and the body was, as it were, covered with a hard skin . . . moreover on the lower part it was formed like a snake, and when it went under water again, it cast itself backwards, and in doing so it raised its tail above the water, a whole ship-length from its body."

Of the sea serpents of legend the most awesome by far was the dreaded kraken. "Amongst the many great things which are in the ocean," wrote Erik Pontoppidan, Bishop of Bergen, in his 1755 *Natural History of Norway,* ". . . is the Kraken. This creature is the largest and most surprising of all the animal creation." According to popular accounts, the surfacing kraken spread itself out over a distance of a mile and a half. Sailors, mistaking its vast form for an island, would land upon it, light their campfires of an evening and prepare to spend the night. At times the kraken would object and sink beneath the sea, leaving the astonished sailors floundering in the water.

Another fearsome sea monster was reported by

An account of Marco Polo's 13th-century travels in India told of dog-headed humans like those shown at left.

Lieutenant Bouyer, commander of the sloop *Alecton*, when he advised the French naval minister of a singular incident experienced during the vessel's passage from Cádiz to Tenerife toward the end of 1861. "On November 30th, 100 miles N.E. of Teneriffe, at 2 PM," wrote the French officer, "we encountered a monstrous animal which I recognized as the *Poulpe géant* whose existence has been so much disputed and now seems to be relegated to the realms of myth." The men of the *Alecton* harpooned the many-tentacled thing and drew a noose around what seemed to be its tail. But with a violent lunge the creature snapped the harpoon and tore itself free, and when the crew hauled in the rope, they found nothing but a 40-pound fragment of the dreadful monster they had pursued.

Yet, reported Bouyer, "we saw the creature at close enough range to give an exact description of it. It was in fact the giant calamary, but the shape of the tail suggested it belonged to a species not yet described. The body seemed to measure about 15 to 18 feet in length. The head had a parrot-like beak surrounded by eight arms between 5 and 6 feet long. In aspect it was quite appalling; brick red in color, shapeless and slimy, its form repulsive and terrible." Unfortunately, the fleshy evidence that might have proved the story rotted before the men of the *Alecton* made home port, and, despite Bouyer's account, the French Academy of Sciences could only conclude that Bouyer and his men had been the unwilling victims of mass hallucination.

Despite official skepticism, accounts of impossible sea monsters persisted. One celebrated tale concerned a mortal struggle between a sea serpent and a whale, occurring off the coast of Brazil and reported by the *Illustrated London News* of November 20, 1875. "Captain Drevar, of the barque *Pauline*, bound with coals from Her Majesty's naval stores at Zanzibar," the story began, "observed three very large sperm whales, and one of them was gripped round the body, with two turns, by what appeared to be a huge serpent. Its back was of a darkish brown and its belly white, with an immense head and mouth, the latter always open; the head and tail had a length beyond the coils about 30 feet; its girth was about 8 feet or 9 feet. Using its extremities as levers, the serpent whirled its victim round and round for about fifteen minutes, and then suddenly dragged the whale down to the bottom, head first."

Less than 20 years after the episode of the *Alecton* and its discredited calamary, indisputable evidence turned up that at least one kind of "impossible" sea monster—the giant squid—did indeed dwell in the deep. The 1870s saw an epidemic of great tentacled carcasses washing up on north Atlantic shores, and at least one of the monstrosities was recovered alive. On November 2, 1878, three fishermen in a boat from Thimble Tickle, Newfoundland, saw an enormous marine animal struggling against the incoming tide. They hooked the

An Eskimo craftsman added a woman's head to the soapstone fish above to symbolize the link between the marine creature and the spirit world.

A carved Aztec turtle has the head and hands of a man.

creature with a barbed grapnel and, as waves bore it onto the beach, tethered it to a tree ashore. The body of the thing measured 20 feet, its tentacles another 35 feet each. The Thimble Tickle squid, with tentacle suckers about four inches across, appeared to be a scaled-down version of the kraken of legend; and although no larger specimens have ever been recovered, whalers have often told of hauling in sperm whales bearing sucker scars nearly 20 inches in diameter, suggesting a true kraken-sized monster of about 250 feet.

Yet by no means do all reported manifestations of sea monsters fit the description of the kraken, nor can the many hundreds of sightings of monsters over the years and around the world be counted as genuine. All the same, it appears that in the majority of reported cases, *something* startlingly unusual was seen. Belgian zoologist Bernard Heuvelmans, author of *In the Wake of the Sea Serpents,* suggests that not one but several different types of unknown animals have been seen and dubbed "sea serpents" for want of any other name.

Heuvelmans painstakingly collected and sifted 587 reports of sea-monster sightings dating from 1639 to 1966. After eliminating probable mistakes, deliberate hoaxes and accounts too vague to be of value, he was left with 358 convincing cases. Putting every detail of the apparently reliable sightings on punch cards, he ran a computer analysis that resulted in the classification of nine distinct types of previously unacknowledged underwater creatures, all outsize and extraordinary yet credible in the watery underworld that is the home of 60-foot squids and 100-foot whales.

As bizarre and frightening as the real or mythical

monsters of the deep may be, they lack a final element of horror that a number of land-borne creatures possess: a disquieting kinship to ourselves. It takes a creature vaguely recognizable as one of *us*—a monster of human or semi-human form—to generate the terrifying aura of true malevolence.

Among the earliest and most persistent manifestations of the man-monster is the shape changer, or were-animal. Be the creature werewolf, were-jaguar, were-panther or were-bear—for the animal characteristic varies with geography—it is a physical projection of bestial human traits. Instead of directing his horrors onto some dreaded predator or dream creature, the individual believes that he himself turns into a monster, assuming the shape, hair, fangs and claws of a beast.

The great majority of werewolf cases have occurred in Europe. To our European ancestors, living in days when the human population was small and scattered and the forests were dense and hostile, the wolf was an immediate and ever-present source of terror. It was known for its unbridled ferocity, bloodthirstiness, cunning and strength. No flight of fancy or slip into psychosis is necessary to invest the wolf with the terrifying characteristics it possesses naturally.

Episodes of werewolfery through history number in the tens and even perhaps hundreds of thousands. Between 1520 and 1630, a peak period, there were 30,000 recorded cases in France alone. A classic case concerns one Pierre Bourgot of Poligny, a shepherd who was tried for a series of atrocities in 1521. Confessing, he testified that 19 years earlier he had been searching for sheep lost in a terrible storm when three black horsemen approached and inquired what troubled him. Bourgot explained, to which one of the horsemen allegedly replied, "Take courage. If you show faith, my Master will protect the straying sheep."

Bourgot apparently showed sufficient faith, for soon he found his flock. A few days later the black horseman reappeared and suggested that Bourgot become a servant of the devil in exchange for protection and wealth. "I fell on my knees and gave in my allegiance to Satan," Bourgot told the court.

In wolf guise, and sometimes accompanied by another werewolf named Michel Verdung, Bourgot committed uncounted savage murders, his favorite victims being young women, including one whose neck he cracked with his teeth before tearing out her throat. The revolting spree came to an end when Verdung, in wolf form, leaped upon a traveler who fought back and wounded him. The wolf loped briskly into the woods, leaving a trail of blood for the traveler to follow. In a hut at the end of the trail the bold fellow found Verdung, in human form, having his bloody wound tended by his wife.

A fascinated court learned that Pierre Bourgot transformed himself into a wolf by stripping off his clothes and rubbing his body with a special ointment supplied by the devil's henchman, whereas Verdung, possessed of a finer natural talent, was said to turn himself into a wolf at will. The two men and a lesser werewolf were executed.

A somewhat similar episode occurred in 1573, when a French village in the vicinity of Dôle was terrorized by a monstrous creature that killed and partially devoured several children. One day when a group of villagers surprised an enormous wolf in the act of savaging a child, they were struck by the animal's strong facial resemblance to a local recluse named Gilles Garnier. When apprehended and tried, the suspect confessed that his poverty and hunger had led him to make a pact with an evil spirit he had chanced to meet on a forest path. The spirit had given him a salve to apply to his body that would change Garnier into a wolf, so that he might satisfy his hunger for meat. After telling his story, Garnier was burned alive.

In the small town of Bedburg, Germany, in 1589, a crowd of 4,000 people gathered to witness another execution, that of the notorious Peter Stubb or Stump, described in a contemporary pamphlet as "a most wicked Sorcerer, who in the likeness of a Wolf, committed many murders, continuing this devilish practice 25 years, killing and devouring Men, Women and Children." Bedburg had been terrorized by what its citizens thought was a lone wolf that killed sheep and cattle on occasion but showed a preference for humans.

Stubb, a brutish woodcutter, had been cornered in a forest ravine by a large hunting party with a pack of hounds. Scrabbling around on all fours, snapping and snarling like a ferocious beast, he had fought with inhuman strength until he had been overcome. Later, on trial in Cologne, he recounted a familiar story of a pact with the devil, who had given him a "girdle of wolf pelt" along with a promise to protect him while he practiced "foul malice on men, women, and children in the shape of somme beaste."

Diabolism features prominently in the story of Jean Grenier, a homeless youth who was brought to trial for werewolfery in Bordeaux, France, in 1603 and who, in a boastful confession attributed his career to a chance encounter with a tall, dark horseman called the Lord of the Forest, an icy-fleshed stranger who had sworn him to service and presented him with the means of changing shape. Transformed by a magic ointment and a wolfskin cloak, the lad had gone hunting on countless occasions with nine other man-beasts of similar persuasion. Even after he was picked up, he ran around on all fours and confessed a preference for the taste of girls. An astonishingly enlightened court found that Grenier was as much a victim as a criminal and sentenced him to confinement in a monastery.

Increasingly, investigators of werewolfery came to believe that its victims suffered from a mental illness

(continued on page 98)

Alexander the Great was said to have slain a dragon, as shown in a 15th-century Italian tapestry.

A dragon and other beasts are cast into Hell in this 14th-century Norman view of the Apocalypse.

An attack by the sea monster *poulpe colossal* was described by French naturalist Denis de Montfort in his *Histoire Naturelle Générale et Particulière des Mollusques,* published in the 19th century.

Fabulous Beasts of Sea and Land

Babylonian legend tells how Marduk slew the dragon armies of an evil goddess, Tiamat, in order to create the universe and set himself at its head. In a Scandinavian saga, Sigurd battled the dragon Fafnir to gain a cache of gold and a cursed ring that in the end unleashed destruction on the world. Christianity has wrestled with its dragons too. Saint George is said to have killed a dragon in order to free a terrified heathen population and convert it to Christianity, and, according to Saint John the Divine's Revelation, dragons and other beasts will ultimately be overcome and pitched into Hell as

the world ends. Even 15th-century Europeans setting out to conquer the Atlantic feared that it might be filled with scaly and terrifying man-eating monsters.

How could tales of such beasts appear in so many cultures and survive for so many centuries when none had ever been seen? Richard Carrington, author of *Mermaids and Mastodons,* suggests that like primitive religion, monsters represent an attempt to deal with "the mystery and immensity of the Universe." Only by characterizing such fears as dragons that might be slain, Carrington says, could man cope with his own apparent insignificance.

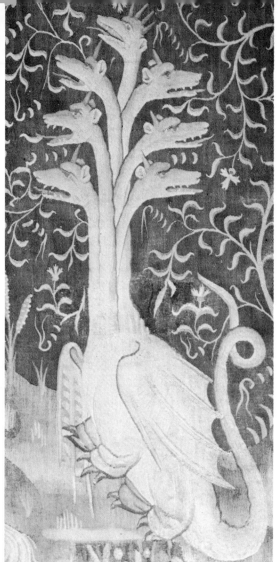

Scandinavian waters boiled with man-eaters, according to Olaus Magnus's 16th-century work on the subject.

Many monsters were said to have seven heads, like the Hydra in this 14th-century tapestry.

An old English ballad tells how More slew the dragon of Wantley.

Andromeda is rescued by Perseus in the Renaissance painting at left.

97

Artist Leonora Carrington's serene, child-like female giant presides quietly over a verdant pastoral scene, a scene that belies the towering menace of almost all legendary giants.

called lycanthropy. The deluded being, usually mentally subnormal and perhaps under the influence of hallucinatory drugs, truly believed that he could change shape. This conviction, laced with a dreadful sadistic craving for flesh and blood, was enough to turn man into monster and, seen through a veil of legend and superstition, was enough to convince witnesses that they were indeed seeing a snarling, four-legged canine creature.

But growing understanding of lycanthropy as a disease has not yet exorcised the werewolf from the human mind or from human society. On a hot summer's night as recently as 1949 the police were called to investigate reports of a werewolf seen in a garden in Rome. A patrol discovered a young man on his hands and knees, howling, mud-drenched, clawing at the ground with long, sharp fingernails. Later at the hospital the man said that he regularly lost consciousness when the moon was full and, upon waking, would find himself stalking the streets, impelled by some unrecognizable urge.

The question that remains is why anyone would wish to be a wolf. John Godwin, author of *Unsolved: The World of the Unknown*, offers a possible explanation: "Individuals driven and tormented by urges they knew to be subhuman may wish to escape from the human shape that bars their fulfillment. By becoming beasts they could shed ingrained taboos and gratify, without guilt or fear, all the warped cravings burning in their minds. For animals human taboos do not apply."

But sometimes the human being needs no transformation into animal to ignore taboos. He is already a monster, an upright beast of prey with no discernible human feelings. Such is the vampire, awakened from the dead and craving blood but with an oddly erotic appeal to his victims.

Opinions vary as to what exactly the traditional vampire is. Some people believe him to be an evil spirit wearing the body of the newly dead; others think he is a corpse animated by his original soul. To sustain himself he must have that most vital of bodily ingredients: blood. "Vampires issue forth from their graves in the night," wrote scholar John Heinrich Zopft in 1733, "attack people sleeping quietly in their beds, suck out all their blood from their bodies and destroy them."

Typically, the captured or disinterred vampire is found to be ruddy of complexion, well-nourished and apparently bursting with health. His appearance, however, is marred by his long, curving fingernails, grown in the grave, and the blood smeared over his mouth. According to most legends, the only way to destroy such a corpse is to drive a stake through its heart, which causes a terrifying screech and an outpouring of purloined blood, and to then burn the blood-drenched remnants of the corpse to ashes.

Legends of vampirism, like those of werewolfery, had their roots in traditional fears and some facts. Such

Giants: Larger Than Life

The human giant is perhaps the most familiar of all the monsters man has created. Fashioned in man's own image, invested with his passions and flaws, but blown up to tremendous size, he appears in legends throughout the world. In the tale of Gog and Magog, for example, these last members of a vanquished race of British giants are forced by Brutus, their conqueror, to stand guard at the entrance to his palace in the newly founded city of London. In Greek mythology the Titans, Cyclopes and Gigantes are the oversize offspring of the Greek gods Uranus (sky) and Gaea (earth). In biblical accounts giants are the malevolent fruit of fallen angels and women, while in Norse myth they are credited with creating the earth and founding the human race. In the *Odyssey* the vile, cannibal giant Polyphemus the one-eyed is easily outwitted by the valiant, resourceful Odysseus. In a parallel biblical tale, David's victory over Goliath symbolizes the triumph not just of intelligence over brute force, but of good over evil, a moralism that survived in medieval Europe.

Fairy tales, too, abound with giants. Psychologist Bruno Bettelheim, in *The Uses of Enchantment,* theorized that children relate easily to small but clever heroes who outwit powerful giants. Bettelheim quoted a young boy who, after hearing "Jack the Giant Killer," said, "There aren't any such things as giants, are there? But there are such things as grownups, and they're like giants."

In real life, genetic giants have been servants, soldiers and sideshow spectacles. Human giants were pressed into service as porters by British rulers from Elizabeth I to George IV and into battle under Russian and Prussian flags. Oliver Cromwell had his own giant, a religious madman named Daniel, who ended his days preaching a wild gospel behind Bedlam's iron bars.

Until the mid-19th century, romanticism and a lack of scientific knowledge worked to obscure the obvious pathology that causes human giantism. Among the first to point out the discrepancy between romance and reality

The malevolent giant that looms over war-ravaged Spain in Goya's large canvas hints as well at the artist's inner fears.

was the French zoologist Isidore Geoffroy Saint-Hilaire, co-founder of the science of teratology (the study of malformation). Geoffroy described a class of giants as "inactive, energyless, slow in their movements . . . in a word, weak in body as well as intelligence." By the middle of the century, the process of bone formation was understood, but scientists had yet to identify the factors that regulated it. When the origins of a disease known as acromegaly were traced to pituitary tumors, their possible links with giantism—many of whose victims displayed acromegalic symptoms such as thickening of the facial features and alarming increases in adult head, hand, and feet size—became apparent.

Estrangement from society and great suffering have characterized the lives of most natural or genetic giants. Victims of their own bodies and of society's cruel regard, they rarely survive beyond early adulthood, and they suffer both physically and mentally. Four Irish giants of the 19th century (three of whom called themselves Patrick O'Brien) lived in terror of being dissected by scientists after death. And the tallest known giant, Robert Wadlow of Illinois, lived in perpetual pain as a result of his unchecked growth. He had reached 6 feet 5 inches by the age of 10; when he died at 22, he stood 8 feet 11$^{1}/_{10}$ inches. As a result, his brain was so far removed from his feet that it could not feel the pain that signaled the final stages of a fatal infection.

In 1936, while he was still in high school, Robert Wadlow was nearly 9 feet tall.

Anna Swann, 7 feet 11 inches tall, appeared in P. T. Barnum's gallery of wonders in 1865.

a fear was that the dead might return to their old haunts, particularly if they had been suicides, lycanthropes, excommunicates or unfortunates buried without appropriate rites. Occasional maniacs afflicted with necrophilia or some other perversion involving the stealing of corpses provided apparent proof that some of the deceased could leave their graves. Other deviants, fortunately even more rare, demonstrated a pathological or physiological thirst for blood, thus contributing another element to the tales of vampirism.

Terrible and mysterious events such as unsolved mass murders and outbreaks of the plague were likely to be ascribed to an uprising of vampires, whose supposed stench was indistinguishable from that of the putrefying bodies of the dying and the dead. People who looked rosy-cheeked and yet were seldom seen by day were likely to be cast as villains; and there were not a few such people. In the late Middle Ages, when the phenomenon of vampirism made its initial appearance in the Slavic regions and Baltic states of eastern Europe, interbreeding among noble Slavs led to a number of genetic disorders, among them a rare disease called erythropoietic protoporphyria. This is a pigment disorder in which the body produces an excess of protoporphyrin, a substance basic to red blood cells. The result is unbearable itching, redness, edema and bleeding cracks in the skin after brief exposure to sunlight. Sufferers naturally tended to avoid day trips and emerged

The cross worn by a young woman does little to protect her from a voracious werewolf in this 18th-century engraving.

only at night. The disease was not diagnosed until the 19th century, and until that time it was not surprising for the afflicted individuals to have been regarded with revulsion bordering on superstitious fear.

But probably the most common source of the vampire concept was premature burial. Comatose individuals, dead-drunks and persons in a state of catalepsy were not infrequently buried alive.

Quite possibly because of such precipitate interments, stories of exhumations provided grisly support for the vampire legend. Early in 1732 an apparent epidemic of vampirism swept the neighborhood of Meduegya in Serbia, precipitating such panic that the government sent a detachment of soldiers, including three army surgeons, to open the graves of the recently dead. The investigating team opened 13 graves. Only 3 exhumed corpses were undergoing the normal processes of decay. The other 10 bodies, some of them longer underground than the decomposing departed, were firm-fleshed and rosy-cheeked and when dissected were discovered to contain fresh blood. All 10 were promptly decapitated and burned until soft gray ash was all that remained of the corpses.

Tales of this episode and others much like it were picked up by travelers and spread throughout Europe. The oral-erotic, repellent-attractive connotations of the death bite were not lost on poets and other writers. Among those inspired to literary celebration of the vampire were Goethe, Tolstoy, the poet Robert Southey, Lord Byron, Théophile Gautier and Alexandre Dumas père. In 1847 a hack novelist by the name of Thomas Prest produced a best seller of the genre (868 pages of purple gore), calling it *Varney the Vampire; or, The Feast of Blood*. After an incredibly long run, this "Romance of Exciting Interest" was unceremoniously shoved into the background with the publication, in 1897, of Irish author Bram Stoker's bloodcurdling *Dracula*, the most famous of all vampire tales.

The fictional Dracula has come to epitomize the vampire. But infinitely more horrible than any bloodsucking Transylvanian count was the historical personage upon whom Stoker based his anti-hero.

Vlad Basarab was born in the Transylvanian town of Schässburg about 1430. His father, notorious for his cruelty, had been known as Prince Dracul, a name that can be variously translated as "dragon," "devil" or "vampire." But if Vlad Dracul was ruthless, he was the merest of tyros compared with the younger Vlad, known as Dracula, son of Dracul.

Dracula was the prince of Walachia, part of what is now southern Rumania, in 1448, from 1456 to 1462 and then again in 1468. Although famed for his courage in battle against the Turks, he earned his nickname not as a warrior but as a depraved killer whose sadistic savagery was considered excessive even by his bloody-minded contemporaries. To them Dracula was known

Nocturnal leaping matches were a feature of many werewolf tales. Maurice Sand's *Légendes Rustiques*, published in 1858, told of a cemetery wall where "some thousands of werewolves come together, that each may try his nimbleness in leaping."

as Vlad Tepes, or Vlad the Impaler, so named for his favorite sport of skewering his victims on stakes.

At the time of Vlad's rule the throne of Walachia was threatened from outside by Turks and Hungarians and from within by power-hungry barons who fought one another with bestial ferocity. Vlad managed to stave off the many threats to his crown by slaughtering his political opponents as well as their families and friends and by betraying colleagues. Holding supreme power for several years and having plenty of captives on hand, he was able to indulge in a pleasure far more exquisite than the thrill of battle: watching terrified people die very slowly. The routine was to select human playthings at random, cut off their hands and feet, then impale the unfortunate beings on sharp wooden stakes. It was nothing for 50 pain-maddened people to thus entertain him at one time; and it has been recorded that during one rampage 30,000 of Vlad's innumerable enemies died on the stakes.

The year 1476 was the climax and the end. Every horror of previous years had been a mere prelude to the hellishness of Vlad's final orgy. There were corpses impaled at every crossroads, corpses spilling out of the palace, piles and tubfuls of severed heads and limbs. Into this nightmarish scene marched Sultan Mohammed II and his army, come not for vengeance nor to destroy an unspeakable monster but to chastise the Walachian for refusing to pay tribute. In the clash of armies Vlad Dracula fell, and his head went to Constantinople, tucked under the arm of a victorious Turk.

Legends of the blood-drenched tyrant drifted down through the centuries, lending something of substance to the fiction that he was a vampire. But he was not; he was a living human fiend who delighted in the shedding of blood but who apparently never entertained the possibility of drinking it. The beautiful Transylvanian countess Elizabeth Bathory, on the other hand, both drank human blood and bathed in it.

Elizabeth was born in 1560 into one of the wealthiest and most illustrious families in Europe. Her first cousin was the prime minister of Hungary, another close relative was a cardinal, and her uncle Steven, Prince of Transylvania, would become king of Poland. On the other hand, another uncle was a diabolist who practiced witchcraft, her brother was a notorious satyr, and a favorite aunt was an equally notorious lesbian.

Elizabeth married in 1575 at the age of 15 and went to live with her dashing husband, Count Ferencz Nadasdy, known as the Black Hero of Hungary for his prowess in battle, in Castle Csejthe in the lonely hill country of northwestern Hungary. Count Ferencz soon went off to the wars, and Elizabeth became restless. Running off with a pale young nobleman, reputed to be a vampire, was but a passing diversion, and upon her return to the castle the bride sought other amusements.

She began to dally with the servants, especially the young females. At first the maids were not much more than convenient playthings, but when Elizabeth was initiated into the arts of black magic and witchcraft by her manservant Thorko and a nurse named Ilona Joo, the games became bizarre rituals.

When, in 1600, the Black Hero died of undetermined causes, Elizabeth threw her despised mother-in-law out of the castle, shipped her four children off to relatives and devoted herself wholly to her macabre pleasures. One day a boudoir maid accidentally pulled the countess's hair while combing it into its usual elaborate coiffure. Elizabeth slapped her so viciously

Though they may be wizened hags in the grave, vampires can appear as beautiful young women searching for blood.

that blood spurted from the girl's nose onto the countess's hand. Elizabeth, who worried about her looks, thought that the skin smeared by the maid's blood was fresher, smoother and more youthful than it had appeared in many a year. Immediately she sent for two of her henchmen, major-domo Johannes Ujvary and the male witch Thorko, who slashed the terrified maid's veins and drained her blood into a vat so that Elizabeth could bathe in it.

The countess's first blood bath was the beginning of an orgy that lasted for 10 years. Male and female accomplices scoured the countryside in search of the unmarried girls whose blood Elizabeth demanded, luring them to Castle Csejthe with promises of jobs as servants. In time Elizabeth grew careless, and instead of burying all the used-up bodies, she took to having them thrown out in the fields for the wolves to find and devour. But one wintry night the wolves were late. Early-rising local inhabitants found four pathetic corpses beneath the castle ramparts and raised an outcry that reached the king himself. One of Elizabeth's own cousins, Count Gyorgy Thurzo, was delegated to lead a detachment of soldiers in a surprise night raid on Castle Csejthe on December 30, 1610.

The raiders broke in on a grotesque, unbelievable scene. In the main hall of the castle one young girl lay dead and bloodless. Another, still living, bore myriad puncture marks on her body, and a third, also barely alive, had been terribly tortured. Beneath and near the castle the soldiers dug up about 50 bodies.

Elizabeth, being a noblewoman and thus privileged, was placed under castle arrest, while some 16 members of her household—her sorcerer and torturer accomplices—were taken to jail in Bitcse. Elizabeth re-

fused to testify or plead when tried for her crimes.

All of the accused were found guilty. Most were beheaded and cremated, but two were burned alive. The countess herself was walled up in her bedchamber with only a narrow slit left open to permit the passage of food, water and air; she survived for four years.

Crimes of that monstrous sort are not, of course, confined to distant centuries. Fritz Haarmann, for example, known as the Hanover Vampire, was tried in Germany in 1924 for the murder of 24 boys, most of whom he killed with one savage bite on the throat. In a somewhat similar case, an Englishman named John George Haigh, who had once been a sweet-faced choirboy in Wakefield Cathedral, was hanged in 1949 for murder. He confessed to killing nine people and disposing of the bodies in barrels filled with sulfuric acid. His main motive, he asserted, had been to drink his victims' blood. His claim to a bizarre thirst earned him the title of the Vampire of London. Such grim cases as these are locked into time and place, and once the perpetrators—human creatures acting out their own monstrous depravity—are jailed or dead, they lose the power to terrify. Monsters that never lose that power are the demonic man-shapes shambling about in the shadows of every human mind. It was a girl barely out of her teens who released one of the most terrifying monsters ever conceived, a thing that had come to her in a waking vision as she sought sleep one night after a disturbing conversation.

"When I placed my head on the pillow," she subsequently wrote, "I did not sleep, nor could I be said to think. My imagination, unbidden, possessed and guided me, gifting the successive images that arose in my mind with a vividness far beyond the usual bounds of reverie. I saw—with shut eyes, but acute mental vision—I saw the pale student of unhallowed arts kneeling beside the thing he had put together. I saw the hideous phantasm of a man stretched out, and then, on the working of some powerful engine, show signs of life, and stir with an uneasy, half vital motion."

Mary Godwin, creator of the legend of Franken-

Vlad the Impaler was a cruel, real-life Count Dracula.

The deranged Elizabeth Bathory bathed in blood.

stein, was born in London in 1797. Her mother was Mary Wollstonecraft, England's most fiery feminist; her father, William Godwin, a radical intellectual. Largely because Wollstonecraft refused to be attended by male physicians until it was too late, Godwin was left a widower 10 days after his baby girl's birth. As soon as the child was old enough to understand, he made it clear to her that she was responsible for her mother's death and would have to atone for it by demonstrating the intellectual brilliance, moral courage and literary skills of Mary Wollstonecraft, by becoming, in effect, a replacement for her own dead mother.

Life became wildly complicated as Mary grew up. In 1814, when she was 17, she eloped with the poet Percy Bysshe Shelley, taking along her half-sister Jane (later Claire) Clairmont. Shelley was married at the time and his wife, Harriet, was pregnant, but no one other than Harriet seemed to care. Mary gave birth to her first child by Shelley in February 1815. The infant girl, premature, died in March. "Dream that my little baby came to life again," Mary wrote in her journal on March 19; "that it had only been cold, and that we rubbed it before the fire, and it lived." But the child did not live. Nor did a boy born the following January.

The young science student Victor Frankenstein was conceived in 1816, and with him his charnel-house monster. Mary, Percy and the tagalong Claire were holidaying in Geneva at the time, staying in a lakeside house a short distance away from the larger Villa Diodati, occupied by the rakish Lord Byron and his friend John Polidori. On fine days the two households converged at the lake and enjoyed the conventional sport of boating, but for the most part the weather was dank and dreary. Incessant rain kept them all indoors for days at a time, usually in the capacious Villa Diodati.

"Various philosophical doctrines were discussed," Mary wrote later, "and among others the nature of the principle of life, and whether there was any probability of its ever being discovered and communicated. They talked of the experiments of Dr. Darwin who [they believed at the time] preserved a piece of vermicelli in a glass case till by some extraordinary means it began to move with voluntary motion." But this did not strike the poet-philosophers as a promising method of creating life. Italian anatomist Luigi Galvani had discovered that the leg muscles of dissected frogs could be made to twitch if the spinal cord was stung by a current of electricity; it followed, therefore, that "perhaps a corpse would be reanimated; galvanism had given token of such things: perhaps the component parts of a creature might be manufactured, brought together, and imbued with vital warmth."

During this same soggy period, Lord Byron began to read macabre tales out loud. One was a German ghost story of an inconstant lover who kissed his bride on their wedding night only to see her metamorphose into the rotting corpse of the woman he had deserted. Another was Coleridge's poem *Christabel*, inspired by the real-life story of Mary and her mother. In Coleridge's poem the enchantress-vampire mother destroys her husband and daughter, Christabel. The stage was thus set for Lord Byron to suggest that each person present should write a ghost story.

As it turned out, the poets soon lost interest in the challenge. Mary, who was to become Mrs. Shelley upon the suicide of Harriet, did not. The twin ideas of death and creation haunted her. She had killed her mother and not replaced her, she had tried to will her dead baby into life, and she had listened for hour after hour to speculations about new forms of immortality contrived by latter-day Prometheans. In addition, she had read about a legendary creature called the golem, a figure made of clay by man and brought to a kind of life by magic means. Psychologically and intellectually she was ready to invent the brilliant young student Victor Frankenstein, who through diligent labors discovered the means of animating lifeless matter—then looked upon what he had wrought and was appalled.

"It was on a dreary night of November that I beheld the accomplishment of my toils," Mary has Victor say of his work. Rain spattered against the windowpanes as the exhausted youth gathered the instruments with which to infuse life into the creature he had made, an 8-foot man-thing constructed of organs stolen from graveyards. "I saw the dull yellow eye of the creature open; it breathed hard, and a convulsive motion agitated its limbs." It was supposed to have been a creature of the utmost beauty, each part lovingly selected for pro-

Elegant vampires of Victorian literature preyed almost exclusively upon young women of great beauty and virtue.

The Little People

Were the fairies real or merely cutouts made by 16-year-old Elsie Wright, who took the picture? This was a question of major interest in England after the photograph above appeared in a 1920 article by Sir Arthur Conan Doyle.

They populate a parallel universe of shifting light and shadow, as familiar as the tales of childhood, yet receding always like a half-remembered dream. Fairies are enchanting folk, fey, beguiling and tricksy, falling midway between demons and ourselves in exceedingly fragile variety. Still, scholars have done their best to classify fairies into two main groups. The first is made up of all who belong to the fairy race or nation, which dwells in a timeless, hidden kingdom, ruled by a fairy king and queen. This is the aristocracy of the species, called good folk or little people by humans. Usually diminutive and delicate—think of Titania, Oberon, Tinker Bell—these winged, laughing creatures dwell amid gold and silver, and dine on matchless food. Unwary humans coming upon them singing and dancing in the moonlight are likely to fall under their gossamer spell, occasionally with bittersweet results: a person who sojourns in fairyland may think he has lingered but a day, while hundreds of years have actually passed, and his mortal life has drifted away. Not that fairies wish such things to happen; they have little cause to trouble humans, and when, of necessity, they kidnap a baby or a mortal midwife, their victims are dutifully repaid with a changeling or a fairy child. The second type of fairy loves to dabble in human affairs, sometimes as benefactor, sometimes as troublemaker. Each has a function, a habitat or a trade: leprechauns cobble shoes in the night, dwarfs mine deep for gold, banshees howl the dying to rest. Brownies and kobolds are household familiars who finish chores while the family sleeps, but are just as likely to hide a broom or upend a flour bin if the mood strikes. Travelers who lose their way are called "pixie-led," while trolls terrify passers-by, and gremlins dance on the wings of airplanes and lure pilots off course. Some would have it that this magical multitude is the last trace of a pre-Adamic race, others that they are fallen angels. Still others know better than to question the ways of fairies; they close their eyes and hope for a visit.

portion and perfection. But—"Beautiful!—Great God! His yellow skin scarcely covered the work of muscles and arteries beneath; his hair was of a lustrous black, and flowing; his teeth of a pearly whiteness; but these luxuriances only formed a more horrid contrast with his watery eyes, that seemed almost of the same colour as the dun white sockets in which they were set, his shrivelled complexion and straight black lips."

Mary Shelley—the writer's name by the time her book *Frankenstein; or, The Modern Prometheus* was published in 1818—had dipped into her private fears and given shape to a grotesque, human-like figure that even today strikes an almost universal chord of horror and revulsion because we continue to fear that the creation of just such a monster is dangerously within man's capability. This suspicion that such things may someday be unleashed by man is fed by the knowledge that nature itself is capable of producing bizarre hybrid creatures, less ghoulish perhaps than the death-sired creation of Mary Shelley but still threatening in their perversion of the human form.

One night toward the end of June 1973, Randy Creath and Cheryl Ray heard something move in the brush nearby. Cheryl reached for a light switch and Randy got up to look. The news story, originating in Murphysboro, Illinois, continues: "At that moment it stepped from the bushes. Towering over the wide-eyed, teen-age couple was a creature resembling a gorilla. It was eight feet tall. It had long shaggy matted hair colored a dirty white. It smelled foul like river slime." After a moment that seemed interminable, the creature turned away and lumbered through the brush toward the Big Muddy River.

Although 17-year-old Randy was the son of a state trooper, his story might not have been believed if he and Cheryl had been the only witnesses. But the creature was seen several times over a period of weeks by a number of people, including three hard-to-fool carnival workers, a fascinated four-year-old and an adulterous couple disinclined to call attention to themselves. Observers—excluding the child, who said he saw "a big ghost"—independently described a creature about eight feet tall and about 300 to 400 pounds in weight, covered with light-colored, mud-matted hair. The entire 14-man Murphysboro police force, guided by a tracking dog and his trainer, pushed through the brush on the track of the unknown monster. They found a rough trail of broken branches and crushed grass. On the grass were gobs of black slime, redolent of the sewage sludge in tanks between Cheryl Ray's house and the river. The trail led the searchers to an abandoned barn, then vanished completely.

Later a screeching cry was heard several times. Peculiar footprints were seen on the muddy riverbank. Dogs picked up an unfamiliar scent, and panicked. Hunters swarmed over the area with rifles and shot-

(continued on page 108)

Bogus Beasts: Man-made Monsters

The 13th-century traveler, having just returned from some 16 or 17 years in China, had stern words for the unsavory industry he had witnessed while passing through Sumatra. "I also wish you to know," wrote Marco Polo, "that the pygmies that some travelers assert they bring from India are a lie and cheat, for I may tell you that these creatures, whom they call men, are manufactured in this island; and I will tell you how."

Marco Polo went on to describe the ingenious doctoring of small monkey corpses that made them seem like shrunken humans, but his indignant warning had little effect on the traffic in Sumatran pygmies. "Give the public what it wants" was as potent a dictum then as now, and one thing the public has always cherished is monsters, bogus or otherwise. Europeans of the 16th century were enthralled by dragons, and dragons they were given—sometimes concocted by mutilating a species of flying lizard imported from the Far East, but most typically made from the pliable carcass of a variety of skate, a flat-bodied, diamond-shaped fish. Even in their natural form, the underbellies of skates and their relatives the rays present markings that bear an eerie resemblance to a human face. Fill one to dragon plumpness, dress it with a spiky spine, dry it in the sun like a prune, and as if by magic there appears a genuine, albeit deceased, "dragon cub."

Such patchwork anomalies are called Jenny Hanivers (the name may come from *Anvers,* French for Antwerp, where some of these creatures were sold), whether they are peddled as dragons or as variants of the dread basilisk, a terrible mythical snake-like monster. American fishermen, apparently oblivious of their distinguished history, were selling homemade Jennys as recently as the 1930s.

The astonishing ease with which the true believer is duped by bogus beasts can be seen by comparing the mermaids of myth and a prototypal composite siren exhibited by P. T. Barnum in the mid-19th century. The Feejee Mermaid, as this fraudulent beauty was called, was really a two-foot-tall mummy-like hybrid, half monkey, half fish. Though its precise origins are unknown, the Feejee maiden is of a type that was turned out regularly by Japanese fishermen, who usually collected twice on their craft: once by charging for a viewing of their hideous handiwork and then by selling charms to ward off illnesses foretold by the creature before her "death."

Jenny Hanivers, such as this one, which was sold in London in 1970, are monsters made from bits of sea animals.

Yet however beguiling such bizarre aquatic specimens may be, all successful hoaxers know that man remains most interested in man. And since the days of Darwin, nothing has so fascinated mankind as news of the discovery of a missing link, a kind of hypothetical first cousin to both man and ape. The Ape Man of Sumatra, or *orang pendek,* as it was called by Dutch colonists, was one of the first lost links to turn up. An anthropoid creature, the Ape Man had for generations been "seen" in the jungle; he was reported to be between two and a half and five feet tall, to have pinkish skin, to be variously hairless and hairy, and to walk upright, although with heels facing forward. A likely specimen was found in May 1932, but on inspection it turned out to be only a lotong, a kind of monkey, shaven and with its cheekbones smashed to sharpen its resemblance to a human. Then there was Piltdown man, fragments of which were discovered in Sussex from 1908 to 1913 and were reportedly verified by scientists of the British Museum as belonging to an intermediate species. Or such was the belief until 1953, when the scientific community was shocked to learn that new tests revealed that the fragments had come from an orangutan and a paleolithic skeleton, their antique tint produced not by oxidation but artificially, probably by the application of the pigment Vandyke brown.

The scientific age is hard on bogus beasts, but they have not become extinct. The Ice Man of Minnesota created a huge stir in the 1960s when he was put on display. This incredible beast was covered with fur like an ape but had a body, including hands and feet, that seemed to be a cross between ape and man. Its exhibitor at first claimed that it had been discovered frozen in a block of ice floating off the coast of Siberia, but later he said that he had shot the creature and frozen it himself. One scientist, after viewing the Ice Man through the block of ice, was so impressed that he declared it a new species, but later students became convinced that it was another example of a bogus beast, this one made of plastic. And not long ago a British woman purchased a "very rare fur-bearing trout," only to be told when she took it to a museum that her trout had been covered with rabbit fur. She quickly offered to donate the furry fish to the museum.

Fact vs. Phenomenon

Marvelous Monsters of the Movies

By the time the movie industry was 16 years old, a vampire had sucked blood on the French screen (*The Devil's Castle*, 1896), Dr. Jekyll had transformed himself into Mr. Hyde in a 1908 feature filmed in Chicago, and Dr. Frankenstein's monstrous creation had flickered before moviegoers in 1910, all thanks to the genius of Thomas Alva Edison. In countless variations, these doughty monsters, together with mummies, werewolves and zombies, have been terrifying audiences ever since. Do we simply love being scared, or is there a deeper significance in our devotion to horror? Certainly, the triumph of good over evil is guaranteed in monster films. But their appeal may be even more basic. For thousands of years man has believed in magic; today, in the darkened confines of the movie theater, even the most rational of men can still indulge in the fantastic.

The murderous Mr. Hyde was portrayed by Fredric March in 1932.

Attending a masked ball disguised as a skeleton is the Phantom of the Opera, a horribly disfigured man who lived in a dungeon beneath the Paris Opera until he fell in love with a beautiful young opera singer.

Bela Lugosi created the first debonair vampire, the elegant Count Dracula, in a 1931 masterpiece.

Lon Chaney as Phantom of the Opera (1925)

Lon Chaney, Jr., as the Wolf Man (1941)

Boris Karloff in *The Old Dark House* (1932)

Boris Karloff's monster of *Frankenstein* (far left) and Max Schreck as Count Orlock in *Nosferatu,* made in 1921.

Lon Chaney played Quasimodo, the deformed bell ringer who fell in love with a Gypsy, in the 1923 version of *The Hunchback of Notre Dame.*

Egyptian mummy Kharis, kept alive by tea made from magic tana leaves, avenges the desecration of his beloved's tomb in *The Mummy's Curse* (1945).

Bela Lugosi as vampire Count Dracula

Boris Karloff's monster in *Frankenstein* (1935)

Lon Chaney in *London After Midnight* (1927)

Christopher Lee as Count Dracula in 1958

guns. But the mysterious creature was never found.

Some investigators believe that a gene deviation in a large ape may be responsible for a family of vertical, shaggy, generally bad-smelling and elusive creatures that bear a strong, if brutalized, resemblance to man and are known by such names as sasquatch, Bigfoot, yeti, Abominable Snowman, Swamp Ape and Skunk Ape. Others incline to theories involving hallucination, strong drink or hyperactive imagination.

In its manifestation as the Abominable Snowman, or yeti, the shaggy hominid has been known to Himalayan villagers for at least two centuries; Tibetans automatically include it in a list of local fauna, along with bears, snow leopards, civet cats and monkeys. The Western world was initiated into the yeti tradition in 1832, when B. H. Hodgson, British resident at the court of Nepal, mentioned in an article that his Nepalese porters had run in terror from a creature they described as upright, tailless and covered with long dark hair. Hodgson himself thought it was an orangutan, but the witnesses insisted they had seen a demon.

It was more than 50 years before another Westerner found some corroborative evidence of an unknown animal in the Himalayas. Maj. L. A. Waddell, a medical officer, Doctor of Laws and Fellow of the Linnaean Society, saw huge footprints in the snows of Sikkim at 17,000 feet: his porters told him they were yeti tracks. In his book *Among the Himalayas,* he discussed the Tibetans' profound belief in a hairy man of the snow, known as the *yeh teh* in the Sherpa dialect. But, he added, he had never actually seen the creature.

Stray discoveries of extraordinary tracks, glimpses of unidentifiable man-beasts and reports of bizarre attacks by alleged yetis slowly increased in the second quarter of the 20th century, but most Westerners believed that the snowman's true habitat was the realm of fantasy. Then in November 1951, British mountaineers Eric Shipton and Michael Ward discovered a set of enormous footprints impressed in mountain snow. The two climbers, returning from an Everest reconnaissance expedition, were exploring the Menlung Glacier at 18,000 feet when they came across fresh tracks extending for a mile along the edge of the ice mass.

As the trail descended into shallow, crystalline snow, the individual prints became increasingly firm and distinct. Shipton selected the clearest and sharpest of the impressions and photographed it twice, using Ward's booted foot as a scale in one photograph and an ice ax in the other. Taken from directly above, perfectly exposed and focused, Shipton's pictures show a five-toed foot more than 13 inches long by 8 inches wide, with an exceptionally broad heel.

If these were not the tracks of the yeti, they were the tracks of some other unidentified upright animal. Shipton, no stranger to footprints in the snow or the effects of melting ice crystals, declared himself convinced of "the existence of a large apelike creature, either quite unknown to science or at least not included in the known fauna of central Asia."

Yeti hunts became the rage during the 1950s and 1960s but fell off when nothing turned up. Then, in 1970, Don Whillans, deputy leader of the British expedition that tamed the south face of Annapurna, found and photographed a mystifying trail of prints at 13,000 feet in Nepal. Later, at night, he looked out from his tent and in the bright moonlight saw an ape-like creature "bounding along on all fours" across the crest of a ridge. He saw it only once, and briefly, but the sighting by a mountaineer of international repute cheered monster lovers everywhere.

Other evidence of something unaccounted for in the Himalayas turned up in December 1972, when

Coelacanths, prehistoric fish dating back at least 350 million years, were long thought to be extinct until fishermen accidentally caught one off the coast of South Africa in 1938.

In the wild, Mexican vampire bats suck the blood of their prey through tubes formed by their tongues and lower lips. Here, they lap blood from a laboratory dish.

members of the Arun Valley Wildlife Expedition made a reconnaissance trip from the rich river valley between Everest and Kanchenjunga up to the as yet unexplored heights around Kongmaa La mountain. On December 17 zoologist Edward W. Cronin, Dr. Howard Emery and two Sherpa assistants made camp at about 12,000 feet. The snow around their two light tents was crisp and firm, and there were no traces of footprints other than their own.

Before dawn on the following day Cronin was aroused by an excited cry from Emery, who had risen very early. A set of fresh footprints, apparently non-human, ran directly between the tents. Investigation indicated that whatever had made the tracks had climbed up an extremely steep and dangerous slope that must have required phenomenal strength and agility to negotiate. Working ahead of the sun, the two scientists photographed the footprints. Later in the day the expedition's mammalogist, Jeffrey McNeely, made plaster casts of the prints. The consensus was that the tracks bore a striking resemblance to the footprint in Eric Shipton's photographs. They looked, in fact, like the tracks of a huge, upright ape.

But was there any reason to regard it as a fearsome monster? Possibly. A creature leaving similar footprints attacked a Sherpa girl near the Everest village of Machermo in July 1974. The girl, Lhakpa Domani, had been tending yaks in a mountain pasture when she heard an odd coughing sound. Turning, she saw an enormous reddish-brown, monkey-like being with large eyes and prominent cheekbones. She screamed in terror and surprise, at which provocation the stranger

Hypertrichosis, a rare disease, can cover the body with hair.

picked her up and threw her roughly aside. The yeti—for that is what the villagers and the police constable declared the creature to be—then turned on the yaks, killing one by punching it and another by twisting its horns to break its neck. The monster then ate some of the meat and shambled away, having added another episode to the growing collection of man-monster tales.

Arguing against the existence of the yeti is the drab fact that not a single specimen has been captured alive or dead. The same lack of hard evidence pertains to its Western counterpart, commonly known as Bigfoot. Indians of British Columbia and the Pacific Northwest call the creature sasquatch, and Americans of various localities give it pet names such as the Skunk Ape of the Everglades and Momo the Missouri Monster, but Bigfoot is Bigfoot under any name.

It is also an enduring as well as a ubiquitous mystery, a part of American Indian tradition for centuries and the subject of 245 legends variously rooted in Canada and the United States. The earliest record of Bigfoot's apparent footprints dates from 1811, when a well-known explorer and trader named David Thompson, attempting to reach the mouth of the Columbia River by crossing the Rockies near what is now Jasper, Alberta, came across a trail of prints measuring an astonishing 14 inches long by 8 inches across. Indians said the tracks must have been made by one of the giants living on Vancouver Island.

Thompson did not encounter a giant, but since his time at least 750 people have seen a creature they believe to be a sasquatch or close member of the family, and probably as many more people have seen large footprints that defy explanation. Sightings have been reported from the Pacific Coast to Michigan, from the Yukon to Mexico; and oversize, shaggy, foul-smelling, two-legged beasts have apparently infiltrated various swamps and mountain areas in Arkansas, Florida, Mississippi, Missouri, Ohio, Oklahoma, Oregon, Washington and even North and South Dakota.

Example piles upon example to confound the skeptic. In 1924 a miner named Fred Beck, working a strike in Washington State's Ape Canyon, about 60 miles north of Portland, Oregon, shot a large ape-like creature that appeared unexpectedly at the canyon's rim. That night a horde of similar creatures attacked the cabin occupied by Beck and several fellow prospectors, pounding on the roof and on the walls in an apparent attempt to break in. Five hours later the frustrated callers went away, leaving hundreds of enormous footprints in evidence of their siege.

In 1962 a retired traffic controller named Harlan Ford and a buddy, Billy Mills, built themselves a hunt-

Such natural, though unusual, genetic deformities as two-headedness, which occurs occasionally among snakes as well as other animals, fascinated early-19th-century Europeans.

ing shack in Honey Island Swamp, a massive mire of wilderness shared by Mississippi and Louisiana. One morning, while taking in supplies, the two hunters saw a bulky shape rooting in the mud some 30 feet away. It rose up on two feet and stared straight at them. Its chest and shoulders were enormous and its body was covered with dingy grayish bristle, but the creature's face looked oddly human. After a moment it turned and disappeared into the bushes.

Ford and Mills were never again able to get close enough to the creature to put a bullet in it. But they found its tracks, many of them, and made plaster casts of yeti-like feet, which baffled investigators. Once they came across a big wild boar in its death throes, its throat ripped out by something that could not possibly live in the swamp—but evidently did. And often at night they and other campers heard the creature utter its cry: a long, high scream, ending in a throaty gurgle.

Not a few alleged Bigfoot prints and plaster casts of enormous tracks have turned out to be fakes. But the primate biologist John Napier is persuaded that the sasquatch probably does exist. One piece of evidence particularly convincing to Napier is a set of tracks spotted at Bossburg, Washington, in October 1969 by a butcher named Joe Rhodes and reported to sasquatch hunters Ivan Marx and Rene Dahinden. Analyzing the material gathered by the two investigators, Napier was struck by the fact that no fewer than 1,089 footprints had been discovered. At 17½ inches by 7 inches, they were large even for a sasquatch, but their most remarkable feature was that they had apparently been made by a cripple. The right foot of the Bossburg sasquatch was a clubfoot, which Napier judged to be the result of a crushing injury to the foot in early childhood. "It is very difficult," writes Napier in his book *Bigfoot*, "to conceive of a hoaxer so subtle, so knowledgeable—and so sick—who would deliberately fake a footprint of this nature. I suppose it is possible, but it is so unlikely that I am prepared to discount it."

If the creature is real, what is it? Perhaps, as suggested by a find in a Chinese drugstore, it is an anthropological dropout or an evolutionary hermit. In 1935 Ralph von Koenigswald, a Dutch paleontologist, entered an apothecary's shop while on a visit to Hong Kong. While waiting to be served, he browsed through the store's collection of fossil bones and teeth, which, pounded into powder, would be sold for their curative powers. In a jar on the counter he found a lower third molar of enormous size, apparently belonging to a primate of some kind but twice the size of the largest ape tooth ever found. The druggist had no idea where the tooth had come from or how long it had been among the family wares, but Von Koenigswald was so fired by his find that he spent much of the next 20 years searching for similar specimens. By 1954 he had 19 of the enormous teeth, and Chinese paleontologists had

For years the 600-pound mountain gorilla seemed to be a mythical beast. But then, in 1903, Oscar von Beringe killed one in Africa and displayed the hide in Europe.

This creature was killed in 1920 along the Colombia-Venezuela border. Unlike any monkey known from South America, it was, claimed its discoverer, five feet tall and tailless.

Hidden away on a farm by its owner and said to be a living specimen, Oliver is alleged to have one less chromosome than apes but one more chromosome than man.

unearthed another 47. Since they were virtually identical to human teeth, but six times larger, Von Koenigswald decided that they must belong to a species of giant ape, which he then dubbed *gigantopithecus*. Further discoveries of fossil specimens in Asia persuaded investigators that they had unmasked a man-ape about nine feet tall and 600 pounds in weight, whose family span began about 8 million years ago but who apparently died out within the last half million years.

But did *gigantopithecus* die out? Some monster enthusiasts think not . . . or maybe not. Zoologist Edward Cronin suggests the possibility that during the middle Pleistocene epoch, Asian *gigantopithecus* sought sanctuary from *Homo erectus* in the valleys of the Himalayas.

As for the American Bigfoot, it may be a variant of the Asian *gigantopithecus,* or it may not. That it too has eluded hunters for so long is not surprising. Peter Byrne, founder of the International Wildlife Conservation Society and director of the Bigfoot Information Center in Hood River, Oregon, points out that sasquatch and its relatives have been glimpsed over an area of about 100,000 square miles, much of which is mountainous or heavily forested land, sparsely inhabited

them. There *is* something remote and incomprehensible about the things that men call monsters, and it *is* more than their physical bodies. Francis Hitching, investigator of the mysterious, concludes that "the more you research this kind of subject, the surer you become that something else is operating in addition to the model of the Universe with which we have become familiar."

That "something else" is the real mystery and the real monster. If all physical manifestations are explained away, we are still left with amorphous terrors of the mind and our own need to give some form to them. Mary Shelley knew this and quoted Coleridge's *Rime of the Ancient Mariner* to express young Frankenstein's creeping "sickness of fear" as he attempted to elude, and at the same time ignore, a stalking horror:

> Like one, that on a lonesome road
> Doth walk in fear and dread,
> And having once turned round walks on,
> And turns no more his head;
> Because he knows, a frightful fiend
> Doth close behind him tread.

Some 20 feet of film were made of this "California sasquatch" (left) in 1967, but many naturalists doubt its authenticity. Other evidence includes numerous casts, such as the one below, with human bones superimposed on it.

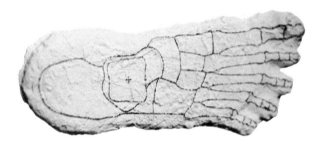

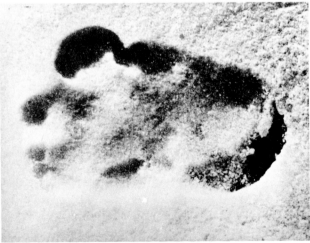

Veteran British mountain climber Eric Shipton photographed this footprint in 1951 in the snows of the Himalayas, home of the legendary but still undiscovered Abominable Snowman.

by humans and in places virtually impenetrable. The Stone Age Tasaday tribe, Byrne notes, lived undetected in the jungles of the Philippines until 1971.

The days of zoological discovery may be numbered, but they are not yet over. It is conceivable that, with 10 percent of the earth's land surface still unexplored, to say nothing of the ocean bottom, many unknown creatures may remain to be discovered: huge mammals or reptiles deep in the waters of the world; hairy man-apes or unimagined quadrupeds hidden in shrinking swamps or remote valleys. Within the last 150 years a great number of ancient myths have become scientific facts. Rumors of such animals as the gorilla, giant panda, pygmy hippopotamus, whale shark, okapi, platypus and the dragon-like lizard of Komodo caused jeers until they turned out to be true.

Yet it does no service to mankind to suggest that all the dark shapes of our fears and fantasies can be dismissed in terms of seagoing cephalopods and gigantic, evil-smelling man-apes. It is unlikely that the rational pursuit of such mystifying creatures will leave the world of monsters populated only by odd-looking natural animals with nothing of the nightmare about

Cameras and Sonar Probe for Nessie

If sighting reports are an indication, one of the largest classes of monsters inhabits neither the oceans nor the land. In a recent survey, British authors Janet and Colin Bord found that aquatic monsters have been reported in no fewer than 265 of the world's lakes and rivers. Of this total, Scotland claims 24 sites, one of which is probably the world's single most famous monster habitat.

Loch Ness is a long, narrow (24 miles by 1 mile) lake that lies in the basin of a great geologic fault that cuts through northern Scotland's Highlands. Despite the cold, the lake never freezes and is exceptionally deep—975 feet in at least one place. Its waters are so clotted with peat that underwater visibility extends only a few feet, but the loch nevertheless sustains an abundance of aquatic life, notably salmon, trout, chars and eels (some of which grow to great size).

No one knows when a monster may first have been sighted in Loch Ness, but as early as A.D. 565 the Irish missionary Saint Columba is said to have narrowly saved the life of one of his retainers who was swimming in the lake when the monster suddenly attacked. Since then, according to one estimate, 10,000 sightings have been reported, and the Loch Ness "beastie" has become a permanent fixture of Scottish folklore, attracting countless visitors to the mysterious site.

The widespread modern fame of the monster may be said to date from May 1933, when a correspondent for the Inverness *Courier* wrote a story based on the then-latest sighting report. The story provoked much local interest and prompted other people to come forward with tales of their own encounters with the monster. Yet another sighting was reported in July, and by October there had been over 20 more. Suddenly Nessie, as the monster was now called, was headline news throughout the world.

An inevitable negative reaction set in during the early months of 1934. Eminent scientists and academicians derided the sighting reports, and in at least one case, circumstantial evidence of Nessie's existence was found to have been faked. Perhaps worst of all, the press was beginning to lose interest in the story. Ironically, it was at just this time—April 1934—that Lt. Col. R. K. Wilson, a London physician, took a photograph allegedly showing Nessie's head and neck (above, right). Although no evidence of tampering could be found, the picture was not taken seriously at the time. Yet it remains one of the best portraits of Nessie to date.

The dark-colored creature shown in Wilson's picture is consistent with most—though not all—of the eyewitness reports before and since. Protruding from

The monster's head and neck seem to loom out of Loch Ness in this shadowy photograph taken in 1934.

what appears to be a large oval body is a swan-like neck surmounted by a small, flat head. In fact, the Nessie of Wilson's picture looks very much like a plesiosaur—a family of large marine reptiles thought to have been extinct for more than 70 million years.

In the years that followed the publication of Wilson's now-famous photograph, sighting reports continued to multiply, but it was not until 1960 that a second equally impressive picture of the monster was taken. In April (apparently a good month for Nessie-watchers) of that year, Tim Dinsdale, an English aeronautical engineer, took 50 feet of 16-mm. movie film showing a large black hump-shaped object moving across the loch at better than seven miles per hour. Dinsdale's film was later analyzed by the Royal Air Force's Joint Air Reconnaissance Intelligence Center, which concluded, "It probably is an animate object."

In 1972 the hunt for Nessie moved into a more sophisticated phase. In August a U.S. team of scientists from the Academy of Applied Science, using an advanced form of underwater stroboscopic camera in conjunction with Raytheon sonar equipment, obtained visual and sonic images of something in the loch. Upon subsequent enhancement by NASA computers, one image appeared to show a flipper attached to a larger object, perhaps a very large animal. Encouraged, the academy sent another expedition to Loch Ness in 1975 and obtained further evidence. According to the lab technician who performed the computer enhancement of the 1975 images, "One picture showed a body with a long neck and two stubby appendages. . . . the second frame appeared to show a neck and head. . . . the neck was reticulated." The academy's conclusion: "There *is* a species of large aquatic creature in Loch Ness."

So great was the excitement about the academy's finds that in 1976 the staid *New York Times* contributed $25,000 in support of a new expedition to the Highlands loch. Yet in spite of additional sonar evidence and photographs, Nessie eluded further detection. Undeterred, the academy explored the possibility of training British dolphins to help extend the search.

Sensational though the 1972 and 1975 findings were, a majority of scientists remain unconvinced. Most reports, they say, are just plain unreliable, and even the best photographs are too ambiguous to constitute proof. Thus the controversy continues, essentially unresolvable until Nessie is actually found. Until that moment, one might do worse than to keep an open mind about the whole affair. As G. K. Chesterton once pointedly remarked, "Many a man has been hanged on less evidence than there is for the Loch Ness Monster."

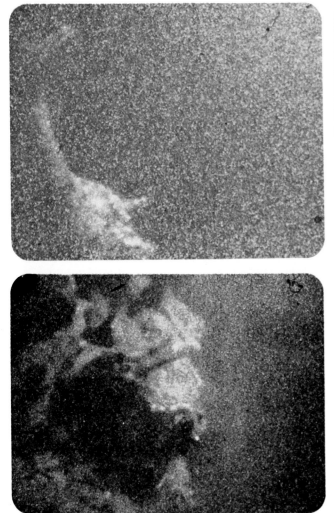

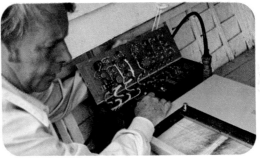

The Boston-based Academy of Applied Science used sonar to search for the Loch Ness monster during its investigations.

An underwater photograph (left) taken by the academy team shows a vague form that might be the figure of Nessie.

This underwater picture may show the creature's head and open mouth, facing the camera. After analyzing this image, naturalist Peter Scott made the painting at right to show how the head might actually look.

The artist's rendering above of the bottom of Urquhart Bay in Loch Ness vividly depicts the labyrinth of deep valleys in which an underwater creature might hide and thus escape electronic detection. The vertical scale in the diagram is exaggerated for greater clarity.

Using animals, exotic cards and
the human body itself, men and women have
long sought to predict the future.

DIVINATION

A French Renaissance tarot card may foretell disaster or change.

In *The Religious System of the Amazulu,* British scholar Henry Callaway quoted a tale told by a South African who was worried about his pregnant goat: "We went to a diviner, the brother of Umatula, who divined with bones. . . . He took a little medicine and chewed it, and puffed [blew] on his bag in which the bones were kept; he rubbed them, and poured them out on the ground; he managed them, and said, 'O, what does the goat mean? There are two kids—one white, and the other, there it is, it is grey. What do they mean?'

"We replied, 'We do not know, friend. We will be told by the bones.'

"He said, 'This goat, which is a female black goat, is yeaning [pregnant]. But it is as though she had not yet yeaned [given birth]. But what do you say? You say, the goat is in trouble. O, I say for my part when I see the bones speaking thus, I see that the young ones are now born. . . . The bones say, "When you reach home the goat will have given birth to two kids. . . ." This is what the bones say.'

"We gave him money and went home," the South African's account continued, "I not believing that there was any truth in it, for the bones did not speak. . . . When we reached home we found the goat now standing at the doorway with two kids—one white and the other grey. I was at once satisfied. We sacrificed and returned thanks to the Amatongo."

Divination, man's effort to know the mysterious present and predict the future, has been practiced throughout the world since the dawn of history. Although rituals of divination have changed with the passage of time, their purpose has remained constant: to gain hidden knowledge, if possible through divine channels, that may help solve the great and small problems of life. Thus, kings have asked oracles to determine the most effective strategy for military campaigns; tribal hunters have tried to discover where game might be most plentiful; and lovers have sought to divine the most propitious time, place and means of winning the affection of their beloved.

Do the divinatory arts bespeak some common intuition that suggests that neither causality nor time is quite as we perceive it?

Poet T. S. Eliot once wrote:
Time present and time past
Are both perhaps present in time future,
And time future contained in time past.
If all time is eternally present
All time is unredeemable.
What might have been is an abstraction.

Eight forces of change, symbolized by the three-line trigrams within the circle on this Chinese panel, combine to tell the future in the *I Ching.* Yin and yang at the circle's center and an egg-shaped tiger represent the melding of opposites.

If this were indeed true, then theoretically divination might work. It would simply be a method of detecting a future that is already adequately defined and firmly embedded in the present. Or does divination, a human activity at once so ancient and so universal, do no more than prove the vulnerability of man's intellect to the incessant proddings of desire and dread? Setting aside such major questions, there is a more basic issue: Does divination work? The record is an intriguing one.

Among the most advanced and literate civilizations of ancient times were those of Greece and China. Two events illustrate the unbroken tradition of divination in these two cradles of so much of modern thought, literature, science and technology. One example is ancient, the other from the present day.

The Greek historian Herodotus recorded the story of a prediction made to King Croesus of Lydia, best known for his fabulous wealth ("as rich as Croesus"). Croesus, before undertaking a military campaign against Persia in the 6th century B.C., wanted to select the most reliable oracle. He tested several by asking them what secret action he was engaged in. The best description came from the Delphic oracle, where one of the priestesses said the king was "boiling a lamb and a tortoise together in a copper vessel with a copper lid." Pleased with the Delphic oracle's response, Croesus then asked for a prediction concerning his planned attack against the Persians. The priestess replied that if he crossed the Halys River, which would be tantamount to launching such an attack, the king would "destroy a great empire." Unfortunately, when Croesus did march his troops against Persia, he succeeded only in destroying his own empire. In truly oracular fashion, the prediction had been correct.

A modern test of divination occurred in July 1976 after a northeastern area of China, including the industrial city of Tangshan, suffered one of the most severe earthquakes in the country's history. Although reported officially only in the vaguest terms, news of the disaster spread throughout China and was widely interpreted as an omen of Chairman Mao Tse-tung's "impending" death and of an aftermath of turmoil.

Peking authorities were alarmed by such tendencies to rely on traditional ways of ascribing supernatural meanings to odd or frightening events. To counter-

In one form of Roman animal augury, a chicken was set loose amid corn scattered near letters set in a circle. Letters left untouched formed the basis of various predictions.

act the trend toward renewed belief in omens, the official press, including the scholarly publication *Scientia Geologica Sinica*, denounced it as an expression of primitive, anti-Marxist superstition. The geologic magazine recalled that following the fall of a meteor in 1064, some disciples of the philosopher-sage Confucius had used the event "in order to confuse the masses with evil rumours." Yet later in 1976, when China's powerful chairman died, a time of extensive turmoil did indeed ensue.

The universal allure of divination is striking. N. Mkele, a South African authority on divination and diviners, has written that "basic to African thinking is the assumption of an ordered nature of things that is amenable to human control." Much African divination concentrates on finding the causes of illness. Among the Xhosas and Zulus, according to Mkele, it is believed that the diviner has "super-normal powers of cognition which enable him not merely to describe the course of a patient's illness, but to tell whether the patient has been bewitched and by whom, or whether the illness is a religious one, or is due to natural causes." The diviner is credited with access to the ancestral gods, and it is believed that "nothing can be hidden from him."

Similar practices are followed among the Nyoro of Uganda. According to John Beattie, the author of a sociological essay on divination in Bunyoro, Uganda, the Nyoro "consult diviners when they are in trouble, and want to know the cause of the trouble, and what they should do about it. The commonest kind of trouble is illness, and most consultations relate to a client's health, or that of his child or other close relative." As with many other African tribes, cowrie shells play a major part in Nyoro divination. Predictive techniques center on the way in which cowrie shells fall on the ground. The diviner may also ask a shell a specific question, then hold it to his ear for a response.

A fascinating link with the divination of antiquity is the Nyoro use of animal entrails (haruspication), known from cuneiform tablets to have been employed in ancient Babylonia. The Nyoro diviner usually uses a chicken, cutting it open carefully so as not to injure its intestines. In general, if internal organs are found to be in good condition, this augurs well; if not, it may mean trouble. Spots on the organs, swellings and obvious disarray are bad signs, but "if there are no spots and the intestines are lying in their normal positions," then "the patient will recover."

There has been speculation among anthropologists that divination by animal intestines and charred bones might have evolved from animal sacrifices. No written record documents this assumption, and yet, as sacrifices were common, it seems possible that augury might have taken place before or after such ceremonies.

Bones may be used to divine in the same way that shells, tea leaves, coffee grounds and dice are employed in different cultural settings. Modern dice in fact may have derived from cubes originally used in the predictive arts. Certain dice found in China have suggested such an evolution, and dice with markings much like those on today's dice have been found in Egyptian tombs dating to 2000 B.C. Yet no one is sure what came first, divination or gaming.

Another divination technique involves liquids and the predictive patterns they may make. In Louisiana today, for example, breaking a raw egg and reading the way the yolk and white separate is still in use. This method has been described by Tracey Peterson, who recalled that her great-grandmother Alexina Charpentier Renaud had practiced this form of Cajun divination. Renaud, who died in 1955 at the age of 87, used to break three eggs into three glasses of water and say that she saw images in the "feelers" of the eggs.

On one occasion Renaud used egg divination to locate her son Randolph, a soldier stationed in France during World War I. He had been writing regularly until the armistice, but then his whereabouts became unknown. His mother decided to "ask the eggs." When she did so, she saw forming in the egg "a tiny image of a train," including miniature passengers with tiny heads. When Randolph returned, he confirmed that at the very time that his mother had practiced her egg divination, he had indeed been "on the East Coast, heading for Louisiana by train."

In central Europe a similar tradition of long standing remains popular even now on New Year's Eve. After the New Year has been rung in, celebrants—particularly youngsters—take lead, melt it in a spoon, drop it into water and then read their fortunes in the odd shapes that the hardened lead has taken. This practice, now undertaken in the spirit of New Year's Eve fun, is believed by folklorists to predate Christian times.

A related procedure substitutes melted wax for liquid lead in a divination technique employed in many parts of the world, including the United States. Instructions on how to use and interpret candle wax were given by James R. Cole in *Fate* magazine, June 1973: "The client lights the candle and at the same time silently asks a question or makes a wish. Then the candle is tilted slightly, so that drops of the wax fall onto the surface of the water in the pan. The drops solidify into tiny spheres about one-eighth inch in diameter and float on the surface of the water. The first drops will go straight to the edge of the pan as if drawn by a magnet and gradually fill out a border. As you continue to drop wax the drops begin to form symbols or patterns on the surface of the water. An inexperienced seer sometimes does not let enough wax fall. The more wax that falls, the more symbols are formed and the more complete the reading will be."

The accumulation of wax at the edge of the pan gives the diviner his first clues. If the border is unbroken, this indicates a positive answer to the client's question; a wavy border suggests doubt; a broken border

(continued on page 120)

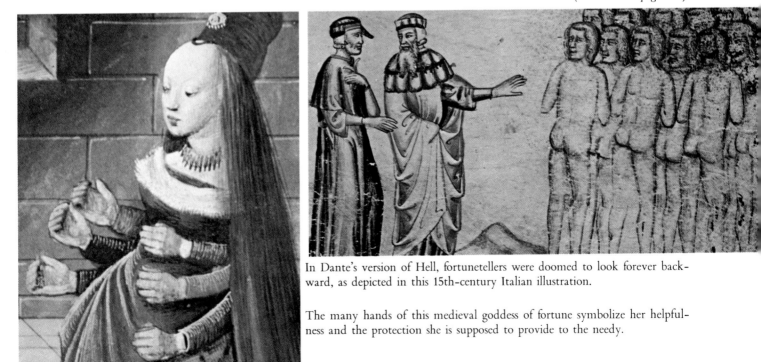

In Dante's version of Hell, fortunetellers were doomed to look forever backward, as depicted in this 15th-century Italian illustration.

The many hands of this medieval goddess of fortune symbolize her helpfulness and the protection she is supposed to provide to the needy.

Aleister Crowley created a tarot pack—one card depicted a goat-devil—to sustain his occult views.

This knight of cups is from an 18th-century Bavarian minor arcana tarot pack.

The high priestess shown at right is part of a tarot pack designed for *Live and Let Die*, a 1973 James Bond movie.

THE HIGH PRIESTESS

The Art of the Tarot

"The Gypsies possess a Bible, yes, this card game called the *Tarot* which the Gypsies possess is the Bible of Bibles," wrote Gérard Encausse in 1889 in tracing the tarot's origin to the Gypsies who wandered from India into Europe. Yet Antoine Court de Gébelin, among the most famous of tarot theorists, wrote in 1781 that the cards' markings distilled all Egyptian knowledge.

In fact, little is known with certainty about the development of the two tarot packs. The minor arcana, the face and number cards from which our modern playing cards derive, seems to represent not only the kings, queens and knaves but also other segments of medieval society: the wand symbolizes peasants; the cup, clergy; the sword, nobles; and the coin, merchants. Yet 19th-century French courtiers saw prophetic power in these symbols as well, the wand foretelling news; the cup, happiness; the sword, death; and the coin, money. Of the major arcana, all that is known is that the design of the oldest existing pack, dating from 1392, has shown little change over the years. Though the tarot's secrets and origins remain obscure, by 1601 at least one person was forced to take the cards seriously. On March 13 of that year, Henry Cuffe, secretary to the Earl of Essex, was found guilty of treason and hanged—and it was rumored that his future had been foretold by the turning of three cards—a man under guard, a judge and a gallows.

Tarot cards were used not only to tell fortunes but to play fashionable card games such as tarocchino, which was introduced by the prince of Pisa in the 15th century.

Italian minchiate cards, such as these from the 18th century, showed virtues, zodiac signs and a sacrificial lamb in a blazing pyre as well as traditional tarot figures.

The hanged man and the chariot above are from the oldest-known tarot pack, one thought to have been made in 1392 for the mad French king Charles VI.

This emperor, representing power, strength and worldly success, is from the French Marseilles deck.

L'EMPEREUR

points to trouble. Every diviner seems to have favorite, strongly indicative symbols. When Cole perceives what appears to be a cat in the melted wax, he regards it as an indication of trickery; a pistol suggests disaster and possible death, an image of Venus points to peace and/or love, a jumping figure indicates change, and a ship portends news from a distance, or a journey.

Cole never melts a black candle because he feels the color has "negative vibrations." Indeed, if colors can be said to contain divinatory symbolism, none can compare with black, the color of darkness and death.

A black raven, celebrated by Edgar Allan Poe, has repeatedly played the role of ill omen. Black birds generally are said to "bring bad luck." The royal house of Hesse, with family links to the British and Russian royal families, has been associated with the raven as a dire omen since the 19th century. Specifically, its castle near the German town of Darmstadt has reportedly been the scene of various raven appearances.

In 1873 two youthful princes were playing together in their chamber within the castle when a raven landed on the window ledge. One of the boys, Prince Frederick, leaned out the window and fell to his death. Five years later another black raven was discovered, this one flying in the sickroom of the Hesse children, who were ill with diphtheria. One of the little girls died shortly afterward. Later that year a black bird was seen again, shortly before the Grand Duchess of Hesse, second daughter of Queen Victoria of England, died at the castle. It is said that the court physician had heard the raven pecking at the window. The bird seems to have appeared at the castle several times thereafter, always as an omen of impending ill fortune or death.

Birds, of course, are only one of many kinds of animals in whose behavior humans have professed to find auguries of the future. Extensive collections of premonitory lore are associated with dogs, cats, goats, sheep, fish, rats, mice and even spiders (a spider seen in the morning, according to an old German saying, brings illness and sorrow; one seen in the evening, health and good fortune). Yet in most cases of this kind, the proposed link between what an animal is doing and what its actions portend is entirely magical—that is, there is no scientifically demonstrable connection whatever. Yet in certain cases this may not be entirely true. For ani-

A wheel for divining by numbers illustrated an 1831 occult work, *Raphael's Witch.*

mals do sometimes show an uncanny ability to perceive the onset of certain large-scale weather changes, natural calamities and the like. Even now scientists cannot fully explain why some animals, hours or even days before the event, seem able to sense the coming of an earthquake, though the matter is being seriously studied. Doubtless the key word in this mystery is *sense.* It is one thing if the animals in question are simply using their five senses, if in much amplified form. It would be quite another if they were making use of special sensitivities researchers know nothing about.

In recent years psychologists and physiologists have devoted a good deal of study to what are called altered states of consciousness (ASC). These are states of mind that differ from what we recognize as normal, and they include various forms of awareness, body control and wakefulness. A person who is asleep is, obviously enough, in a quite different form of consciousness from someone who is awake. But there are many related stages, including differing degrees of hypnosis, trances and pre-sleep consciousness. Ancient oracles may have achieved such an altered state by breathing noxious fumes from the earth, as at Delphi. Other forms of disassociation may be achieved by autosuggestion, often by gazing intently at a bright object, such as a fire, candle or crystal ball, or possibly by staring at the sun.

In the history of divination, the *I Ching,* or *Book of Changes,* has a unique place. It is both ancient and modern, primitive and sophisticated: the system has been used in China for thousands of years, and it has enjoyed remarkable favor in the Western world in the 20th century. The *I Ching*'s basic technique, the throwing of sticks, has much in common with simple divination methods, yet through the sticks a diviner is linked with a series of complex philosophic principles.

While the history of the *I Ching* is unclear, the *Book of Changes* that outlines it has been attributed to the Chinese emperor Fu Hsi, himself a legendary figure. Such an association would date the *I Ching* to the 3rd millennium B.C. The *Book of Changes* was streamlined by King Wên Wang around 1100 B.C. and altered by his son the Duke of Chou. Around the 5th century B.C. it was interpreted by Confucius, the sage who is said to have used the system throughout his life. Confucius is credited with saying that the book has "as

Reading the Body's Signs

Of man's many exercises in self-interpretation, perhaps none exceeds in earnestness the practices he has invented to divine his future and character by reading various parts of the body. The best known and most widely practiced today is palmistry, the study of the hand, but there is also phrenology, the study of the shape of the skull; physiognomy, the study of the features and structure of the face; and moleosophy, the study of moles on the body.

The origins of palmistry are unclear, although it is believed to have started either in India or in China, where it is said to have been in use as early as 3000 B.C. It is still practiced widely among the people of the East and Middle East, and is sometimes combined with podoscopy—divination by analysis of the feet.

Palmistry begins with the obvious and proceeds—by innumerable intricate steps of judgment and interpretation—to extreme detail. Its conclusions are couched not in terms of certainty but of probability and tendency. A serious palmist will begin by examining both hands: with a right-handed subject the left is considered the "birth" hand—that which shows inherited predispositions of character—while the right hand is thought to reflect individuality, flexibility and potential. For the left-handed subject, the opposite would be true.

To the palm reader, overall formation of the hands is a first clue to character and destiny. A square hand identifies the practical person, someone forceful, purposeful, capable of achieving success. The tapering hand, called conical in palmists' parlance, is likely to belong to an artist, a convivial, enthusiastic and sensitive soul. The spade-like hand appears to be in motion even at rest and denotes an energetic owner with a need for positive action. The pointed hand belongs to the idealist, the sometimes impractical lover of beauty. The long hand, knotty at the joints, is that of the thinker, or philosopher. Most people have a mixed hand, displaying features of two or more classic shapes. Besides shape, there is also flexibility to be considered. Moderate flexibility tells of a reasonable personality, while great flexibility indicates unconventionality, and great stiffness shows stubbornness.

Thumbs and fingers are considered as well. A thumb set low, at a wide angle to the hand, bespeaks a careless type, while a thumb set high on the hand indicates a

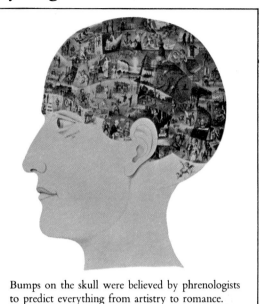

Bumps on the skull were believed by phrenologists to predict everything from artistry to romance.

cautious, possibly even unyielding character. Long fingers suggest a fondness for detail, short fingers an impetuous, impatient personality. (Fingers are considered long if the length of the second finger exceeds the distance from its knuckle to the wrist; if the distance is less, they are short; if equal, average.)

Palmists consider all these facets of the hand and more before arriving finally at palmistry's lodestone: that richly articulate assemblage of planes, bumps, lines and markings that form the palm itself. The landscape of the palm is dominated by mounts, fleshy swellings that lie at the base of each finger, at the base of the thumb and along the palm's outer edge. Critical, too, are the palm's three major creases, which extend across it and are called, from the top down, the line of Heart, the line of Head and the line of Life. Palmistry's links to astrology are evident in the naming of the mounts and regions of the hand. From the mount just below the first finger outward they are: Jupiter, representing ambition; Saturn, sobriety; Apollo, artistic talent and appreciation; and Mercury, hope and intelligence. Upper Mars, just below Mercury, represents perseverance; Luna, lying along the heel of the hand, the creative forces, imagination and intuition; Venus, at the lower base of the thumb, love and passion; and finally Lower Mars, above Venus, tells of coolness and calculation. In the center of the hand is the Plain of Mars, representing emotional control, nervousness or negativeness, depending on its form.

Beyond such complexities, the permutations of markings in a given hand—circles, stars, crosses and squares—begin to flow into infinity. Yet it is just this infinite number of possibilities that the seeker of a reading pursues: not necessarily for knowledge of the future or of hidden character, but for confirmation of his personal uniqueness.

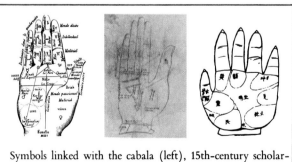

Symbols linked with the cabala (left), 15th-century scholarship, and the *I Ching* have influenced palmistry.

121

many layers as the earth itself," and many contemporary students of the system will eagerly testify to the accuracy of this description.

Yet even if one allows for the complexity of philosophic wording and the intricacies of translating from a language that is archaic as well as vastly different in structure, the *Book of Changes* remains difficult to comprehend. As a result, while scholars have interpreted its meanings in myriad ways, the work's very elusiveness has added to its mysterious attraction.

Much of the book's present popularity is due to the enthusiasm of the Swiss psychologist-philosopher Carl G. Jung, whose system of analytical psychology contains the concept of synchronicity, or meaningful coincidence. In his forward to Richard Wilhelm's translation of the *Book of Changes,* Jung noted his life-long interest in "this oracle technique, or method of exploring the unconscious" and its relation to his synchronicity concept. He said that use of the *I Ching* parallels "the coincidence of events in space and time as meaning something more than mere chance, namely, a peculiar interdependence of objective events among themselves," as well as with the subjective psychological states of "the observer or observers."

The *Book of Changes* can be consulted in several ways. According to the classic method, 50 yarrow sticks are divided into random piles and then counted. The numbers derived from repeated countings tell what hexagram, or figure of six parallel lines, to consult in the book. Each of 64 possible hexagrams refers to one or more enigmatic sayings from which an advisory message can be surmised. A popular modern technique for consulting the hexagrams is to cast three coins. They must be thrown a half-dozen times in all to obtain the six lines of the figure.

Traditionally, the *I Ching* is used in a way that encourages deep thought and self-examination. It may even be used to induce a state of consciousness similar to meditation. Concentration is essential, experts advise, because the sayings to be interpreted may be obscure; for instance, the 14th hexagram, Ta Yu (Abundance), says that "there will be great progress and success," and "the Superior Man represses evil and gives distinction to what is good." It is the reader's wisdom and thorough knowledge of centuries-old interpretations, believers feel, that are the key to a successful reading.

The Western parallel of the *I Ching* is a unique group of playing cards known as the tarot. Although they bear some of the symbols familiar in modern playing cards, tarot cards possess a special element, a sense of the ancient and fear-inspiring. Their medieval designs seem sometimes deliberately shocking—death, the devil, the hanged man—though some are more engaging, such as the lovers, the juggler, the chariot, justice, the wheel of fortune, the sun, moon and stars. In any event, as playing cards evolved, the swords found on early tarot sets became spades, cups turned into hearts, coins into diamonds, and wands into clubs. Thus just as modern dice probably have fortunetelling cubes as their antecedents, so do modern cards reflect the existence of earlier symbols. According to occult tradition, the tarot may have originated in Egypt, or the cabalists in northern Africa may have designed the cards in A.D. 1200. It is possible as well that Italian, perhaps Venetian, occultist-designers superimposed their own ideas of ancient symbols on cards that may have been used in connection with alchemy or for more mundane purposes, but no one knows with certainty.

Richard Cavendish, in *The Black Arts,* has written that "there is something extraordinarily fascinating about the Tarot. It opens strange windows into a world in which things are never quite what they seem, can never quite be grasped, a sunlit medieval landscape of tiny figures moving like marvellous toys—the Fool with cap and bells, the Emperor and Empress with a

The mythical Li T'ieh-Kuai, immortal but living as a crippled beggar, illustrates the merging of opposites, the philosophy upon which the *I Ching* is based.

豫

*Yü
Enthusiasm*

☷☳

Enthusiasm. It furthers one to install helpers and to set armies marching.

未濟

*Wei Chu
Before Completion*

☲☵

Before completion. Success. But if the little fox after nearly completing the crossing, gets his tail in the water, there is nothing that would further.

glittering cavalcade, Death at his reaping, the Hermit with staff and lamp, the Hanged Man swinging from his gibbet, the pale Tower falling."

The standard pack of tarot cards today is composed of four suits of 14 cards each. These 56 cards make up the minor arcana. The major arcana, or trumps, contains an additional 22 cards decorated with figures representing natural laws, elements, virtues and vices. The unnumbered figure of the fool has come down to us as the joker in everyday playing cards.

While experts recognize many existing versions of the accurate order of the trumps, the following is one that is widely accepted: 0 The fool; 1 The juggler; 2 The female pope; 3 The empress; 4 The emperor; 5 The pope; 6 The lovers; 7 The chariot; 8 Justice; 9 The hermit; 10 The wheel of fortune; 11 Strength; 12 The hanged man; 13 Death; 14 Temperance; 15 The devil; 16 The falling tower; 17 The star; 18 The moon; 19 The sun; 20 Judgment Day; 21 The world.

Divining by tarot cards is as individual as crystal gazing or any other form of popular fortunetelling. No single authoritative book of instructions exists, although numerous volumes on tarot techniques have been published. The personality, attitude and inclination of whoever reads the cards come into play when the tarot cards are laid out and divination begins. As in every other method, an altered state of consciousness seems a valuable adjunct to interpretation. The British author Colin Wilson says in *The Occult* that the reader should seek a medieval mood, his mind filled with images of Gothic cathedrals and stained glass, "small towns surrounded by fields, and artisans at their everyday work."

A reader consults the *I Ching* by repeatedly dividing and counting groups of yarrow sticks. The resulting numbers determine which of 64 six-line hexagrams (four are shown at left with their meanings) bear advice for the future.

Chung Fu
Inner Truth

Inner truth. Pigs and fishes. Good fortune. It furthers one to cross the great water. Perseverance furthers.

Pi
Grace

Grace has success. In small matters it is favorable to undertake something.

Readers have their own preferences on how best to place the cards before them. One of the most popular methods is the seven-card spread. Basic interpretations of the value of individual cards may be found, but there is no general agreement on their meaning in all situations. The fool may be seen as the eternal symbol of folly; the juggler, or magician, as a primitive life force (or, in modern psychological terms, as the ego); and the female pope, or high priestess, as feminine duality—the balancing of opposites through the use of common sense and wisdom. The seven-spoked wheel of fortune is often perceived as a symbol of birth and rebirth, the ever-renewing cycle of nature. Justice, a female figure who holds scales, exhibits neither fear nor favor. The hanged man is perhaps the most controversial of the cards: students of the tarot have suggested as alternatives to its macabre image the themes of renewal and resurrection.

Tarot cards differ from playing cards in that their upper and lower halves have different values. The pictures if placed right side up have one meaning; if placed upside down, the meaning is reversed. Thus, Angus Hall, in *Signs of Things to Come,* gives this interpretation for the world card when it appears turned right side up: "attainment; ultimate change; completion; success; the admiration of others. Triumph." He interprets the same card when placed upside down as symbolizing "imperfection; lack of vision. Failure to finish what has been started."

Yet for all its antiquity and prestige, the tarot probably must yield pride of place in the West to another form of divination: crystal gazing, best known for its basic tool, the crystal ball. Cartoonists often portray fortunetellers, complete with turbans and exotic furnishings, recounting something startling or baffling to their clients, a crystal ball on the table between them. In fact, crystal gazing seems to have derived from something even more ancient: the haunting quality of reflected images. The ancient Greeks used the calm surface of water, and later a mirror, as a means of entering a trance, which enabled them to "see" their fortune or that of someone else. Any reflective surface might create such a state of transient consciousness, and Arab tradition has it that warriors used the polished surfaces of their swords for this purpose.

The use of a mirror as a divinatory tool is part of universal folklore. The fairy tale "Snow White," based on European folk tradition, portrays the wicked stepmother as asking, "Mirror, mirror on the wall, who is the fairest of them all?" As long as the mirror announces that she is the most beautiful of women, all is well; but when the mirror replies that Snow White has grown to be the fairest, the stepmother tries to destroy the girl by giving her a poisoned apple.

To reflect the gleam of spring water, the ancient

Gazing into a crystal's twisted images, like those shown in this 17th-century ball, may alter the mind's perceptions.

Greeks lowered a mirror toward the water's surface, the better to trap an image appearing there. Pausanias reported in *Description of Greece* that there was a spring near Patrai, or Patras, where people used to "tie a mirror to a fine cord, and let it down so far that it shall not plunge into the spring, but merely graze the surface of the water with its rim. Then, after praying to the goddess and burning incense, they look into the mirror, and it shows them the sick person either living or dead. So truthful is the water." Nostradamus (Michel de Nostredame), the famous 16th-century French physician and seer, also used both water and mirrors for divination. He often stared at the surface of water in a bowl until he believed he saw images of future events.

Divination by means of gazing into any reflector, such as water, a mirror or a crystal ball, is known as scrying (from the archaic English word *descry,* which means "to see"). Arabic tradition, which in many ways served as a cultural bridge between antiquity and the Renaissance, includes various forms of scrying. A 14th-century writer, Abd al-Rahman ibn Muhammad ibn Khaldun, spoke of "those who gaze at diaphanous bodies, such as mirrors, basins filled with water and liquids." He described as "mistaken" the diviners who believed that the image they saw actually "appears on the surface of the mirror." Rather, he felt, "the diviner looks fixedly at the surface until it disappears and a fog-like curtain interposes itself between his eyes and the mirror," and "on this curtain the shapes that he desires to see form themselves."

Andrew Lang, writing in the *Encyclopaedia of Re-*

"Seeing" With Trembling Hands

The Navaho Indians in the United States practice one of the most mysterious of the many forms of divination, a technique that depends upon a trance-like state of physical decontrol known as hand trembling. The American anthropologist Dr. Clyde Kluckhohn studied and reported on his personal experiences with one hand trembler, a particular Navaho diviner by the name of Gregorio.

Kluckhohn and his wife visited a Navaho reservation on a field trip. Once there, having heard about Gregorio's skill, they decided to combine the practical with the scholarly and asked him to attempt to locate a handbag that Mrs. Kluckhohn had lost only a few days before. After listening to the Kluckhohns, Gregorio rolled up his sleeves, carefully washed his arms and hands and climbed slowly to the top of a hill. While facing north, he sprinkled corn pollen on his right hand, which began to tremble. Next he rubbed the palms of both hands together, and in a short while his left hand began to tremble as well. Gregorio continued this ritual several times with his eyes closed. He then slowly moved both hands as if to form the outlines of the missing bag. Finally he explained to the Kluckhohns that the missing bag could be found at the local trading post. And there it was.

Diviners such as Gregorio, the Kluckhohns found, regard their trembling hands as something that exists beyond their personal powers and control. And whatever the validity of their accomplishments, their skill seems very much alive and often impressive in its achievements. Richard Reichbart, writing in the *Journal of the American Society for Psychical Research* in 1976, reported that hand trembling "continues to flourish" to a remarkable degree on the 22,000-square-mile Navaho reservation that straddles northeastern Arizona, northwestern New Mexico, southeastern Colorado and a piece of southern Utah. He noted as well that the region's "extreme isolation has permitted the continuance of traditional Navajo customs, perhaps more so than in the case of customs of less isolated tribes."

Hand trembling, like many other methods of divination, is most often used for practical purposes, such as finding stray horses or sheep, missing people, stolen or misplaced items. Visitors among the Navaho have reported the recovery of valuable jewelry, saddle horses and a stolen necklace. Yet treatment of illness is also included among the Navaho hand trembler's arts, and tribesmen consult hand tremblers when faced with fearful precognitive dreams. Simply reporting a bad dream to a hand trembler is believed to forestall its consequences, or the trembler may advise that a special ceremony be performed. Hand trembling's link with dowsing is obvious and in the past was remarkably direct: hand tremblers, once in their state of apparent physical decontrol, were often used to divine the presence of underground water.

ligion and Ethics, described the procedure in similar terms: "In practice the easiest method is to look steadily, for perhaps five minutes, at a glass or crystal ball laid on any dark surface, at the distance from the eyes of a book which the experimenter might be reading. If the gazer has the faculty, he usually sees a kind of mist or a milky obscurity cover the ball, which then seems to become clear and black; pictures then emerge. Sometimes the ball ceases to be present to the consciousness of the gazer, who feels as if he were beholding an actual scene."

If everything from melted wax to tarot cards and crystal balls can serve the divining arts, where can one find a common denominator? To begin, one must face the reality that a good deal of what is called divination is deception designed to extract money from the gullible, the desperate or the curious. Those who seek the guidance of a fortuneteller are often motivated by nothing more than what the British poet and playwright John Dryden expressed with these words: "With how much ease believe we what we wish." All too many people are eager to read significant meanings into bland generalities that might be interpreted in a variety of ways. Self-styled diviners are often highly skilled at asking provocative questions, at aptly assessing clients' reactions and at telling them what they want to hear.

Dr. Ray Hyman, a psychologist at the University of Oregon, has actually analyzed the methods of cold reading—the technique by which a fortuneteller reads a client from his or her appearance and speech cues. He outlined his findings in an article called "'Cold Reading': How to Convince Strangers That You Know All About Them." In the article he mentions a "stock spiel" developed by his colleague Norman D. Sundberg, a bland form of "character reading" that might be applied to most male college students. The subject is

(continued on page 128)

Her 200-year-old crystal ball stolen, British psychic Mme. du Barry used a spare to foretell the return of her lost globe.

Ngombe Francis, a medical doctor in Zambia, uses a crystal ball in his work.

Dowsing's Inexplicable Success

"At first sight," wrote Sir William Barrett, professor in 1897 at the Royal College of Science in Dublin, "few subjects appear to be as unworthy of serious notice and so utterly beneath scientific investigation as that of the divining rod." But even as he wrote this, Barrett, a sometime skeptic, was in the process of becoming a convert to the mysterious art.

At the urging of a colleague, he had undertaken a "scientific" study of the ancient practice of dowsing in, as he put it, a spirit of "reluctance 'and even repugnance'" and with the hope that he could soon consign the whole subject to that "limbo, large and broad, since called The Paradise of fools." Instead, what he found both astonished and baffled him. He was particularly impressed by the work of a dowser named John Mullins, who, in 1889, had been hired by the Waterford Bacon Factory to locate underground water on its property. Professional geologists had already failed in this enterprise, even after sinking numerous boreholes to depths of up to 1,000 feet. When Mullins arrived at Waterford, he walked about the property at random, holding a forked twig in front of him. At a spot only a few feet from a previously drilled hole the twig twisted so violently that it broke. Here, Mullins told witnesses, at a depth of 80 to 90 feet, the factory owners would find water. And so they did.

No one knows when the first dowser—one who, by unexplained means, could locate underground water, minerals, oil, treasure or even lost persons—began to practice his art. A cave painting in the Sahara from about 6000 B.C. shows a figure holding what appears to be a divining rod, but one cannot be sure. Equally uncertain is whether dowsing was performed in classical times. Greek and Roman literature contain many references to rhabdomancy—divination by use of rods, staffs and arrows—but whether this was the same as contemporary dowsing is debatable. What is not debatable is that dowsing, virtually in its modern form, began to turn up in written and graphic records in the Middle Ages. We know, for example, that prospectors in 15th-century Germany used dowsing to locate minerals in the Harz Mountains, that Martin Luther condemned the practice as smacking of witchcraft, and that Georg Agricola both discussed and illustrated it in his 1556 treatise on mining and metallurgy, *De Ra Metallica*. At the end of the 17th century, French police asked a dowser to help them solve a grisly ax murder and theft in Lyons. The dowser led them to a far-off town and there identified a petty criminal, who later confessed to having a part in the crime. In recent times

a U.S. dowser has employed his dowsing rod to diagnose engine troubles at his Connecticut service station.

Yet dowsing remains a mystery to 20th-century science. Not only does it fail to conform to any known physical principle, but dowsers themselves are often indifferent to theories attempting to explain their art. "The reasons that the . . . procedures work," a handout of the American Society of Dowsers notes, "are entirely unknown." The standard practice is for the dowser to walk slowly over the ground to be surveyed, holding in front of him a forked stick, a pair of rods or a plumb line. (By tradition, the stick or rods should be made of hazelwood, but modern dowsers use almost anything, including metal coat hangers.) While walking, the dowser is supposed to be concentrating on—and, preferably, saying aloud—the precise nature and depth of the thing he is looking for. When he finds the right spot, his stick will suddenly bend down; or if he is carrying rods, the rods will either cross or diverge; or his plumb line will begin to swing erratically.

Skeptical observers, from Barrett on, have noted that the movement of stick, rods or plumb line probably results from involuntary muscle contractions in the dowser's arms and hands. Most dowsers readily admit this: it explains almost nothing. The central mystery concerns the dowser himself. Is he, as some have speculated, sensitive to small electromagnetic variations that hidden substances may produce? Can he detect subtle changes in ground temperature? Is he relying on some combination of the five senses, or is some other, as-yet-unknown instinct or sense involved?

At least one form of dowsing can be explained only in terms of extrasensory perception. This is map dowsing—a procedure in which the dowser holds a plumb line or some other indicator over a map of the terrain to be explored. Perhaps the most famous map dowser is Henry Gross, celebrated in articles and books by his even more famous acolyte, the novelist Kenneth Roberts. Gross performed one of his best-known feats while at a late-night gathering of friends in Maine in October 1947. Conversation centered around Bermuda, and someone mentioned that geologists had determined that no fresh water existed on the island. Gross asked for a map of Bermuda, spread it out and, after making a few passes with a divining rod, indicated four places where fresh water might be found. Within the next few months, during a period of major drought, fresh water was discovered in three of the four locations that Gross had marked on the map.

The fact that science cannot explain dowsing—let

alone map dowsing—has done little to discourage either dowsers or their clients. The American Society of Dowsers, which boasts more than 2,000 dues-paying members, estimates that there are at least 25,000 practicing dowsers in the United States. And in many cases they have been successful. Dowsers, Christopher Bird pointed out in *The Divining Hand,* have even been used to discover oil. "It's a fact," he said, "that the Occidental Petroleum Corp. got its start in the petroleum industry when it bought ten producing wells that had been successfully dowsed."

Even the U.S. Marine Corps has made use of dowsing. In 1967, Hanson W. Baldwin, the *New York*

Times' military correspondent, filed a story from Camp Pendleton, California, describing how marines of the 5th Division's 13th Engineer Battalion were being given a demonstration in the use of divining rods. Baldwin reported, "The unofficial use of the device has spread and the Marine .engineers here at Camp Pendleton swear by it. They do not know why it works either, but they are convinced that it does."

Are dowsers something more than natural-born geologists? This and similar questions continue to be hotly debated. Yet one thing is certain: on the basis of performance, no other form of divination has so severely challenged its scientific doubters.

Methods of using a traditional dowsing rod, a forked stick (far left), were described in the 1693 French work *Treatise on the Divining Rod.*

A dowser looks for water by holding a pendulum over a map, a technique that defies explanation but has reportedly worked.

An Indian dowser uses no rod but suffers painful "shocks" when he walks over a promising water site. Water is poured over his feet to ease his pain.

The Washington State well driller at far left, who found that dowsing was an important part of his business, shows a client how to look for water with a rod.

Cold Reading Customers

"You have to look at the whole person," Zingara the fortuneteller said. "Fat or thin? Where is the fat? What about the feet? Do the feet show vanity or trouble? Does she stick out her breast or curl her shoulders to hide it? Does he stick out his chest or his stomach? Does he lean forward and peer, or backward and sneer? . . .

"The face comes last. Happy? Probably not. What kind of unhappy? Worry? Failure? Where are the wrinkles? You have to look good, and quick . . . Tell them pretty soon that they're worried. Of course they're worried; why else would they come to a mitt camp [fortuneteller's tent] at a fair? Feel around, and give them a chance to talk; you know as soon as you touch the sore spot."

Although Zingara herself is fictional, a character in a story by Canadian writer Robertson Davies, her description of how a seer sums up a client from the boardwalk—what palm readers, psychics, carnival operators and professors of psychology alike call cold reading—is perfectly put.

A cold reading is a professional seer's craft and his meal ticket. It is based on careful observation and shrewd interpretation of the obvious, and it reflects at least three assumptions about human nature: first, that most people are unwitting advertisements of their class, income, education and cultural background and through their gestures, mannerisms and dress betray a wealth of information about themselves; second, that most people hear what they want to hear rather than what is said; and third, as Zingara observed in *World of Wonders,* that "people are much more like one another than they are unlike."

Before a client has warmed his visitor's chair, a skilled cold reader has made mental note of a dozen clues and deduced enough probable facts to start fishing. Such stock phrases as "Your true talents have yet to be tapped" or "You are cautious about revealing your true feelings" are meant to draw the client out. Topics that fall flat are abandoned, while those that elicit an eager nod or nervous twitch are pursued; a suitable subject is easily found: who is not concerned with affairs of the heart, health or success? And while the seer is muttering generalities, the client can be expected to tailor them to his needs. The seer subtly intimates; the client does the rest.

Cold readings are astonishingly easy to perform, and not just on the carnival circuit. In tests by psychologists, subjects were lulled into thinking that generalized character sketches had been individually prepared. In one classic example, a roomful of students was asked to rate a character description made up piecemeal from an astrology book. Sixteen of 39 students rated the generalized sketch a near-perfect assessment of their characters. Only 5 of the total group assessed it as a less-than-suitable description of themselves.

simply told: "You are a person who is very normal in his attitudes, behavior and relationships with people. You get along well without effort. People naturally like you and you are not overly critical of them or yourself. You are neither overly conventional nor overly individualistic. Your prevailing mood is one of optimism and constructive effort, and you are not troubled by periods of depression, psychosomatic illness or nervous symptoms."

College females, Sundberg found, responded "with even more pleasure" to a somewhat-different character sketch: "You appear to be a cheerful, well-balanced person. You may have some alternation of happy and unhappy moods, but they are not extreme now. You have few or no problems with your health. You are sociable and mix well with others. You are adaptable to social situations. You tend to be adventurous. Your interests are wide. You are fairly self-confident and usually think clearly."

Sundberg also discovered that, to quote Hyman, "a fake, universal sketch can be seen as a better description of oneself than can a uniquely tailored description by trained psychologists based upon one of the best assessment devices we have." Sundberg had given a well-known personality test to a group of students and had then offered them assessments, based upon the test, of themselves. When asked whether the assessment or a stock spiel fitted them better, 26 of 44 students (59 percent) made a remarkable choice: they picked the stock sketch. Hyman commented, "Clients are not necessarily acting irrationally when they find meaning in stock spiels or cold readings. Meaning is an interaction of expectations, context, memory, and given statements."

Beyond manipulation and fakery, no matter how common, one must consider deeper reasons to explain the timelessness of divination. Several authorities ascribe the universality of divination, in one form or another, to one of the most basic of human desires: foreknowledge of and thus control over personal destiny.

Yet this merely suggests why people might want to have knowledge of the future. What of the diviner himself? The one common denominator that exists—most clearly in the case of crystal gazing—is the diviner's use of a tool to achieve a trance-type state of consciousness. Even of the tarot, Douglas Hill and Pat Williams, in *The Supernatural,* wrote that the cards stimulate the "unconscious of the person attempting the divination. . . . This can be said to be the basis of all divinatory methods. The most successful operator is often, for this reason, a clairvoyant who uses cards, words, handwriting, palms, or horoscopes as a focus and a mediating channel between his 'intuition'—the unconscious mind—and the world outside."

If this interpretation is correct, then most of the elaborate paraphernalia of divination—the cast bones,

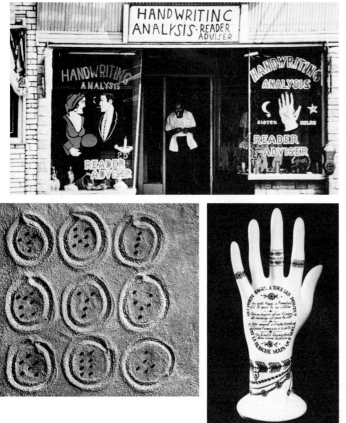

Constantly adapting to modern times—and the human compulsion to know the future—the art of divination flourishes everywhere. For the curious in New York, storefront advisers offer handwriting analysis; in Paris palm and card readings were available to the clients of Mme. Athena in the 1930s. In India, Hindus seek the guidance of a deformed bull that answers yes or no by touching its muzzle to a questioner's left or right fist; in Madagascar, diviners read the future in seed patterns. Seemingly everywhere, belief in omens survives, including a folk tradition that weds steadfastness in love with the finger on which a ring may be worn.

the hot lead, the steaming entrails, the animals, the yarrow sticks and enigmatic phrases of the *I Ching*—are essentially beside the point. If human beings have the capacity to read the future, that ability lies in their minds, not in external symbols; it is to be found, as Shakespeare put it, "not in our stars, but in ourselves."

But does such a predictive capacity exist in the human mind? The chronicle of divination provides many intriguing hints but no certain answers. If answers there are, it may be that the rambling methods of traditional divination are less likely to isolate them than is ongoing research in parapsychology and extrasensory perception. Science's organized efforts may yet confirm a truth that early diviners simply sensed. Or, equally possible, the story of divination may prove to be another chapter in the history of human absurdity.

If one adopts the alternative that it is absurd, is there nothing valid at all to be said of divination? There is at least one positive point to make. Divination, odd as it may seem, may have contributed to the development of the scientific method. In the two societies to which we can most effectively trace the roots of modern civilization, ancient China and Mesopotamia, divination was sustained by a relatively educated elite, a group that not only developed ritual but provided an early structure, whether rational or pseudorational, for predicting events significant to society. Such pursuits encouraged observation, recording, calculation and analysis. They created a framework of apparent cause—and effect.

And perhaps they did something more. Dr. George K. Park, writing in the *Journal of the Royal Anthropologi-*

cal Institute on divination and its social contexts, noted that some social systems still hinge in a "critical way upon the performances of its diviners," for divination facilitates "decision upon some plan of action which is not easily taken." Studies have shown that many societies rely upon divination not simply because their members are superstitious or easily deceived. In fact, in such cultures a client is not likely to blindly follow a fortuneteller's directives concerning his day-to-day existence. Instead, he consults a respected, tribal diviner when some difficult problem must be resolved and seeks council—from one or several sources—until he hears the advice that seems most practical and useful in terms of his situation. In such a system, consulting a diviner is a means of seeking a broad range of opinion from the people who have been judged wisest in the community. And the diviner's council has an added advantage. Once a decision has been reached, it can be readily justified in the eyes of society, for it has been directed by the pattern of the palm, bones or seashells—and not by whim.

In short, divination helped and still helps, in varying degrees, people make up their minds. And as every modern executive knows, all truly difficult decisions have to be made on the basis of inadequate data. In the end, the executive's intuition, coupled with a readiness to act, may count for more than all available evidence bearing on the unresolved issue at hand. In this sense, divination may be more widely practiced today than any of us realize. Perhaps we simply refer to it by another name: decision making.

Prophecy: Haunting Hits and Misses

The jousting tournament celebrating two marriages within the French royal family was in full swing on July 1, 1559. As the sun was setting, King Henry II rode his magnificently draped horse against Gabriel de Lorges, Count of Montgomery. The encounter was judged a draw, but Henry insisted on a return bout. Moments later the lances of the two contestants struck and splintered, and Montgomery's lance pierced the king's golden visor, entering his eye. The king died nine days later.

In the hush that followed the tournament's fateful end, a member of the royal entourage, Constable Anne de Montmorency, cried out, "Cursed be the divine who predicted it, so evilly and so well!" There was little doubt as to the identity of the man against whom the curse was directed. His name was Michel de Nostre-dame (1503–66), or more simply Nostradamus. He has since become history's best-known prophet.

In actuality, Nostradamus during his lifetime published 10 volumes of four-line prophetic verses, or quatrains, 942 verses in all. He had planned that each volume would contain 100 verses and referred to the volumes as *Centaines,* now popularly called *Centuries.* The 35th verse in the first *Century,* published four years before the royal jousting match, carried this extraordinary message:

> The young lion will overcome the old one
> On the field of battle in a single combat:
> He will put out his eyes in a cage of gold:
> Two wounds, and then to die a cruel death.

Even before King Henry II's death, Nostradamus, because of his striking prophetic gifts, had been inter-

Nostradamus predicted the great fire of 1666, according to Erika Cheetham, a student of his work. "The blood of the just will be demanded of London," he warned, "burnt by fire in three times twenty plus six."

mittently held in awe or contempt and subjected to ridicule. After the king's death, crowds in a Paris suburb angrily burned Nostradamus in effigy and demanded that the prophet of disaster himself die by fire at the stake. Yet very few of the hundreds of prophetic quatrains written by Nostradamus were as precise, or could have been interpreted with such exactitude, as his verse prophesying the king's death in a duel. For as happens frequently in instances of prophetic success, the enigmatic phrasing of Nostradamus's quatrains along with the great number of prophecies he did make added to the likelihood that at least some of his forecasts would turn out to be impressively accurate.

There is no doubt, however, about Nostradamus's skills as a physician, notably during repeated plague epidemics in the south of France, nor about his scholarship and skills as a prolific writer. Aside from his 10 *Centuries,* he published widely read almanacs, drew horoscopes and concocted cosmetic preparations for a group of admiring and wealthy patrons.

Over the centuries, constant reinterpretation has

enhanced the allure of Nostradamus's prophecies. In *Nostradamus: Life and Literature,* Edgar Leoni suggested that Nostradamus himself encouraged the legends that cloak his work, claiming modestly that his prophecies would remain valid through the year 3797. Leoni also commented on the invaluable ambiguity of the French physician's creations, noting that "many of his prophecies lend themselves to repeated interpretations, so that they never seem to be out of date."

The word *prophecy* comes from the Greek and means, in general terms, "speaking before." Today, in many instances, the terms *prophecy* and *divination* are used loosely and often synonymously, referring to forecasts of events yet to come. Originally, however, *prophecy* had a more basic meaning, one distinctly removed from the trappings and devices employed by diviners past and present. In biblical times, prophets functioned not as interpreters of the future but as direct representatives of and spokesmen for a god, most often Yahweh, the God of Israel.

Armed with the force of such direct communication, biblical prophets often served as advisers to kings and courts. The Old Testament frequently cites such prophets, adding that their prophetic messages "came to pass," an apparent indication that a particular prophecy, like that concerning the young and old lion, turned out to be correct. Prophets also warned of disasters, especially when monarchs or the common man seemed to fail in sustaining the Divine Word. Jeremiah, for example, the "prophet of doom," forecast Israel's destruction and eventual Babylonian rule.

Although the theme of divine inspiration carried over into the classic period, Greece and Rome developed forms of prophecy that had distinctly secular applications. Biblical prophets were usually men; but as Richard Lewinsohn observed in *Science, Prophecy and Prediction,* in Greece, "where women normally lived such retired lives, it was they who were chosen for the high office of official prophet." The Pythia, priestess of the Delphic oracle, had to be celibate, a precondition found elsewhere in the ancient world. Lewinsohn wrote that in Egypt "priest-prophetesses were among the highest state dignitaries, and in Babylonia and other

Another of Nostradamus's prophecies was fulfilled in 1936, some believe, when Edward VIII abdicated: "For not wanting to consent to the divorce which . . . will be recognized as unworthy, the King of the Islands will be forced to flee."

Prophecy: Haunting Hits and Misses

countries of the Near East, prophetesses were a common phenomenon."

During the Dark Ages in Europe, prophecy, less concerned with divine revelation yet still largely unencumbered by the trappings of divination, became once again the province of men, occasionally with startling results. In a truly remarkable and little-known prophetic outburst, the scientist-monk Roger Bacon startled later English necromancers with a forecast of the development of "seagoing ships" that will move "with one man to steer, and at a greater speed than if they were full of men working them." He also anticipated the existence of vehicles "without animals to draw them" and "flying machines" with "a man sitting in the middle of the machine." In other prophecies Bacon envisioned the creation of both the microscope and telescope. Nearly two centuries later Leonardo da Vinci translated Bacon's visions of architectural and engineering triumph into highly specific designs, correctly anticipating a remarkable array of future weapons, vehicles, machines and buildings.

Over the centuries two themes have appeared again and again in the broad text of prophetic expression: catastrophe and inventions. In 1661, for example, Englishman George Fox predicted the plague that swept London in 1665. In 1856 in his book *Penetralia*, Andrew Jackson Davis forecast in detail both the automobile and an exotic kind of typewriter. These were the words he used to describe his writing machine: "I am almost moved to invent an automatic psychographer—that is, an artificial soul writer. It may be constructed something like a piano, one brace or scale of keys to represent the elementary sounds; another and lower tier to represent a combination, and still another for a rapid recombination so that a person, instead of playing a piece of music may touch off a sermon or a poem." War, disaster and the death of heads of state have long been subjects of prophetic activity. In 1853 a nine-year-old boy, Daniel Offord, predicted a cholera epidemic within two months; the Yorkshire *Spiritual Telegraph* reported: "Exactly two months to a day the official notification appeared." The assassination of President Lincoln was predicted by Daniel Home at Dieppe, France, in 1863, and the deaths of the king and queen of Serbia in 1903 were foreseen by a Mrs. Burchell, a Yorkshire prophet. In February 1914, Sir Arthur Conan Doyle, who was fascinated by the occult, received this message from an Australian medium: "Now, although there is not at present a whisper of a great European war at hand, yet I want to warn you

that before this year, 1914, has run its course, Europe will be deluged in blood."

While it did not involve war or the death of a head of state, a 19th-century novel turned out to be startlingly prophetic. *Futility,* by Morgan Robertson, was published in New York in 1898. Robertson, in effect, predicted in great and telling detail the sinking of the S.S. *Titanic* 14 years later, on April 14, 1912. As in the actual disaster, the ship in the fictional account had been regarded as unsinkable and yet sank during the month of April. In Robertson's novel the number of people aboard was 3,000; in actual fact there were 2,207. In the novel the lifeboats numbered 24; in fact there were 20. The story had the ship traveling at a speed of 25 knots; in real life the speed was 22.5 knots. In the story the ship was 800 feet long; in fact the *Titanic* measured 882.5 feet.

In the late 18th and early 19th centuries, prophecy during hypnosis was launched by mesmerism, the technique pioneered by the Austrian Franz Anton Mesmer. One of Mesmer's pupils, the Marquis de Puységur, was able to induce what he called "artificial somnambulism." He placed a young girl from the Black Forest region of Germany in a prophetic trance, thus reportedly enabling her to predict the violent events that later accompanied the French Revolution. Nearly 100 years later the American Edgar Cayce became famous as "the sleeping prophet." Cayce, who spent most of his life at Virginia Beach, Virginia, produced personal forecasts about the health and career of individuals who consulted him, as well as utterances that predicted long-range geologic changes of continental magnitude. For a period ending in 1998, Cayce's geologic prophesies included a breakup "in the western portion of America," and changes in "the upper portion of Europe," while "the greater portion of Japan must go into the sea."

One of the 20th century's most dramatic prophecies, however, was made by Jeane Dixon of Washington, D.C. It was the basis for a story in the Sunday newspaper supplement *Parade* of May 13, 1956: "As for the 1960 election, Mrs. Dixon thinks it will be dominated by labor and won by a Democrat. But he will be assassinated or die in office 'though not necessarily in his first term.'" This remark was recalled when Presi-

dent John F. Kennedy was assassinated in Dallas on November 22, 1963. Dixon made numerous other dramatic prophecies, however, some of them obviously errant. Among these was the forecast that Communist China would "plunge the world into war" in 1958; that the Soviet Union would invade Iran in 1953; and that Premier Fidel Castro of Cuba was "either in China or he's dead" in 1966.

However, as in the case of Nostradamus's prediction of King Henry's death, Dixon's prophecy of President Kennedy's assassination has remained fixed in public memory. The "death of kings" does tend to attract, and often seems to vindicate, prophets. However, certain anecdotal incidents can be even more baffling than death prophecies. When, for example, the American Society for Psychical Research undertook a survey of spontaneous psychic phenomena, including precognitive cases, a strangely prophetic adventure was reported by Mrs. Paul H. McCahen of Inglewood, California. In the evening twilight of their visit to the Grand Canyon on September 4, 1956, Mr. and Mrs. McCahen saw a woman walking up to one of the cabins, accompanied by a man and a boy. Mrs. McCahen said to her husband, "There is Mrs. Nash, a lady I served jury duty with a year ago. Her husband has one arm. But I will see her in the morning, as she is probably tired."

In her letter to the psychic research society, Mrs. McCahen added, "The next day I saw her sitting on the veranda, and I went to talk to her. Our husbands met each other and we had a pleasant chat until I mentioned I had seen her the evening before, but didn't speak then. Mr. and Mrs. Nash both looked astonished and said they had just gotten there with a busload of tourists. He doesn't drive far, because of his arm."

Mr. McCahen confirmed his wife's account, saying that his wife had pointed out Mrs. Nash to him the day before, and that they met the couple the following noon, although Mrs. Nash said "that was impossible because they had arrived only that morning."

Is there a reasonable explanation, one that might not distort existing scientific principle, for such seemingly inexplicable incidents involving future time and coincidence? In his book *Prophecy in Our Time,* Martin Ebon, a prolific writer on paranormal subjects, offered a possibility that is as intriguing as it is comprehensible: "There is a simple analogy about prophecy," Ebon wrote. "If you are in a helicopter, circling over a mountain, and you can see two trains on opposite sides of the mountain but heading toward each other—you can then foresee a collision as if you had superhuman knowledge, at least in contrast to the passengers and engineers on the two trains. It is a neat analogy. It does not demand basic readjustments of traditional concepts of time and space. But can we achieve helicopter-like perception of our own future? Yes, certainly, to the degree to which each of us gains greater insight into himself—because we are not so much masters as, unconsciously, the magnets of our fate."

Astrologer Jeane Dixon claims to have learned of John Kennedy's assassination in "visions" experienced some 13 years before the event and to have forecast Franklin D. Roosevelt's death when asked by him how much longer he had to live.

The orderly traffic of the heavens
has beguiled the perceptions of observers
for at least 50 centuries.

ASTROLOGY

The zodiac sign for Taurus is shown as a Brahman bull in the horoscope of a 19th-century Indian prince.

A lone among living things, humans are haunted and enriched by a knowledge of the future. For men and women possess a sense of the passage of time and the means to measure hours, days and even years with second-splitting accuracy. Yet despite man's superior temporal sensitivities and ever improving technologies, his intricate planning and major projections, the exact nature of the future eludes definition. We do not know and as a result we wonder constantly about future matters both large and small.

Yet in broadest terms, mankind's struggle to foretell and thus control the future is probably as old as society itself and surely older than any orderly system of science. Fresh anthropological evidence suggests that 32,000 years before the birth of Christ, Cro-Magnon man read the sky and marked the seasons by carving notches in bone. It is possible that such carvings allowed him to follow the migrations of animals and plot the growth of plants. In a hostile world, such calculations would have been invaluable.

In a sense then, Cro-Magnon man may have practiced astronomy, the science devoted to the study

of the heavenly bodies. What researchers cannot know, however, is what sort of connection he may have made between what he saw in the sky and what he observed in the world around him. He probably did chart the passage of time, and he did create magical stories about his world in paintings on the walls of caves. Yet did he come to believe that a certain number of full moons was necessary to *make* reindeer migrate and plants grow? If so, Cro-Magnon man may have been among the earliest recorded astrologers and, as such, a practitioner of an art that has caught the attention of learned as well as common men ever since.

Even in this age of science, it is impossible to ignore astrology—the belief that the movements of the sun, the planets and the stars influence events on earth. In 1978, for example, according to one Gallup poll, 1,200 of 1,750 U.S. newspapers carried horoscope columns. Above all, astrology is a hardy system of belief, and as modern and scientific as we may be, there is still something in many of us that responds to the temptation of reading the future in the skies.

"Let there be lights in the firmament of the heavens . . . and let them be for signs and for seasons."
—Genesis 1:14

To the profound consternation of doubters, astrologers have been known to read the portents of the heavens with remarkable accuracy. How else but by

A 17th-century map of the heavens is surrounded by Ptolemy's view of the universe (top, right), a Roman astrological globe, a 15th-century French illumination linking planets to signs, and a Greek coin showing signs of the zodiac.

An astrologer's magic symbols, a monster and a skull and crossbones, appear in Campagnola's 16th-century print.

successful astral readings might one explain, for example, the amazing insights of Evangeline Adams? A descendant of President John Quincy Adams, she was born in Boston and, following the advice of her own horoscope, moved to New York City in 1873. The very day she took up residence in a local hotel, she informed the proprietor that disaster would soon occur. A day later the hotel burned down; Adams's name was emblazoned across the front pages of newspapers, her story spread, and she was on her way to becoming one of the most noted of modern U.S astrologers.

Fame did not protect her, however, from being arrested in 1914 for the crime of fortunetelling, though her astrological skill saved her from conviction. Testifying in court, she first described in detail how she arrived at her predictions. She then offered to be tested. She would, she said, read the horoscope of a stranger as a demonstration; no name was necessary. The trial judge sensibly volunteered his own son and was so beguiled by the accuracy of the resulting horoscope that he ruled: "The defendant raises astrology to the dignity of an exact science." Adams was released to continue her science and soon set her talents to work for such illustrious clients as J. P. Morgan, Enrico Caruso, the Duke of Windsor and actress Mary Pickford.

In 1931, Evangeline Adams made a startling prediction—that the United States would be at war in 1942—but she did not live to see her prophecy fulfilled. She died in November 1932 at the age of 59, having refused a lecture tour scheduled for the fall. She turned down the tour because, it has been said, her astrological chart had indicated that her imminent death would make such a trip impossible.

Adams's record was an exceptional one, however, for the history of astrology is rife with predictions that have not come true. When Alfred Witte, an astrologer from Hamburg, was drafted into the German Army at

Varying Views on Astrology

Astrology is one of those subjects, like religion and politics, on which almost everyone is eager to express an opinion. What's more, it seems to inspire excess and poetry in both believers and doubters.

According to John Calvin, for instance, anyone who believed that "happiness or misery depends on the decrees and presages of the stars" was an infidel, while Puritan Increase Mather saw God's hand at work in a brilliant comet passing over New England in 1682 and wrote that it "does portend a cold and tedious Winter, much Snow, and consequently Great Floods."

Separated by nearly 2,000 years, Roman poet Juvenal and 20th-century writer Aldous Huxley both indicated that a woman's character might be inferred from her belief in astrology. "Flee the dame whose Manual of Astrology still dangles at her side, smooth as chafed gum, and fretted by her everlasting thumb!— Deep in the Science now she leaves her mate to go, or stay; but will not share his fate" is the way Juvenal put it. In *Crome Yellow,* Huxley invented the "gay and gadding" Priscilla, whose "days were spent in casting the horoscopes of horses" so as to invest "her money scientifically, as the stars dictated."

In *King Lear,* Shakespeare had one of his characters make a shrewd jibe at astrology. "This is the excellent foppery of the world," Edmund says, "that, when we are sick in fortune—often the surfeit of our own behaviour—we make guilty of our disasters the sun, the moon, and the stars . . . an admirable evasion of whoremaster man, to lay his goatish disposition to the charge of a star!"

Renaissance scholar-magician Cornelius Agrippa renounced astrology after years of earnest but ultimately disappointing experiments led him to conclude that it "was built upon no other foundation, but upon mere trifles and feigning of imagination."

In his 1946 book *The Royal Art of Astrology,* Robert Eisler alluded to the art's appeal, even as he pinpointed its emptiness, when he termed it the "stale, superstitious residue of what was once a great, pantheistic religion and a glorious philosophical attempt to understand and rationally to explain the universe."

Years of such criticism have been heaped upon the resilient catechism of astrology, yet belief in it persists. What must be among the most astonishing modern remarks made about the art were reported in the Washington *Post* in 1974, as part of an exposé on job discrimination by members of Congress. To hire their staffs, congressmen telephone a placement office, where their preferences, including job qualifications and disqualifications, are noted. One congressman specified "No Water Signs," explaining that these were Scorpio, Pisces and Cancer. Another called for someone "attractive, smart, young and No Catholics or water signs." It seems that there will always be those who prefer to view the world through astrology's prism.

the outbreak of World War I, he lost no time in putting his art to use trying to stay alive. He attempted to plot the arrival of Russian artillery fire by studying the astrological circumstances associated with the hostile barrages. When his first predictions proved insufficiently accurate, Witte returned to his charts and tables, eventually determining that an unknown planet named Cupido was distorting his calculations. Cupido, Witte thought, lay beyond the orbit of Neptune. Many years later, in 1930, astronomers identified a new planet, indeed beyond Neptune, and labeled it Pluto.

Witte's seeming triumph was not without its flaws, however. For one thing, Pluto's path differs greatly from the orbit calculated for Cupido. Even worse for Witte's record is the fact that, after inventing Cupido, he and a colleague, Friedrich Sieggrün, identified seven other unknown planets: Hades, Zeus, Chronos, Apollo, Admetos, Vulcan and Poseidon. No trace of these celestial wanderers has ever been detected.

Nevertheless, Witte used his Cupido calculations to refine his forecasts of Russian shelling, and he claimed that his accuracy improved substantially. He never reached the level of infallibility, of course, but he did survive the war to found a new kind of astrology, which is called the Hamburg School. Witte's system, which includes the influences of his eight new planets in its astrological forecasting, is still in use, especially in Austria and Germany. In the late 1950s Ludwig Stuiber, a disciple of Witte's, published examples of the system's accuracy. In one case, a Hamburg School astrologer was told the time, date and place of birth of an unknown woman and was asked what had happened to her in Vienna at 4 p.m. on March 4, 1954. The astrologer put the data through Witte's system and replied that she had been shot in the back. He was, claimed Stuiber, absolutely correct in his evaluation.

Such feats—and there are many of them—are one reason that belief in astrology has survived. Another reason is that astrology for the most part has shown a vigorous—some would say uncanny—ability to adapt itself to new trends and discoveries in the realms of religion and science. Indeed, there was a time when it was impossible to distinguish among religion, astrology and science, which together formed but one, seemingly indivisible body of knowledge and belief.

As a result, as much as modern astrologers would like to base their practice on a fixed set of ancient principles, scholars have been unable to pinpoint where those principles originated. Some attribute the earliest systemization of astral observations—both the science of astronomy and the art of astrology—to the Babylonians. Others argue that astrology is the legacy of an earlier Mesopotamian people, the Sumerians, who believed that the heavenly bodies were representations of their gods. There is agreement among many scholars, however, that a successor tribe to the Sumerians, called the Chaldeans, did practice a recognizable form of astrology. Installed atop watchtowers called ziggurats (one of which, the biblical Tower of Babel, reached a height of 300 feet), Chaldean astrologer-priests studied the skies and made predictions for their kings. Theirs was what astrologers call mundane astrology, concerned with the fate of nations and crops and rulers; it was not yet the comforting companion of the individual.

Wheels hidden beyond the limb of the universe mechanize the sun, moon and stars in this 16th-century German view.

Ancient pagan philosophers, including Seneca, are shown to be closely aligned with the cosmic power of various heavenly bodies in this 14th-century manuscript illumination.

Zodiac signs surround an Egyptian goddess on this 2nd-century mummy case.

While most scholars consider the Chaldeans to be the intellectual founders of astrology, other forms of the art sprang up elsewhere in the world. The early Egyptians, whose survival depended on the flooding of the Nile, which fertilized their lands, were quick to notice that the water's rise coincided with the rise of the star Sirius in tandem with the ascension of the sun. In Indian religion and philosophy, too, can be seen some element of astrological thought, while the emperors of China, around 2000 B.C., were known as sons of Heaven. The Chinese rulers ritually moved from one corner of their square palaces to another in the belief that the four points of the compass were strongly related to the four seasons. They lived in the east in spring, the south in summer, the west in fall and the north in winter.

As with the Chaldeans, the Mayan civilization of Mexico produced a class of astronomer-priests, but it was the ancient Greeks who, in expressing their democratic ideals, made astrology available to all. No longer was a horoscope the exclusive purchase of a king; every citizen might have one cast if he cared to pay for it. With their restructuring and repackaging of the art, the Greeks launched what was to become astrology's centuries-long struggle for acceptance.

As Lawrence E. Jerome, an outspoken critic of astrology, put it in his book *Astrology Disproved*, "The Greeks saw the universe as a cosmological whole, a single living organism growing, as it were, out of the Primal Egg. . . . Every part of the cosmos was supposedly linked to every other part through correspondences between high and low, between heaven and earth. . . . the Greeks imposed a mathematical geometry on the system, attributing the correspondence to physical interactions and interconnections between the various celestial spheres and the earth."

In addition, the democratic Greeks decided that the portents of astrology did not rule but merely influenced human existence, suggesting, for instance, favorable times for projects but not guaranteeing their success. One byproduct of the Greeks' system, which was called catarchic astrology, was an avoidance of

conflict with later theologians and philosophers. The system survived and is practiced today, and because of it—especially when a prediction goes sour—astrologers can say, "The stars impel; they do not compel."

Like many other products of Greek culture, astrology traveled well to Rome. The use of horoscopes was common among all classes. Augustus, the first Roman emperor, was a true believer, encouraged in his conviction by a forecast made when he was born. According to an astrologer named Nigidius, Augustus would be "master of the world," and becoming emperor of the Roman Empire seemed to fulfill the prophecy. Impressed with the prediction's success, Augustus issued coinage struck with his birth sign, Capricorn.

The most important book on astrology was written in A.D. 200 by the major astronomer of the time, Claudius Ptolemaeus, called Ptolemy, who in the four volumes of *Tetrabiblos* set down all that was thought to be known about the art. Ptolemy regarded astrology as the equal and legitimate partner of astronomy, and his charts and descriptions of planetary influences were to be accepted, virtually without alteration, until the 17th century. In fact, much of what astrologers believe and practice today is based on Ptolemy, who wrote, "That certain power, derived from the aetheral nature, is diffused over and pervades the whole atmosphere of the earth, is clearly evident to all men."

The moon is entwined with Cancer, the crab, in an Arabic edition of a 9th-century Iraqi astrological manuscript.

Pisces is one of the 12 astrological signs that, along with scenes of laborers, decorate a stained-glass ambulatory window in the 13th-century cathedral at Chartres, France. The window was donated by a local count and an association of vine growers.

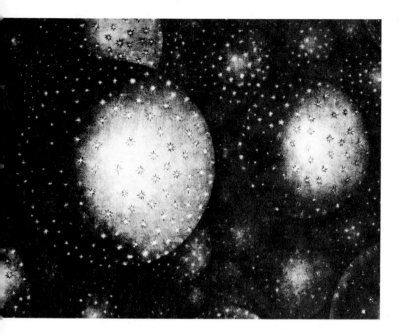

But what was obvious to Ptolemy was not so to the bishop of Hippo, better known as Saint Augustine. In the 4th century A.D., he struck astrology a blow that sent it reeling for centuries. In Augustine's day, Christianity was the official state religion of the Roman Empire, and his views on religious matters carried nearly the force of revelation. As a young man he had believed in astrology, but by the time he wrote *City of God,* his outlook had changed: "Those who hold that stars manage our actions or our passions, good or ill, without God's appointment, are to be silenced and not to be heard . . . for what doth this opinion but flatly exclude all deity?" Thus to accept planetary influence, according to Augustine, was to deny the power of God.

His theology aside, Augustine had arrived at his stern view of astrology through careful reasoning. He believed, for example, that astrological theory indicated that children born at virtually identical times would lead nearly parallel lives. Such children are today called astral twins. Considering the simultaneous births of a nobleman's child and a slave's, Augustine saw little parallel in the lives the two might lead. His resulting pronouncements were taken with great seriousness, and the practice of astrology dwindled. It was not to reappear with any impact until the 12th century, when European scholars began translating Arabic texts on the subject.

In the 16th century Johannes Kepler, one of the greatest astronomers of the Renaissance, struggled to reconcile astrology and astronomy. Copernicus had already begun to undermine ancient astrological views by suggesting that the earth was not the center of the solar system. Kepler (who worked as an astrologer himself, perhaps because he needed the money rather than out of conviction) made a resolute stab at describing the motions of the planets in terms of geometric relation-

ships. He failed but went on to formulate his laws of planetary motion. Then came Newton with his description of gravity, Darwin and his theory of evolution, and Gregor Mendel with his genetic laws. Each scientist, with each discovery, sent astrology—and magic—into further disrepute.

Today most people think of astrology in terms of sun signs—the traditional signs of the zodiac. These are Aries, Taurus, Gemini, Cancer, Leo, Virgo, Libra, Scorpio, Sagittarius, Capricorn, Aquarius and Pisces. Astrology columns in newspapers commonly provide advice and warnings based on sun signs alone. Yet for a knowledgeable astrologer, to characterize a person by his sun sign, without using the full range of astrological influences, is close to blasphemy. In truth, fully developed horoscopes are based upon the relative positions of hundreds of stars and planets at any given moment. And it may be because of this link with astronomy that astrology, of all the predictive arts, has been so long-lived and persistent in attracting public attention.

This persistence has frightened some scientists. In 1975 a distinguished group of 186 of them, including several astronomers, felt the need to issue a public statement decrying the works of astrologers: "We believe that the time has come to challenge directly, and forcefully, the pretentious claims of astrological charlatans." In a companion article, however, one of the signatories also said, "I have come to realize that astrology cannot be stopped by simple scientific argument only. To some, it seems almost a religion."

Many astrologers would agree, pointing out that most scientists are unaware of the full implications of an astrological reading. Some astrologers, in fact, see their work as akin to psychiatry. Others describe it as supporting an individualistic search for the future or a

In the Age of Reason some thinkers tried to reconcile scientific and religious belief. British natural philosopher Thomas Wright, for instance, contended in 1740 that innumerable spheres, shown in the engraving at the far left, surrounded a divine center, or region, where God was believed to exist.

When the map at left was published in 1660, Copernicus's view that the earth revolved around the sun had only recently been accepted, superseding Ptolemy's belief in an Earth-centered universe.

Galileo, in his 1610 work *The Star Messenger,* shown at right, explained how, with the aid of the telescope, he had perceived many new stars and four new planets (later found to be moons of Jupiter). All had been unknown to the ancients and unaccounted for by their astrological theory.

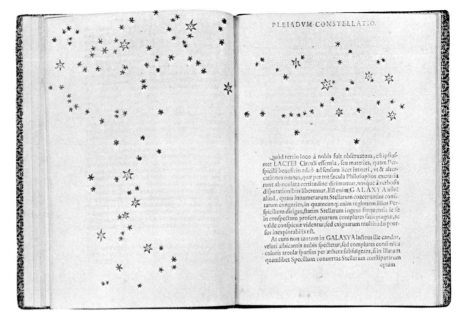

kind of reassurance of one's personal uniqueness and identity. As one observer of astrology has speculated, "If newspapers were to publish a horoscope in which all the fortunes or forecasts were the same, the readers of those horoscopes would feel cheated and abused, regardless of the astrological reasoning that might be advanced to justify that uniformity. They read those horoscopes not to learn their future, but to come into contact with a framework that supports the intuition that their future is a distinctive one—as, of course, it is. In this sense astrology is a kind of instant ethnicity, and serves the same purposes as an assertion of cultural and ethnic particularism."

Yet more than methodology, it is the premises of astrology that scientists condemn. One central premise, for example, is that the planets exert their influences at the moment of birth. But when a scientist attempts to measure those influences, he discovers that, of the forces he has been able to measure—gravity, for instance—the doctors, nurses and equipment in the delivery room all exert much more influence than the heavens. And why, asks the scientist, is the instant of birth of such great concern? Isn't the time of conception a more likely moment for the stars to intervene?

The discovery of Uranus, Neptune and Pluto in 1781, 1846 and 1930, respectively, poses another potential problem. New influences have been assigned to these newly discovered planets, and they are now used in casting certain horoscopes. Little has been said, however, about the validity of older horoscopes, which did not take them into account.

Occasionally, however, scientific study has produced surprising results. Using statistical techniques, Michel Gauquelin, a French psychologist and statistician, analyzed traditional astrological associations and found no support at all for them. Nonetheless, in compiling his research he made an unexpected discovery. He found what seemed to be a strong relationship, well beyond chance, between certain planetary movements and particular occupations. Scientists and doctors, he found, appeared to be born more frequently during the rise or zenith of either Mars or Saturn than of other planets. Similarly, Jupiter was often rising or at its zenith at the births of team athletes, soldiers, ministers, actors, journalists and playwrights.

Gauquelin's astonishment remained when others checked his figures and found them correct and when further studies produced the same results. Yet even with such compelling figures in hand, he could not believe that the planets "caused" the selection of professions. He began to think, instead, about the relationship between genetics and the professions.

After five more years of research, Gauquelin produced his hypothesis of "planetary heredity," which said that, in effect, some unknown inherited factors may influence both what profession a child eventually chooses and the time when he is born. Explained Gauquelin of such tendencies in choice of profession, "The reason would appear to be, simply, that such people have inherent constitutional (and therefore hereditary) elements which lead them by a natural tendency to a certain way of life which suits them particularly well."

A last and most difficult question remained: if hereditary elements may lead one in the direction of a particular profession, how, in addition, can they influence when a child is born? Gauquelin's highly speculative response reversed traditional astrological thinking and suggested that somehow an unborn child of a particular genetic makeup may perceive the movement of compatible planets and thus, perhaps with hormonal

(continued on page 144)

The Intricate Art of Horoscope Casting

To cast a modern horoscope is in many ways to step back in time to an ancient Mesopotamian observatory where stargazing priests believed that they stood at the center of their universe. Although that assumption was wrong, the celestial alignments they charted are still clearly visible today. And behind all the charts and tables that are the modern astrologer's basic tools, it is these heavenly phenomena that, to those who believe in astrology, seem to influence human destiny.

Like modern astronomers, the ancients mapped the heavens as though all the stars were on the surface of a single transparent sphere. The 12 houses of the zodiac that astrologers consult today are the work of early astrologers, who marked off segments of the sky by dividing the entire sphere into wedges like those formed by the sections of an orange. From any point

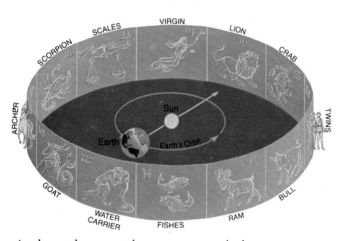

As the earth moves, the sun, moon and planets appear to pass through the constellations of the zodiac band. This apparent movement is the basis for astrological prediction.

on earth, the houses were often numbered starting at the eastern horizon, with the first house sitting just below the horizon, and the rest numbered downward below the earth and up to the western horizon, continuing overhead until they reached the eastern horizon. Thus they extended around the sphere, dividing the whole into 12 sections. These 12 celestial sections, or houses, form a backdrop: the planets and signs are said to move through them. At the same time, each house deals with some aspect of life. The first house, for instance, represents personality; the second, money and wealth; the third, peer groups; the fourth, family.

The ancients also divided the earth's orbital plane, called the zodiac, into 12 equal sections of 30° each. Each section was given a sign that was thought to project certain influences: Aries, Taurus, Gemini and the rest. (The names of the signs were derived from the names of the constellations.) The apparent movement of the zodiac band around the earth (a result of the earth's revolving) determined one of the most important elements in the horoscope: the rising sign—the sign appearing on the eastern horizon at the moment of birth. Not only would an individual be destined to express many of its qualities, it was believed, but it would lend its power to his first house. Thus if the rising sign was Taurus, associated with sensibility and persistence, then an individual's personality, represented by the first house, ought to be orderly and tenacious. The second house, which represented money matters, would be ruled by Gemini, and the remainder of the houses would each be ruled, in turn, by a subsequent sign.

Just as important as the rising sign, however, was the sun sign. Sun signs came into being because the ancients saw the sun moving through the heavens

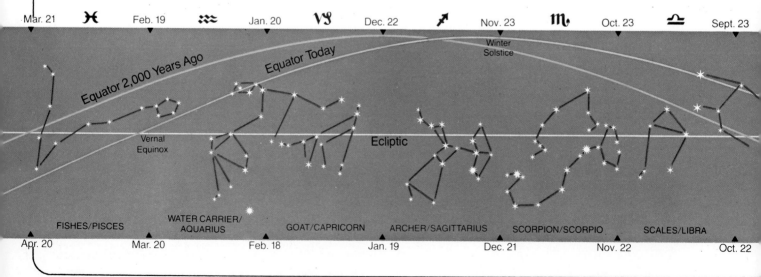

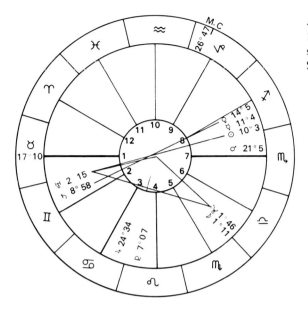

A horoscope cast for the nuclear age, born on December 2, 1942, with the first self-maintaining nuclear chain reaction, shows Taurus as rising sign and first house. The relationship of Saturn and Uranus with Neptune and the Moon bodes well.

along the same path as the zodiacal constellations, and they calculated that the sun passed from one to the next in about a month. Thus whatever sign the sun seemed to be passing during the month of a person's birth became an additional element in his horoscope, his sun sign, the sign that most people know today.

Now, however, the signs and stars no longer align exactly as they did in ancient times. Nonetheless, most modern astrologers calculate that the sun enters the first sign, Aries, on about the first day of spring (the spring equinox), just as the ancients did. But due to a gradual shift in the earth's axis, called precession, this is no longer true. The result: the first day of spring comes not when the sun is entering Aries but when it is entering Pisces. In fact, because of precession, the sun actually passes through each constellation about a month later than it did in ancient times. And while a few astrologers do base their calculations on existing earth-star relationships, most deal with the zodiac as determined thousands of years ago.

Like the sun, the moon and planets are thought to

rule one or more signs and are thus factors in the mechanics of astrology. Ancient astrologers calculated and considered the angles (called aspects) that the planets formed with the earth as the vertex. For instance, two planets 60° apart or 120° apart were held to be mild in influence. But bodies in square (90°) or in opposition (180°) were considered ominous. Two planets in conjunction (an aspect of 0°) reinforce their powers if compatible but could cause conflict if not.

Most modern astrologers calculate and ponder all these heavenly relationships—signs, planets, houses and other factors—not by looking into the heavens but by consulting astrological charts and tables. They are likely to record the information on a round diagram that has been subdivided into the 12 houses. But with so many heavenly alignments to consider, and because each alignment is said to imply and suggest but not to unequivocally predict, interpretation is crucial to the subjective art of astrology. Even more essential to astrological activities, of course, is another assumption: that life is in fact influenced in some manner by the heavens. Nonetheless, astrology's attraction remains powerful, drawing the attention not only of thousands of true believers but of millions of casual followers who, though they may not guide their lives by astrological counsel, cannot help but wonder if heavenly cycles do in fact carry some message for them.

The constellations below, shown as they appear from earth, are those of the zodiac band. About 2,000 years ago the sun entered Aries on March 21, as shown by the dates given above the band. Today, however, the sun actually enters Aries on April 20, as shown by the dates given below the band.

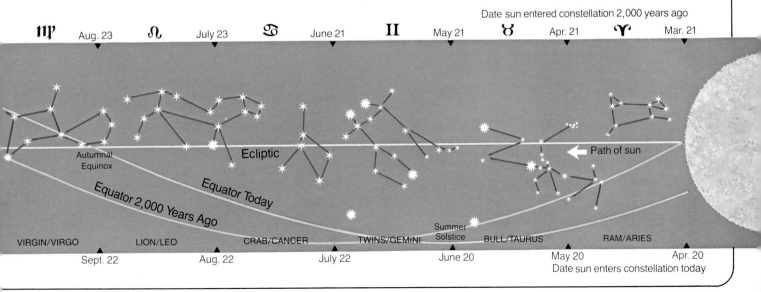

Date sun entered constellation 2,000 years ago

Date sun enters constellation today

Arrested in 1914, Evangeline Adams (above, left) so impressed a judge with her astrological skills that he released her. Some 40 years later, Michel Gauquelin found statistical correspondences between the sky at birth and occupation.

secretions, influence the timing of its own birth.

Not surprisingly, Gauquelin would be the last to claim predictive value for his highly complex theories. "There is not, and there never will be, any 'planet of the professions,'" he wrote, "nor even a 'planet of character,' but only cosmic clocks or 'time-keepers' which operate in a way which is still unknown but seems to be connected with the earth's rotation. . . . We are surrounded by mystery and can only advance gropingly. Our position is a little like that of a prisoner who, having made a hole in the wall of his cell, is still uncertain whether this opening will lead to the way of freedom or whether it will lead to the warden's office."

The statistical opening developed by Gauquelin seemed to lead back to the mathematician's blackboard. And in 1975 Lawrence E. Jerome published an article that attempted to explain what he saw as Gauquelin's mistakes. His statistical manipulations were acceptable, claimed Jerome, but he had misapplied certain probability statistics, "thus arriving at odds against chance on the order of one hundred thousand to one for statistical fluctuations that are actually well within chance level." Although Gauquelin's claims remain controversial—subsequent studies have done little to prove or disprove them—Jerome's conclusions were harsh: "Legitimate statistical studies of astrology have found absolutely no correlation between the positions and motions of the celestial bodies and the lives of men."

Over the centuries, Jerome also wrote, the adaptability of astrologers has meant that magical assumptions, such as "the principle of correspondences," have been covered up. "This confused state of affairs," claimed Jerome, "is precisely the astrologers' aim: as long as they can obscure the fact that astrology is nothing more nor less than magic and totally unrelated to physical science, they can continue to find customers willing to part with hard-earned funds. For, after all, astrology *is* a practical 'art'; it has provided many an astrologer with a lifelong living."

Horoscopes by Mail

Astrology in the United States may be big business these days, but it still operates more like an 18th-century cottage industry than a modern conglomerate. Thousands of independent astrologers ply their popular trade from storefronts, newspaper columns and paperback bookstalls, but an astonishing number woo clients with three- and four-line advertisements in the classified sections of national tabloids.

"The secret to a happier, more successful life lies in the stars. Call or write Naru now! . . . $3.00." "Astrology readings . . . Remarkable results . . . Sister Anna . . . Call or Write . . . $3.00." "Psychic astrologer from India. Mother Ora reveals your future even though miles away. $4.00." Assuming one is indeed in search of a "happier, more successful life" or even of "remarkable results," who would bet on achieving either by means of a long-distance correspondence with Naru, Sister Anna or Mother Ora? Even many believers in astrology would doubt that satisfaction was to be had at such a price and from such sources. But when a pair of psychologists at Northwestern University decided in 1968 to find out what three or four dollars would buy on the mail-order market, they turned up some surprisingly good news.

Profs. Lee Sechert and James H. Bryan confined their investigation to a single question—whether to go ahead with a proposed marriage—then identified 18 astrologers whose advertisements indicated a specialty in marital matters. They carefully composed three types of letters to be sent under a variety of names. The first type was neutral, providing only basic information—age, birthplace, hour of birth and so on of the prospective bride and groom—but giving no clue to the writer's state of mind regarding the impending nuptials. The second and third letters indicated either a positive or a negative attitude on the part of the clients. Each astrologer was sent a neutral letter and either a positive or a negative one. To the delight of the researchers, whose main concern was the quality of advice dispensed, the responses that came back were remarkably free of astrological theory and jargon. The advice relied not just on astrological charts, but took into account the negative or affirmative slant of the clients' letters and measured positively on the six criteria the professors had established for "good" personal counseling. The advice was generally prompt, relevant and practical, credible, sound, inexpensive and, most important, friendly and concerned. It was also weighty and thorough on occasion, with one practitioner typing a 450-word reply to one query and a 750-word answer to the second, each for a fee of only 50 cents. Only one mail-order astrologer framed his answer in purely astrological terms, but another more than compensated by actually scolding his client to "give up this crazy plan. Marriage is a personal thing and can't be foretold by the stars!"

Jerome's critical statement emphasized astrology's magical roots, and even now many of us do cling to some portion of a belief that the heavens rule. A question about a stranger's birth sign enlivens conversation, and the generalizations published in newspapers are fun to read; glimmerings of apparent truth can often be found in their broad predictions. Nor does it especially matter that many of us consult the wrong sign in the newspapers. This is because many astrologers are still using celestial charts based on 2nd-century calculations, not charts that depict the sky at the moment of a 20th-century birth. The reason: the earth is not a perfect sphere; it is flattened at the poles and consequently "wobbles" slightly on its axis. The result is a process called the precession of the equinoxes, and over thousands of years it has created crucial changes. The effect is as if the belt of the zodiac circling the earth were slipping, so that at the start of the spring equinox—the beginning of the belt, by ancient definition—the sun is no longer entering Aries but Pisces instead. Thus the

The western portion of the United States, where one Californian went so far as to embellish his swimming pool with signs of the zodiac, led the nation in belief in astrology in 1975. Other areas of the country, it was found, were not far behind.

Star Power: It's in the Polls

In 1976, soon after a group of 186 scientists, including 18 Nobel Prize winners, issued a statement declaring astrology to be utterly without scientific merit, the Gallup poll announced the results of a survey of U.S. beliefs about astrology. The findings must have made some scientific hearts sink, for almost one-quarter of the U.S. public confessed to believing in the influence of the stars. This was a decline from one year earlier, when, according to a Roper poll commissioned by the *National Enquirer,* 45 percent of those questioned said that they believed in astrology or some aspect of the art. But by 1978 when Gallup undertook a broad survey of U.S. belief in a wide range of paranormal phenomena, fully 29 percent of the U.S. public said they believed in astrology.

So saturated has the popular culture become with astrological lore that in 1976, Gallup found that 76 percent of the population could name their sign. Belief was highest among women (26 percent versus 18 percent for men), non-whites (41 percent versus 20 percent) and graduates of high school but not college (26 percent versus 14 percent of college-educated respondents and 21 percent of those who completed only grade school). Westerners believed in greater numbers (25 percent) than any other regional group, with midwesterners being the most skeptical (19 percent). The most credulous by age were 18- to 24-year-olds, the least credulous those between 30 and 49. As income rose, belief declined: 36 percent of people earning less than $3,000 a year said they believed, while only 17 percent of those earning $20,000 or more did. Democrats outflanked Republicans 26 percent to 14 percent. Religion seems, to a few, to be no obstacle to belief in the influence of the stars, with 19 percent of respondents saying they both believed in astrology and attended church regularly. Furthermore, Catholics (21 percent) and Protestants (22 percent) reported almost equal rates of belief. More manual workers than professionals acknowledged following the stars and more city folk than country folk. Almost twice as many single (33 percent) as married people (18 percent) believe, although Gallup did not ascertain how soon after marriage disinterest set in.

Involvement and interest in astrology is not unique to the U.S. public. In 1960 the Japanese purchased 8 million copies of horoscopes, or Koyoni. And among West Germans, some 30 percent were found to be believers, according to a study conducted in the mid-1950s. Seemingly most interested of all, however, are the French, a full 53 percent of whom admitted to reading their horoscope regularly during 1963.

zodiac has slipped backward, so that to some astrologers yesterday's Leo is really a Cancer, and a Scorpio is actually a Libra. Some astrologers have attempted to compensate for such celestial slippage by using a movable zodiac in their calculations, but the idea is not accepted in most astrological practices. Dane Rudhyar, a leading U.S. astrologer, offered this argument against it: "I do not believe that this type of astrology is what we need today—that is, it does not fill the psychological need of our present humanity."

Predictably, psychologists have invaded the astrological realm in an attempt to explain why people continue to believe in the face of so much contradictory evidence. In a 1964 study French psychologist L. H. Couderc offered through advertisement his services as an astrologer. To each respondent, he sent back a single, deliberately general and ambiguous horoscope. He received more than 200 replies to thank him for his vision and accuracy. A study conducted 10 years later by clinical psychologist C. R. Snyder at the University of Kansas showed that the more exacting the information a client is asked to provide, the more likely he is to believe the predictions that result. A horoscope presented as "generally true for most people" who have a particular sun sign is not as credible to a customer as one claimed to have been tailored specifically for him. Perhaps because they have an intuitive understanding of this phenomenon, many modern astrologers demand not just the year, month, day and location but also the minute of a customer's birth.

Astrology's basic concept has always been buoyed by new ideas, however tangential. Today, for example, a field that is providing intriguing research is the study of the physical influences of heavenly bodies on earthly life. This study does not support the proposition that the planets influence human destiny, but it has suggested that celestial bodies do more to earthly life forms than has heretofore been suspected.

Consider the story of the careful calculations of a Japanese doctor, Maki Takata. Before World War II, he had worked out a technique to determine where a woman was in her cycle of ovulation by means of a delicate measurement of the chemical changes in the

A U.S. Naval Observatory photograph records the path of a satellite crossing in front of the stars of Sagittarius and the galactic clouds that mask the heart of the Milky Way.

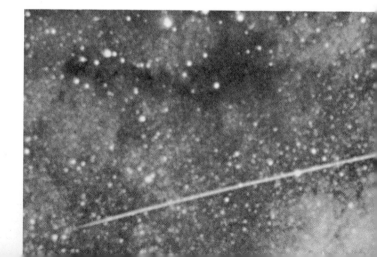

blood. In women such changes occur regularly during each month, while the blood chemistry of men is without variation. The Takata Reaction was thus useful to gynecologists and applied exclusively to women. It is no wonder, therefore, that Takata was astonished by reports that poured in from around the world in 1938: his test was useless because the blood chemistry of women—and men—was not behaving as it should.

Takata studied the sudden changes in the blood chemistry of men and established that they occurred at the same time everywhere. The cause, he reasoned, had to be extraterrestrial. But what could it be? His conclusion, after 17 years of research, was: "Man is a kind of living sundial." For Takata discovered that the measured changes in men's blood varied with the movements of sunspots toward the sun's central meridian. The closer to the sun the men were, the more their blood was changed; Takata checked the phenomenon by sending a relative up in an airplane to provide blood samples at various altitudes. Why, then, had Takata's results been so reliable at first? A possible explanation is that in 1938, the year when blood changes became so noticeable, the level of solar activity, particularly the movement of sunspots, increased dramatically.

Takata's experience was far from unique. Man has known for centuries that the sun plays a major role in the changes of seasons, weather, the growth of vegetation and much that follows from these events. The moon and, to a lesser degree, the sun push and pull the tides of our oceans. But what is to be said of John H. Nelson's findings about the way in which the positions of the planets seem to influence the movement of radio waves passing through space?

Nelson, an engineer for the Radio Corporation of America, learned in the early 1950s that disturbances in radio transmission occurred when two or more planets formed a 90° or 180° angle with the earth. This, surprisingly enough, fits neatly with the astrological idea that such angles are bad omens. To make matters even more puzzling, radio transmission was found to be easier when the planets were in the angular relationships that astrologers consider to have a benign influence. And why, to raise another scientific puzzle, should the behavior of bacteria in test tubes change with variations in the sun's rays? And why should such changes occur even when the bacteria are shielded from such obvious forces as atmospheric temperature and pressure changes?

Despite its major and minor flaws, however, one should not assume that astrology will vanish. The human need for belief is too real, though offered with an apologetic laugh or played out as a cocktail-party ploy. As recently as World War II, for example, British leaders, believing that Adolf Hitler might be consulting astrologers, hired their own to try to discover what kind of predictions were being made in Germany.

It was not the first time that Hitler had been linked with astrology. In 1923 astrologer Elsbeth Ebertin wrote in an almanac called *A Glimpse Into the Future:* "A man of action born on April 20, 1889, with Sun in the 29th degree of Aries at the time of his birth, can expose himself to personal danger by excessively rash action and could very likely trigger off an uncontrollable crisis. His constellations show that this man is to be taken very seriously indeed. He is destined to play a 'Führer-role' in future battles. . . . The man I have in mind, with this strong Aries influence, is destined to sacrifice himself for the German nation, and also to face up to all circumstances with audacity and courage, even when it is a matter of life and death, and to give an impulse, which will burst forth quite suddenly. . . . But I will not anticipate destiny. Time will show."

Soon after the prediction, Hitler—birth date, April 20, 1889—tried to overthrow the German government in his Munich *Putsch.* He went to jail, but Führer and creator of uncontrollable crisis he came to be.

And so the flickers of insight continue to taunt the imagination. Was it with resignation or triumph that Michel Gauquelin wrote: "For them [20th-century astrologers], astrology is no more than an echo, a dead idea. The majestic river which was man's early thought about his universe has been swallowed up in a desert of foolishness. However, such as it is, and dead to our way of thinking, astrology should still be respected. Those who have passed away are owed respect. Let us honor the memory of this old and slightly crazy lady who was lively enough in her time"?

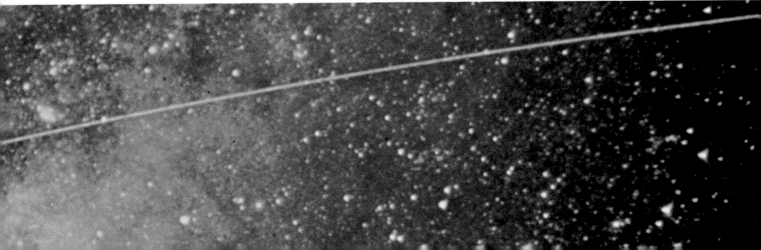

Fact vs. Phenomenon

Enigma of Lunar Lunacy

Oscar Collier was for many years one of New York's most distinguished literary agents. Whenever Collier held an important auction, in which publishers were asked to bid competitively for a promising new manuscript, he invariably tried to do so on a day when the moon was full. "I'm not a believer in the occult," says Collier, "nor do I have any scientific theory whatever about how the moon may influence people. The way I scheduled my auctions was entirely pragmatic. Over the years I found that the bidding was always livelier and the final selling price was always higher at the time of the full moon. I can't explain it, but I would have been foolish to ignore it."

Many people share Collier's belief. It is, for example, a commonplace among policemen, firemen and ambulance drivers that their busiest days—and, more specifically, nights—occur when the moon is new or full, for these are the times when suicides, crimes of passion, arson and all manner of aberrant human behavior seem to crest. "On those nights, there is a holy mess of violent crimes and accidents," a New York ambulance driver told psychiatrist Arnold L. Lieber, author of *The Lunar Effect.*

There is nothing new about the idea that the moon can have baneful effects on human behavior. It is an immemorial part of Eastern and Western folklore; it is mentioned in the Bible, the Talmud and the Koran, and it has been a fixture in Western medical and philosophical literature since at least 400 B.C., the time of Hippocrates, the father of medicine. Indeed, the very word *lunacy* derives from the Latin word for the moon: *luna.* And until fairly recently, the moon was even accepted in law as a cause of insanity. Thus the great 18th-century English jurist Sir William Blackstone wrote: "A lunatic, or *non compos mentis,* is one who hath . . . lost the use of his reason and who hath lucid intervals, sometimes enjoying his senses and sometimes not, and that frequently depending upon the changes of the moon." In a 19th-century homicide trial, so the story goes, Charles Hyde, the defendant, pleaded innocence on the grounds that the new and full moons regularly drove him mad. Hyde supposedly lost his case but achieved an immortality of sorts; Robert Louis Stevenson may have used him as a model for Dr. Jekyll's murderous alter ego.

In folklore the moon's capacity to affect human beings in unpleasant ways is perhaps best encapsulated in werewolf legends, the vivid metaphors (if they are nothing more) of what is supposed to be the moon's subtle power to unleash all that is beastly and irrational in man. Who wouldn't believe in such things, having watched at the movies dreadful scenes of men, at full moon, turning into preying wolves? Some may even recall the rhymed warning the sinister Gypsy gave Lon Chaney, Jr., in *The Wolf Man* (1941):

> Even a man who is pure at heart
> And says his prayers by night
> May become a wolf when the wolfbane blooms
> And the moon is full and bright.

The moon may precipitate not only romantic poetry but also, according to certain controversial studies, dramatic increases in violence, madness and suicide.

Considering how many people, for how many centuries, have believed in moon madness, one might reasonably expect modern science to have made some definitive pronouncement on the subject. In fact, science has shown that some living organisms do respond to the moon's phases: fiddler crabs, for example, change color in relation to the moon's position, and the feeding cycle of oysters is also influenced by lunar change. Yet the verdict of science on man's lunar sensitivities is at best ambiguous. Probably the chief proponent of the moon-madness theory—or, as some like to call it, the "Transylvanian hypothesis"—is psychiatrist Arnold Lieber. In *The Lunar Effect,* Lieber suggests that lunar gravitation may somehow affect our internal biological "tides" in ways similar to its effects on the oceans. He also suggests that the moon's influence on the earth's electromagnetic field may have some unknown consequences for man. Thus, he speculates, the moon might indeed influence not only our emotions but our metabolism and fertility as well.

Speculation aside, the chief evidence Lieber has adduced is from two statistical studies he conducted with Dr. Carolyn Sherin. The pair tabulated homicides occurring in Dade County, Florida, between 1956 and 1970 and in Cuyahoga County, Ohio, between 1958 and 1970. In the Florida study the researchers found what they called "a statistically significant lunar periodicity," in that more murders took place at times of the new and full moons than at other times. That they found no "significant lunar periodicity" in the Ohio study, Lieber and Sherin also took to be encouraging because, they claimed, the intensity of lunar effect was likely to vary with location.

Lieber's scientific critics have tended to avoid discussing many of his theories, but they have been both vocal and harsh in dealing with the statistics he gathered in Dade and Cuyahoga counties. The data, they have argued, were defective. And even if the figures were not, Lieber's statistical method was so weak, they have claimed, that results he called "significant" were nothing of the kind. Worst of all, attempts to replicate his study—whether with respect to homicides, hospital admissions or the frequency of telephone calls received by a psychiatric counseling service—have produced negative or, at best, hopelessly ambiguous results. As far as these researchers are concerned, Lieber's efforts to verify what every policeman "knows" have failed.

Is the idea of moon madness, then, nothing more than an ancient popular delusion? Not even Lieber's most vehement critics go that far, for most agree (however reluctantly) that many more carefully controlled studies would have to be conducted before the matter could safely be called either proven or disproven. Meanwhile, as it has done for eons, the vagrant moon will continue to ride the night sky, holding in thrall, if not our sanity, then our imagination. And in that realm, if nowhere else, lies the answer to Keats's question: "What is there in thee, moon, that thou shouldst move my heart so potently?"

A need to believe and a lack of conclusive
proof are the antagonists in man's eternal struggle
to investigate rebirth after death.

REINCARNATION

On an ancient Greek grave-
stone a soul is shown wandering through the nether world.

When the little Indian girl Shanti Devi was just three years old, she startled her parents with her matter-of-fact chattering about her husband and children. Finally, her mother asked who this husband was of whom the girl spoke so often. Though the girl had, in fact, been born in Old Delhi, India's capital, in 1929, she answered without hesitation, "My husband's name is Kendarnath. He lives in Muttra. Our house is yellow stucco, with large arched doors and latticework windows. Our yard is large and filled with marigolds and jasmine. Great bowers of scarlet bougainvilleas climb over the house. We often sit on the veranda, watching our little son play on the tile floor. Our sons are still there with their father."

The child, of course, did not use these exact words or possess such a sophisticated vocabulary. The words are probably the work of the Indian press, which later reported at great length on the case and re-created many conversations between the girl and her parents. As a result, Shanti Devi became one of the most-talked-about cases of reincarnation in modern India. And yet beneath the popularization of Shanti's accounts of her earlier life there exists a body of haunting circumstance and compelling coincidence that is as fascinating as it is difficult to explain. For according

Buddhists believe that the soul is reincarnated through many realms, symbolized in the six scenes on a Tibetan wheel of life; ultimately, the soul is freed and may attain perfection.

to both her parents and the family's physician, the little girl provided an extraordinary amount of detail about her alleged earlier existence. Shanti said, for example, that her name during a previous life had been Ludgi, that she had died giving birth to a child of her own, and that she had "a difficult pregnancy." She told how she felt "worse and worse," and when the baby came, "it was a breach birth. The baby lived but the delivery killed me."

For four years Shanti's parents lived with the troubling paradox of the girl's accounts of her life in Muttra, her final pregnancy and her death. And then a close relative, Prof. Kishen Chand, decided to challenge the girl's apparent fantasies by addressing a letter to her alleged widower. This man, Kendarnath, suspecting a mercenary maneuver, asked a cousin in Delhi to look into the matter. But when the cousin called on the Devi family, Shanti greeted him with great delight. She then not only identified the man correctly but also mentioned this mundane, yet compelling fact: he had moved from Muttra to Delhi during her years as Kendarnath's wife. The next encounter in Shanti's chronicle—a visit by Kendarnath himself, accompanied by his son, to the Devi household—was even more remarkable. For during this reunion, if indeed it was such, Shanti acted as both a dutiful wife to Kendarnath and loving mother to his son.

Soon enough, word of Shanti's case spread, and the All-India Newspaper Association arranged for a firsthand investigation. Under the direction of the association's head, parliamentarian Desh Bandu Gupta, the

Delhi family was transported to Muttra, accompanied by a committee of experienced observers.

Upon arriving in Muttra, Shanti passed one crucial test. She was able to lead the group from the train station to the house that she claimed had been her home during her earlier life. Looking at the house, she reportedly said, "In my days it was yellow; now it is white." Shanti's story of her previous life and details concerning her home, her children and the town itself were checked against the facts and found to be substantially correct. And so for better or worse, because of the human fascination with the possibility of life after death and in order to boost newspaper sales, Shanti Devi became a nationwide celebrity.

Decades after she had been a much-publicized child, Shanti Devi was asked how she felt about her memories. "I do not wish to revive my past lives," she told visitors, "either this one or my previous existence in Muttra. It has been very difficult for me to bury my desires to return to my family. I do not want to open that closed door again."

Yet however dramatic the Shanti Devi case may have been, it is but one of thousands that have been documented in recent decades. And while northern India is particularly rich in such reported cases, accounts of remembered past lives have been reported in many parts of the world, including Latin America, western Europe, southern Asia, sections of the Near East and the United States. There are even indications, based on folkloric tradition, that tales of reincarnation, in the form of myth and legend, may actually predate the establishment of the world's major religions.

Essential to all such concepts, both modern and preliterate, Eastern and Western, is a belief that some essence of individual life exists after death, that it may leave the corporeal form that has perished, and that it may re-enter the known world in a similar or different physical guise. Hinduism is pre-eminent among organized religions in its belief in reincarnation, a belief that probably originated in India about the 6th century B.C., possibly when people there adapted older traditions concerning souls and the cycle of existence. Fundamental to the Hindu creed is the idea of karma, which suggests that each rebirth may be either a punishment or a reward for deeds done in a previous life. The Hindu also believes that the soul may increase in purity during successive existences until it ultimately reaches a divine world.

Asian belief in reincarnation may have been transported to North America by migrants who crossed the Bering Strait thousands of years ago, when either the strait was narrower than it is now or a land bridge linked Siberia with North America. Dr. Ian Stevenson, director of the Division of Parapsychology of the Department of Psychiatry at the University of Virginia and one of the leaders in modern-day reincarnation

research, emphasized this point in his book *Twenty Cases Suggestive of Reincarnation*. Ethnologists, he pointed out, generally agree that "the ancestors of the Indians of the northwest coast of America, including the Tlingit Indians, were the last migrants from Asia." He also noted that the Tlingits' belief in reincarnation did not result from European influence but does include "a concept somewhat similar" to the Hindu karma. In his studies among the Tlingit Indians of southeastern Alaska, Stevenson uncovered a case that is provocative in both Hindu and Western terms. It involved an instance of "a prediction of rebirth prior to death." An Indian named William George, Sr., a celebrated fisherman, once told his son George and his daughter-in-law, "If there is anything to this rebirth business, I will come back and be your son." He also told them that they would be able to recognize him "because I will have birthmarks like the ones I now have."

As it happened, events seemed to bear out the words of William George, Sr. In August 1949, William George disappeared on a fishing trip and was presumed dead. Soon thereafter his daughter-in-law became pregnant and gave birth to a boy. The baby had pigmented birthmarks on his body that resembled those of his grandfather; not surprisingly he was given the name William George, Jr. As the child grew, his parents felt that they observed in their son certain characteristics that, in Stevenson's words, "strengthened their conviction that William George, Sr., had returned." For example, the child walked with a limp, much as his grandfather had moved as the result of a basketball injury. Like the elder William George, the boy tended to fret and to warn other people of various dangers, and he "showed a precocious knowledge of fishing and boats" and "exhibited a knowledge of people and places that, in the opinion of his family, transcended what he could have learned through normal means."

The Egyptians believed the soul, shown as a bird in this painting, departed the body at death but continued to require food and other earthly ministrations in the afterlife.

The Chinese of the 2nd century B.C. sought to preserve the dead by encasing their remains in jade and gold—both associated with yang, the active principle of the universe—as in this funeral suit made for a queen.

Another strange element in the case was that before he died, William George, Sr., had given his son, the boy's father, a gold watch. One day when his mother was sorting through her jewelry, the boy saw the watch and seized it, saying, "That's my watch." He clung desperately to the watch, and it took the boy's mother a long time to persuade him to release it. Even so, the boy remained emotionally attached to the watch into his teens, when, Stevenson observed, he had "largely lost his previous identification with his grandfather."

Modern researchers seek to verify reincarnation accounts by corroborating—through interviews and historical records—reported memories of the former life. Stevenson, who introduced quantitative evaluation to the field, published the Tlingit case together with a tabulation of nine major points of correlation. For purposes of verification he painstakingly matched statements such as those referring to birthmarks and moles in grandfather and grandson. Such comparisons, however, can never really be complete or conclusive. As Stevenson has said, "I can imagine the 'perfect case,' but have no expectation of finding it."

A quite different and more contemporary case, though hardly a perfect one, involved Mrs. Dolores Jay, then of Greenbush, Ohio, who, on April 21, 1970, began to have visions of herself in a previous life. Her earlier incarnation, she believed, was as Gretchen Gottlieb, who had lived in Germany during the 19th century. The incident began when Mrs. Jay's husband, the Reverend Carroll E. Jay, a Methodist minister who had used hypnotherapy to ease his wife's back pains, heard her speak one night in a "strange, alien voice" in a language that turned out to be German.

The resulting conversation, and many subsequent ones, suggested that Mrs. Jay perceived herself as Gretchen, daughter of Hermann Gottlieb, mayor of the German town of Eberswalde. The Gottlieb family had

Australia's aborigines believe that the soul will reach the land of the dead after confronting many obstacles on the pathway to the afterlife, as depicted in the bark painting above.

been at odds with the Federal Council (Bundesrat) of Germany, and the daughter had been murdered. Dolores Jay's vision of herself as Gretchen, however, was, as the Reverend Mr. Jay wrote in his book *Gretchen, I Am,* of an attractive, small girl, brown hair braided in a bun, who "rode a beautiful bay mare side-saddle, her long dark skirt draping to her ankles."

Early Christians castigated Origen for doubting a soul could be eternally damned.

Researchers, including Stevenson, were impressed with the relatively sophisticated German spoken by Mrs. Jay and with her ability to comprehend questions in German and to answer them correctly. Yet the experience, though it seemed to be spontaneous, disturbed and disrupted the Jay household. Early attempts to track down and verify the Gottlieb data in Germany were unsuccessful; although there were several towns with names similar to Eberswalde, none listed a Hermann Gottlieb as mayor in its municipal records. Finally, the Jays traveled to Germany to trace "Gretchen's roots," and there they found certain correlations between local place names and family names and those mentioned by Gretchen in her fragmentary, anxious way. In spite of the limited success of their search,

Origen suggested that the Scriptures might tell whether the Jews believed John the Baptist, shown in a Russian view from around the 16th century, to be Elijah reincarnate.

however, the Reverend Mr. Jay announced that "the search for proof of exact dates and places must go on."

Later, after moving from Ohio to become pastor of the Anderson Memorial United Methodist Church in Gretna, Virginia, Jay did admit that in the Gretchen case, "first observations seem to indicate reincarnation." He said, however, that he had also considered the possibility that Mrs. Jay had been possessed by the restless spirit of Gretchen. Mrs. Jay herself could explain no more but concluded, "Gretchen is a part of my life. I did not ask her to come, but she has been with us so long, she now seems like a part of the family."

Such are the problems with reincarnation, a field that even now is shunned by many parapsychology researchers. Spirit possession, spirit-to-living telepathy and even poltergeist activity (physical disturbances attributed to restless or mischievous spirits) have all been suggested as alternative explanations for reincarnation-type phenomena. Sometimes these explanations are offered in combination and sometimes, as in the case of Mrs. Jay's possession, individually. Religious and cultural beliefs also have had great influence on the manner in which the theories and even the facts of reincarnation cases are expressed. In his research, for example, Stevenson has found that the interval between death and alleged rebirth varies from country to country, with cases in Turkey averaging about 9 months, in contrast to those in Sri Lanka (21 months), India (45 months) and among the Tlingit Indians in Alaska (48 months). In addition, although a high incidence of violent death appears among alleged previous personalities, the percentage rises from about 40 percent in Sri Lanka to nearly 80 percent in certain areas of Lebanon and Syria. Sex change in the course of reincarnation and the frequency of "announcing dreams," in which a pregnant woman reportedly receives a communication from a discarnate spirit announcing its intention to return as her child, also reflect cultural influences.

Yet there are constants in the field, elements that occur with near universality and suggest to some researchers that the body of reincarnative lore, even without conclusive proof or a good chance of obtaining it, reflects common human experience and thus cannot be ignored. Such recurring features include the extremely early age (two to four years) at which many subjects express their feelings about apparent past lives, the age (five to eight years) at which they tend to stop such communications, and the intensity of memories related to the death of the alleged previous personality. The pervasiveness of such themes was emphasized by Prof. C. J. Ducasse of Brown University in a paper, "The Doctrine of Reincarnation in the History of Thought," in which he wrote that the idea of reincarnation has "commended itself to a number of most distinguished thinkers from ancient times to the present." In elemental biological terms, the same concept

According to Christian belief, a soul cannot be reborn but is either damned or ascends to meet with God and his angels, as depicted in Hieronymus Bosch's 16th-century painting.

may reflect man's unique sense of self-consciousness and his reluctance to believe that such neurophysiological triumph could be terminated by death.

Greek ideas on reincarnation, possibly evolved through contact with India, were already well developed several centuries before the birth of Christ. Pythagoras, who lived during the 5th century B.C. and is best known for his mathematical concepts, is said to have told a man who was beating a puppy, "Do not hit him, it is the soul of a friend of mine. I recognized it when I heard it cry out." Ducasse helped explain Plato's ideas about reincarnation by summing up the message of the *Phaedrus:* "The soul which has seen most of truth shall come to the birth as a philosopher or artist, or musician or lover; that which has seen truth in the second degree shall be a righteous king or warrior or lord; the soul which is of the third class shall be a politician or economist or trader; the fourth shall be a lover of gymnastic toils or a physician."

The final, or ninth, degree of the soul, according to Plato, is the tyrant. Professor Ducasse, in paraphrasing Plato's ideas about degrees, added that "all these are states of probation, in which he who lives righteously improves and he who lives unrighteously deteriorates his lot." Ducasse also noted that Plato thought that a human soul "may pass into the life of a beast, or from the beast again into the man."

The application of this concept in later centuries, when religion and philosophy in the West had evolved from Judeo-Christian tradition, prompted much theological discussion. The Old Testament contains only peripheral references to reincarnationist beliefs. Such views are alluded to more frequently in the New Testament, but much depends on context and interpretation. This was acknowledged by Edgar Cayce, the self-styled clairvoyant whose readings of individuals' previous lives did much to popularize reincarnation in the United States in the early decades of the 20th century. Cayce said, "I can read reincarnation into the Bible, and you can read it right out again."

In contrast to the reincarnation concept that the soul is purified during successive incarnations and finally reaches a divine world, most of Christianity holds that the dead will arise on Judgment Day and will join with Jesus Christ. Historians see a crucial turning point in Christianity's view of reincarnation in the Second Council of Constantinople (the Fifth Ecumenical Council of the Church) in A.D. 553, during the reign of Byzantine emperor Justinian I. One of the council's 14 anathemas, or denunciations, stated, "If anyone asserts the fabulous pre-existence of souls, and shall assert the monstrous restoration which follows it, let him be anathema." Modern theologians, however, have expressed doubts as to whether the anathemas announced by the council should be considered binding by contemporary Christian denominations.

Much of the Second Council's attention was directed at the early Church theologian Origen, who was accused of having advocated a variety of concepts at variance with true Church doctrine. As Origen's writings, to the degree that they can be traced today, were voluminous, discursive and highly tentative, his critics appear to have accused him of views that he may have discussed and tolerated but neither fully accepted nor endorsed. Among these, reincarnation was prominent, although Origen at one point referred to it as "the false doctrine of the transmigration of souls into bodies." According to Dr. Geddes MacGregor, Distinguished Professor of Philosophy Emeritus at the University of Southern California, Origen may have gone so far as to attack "the widespread notion of his day that the soul of a human being could ever be imprisoned in the body of a beast (which he considers unfitting for a creature made in the image of God)."

MacGregor, in his book *Reincarnation in Christianity,* wrote that Origen seems to have been "attracted to reincarnationism, but that some forms of it with which he was familiar are suspect in his mind." MacGregor noted that Origen discussed the "alleged identity" of John the Baptist with Elijah, whose return was expected. The idea that John was a reincarnation of Elijah is based on the New Testament accounts of the reception John the Baptist received when he came to witness for Christ (John 1:19-28) and was asked whether he was Elijah. The Reverend Leslie Weatherhead, Methodist minister of the City Temple, London, from 1936 to 1960, cited this biblical passage in his booklet *The Case of Reincarnation.* Christ had never taught reincarnation directly, the minister wrote, but "seemed to have referred to it as though it were part of the accepted ideas of His day" and had "never repudiated or denied it, or taught that it was false."

Weatherhead also referred to a passage in John 9, "where we read that a man *born blind* was brought to Jesus with the question: Rabbi, who sinned, this man or his parents, that he was born blind?" Of this passage Weatherhead commented, "We must not stay with the answer, but we must note the currency of the idea of reincarnation. If it were contemplated that a man *born* blind was being punished by blindness for sin committed, then the sin committed must have been done in an earlier life before he was born into this world." This interpretation suggests that concepts akin to karma, whereby sins in one incarnation are atoned for in a later one, were, to some degree, current and acceptable during the time of Christ.

Origen appears to have been influenced by Plato,

Tibetan god Vajrapani is a protector of hidden wisdom.

and included a leading Neoplatonist, Plotinus, among his fellow students in Alexandria, Egypt, the metropolis of learning. According to Plotinus, different types of experiences help to perfect the soul, as "the experience of evil produces a clearer knowledge of good," particularly in the lives of those who "cannot, without such experience," comprehend what is best.

The desire for continuity after death, for a "second chance," is clearly a human need that reincarnation doctrine appears to meet. People who live drab lives may derive emotional sustenance from the belief that they lived dramatic lives during previous incarnations or that future lives will reward them with wealth and prominence for present suffering. Yet as Daniel Dunglas Home, the British medium, is quoted as saying with great pertinence—as well as impertinence—"I have had the pleasure of meeting at least twelve Marie Antoinettes, six or seven Marys of Scotland, a whole host of Louis and other kings, about twenty Great Alexanders, but never a plain John Smith. I, indeed, would like to cage the later curiosity." Another question that reincarnation appears to answer, however speculatively, is that raised by the appearance of infant prodigies who display skills that might normally require a lifetime of training. Thus children who perform unusual feats of memory or complicated mathematical calculations or who display linguistic versatility or awesome talent in music are frequently cited by reincarnationists as living proof of the doctrine of rebirth. Most often mentioned are Wolfgang Amadeus Mozart, who composed simple music at about the age of four, and the 17th-century mathematician Blaise Pascal, who had outlined a new geometric system by the time he had reached 11 years of age.

Today, controversy over the techniques used to summon up reincarnation information involves both the validity of the information gathered and the possibility that such techniques may produce damaging psychological side effects. Drugs, hypnosis and meditation have all been employed to help induce the recall of alleged reincarnation experiences. Great public interest arose in 1956, for example, when a corporation executive, Morey Bernstein, published a book called *The Search for Bridey Murphy,* which alleged that a hypnotized Colorado housewife had furnished information that she had lived as Bridey Murphy in Ireland a century earlier. The housewife, Virginia Tighe, had been regressed by Bernstein while she was under hypnosis, and in that state she seemed to remember exact details of her former life as a girl who married at an early age, remained childless and died at the age of 66.

Extraordinary Search for the Dalai Lama

In the year of the water bird, after a long and fruitful reign as the spiritual and temporal leader of Tibet, Thupten Gyatso, the 13th Dalai Lama, died at his summer palace in Lhasa, the capital city. It was 1933 in the outside world, and the death of the Dalai Lama set in motion a long, sacred search for the child that Tibetans believed would be born soon afterward as his reincarnate successor, the latest in a line that had continued uninterrupted since 1391. In the interim the country was to be ruled by a regent.

The high lamas whose task it was to locate the new leader consulted oracles, interpreted their visions and looked for hopeful omens to direct their search, but their first clues were close at hand. At the Dalai Lama's death his body had been placed in a throne chair facing south within a pavilion-like shrine. A few days later it was observed that his face now inclined to the east and that a large, star-shaped fungus had appeared on a wooden pillar at the northeast corner of the shrine.

As the 14th Dalai Lama later wrote in his autobiography, *My Land and My People*, these two omens suggested that the little boy who had become the latest incarnation of the "Ocean of Wisdom" was to be found northeast of Lhasa. In 1935 the regent traveled to the sacred lake of Lhamoi Latso to seek a vision in the water's surface. After a time of prayer and meditation he had visions of three Tibetan letters: *Ah, Ka* and *Ma*. He also envisioned a monastery with roofs of jade green and gold, as well as a house with turquoise tiles.

The Dalai Lama addressed seminarians during a 1979 visit to San Francisco.

The regent's visions served as a guide to the high lamas and other dignitaries who traveled throughout the Tibetan countryside in search of such a monastery and house. In 1936, three years after the death of the 13th Dalai Lama, a team of investigators journeying northeastward reported the discovery of the green and golden roofs on the Kumbum monastery, and a house with turquoise tiles in the nearby village of Taktser. In the house lived a couple and a boy who was not quite two years old.

A group of wise men visited the family, making every effort to hide the importance of their inquiry. A junior member of the group, Losang Tsewang, pretended to be its head, while its real leader, the lama Kewtsang Rinpoché from the Sera monastery, dressed and acted like a servant. The 14th Dalai Lama described their visit:

"At the gate of the house, the strangers were met by my parents, who invited Losang into the house, believing him to be the master, while the lama and the others were received in the servants' quarters. There they found the baby of the family, and the moment the little boy saw the lama, he went to him and wanted to sit on his lap. The lama was disguised in a cloak which was lined with lambskin, but round his neck he was wearing a rosary which had belonged to the Thirteenth Dalai Lama. The little boy seemed to recognize the rosary, and he asked to be given it. The lama promised to give it to him if he could guess who he was, and the boy replied that he was *Sera-aga*, which meant, in the local dialect, 'a lama of Sera.' The lama asked who the 'master' was, and the boy gave the name of Losang. He was also able to provide the name of the real servant, which was Amdo Kasang.

"The lama spent the whole day in watching the little boy with increasing interest, until it was time for the boy to be put to bed. All the party stayed in the house for the night, and early next morning, when they were making ready to leave, the boy got out of his bed and insisted that he wanted to go with them."

The search party returned a second time to conduct further tests and watched as the child successfully selected rosaries, a drum and a walking stick that had belonged to the Dalai Lama. As for the regent's vision of the three Tibetan letters, this was interpreted as referring to the *Ah* in Amado, the name of the district in which the boy's family lived; *Ka* for Kumbum; or *Ka* and *Ma* for the nearby monastery of Karma Rolpai Dorje.

After long delays dictated by caution and political maneuvering, the little boy was transported to Lhasa in 1939, escorted by a caravan of 50 people and 350 horses and mules. The Lhasa assembly agreed that the search had been "in accord with the advice of the leading oracles and lamas" and with the 13th Dalai Lama's indications "of the place where he wanted to be reborn." On the 14th day of the first month of the year of the iron dragon (1940), the child was placed on the Lion Throne.

In talking to Bernstein while hypnotized, Tighe replied in a voice accented by a brogue and said that as Bridey she had been born to Kathleen and Duncan Murphy in Cork on December 20, 1798. The family had lived in a farmhouse called Meadows, and her father had practiced law. As a girl she attended Mrs. Strayne's Day School and studied "house things, proper things." Among other reported memories, she recalled a party for a friend by the name of Genevieve.

Bridey met her future husband, Brian MacCarthy, Tighe said, when she was 17 years old and he was 19. Three years later they married, but her parents "were unhappy about it" because they felt "they were losing me." The couple settled in a small cottage in Belfast, behind a house that belonged to MacCarthy's grandmother. Bridey's husband practiced law, taught at Queen's University and contributed articles to the Belfast *News-Letter*.

Of the details of her married life Bridey spoke with less sprightliness, perhaps with good reason. For the hypnotized Tighe reported that as Bridey MacCarthy she often cooked her husband's favorite dish, boiled beef with onions; and there appeared to be little diversion in the couple's life, although Bridey did recall dancing the sorcerer's jig with her husband. Father John, the family confessor, she recalled, had visited the family fairly frequently.

As recorded on tape by Bernstein, the Bridey personality remembered that she had fallen down the stairs in the MacCarthy home, had broken her hip, and had felt like a "burden." In such a depressed state she "sort of withered away," and one Sunday, while MacCarthy was off "to church," Bridey died.

Because of the mass of seemingly hard evidential detail that emerged from the six tape-recorded sessions with Virginia Tighe, several investigators, including a number of journalists, traveled to Ireland to seek confirmation of the Bridey data. Yet the information they gathered was at best circumstantial. And while "Come As You Were" parties and popular songs echoed the enormous public interest in the United States in the case, the evidence did little more than convince those inclined to regard Bridey's reincarnation narrative as genuine that it was so. For those who did not believe Bridey's accounts or accept the validity of hypnotic regression techniques, the case of Bridey Murphy remained unproven. One investigator suggested that the story was based on the life of an Irish family Tighe had known as a child.

Nevertheless, the technique of eliciting reincarnation data from a person under hypnosis continued to be popular and is still so today in many paranormal investigations, including the recall of incidents of personal contact with unidentified flying objects. With hypnosis it is possible to regress subjects to an earlier time in their lives, so that they may seem to recall forgotten or sup-

pressed events, possibly of a traumatic nature. To hypnotically regress them to an alleged previous life is also relatively easy to do. Yet the material that emerges in a hypnotic trance, as in the Bridey Murphy case, in no way proves the existence of reincarnation and, indeed, may be colored by a subject's tendency to fantasize, if only to please the temporarily dominant hypnotist.

Because of Stevenson's prominence as a reincarnation researcher, he has received numerous inquiries on the question of hypnotic regression. Such inquiries have prompted Stevenson to write that "many persons who attach no importance whatever to their dreams—realizing that most are merely images of the dreamer's subconscious mind without correspondence to any other reality—nevertheless believe that whatever emerges during hypnosis can invariably be taken at face value." Yet in Stevenson's words, "The state of a hypnotized person resembles in many ways—though not in all—that of a person dreaming. The subconscious parts of the mind are released from ordinary inhibitions, and they may then present in dramatic form a new 'personality.' If the person has been instructed by the hypnotist—explicitly or implicitly—to 'go back to another place and time' or given some similar guidance, the new 'personality' may be extremely plausible both to the person and to others watching him or her."

Such a hypnotically evoked "personality" is, in Stevenson's view, nearly always "entirely imaginary, as are the contents of most dreams." Stevenson noted, however, that some accurate historical details may emerge, though these may be based on information acquired through reading, listening to the radio or watching television. The researcher-psychiatrist added an additional caveat: "There are some hazards in this procedure of regression to 'previous lives.' In a few instances the 'previous personality' had not 'gone away' when instructed to do so, and the subject in such cases has been left in an altered state of personality for several days or longer before restoration of his normal personality."

Nonetheless, in an article, "Artificial Reincarnation Through Hypnosis," a Russian physician, Dr. Vladimir L. Raikov, has reported that "the hypnotic phenomenon of mental suggestion can be utilized in teaching." Raikov called his method artificial reincarnation because he induced his hypnotized subjects to act as if they were the historical personalities with whom they had been matched. He cited the example of a young woman who was studying the violin and was told that she was, in fact, the virtuoso violinist Fritz Kreisler. Raikov observed that "her manner of playing"

India's supreme god Vishnu in his eighth incarnation is the god Krishna, famed for his ability to love and to inspire love, especially in the beautiful shepherdess Radha. He is portrayed with her in the 18th-century Indian painting at right.

under hypnosis became "reminiscent of that of Kreisler." Another subject was an aviation engineer who, when informed that he was a famous Russian painter, managed to paint with superior skill while under hypnotic influence. Conversely, a student who was advised that he was a five-year-old boy succeeded only in making a naive, childish drawing of a man and a cat.

The United States has emerged as a country with a wide academic and popular interest in reincarnation. On the one hand, Stevenson's type of exacting research has emphasized a degree of scholarship that deals largely with data that are "suggestive of reincarnation." On the other hand, newspapers and weekly tabloids regularly feature colorful accounts of previous-life experiences. A third field concerns the therapeutic application of reincarnation claims and fantasies.

Writing in the *Newsletter* of the Association for Transpersonal Psychology in 1978, Dr. Arthur Hastings reported that "the trend of current interest is more popular than scholarly." He added, "One facet of this is curiosity and perhaps ego-gratification. To learn that you were once a princess in Egypt, or a Sufi teacher, may give you a thrill, add spice to your self-concept, or confirm that your life has a particular meaning."

Hastings then described the two major channels through which people seek information concerning their past lives. "In our contemporary life, information about 'one's past life' is usually given by someone claiming to be 'psychic,' or is evoked within a light trance guided by a leader, in which the participant 'remembers' experiences that are interpreted as coming from a past life. These experiences are often vivid and plausible, but I think we must say that there is usually no reliable proof that they *are* memories of a past life. They could equally well be constructions of one's imagination in response to the leader's request in the suggestible state of relaxation or guided fantasy. In the same manner, a psychic may be constructing an experience or a personality based on his or her perception of the other individual, but interpreting the construction as a past life rather than as a current creation."

Hastings referred to the second category in this manner: "Psychotherapists . . . have reported that traumas or neurotic problems of some of their patients have been resolved when the patient remembered a traumatic incident which apparently happened in a past life." He explained his reference this way: "One patient who had a fear of leaving his house recalled a 'past life' in which he as a frontiersman left the house and returned to find his wife and family had died in a fire. Becoming aware of this 'event' enabled him more consciously to release the programed fear."

Hastings noted as well that most therapists are less interested in theories concerning reincarnation than in producing therapeutic change. They also, perhaps alarmingly, seem not to share Stevenson's view that re-

Dr. Ian Stevenson has attempted to verify details of accounts of earlier lives.

Dr. Leslie Weatherhead searched the Bible for signs of belief in reincarnation.

incarnation evidence when elicited under hypnotic regression is no more reliable proof than a dream of a previous life. Yet Hastings reported that such techniques "may have therapeutic value, regardless of the 'reality base' of the memory" because any past-life memory could well have "symbolic value that relates to *current* life experiences."

Morris Netherton, Ph.D., in his book *Past Lives Therapy*, written with Nancy Shiffrin, claimed that "almost invariably my patients have found that their mental anguish in this life could be pinpointed to a physical situation in a past life." If a patient of Netherton's suffers from an acute fear of heights, chances are the patient "will discover recurring past-life situations where he died by falling long distances." While such visions of the past could be "creative daydreams," Netherton admitted, he personally believed that "reincarnation does in fact take place."

Similarly, Dr. Edith Fiore wrote in *You Have Been Here Before* that she became increasingly convinced that her patients' memories were not mere fantasies. Fiore's basis for such belief was that the "remission of symptoms" in her patients provided "almost conclusive proof" of reincarnation. Fiore also dealt with the delicate question of how person-to-person relationships in a previous life may affect present marriages and sexual interactions. She wrote, "In my work, one of my patients found that in his former life he murdered his wife after she flaunted extramarital affairs in his face. He stays with her now [in his current life], despite tremendous marital difficulties. He owes her a debt."

Other researchers have reported that past-life recollections may actually create marital difficulties, in that alleged relations in previous lives may be used to justify extramarital relations in the present. Netherton, in fact, suggested that people who are untroubled by behavioral disorders ought to leave the question of past lives alone and their "unconscious mind undisturbed."

Psychologist Helen Wambach of Walnut Creek, California, regards the use of hypnotic regression as a valid means of discovering and studying accounts of earlier incarnations. After examining more than 1,000 descriptions of previous lives, gathered from 1,000 subjects, she reported that some 90 percent of her hypnotized subjects had been able to "vividly recall scenes and emotions from past lives."

Wambach undertook her study in the hope that by examining a large number of hypnotically induced accounts of former incarnations, she might find evidence that these tales were more than fantasy. She began her experiments by hypnotizing a number of people simultaneously and asking them which of several dates she mentioned brought to mind a vivid picture or image. On other occasions she asked subjects to look at a map and choose whatever spots seemed to have particularly strong appeal. Then she would urge her subjects to describe what they saw and felt. She sought detailed information that was unlikely to be found in books, magazines or films, inquiring, for instance, about landscape and climate. She also looked for descriptions of personal appearance, eating utensils, clothing and money, and home and village life.

While the vividness of her subjects' descriptions was not necessarily surprising—it is to be expected that a hypnotized subject will imagine graphically whatever a hypnotist suggests—the fact that many of the details proved to be historically or archeologically accurate was, to Wambach, highly significant.

In some instances, subjects were troubled because, on the basis of their general knowledge, they were convinced that their descriptions had to be wrong, though later research proved that this was not the case. In an instance of special interest to Wambach, several subjects described themselves as blond and fair-skinned although

they believed that they were living in regions around the Caucasus. Only later did these people learn that over the centuries, the Caucasus had been the home of a variety of physical types.

Wambach was also impressed that the 1,088 past-life descriptions she collected accurately reflected estimates of components of the world's population. For instance, men and women were always nearly equally represented in the hypnotically induced past-life tales, whether or not there were equal numbers of male and female subjects in the group that had been hypnotized. Socioeconomic data, too, seemed to correspond to actual populations. Statistical analysis showed that only 10 percent of the past lives described were of upper-class people, while the great majority—from 60 percent to 77 percent, depending upon the century being described—were of people from the lower classes, many of them farmers. The great majority of descriptions collected told of simple, difficult lives involving poor food and shelter. Interestingly enough, the percentage of descriptions of middle-class lives varied, growing larger as the centuries passed and the world as a whole became more prosperous. Only a handful of subjects reported former lives as leaders, and these were as tribal chiefs and obscure kings or princes; and only one reported a life as a famous person, U.S. President James Buchanan.

The number of past lives in various ages also seemed to reflect the gradual growth of the world's population. Twice as many past lives were reported from the years around 1500 as from the years around

Annie Besant (right), a 19th-century feminist and leader in London's Theosophical Society, was convinced that she would be reincarnated.

Under hypnosis, Dolores Jay said she was a 19th-century German girl who was murdered at age 16.

George Patton believed he was a Roman warrior in a previous life.

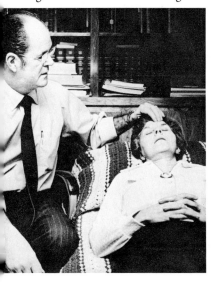

Child prodigies, such as Mozart (right), may be reincarnations of talented people from an earlier time, some believers feel.

Colorado housewife Virginia Tighe said that she had been a 19th-century Irishwoman in a previous life.

161

Real Roots of Past Lives

How solid are the foundations of reincarnation experiences? Dr. Edwin S. Zolik, then an assistant professor of psychology at Marquette University, undertook in 1956 an investigation designed to link crucial elements of "previous-existence" fantasies with unconscious memories related to a subject's personality. Under hypnosis, one subject saw himself back in 1875 as a man named Dick Wonchalk, piloting a flat-bottomed boat on a river. He portrayed himself as an outdoorsman who did "nothing much, just live off the land," and as very much alone.

The subject described Wonchalk as having been born in 1850, living without any close friends all alone on the river, hunting with a "Baldwin cap squirrel rifle," and only occasionally sitting around in taverns "down the river" when it was cold. As he recalled his "previous existence," he had died in 1876, having been sick for a month, with no one to look after him. He missed not having made "enough friends" and not "mingling with people."

Ultimately, Zolik matched this account not with an earlier life but with a movie the subject had seen (the subject even remembered the movie house where the film had played), and found that "the plight of the movie's main character," who lost his parents during an Indian raid, "generated a strong initial emotional identification, further strengthened by the plot's components of solitude, loneliness and independence." The subject had felt isolated from his parents since childhood, although they were still alive. In his study, Zolik concluded that the subject was "concerned about being lonely and being accepted by people" but also had very real fears of "being sort of left out," and thus his reincarnation fantasy served to dramatize this real-life view of himself.

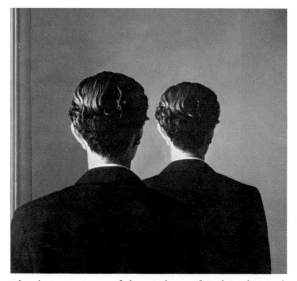

The aberrant powers of the mind, as reflected in this work by René Magritte, can heighten belief in stories of past lives.

A.D. 100. Past lives of the 19th century were twice as numerous as those of the 16th century, while past lives of the 20th century were four times as frequent as those of the century before.

Eventually, Wambach began asking her subjects about their existence between lives. Nearly 40 percent had no recollection of such a period of transition and either did not answer her questions or fell into a sleep-like state. Yet of the others, fully 95 percent thought that they had chosen to be reborn, possibly as part of a kind of gradual spiritual improvement. Many felt that although they had not actually looked forward to re-birth, they had been helped in choosing it by kindred spirits, friends and teachers. They had re-entered the world, some said, with a feeling of compassion for those who had no knowledge of another realm.

Like Stevenson, Wambach believes that earlier incarnations might help to account for existing emotional disturbances. She reported, "For example, people who committed murder in a previous life often feel emotionally disturbed. Once their past is revealed, and they see the reason for their trauma, they lose their guilt feeling and can lead a normal life." Although her approach differed substantially from that of Stevenson, who has studied many cases of children who claim to recall past lives, Wambach shared his view that such memories tend to fade. She found that "children under five can often recall past lives" but that "this recall is usually lost by the age of six or seven, and in adulthood it is lost altogether." She speculated that very young children "are just much closer to the people they once were—in another place, another time."

Stevenson has used certain reincarnation cases in an especially fascinating manner: to help interpret what he regards as "several features of human personality and biology that currently accepted theories do not adequately clarify." He cited cases that might explain unaccountable childhood fears and preferences, skills not learned in early life, abnormalities in child-parent relationships, childhood sexuality and gender confusion, birthmarks and congenital deformities, personality differences between identical twins, and even abnormal maternal appetites during pregnancy.

In addition, Stevenson has made this dramatic suggestion—that the formation of the human personality may extend "much further back in time than conception and birth." Stevenson emphasized that he did not offer reincarnation as an explanation for "everything we need to know about child development and human personality" but as a supplement to "knowledge in these areas." He regarded it as a third factor to be considered in addition to genetic and environmental influences.

Over the years, Stevenson has investigated many such cases. He has found, for instance, fear of water among several people who reported that they had drowned in previous lives. As an example of powerful, unaccountable fascinations, he cited the cases of two individuals with strong religious involvement "who claimed to remember the previous lives of women who had been unusually pious and active in religious activities." He also chronicled compulsions of a harmful sort, including the existence of "surprising appetites for alcohol" among small children who "claimed to remember their previous lives as heavy consumers of alcohol."

As examples of skills that might have been acquired in an earlier life, Stevenson noted cases of expertise with marine engines, singing and dancing, use of a sewing machine, and the weaving of coconut palm fronds for inclusion in thatched roofs. Stevenson also found among his cases suggestive of reincarnation a "high incidence of violent death in the previous personalities." Such cases, he feels, may lead to a desire for vengeance in children born, as many are, "within the same culture and near the community where the related previous personality has lived and died."

In addition, Stevenson believes that genetics cannot always completely explain specifically located birthmarks but that reincarnation, "in some cases, may." Stevenson examined at least 200 such birthmarks found on the bodies of subjects where "bullets or bladed weapons fatally wounded them in the previous lives which they seem to remember." These, he said, are usually much larger than common freckles or flat moles; they often resemble the scars of acquired wounds.

Yet in regard to the widely held view among reincarnationists that infant prodigies may be explained by rebirth and that karma is an integral part of the concept, Stevenson's findings were compelling—and negative. For he noted that "no Western child prodigy has ever claimed to remember a previous life." He also uncovered little or no sign of "any empirical basis for the concept of retributive karma." When comparing previous and current personalities, Stevenson did not encounter "degrees of evil or goodness which allow us glibly to account for the great differences between the subject's circumstances and those of the related previous personality." He emphasized that Western observers who regard reincarnation and karma as inseparable are unaware that many groups who believe in reincarnation "have no concept about it corresponding to the idea of karma found in Southeast Asia."

Thus after examining some 1,600 past-life claims, Stevenson, certainly a controversial figure in the field, has formed this view of reincarnation: "We can never show that it does not occur; nor are we ever likely to obtain conclusive evidence that it does occur. All the cases I have investigated so far have some flaws, many of them serious ones. Neither any single case nor all the investigated cases together offer anything like a proof of reincarnation. They provide instead a body of evidence suggestive of reincarnation that appears to be accumulating in amount and quality."

Reincarnation and *Déjà Vu?*

Does reincarnation have anything to do with *déjà vu* (already seen), the feeling that one has been in a certain locale previously, perhaps, as believers in reincarnation suggest, during an earlier incarnation? Neurological explanations for such feelings are fascinating. Yet they seem inadequate in accounting for stories such as this one reported by the writer William Chapman White. It involved a Midwestern couple, Mr. and Mrs. Bralorne, who left their cruise ship in Bombay, India, and had an odd experience.

Mr. Bralorne said, "Never having been out of America before, obviously I'd never seen Bombay, but as soon as we landed I had a strange feeling. As my wife and I started to walk the streets, I said, 'When we round that corner we'll come to the Afghan church,' and a little later, 'Two streets down and we'll find De Lisle Road.' My wife gave me a funny look and said, 'You certainly know your way around. Or maybe you feel that you've been here before.'

"I was astonished at that. It was precisely what I did feel. I cannot tell you how our bewilderment grew during the day. We went around the city as if we had known every street and every old building all our lives or in some other life."

When the Bralornes took another walk in the city, they asked a policeman whether there was a big house at the foot of Malabar Hill, with a big banyan tree in front. The police officer told them that such a house had been on that very spot but had been torn down 90 years before. The policeman's father had been a servant in the house, which had belonged to the Bhan family. And yes, there used to be a large banyan tree in front of it. It was at this point that the Bralornes recalled that they had named their son Bhan Bralorne because "at the time it seemed most fitting."

The sense of *déjà vu,* expressed graphically by the French artist above, is explained by some in terms of reincarnation.

Fact vs. Phenomenon

Charles Fort and Forteana: Why Not?

The frog at left was found, apparently mummified, in a lump of coal. The toad above is said to have survived for five weeks after its release from a similar lump of coal.

I n two words: im-possible." Most people would find themselves quoting movie producer Samuel Goldwyn if faced with reports of rains of frogs and fish, spontaneous human combustion, teleportation of animals and humans, fireballs, stigmata and ghosts. Not the indomitable Charles Fort. Though Fort would never have gone so far as to say he believed, he was given to phrases like "Could be," "Who knows?" and "Why not?" when confronted by such peculiarities.

Charles Fort was a connoisseur of the impossible and the father of modern phenomenalism. He considered with a firmly open mind just such miscellaneous, unconnected and unexplained phenomena as rains of frogs. Appropriately enough, these and other such natural and "unnatural" anomalies are often called Forteana by modern students of such bizarre and beguiling, if usually unprovable, occurrences.

Fort in fact was fascinated by all that science "damned," all, that is, that science could not explain in its own terms. To counter pronouncements that certain phenomena were categorically ruled out by the known rules of physics, Fort would suggest the existence of a set of *unknown* rules of physics. As impatient with the explanations scientists offered to force phenomena into accepted and acceptable niches as he was with scientific skepticism, Fort periodically challenged traditional researchers by concocting satiric explanations of his own. To account for the frequently reported rains of creatures and debris that scientists variously attributed to whirlwinds or volcanoes, Fort invented the Super-Sargasso Sea, a zone located somewhere above the earth to which all kinds of matter were unaccountably attracted, only to be flung back to earth in storms and showers at some later time.

Born in 1874, Fort began his extensive cataloging of phenomena at the age of 42, after a modest inheritance freed him from the necessity of making a living as a journalist. Working in the British Museum and the New York Public Library, he searched for 27 years, combing scientific and popular accounts for tales of anomalies and whatever unconventional explanations might be offered for their occurrence.

Any student of Forteana understands implicitly the need for the Super-Sargasso Sea, as rains of creatures and objects are a staple of phenomenalism. To wit: The New York *Sun*, in 1892, told of a rain of eels in Coalburg, Alabama. The Philadelphia *Times* reported in 1896 that the city of Baton Rouge had been showered with dead birds one clear day. Nor were they birds of a feather, but included wild ducks, catbirds, woodpeckers and an unidentified covey that resembled, but were not, canaries. Twenty years earlier, *Scientific American* had reported a shower of meat flakes in the sky over Kentucky. The still-fresh squares of flesh floated down into a 100-yard-long field, where one bold observer chanced a bite and said the meat tasted like venison or mutton. Then there was the astonishing appearance of snakes—thousands of them concentrated in a two-block area—after a heavy rainstorm in Memphis, Tennessee, in 1877. The *Monthly Weather Review* covered that story. Fort's favorite phenomenon was the frog fall, and he was able to collect a wealth of examples before he died in 1932. Were he still around, he would not want for additional entries: Birmingham, England, according to a witness from Sutton Park, was the site of a spectacular frog shower in 1954, and the Camden *News,* in Arkansas, printed the report of a local caddie in January 1973 of a "shower of tiny frogs about the size of nickels" that fell on the golf course during a cloudburst. One of the curious things Forteans note about such rains is their purity: frogs are never accompanied by the slimy residue of ponds, nor fish (which are every bit as ubiquitous as frogs) by seaweed and algae. Both species, however, must compete for space with a motley assortment of anomalistic rains, including showers of jelly-like blobs, mussels, Judas tree seeds, blood, and stones, as well as fragrant downpours smelling of sandalwood and bay rum, to list but a few of those on record.

Much Forteana would seem to fit religious definitions of the miraculous. Stigmata, the seemingly preternatural replication of the wounds of Christ, are generally attributed in modern times to religious hysteria or morbidity. Forteans draw no conclusions but point to episodes not related to Christian doctrine—an outbreak of slash marks across people's necks in Japan,

Charles Fort amassed thousands of incredible tales in the 27 years he spent combing libraries for stories like those of worms raining on Sweden and showers of exploding hailstones falling in Missouri.

In one version of the Indian rope trick, a boy and knife-wielding magician seem to ascend a rope and vanish. After bloody limbs fall, magician and boy reappear intact. Mass hallucination has been suggested as an explanation for this illusion.

Stones on India, bullets on South Carolina, metallic objects on Russia and a salty, snow-like substance on Turkey are among the thousands of things alleged to have tumbled from the heavens. The cannonball-like sphere below, found in New Zealand in 1972, is said to have fallen, too.

for example, and a pigeon in the Philippines that seemed to develop stigmata matching the marks on another bird that had been stabbed. An astounding modern stigmata case is that of a 10-year-old Protestant girl in Oakland, California, who bled spontaneously from her palms for 17 days before Easter in 1972. Two related phenomena are of equal interest to Forteans and religious believers. The phenomenon of weeping, sweating or bleeding images is one that has been recorded at least since the time of ancient Greece and that has been commonly reported in this century. The weeping Madonna of Sicily and the bleeding statue of Christ in Pennsylvania are but two of hundreds of supposedly reliably witnessed instances. Humans who radiate light have been similarly documented throughout history. Halos are popularly attributed to saints and prophets (the Bible says that after Moses received the commandments, "the skin of his face shone"). Humbler souls have been known to radiate light as well: there was a remarkable woman in the United States in the late 19th century whose toe lit up for nearly three-quarters of an hour before fading to its normal fleshy tone.

No one has yet come up with a scientifically acceptable explanation for those floating balls of light that are sometimes called ball lightning and sometimes will-o'-the-wisps. Nonetheless, they have won the credence of scientists, who formerly thought them humbug.

Possibly the grisliest item of Forteana is the freakish fate recounted in Dickens's *Bleak House:* spontaneous human combustion, or, as phenomenalists say, SHC. SHC is the high-speed consumption of the human body by intense heat but with no apparent outside cause. It might be a form of autoincineration, some have suggested, yet it remains totally inexplicable. In one well-documented and typical case that occurred in 1951, a 67-year-old Florida woman was found reduced to a pile of ashes and fragments of bone, although the rest of her apartment was unscorched and a stack of newspapers nearby had been left intact.

The world of Forteana also includes "electric people," who are reportedly capable of causing compasses to malfunction and objects to retreat at their approach. It includes as well a frog that survived embedded in coal, presumably but impossibly embalmed at a depth of more than 300 feet for millions of years, before it went on display at the Great Exhibition of London in 1862. And it also takes in rolling stones, dancing fits that beguile entire towns, and dozens more impossible things, all designed to evoke one of Charles Fort's favorite refrains: "Why not?"

Tales of apparitions, restless spirits
and phantom forms have expressed mankind's
fear of death for thousands of years.

GHOSTS AND SPIRITS

Bizarre fires, such as this one on a French farm, are sometimes attributed to evil spirits.

Let me say at once that I am incredulous by nature, and as unsuperstitious as they come. I have never bothered about the number 13 . . . or any of the current superstitions which may occupy the human heart in the absence of faith. . . .

"But the late C. S. Lewis, whom I did not know very well and had only seen in the flesh once, but with whom I had corresponded a fair amount, gave me an unusual experience. A few days after his death, while I was watching television, he 'appeared' sitting in a chair within a few feet of me, and spoke a few words which were particularly relevant to the difficult circumstances through which I was passing. He was ruddier in complexion than ever, grinning all over his face, and, as the old-fashioned saying has it, positively glowing with health. The interesting thing to me was that I had not been thinking about him at all. . . . A week later, this time when I was in bed reading before going to sleep, he appeared again, even more rosily radiant than before, and repeated to me the same message, which was very important to me at the time. I was a little puzzled by this, and I mentioned it to a certain saintly Bishop who was then living in retirement in Dorset. His reply was, 'My dear J . . . , this sort of thing is happening all the time.'"

One of the most famous of alleged spectral photographs (inset) was taken at Raynham Hall (left) in England in 1936. The ghostly figure is called the Brown Lady of Raynham.

Whatever "this sort of thing" may have meant to the bishop, to Church of England canon J. B. Phillips, D.D., a prominent writer on theology, it meant one thing: in 1963 he had seen a ghost.

Nathaniel Hawthorne saw them too. In fact, the U.S. writer saw several ghosts in his lifetime and believed that the house he lived in was haunted. Yet the ghostly form he perceived most often was that of the Reverend Dr. Harris, an elderly clergyman who had shared Hawthorne's fondness for the reading room in the Boston Athenaeum. One evening Hawthorne was surprised to learn that Harris had recently died; he was certain that he had seen the old gentleman at the Athenaeum that very day. The next morning Hawthorne returned to the reading room and there again beheld Harris quietly reading before the fire. Hawthorne sat down across the room and observed Harris surreptitiously for a while to make certain that it was he and no other. He noticed that no one else in the room, including a number of Harris's close friends, seemed to be aware of the ghost that sat among them. The apparition's daily visits continued for weeks, but as far as Hawthorne could tell, he was the only percipient. He first considered, then rejected, various means of testing his vision. As he later wrote, "Perhaps I was loth to destroy the illusion, and to rob myself of so good a ghost story, which might probably have been explained in some very commonplace way." Although Hawthorne gradually became conscious of more direct interest on the part of Harris's ghost and

167

began to suspect that a message was forthcoming, both the living man and the specter continued to observe the traditions of the room in which, as Hawthorne noted, "conversation is strictly forbidden and I could not have addressed the apparition without drawing the instant notice and indignant frowns of the slumbrous old gentlemen around me. . . . And what an absurd figure should I have made . . . addressing what must have appeared in the eyes of all the rest . . . an empty chair! Besides, I had never been introduced to Doctor Harris." It does seem that ghosts appear to whom they will, whether friends, family, acquaintances or even strangers.

In preparing to research *The Stately Ghosts of England,* author Diane Norman wondered whether a promising haunt for ghosts might not be some of England's oldest mansions. To test her theory she wrote to 30 owners of such stately homes, asking if they had any ghosts about the place. Among the 28 who replied seriously and positively were the then-current owners of Brede Place, in Sussex.

The ancestors of Roger and Alexandra Moreton-Frewen had lived at Brede for well over 200 years. The estate itself dated to 1350, but only after the first Frewens took over in 1708 had Brede begun to acquire its reputation as a "haunted" house. Its grisliest tales concerned a giant's ghost, reputed to gobble up local babies at night, but it had long been suspected that the giant was the invention of a local smuggler who hoped to keep his curious neighbors at a distance. Other tales were taken more seriously. Almost every member of

the family felt dread about some corner of the estate. One uncle avoided certain upstairs rooms at night; owner Roger Frewen's father would not speak of what he had seen in the cellar, nor would Frewen's grandfather stroll through the garden after dark unless someone watched from the front door. Visitors were not immune either. One young boy reported being awakened in the pre-dawn hours by a woman in a "large dress and a ruff around her neck." And Lady Randolph Churchill, Sir Winston's mother, found one guest room so oppressively occupied by an unseen and unhappy other that she fled it in the middle of the night and moved in with her sister Clara. But it was Frewen's cousin Margaret Sheridan who had had one of the strangest encounters with ghosts.

Sheridan met her first ghost not at Brede, but at Frampton, the estate of her father's family. Her mother had taken her and her brother there to await news of their father, a British Army officer serving at the German front in World War I.

"On my way down to the drawing room at tea time," Sheridan would later write, "I met a little boy on the stairs. He was wearing a white sailor suit, with a round straw hat on the back of his head. He looked at me, and I looked at him. We passed each other without a word. Nanny had always impressed upon me that I must never speak to strangers; I assumed, nevertheless, that he had come to play with me.

"As soon as I got into the drawing room, I announced with shrill anticipation: 'I saw an itty sailor

Ancient tribal shamans danced and sang in order to induce in themselves the trance-like state necessary to overcome the ghosts that they believed were haunting them, as shown in this illustration from a 15th-century Turkish manuscript.

boy.' I waited for an explanation. 'An itty sailor boy,' I repeated. In the ashen silence which followed, my grandmother directed my attention to the dish of buttered toast. Her hands were trembling. I was not to know, until much later, that the Sailor Boy was a visitor of ill-omen in the Sheridan family. In life he was an ancestor who had been drowned at sea as a midshipman. He appeared at Frampton only before the death of the heir. The strange part was that the portrait of him was that of a young man of sixteen or seventeen, yet what I saw—and saw clearly—was a child about my own age.

"Shortly afterward the letter came." Margaret Sheridan's father had been killed at the front.

When Diane Norman and her collaborator on *Stately Ghosts,* "psychic" Tom Corbett, visited the Frewens at Brede in 1969, they were invited to inspect the house before discussing the various ghosts the family had identified on its own. After making a complete tour, Corbett volunteered his opinion that at least three ghosts were in residence: a man and a woman who haunted the bedrooms in the eastern half of the house and a man—Corbett believed him to be a priest—who seemed to occupy both the chapel on the west side of the house and the little room built over it. It was the priest whom Corbett judged to be the "main influence in the house, and a very good influence."

Pronouncing Corbett's assessment to be absolutely accurate, Roger Frewen produced a thicket of family records attesting to the Frewens' long familiarity with these three ghosts and several more besides.

While the English may meet their ancestors in ancient corridors, every culture has its seen and unseen spirits. In 1976 a highly praised book by a young Chinese-American woman appeared, called *Woman Warrior.* It was subtitled *Memoirs of a Girlhood Among Ghosts.* Showing no inclination to explain, the author, Maxine Hong Kingston, recalled the fierce nocturnal struggle her mother, Brave Orchid, had once had with a dread Sitting Ghost, one of a host of Chinese spirits that includes both the ghosts of recognizable ancestors and a pantheon of frightening ghosts more akin to monsters than to human phantoms.

"It was bigger than a wolf," Brave Orchid told her daughter long afterward, "bigger than an ape, and growing. I would have stabbed it. I would have cut it up, and we would be mopping blood this morning, but—a Sitting Ghost mutation—it had an extra arm that wrested my hand away from the knife. At about 3:00 A.M. I died for a while. I was wandering and the world I touched turned into sand. . . . For ten years I lost my way. I almost forgot about you. . . . But I returned. I walked from the Gobi Desert to this room in the To Keung School. That took another two years, outwitting Wall Ghosts en route."

While Brave Orchid's account is as much an allegory as a description of a remembered ghostly encounter, one important thing is clear: for her and for her modern daughter, Sitting Ghosts and Wall Ghosts and the countless other ghosts capable of making them-

In this 19th-century scene a Japanese monk who has become a ghostly rat eats the scriptures of a rival temple.

In a haunting portrayal by Frederic Remington, a French-Indian guide is led through the cold by the ghost of an Indian maiden who tempts him with a pot of hot stew.

selves unexpectedly visible are real. And as in so much of the abundant literature on ghosts, the woman's encounter with one was a singular and resonant experience.

Allegory, romanticism and good stories aside, is not the very notion of ghosts a challenge to rational concepts of reality, as well as to modern Western convictions about the mind, the body, and life and death? How is it possible for the dead to appear to the living? And what do we really mean when we say we have seen a ghost? Even now it is hard to imagine how these questions might be satisfactorily answered.

Of all the sciences, only psychiatry has offered a plausible explanation. Ghosts, it suggests, are manifestations of assorted unconscious wishes, unresolved guilts, patchwork imaginings. So convinced have we grown of the power of the unconscious mind to influence our conscious behavior that it seems entirely possible that a distraught and lonely widow might conjure up a two-dimensional image of her dead husband on an inclement night or, equally, that a troubled, alienated adult might summon in a moment of crisis the "ghost" of a beloved parent long dead.

But what would make the sensible Canon Phillips conjure up C. S. Lewis dressed not in clerical robes, as on the one occasion the two men met, but in the "well worn tweeds" that Phillips only later learned reflected Lewis's customary costume? In pondering his experience, Phillips acknowledged a mixed personal sympathy with Lewis as someone he had admired yet whose opinions were often hard to take. And he volunteered, too, that at the time of the apparitions he was going through an unsettling letdown after completing a long and consuming writing project. Did his mood impel him to choose Lewis as the subject of a comforting hallucination, or was it perhaps the other way around? Did Lewis somehow choose Phillips as a suitable percipient because of the canon's temporary sensitivity? If so, why? What was Lewis's intent?

One might ask the same questions about Nathaniel Hawthorne's experience: What unconscious need or wish would cause him to persist day after day in hallucinating a man he hardly knew? Hawthorne himself later wondered if love of a good story might have been reason enough, but Hawthorne's imagination could surely have provided a more satisfactory conclusion to the episode than the one he reported. And what unrecognized longing in three-year-old Margaret Sheridan could have successfully materialized a chronic family ghost about which she knew nothing?

One possible explanation for the child's apparition rests on current theories about the highly controversial subject of telepathy. Perhaps, such a theory suggests, either the mother or grandmother or both, dwelling subconsciously on dreaded family superstition but desperately trying to suppress it, succeeded instead in transmitting the fable intact to an impressionable child, who then transformed the sailor into a child of her own

The phantom of Anne Boleyn, whose portrait this may be, is said to haunt the Tower of London, including the chapel shown below.

Clara Jerome Frewen (top) and her granddaughter (above) believed their ancestral home, Brede, to be haunted.

The specter of Lady Louisa Carteret is said to stalk the passageway shown below, where her lover met his death in a duel.

Defoe's Factual Ghost Story

Daniel Defoe, shown pilloried for his religious views, may have based a bizarre ghost story upon an obscure newspaper account.

The story is both ghostly and factual, and when Mrs. Bargrave told it later on, the most impressive detail involved a handsome dress her old friend Mrs. Veal was wearing the day she stopped in for a visit. The dress was new since the two women had last met, and it was made of scoured silk. Several times in the nearly two hours the friends talked she leaned forward to feel the material.

The two women had been close friends in Dover but had been out of touch for two and a half years. In the meantime Mrs. Bargrave had moved to Canterbury. Mrs. Veal apologized for her neglect and explained that she had come by that day because she was leaving on a journey and wanted to renew their friendship. Mrs. Bargrave was surprised by this news, since she knew that her friend was prone to epileptic fits and rarely traveled except when her brother was free to accompany her. When she remarked on this, Mrs. Veal replied oddly, "Oh, I gave my brother the slip."

The two women talked of their past adversities, the comfort they had given each other, and their health. Mrs. Veal anxiously asked whether Mrs. Bargrave didn't think that she, Mrs. Veal, had declined terribly since they had last met. Mrs. Bargrave answered, "No, I think you look as well as I ever knew you." Mrs. Veal then asked after Mrs. Bargrave's daughter, and her friend went off in search of the girl. Mrs. Bargrave returned without her daughter to find Mrs. Veal waiting, ready to leave.

Mrs. Veal then walked off down the street, and Mrs. Bargrave watched until she had turned the corner. The clock had struck noon when Mrs. Veal first appeared; it was now 1:45. It was a Saturday, September 8, 1705.

Two days later, Mrs. Bargrave paid a call on Captain and Mrs. Watson, relatives of Mrs. Veal's. The Watsons had just learned that Mrs. Veal had died about noon on the previous Friday, some 24 hours before she appeared at Mrs. Bargrave's house. Astonished, Mrs. Bargrave described the visit and made a point of mentioning the dress her friend had worn. Mrs. Watson knew it well; she had helped Mrs. Veal make it, and only the two of them had known that the silk was heavily washed, or scoured.

This modest ghost story, first published anonymously as "A True Relation of the Apparition of one Mrs. Veal" in 1706, was the work of Daniel Defoe. Like his other, larger works, *Moll Flanders, Robinson Crusoe,* and *A Journal of the Plague Year,* "Mrs. Veal" was widely read in the 18th century and was presumed to be pure fiction.

In fact, Defoe based his writing on real-life models, and much academic research has been carried out to uncover the origins of his greatest characters. However, it was not until 1955 that a professor of English literature happened on a certain London tabloid from Defoe's day. The copies he found covered only four months, from November 1705 to March 1706, but there on one side of the December 24 copy of the *Loyal Post* was a story about Mrs. Veal's visit to a Mrs. Bargrove. The essential facts, including the crucial 24-hour gap, matched those in Defoe's account, but while Defoe invented suitable conversations between the women, the *Loyal Post* had paid particular attention to the description Mrs. Bargrove gave of the scoured silk dress her friend had worn.

Ghostly Animals and Things

One of the oldest and strangest legends of the sea tells of the Flying Dutchman, a spectral ship condemned to an eternal voyage, with a single skeleton for a crew, because its captain attempted to round the Cape of Good Hope in defiance of a divine warning to turn back. The Dutchman, however, is but one of a number of phantom ships to have been sighted, for the perception of ghosts of inanimate things on both sea and land is not uncommon. Though less numerous than their human counterparts, ghosts of things—ships, buildings, castles, lakes, violins, horse-drawn carriages and cars—abound. So do ghosts of animals, a relatively popular species of phantom.

Such irregular ghosts can be every bit as unsettling as an unexpected human apparition, and now and then perhaps even more so. After all, there is an appropriateness about human ghosts—man may hope to exist beyond his mortal years; but extending the privilege to cats and dogs and horses? And mortar and bricks? Unthinkable perhaps, and yet such stories do appear and persist.

In 1892 a woman reported that after deciding to put a sick cat out of its misery by drowning it, she was horrified to see the gray-and-black-striped creature reappear "thinner and dripping with water" at her door. She ordered a servant to remove it, but the servant replied that she saw no cat and told her mistress of having already witnessed the animal's burial.

In another case a man was walking through an unfamiliar part of the Australian countryside when he happened on "a collection of grey buildings and pipes" and heard "the sound of water gushing forth." He mentioned what he had seen to his father, who returned to see for himself and found only "a dry, rocky gully." The man was bewildered by his vision for several years, until, as he told it, "a local resident informed my mother that there had been just such an installation as I had described back in the old mining days."

Writer Barbara Cartland and her brother came upon "a story-book castle complete with spires and turrets" while walking in the countryside of Carinthia in southern Austria. After the walk they mentioned their discovery in a local village and were told that the castle had long ago been destroyed.

In 1910 several members of the Tweedale family in Yorkshire, England, shared a vision of an aunt who had died years earlier. Later, Mrs. Tweedale reported that the specter had as a companion a nervous, short-haired white dog. The aunt had indeed owned such a dog, although none of the family had ever seen it.

Is it all possible? Are the ghosts of buildings, nervous dogs and drowned cats suitable phantoms to ponder? As with ghostly humans, the apparitions of things and animals may exist only in the human mind; or the universe may be infinitely more cluttered than we can perceive or dare imagine.

age. That leaves only the troublesome climax to the story: the heir, in fact, died.

Telepathy has also been proposed to explain an incident that occurred in 1964 at an automobile plant in Detroit. A motor fitter working on an assembly line narrowly escaped being crushed to death when an enormous piece of machinery accidentally set in motion started to bear down on him. As he explained to his fellow workers afterward, he had been suddenly pushed to safety by a tall black man with a scarred face. The man was now nowhere to be seen, nor had the fitter ever seen him in the plant before. But several of the older workers had; they recognized the fitter's rescuer as a worker who had been decapitated on the job 20 years before, in the same section of the plant, after he had become drowsy while working long stretches of overtime during the war. The fitter had never heard the wartime story, had never heard of his phantom savior's death. Proponents of a telepathic theory suggest that one of the older workers on the line, spotting the fitter's predicament but unable to save him himself, had somehow telepathically conveyed such a powerful image of the earlier victim that the fitter was thrust out of harm's way. But what of the fitter's conviction that he had been physically shoved? He recalled that his rescuer had "enormous strength and just pushed me out of the way like I was a featherweight."

While it should not be surprising that patterns of the past recur conspicuously in encounters with ghosts, the precision with which ghosts preserve the circumstances of their own time can be astonishing. British writer Paul Bannister, in his book *Strange Happenings,* told of a remarkably anachronistic appearance by a Roman legion. Constable Harry Martindale, Bannister wrote, "is a man of whom the British police force can feel proud. A big man, six feet four inches and 250 pounds, Martindale has hands like shovels and a careful, even ponderous manner. He prides himself on being unimaginative, for he is solid and unshakeable." At the time of the incident, Martindale, then a heating engineer, was repairing pipes in York's Treasurer's House. It was in the cellar of this medieval building that he heard "a sort of tinny trumpet call."

As Martindale told Bannister, "I looked around and a smallish soldier wearing a kilt and carrying a sort of trumpet came out of that wall over there. He ignored me and shuffled diagonally across the cellar toward the opposite wall. But before he disappeared, another soldier, on a ragged looking pony, followed him. Behind them came about fourteen or sixteen more men, in double file. I fell from my stepladder and cowered against the corner, but they ignored me.

"The oddest thing was that they were all marching thigh-deep in the floor. Only in one spot, where someone had dug away a part of the floor could I see their feet."

The constable's description of the soldiers was meticulously detailed. They carried round shields and all manner of weaponry, from short swords to long spears. They wore "hand dyed kilts of streaky green" and most had on leather helmets; the man on horseback wore plumes in his. They were all shod in sandals whose thongs extended to the knees. And the trumpet carried by the "smallish" fellow was long and curving; Martindale guessed that it was made of brass. "They sort of shuffled along dispiritedly," is the way Martindale described the scene. "I reckoned they were Roman soldiers but they didn't look like Charlton Heston."

A few days afterward the still-edgy Martindale unburdened himself to a local historian, who happened to know that the hole in the cellar had been made by archeologists digging down to a section of the old Roman road underneath. But on the basis of one of Martindale's carefully remembered details, the historian concluded that the collective apparition had to have been imagined. Because while the pipe fitter's soldiers carried round shields, Roman soldiers never did.

Martindale pursued it no further, but seven years later a pair of archeologists working in the same cellar experienced an identical apparition, complete with trumpet blast. The event prompted the recollection of Martindale's story, but this time there was an additional piece of historical information against which to measure it. Between the two sightings, it had been established that when the 6th Roman Legion was moved out of York during the 4th century, it had been supplemented by auxiliary troops who carried round shields.

Martindale had never really doubted his vision: "I believe I saw a troop of those auxiliaries," he told Bannister, "marching out in some hopeless foray in which they were all to die." And while for historians the validity of his account hinged on those 1,500-year-old shields, for Martindale the telling detail was their sunken path. "The reason I saw them thigh-deep in the floor was because their spirits were still marching on the surface of the now-buried road."

Similar examples of verisimilitude abound in reports of apparitions to such an extent that it begins to sound as though ghosts are spirits preserved in some kind of time-lapse gel. F.W.H. Myers's studies on the subject led him to define a ghost as "a manifestation of persistent personal energy . . . some residue of the force or energy which a person generated while yet alive." Oxford philosopher H. H. Price postulated that such impressions might survive because all matter and space were permeated by an unseen substance capable of retaining indefinitely the impressions made by the living. He called the substance "psychic ether." Recordings, made during some traumatic moments, would remain suspended in the time-indifferent substance, where they would later be perceived by sensitive recipients. Frank Smyth pointed out in *Ghosts and Poltergeists* that the presence of "psychic ether" might even explain the occasional appearance of ghosts on photographic film.

Anthropologist Margaret Murray offered a similar *(continued on page 176)*

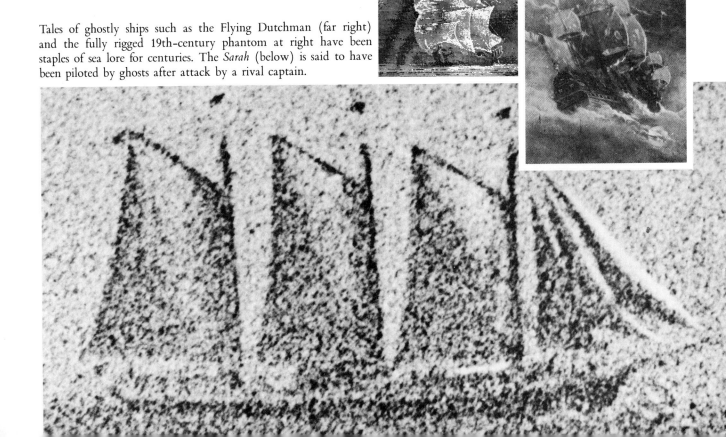

Tales of ghostly ships such as the Flying Dutchman (far right) and the fully rigged 19th-century phantom at right have been staples of sea lore for centuries. The *Sarah* (below) is said to have been piloted by ghosts after attack by a rival captain.

Fact vs. Phenomenon
Spirit Photography

Extras—strange faces and figures that are not seen when a picture is taken but are clearly visible when film is developed—have created a controversy within an already controversial subject: the existence of ghosts. Some investigators claim that the spectral figures do prove that ghosts are real. Others make a different point—that the images may be the work of unseen forces out to create a false impression of the spirit realm.

In fact, from its birth in the 1860s, spirit photography has been a lucrative profession, and the vast majority of spirit photographs can be traced to human deception and avarice. With hidden lenses or double exposures, so-called photographer-mediums have produced hundreds of portraits containing likenesses of dead friends or relatives. And yet there have been cases in which fraud would seem an unlikely, though possible, accomplishment. Mary Todd Lincoln, for instance, used an assumed name when sitting for William Mumler, often considered the first spirit photographer; nonetheless, the picture that resulted included a misty likeness of her dead husband, the President. And even today, with spirit photography so lightly regarded that many researchers shun it, a mysterious extra does turn up occasionally on film.

With no known natural causes to explain it, the bizarre ball of light above, which appeared and was photographed in Basel, Switzerland, in 1907, became known as the "ghost light."

A hooded figure seems to float on the steps of the altar at England's Newby Church in the photograph at right, taken in the 1960s by the Reverend K. F. Lord. Lord reported that he saw no such figure at the altar.

At the far right, a semi-transparent image, one that seems to show a man in priest-like robes, was recorded on film in front of the altar of St. Nicholas's Church in Arundel, England.

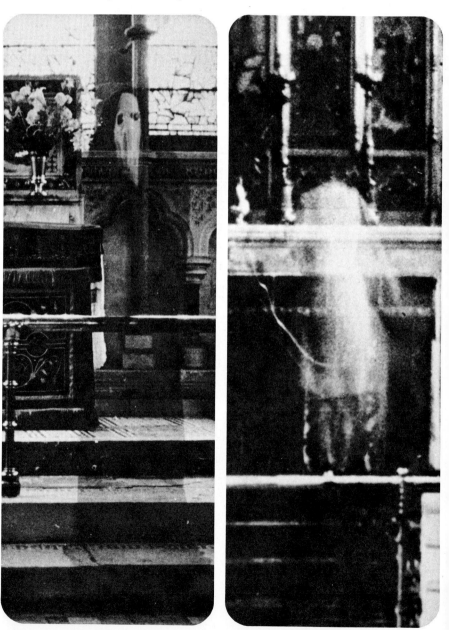

Three faint but still identifiable images of young Bill Watkins appeared mysteriously on Polaroid film, although the boy had not been the subject of the picture (left) taken by his brother. Shortly thereafter Bill was involved in a car accident.

In a photograph of alleged poltergeist activity, a "jumping stick" is shown seemingly suspended in midair. Many witnesses in the Yorkshire, England, community where the picture was taken said they had seen the stick floating.

The picture at left, published in 1959, is said to have been made during a visit by the photographer to his mother's grave. Yet upon development the photograph seemed to show the mother seated in the back of a car.

The Reverend R. S. Blance was photographing an abandoned ceremonial site in Australia in 1959 when he made this picture. The man appeared only on the developed film, Blance said.

theory in *My First Hundred Years*. After announcing that "I believe quite seriously in apparitions," Murray, who died in 1963, proposed as a "working hypothesis" that ghosts are "a form of photograph" or "a writing caused by light on some . . . constituents of the air." In comparing the process to the workings of a camera, Murray wrote: "It should be remembered that, though the light waves are recorded on a prepared surface, the result is not visible till the surface is specially treated, otherwise, the surface . . . remains blank. I suggest that this is also the case with apparitions. . . . Another point . . . is the very restricted area in which the ghost is seen. . . . You would never meet a ghost a quarter of a mile from its natural haunt. The suddenness of its disappearance suggests a current of air blowing away the particles on which it is imprinted. Also similar to a photograph is the fact that it appears to fade in course of time, appearing less frequently. Towards the end of its 'existence,' it will only appear in exceptional atmospheric conditions, such as just before an electrical storm."

The persistence of the idea that every ghost somehow transcends time as it is perceived by the living may be traced in part to our incomplete understanding of the meaning of time itself. Throughout most of history, man has conceived of time as an absolute continuum, a steadily flowing river in which the past lies somewhere downstream, the future upstream, and the present wherever we happen to be standing on the riverbank. Yet Albert Einstein demonstrated in the theory of relativity that time changes in relation to space and motion, that it flows at a different rate according to whether the observer is stationary or in motion. Thus if one thinks of the dead in a moving system and the living in a stationary system, then it is possible to imagine the dead lingering beyond the artificial time of death as understood by the living.

Interestingly enough, one of the most commonly reported types of ghosts—called a crisis apparition—seems to become visible when a person has recently died or is on the verge of death. The poet Robert Graves was visited by such a ghost during World War I. As he wrote in *Good-bye to All That*, "I saw a ghost at Béthune. He was a man called Private Challoner who had been at Lancaster with me, and again in F Company at Wrexham. When he went out with a draft to join the First Battalion he shook my hand and said: 'I'll meet you again in France, sir.' He was killed at Festubert in May and in June he passed by our C Company billet where we were just having a special dinner to celebrate our safe return from Cuinchy. There was fish, new potatoes, green peas, asparagus, mutton chops, strawberries and cream, and three bottles of Pommard. Challoner looked in at the window, saluted, and passed on. There was no mistaking him or the cap-badge he was wearing. There was no Royal Welch battalion billeted within miles of Béthune at the time. I jumped up and looked out of the window, but saw nothing except a fag-end smoking on the pavement. Ghosts were numerous in France at the time."

Other examples, collected from the files of the British Society for Psychical Research by Thelma Moss

In the British lane below, known as Cranbourne Chase, a ghost from pre-Roman times is thought to roam. The specter, wearing a gray cloak, rides a horse without bridle or stirrups.

The ghost of Scotney Castle in Kent, England, haunts not the land but the murky waters of the castle's moat, rising in times of crisis to hammer on the stone structure's great door.

for her book *The Probability of the Impossible,* further demonstrate the ubiquity of crisis apparitions. In one case, a woman in Italy looked up from her housework to be met by the specter of her mother's body, laid out as if for burial. Greatly upset, she immediately wrote to her mother (the year was 1869) to inquire about her health. By return post came news that her mother had died without warning; she had been buried the day of her daughter's vision.

A Chicago woman awoke one morning in 1890 feeling depressed without any clear cause. She entered her pantry to make a cup of tea and was met by an astonishing sight. "My brother Edmund—or his exact image—stood before me and only a few feet away . . . with back toward me, or, rather, partially so, and was in the act of falling forward—away from me—seemingly impelled by a loop of rope drawing against his legs. The vision lasted but a moment, but was very distinct. I dropped the tea, clasped my hands to my face and exclaimed, 'My God! Ed is drowned.'" In fact, six hours earlier, the woman's brother, a stoker on a tugboat, had been dragged overboard and drowned.

A young English matron stationed with her husband in India was dressing her infant on the morning of March 19, 1917, when she felt compelled to look behind her. Turning around, she saw her brother, a pilot, standing in the room. Assuming he had been newly posted to India, she was thrilled and was about to greet him when she remembered her baby lying on the bed. She turned away to make sure her son was safe and then turned around again, intending to welcome her surprise visitor. But her brother was gone. She searched the house for him, thinking he must be playing some sort of joke on her, but he was nowhere to be found. The day of the apparition, she later learned, he had been killed in an air battle.

Whether these stories can be explained as a soul's final visit to a far-off loved one or as a form of mental telepathy, it is impossible to say. Even the most scientifically conservative explanation—the unconscious mind's response to loneliness and worry, punctuated by bizarre coincidence—seems all but impossible to comprehend. Yet the role of the mind in such ghostly encounters must not be underestimated.

One of the most horrifying manifestations of the strange interaction of mind and circumstance occurred in the early 19th century in the United States. There, over a four-year period, a prosperous farmer and his family in Tennessee were tormented by a malevolent force that came to be known as the Bell Witch.

The strange protracted episode began with a series of seemingly unrelated sightings. One day John Bell, the head of the family, noticed a peculiar-looking dog in his cornfield. He shot at it, but when he went to retrieve the animal, he could find no trace of it. A few days later two of Bell's sons were with him when he

Paul Bannister and English policeman Harry Martindale inspect a wall through which, according to Martindale, phantom Roman soldiers walked in kilts, sandals and helmets.

spotted a strange bird high in an oak tree. It was bigger than a turkey and unfamiliar to the region. Bell took aim, the bird seemed to fall, but when his boys rushed forward, they could find nothing on the ground. Not long afterward, Betsy, Bell's youngest daughter, reported that when passing the same tree, she had seen a girl "swinging to a limb of [the] tall oak." The girl wore a green dress and seemed to be about Betsy's own age, 12. Betsy tried to make friends but as she approached the tree, the girl disappeared. A fourth phantom, a snarling black dog, was regularly sighted by one of the Bells' slaves, who reported that the dog vanished when threatened by a stick.

This cycle of events was followed by a siege of increasingly ominous auditory disturbances: the rattling of windows, a rapping at the door, relentless clawing on the floor, then the low growling of what seemed to be two dogs fighting. Every day, additional sounds were heard—choking and gurgling, the scraping of furniture across the floors, the clanking of chains being dragged through the house. The bedposts showed signs of having been gnawed by rats in the night.

Soon members of the family were being attacked as they slept. Covers were yanked off in the middle of the night, and any opposition was met with a powerful slap from an unseen hand. Someone or something frequently pulled at the children's hair in the darkness, though Betsy Bell appeared to be victimized with particular ferocity. At night she could be heard screaming in her bedroom.

Although she was still very young, Betsy Bell was being courted by two suitors who hoped for an early and provident match with the daughter of one of the county's most prominent citizens. One of her suitors was an older man, Richard Powell, the town schoolmaster; the other was closer to her own age, a man named Joshua Gardner. Betsy seemed to be inclining toward her contemporary, but his visits began to have unpleasant consequences; every call he paid to Betsy would be matched by a visit from the Bell Witch.

As the attacks on the girl grew more and more violent, her family became alarmed about her health. Hoping to remove her from the witch's influence, the Bells sent Betsy to stay with friends, but the witch

Distraught Betsy Bell, as depicted in an 1894 book.

followed, and the assaults grew more terrifying. Betsy said she felt as though she were being suffocated, complained of lack of breath and suffered from fainting. Her face was frequently streaked red, as though she had been slapped hard. She spoke of feeling pins and needles all over her body and once seemed to spontaneously vomit a stream of the sharp objects.

The Bell family horror soon became a regional fixation. Exorcists and spiritualists flocked to the tiny town of Adams from all over Tennessee and from neighboring Kentucky. The chorus of earnest voices they raised eventually succeeded in eliciting a response from the unseen tormentor, a response that, like the first contact with the family, grew more pronounced in stages. First the unseen force rapped out indistinct answers to questions, then it whistled, then it developed an unmistakable whisper, which grew daily more comprehensible to those listening. In time the voice grew bold and clear, although the witch refused to answer the direct questions put to it about its origins and intent. "I am a spirit from everywhere, Heaven, Hell, the Earth," it declared in stilted speech. "Am in the air, in houses, any place at any time, have been created millions of years; that is all I will tell you."

Harry Price's Great Ghost Hunt

By the time ghost investigator Harry Price finished with Borley Rectory, he called it "the most haunted house in England." The ghosts and specters he cataloged there included a nun who, according to legend, had been "bricked up alive" in a convent wall, a headless man, a coach and horses, and the Reverend Henry Bull, who had built the gloomy house in 1863.

During his lifetime, Price was probably the most technically accomplished and best known of the early-20th-century ghost hunters who attempted to prove, through practical methods and modern technology, whether ghosts were real. Price's "ghost-hunter's kit" included felt overshoes for "creeping unheard about the house"; steel tape measures to check the thickness of walls in search of secret chambers; a still camera equipped for indoor and outdoor photography; a remote-control movie camera; fingerprinting equipment; and a portable telephone for instant communication with other investigators.

Borley Rectory's reputation for being haunted had been of relatively ordinary magnitude by English standards until Price took an interest, and even then, the ghosts he identified were of an entirely predictable character. What first attracted Price's attention, in 1929, were the complaints of the current tenants, the Reverend G. Eric Smith and his wife, who for some time had been disturbed by moving furniture, keys falling out of locks, the sounds of footsteps and a woman's voice. Price under-

took three days of careful study and claimed to have found no natural explanations for any of the unusual phenomena. He also announced that he had observed a shadowy figure that might have been the nun and had made contact with the deceased Reverend Mr. Bull.

Price began another investigation of the rectory a year later, after the Smiths were replaced by the Reverend Lionel Algernon Foyster and his wife, Marianne. As soon as the Foysters settled in, what seemed to be a poltergeist, or noisy ghost, became active. People were locked out of rooms, household items vanished, windows were broken,

Borley Rectory, site of Harry Price's most extensive ghost hunt, was gutted by fire just before his findings were published.

Nor could the witch's purpose be determined from its conflicting behavior. Early on, it was given to repeating with uncanny accuracy the recent sermons of the two local preachers; later it adopted an obscene vocabulary that horrified the pious Bible belt community. And although initially it seemed indiscriminate in its treatment of members of the family, incidents soon made it clear that the witch had a special favorite. Its attitude toward Lucy Bell—Bell's wife and Betsy's mother—was noticeably solicitous and kind. Lucy was always treated respectfully by the witch, who was soon to torment not just Betsy but John Bell as well. To the astonishment of a group gathered in the Bells' kitchen one evening, the witch announced, "I am determined to haunt and torment old Jack [John] as long as he lives."

Thus the witch turned its malevolent attentions from Betsy to her father, visiting upon him maddening afflictions. His tongue swelled to such size that he could neither eat nor talk, and its great growth so changed his mouth that his entire face seemed distorted. A facial tic, which he realized had begun to bother him at the first manifestation of the witch, now worsened. He was subjected to vile shouted curses as he went about the farm. The attacks of swelling grew ever more frequent and debilitating, forcing Bell to abandon his work and all activity for days at a time. In mid October 1820, just as Bell recovered from a siege that lasted several days, he was freshly assaulted in a most violent manner by the unseen force.

As the farmer walked along the dirt road from the house to the pigpen with his youngest son, Richard, who later told the story, John Bell's shoe suddenly flew off his foot. It was replaced and tightly tied, and a few moments later, the other shoe flew off. It, too, was replaced and secured. Father and son continued along in this way, the father's shoes inexplicably flying off, "notwithstanding," the son wrote, "his shoes fitted close and were a little hard to put on." After tending the pigs, they started back home and the whole sequence began again. This time the flying shoes were accompanied by a terrific blow to the face that forced Bell to stop and rest. He sat down on a log and "then his whole face commenced jerking with fearful contortions, soon his whole body," Richard recollected. In a short while the frenzy was intensified by the "reviling sound of derisive songs piercing the air with terrorizing force. As the demoniac shrieks died away in triumphant re-

furniture was tossed about, strange smells filled the air and strange noises resounded. But all the worst incidents seemed to involve Mrs. Foyster. She was thrown from her bed in the night, slapped by an invisible hand, given a black eye, and once was nearly suffocated by a mattress. And then there began to appear on various walls of the rectory plaintive, nearly indecipherable, scrawled messages, such as "Marianne

Please help get" and "Marianne light mass prayers."

Mrs. Foyster sought clarification of alleged ghostly scrawls.

Harry Price, shown at left with a telescope, applied technology to ghost hunting.

case of haunting in the annals of psychical research."

Although he did have many detractors, Harry Price was widely respected for both his imaginative and resourceful methods and his honesty. And because he had spent some 40 years investigating psychic phenomena, it was a scandal of major proportions when, after his death in 1948, criticism began to seriously undermine his reputation. A newspaper reporter claimed to have caught Price faking evidence, and Mrs. Smith wrote that neither she nor her husband had ever believed the rectory to be haunted. Then in 1956 three investigators for the Society for Psychical Research reported that their interviews with the people involved at Borley and an exhaustive study of Price's own research notes had demonstrated that he had manipulated certain facts. Borley was supposed to be Price's masterwork, and yet despite his sophisticated methods, he never fully proved that there were ghosts there. Possibly because he was unwilling to have his labors remain unresolved, Price enhanced his own interpretation of the unknown.

Because almost all of the poltergeist activity occurred when Mrs. Foyster was either absent or alone, Price was inclined to attribute it to her manipulations; yet he continued to believe in the possible authenticity of the nun and the Reverend Mr. Bull. Thus when the rectory again became vacant, Price seized the chance to lease it and turn it into a laboratory for the study of the supernatural. Working with 48 volunteers, he conducted the elaborate tests for which he was famous, and concluded in *The Most Haunted House in England,* published in 1940, that Borley is "the most extraordinary and best-documented joicing, the spell passed off, and I saw the tears chasing down father's yet quivering cheeks."

The attack left John Bell in despair. "Oh, my son, my son," he cried to Richard, "not long will you have a father to wait on so patiently. I cannot much longer survive the persecutions of this terrible thing. It is killing me by slow tortures, and I feel the end is nigh."

Bell was put to bed that day and he never got up again. Weeks passed and his strength drained steadily away, until one December morning his family discovered him in a near coma, his body twisted upon the bed. A doctor was summoned, and as he leaned over the sick man, the familiar voice of the witch filled the room. "It's useless for you to try to relieve old Jack," it shrieked. "I have got him this time."

Just before the doctor's arrival, one of Bell's sons had discovered a foreign-looking vial of liquid among his medicines. No one had been able to identify it, and now one of those present addressed the witch, asking, "What is this vial?" The witch answered that it had produced the mixture and fed some to Bell during the night, "which fixed him." The substance was fed to a cat, which jumped and whirled over a few times and died. Bell survived until the next morning.

The Bell Witch took its leave of the family soon afterward but not before interfering in one more life and making a final threat. Betsy Bell, who was now

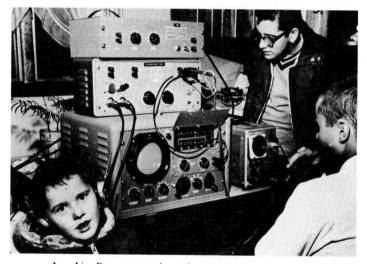

An Air Force crew investigated the strange whirring sound that a family from New York State said was haunting their home.

Finding no explanation for the 39 panes broken in the home of this Massachusetts woman, neighbors attributed the damage to spectral forces.

16, had finally accepted Joshua Gardner's offer and was making plans to be married when the witch turned its attention to her again. The torment took the form of a plea. "Please, Betsy Bell, don't have Joshua Gardner," the witch wailed repeatedly, until the girl could stand it no longer and called the wedding off. She later married the schoolmaster, who died when she was in her early thirties. She remained a widow until her death at the age of 86, in 1890.

The witch's final communication with the family took the form of a promise to return after seven years. When it happened, only Lucy Bell and two of her sons were still living in the house, and the visit was marked by a spurt of harmless poltergeist activity, nothing like what had gone before. It was the last time the Bells were to experience the witch's direct wrath, although some among the numerous descendants of John Bell have chosen to attribute their assorted misfortunes to the intervening malice of the 19th-century spirit.

The ordeal of the Bell family has been the focus of much study and speculation over the years as an especially rich and complex instance of paranormal activity. For one thing, as Frank Smyth pointed out, "it seems certain that the principal phenomena did take place," and indeed, they were witnessed by dozens of observers, including many outside the family who were presumably of objective dispositions. The witch was extensively "interviewed" by a committee of God-fearing neighbors, and both Betsy and John Bell, the primary victims, were examined by the family doctor, who could find no natural causes for their suffering. Betsy was for a while suspected of ventriloquism, but after one occasion when the doctor placed his hand over her mouth while the voice was speaking, the suspicion was dropped. In the world of the Bells, a remote rural corner of the Bible belt in the early 19th century, there could be but three possible explanations for the Bell Witch: it had to be a fraud, the devil or a ghost. The consensus of the community was that the Bell Witch was some sort of combination of the last two, an evil visitation against which there was no defense.

In the post-Freudian world in which we live, the most plausible explanation for the disaster that overtook the Bells may well be that suggested by psychoanalyst Nandor Fodor in a book entitled *Haunted People.* In his study of the Bell case, Fodor noted that the symptoms manifested by Betsy—swooning, fainting, dizzy spells—are those ordinarily experienced by someone entering a trance, in other words, someone who is leaving her conscious self behind. And he observed that John Bell's ailments—nervous tic, inability to eat or speak, withdrawal from all normal contacts and activity—are commonly associated in modern psychiatric theory with severe feelings of guilt. Fodor further recalled that the behavior of the witch was capricious, adolescent, *human,* and that while the witch was almost

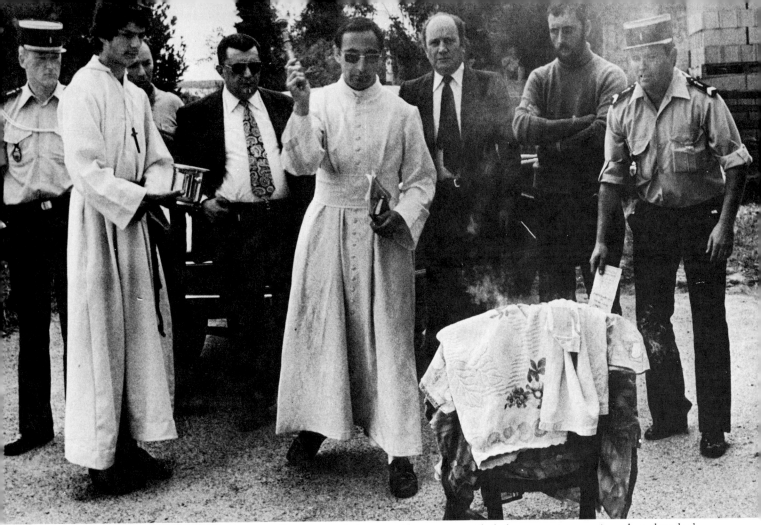

Plagued by more than 80 fires of unexplained origin at their farm in one month in 1979, the Lahore family in France asked a priest to try, with holy water, to exorcise what they had come to believe might be the evil powers causing the blazes.

uniformly malicious, it did act in a kindly manner toward one person in the family, the mother, Lucy Bell. After analyzing these and other elements in the case, Fodor came to the fascinating, if highly speculative, conclusion that the Bell Witch was the expression, possibly through the power of the mind, of Betsy Bell's intense but impossible-to-acknowledge hatred for her father. Such hatred, Fodor theorized, might have been engendered by sexual advances made by the father or by some form of incestuous relationship between father and daughter. As a result, according to Fodor, Betsy was incapable of dealing with her emotions consciously, and when they were stirred by the attentions of two suitors, Betsy's personality split in two—the split including, perhaps, "the girl in the green dress" swinging from the oak tree. Part of her personality then proceeded to attack her father.

Of course, Fodor's version of the origin of the Bell Witch is only psychological conjecture offered a century and a half after the fact, there being no possibility of proving his theory. The subject of ghosts is no easier to resolve. It may be, as many believe, that ghosts are simply the distillation into familiar forms of our deepest wishes and fears; they may be hallucinations, pure and simple; they may be waking dreams; they may be serendipitous electrical reactions; or they may be the visible edge of a phenomenon as yet beyond the range of human comprehension. After all, when one realizes how dim an understanding most people have of recently explained phenomena, such as radio and television waves, it is not difficult to believe that the universe may harbor additional secrets as well.

In the end, it matters little to those who have seen ghosts whether others believe in them or not. For those who have seen them, ghosts just *are*. Long after Robert Graves let it be known that he had seen the ghost of young Private Challoner, he was asked to elaborate on the likelihood of such an event. His response to the question was at once unexcited and provocative.

"I think," he wrote, "that one should accept ghosts very much as one accepts fire—a more common but equally mysterious phenomenon. What is fire? It is not really an element, not a principle of motion, not a living creature—not even a disease, though a house can catch it from its neighbours. It is an event rather than a thing or a creature. Ghosts, similarly, seem to be events rather than things or creatures."

A Man-made Ghost Named Philip

Ghostly rapping sounds, mysterious knocking noises and the tipping of heavy tables were considered the work of spirits by 19th-century spiritualists. Some modern parapsychologists, however, are inclined to suspect the intervention of the unconscious mind in such matters. And to study the mind's potential influence over inanimate objects, a group formed by the Toronto Society for Psychical Research in Canada, began a remarkable experiment. In the early 1970s the eight-member group invented a non-existent figure from the past, then actively concentrated on making the invented ghost manifest itself.

In his introduction to *Conjuring Up Philip*, the group's scientific adviser, Dr. A.R.G. Owen, a member of the Department of Preventative Medicine and Biostatistics at the University of Toronto and a psychic researcher specializing in poltergeist cases, wrote, "It was essential to their purpose that Philip be a totally fictitious character. Not merely a figment of the imagination but clearly and obviously so, with a biography full of historical errors." Or, as the book's co-authors, Iris M. Owen and Margaret Sparrow, put it, the ghost had to be someone who, as every member of the experimenting group knew, "had never existed in real life."

One of the group members, identified only as Sue, the mother of three boys and a former nurse with the Canadian armed forces, was given the task of concocting the basic life story of the Philip personality. She wrote, "Philip was an aristocratic Englishman living in the middle 1600s at the time of Oliver Cromwell. He had been a supporter of the king and was a Catholic. He was married to a beautiful but cold and frigid wife, Dorothea, the daughter of a neighboring nobleman. One day, when out riding on the boundaries of his estates, Philip came across a gypsy encampment and saw there a beautiful dark-eyed, raven-haired gypsy girl, Margo, and fell instantly in love with her.

"He brought her back secretly to live in the gatehouse near the stables of Diddington Manor—his family home. For some time he kept his love nest secret, but eventually Dorothea, realizing he was keeping someone else there, found Margo, and accused her of witchcraft and of stealing her husband. Philip was too scared of losing his reputation and his possessions to protest at the trial of Margo, and she was convicted of witchcraft and burned at the stake. Philip subsequently was stricken with remorse that he had not tried to defend Margo and used to pace the battlements of Diddington in despair. Finally one morning his body was found at the foot of the battlements where

The sketch above, drawn by one of the Philip experimenters after lengthy group discussion seemed to help focus attention and produce manifestations of the totally fictitious figure.

he had cast himself in a fit of agony and remorse."

Although there exists a place named Diddington Hall in Warwickshire, England, the manor was pure fiction. The experimenters made sure that the real history of Diddington did not "bear any relationship to that related in the story of Philip." And error was compounded by contradiction, with Philip being described both as having been reincarnated several times and as having appeared on the battlements of Diddington "once every century or so."

The group members memorized the fictitious biographical data about Philip, thought up still more details, studied the period during which he was supposed to have lived, and even acquired photographs of the real Diddington Hall and of the surrounding countryside. They sought to create a "collective hallucination" of Philip by describing his appearance, food preferences, and "especially his feelings toward Dorothea and Margo, until they had created a complete mental picture of him to which they could all subscribe."

For months on end, the group of five women and three men did their best to conjure up their fake spirit. They placed a drawing of their would-be ghost in the center of their circle and meditated on his image. Later, imitating the manner in which Victorian spiritualists sought to create a receptive atmosphere, they adopted a more "relaxed and jolly" attitude.

The group's first ghost-like manifestation was a table knock that was felt rather than heard; all the participants noted a vibration. Next came a number of

Members of the Philip group used colored lights and candles but never sat in total darkness. When they adopted a relaxed attitude, they reportedly felt their first manifestation, a tabletop vibration.

raps, as if someone had hit the table. At first, the participants suspected themselves of having inadvertently caused the knocks. But then as the table started to move around the floor in an irregular, apparently aimless manner, they started questioning one another. Finally, a member asked, "I wonder whether Philip is doing this?" In response, there was a very loud knock. The imaginary ghost, it seemed, had finally arrived.

By asking questions and accepting one rap for yes and two raps for no, the group was soon enjoying a relatively rapid dialogue with the entity it had seemingly conjured up. The bizarre adventure quickly escalated: one room in the house was set aside for "Philip," and the ghostly personality was accepted as a distinct entity that exhibited likes and dislikes, had strong views on some subjects and was hesitant on others.

When "Philip" was asked whether his wife, Dorothea, refused to have children, scratching sounds were heard. One of the group said, "Perhaps he's trying to tell us we are getting too personal. Perhaps he doesn't want us to discuss all these personal details?" The reply was a loudly rapped yes.

Mrs. Owen and Sparrow noted that "the raps and movements of the table seemed to be very closely related, if not actually activated, by the knowledge, thoughts, will, moods and power of concentration of each member of the group." If the group agreed on the answer to a question, the affirmative rap was quick and loud; when some members were in doubt, there was hesitation. As a rule, the raps occurred directly

Though the fictitious Philip lived his tragic life at Diddington Manor, there is a real Diddington Hall in England. It is shown above in a photograph taken by a participant in the project.

under the hand of the person asking a question.

As the group became relaxed and started to enjoy their encounters with "Philip," they began to react "entirely as if he were another member of the group." They teased him, joked and flirted. But when "Philip" was told that if he did not reply, "we can send you away and get somebody else," the raps stopped, and it was difficult to restore rapport. Nonetheless, the rapping and table movements continued, with the table reportedly rushing up to latecomers and occasionally trapping group members in a corner of the room.

In sum, the experimenters had succeeded beyond all expectation, although none understood how or why. As Mrs. Owen put it, "We clearly understand and have proved that there is no 'spirit' behind the communications; the messages are from the group subconscious, but it is the physical force we need to know more about."

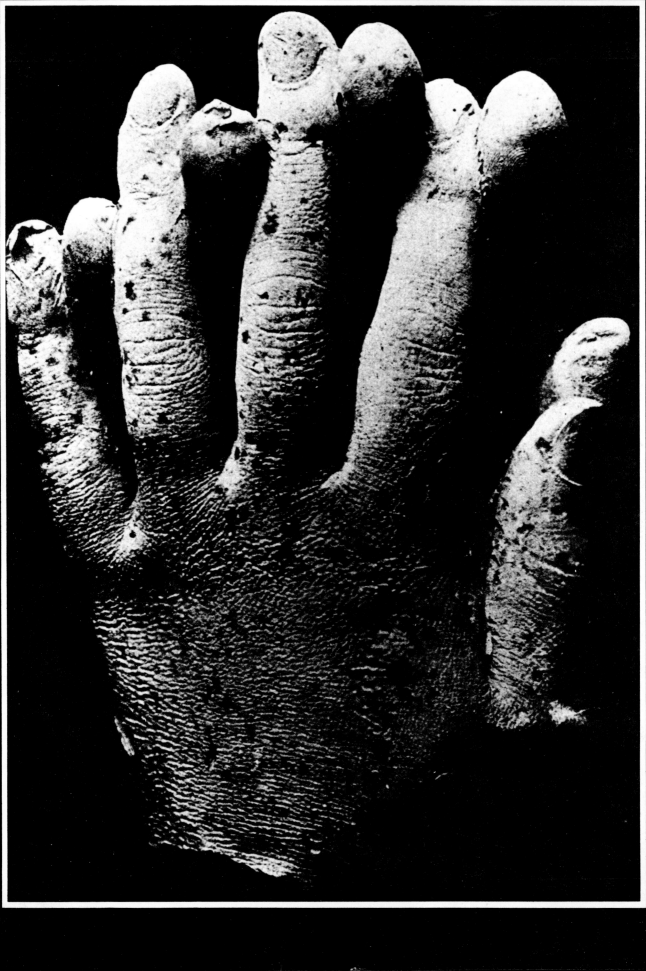

Hope, controversy and fraud have long
surrounded the persistent human belief that
the living can communicate with the dead.

SPIRITUALISM

Spiritualism in modern times began with the Fox sisters' claim of contacting "Mr. Splitfoot."

Modern spiritualism, the belief that the living can communicate with the dead, began in a cottage in Hydesville, New York, on March 31, 1848. Although mankind's efforts to contact spirits can be traced to much earlier times, alleged direct dialogue with the dead had its contemporary beginning that Friday night in upstate New York. The occupants of the cottage were John and Margaret Fox and their two youngest daughters, Margaret and Kate, about 15 and 11 years old, respectively. The Foxes had moved into the house, which already had a reputation for being haunted, in December 1847; three months later they began to hear odd nocturnal noises that so frightened the girls that they asked to sleep in the same room with their parents. On the night of March 31, Kate finally responded to the ghostly rappings. She snapped her fingers in the dark. "Mr. Splitfoot, do as I do," she called out, and clapped her hands several times. The pattern of her clapping was echoed instantly. Then her sister Margaret took a turn. "No, do just as I do," she commanded. "Count one, two, three, four." She clapped four times and stopped. The family heard four answering raps.

Mrs. Fox then asked the invisible force to rap out the ages of all her children, and "instantly, each one of my children's ages was given correctly, pausing between them sufficiently long enough to individualize them until the seventh—at which a longer pause was made, and then three more emphatic raps were given, corresponding to the age of the little one that died, which was my youngest child."

When Mrs. Fox asked, "Is this a human being that answers my questions correctly?" there was no reply. But when she said, "Is it a spirit? If it is, make two raps," two sounds were "given as soon as the request was made." Further communications led to the identification of the unseen rapper as the spirit of a man who had been murdered in the house years before (and, in fact, a skeleton of a man was unearthed by investigators 50 years later).

Word of these otherworldly conversations traveled rapidly, and the Fox sisters soon became famous. In November 1849, they gave a public demonstration of their abilities before an audience in Rochester. The following summer, the New York *Tribune* reported on their séances at the Barnum Hotel. Horace Greeley, the paper's publisher-editor, even took the pair into his home in order to better observe their feats.

The Fox sisters' claim that they had directly communicated with the dead had an astonishing effect on the public. It was as though a trigger long set had finally been released; virtually overnight, spiritualism exploded into a full-blown movement, complete with practitioners, followers and a rapidly growing code of

Franek Kluski, a Polish medium active in the 1920s, offered as proof of the existence of spirits these wax gloves, produced, he said, when a spirit thrust its hands into molten wax.

Swedenborg's Visions

Although his parents are said to have thought that the "angels spoke through him" during his youth, almost every indication in Emanuel Swedberg's early life and young manhood seemed to point in one direction: the achievement of great distinction as a scientist in his homeland, Sweden.

Emanuel Swedenborg's remarkable visions foreshadowed belief in spiritualism.

Swedenborg, as he came to be known early in his adult life when his family was elevated to the nobility, was born in 1688 in Stockholm, the son of a Lutheran bishop and professor of theology. He was educated at the University of Uppsala, where he learned Latin, Greek and Hebrew, along with the mathematics and science that formed the basis for his fame as a scholar and engineer, and at the time "heaven opened to him" he was considered one of the most learned men of his day.

Then, beginning at the age of 55 and continuing until his death at 84, the scientist experienced a series of visions and waking dreams that convinced him totally of the existence of a vast hereafter accessible to the living. Swedenborg's detailed accounts of his "journeys and conversations in the spiritual world," of time spent among the spirits of kings, figures from the Bible and inhabitants of the Moon, Venus and Mars, formed a startling prelude to the spiritualist movement.

Swedenborg's clairvoyant "journeys," including his accurate report, from a distance of 300 miles, of a fire that ravaged Stockholm, were completely unlike the accounts of traditional mystics or mediums. "What I relate comes from no mere inward persuasion," he wrote, "I recount the things I have seen. . . . I have proceeded by observation and induction as strict as that of any man of science among you. Only it has been given me to enjoy an experience reaching into two worlds—that of spirit as well as that of matter."

From the mass of otherworldly "data" he collected, Swedenborg constructed a doctrine of "correspondences," a comprehensive system that linked every aspect of earthly life to the spiritual realm. Swedenborg's legacy was the New Church or New Jerusalem Church, a non-exclusive communion that his followers founded and that members of all Christian sects are invited to join. The spiritual traveler never advocated interdimensional traffic for others; his experiences were personal and prophetic, not exemplary. And the man himself? Even if he was, as is always a possibility with visionaries, self-deluding or hallucinatory, he was nonetheless an extraordinary spiritual pioneer.

conduct for séances. Self-described mediums by the hundreds began to demonstrate their purported powers in New York City, elsewhere in New York State and in a number of Middle Western towns. Philadelphia spawned an inordinate number of mediums, and the craze to converse with spirits leaped the Atlantic to Europe, with particular strength in England.

Whatever the Fox sisters' abilities, whether genuine or fraudulent, the spiritualist movement they began clearly filled a need for many people. For a number of the period's most intelligent and curious minds the prospect of communication with the dead offered new directions for intellectual inquiry. For the layman, spiritualism's promise was the incomparable consolation of communication with lost loved ones.

Spiritualism's golden age lasted little more than 50 years, drawing to an end in the early part of the 20th century. The efforts of psychic researchers, including scientists and philosophers, to substantiate its claims had by then repeatedly yielded inconclusive results, and with the opening of more promising avenues of investigation, academic interest declined. As a popular phenomenon, however, spiritualism persists even to this day. It is often suggested that any sudden increase in premature deaths is still likely to inaugurate a spurt of activity, just as it did in France immediately after World War I. Spiritualism thrives in Brazil, and its continuing appeal in the United States was illustrated in dramatic fashion as recently as the 1960s when the former Episcopal bishop of California James L. Pike confirmed that he had spoken to the spirit of his dead son, Jim, through the mediumship of Arthur Ford, one of the 20th century's most prominent "psychics."

The Pike séance took place in the studios of a Toronto television station, on September 3, 1967. Ford had come to public attention several times before then, notably when he claimed to have learned from the spirit of stage magician Harry Houdini the secret code Houdini had used with his wife, Beatrice, in their mind-reading act. The Toronto television séance was intensely dramatic because the younger Pike had committed suicide in February 1966, casting tragedy over his father's life, beliefs and career.

During the séance, Arthur Ford, in a trance, spoke in the voice of Fletcher, his "spirit control," who was said to have been Ford's playmate in his youth but had died decades earlier. The spirit voice that seemed to emerge from the entranced medium said that it was in contact with someone "with a name like Halverston, or Halbertston." Pike identified this as Marvin Halverson, with whom he was familiar. Next, two entities identified as Louis Pitt, dean of the Virginia Theological Seminary, and George Zobrisky, a lawyer, were heard.

The medium then communicated a message from Pike's son: "Jim says he wants you to definitely understand that neither you nor any other member of the

"Mr. Splitfoot, do as I do."

"Mr. Splitfoot"—this was the name the Fox sisters used to address the spirit with whom they claimed they could communicate. The spirit's raps and knocks, reported to the world from the Foxes' clapboard home (above) in Hydesville, New York, began the spiritualist movement. At one point, Kate (above) repudiated spiritualism, while Leah (top picture) remained a famous medium somewhat longer.

family have [*sic*] any right to feel any sense of guilt or have any feeling that you failed him in any way." Pike answered, "Right, right. Thank you, Jim."

The entranced medium then spoke in behalf of several other entities purported to be the spirits of former friends of Pike's. After the television séance, Bishop Pike confirmed that he felt he had indeed spoken with the spirit of his dead son, saying, "To me, this is the most plausible explanation of the phenomena that occurred." But after the senior Pike's death in 1969 and that of Arthur Ford in 1971, doubts about the genuineness of the Toronto séance mounted. Had Bishop Pike really spoken to the spirit of his son and to other discarnate men he had known? Or had it all been clever ruse, devised by the controversial and flamboyant Ford? In its dubious authenticity as in its varied particulars, the Pike séance dovetailed with the spiritualist pattern.

Because it was born in an age of scientific self-consciousness, modern spiritualism was controversial from the start. The Fox sisters did little to resolve the matter. After years on the séance circuit (where they were eventually joined by a third sister, Leah), they confessed to having faked the original rappings, then confused things further by retracting

This monument stands in front of a replica of the Fox cottage.

their confession. It little mattered by then; spiritualism had already produced a collection of more compelling representatives.

By far the most impressive of these was Daniel Dunglas Home. Born in Scotland in 1833, Home grew up in the United States but achieved his greatest fame as a medium and psychic extraordinaire in England and continental Europe. He was an engaging, handsome figure whose personality and unusual abilities led Robert Somerlott, the author of *"Here, Mr. Splitfoot,"* to call him "the most charming figure in psychic research." In his entire career, it is said, Home was never caught using stage conjuring maneuvers or trickery.

A typical Home séance was nothing short of spectacular. It might include the appearance of disembodied hands, the sight and sound of an accordion being played although no fingers were visible on its keys, and the elongation of the medium's body—all in well-lighted rooms. Yet Home's most incredible demonstration may have been one that took place in 1868. It was described in detail by Lord Lindsay, later the Earl of Crawford, to the Committee of the Dialectical Society in London: "I was sitting with Mr. Home and Lord Adare and a cousin of his. During the sitting, Mr. Home went into a trance and in that state was carried out of the window in the room next to where we were and was brought in at our window. The distance between the windows was about seven feet six inches, and there was not the slightest foothold between them, nor was there more than a twelve-inch projection to each window, which served as a ledge to put flowers on. We heard the window in the next room lifted up, and almost immediately after we saw Home floating in the air outside our window. The moon was shining full into the room; my back was to the light, and I saw the shadow on the wall of the window sill, and Home's feet about six inches above it. He remained in this position for a few seconds, then raised the window and glided into the room feet foremost and sat down."

Lady Crookes, wife of the eminent physicist Sir William Crookes, described another of Home's feats, the appearance of a mysterious accordion-playing phantom: "As the figure approached I felt an intense cold, and as it was giving me the accordion I could not help screaming." As she screamed, "the figure seemed to sink into the floor leaving only the head and shoulders visible, still playing the accordion."

Sir William Crookes was also impressed by Home but devoted most of his attention to another famous turn-of-the-century medium, Florence Cook, and Cook's beautiful "spirit materialization," Katie King. Because Katie King resembled Cook and generally appeared only after Cook had entered a trance state inside a carefully curtained cabinet, medium and spirit were frequently accused of being one and the same. Crookes became fascinated and tried desperately to prove otherwise. He performed a variety of tests, including tying and gagging the medium and wiring her to a galvanometer; he also took some 40 photographs of Katie King. Yet the scientific community remained skeptical, and one historian has accused Crookes of having used the séances as camouflage for his romance with Florence Cook.

Despite official skepticism, however, physical mediumship flourished, and mediums developed a number of incredible phenomena that, so they claimed, were made possible by communication with spirits of the dead. A simple cone-shaped trumpet, for example, might seem to float in a darkened room and to convey the voice of a spirit directly, or an entranced medium might speak as if his or her vocal cords were being activated by a spirit.

Table tipping, where each tilt was part of a code,

was another means of communication. Some mediums materialized apports, such as flowers or perfume, which were supposed to be gifts from the spirits. Certain mediums developed specialties. Franek Kluski, a Polish-born medium who practiced in France, is said to have materialized a lion and a hawk or buzzard that "flew around, beating his wings against the walls and ceiling," and something called a Pithecanthropus, a hairy, ape-like creature that "smelled like a wet dog." Others drew spirit likenesses or communicated with medical "guides" who made diagnoses and suggested remedies. A present-day British medium, Rosemary Brown, plays piano compositions that she says are sent to her by the spirits of composers including Liszt and Beethoven.

Mediums have also communicated via the talking board, known commercially as the Ouija board. The Ouija (from the French and German words for *yes*) is

Medium Florence Cook (above) used Katie King as her so-called spirit control.

Katie King is shown appearing during a séance, possibly from the dark cabinet behind her, in a photograph by Sir William Crookes.

spotted with letters and numbers, so that its users, with hands resting on a guiding device, can observe as the device moves from letter to letter, spelling words and sentences. Related to this technique is automatic writing, in which a person's hand seems to be controlled by what is presumed to be a spirit; certain authors claim to have written whole books under spirit influence.

One of the best-explored and most provocative cases of automatic writing and other forms of spirit communication involved the beautiful young medium Hélène Smith. Smith's séances, held in Geneva, included such typical manifestations as levitating tables, apports, spirit voices and extensive automatic writing. The medium claimed that spirits guided her hand to write in Arabic and an unknown Martian language, as well as to draw pictures of Martian landscapes that she said she had visited with her spirit guides. These séances were attended by some of Geneva's best-known spirit investigators, but they were made famous by a Swiss professor of psychology, Théodore Flournoy.

In the late 1890s Flournoy brought psychoanalytic techniques to the study of Smith's spiritualist phenomena. He sat in on séances for some five years, investigated Smith's past, tried to corroborate the historical data that she said came from her spirit contacts and visited sites she claimed to have seen in visions. He also induced specialists to examine the various languages that she used. His conclusion was that her visions and trance-state "journeys" were, in fact, ingeniously amplified and elaborated memories. He acknowledged her Martian language as an incredible mental feat but claimed that the words were of earthly derivation. In the end, a Sanskrit expert wrote that 98 percent of the words could be traced to known languages. Flournoy

Crookes, with "materialized" Katie King on his arm, was suspected of being romantically involved with the lovely Florence Cook.

Despite links with spiritualism, Crookes was known as one of the great scientists of his time.

did allow, however, that "I believe I have actually found a little telekinesis and telepathy."

Flournoy's evaluation, published in 1899 in *From India to the Planet Mars*, was not well accepted. It was refuted by spirit investigators who claimed that Smith's unknown language was truly Martian and that many of her feats and her detailed knowledge of past existences could be explained only in terms of spirit manifestations. Flournoy was barred from his subject's séances; Smith, on the other hand, became famous and received an income from a wealthy benefactor. So great, in fact, was the general fascination with spiritualism that Flournoy's book, an attempt to explain spiritualistic phenomena in psychological terms, actually drew to Hélène Smith many new patrons and she was able to prosper as a full-time medium.

In truth, some of the greatest minds of the day

believed spiritualism to be at least possible. Among those who showed interest were French Nobel Prize winner Dr. Charles Richet, who discovered that microbes may become at least partly immune to medicines designed to fight them; French astronomer Camille Flammarion and Italian criminologist and psychiatrist Cesare Lombroso. As U.S. historian R. Laurence Moore described the period, nearly everyone, including "important men of business, politics, the arts, and journalism," talked "with dead earnestness" about the implications of spiritualism.

By the end of the century, however, most serious investigators were focusing less on supposed communication with the dead and more on the possibility that spiritualist phenomena might represent unexplored mental powers. Investigation of spiritualism as possible evidence of the "supernormal" powers of the human mind had begun with the establishment of the Society for Psychical Research (SPR) in London in 1882. Three years later the American Society for Psychical Research (ASPR) appeared and, after that, the Institut Metapsychique International in Paris. Similar groups sprang up elsewhere in Europe and in Latin America. Within these organizations researchers were beginning to wonder whether mediums might obtain their information not from spirits but by what has since come to be known as extrasensory perception.

Dr. John Beloff, a psychologist at the University of Edinburgh, has reported that "this shift was well illustrated by the career of Leonora Piper, a brilliant medium from Boston, who was discovered by no less a person than the great William James." James was the leading figure in U.S. psychology. Nonetheless, James's fascinating study of Piper's mediumship reflects the ambiguity experienced by most serious researchers in the field, and his accounts display the mixture of enthusiasm and caution, conviction and frustrating doubts, that he continued to feel in regard to the subject throughout his career.

James first visited Piper in 1885 at the urging of his wife and his mother-in-law, and later wrote that Piper had been remarkably accurate in references to family matters she could not possibly have known about independently. At the time, Piper operated in a trance, during which a spirit control named Phinuit spoke through her in what listeners believed to be a French accent. The entity claimed to have been a physician in France during its lifetime, although no record of such a person has ever been found, and there were additional discrepancies in the character the entity outlined. James complained that "Phinuit himself . . . bears

Medium Hélène Smith sketched "houses" that she said she had seen when, during a trance, her spirit traveled to Mars.

Smith drew the "plant" above as an example of the Martian flora she had seen.

Théodore Flournoy, who investigated Smith, found her alleged "Martian language" to be derived from French.

Flournoy cited the childishness of Smith's depictions, including the "cityscape" shown above, as evidence that her journey to Mars had actually been based on subconscious memories.

every appearance of being a fictitious being. His French, so far as he has been able to display it to me, has been limited to a few phrases of salutation . . . he has never been able to understand *my* French." Furthermore, much that the control had to say was simply not worth hearing, and James spoke at one point of Phinuit's "tiresome twaddle."

Yet the result of months of observation of Piper by James was an extraordinary degree of acceptance. "Taking everything I know of Mrs. P. into account," James wrote, "the result is to make me feel as absolutely certain as I am of any personal fact in the world that she knows things in her trances which she cannot possibly have heard in her waking state."

What James failed to ascertain was the source of her knowledge, whether from fraud, spirit control or by an unconscious reading of a sitter's mind, something James referred to as thought transference. In general, however, Piper's séances were without displays of physical phenomena, although she was reportedly able to make flowers wilt and lose their scent.

In 1887, when James's other responsibilities forced him to forgo his study of Piper, he recommended that Dr. Richard Hodgson, a prominent member of the SPR in London and at that time its representative in the United States, take over. Hodgson had a reputation for being a ruthlessly thorough and cautious investigator, and in his work with Piper, he instituted a regimen of the strictest controls to guard against any leaks of information, trickery or collusion. His precautions reached their height during the winter of 1889-90, which Piper spent in England, where she knew no one. At Hodgson's behest, all sitters came to her anonymously, her comings and goings were checked by a detective, and even her mail was scrutinized. During this period the Phinuit personality did, indeed, seem to be more wraith than physician. Nonetheless, the accuracy of the information he relayed continued to astonish investigators and casual visitors.

Yet the question of whether spirits were involved or whether Piper practiced particularly effective forms of telepathy, clairvoyance or fraud was never solved. Phinuit faded out, and a communicator who called himself George Pelham took over the Piper trances, remaining her major communicator until 1897, when he was replaced by a group of alleged spirits with such pseudonyms as Imperator, Rector and Doctor.

In 1905, Hodgson died suddenly while playing handball. By then, Prof. James H. Hyslop, a professor of logic and ethics at Columbia University, had begun to take a keen interest in the Piper mediumship. At first, as a precaution, he went so far as to disguise his identity by wearing a mask when visiting Piper. He too was disturbed by the sometimes astonishing personalities of alleged spirits, but he weighed the various alternatives, including telepathy and the psychological hypothesis that the entities were secondary personalities of the medium. After 12 sittings he said, "I prefer to believe that I have been talking to my dead relatives in person; it is simpler." In a report on the Piper mediumship to the psychical research society, Hyslop concluded, "I give my adhesion to the theory that there is a future life and persistence of personal identity."

In spite of Piper's reputation for being what Hereward Carrington, a psychic researcher and writer, called "the greatest mental medium of all time," researchers were nonetheless startled by the claim that none other than Hodgson, shortly after his death, became the latest of Piper's spirit controls. As late as 1924, Piper gave a series of sittings for Dr. Gardner Murphy, the noted U.S. psychologist and parapsychologist. In any case, Piper was not perfect. Carrington, who wrote that there could be no doubt about the significant phenomena she produced, only about an explanation for them, noted that even her outstanding mediumship did not exclude half-truths, inaccuracies and total falsehoods. Yet he believed that anyone who had ever met

A spirit guiding the artist's hand was thought to be the true creator of the delicate tracery at left by Anna Mary Howitt Watts, an amateur artist of the late 19th century. The tableau above was executed by Madge Gill, a London housewife who made hundreds of "automatic paintings" before her death in 1961.

191

Leonora Piper (left), born in the United States, and Eusapia Palladino of Italy were among the most famous and rigorously investigated of turn-of-the-century mediums. Many of their feats have never been completely discredited.

her would have been impressed by the supernormal quality of her mind.

Quite different in temperament and performance was another medium whom Carrington and others investigated on both sides of the Atlantic: Eusapia Palladino. Palladino was first discovered by Italian researchers and subsequently studied by French, British and U.S. investigators, who were baffled, intrigued and exasperated by her personality and mediumistic phenomena. She combined what appeared to be startling and apparently genuine physical phenomena with obvious and crude attempts at fraud. She had a fierce temper, as well as a wide range of phobias and superstitions. Palladino's most controversial series of sittings took place in Cambridge, England, in August and September 1895. Frederic W. H. Myers, a leading member and co-founder of the SPR, at whose home the tests took place, had previously been much impressed with the medium's demonstrations in France. But after the Cambridge séances he wrote, "I cannot doubt that we observed much conscious and deliberate fraud, of a kind which must have needed long practice to bring it to its present level of skill."

Some who had not participated at the Cambridge sessions but observed Palladino elsewhere did not agree with Myers. Hereward Carrington, who was instrumental in transporting the medium to New York in 1909, was caught in a cross fire of charges. During tests at Columbia University, several participants, prominent among them the psychologist Prof. Hugo Münsterberg, claimed that the medium had been caught slipping one foot out of a shoe in order to cause a table to move. Carrington wrote, "It is

The charming "psychic" D. D. Home introduced spiritualism to royalty and the well-to-do.

true that Eusapia resorted to trickery at times, and in this she was caught, both by ourselves and others." But he also insisted that many of her phenomena were genuine. He described a typical performance as beginning with table liftings and rappings, invisible hands playing a mandolin, "bits of bodies" forming in space, including heads and "hands firm and solid enough to push and pull sitters out of their chairs, or grasp them with a firm touch."

Carrington tried to explain the Palladino enigma: "Why, it may be asked, should she ever resort to trickery if she could produce genuine manifestations such as I have described? Is it not possible that all her phenomena might have been due to trickery?" It was his view that Palladino was simply her "mischievous, impish self" when trying to "pull something" on researchers but subsequently reverted to producing genuine phenomena. He concluded, "I have seen more or less the same thing happen over and over again, and know that, while she occasionally tricked, she was also capable of producing amazing genuine phenomena which have never been explained."

A more sedate successor to Eusapia Palladino's mediumship was Gladys Osborne Leonard, who in 1931 recorded her experiences in an autobiography titled *My Life in Two Worlds*. She attributed her choice of profession to the influence of a number of factors, including that as a young woman she had had an early-morning vision of her mother in a circle of light and later the same day received a telegram saying, "Mother passed away two o'clock this morning."

Leonard helped provide assurance, however unfounded, to many bereaved parents and wives in England during World War I that their sons and husbands, who had died fighting, continued to live after death. Among those whom her séance messages comforted was the noted physicist Sir Oliver Lodge. In his introduction to Leonard's autobiography, Lodge wrote that "to communicate with the spirit world" is "not out of accord with the doctrines of modern physics."

Investigators for the SPR even designed tests, suggested by Leonard's spirit control, Feda, that indicated that discarnate entities could pinpoint books in languages that a medium did not know and thus would not be able to select telepathically. Feda told one sitter, Mrs. Hugh Talbot, that she would find a small book, bound in dark leather, about 8 to 10 inches long, among her dead husband's possessions. Feda rejected Talbot's suggestion that this might refer to her husband's red log book. Feda said, "It's not exactly a book. It's not printed. . . . It has writing in."

(continued on page 196)

Tragic Crash of the R101

Forty-six people died in the tragic voyage of Britain's experimental dirigible the R101. Yet according to medium Eileen Garrett (right), the spirit of the ship's captain was present at her séances. She believed that he was trying to provide crucial information concerning the disaster.

Its floating salons and staterooms were equal to those of any of the great ocean liners; from a deck chair on the promenade, passengers could look down upon the earth as it passed underneath. The R101 was the largest dirigible ever built; and its maiden voyage, begun on the evening of October 4, 1930, was, appropriately enough, a passage to India. Yet before the next day dawned, at 2:08 on the morning of October 5, the R101 foundered in a severe storm and crashed and burned on a hillside north of Paris. Six crew members survived; 46 passengers and crew died.

Back in England at the time were two women who had tried to prevent the tragedy. One was Emilie Hinchliffe, the widow of a pilot lost over the Atlantic two years before; the second was Eileen Garrett, a medium, through whose spirit control Mrs. Hinchliffe's dead husband had reportedly warned of the disaster, and who, in addition, had experienced three premonitory visions of a smoking blimp falling from the sky. After many sessions in which she heard various dead aviators express doubts about the R101, Mrs. Hinchliffe had finally reported her fears and their source to a Lieutenant Johnston, a friend of her husband's who was involved in the R101 program. Johnston was courteous but discouraging. Months later, while serious problems with the airship were being discovered, Garrett delivered Captain Hinchliffe's warning to Sir Sefton Brancker, Director of Civil Aviation. Despite the warning, Brancker said the airship would be launched and he would be one of its passengers.

If the matter had ended there, the case of the R101

would probably not be considered a spiritualist's classic. But two days after the crash, an unexpected presence made itself known at a Garrett séance. Claiming to be Flight Lt. H. C. Irwin, captain of the doomed ship, the communicator produced an account of the crash, including details of navigation, structure and topography that dumbfounded those in attendance.

The transcripts from the Garrett sitting were shown to a Mr. Charlton, a worker at Cardington and a spiritualist, who obligingly verified the Irwin spirit's technical information. In a parallel development, a Major Villiers, who had known R101 crew members, participated in a series of séances, though not with Garrett, during which he, too, "conferred" with the Irwin figure, whose accounts he declared plausible. In his 1979 book on the R101, John G. Fuller relied heavily on these two authorities; yet he also credited a close friend of Garrett's, a man named Archie Jarman, as knowing more about the entire episode than any other living person. So it is of significance that in early 1980, Jarman, who conducted an exhaustive study of the case, issued a detailed refutation. His point-by-point technical challenge of the "expert" opinion of Charlton, who was but an ordinary ground worker at Cardington, and Villiers, a well-meaning man who knew little of the R101, effectively silenced the Irwin account. As a result, it seems clear that though the R101 was a great and romantic enterprise, its disastrous end came in inglorious fashion, the result of bureaucratic bungling.

Uncanny Powers of Mme. Blavatsky

At one time or another a great many people took Mme. Helena Petrovna Blavatsky very seriously. Among her admirers were Thomas Edison; scientists Alfred Russel Wallace and Sir William Crookes; poets William Butler Yeats and Alfred, Lord Tennyson; Abner Doubleday, the putative inventor of baseball; and even the wife of the Archbishop of Canterbury. And when Blavatsky died in 1891, Theosophy, the mystical religion she founded, numbered about 100,000 adherents; some 35,000 believers persist to this day.

Yet in appearance this remarkable woman must have seemed an unlikely vehicle for such persuasive powers. For in her heyday she was plain-faced, capable of swearing like a trooper, inclined to be fat (once she weighed 232 pounds), a sloppy dresser, bad-tempered, a drug user and an inveterate chain smoker who rolled her own cigarettes. Perhaps her only redeeming physical attributes—in later years, at least—were her startling, almost hypnotic azure eyes. As a result, it was personality, not appearance, that accounted for Blavatsky's allure. And according to those who knew her, she was electric, imaginative, daring, masterful and cunning. She was, as one young female admirer noted in 1873, "like a magnet, powerful enough to draw around her everyone who could possibly come."

Any hopes of accurately reconstructing the details of her early life were dashed by Blavatsky herself, for she lied copiously about her experiences and actively tried to suppress all biographical evidence she found uncongenial. Researchers know that she was born in 1831, the child of a family of lesser Russian nobility. In 1848, Helena's kin married off their (by all contemporary accounts) self-willed, reckless and erratic 16-year-old charge to one Gen. Nicephore Blavatsky, a man considerably her senior. (She later claimed he was over 70 at the time; actually he was about 40.) The young wife soon deserted her husband and fled to Constantinople. What happened after that is largely a matter of conjecture. By some of her accounts, she traveled the world, to Tibet, Mexico, India and Egypt; was a circus trick rider; managed a factory in Tiflis; traded in ostrich feathers in Africa; fought with Garibaldi in Italy; ran a magic show in Cairo; and was one of a handful of persons to survive the explosion and sinking of the S.S. *Eumonia*.

Whatever the truth about Blavatsky's wanderings, she re-entered documentable history on July 7, 1873, when, as a steerage passenger, she sailed past the Statue of Liberty and stepped ashore in New York City.

At first, like many new immigrants, she lived in a Lower East Side tenement and worked in a sweatshop making artificial flowers. But she was not long in reaping the benefits of the land of opportunity. In October 1874, bizarre occurrences at the Chittenden, Vermont, farm of the Eddy brothers, William and Horatio, attracted many of the growing number of people interested in the practice—or exposure—of spiritualism. Blavatsky—H.P.B., as she then called herself—appeared and announced that she had dedicated her life "for the sake of the blessed truths of spiritualism." Spiritualistic occurrences in Chittenden to that point had involved little more than the crude tricks of a medium who claimed she was an old Indian squaw. H.P.B. promptly produced a glittering international cast—a Georgian, a Kurd, an Islamic scholar and several Indian sages.

One of the witnesses to these wonders was Col. Henry Steel Olcott, an impressively bearded "serious

student" of the occult, whom, many years later, H.P.B. would characterize as a "baby," a "blockhead," and a "windbag full of vanity, conceit, and silliness." Olcott was enormously taken by H.P.B., and she instantly recognized in the credulous colonel precisely the kind of front man her New World enterprise would need. Together they organized the Brotherhood of Luxor, which, in 1875, became the Theosophical Society. The aims of the society were spelled out in H.P.B.'s ponderous 1,200-page book *Isis Unveiled*, "dictated to her by the Masters of Wisdom via astral light and spirit guides." Variously described by critics as a "heap of rubbish" and "plagiarized poppycock," *Isis* is a hodgepodge of doctrines taken from the cabala, Agrippa, Pythagoras, Buddhism, Hinduism and Taoism, as well as some weird inventions supplied by H.P.B. herself. (For example, her celebrated "root races" theory traces mankind's predecessors from hyperborean creatures composed of fire and mist through the inhabitants of Atlantis and Lemuria down to the strangely colorless present-day inhabitants of our planet.) Yet Theosophy's muddled precepts were anything but objectionable. They embraced the universal brotherhood of man,

encouraged the study of comparative religion and proposed the investigation of the unexplained laws of nature and the positive powers latent in all men.

Three years after the founding of the society and after the establishment of a branch in London, H.P.B. moved its headquarters to its spiritual home, India. Here, visitors were treated to an endless stream of small-scale miracles. Once, when a delicate china pin tray was accidentally broken, the collected pieces were magically restored. Another time, a guest mentioned a favorite brooch she had lost some years before because its clasp had broken. Over dinner, H.P.B. directed the guest to dig in a certain flower bed. She found the brooch, with its clasp intact.

But the main purpose of the pilgrimage was to participate in the correspondence that H.P.B. maintained with her invisible spiritual masters, including Koot Hoomi Lal Singh, whose knowledge was said to have been accumulated during a long chain of reincarnations. Messages from Koot Hoomi might materialize almost anywhere: under pillows, in luggage and occasionally in the morning mail.

In 1884 the London Society for Psychical Research offered to look into H.P.B.'s astral post office—an offer that, because much of her financial support now came from England, she could hardly refuse. In due course, the society reported its conclusion that "we regard her neither as the mouthpiece of hidden seers nor as a mere vulgar adventuress; we think she has achieved a title to permanent remembrance as one of the most accomplished, ingenious and interesting impostors in history."

They may have given her too much credit. The miraculously restored china pin tray was one of a pair; a record of their sale was found in the store's receipt book. The missing brooch had indeed been lost by its owner, but it had found its way into H.P.B.'s hands with the help of a pawnbroker. (There was even testimony from the Bombay jeweler who had repaired the clasp for her.) One of the messages received from Koot Hoomi was shown to have been published almost verbatim a year earlier in a U.S. spiritualist magazine.

Yet for the faithful, the hypnotic powers of Helena Blavatsky's personality transcended evidence of trickery and cynicism. "It is all glamor," she once said. "People think they see what they do not see. That is the whole of it." On another occasion she confessed to a friend, "What is one to do, when in order to rule men, it is necessary to deceive them? . . . For almost invariably the more simple, the more silly, and the more gross the phenomenon, the more likely is it to succeed."

Despite her frauds, the nearly hypnotic intensity of Helena Blavatsky (left) attracted thousands to her Theosophical Society. She claimed guidance in her work by mahatmas, or great souls, such as Koot Hoomi (above, left) and Morya (above, right).

The control entity insisted that the book's binding was darker than that of the log book and that Talbot should look at pages 12 and 13. Feda elaborated, "There are two books. You will know the one by a diagram . . . in the front . . . Indo-European, Aryan, Semitic languages . . . a table of Arabian-Semitic languages . . . There are lines, not straight, going like this." As Rosalind Heywood, the British author and "psychic," wrote in *Man, Myth and Magic,* "Mrs. Talbot was so sure that Mrs. Leonard was talking rubbish that on her return home she could scarcely be persuaded to look for the book. Eventually she did so and found, right at the back of a top book shelf, a shabby black leather book of the shape described by Feda. To her great surprise it contained a 'Table of Semitic or Syro-Arabian languages' and on page 13 there was a long and apt extract from an old book entitled *Post Mortem,* describing the blissful situation of the author after death."

Heywood wrote in addition that "she did not wish to create the impression that Mrs. Leonard never gave vague or indecisive sittings," adding that "no medium can be on top of her form on every occasion and with every sitter." Nevertheless, Leonard's "integrity was unquestioned," and "she produced a great deal of material which cannot reasonably be ascribed to normal sources."

The last phase of serious scientific inquiry into mediumship included an extended episode that was in most respects as bizarre as any séance recorded by a psychic researcher. Yet as with previous attempts to establish "proof" of communication between living and dead, these now-famous cross-correspondences ultimately proved inconclusive. The cross-correspondences were a series of automatic scripts and markings produced by a group of about 15 mediums—only one of whom, Leonora Piper, was a professional—and automatists over a 30-year period following the death in 1901 of Frederic Myers. During his lifetime, Myers had frequently discussed the prospect of transmitting various kinds of evidence from beyond the grave if it turned out to be possible, although cross-correspondence had not been envisioned. Later, the recipients of the messages in the actual cross-correspondence series said their sources included Myers as well as his two deceased SPR co-founders, Henry Sidgwick and Edmund Gurney. The messages transmitted, however, were of an im-

HOUDINI

Exposes the tricks used by the

Boston Medium "Margery"

to win the $2500 prize offered by the Scientific American.

Also a complete exposure of

ARGAMASILLA

The famous Spaniard who baffled noted Scientists of Europe and America, with his claim to

X-RAY VISION

PRICE, ONE DOLLAR

Master escapist Harry Houdini made a pact to contact his wife if his spirit survived in some form after his death.

penetrably abstruse nature, filled with complicated Greek and Latin references that had to be pieced together and decoded before they could be read.

By the time the last message of the cross-correspondence had been received, however, the standing of spiritualism had changed decisively. Serious researchers had begun to look elsewhere for answers to questions about the operations of the mind and the possibility of communicating with entities of some unknown dimension or reality. At the same time, public interest in spiritualism seemed to be focusing more on the issue of fraud.

Two public figures with powerful egos and interests personified the controversy at its peak. On one side stood Sir Arthur Conan Doyle, the creator of Sherlock Holmes and a combative spiritualist. Opposed to Doyle was the flamboyant stage magician and escape artist Harry Houdini, whose opposition to and campaign against mediums reflected the position of many professional magicians who were offended by repeated demonstrations of fraud practiced on a gullible public.

Houdini and Doyle engaged in fierce public battle over the issues of spiritualism and mediumship. They traveled, they lectured, they debated, they published books. As one respected U.S. psychic researcher of the time, Dr. Walter Franklin Prince, pointed out, the two men "resembled one another," since with both of them, "propaganda in relation to Spiritualism partook of a religious nature." Prince wrote in *The Enchanted Boundary,* "Both men carried on their propaganda with apostolic zeal, one to preach the gospel of Spiritualism, the other to banish the superstition of Spiritualism."

Houdini had made his case in *A Magician Among the Spirits,* while Doyle had expressed his view in *History of Spiritualism.* Prince dissected them both in his book, listing errors of fact, pointing to gaps in documentation or actual distortion of known events. He agreed with Doyle that Houdini "stuffed so many errors into his book" that it showed "extraordinary bias on the whole question," but he also noted that Doyle's bias manifested itself "by the ingenuity of the devices through which he persuades himself that mediums of extremely doubtful character are or were genuine."

Eventually, however, Prince himself was to be drawn into the fray as a result of the controversy surrounding Mina Crandon of Boston, popularly known as Margery the Medium. Indeed, the debate over Cran-

Unlocking the Houdini Code

When Harry Houdini, the world's most celebrated stage conjurer and escape artist, died in 1926, he left behind a challenge to bring back his spirit and with it the secret code that his wife, Beatrice, and he had used in their mind-reading act. The challenge was ironic, for during his lifetime, Houdini had been devoted to exposing mediums.

Nonetheless, on February 8, 1928, Fletcher, the supposed spirit control of medium Arthur Ford, announced during a séance that a woman who "tells me she is the mother of Harry Weiss, known as Houdini," wanted to pass along a message. Speaking for the woman, Fletcher said, "For many years, my son waited for one word which I was to send back. He always said that if he could get it he would believe. Conditions have now developed in the family which make it necessary for me to get my code word through before he can give his wife the code he arranged with her. . . . His wife knew the word, and no one else in all the world. . . . Ask her if the word which I tried to get back all these years was not 'FORGIVE!'"

When informed of the message, Beatrice Houdini confirmed that the word *forgive* was one her husband had "awaited in vain all his life." She noted "one or two trivial inaccuracies" in the message but affirmed that this was "the first message which I have received among thousands which has an appearance of truth."

In a later Ford séance the Fletcher entity announced, "A man who says he is Harry Houdini, but whose real name was Ehrich Weiss, is here and wishes to send to his wife, Beatrice Houdini, the ten-word message which he agreed to do if it were possible for him to communicate. He says you are to take this message to her and upon acceptance of it, he wishes to follow the plan agreed upon before his passing."

The message read as follows: ROSABELLE ** ANSWER ** TELL ** PRAY—ANSWER ** LOOK ** TELL ** ANSWER—ANSWER ** TELL.

After this information was conveyed to Houdini's widow, she decided to have a Ford séance in her home. During the sitting the Fletcher personality asked Mrs. Houdini whether the words were correct. She said, "Yes, they are." Fletcher then said that Houdini wanted his widow to take off her wedding ring and tell the group just what *Rosabelle* meant to her.

Mrs. Houdini did as Fletcher asked, singing four lines from the song. Through Fletcher, Houdini allegedly replied, "I thank you, darling. The first time I heard you sing that was in our first show together years ago."

Fletcher then explained that the words of Houdini's code, making up the first 10 letters of the alphabet, were: 1 *pray*, representing A; 2 *answer*, B; 3 *say*, C; 4 *now*, D; 5 *tell*, E; 6 *please*, F; 7 *speak*, G; 8 *quickly*, H; 9 *look*, I; and 10 *be quick*, J. Fletcher added in explanation, "The second word in our code is *answer*. B is the second letter in the alphabet, so *answer* stands for B. The fifth word in the code is *tell*, and the fifth letter of the alphabet is E. The twelfth letter in the alphabet is L, and to make up twelve we had to use the first and second words of the code." To represent V, the code used *answer* twice (2 and 2), thus producing the 22nd letter of the alphabet.

As a result, according to Fletcher, "The nine words besides 'Rosabelle' spell out a word in our code." The word, as based on the code values, was *Believe!*

That the code had been broken seems clear, but exactly how remains in dispute. The séances had always been controversial, and ultimately they were discredited. Though Beatrice Houdini wrote at the time that she had received "the correct message pre-arranged between Mr. Houdini and myself," she later denied any breakthrough. In the end, Houdini's code left spiritualism where it had been almost from the beginning, with well-meaning inquiry engulfed by fanfare and controversy.

In 1936, Harry Houdini's widow (inset) held the final séance (above) in her 10-year-long attempt to contact her husband.

don within the ASPR grew so intense that Prince had to resign his position as their top research officer.

Margery was unusual among mediums in that she was neither frumpy nor eccentric in a socially unacceptable way. Her husband, Dr. L.R.G. Crandon, served as professor of surgery at the Harvard medical school and was the author of a standard textbook on post-operative treatments. If Margery was fraudulent, it seemed likely that the respectable surgeon would have been her accomplice, a possibility hard to imagine. Beginning in 1923, the Crandon house became a psychic salon and a center of spiritualistic pilgrimage. The medium's powers revealed themselves in virtually classic succession, beginning with table tilting, automatic writing and the sound of ethereal music and eventually progressing to direct-voice communications. Invisible hands played havoc, with rappings and poltergeist-type phenomena occurring all over the house.

When the Crandons visited Europe in 1923, they created a great stir in spiritualistic and psychic-research circles. That same year *Scientific American* offered a sizable sum of money to any medium who could convince a committee of scientists of his or her authenticity. Several were tested and pronounced fraudulent. When it came to Margery, the committee, which included Prince and Houdini, soon split on the issue of controls and evidence. Houdini charged fraud and collusion. Yet the skeptical research officer of the London society, Eric J. Dingwall, visited the Crandons and came away declaring the Margery mediumship "one of the most remarkable in the history of psychical research." He later equivocated, saying that her mediumship "may be classed with those of Home . . . and Palladino as showing the extreme difficulty of reaching finality in conclusions." Prominent in Margery's séances were the so-called spirit entity of her late brother, Walter Stin-

---

Voices on Tape: Sounds From the Spirit World?

When Swedish documentary film maker Friedrich Jürgenson announced that in the course of recording bird calls on tape, he had accidentally picked up voices of several deceased friends and relatives, researchers were eager to hear what they hoped might be proof of spirit communication. Unfortunately, proof has remained elusive, for analysis of such recorded sounds has turned out to be an extremely subjective art.

Jürgenson's first recordings were made in 1959; in the more than 20 years since, while the number of proponents and students of "voices on tape" has proliferated, the thousands of "messages" collected electronically have largely proved to be controversial and inconclusive.

The theory of the voice phenomenon, as it is called, is that spirit entities address their living audience through the medium of the modern tape recorder. This form of communication is not undertaken in a direct manner, by imprinting an articulate, spoken message on a clean tape, but seems invariably to take the form of noise fragments that require hours of repeated listening and highly imaginative interpretations in order to be understood as words at all. It is not unusual, for example, for a series of words recorded on a single tape to be identified as being from several different languages. Both Jürgenson and his best-known disciple, Latvian-born Dr. Konstantin Raudive, regularly produced tapes that, they claimed, contained short, cryptic phrases, combining many different languages.

Although Raudive's extensive experimentation in the field is generally regarded as having been honestly conducted, his methods of control and evaluation have been heavily criticized. D. J. Ellis, who undertook a study of Raudive's tapes, pointed out that they were made without adequate protection against inadvertent registering of

shortwave radio and police transmissions, and even extraneous sounds and voices in the recording room. The improbability of some of Raudive's interpretations has also strained credibility. For example, one test recording produced the following jumble: "Au combat! Longue vita flieht. Han netic man!" To the ordinary ear, it was meaningless. Yet to Raudive, it was a message delivered in five languages—French, Italian, Swedish, German and Latvian—and it meant, "Into battle. The long life flees. He does not believe me."

Much of the research concerning the voice phenomenon has been conducted by electronics engineers using elaborate scientific equipment, but the basic process is relatively simple. A fresh tape is inserted into an ordinary tape recorder and the *Record* button is depressed. When the tape has wound through, it must be rewound and the *Play* button activated. In a more complex process a tape recorder is used along with a radio. Even so, no more than 10 or 15 minutes of recording, experts advise, may produce sounds requiring several hours to analyze.

Despite the ambiguity of the evidence accumulated to date, psychic researchers stop short of totally condemning the voice phenomenon. Some of the experiments conducted by reputable professionals have produced sounds that have not been fully explained except as being of possible paranormal origin, although what that origin might be is still unknown. Some researchers believe that psychokinesis may be involved, others support the idea of auditory hallucination.

British researcher Richard K. Sheargold, who originally regarded the voice phenomenon with great enthusiasm, was quoted in the London *Psychic News* of September 2, 1972, as saying, "There is no longer room ton, and what was supposed to be a unique physical manifestation, Stinton's fingerprints on wax. The fingerprints were offered as proof of Margery's authenticity. Late in the controversy, however, the famous prints were identified as being those of an early participant in the Margery circle, thus lending support to the anti-Margery faction of the ASPR.

Mina Crandon was a woman of vivaciousness and charm. The Boston house, with Dr. Crandon as host, offered gracious hospitality. Visiting researchers clearly enjoyed the ambiance and excitement that a stay with the Crandons offered. Nevertheless, publicity and criticism created periods of strain. Houdini's efforts to discredit Margery, seemingly without restraint, were particularly erosive. The supporters of Mrs. Crandon accused the magician of planting evidence against the medium during a crucial test. After her husband's death, the strain became too much for Margery, and her controversial talents faded away. It took several years for the ASPR to close ranks again, and no final judgment on Margery's mediumship was ever passed.

Among the critics of the Crandon phenomena was Dr. Joseph Banks Rhine, who was to become the world's leading proponent of experimental parapsychology. As part of his work at Duke University's Parapsychology Laboratory, Rhine tested several mediums; but eventually, as he told an interviewer for *Psychology Today*, he was forced to "back away from the problem of post-mortem survival and turn to things we could do experimentally with living people." Toward the end of his life, however, Rhine suggested experimentation "that would allow the long-range study of gradually lowered states of consciousness, and eventually of the terminal stages of life." He hoped, quite clearly, that the experimental laboratory might succeed where, by academic standards, the séance room had failed.

for doubt that the science of psychics has at last achieved its first real breakthrough."

A few years later, after intensive experimentation in the field, Sheargold advised Susy Smith, author of *Voices of the Dead?*, that he had become "ever more skeptical" of the "weak and ambiguous results" that he and others had achieved. Although he continued to believe that "the electronic voice phenomenon is beyond any doubt objective," he warned that repeated, intensive listening to the "very weak voices" was "most unwise." It prompted "great mental strain," Sheargold said, and left the listener prone to "misinterpretation due to wishful thinking."

Parapsychologist Hans Kennis (right) and Jos Spijkstra use tape recorders in attempting to detect voices "from the other side." The voices, the researchers claim, are usually rhythmic, high-pitched, metallic and echoing and can be heard only on the tapes.

Fact vs. Phenomenon

Pioneers of the Unknown

As one of the most influential U.S. thinkers of his generation, a seminal figure in philosophy as well as in early psychology, William James was perhaps the most remarkable pioneer ever to explore the wilderness of psychic research.

Although James did not turn his attention to the study of psychic phenomena until his mid-forties, by which time he had already consolidated many of the philosophical and psychological principles for which he is known, he brought to his investigations a mind free of intellectual prejudice and a habit of imaginative inquiry. Indeed, one of the most remarkable aspects of James's interest in psychic phenomena is that he was willing to publicly embrace so unorthodox a subject.

Near the end of his life, after a quarter century of reflection on a variety of psychic phenomena and a firsthand investigation of Leonora Piper, a medium widely judged to be both genuine and gifted, James pronounced himself "baffled" by what he called this "department of nature." Yet he continued to believe that enlightenment might be around the corner, and that there existed a "continuum of cosmic consciousness, against which our individuality builds but accidental fences, and into which our several minds plunge as into a mother-sea or reservoir."

James came by his intellectual expansiveness naturally. He was the oldest of five children of Henry James, Sr., an eccentric, energetic and curious dilettante and admirer of Emanuel Swedenborg. Along with his brother, Henry, the novelist, and the others, William was the beneficiary of an irregular but stimulating family life. Born in New York in 1842, he made his first trip to Europe before he was three. By the time he was of college age, he was fluent in French and German, had already considered and rejected careers in mathematics and logic, and had settled on becoming a painter. After a year's study, he dropped art and enrolled as a chemistry major at Harvard. He entered Harvard medical school in 1864. Shortly after receiving his medical degree and following the death of a close family friend, James slipped into a state of severe depression and anxiety. He experienced a terrifying hallucination of an imaginary alter ego in the form of an epileptic patient he had once seen in an asylum. He later wrote of this period: "After this the universe was changed for me altogether. I awoke morning after morning with a horrible dread at the pit of my stomach, and with a sense of the insecurity of life that I never knew before and that I have never felt since."

James emerged from this prolonged crisis with a

William James, world famous for his pioneering work in both philosophy and psychology, turned his brilliant mind to questions of survival after death and the alleged powers of mediums.

new belief in "my individual reality and creative power," and with the hopeful conviction that his life was his to make. Becoming an instructor in physiology at Harvard in 1872, at the age of 30, he embarked on a 35-year association with the college, during which he would become its pre-eminent lecturer in both psychology and philosophy and produce a landmark work in each discipline: *The Principles of Psychology* appeared in 1890 and *Pragmatism* in 1907. During his career, James linked these disciplines with elements of the supernatural in his search for understanding. He combined the contradictory roles of catalyst and mediator in an effort to broaden the boundaries of scientific inquiry, continually seeking to demonstrate the interconnectedness of the mind, the body and the spirit. He even dared to suggest that the universe as we perceive it might be but "a mere surface veil of phenomena, hiding and keeping back the world of genuine realities."

It was the vision of this yet-undiscovered reality that drew James to the study of psychic phenomena. Though he was to die without satisfying himself and with a nagging suspicion that the field of psychic research might ultimately prove barren, he left behind an invaluable example of passionate, imaginative inquiry.

Mr. Edison and Life and Death

Scientific American quoted Thomas Edison as having said that he could create a device of such sensitivity that "personalities which have passed on" might employ it as a means of communicating with the world of the living.

Mr. Edison," the reporter for *Scientific American* wrote, "does not believe in the present theories of life and death. Long ago he turned his back on the various old and accepted theories because he felt that they were fundamentally wrong. And just as he experimented with one substance after another without ever becoming discouraged in his search for the filament of the first successful incandescent electric lamp, so he has searched and reasoned and built up a structure which represents his theories of what is life."

"I believe that life, like matter, is indestructible," the *Scientific American* quoted Edison as saying. "There has always been a certain amount of life on this world and there will always be the same amount. You cannot create life; you cannot destroy life; you cannot multiply life."

The year was 1920, and the occasion for this reverent attention to the aging Thomas A. Edison's private cosmology was the electrifying news that the inventor was reported to be hard at work on an "apparatus" intended to facilitate communication with the dead. Did the 73-year-old genius mean to say that he believed such communication possible?

"Now follow me carefully," Edison instructed the man from *Scientific American*, one of dozens of writers who had appealed for an audience to discuss the great man's plunge into psychic hardware. "I don't claim that our personalities pass on to another existence or sphere. I don't claim anything because I don't know anything. . . . For that matter, no human being knows. But I do claim that it is possible to construct an apparatus which will be so delicate that if there are personalities in another existence or sphere who wish to get in touch with us . . . this apparatus will at least give them a better opportunity . . . than the . . . crude methods now purported to be the only means. . . . Why should personalities in another existence . . . waste their time working a little triangular piece of wood over a board with certain lettering on it?" Why indeed, when a device designed and patented by the world's most famous inventor might soon be on the market?

At one time or another the unsolved riddle of death and the hereafter has become the natural preoccupation of almost every serious mind. And though spirit contact may be generally regarded today with skepticism, in its heyday it drew the interest of many eminent thinkers, each of them hopeful of penetrating, by means of the art in which he was fluent, the boundaries that separate the living from the dead. Edison seems to have tried to use his scientific knowledge. He speculated that perhaps submicroscopic living "entities" were what built and rebuilt life-forms and that the effort to rebuild was directed by a small number of "master entities" that, working together, formed the personality. If these master entities remained together after death, the inventor reasoned, the personality might survive and try to contact the living through Edison's highly sensitive machine. For Edison, nearing the end of a life of solving mysteries through practical application, this last mystery must have had a special pull, and even the dim suspicion that he might succeed in surprising fate as well as his adoring public must have been thrilling to this ingenious and creative old man.

And although his interest in psychic phenomena seemed newfound, actually Edison had long believed in telepathy and had participated in several experiments with an alleged clairvoyant, Bert Reese. In fact, so convinced by Reese's abilities was Edison that he publicly defended him when Reese was later accused of fraud.

Ultimately, Edison's efforts to build a mechanical or electrical "medium" were unsuccessful, for although he remained to the very end a man with his mind wide open, the apparatus was probably never completed and the crucial connection never made.

Modern attempts to prove the existence
of extrasensory powers have produced extensive
research, some evidence and much controversy.

PSI AND SCIENCE

J. B. Rhine's efforts to find statistical support for ESP helped launch modern psi research.

Colleagues from those early days of research at Duke University in the 1930s could hardly forget the novel faculty card parties given by the young psychology professor and his wife. Though gambling in any form would have quickly brought disapproval in the conservative community of Durham, North Carolina, these were no ordinary poker parties, and the deck of cards being shuffled and stacked was in no way familiar. For one thing, it consisted of only 25 cards; for another, each card was imprinted with one of five seemingly strange symbols—a star, a circle, a rectangle (later to become a square), a cross and wavy parallel lines. During play the dealer would carefully shuffle the cards, then place the deck behind a small screen. The purpose of the game was as simple to grasp as it was difficult to effect: to guess the order in which the hidden cards were stacked. The guest with the highest number of hits, or correct guesses, won the evening's prize.

There was, however, an additional purpose in these card parties, one that, had the neighbors known of it, might have shocked them considerably more than an evening of poker. For the young psychology professor, Joseph Banks Rhine, was looking for evidence of

a strange and remarkable capability that he called extrasensory perception, or simply ESP. As the name implies, ESP is perception that is presumed to be completely independent of the known senses, such as sight and hearing. And with these same specially marked cards, Rhine, along with his wife, Louisa, was conducting in his Duke laboratory the first important scientific experiments aimed at discovering whether ESP might or might not be real. In particular, Rhine was testing for three extrasensory phenomena—phenomena that appear to be interrelated and are thus often hard to separate—that had seemed to exist previously, if indeed they had, only in an abundance of unverifiable anecdotal reports. They were
• Telepathy, or so-called mind reading—direct mental communication between two persons.
• Clairvoyance, or second sight—the specific perception of an event or object through means that do not involve the known senses.
• Precognition—the perceiving of future events without deducing their occurrence from existing knowledge.

To these three areas of investigation Rhine later added a fourth, psychokinesis—the use of the mind's powers to effect change in external matter. Together, these four areas have come to constitute what is now called psi, a word derived from the 23rd letter of the Greek alphabet, which is sometimes used in scientific equations to stand for an unknown quantity.

With his psi research, Rhine confronted a crucial

His normal senses partially restricted, a subject participates in a research project designed to study and perhaps even display direct brain-to-brain communication, or telepathy.

problem, one that is central to all studies of the paranormal: how best to explore seemingly impossible phenomena by using scientifically acceptable tests. This is of essential importance because, with its revolutionary element, the paranormal often seems to defy the known laws of science. And yet, as history has indicated, scientific laws can change. The 18th-century physics of Sir Isaac Newton, for example, was extended by the 20th-century physics of Albert Einstein. As Rhine wrote in 1937, "In the history of more than one branch of research a long-unrecognized phenomenon has turned out to be the key to a great discovery. The stone which a hasty science rejected has sometimes become the cornerstone of its later structure."

Yet to rewrite scientific laws, Rhine realized, would require more than an accumulation of anecdotes about unusual psi experiences. The trouble with anecdotes and stories, no matter how well-authenticated, wrote Rhine, is that "there is no way of coming to grips with them. They happen and are gone, leaving nothing but memory, none of the hard reality of a meteorite or a fossil." It seemed to Rhine that the best route toward understanding psi phenomena would be to design a series of sound, replicable experiments, such as those with the cards, in an effort to measure as exactly as possible the unexplained forces at work.

An important question remained, however: Are conventional methods of scientific investigation appropriate in examining paranormal subject matter? Is, for example, a statistical analysis of the incidence of clairvoyant ability in a sample population likely to reveal anything but that most people do not seem to have the gift and that a few people may exhibit it occasionally? More succinctly, is it not possible that the act of scientific investigation might, in such cases, deform the very thing being studied? These were but some of the crucial issues Rhine and other researchers dealt with as they began to probe the unexplained world of psi and its potentially awesome forces.

Rhine, however, was not the first scientist to try to trap psi in the laboratory. Charles Richet in Paris, who introduced statistical analysis to such investigations, John Coover at Stanford University, and George Estabrooks and William McDougall at Harvard University had all attempted to examine psi phenomena under controlled conditions. And in the 1920s the author Upton Sinclair, with his wife, Mary, as the percipient, had attempted to demonstrate what he called "mental radio"—telepathy. The book they published describing their research included about 100 simple drawings that Sinclair had tried to transmit telepathically to his wife and the surprisingly parallel sketches and comments she had been able to make in response. In the preface to the book Albert Einstein attested that Sinclair's good faith and dependability should not be doubted. Even Sigmund Freud had noted wistfully in 1921, "If I had my life to live over again, I should devote myself to psychical research rather than to psychoanalysis." Few researchers, however, brought to the task such formidable tenacity and devotion as that possessed by J. B. Rhine.

Rhine had studied theology and psychology but, after receiving a Ph.D. in plant physiology in the 1920s, had moved on to psychic research. As a young researcher, Rhine had read and heard many well-authenticated anecdotes of alleged psi-related experiences. Yet it was a story that he encountered while a graduate student that most impressed him with the necessity for careful research in the area. The story had been told during a lecture by a man whom Rhine called "one of my most respected science professors." The professor said that when he was a young boy, his family had been awakened in the middle of the night by a neighbor wishing to borrow a wagon. The neighbor's wife, it seemed, insisted upon driving immediately to see her brother because she had just dreamed that he was committing suicide. Upon arriving at the brother's farm, the neighbor found the man dead in the barn, lying just as his sister had envisioned.

As Rhine recalled the story many years later, what had concerned him the most at the time was that the respected professor, "though clearly impressed by the occurrence, had no explanation whatever to offer."

In 1928, Upton Sinclair tested his wife, Mary's, apparent ability to read people's minds by asking her to reproduce drawings he had made and she had not seen. Sinclair reported a high degree of correspondence, as shown in the drawings below (his wife's re-creations are on the right).

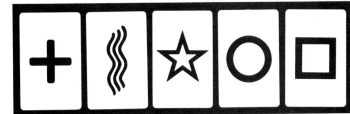

J. B. Rhine (right in picture at left) tested Hubert Pearce's ability to predict which of the ESP cards above would appear next. For one test, Pearce and the cards were 100 yards apart (at A and B below). A score card is at right.

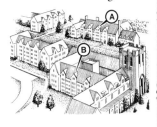

Rhine realized that no matter how compelling the event, the impartial mind could not be forced to assume from an anecdote that psi powers had been at work. To make that crucial leap, he knew, more would have to be discovered—by experimentation and testing. Rhine's interest in psychic research was also sharpened by a lecture on spiritualism given by Sir Arthur Conan Doyle, the creator of Sherlock Holmes. And at Harvard and after moving to Duke in 1927, Rhine attempted to investigate the powers of several persons said to be able to communicate with the dead. It soon became evident to Rhine, however, that the intimate knowledge of the dead revealed by such mediums might have been gained in a quite different manner—from the survivors of the deceased, perhaps through telepathy.

To test for telepathy and other psychic abilities, Rhine recruited subjects largely at random, including Duke faculty members and students who, for the most part, laid no claim to any special capabilities for extrasensory perception. His experimental methods were not unlike those that provided the entertainment at his parties, focusing on Zener cards, which he had developed in conjunction with Karl Zener, a fellow member of the Duke psychology faculty. In telepathy experiments the sender concentrated on the symbol of a card he had turned up, while the subject—sometimes in the same room, sometimes in a separate building—recorded his impression of the symbol. In clairvoyance experiments the subject attempted to directly perceive either the card being turned over out of his sight or the order of the cards in a shuffled deck. In tests of precognition the subject attempted to determine the order the cards would take after they had been shuffled.

Rhine did not expect subjects to score hits on every card but relied instead on the statistical methods widely used in psychology and other experimental sciences. According to the mathematical theory of probability (and the statistical table developed for use in this type of experiment), chance would indicate that one of Rhine's subjects was likely to score five correct guesses in a single run through the 25-card Zener deck. Since a subject would not score exactly five correct guesses in every run, the statistical table also indicated when experimental results were within an acceptable range of the chance number. Results that varied too far from chance, on the other hand, were considered "statistically significant"—and hence suggested that something other than chance had been at work. In a 25-card run nine hits would be considered a statistically significant variation from chance because the odds against such a score are approximately 20 to 1.

Although positive results were elusive, by 1932, after about two years of work with the Zener cards, Rhine had found eight subjects who regularly scored above chance on the tests for telepathy and clairvoyance. The eight subjects, Rhine reported, underwent a total of 85,724 trials and achieved 24,364 hits. This was 7,219 more hits than might be expected by chance.

The most successful of these high-scoring subjects was Hubert Pearce, a divinity student at the Duke School of Religion. Besides consistently scoring above chance in the normal experimental situation, Pearce took part in 1933 and 1934 in a series of long-distance tests that still rank among the milestones of paranormal research. The experimenter was J. Gaither Pratt,

Remote Viewing: The Search for Second Sight

"I see a little house covered with red, overlapping boards. It has a white trim and a very tall, pointed roof. But the whole thing feels fake, like a movie set."

This was the first description Hella Hammid produced as a participant in research into a kind of clairvoyance and telepathy known as remote viewing and conducted by a pair of physicists at the Stanford Research Institute (SRI) in Menlo Park, California. The structure she "saw" was a 15-foot-high model of an old-fashioned little red schoolhouse at a miniature golf course in the vicinity. This test was a prelude to an experiment in which Hammid would attempt to describe nine separate targets within a half-hour's drive of the research laboratory. The preliminary schoolhouse test was made to coax a doubtful Hammid into a more receptive attitude toward remote viewing or, as Russell Targ and Dr. Harold Puthoff wrote in their account of the study, *Mind-Reach,* to demonstrate "the *non*uniqueness of the ability; in our research, paranormal functioning appears to be a latent ability that all subjects can experience to some degree."

Puthoff and Targ conducted their first series of remote-viewing experiments from 1972 through 1975. The procedure generally followed in Menlo Park was simple: while the subject was monitored at SRI, two to four outbound experimenters went to a site picked at random from 100 previously selected target locations. The outbound experimenters then remained at the target site for 15 minutes to a half-hour, moving about and closely examining their surroundings. At the same time, the research subject began to describe and sketch what he visualized. The descriptions were tape-recorded, and transcripts, along with the drawings, were given to an independent judge who was an SRI professional otherwise unconnected with the experiments. The judge was then asked to travel to all the target locations and attempt to match them with all the subject's unlabeled descriptions. He was to give each description a ranking with respect to each possible target: a ranking of one meant he felt that the description was most likely to correspond to the target; two was second most likely and so on. When a judge gave a ranking of one to a description that in fact corresponded to the target, that was called a direct hit. In the Hella Hammid series, the judge recorded direct hits on five out of nine targets and gave rankings of two to the remaining four. The odds against such a close corroboration's occurring as a result of chance were, the researchers maintained, 500,000 to 1. On the basis of more than 100 tests of 20 subjects, Targ and Puthoff concluded that the phenomenon seemed to be unaffected by distance or electrical shielding and to be a non-analytical skill, possibly a function of the brain's right hemisphere.

A small band of scientists has continued to investigate remote-viewing phenomena. Unfortunately, many investigators have not been able to duplicate Targ and Puthoff's results. In fact, close study of their methods has resulted in some serious criticism, especially of procedures involved in the judging process. New Zealand psychologists David Marks and Richard Kammann have pointed out that almost anyone would tend, perhaps unconsciously, to look for similarities and ignore differences in comparing descriptions and targets. This, coupled with methodological problems in the Targ-Puthoff procedure, problems involving unedited cues in the transcripts, could have helped the judges choose the correct description even without visiting the target.

None of the proponents is yet able to offer answers to the questions why and how. Targ and Puthoff have suggested hypotheses involving quantum physics, the theory of relativity, and time being altered when one is dealing with atomic matter. Psychologist Charles T. Tart, who has attempted to replicate their work, has theorized that the overdevelopment in Western man of the left side of the brain may be involved and has suggested that remote viewing may be a faculty once exercised by everyone.

In Puthoff (below, top picture) and Targ's remote-viewing experiments, a subject described the model schoolhouse below as "a little house covered with red, overlapping boards," and drew a series of inset boxes to depict the lines of a pedestrian overpass.

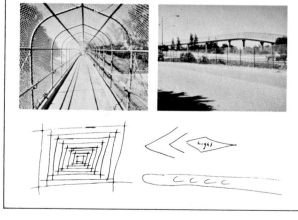

a graduate student who later became a leading parapsychologist. Pearce and Pratt operated in different buildings in carrying out the series of experiments. In one building, Pratt would lift a card from the deck and carefully place it face down at a prearranged time. Pearce, in a cubicle in the library, either 100 or 250 yards away from Pratt, depending on the building the researcher was in, recorded his impression of each card. Since Pratt did not look at the faces of the cards until the end of the test and hence did not know the order until after Pearce had recorded his guess, this was basically a test for clairvoyance. The results were truly startling. In the 1,850 trials conducted over an eight-month period, Pearce achieved so many hits that the odds against his doing so by chance were represented by a number consisting of 10 followed by 21 zeros to 1. As even critics would later concede, something besides coincidence seemed to be operating.

Rhine published these impressive early results in 1934 in what he later characterized as "a modest little monograph," *Extra-Sensory Perception.* The modest little monograph understandably created widespread interest—and equally understandably triggered fierce controversy. For one thing, Rhine's results defied the laws of physics. For another, the scientific community was being challenged by a scientist of solid reputation, and critics of Rhine's work did not hesitate to voice their concerns. At first, Rhine's method of using statistical probability was questioned, but such criticisms were for the most part refuted. The larger questions, some of which still linger, involved the design of Rhine's experiments and the methods he used. A critic later wrote that given the implausibility of psychic phenomena, "it is best, first, to assume that ESP is impossible and then to seek some explanation to account for the results in terms of well established processes."

Critics sought such explanations in several areas of the Rhine experiments. One methodological weakness often cited was that the Zener cards were shuffled by hand rather than in a way that guaranteed scientific randomization. Another criticism focused on the possibility that subjects might have gained knowledge of the cards' markings through some ordinary sensory means. An experimenter who was visible to a subject, for example, might unconsciously have given away the correct answer through a nod of the head or changes in body position. In fact, the cards themselves may have

Dr. Gertrude Schmeidler, of New York's City College, found that believers in ESP did better in her clairvoyance experiments than non-believers.

been a giveaway. Some of the subjects had handled the cards, and after Zener cards went on sale to the public in 1936, it became apparent that under certain lighting conditions, the Zener symbols could be ascertained from the backs of the cards and even from the sides. There was also the possibility that conscious—or, more likely, unconscious—errors had occurred in recording the results.

C.E.M. Hansel, a British psychologist and one of psi research's most active opponents, went even further in his criticism, suggesting that if something were operating other than chance, that something might be fraud. In his book *ESP: A Scientific Evaluation,* Hansel insisted that trickery could not be ruled out even in the Pearce-Pratt experiments. This is because the percipient Pearce, Hansel pointed out, would have had time to leave the library and spy through an office transom while Pratt recorded the order of the Zener cards. For Hansel, the very possibility of fraud—there is no actual evidence of it in the Pearce-Pratt testing—was enough to invalidate the highly positive results.

It is to guard against such charges of fraud or erroneous interpretation that science insists upon replication of experiments. Independent researchers, using the same basic experimental design, attempt to achieve the same results as other investigators. Successful replication helps corroborate earlier work. As psi research proliferated in the United States and abroad in the wake of Rhine's claims, replication became a central and highly controversial issue. During the late 1930s some researchers felt that they had successfully reproduced the Rhine findings; others were unable to do so. Even Rhine himself achieved only mixed results when he painstakingly repeated his own experiments.

Thus the battle lines between psi and science were clearly drawn. Most conventional scientists saw in the failure to obtain consistent replication a reason to ignore or reject Rhine's findings. Rhine and other parapsychologists interpreted the failure to replicate as a clue to the essential nature of psi—elusive, unpredictable, prey to the mood of both subject and experimenter, but quite real nonetheless. Indeed, the breadth of this schism was already evident in 1935 when Duke established a parapsychology laboratory with Rhine as its director; the new laboratory was carefully separated from psychology and other departments of traditional science.

Few modern scientists have encountered such re-

The Psi Sensitive

So much of serious psi research has depended on the cooperation of a handful of "psi-gifted" subjects that psi seems at first glance to be a rare and restricted capacity. Such, certainly, was the view of Andrew Greeley, a sociologist at the National Opinion Research Center in Chicago, until several questionnaires he prepared turned up evidence of surprisingly widespread belief in the supernatural. Greeley was so intrigued by the unexpected findings that when he and a colleague, William McCready, were commissioned to do a study of basic belief systems in the United States in 1973, they included questions about mystical experiences. In addition, McCready suggested that for clarity's sake, they also enter questions on psychic experiences. When the questionnaires came back, the researchers were "astonished" by the answers. "Almost a fifth of the American population reports frequent paranormal experiences," Greeley wrote in *The Sociology of the Paranormal,* a "finding that dazzles our social science colleagues as it does us."

Dazzled, but not overwhelmed, Greeley and McCready attempted to construct a profile of individuals who ranked high on what Greeley calls the psi scale—an estimated 15 percent of the U.S. population, or 30 million people, who " 'often' experience ESP, or déjà vu, or clairvoyance." Despite the fact that many people equate psi with superstition and ignorance, Greeley found that people "high on the psi scale" tended to be "younger, better educated, more likely to be affect prone [sensitive to events around them], more liberal racially, and both more confident and more agnostic religiously." While psi-types are "slightly less likely to go to church than the average American," Greeley found, they are also "more likely to believe in human survival, to have certainty about fundamental religious beliefs, and to be religious optimists."

While people high on the psi scale fell into almost every possible age, race and socioeconomic bracket, Greeley found that slightly more white women and black men than black women and white men reported psi experiences, that more men who reported bad marriages than happy ones claimed them, and that a history of family tension tended to increase the incidence of psi experiences. The sociologist speculated that high levels of family tension among those who told of frequent psi encounters might mean not so much that these people had poorer-than-average family relationships but that they were "better in touch with their emotions." Their "emotional sensitivity," Greeley reasoned, might account for a heightened awareness of psi.

After weighing all of the variables, Greeley concluded that people who experience psi frequently are people who, because of a combination of personal and social factors, develop an exceptionally high "level of emotional resonance." They are, perhaps, "more likely to be attuned to tensions, as well as to psi factors."

sistance from their colleagues on the one hand and, on the other, such cantankerous subject matter as did Rhine and other pioneering parapsychologists. It soon became clear, for example, that the three ESP phenomena—telepathy, clairvoyance and precognition—could not easily be separated. What appears in one instance to be telepathy might well be clairvoyance; perhaps a subject was perceiving the identity of Zener cards directly instead of through the mind of the sender. Or hits might be the result of precognition; perhaps the subject was anticipating the card that was coming next in the deck. The fact that Rhine and other researchers sometimes scored well when they served as subjects in ESP tests further complicated matters. What if they were unconsciously influencing their own experiments through psychokinesis—mind over matter?

Imperturbable in the face of criticism and of the complications of experimental psi, Rhine plunged relentlessly ahead. Over the next three decades, he trained scores of enthusiastic new psi researchers. He continued his work with Zener cards, or ESP cards (as they were now being called), tightening up procedures with devices such as an automatic card-shuffling machine. He also began testing subjects for psychokinesis by attempting to determine whether they could mentally influence the way dice fell when they were rolled. Other researchers introduced so-called free-response ESP tests in which subjects were asked to duplicate an unseen drawing or to describe a randomly selected distant scene about which they had no sensory knowledge. To ensure randomization in experiments, researchers began using number generators that were based on the rate of radioactive decay of atomic nuclei.

For years, psi researchers gave the appearance of being in a race to refute the skepticism of conventional scientists—tightening their methods in response to each new complaint and criticism. Increasingly, however, Rhine and other parapsychologists looked beyond merely proving the existence of psi—after all, they had continued to publish highly positive results. Now they began to explore its maddeningly elusive subtleties, trying to find out why psi, as one writer described it, "is like something seen out of the corner of your eye that vanishes when you turn to look at it."

One frustrating example of psi's elusiveness had been evident since the early days of research. This was the so-called decline effect. A subject might score well in early trials and then, as the experiment wore on, his scores would fall to chance levels. The decline effect provided additional ammunition for critics. To psi researchers, however, it suggested that psi ability simply fluctuated with the subject's mood, declining as he became tired or bored with the experiment.

A possible way to prevent the decline effect has been studied by Charles T. Tart, a psychologist at the University of California at Davis. In typical psi experi-

Olof Jonsson (above), a drafting engineer, uses ESP cards to demonstrate what he claims is his special telepathic ability to transmit or receive specific images over the telephone.

A triple-exposure photograph (above, left) of an experiment in precognition at the Institute for Parapsychology in North Carolina depicts the uncertain nature of future-time probes.

Self-described psychic Lalsingh Harribance (left) of Trinidad showed variations in alpha brain waves during psi performances.

A sender (below) tries to transmit telepathically a picture of a pair of chimpanzees to a subject whose physical senses are shielded (inset), in an experiment conducted at the Maimonides laboratories.

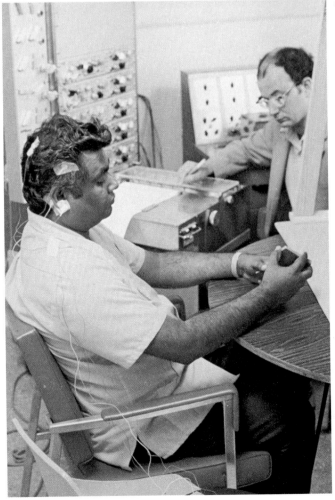

ments, Tart pointed out, the subject does not find out how well he is doing until the end of a 25-card run. This may make it difficult for the subject to recognize psi if he is indeed expressing it. In the early 1970s, Tart devised an experiment that provided immediate feedback to the subject. He set up a console consisting of 10 lamps connected to an electronic number generator, which controlled the random lighting of the lamps. The subject was instructed to push the button adjacent to the lamp he thought would light up next. Then, whichever lamp the number generator had selected would go on, telling him whether or not his guess was a hit. With the aid of immediate feedback, Tart's 10 subjects scored 722 hits in 5,000 trials—significantly above the 500 hits expected by chance.

Tart's research and that of others support a startling contention that is widely held among many parapsychologists: everyone may have some psi ability. Even animals, some believe, are capable of psi. Public opinion surveys tend to buttress parapsychology's belief in the ubiquity of psi. In various surveys, from 10 to 58 percent of U.S. residents have reported having personally experienced a psi phenomenon. According to a recent sample of 1,460 U.S. residents taken by Andrew Greeley, a prominent sociologist, 58 percent felt they had experienced some form of telepathy and 24 percent thought they had experienced clairvoyance. "Greeley's survey," says Tart, "indicates that it is normal to have apparently paranormal experiences."

Why some people seem to experience psi and others do not has been an important focus of research since the 1940s. A number of experiments suggest that a person's attitude toward psi may be an important factor. Psychologist Gertrude R. Schmeidler of City College in New York found what she labeled the "sheep-goat effect." Subjects who believed they would score well on psi tests did score well. Schmeidler called them sheep because they "accepted the possibility of paranormal success" in the experiment. By contrast, subjects who did not believe they would score well tended to fall

In a Japanese experiment, when a psychic began meditation, changes (red line) in body volume, breathing and skin resistance were recorded in a subject in a nearby room.

below chance. Schmeidler called them goats because they balked at the possibility of demonstrating positive psi results and erred in the opposite direction—below chance. When subjects score significantly below chance, it is said to be an instance of "psi-missing." The assumption is that something other than chance is operating. Schmeidler theorized that her goats were unconsciously "avoiding the assigned target."

In fact, the hidden workings of the unconscious are a focal point for many parapsychologists. According to this view, conscious psi experiences constitute only the tip of an iceberg. Beneath the surface, in the unconscious, they say, all humans are constantly being bombarded with psi signals. Such signals would be so faint, however—what Tart calls "a still, small voice within"—that they would seldom reach conscious awareness.

The theory that psi resides largely below the threshold of conscious awareness has been tested indirectly in several experiments. Such experiments attempt to detect a psi-induced physical reaction of which the subject would otherwise be unaware. For example, two physicists at the Stanford Research Institute (SRI) in California, Harold Puthoff and Russell Targ, used an electroencephalograph to monitor the brain waves of a subject during a telepathy experiment. The sender sat in another room in front of a strobe light that flashed on and off in his eyes. When the recipient, a woman, was asked to guess when the light was flashing in the sender's eyes, she tended to score at only chance levels. But her brain-wave response changed, registering fluctuations on the electroencephalograph when the light flashed in the other room. These fluctuations were interpreted as suggesting that something was happening in the subject's brain even though she was not aware of it.

Presumably, certain types of psi information may be so potent that they can break through and enter consciousness. If so, then sexual matters might constitute such a kind of strong psi material. To test this theory, researchers asked male college students to attempt to match standard ESP cards against concealed cards of the same type. Unknown to the subjects, however, half of the concealed cards had enclosed with them other cards portraying human sexuality. The students proved to be significantly more accurate in matching the ESP cards that had erotic images enclosed with them.

If the potency theory is correct, then information about danger might also be expected to break through to consciousness. Earthquakes, airplane crashes and other disasters often are accompanied by stories of psi experiences. Reports of such spontaneously occurring events are seldom subject to verification by experiment, of course, yet these incidents can be suggestive of possible psi activity. For example, one study of railway accidents in the United States led to the conclusion that most of the trains involved actually carried fewer passengers on the day of the accident than on an average

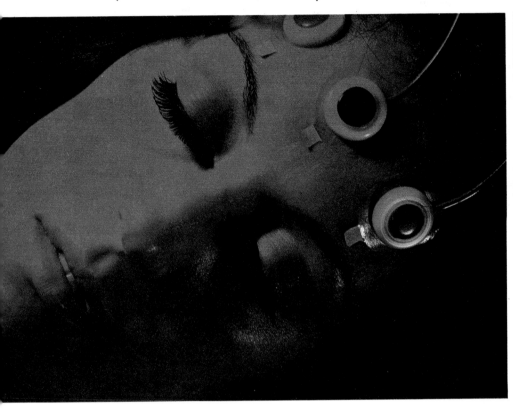

Psi experiments, many researchers feel, are more likely to succeed when a subject's brain waves resemble those in the alpha state, a state that helps biofeedback patients control such normally involuntary functions as heartbeat and blood pressure. The pattern shown in red above is a 30-second record of alpha waves.

of 10 other days. To psychic researcher W. E. Cox, the author of the study, this suggested that many people might have had unconscious premonitions and thus not taken the trains in question.

Perhaps the most fascinating study of psi associated with a major disaster was conducted by Ian Stevenson, a psychiatrist and parapsychologist at the University of Virginia. Stevenson found no fewer than 19 instances of seeming telepathy, clairvoyance and precognition related to the sinking of the ocean liner *Titanic* in 1912. Some of the people whose tales were collected had loved ones aboard the ship; others had no apparent connection. Their alleged psi experiences took the wide range of transmission forms typically reported: from dreams and waking hallucinations to an 11-year-old English girl's "strange sense of doom" about her mother, a stewardess who survived the sinking.

Stevenson's study of the *Titanic*, like other surveys of spontaneous experiences, turned up evidence that dreams may be a route through which psi phenomena can penetrate conscious awareness. In addition to studying dreams, parapsychologists have investigated other mental states that, in theory at least, might allow suppressed psi abilities—if they are there—to surface.

Psi research in this area has coincided with a new interest by conventional psychologists in the so-called altered state of consciousness (ASC). Parapsychologists have noted, for example, that ASC's such as meditation and even drug-induced states sometimes seem to facilitate high psi scoring during experiments. Psi researchers are particularly interested in an ASC that most people experience at some time or another—the calm, relaxed, yet alert state that is linked with a kind of brain wave known as alpha. During the 1960s a San Francisco brain researcher, Joe Kamiya, discovered that subjects could learn to generate alpha waves at will through a teaching technique that was both simple and radically new. Every time a subject succeeded in producing alpha waves, as registered on an electroencephalograph, Kamiya provided him with direct feedback by sounding a tone. This discovery, part of the new branch of science known as biofeedback, which enables people to exercise some control over internal processes such as brain waves and blood pressure, is of special interest to parapsychologists. This is because the alpha state closely resembles the kind of mental state that long has been alleged to be the optimum for getting positive results during psi experiments. Psychologist Lawrence LeShan notes that psychics often have described this state as a mood in which "no two entities

211

are separate because everything flows into everything else." Experiments suggest that while the alpha state does not guarantee psi performance, it is sometimes associated with high test scores.

Another possible road to the unconscious and heightened psi sensitivity has been suggested by Charles Honorton, a parapsychologist formerly at Maimonides Medical Center in Brooklyn. In 1974, Honorton reported significant results from a study of 30 subjects who were isolated from distracting sights and sounds. A subject was left alone, seated in a lounge chair in a soundproof room, his eyes shielded with translucent covers, his hearing restricted by earphones transmitting soothing recorded sounds. The subject was then instructed to talk into a microphone for 35 minutes, describing all the images, feelings and fantasies that entered his stream of consciousness. During this period an experimenter in another room concentrated on one of a group of 31 numbered picture reels chosen by drawing a card at random from a deck of 31 correspondingly numbered cards that had been shuffled and cut. One reel, for example, showed buildings and nightclubs in Las Vegas. As the sender looked at these transparencies, the subject, a 28-year-old psychiatric nurse named Ellen Messer, reported, "I'm floating over some kind of a landscape. It's surrealistic. . . . And marquees—nightclub marquees. Just seeing them. Nightclub marquees . . . in Las Vegas."

Improved psi results also have been reported from experiments in the United States, Finland, the Soviet Union and other countries using an altered state of consciousness that long has baffled science—the hypnotic trance. During hypnosis, some psychologists believe, dissociation takes place: certain mental processes split off from consciousness. This seems evident in conventional experiments in the psychology laboratory. Under hypnotic suggestion, the subject puts his hand in a basin of cold water and reports feeling no discomfort. If he is asked to write about his experience, however, he typically reports having felt pain. In short, at least two different levels of consciousness seem to be at work. Something of this sort may be in operation in unusually gifted psychics who perform their feats in a trance-like state. Through dissociation, submerged levels of awareness may rise and, with them, greater sensitivity to and consciousness of psi information.

Extraordinary results using hypnosis in psi research were reported from Prague in 1962 by a government biochemist, Milan Ryzl. Instead of employing hypnosis in experiments, Ryzl used it as a means of training subjects in the development of their psi potential. Hypnosis, Ryzl contended, helped subjects ignore distractions, motivated them to want to pursue psi consciousness and trained them in the heightened mental visualization often associated with psychic experiences. Ryzl's star pupil was a young Czech librarian named Pavel Stepanek. In a series of tests for clairvoyance—guessing whether the face of a card concealed inside a cardboard cover was green or white—Stepanek scored at odds against chance of 500,000 to 1. He repeated impressive scores for visiting researchers from half a dozen countries, including Great Britain, Japan and the United States. Yet when this particular ability seemed to desert Stepanek, he demonstrated another talent: he would consistently make the same guess, right or wrong, for the same card each time, even though the cards reportedly were well concealed. The fact that Stepanek could see and handle the cardboard covers seemed suspicious to some critics; nonetheless Ryzl's account of his work with Stepanek was published in *Nature*, a prestigious British science magazine. Stepanek was tested for more than a decade; the U.S. parapsychologist J. Gaither Pratt described this as "the largest number of trials and the longest period on record of a successful demonstration of ESP by a subject in laboratory tests."

In other research, a Swedish psychiatrist, John Björkhem, worked extensively with a variety of subjects to see if they might perform a kind of "traveling clairvoyance" under hypnosis. In this procedure the subjects were hypnotized and then attempted to perceive and report on various aspects of a distant scene. Björkhem's work produced mixed results; in some cases subjects reported in great and believable detail *inaccurate* information, while in others they produced details of distant scenes that were astonishingly correct.

In addition to probing the unconscious, parapsychologists have investigated the role of emotional

Details in Morgan Robertson's 1898 story, *Futility,* in which a supposedly invulnerable ship struck an iceberg and sank, were remarkably like those of the *Titanic* disaster 14 years later.

According to one study, some trains involved in wrecks have carried fewer passengers than would ordinarily be expected, suggesting to one psi researcher that premonitions might have played a part in causing people to avoid such ill-fated carriers.

rapport in the reported communication of psi. Stories of spontaneous telepathy in everyday life seldom involve strangers; the participants typically are friends, relatives, loved ones who are bound by emotional ties. Moreover, there is experimental evidence to suggest that elementary-school children who like their teacher score higher in ESP-card testing than students who feel no such emotional rapport. Students whom the teacher regards highly are also likely to have high scores, despite repeated experiments showing that psi ability is not related to intelligence. Even in the intent and physical world of professional sports, extrasensory communication sometimes seems to occur. Former Los Angeles Dodger pitcher Sandy Koufax recalled a moment of apparent telepathic rapport with catcher Johnny Roseboro during the 1963 World Series against the New York Yankees. Virtually at the same moment, both Koufax and Roseboro decided that the next pitch to Mickey Mantle, the Yankees' center fielder, should be a slow curve, even though Mantle ordinarily hit such pitches out of the ballpark. The telepathic communication, if that is what it was, seems to have worked. Mantle struck out on the next pitch.

Such reports can be interpreted in at least two ways by psi proponents. On the one hand, they may offer evidence in support of the theory that psi ability is ordinarily trapped in the unconscious, rising to conscious awareness in situations that are emotionally charged or otherwise conducive to its appearance. On the other hand, as has been suggested by a number of researchers, people may consciously experience psi most of the time but simply are not aware of it. This theory might explain the high incidence of psi reports involving friends and relatives. People with such ties are in normal contact and would tend to communicate with one another, thus bringing to light and confirming random

telepathic experiences. Strangers, by contrast, are unlikely to discover that they may be exchanging thoughts.

Among the strongest of human emotional ties are those that bind parent and child. The potential role of psi in this relationship has come under the close scrutiny of several investigators trained in Freudian theory, which traditionally emphasizes the parent-child bond. Psychiatrist Berthold E. Schwarz has studied instances of apparent telepathy in the communication patterns of his own family. In his book *Parent-Child Telepathy,* Schwarz records in detail 505 such episodes that occurred during a nine-year period and that involved Schwarz or his wife, Ardis, and their two young children, Lisa and Eric. Telepathy, says Schwarz, is "the missing link"—the neglected key factor—in communication between parent and child. Reports of telepathic episodes between parent and child may be most frequent in crisis situations—a mother, for example, somehow senses that her absent child is in danger. What lends fascination to Schwarz's account is that the episodes described often involve trivial, but nonetheless intriguing incidents from everyday life. Typical is the following example, which occurred when Lisa was not yet three years old:

"July 21, 1959, Tuesday, 6:00 P.M. I was taking a walk in the backyard with Lisa after dinner. While going down the hill and holding on to her hand, I noticed a few stray leaves on the ground from the pear and apple trees. The thought crossed my mind, 'I wonder if the pear tree will die with these leaves coming down?' Lisa then verbally repeated the same words. When I asked her why she thought that, she said, 'Mommy said so.' I later checked with Ardis, who said she has never commented on the pear tree or any other trees to Lisa. During this walk Lisa was very affectionate."

Another investigator, the psychiatrist Jan Ehrenwald, suggests that telepathy may commonly occur between mother and infant. Mothers, he says, seem to understand the needs of the young infant "in a way which is difficult to account for in terms of the 'ordinary' means" of pre-verbal communication, such as gestures, crying, smiling and other social signals. During the period before it acquires language, an infant is helpless and dependent upon the mother or other care giver for survival. In Ehrenwald's view, telepathy may have evolved in the human organism to bridge the communication gap that exists before the infant can speak—"a makeshift expedient hit upon by the evolutionary process to bail man out from a temporary embarrassment in the early postnatal phase." Once the child acquires language, says Ehrenwald, the lines of telepathic communication are no longer essential for survival, and the ability is either suppressed or lost.

If Ehrenwald's theory is correct, then children who remain in a close, symbiotic relationship with their mothers longer than normal because of physical or mental handicaps might demonstrate some evidence of psi. In fact, several cases have been reported in which telepathy from a mother has in fact been thought to be responsible for the behavior of a child. In one case a young boy whose vision was seriously impaired by cataracts could read the doctor's vision-testing chart only when his mother stood where she could also see the chart. In another case a retarded boy was believed to be a "lightning calculator" because he could do complicated mathematical calculations in his head. It later developed that he could perform the feats only if his mother was also doing them. In 1935 a German professor of forensic medicine, Ferdinand von Neureiter published the case of Ilga K., a nine-year-old girl who

suffered from a severe reading disability. The details are intriguing: Ilga could not read unless her mother was perusing the same material at the same time—even in a separate room. A later investigation showed that the mother's lips "were often moving simultaneously with the child's utterances." This case and others like it involve mothers who had, in Ehrenwald's words, "powerful motivation to compensate, through their own efforts, for their offsprings' disabilities: They tried to function vicariously in their behalf."

Though Ehrenwald's mother-child theory of telepathy has not been directly tested in the laboratory, it has received indirect support from work done at the University of Montana. The Montana experiments measured the physical reaction of mothers to a frightening situation encountered by their daughters. The measure of physical reaction was galvanic skin response (GSR), which is also used in lie-detector tests; it monitors subtle changes in the body's rate of perspiration, changes that are indicative of emotional response. In the Montana tests, the GSR of various mothers was recorded while their daughters—out of sight and out of earshot—encountered a frightening situation: blank cartridges were fired in front of them. The GSR of mothers whose daughters had been frightened changed more appreciably than that of a control group of mothers whose daughters were not subjected to the firing of cartridges. Here, two elements that often appear to be associated with psi—the parent-child relationship and a frightening situation—may have combined. Together they produced evidence for some degree of possible mother-child telepathy.

Twins, both identical and fraternal, represent another kind of family pairing with, many researchers

In a telepathy experiment a scuba diver off Florida transmitted sufficient information to a recipient in Zurich to cause measurable changes in blood-vessel constriction. Less successful but still intriguing have been studies of the behavior of twins: the Van Arsdales, for example, compiled remarkably similar professional basketball records.

feel, psi potential. Yet laboratory work with twin pairs has been generally as inconclusive as anecdotal accounts of twin communication have been intriguing. One of the most provocative stories involved a pair of identical twins in California. After one examination, teachers at the boys' school became worried that the boys had cheated. Their answers on a particular test were nearly identical. As a result, the boys were placed in different rooms for a second test, one dealing with Vergil's *Aeneid*. One of the twins, seated in a teacher's office, hesitated, however, and would not begin until his brother had been given his test paper. When the test was over, the papers were once again nearly identical, showing close correspondences in syntax, grammar and even mistakes. Clearly, the boys could not have communicated by normal means. Thus, the possibility of telepathic interaction seemed strong, if entirely circumstantial.

When interviewed, twins often speak of reading each other's minds or communicating in other nonverbal ways. Yet the few studies that have attempted to test for telepathic communication between twins seem to bear out the conclusions of an investigation conducted at Fordham University more than 40 years ago, one that involved six sets of twins and more than 20,000 trials. The report concluded, "On the whole, the results of these experiments are not significant. In particular, they do not show that as the test was made, any telepathic connection exists between the twins."

(continued on page 218)

Dr. Berthold Schwarz (below) believes members of his family have communicated telepathically. In an apparent mind-to-mind exchange, Dodgers Sandy Koufax and John Roseboro decided to gamble on a slow curve to Mickey Mantle.

Psi Try on *Apollo 14*

Ex-astronaut Edgar Mitchell founded an institute to study psychic phenomena.

What *Apollo 14* astronaut Edgar D. Mitchell saw as "a blue and white jewel suspended against a velvet black sky" was the planet Earth viewed from the depths of space. At the euphoric moment of that first glimpse, says Mitchell, "the presence of divinity became almost palpable and I *knew* that life in the universe was not just an accident based on random processes. This knowledge came to me directly—noetically."

Other returning astronauts have described somewhat similar sensations, but probably no space voyager before or since had been as psychologically ready as Mitchell to interpret such an experience of "instant global consciousness" in mystical terms. In the four years prior to his January 31, 1971, liftoff, for example, Mitchell had become increasingly engrossed in parapsychology. Although he later claimed that when he went to the moon, he "was as pragmatic a test pilot, engineer and scientist as any of my colleagues," it now appears Mitchell was already looking beyond conventional science, religion, and philosophy. As part of his search and without the sanction of his NASA superiors, Mitchell planned to conduct the world's first deep-space ESP experiment. He had made arrangements with four earthbound recipients so that they might attempt to receive telepathic messages—in the form of sequences of Zener symbols—transmitted by him during six of the mission's scheduled rest periods.

The conditions of the experiment began to degenerate almost at once. Liftoff was 40 minutes late, thus altering the timing of the rest periods; and during the mission, Mitchell was able to use just four of the six designated periods for his attempts at telepathic transmission. Thus the results of the experiment were reduced to a nearly meaningless jumble.

Two of the recipients, for example, logged in 51 correct answers out of 200 guesses (chance would have called for 40), but because of the skewed timing, this slightly positive result would have to be more the product of precognition than of telepathy. In all, the four recipients scored with so little success that their cumulative result was negative: 3,000 to 1 *against* what chance would have predicted. Attributing the results to psi-missing, Mitchell remained undismayed. He went on to found a center for the scientific study of psychic phenomena and to collaborate on *Psychic Exploration*, a book that included a report on his struggle to probe the unknown.

How to Test for ESP Power

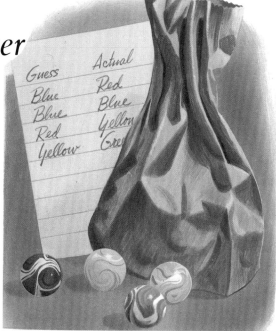

Telepathy To test for telepathy, have a friend shuffle a pack of Zener cards. Then synchronize watches, and at intervals of 30 seconds, let the friend turn over the cards, concentrate on each face, record it, then place it face down. Meanwhile, write down the order of the cards as you perceive them. Reshuffle the pack and repeat the test four more times, for a total of 125 tries. Chance should give you close to five correct answers for each run through the deck. A consistent scoring average of 6.5 cards over many hundreds of individual 25-card runs would put you in much the same telepathic category as many of J. B. Rhine's early successful test subjects.

Clairvoyance To test for clairvoyance, place 20 marbles, five each of four different colors, in a bag. Then let a friend remove the marbles from the bag one at a time, keeping each marble hidden from both of you. As each marble is removed, you guess its color and your friend records the guesses. Only after each guess should the marble be looked at and its actual color be recorded; then it should be returned to the bag. Continue the testing procedure until 20 guesses have been made. Repeat the sequence four more times, for a total of 100 guesses in all. By chance, the expected number of correct guesses is 25. But a very good score, at odds of approximately 1 in 100, would be 34.

Statistics and Psi

In the last 50 years psi research has achieved considerable respectability, and a major, if controversial, contributor to this changed status has been the use of statistics. Only by statistics can experimenters in any field gain some understanding of whether their results are really different from what would be expected to occur by the laws of chance. For parapsychologists such a measure is essential because the forces they have been attempting to quantify have proved to be so elusive.

Simple chance, though it is hardly simple, is determined by the number of possibilities available in a given situation: if you have to choose between two doors, the chances are 1 in 2 that you will choose the correct one; if you have to select among four shells, the chances are 1 in 4 that you will pick the right one. With dice, the chances are 1 in 6 that a roll of a six-sided die will turn up a given number, and with playing cards, the chances are 1 in 52 that a card slipped from a deck will match the number and suit of a card previously selected. In some of the earliest psi experiments, J. B. Rhine at Duke University used a pack of 25 Zener cards. The Zener pack was made up of five sets of five cards each, with each set bearing a separate symbol: a star, a rectangle, a circle, a cross and a trio of wavy lines. By the laws of chance, a subject could be expected to pick the appropriate card 5 times out of 25 opportunities, a mathematical extrapolation from the odds for a single trial: 1 to 5. This is not to say that the subject would pick exactly five correct cards each time; he might pick four one time and five the next, or even three on one occasion and seven on the next. But over time and most times, the number of correct guesses would average around five. This average, based on a substantial num-

Precognition To test for precognition, let a friend remove the four aces from an ordinary pack of playing cards. Then, on a sheet of paper, write down the order in which you feel the deck's remaining 48 cards will fall after a thorough shuffling. Let your friend shuffle the pack. Then let the friend turn the cards over one at a time and record the number and suit of each one next to your guesses. By chance you should expect to have one correct match. A score of two or more matches reflects chance at about 1 in 4, a level not considered to be especially significant statistically. A score of four or more correct matches becomes an intriguing precognition long shot of about 1 in 50.

---

ber of attempts, is known as chance expectation.

It is when the number of correct guesses made by a subject over an extended series of attempts, or runs, consistently exceeds or falls below chance expectation that the possibility of some undetermined outside influence is most strongly raised. And if the experiment has been designed—and executed—in a manner that excludes all other influences, then a psi factor, or possibly some other unknown, may be suspected.

Once such a deviation from chance expectation has been observed, a second difficult question must be answered: How likely is it that the observed deviation is itself the result of chance? To answer that question statisticians turn to a table of mathematical probabilities. When they find that the deviation from chance odds is outside of the range that might be expected by chance, they call the results "statistically significant." Statistical significance is a concept that is indispensable to the assessment of scientific data in many areas of research. As a method of evaluating findings, it is as useful to economic analysts as to biochemists, and it has proved to be the premier tool of parapsychologists.

Statistical significance is not the same as hard proof. Rather, it compares the score actually achieved in an experiment with the chance of achieving that or an even better score. If the chance of that or a better score is very slight, the achieved score is considered a "significant" deviation from chance. Although scientists speak informally of results being "just significant" or "highly significant," the level of significance is more usually expressed in precise mathematical terms, with the lowest acceptable limit reflecting statistical chance of 1 in 20. The scientist divides 1 by 20 to express chance as $P=0.05$, with P standing for probability. Thus when the chance of a particular result's occurring is 1 in 20, its actual occurrence is said to be significant at the 0.05 level. If the chance is 3 in 1,000, its occurrence is said to be significant at approximately the 0.003 level. The smaller the decimal figure, the greater the suspicion that the results are not simply the workings of chance.

Size of the sample, too, is taken into account in the concept of statistical significance. If, for example, in four runs through a Zener pack of 25 cards, a subject were to make 30 correct guesses, or 10 over chance expectation, that would constitute a "just significant" finding at about the 0.004 level. This means that the chance of making 30 or more correct guesses for the four runs is about 1 in 250. If, however, the same sequence of four runs were to be repeated 50 times, the chance that the subject would produce at least 30 correct guesses during one or more four-sequence runs within the total 50 increases to about 1 in 5.

Calculations of chance likelihood become even more complex when other factors, such as feedback during the testing sequence, are introduced. Obviously, if a subject learns after each call what card was, in fact, turned, his chance of success in subsequent calls can improve markedly, much as a bridge or poker player's chance of winning improves if he keeps track of which cards have been played. But odds can also be affected when cards are not revealed by telling the subject whether each call is right or wrong. The problem of calculating likelihood and statistical significance in such cases is mind boggling and explains why statistics can become the focus of much controversy even with the help of computers. Nonetheless, such calculations can be invaluable, and by using them, modern psi researchers seek to discover the truth about psi.

Margaret Mead encouraged acceptance of parapsychology by U.S. scientists.

Several investigations by parapsychologists have sought to isolate the physical properties of psi. Can it, if it exists, be blocked by concrete walls or electromagnetic shielding? It cannot, at least according to experiments carried out by Soviet and U.S. researchers. Do psi signals decrease in intensity over distance as do known forms of physical energy such as radio waves? Not if one is to believe the results of a number of experiments, including one particularly bizarre test of long-distance telepathy. In the test a percipient in Zurich, Switzerland, was monitored by a device that measured blood-vessel constriction. The sender was some 5,000 miles away, off the coast of Florida, and, extraordinarily enough, scuba diving as well. When the sender, swimming underwater, concentrated on names that were important to the percipient in Zurich, significant changes in the percipient's blood vessels were recorded.

Such has been the accumulation of laboratory work supporting the existence of psi that, before J. B. Rhine died in 1980 at the age of 84, the grand old man of parapsychology could look back with pride on a half-century of impressive results. Thousands of volunteers in millions of trials with ESP cards, random-number generators and dozens of other devices had recorded significant scores in telepathy, clairvoyance, precognition or psychokinesis. So convinced was the Parapsychological Association that in 1971 it concluded, by an overwhelming vote, that further tests designed merely to prove ESP's existence would be both boring and time-consuming. Members talked of changing the name of their profession to psychotronics or psychophysics in order to reflect either the existence of the electronic techniques that had largely replaced ESP cards or the fascination of many researchers with the world of physics. Even the American Association for the Advancement of Science had voted grudgingly—after a plea by anthropologist Margaret Mead—to grant affiliation to the Parapsychological Association. All of this was a tribute to J. B. Rhine—to his integrity, to his zeal in attempting to link psi with the scientific method, and to his efforts to free such research from what he called "its fringe of unsavory cultist associations."

Despite such progress, however, psi research remains outside the mainstream of science. Scientific journals still largely exclude psi articles from publication.

Extrasensory Success?

Alfred P. Sloan, Jr., late president of General Motors, once remarked that William C. Durant, the giant automobile company's founder, "would proceed on a course of action guided solely, as far as I could tell, by some intuitive flash of brilliance. He never felt obliged to make an engineering hunt for the facts."

Durant was far from being the only big-business man to operate on hunches. Conrad Hilton, creator of the vast Hilton Hotel empire, described his *modus operandi* this way: "I know when I have a problem and have done all I can—thinking, figuring, planning—I keep listening in a sort of inside silence 'til something clicks and I feel a right answer."

Tales of Hilton's dazzling guesswork can be matched by thousands of similar examples from every precinct of the business community. Possibly the most famous is the celebrated case of Tract 57. In 1969 two huge oil combines were competing in a sealed-bid auction to obtain drilling rights to what in the end proved to be a fabulously oil-rich four-square-mile area on the North Slope at Prudhoe Bay, Alaska. Though the site's value was as yet unknown, both groups, Mobil-Phillips-Standard of California and Amerada Hess-Getty, submitted bids of $72.1 million. Then, on the weekend before the bids were to be opened, Leon Hess got a hunch that his bid would lose. Accordingly, he revised it to $72.3 million, thus winning the prize site by a scant $200,000.

That top executives should ever permit themselves to be guided by intuition is not surprising. But to what extent might that intuition be influenced by psi? Two researchers who had a chance to find out were Douglas Dean and John Mihalasky, who, in 1962, undertook a series of studies known as the PSI Communications Project. Subjects in these studies were asked to record a 100-digit number by punching holes in computer cards. The computer then formulated another 100-digit number and compared it with the cards: by chance, 10 digits might be expected to match. More matches were considered evidence of possible psi ability. When this test was administered to business executives, Dean and Mihalasky found a correlation between possible psychic ability and business success. The test also showed that subjects who conceived of time as a dynamic, moving entity scored significantly higher than those who saw it as quiet and still. These results held true regardless of whether subjects believed in ESP, although, interestingly enough, a high proportion of the executives thought it might exist.

How significant are Dean and Mihalasky's results? Their sample was small and their statistical spreads narrow. Other forces, including subconscious associations and coincidence, must certainly be at work in businessmen's hunches. Yet the executives themselves seemed to accept the possibility of psi. As one told Dean, "I believe in ESP for one reason—because I use it."

Only a handful of universities are willing to fund psi research or to give faculty status to parapsychologists. Even Duke University withdrew its support for parapsychology after Rhine's retirement in 1965.

One reason for the continued schism is the suspicion of fraud that long has tainted psi research. Parapsychology has had its share of falsified experimental results, of course—about a dozen or so cases have been uncovered during the first half-century of modern psi research. No branch of science is immune to such fraudulent practices. Yet parapsychology, because of continuing difficulties in replication of positive results and because of the nature of the phenomena being explored, is a highly vulnerable target.

The fragility of the field's foundations was revealed again recently when doubt was cast upon a group of 40-year-old experiments that long were considered bedrock evidence for the existence of psi. In those experiments, carried out by the British pioneer in psi research, S. G. Soal, a professional photographer named Basil Shackleton achieved extraordinarily high scores in card-guessing over a two-year period beginning in 1941. Yet a painstaking computer analysis by Betty Markwick, a British researcher, turned up evidence that has discredited the experiments and, by implication, the remainder of Soal's positive results. Consciously or unconsciously, Markwick concluded, Soal manipulated the results of his epic experiments with Shackleton. Interestingly enough, Markwick reported that the inspiration to investigate Soal's work came to her in a dream, which she suspects may have involved some form of ESP.

The biggest barrier to acceptance of psi by conventional science, however, involves neither disputes over methodology nor the suspicion of fraud. It is centered instead on the very real failure of parapsychology to develop a plausible theory to account for phenomena that appear to transcend our concepts of time and space. For science requires not only facts but also a way of explaining them. Thus far, there has been no want of speculation: to explain psi, various theorists have invoked virtually every possibility, from electromagnetic fields generated by the brain to the seemingly chaotic dance of subatomic particles. Yet no researcher has come up with a coherent theoretical framework in which to fit all the fragments of psi research.

A century ago the Nobel Prize–winning physiologist Charles Richet said of the evidence for precognition, "I will not say that it is possible. I will only say that it is true." Modern parapsychologists believe they have proved the existence of psi beyond reasonable doubt. Yet unless such researchers can experimentally demonstrate psi on demand, they must at least develop a plausible theory of psi operations. Until then, the field is likely to remain, as one critic put it, "a no-man's land between the lunatic fringe on the one hand and the academically unorthodox on the other."

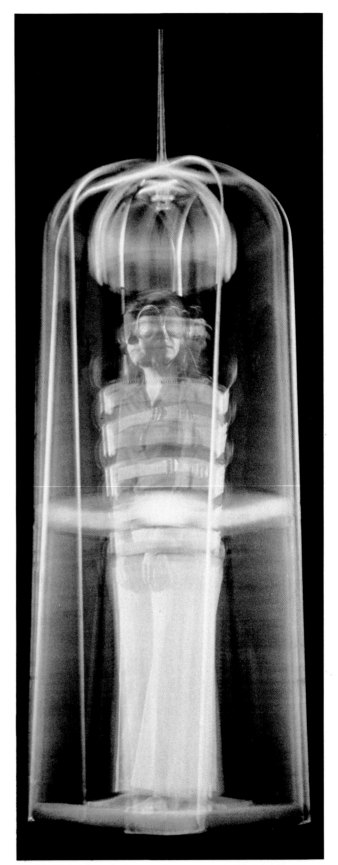

Researchers have used a modern version of a "witches' cradle" to disorient subjects in an effort to determine if, in such a state, they might be more receptive to ESP communication.

The Frustrating Case of Psychics and Crime

Psychic solves murder that baffled cops. Those who are skeptical are quick to suggest that the affinity of famous psychics for criminology may have more to do with showmanship than psi, but practitioners of the art insist that the dark passions involved in the commission of crimes—especially crimes of violence—create exactly the kind of intense signals easiest to detect by extrasensory means.

Though it ought to be easy to evaluate the claims of psychic detectives on the basis of their actual performance, as with most things having to do with the paranormal, it is not. One problem is that records, where not actually falsified, are often muddled, distorted or incomplete, and their meaning is in almost every case open to interpretation. For example, it is popularly held that in 1888 a famous London medium named Robert James Lees led police to the house of a well-known physician who was in reality Jack the Ripper. After damning evidence was discovered in the house, Lees's story goes, the doctor was secretly arrested, adjudged insane by a specially formed commission on lunacy and anonymously committed to an asylum for the remainder of his days. In fact, the London police claim never to have made any arrest, and at one point the head of Scotland Yard's Criminal Investigation Division not only named the leading suspects in the Ripper investigation but indicated that the prime suspect had been a lawyer. Yet until the Yard's files on the case are made public in 1992, Lees's story cannot be judged.

Better documented, but still far from satisfying, is the case of August Drost, a psychic active in efforts to solve a number of criminal cases in Germany in the early 1920s. Most of the surviving evidence on Drost, however, comes from the records of his own trial: in 1925 he was arrested on charges of defrauding the victims of crimes by offering them psychic assistance for a fee. The prosecution's case foundered on the unwillingness of witnesses to testify against Drost—most said he had helped them. If their testimony is to be believed, some of Drost's psychic sleuthing was astonishingly effective, but official corroboration is lacking.

The detective feats—and failures—of two Dutch psychics who gained fame in Europe in the decades following World War II are better documented. Peter Hurkos's crime-solving career began in 1946 when he reportedly correctly informed the police in the town of Limburg of the whereabouts of a piece of evidence needed to complete a case against a suspected murderer. A few years later he is said to have correctly identified an arsonist by selecting a picture from a batch of more

The psychic powers of the late Gerard Croiset (above) were closely studied by Dutch parapsychologist W.H.C. Tenhaeff. Although Tenhaeff found Croiset's abilities to be remarkable, subsequent investigators remained unconvinced.

than 500 of local youths, most of whom had no police record. But when Hurkos went to the United States in 1959 to investigate a multiple murder committed in Virginia, he identified the wrong man.

One of the best-known cases involving Hurkos's famous compatriot the late Gerard Croiset indicates how tales of psychic detection become muddled in the retelling. On the evening of December 5, 1946, in the village of Wierden, the Netherlands, a 21-year-old woman was attacked by a hammer-wielding assailant. Though injured, she managed to wrench the hammer from her attacker's hands, whereupon he fled. She never saw his face, and there were no witnesses.

According to a reporter for a U.S. magazine, Jack Harrison Pollack, the Wierden police contacted Prof. W.H.C. Tenhaeff, former director of the Parapsychology Institute at the University of Utrecht, who then brought in Croiset. Since the young woman was said to be in the hospital, Croiset decided not to interview her. Instead, picking up the hammer, he concentrated on it for a moment and then told the police that the man they sought was tall, dark, about 30, and had a deformed left ear (Pollack called this the "key clue" in the case). Several months later, when police arrested

Psychic Peter Hurkos is shown below at the site of the brutal 1969 murder of actress Sharon Tate. Hurkos's contributions to the case, as in other cases in which he claimed an important role, were later minimized by investigating police officers.

Housewife Dorothy Allison has allegedly helped trace more than 26 missing people and six murderers. Many of her visions, however, are too enigmatic to be useful.

just such a man on a morals charge, he confessed to being the hammer-wielding attacker.

In 1961, however, C.E.M. Hansel wrote to the police of Wierden asking them to confirm the details of this story. The police forwarded the letter to the town's mayor. According to him, and contrary to Pollack's account, the Wierden police called neither Tenhaeff nor Croiset (Croiset, who lived less than 17 miles away, had been brought in by an elderly landlord). Furthermore, the young woman had been at home, not in the hospital, and nothing whatever was found to be the matter with the ears of the man who was arrested.

Dorothy Allison's rise to fame began in December 1967, when the housewife from Nutley, New Jersey, told police that she had dreamed that she saw the body of a small boy wedged in a drainpipe. He was dressed in green, she said; his shoes were on the wrong feet; and in the background were a gray wall, a building with gold lettering on it, and the number eight. Two months later the police discovered the body of five-year-old Michael Kurcsics in a drainpipe in Clifton, New Jersey. He was dressed in a green snowsuit; his sneakers were on the wrong feet, and nearby were a gray building, a factory with gold lettering on the door and the P.S. 8 elementary school.

According to *People* magazine, which ran a profile of Allison in 1979, she subsequently provided psychic assistance in locating 26 missing persons and solving six murder cases. So impressed with her abilities was Nutley police detective Salvatore Lubertazzi that he volunteered to become Allison's liaison with police all over the nation. He admits, however, that her pronouncements are often so obscure that they cannot be readily interpreted. As one police officer who worked with Allison said of her allegedly psychic descriptions, "She said a whole lot of things, a whole lot of opinions, partial information and descriptions. She said a lot. If you say enough, there's got to be something that fits." Lubertazzi himself says, "Sometimes it gets very frustrating."

Frustrating is a word that the subject of psychic crime-solving brings readily to mind. The technique seems to have been effective in some cases, yet even its most apparent successes are hedged with doubts and unanswered questions. For one thing, as most psychics are willing to admit, their methods of sleuthing are subject to errors of interpretation, either by the psychic himself or by his auditors, which is why testimony based on alleged psychic knowledge is barred from U.S. courts and almost all others around the world. And even before a criminal case comes to trial, it is possible that a psychic's advice might actually impede the investigation of a crime by sending police off on a wild-goose chase. Finally, and most seriously, psychic investigation poses something of a threat to innocent people whose reputations and freedom might be jeopardized by a psychic's misunderstood—or mistaken—observations.

The sleeping mind, especially during dreams,
may be uniquely receptive to messages that challenge
the boundaries of time and space.

POWER OF DREAMS

To Sugar Ray Robinson, the dream that awakened him just before his 1947 welterweight title fight with Jimmy Doyle seemed a clear and terrifying warning. "Doyle was in the ring with me," Robinson recalled in his autobiography. "I hit him a few good punches and he was on his back, his blank eyes staring up at me, and I was staring down at him, not knowing what to do, and the referee was moving in to count to ten and Doyle still wasn't moving a muscle and in the crowd I could hear people yelling, 'He's dead, he's dead.'"

Distressed by the dream, Robinson told his trainer George Gainford and promoter Larry Atkins that he wanted to call off the bout. Both men told him that he was being foolish. "Don't be ridiculous," said Atkins, "dreams don't come true. If they did I'd be a millionaire." Robinson persisted until a hastily summoned priest persuaded him to go ahead with the fight.

Champion and challenger slugged it out for seven rounds that night before Robinson saw his opening. Then in the eighth, he dazed Doyle with a double right to the belly and head and then floored him with a left hook to the jaw. Doyle toppled like a falling tree, striking the back of his head on the floor. Robinson

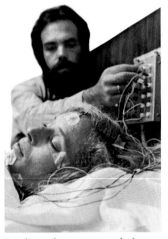

Modern dream research began with the discovery of rapid eye movement during sleep.

stood over him and stared down as he had in the dream. Doyle's hand fluttered toward an unreachable rope at the count of four, but after that he was still. He died the next afternoon.

Stories like this one have been part of popular folklore since time immemorial. Yet they are only one aspect of that disoriented theater of the sleeping mind in which, nightly, the dreamer is at once both observer and actor. Heavily influenced by memory, dreams are plainly much more than memory, for they regularly deal with events that have not happened, in places that are not real. Dependent on imagination, dreams are yet far more vivid, emotionally intense and uncontrolled than any waking fantasy. And though dreams are not like everyday reality, they often seem strangely real and tangible.

Small wonder, then, that people have persistently felt that dreams could be understood as messages. But messages from where? From ourselves? From other minds? From the gods? From the dead? And, perhaps most importantly of all, from whatever source, how best might such messages be interpreted?

The richly documented phenomenon of the "creative" dream illustrates the mystery that even today surrounds the sources of dreams. The lore of dreaming is replete with examples of poets dreaming verses, writers conjuring up plots, musicians discerning melodies and scientists discovering truths that had eluded them during their waking labors. The result, apparently a

The haunting images of dreams, as fleeting as the fantasy forms in a Chagall painting, may express deep-seated wishes and fears and may play a role in ESP communication.

223

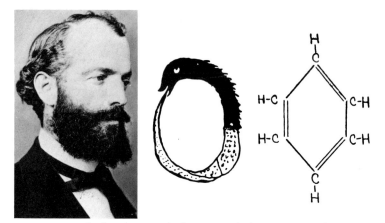

Friedrich August Kekulé perceived the structure of the benzene ring after dreaming of a snake biting its own tail.

kind of synthesis of thought and unconscious reverie, has often been a gloriously original burst of creativity.

The great English poet Samuel Taylor Coleridge dozed off one afternoon after taking opium as a sedative. The last words he read before he fell asleep were: "Here the Khan Kubla commanded a palace to be built." Coleridge awoke three hours later with some 200 to 300 lines of poetry in his head. The poetic images appeared to him "as *things*," he wrote, "without any sensation or consciousness of effort." Quickly he penned the majestic opening lines of "Kubla Khan":

> In Xanadu did Kubla Khan
> A stately pleasure-dome decree:
> Where Alph, the sacred river, ran
> Through caverns measureless to man
> Down to a sunless sea.

Coleridge had written 54 lines when he was interrupted by a visitor. Returning to work an hour later, he found that his original inspiration had vanished "like the images on the surface of a stream." He wrote no more. His masterpiece was finished.

A creative dream experienced by the 18th-century Italian composer Giuseppe Tartini refutes the notion that the opium and not Coleridge deserved the credit for "Kubla Khan." Tartini dreamed that he made a Faustian compact with the devil and then handed Satan his violin. "How great was my astonishment," he wrote, "when I heard him play with consummate skill a sonata of such exquisite beauty as surpassed the boldest flights of my imagination." When he awoke, he grabbed his violin and "tried to retain the sounds I had heard. But it was in vain. The piece I then composed, however, 'The Devil's Sonata,' [also called 'The Devil's Trill,'] was the best I ever wrote, but how far below the one I had heard in my dream!"

A dream of a snake, one of the most widely known dream symbols, helped the German chemist Friedrich August Kekulé complete a long quest to understand the molecular structure of the chemical

Tribal Magic: Dream Analysis

Though surrounded by warlike tribes in Malaysia's mountainous jungles, the Senoi people are left alone by their hostile neighbors. And for good reason: they are so peaceful that they are believed to possess protective magic. In a sense they do, in the form of a philosophy based on dreams and their interpretation. For dreams dictate the timing and conduct of every important event in Senoi life, and the interpretation of dreams is the major business of the tribe. The result, according to studies conducted by a number of researchers, is a society in which personal aggression and violence are almost unknown.

Even Senoi toddlers are encouraged to report their dreams and are instructed in the techniques of dream control, by which it is believed that the Senoi ultimately achieve their psychological and social stability. As described by Patricia Garfield in *Creative Dreaming,* these techniques focus on three principles: to "confront and conquer danger," to "advance toward pleasure" and to "achieve a positive outcome."

The first principle helps the dreamer overcome fears. For example, a child who reports a dream in which he flees in terror from a tiger is instructed to try to re-create the dream, and he is told that in the re-creation he must stand his ground and attack the tiger directly. If necessary, he may enlist the aid of dream friends, but he must never run away. Thus a child learns to transform a nightmare into a constructive lesson in self-confidence.

By accepting the second principle, the pursuit of pleasure, the dreamer can turn fearful experiences into exalted ones: the common and terrifying sensation of falling, for example, is converted by the Senoi into the liberating and expansive sensation of flying. Sexual satisfaction is specifically promoted by this rule. Because the Senoi accept the vagaries of the unconscious as natural and view dream images as aspects of the self that need to be integrated, no dream partner is unacceptable and no dream act improper.

The third principle, achieving a positive outcome, encourages the dreamer to turn adversity into advantage: if he is wounded by an enemy in his dream, he can take heart from knowing that he has used up some of the enemy's strength. Psychologists and psychiatrists still debate whether modern man might change his life style by manipulating his dreams as do the Senoi. One enthusiast, California psychologist Eric Greenleaf, has founded a dream workshop where Senoi techniques are used. Dreamers in the workshop help one another to adopt a gentle, questioning attitude in the face of frightening dreams. They are encouraged to fantasize about alarming dream figures in order to bring them into new dreams where they may be questioned further and confronted constructively. If such techniques can help people with their fears, dreams might indeed prove to be a balm to modern man.

compound benzene. The atoms, dancing in his dream, suddenly formed themselves into a snake with its tail in its mouth, and Kekulé awoke—"as if struck by lightning"—to the realization that the structure he sought was in the shape of a ring. The U.S. Assyriologist Hermann Volrath Hilprecht arrived at a similar breakthrough while he slept. Unable to identify two ancient fragments of agate that bore a peculiar inscription, he dreamed of a conversation with a Babylonian priest that provided the answer: the two fragments were part of the same piece. Hilprecht later joined them together and deciphered the inscription.

The writer Robert Louis Stevenson attributed many of his literary achievements to an active collaboration between his dreaming and waking mind. Stevenson claimed that he could dream in sequence, picking up a story where it had left off the night before, and also that he could dream stories on demand when he needed a salable work. His great tale "The Strange Case of Dr. Jekyll and Mr. Hyde" was the result of just such an opportune dream. The author wrote later that he had long been searching for a work illustrating "that strong sense of man's double being. . . . Then came one of those financial fluctuations." As if on cue, the dreaming Stevenson created the fiction, including a scene in which Hyde ingests a powder and undergoes a metamorphosis in the presence of his pursuers.

The angel of dream-borne creation, to be sure, can occasionally stray off course. A scientist seeking a title for his book on organic chemistry once excitedly awoke with the dazzling inspiration *Twelve Bedsteads in Search of an Answer*! And the philosopher William James once bolted from bed in the belief that he had solved the riddle of the universe in a rhyme he had jotted down during the night. On his note pad he found the following:

> Higamus, hogamus,
> Women are monogamous;
> Hogamus, higamus,
> Men are polygamous.

Are such dreams examples of messages sent by the dreamer to himself? That, certainly, is an explanation widely accepted today, for it is hard to imagine how stories can be written and scientific problems solved beyond the limits of the mind.

The problem of understanding dreams is, of course, greatly compounded by those dreams that appear to be prophetic. If such dreams actually do exist, it seems reasonable to consider influences outside the dreamer's own mind. One serious and well-educated man who claimed to have had many prophetic dreams was the pioneer British aviator and aeronautical engineer J. W. Dunne. Dunne was camped with his Army unit in South Africa during the Boer War when he had the dramatic dream he later recounted in a best-selling book. In the dream he was standing on a hill and gazing in horror at a volcano that appeared to be about to erupt. Vapor billowed up from the ground

"The Devil's Trill," generally considered Giuseppe Tartini's greatest work, was written after a dream in which the composer heard the devil play. Tartini's attempt to recapture the sound could not compare, he said, with the music of his dream.

around him. Dunne then saw himself at a neighboring island, pleading desperately with French officials to send ships to rescue the victims, whose number he saw as 4,000. He was still pleading when he awoke.

The next shipment of English newspapers to Dunne's outpost brought word of a catastrophe with stunning parallels to his dream. "Volcano Disaster in Martinique," a headline in the *Daily Telegraph* blared. An eruption on the French-held West Indian island, the paper said, had caused some 40,000 deaths—one zero more than the figure in Dunne's dream; the survivors, of course, were removed by ship.

Dunne, whose credibility was attested to by almost all who knew his work, related several such incidents in his book. One night he dreamed that he was near Khartoum, in the Sudan, when three raggedly dressed Englishmen appeared and announced that they had come all the way from the southern tip of Africa; next morning he read in the *Daily Telegraph* of the arrival in Khartoum of the British "Cape to Cairo" expedition. Dunne had not previously known about the expedition. In another predawn drama he saw a train that had plunged over an embankment near Forth Bridge in Scotland; this time there was a lapse of several months before a famous train called the *Flying Scotsman*

went over an embankment 15 miles from Forth Bridge.

Dunne considered the argument of some of his detractors that upon reading the newspaper accounts he somehow imagined that he had had strikingly similar dreams. He even wondered whether he had learned of the stories by telepathic communication with *Daily Telegraph* reporters. In the end, however, he concluded that while such factors might come into play, dreams could in fact be prophetic; all that was necessary, he believed, was the training of oneself to remember dreams and to keep a record of them. A series of tests was carried out to corroborate this theory, but the tests proved inconclusive.

Why dreams that appear to be prophetic should so often be the bearers of tragic tidings, particularly death, is a baffling unknown; perhaps it is because the most vividly disturbing dreams are the ones that linger longest in the memory. The 17th-century French actor Champmeslé, for example, was stunned by a dream in which he saw his dead mother beckoning to him. Instantly divining that the scene foretold his own death, he mentioned it to friends and promptly organized and paid for his own funeral Mass. At the conclusion of the Mass he walked out of the church and dropped dead.

Mothers have frequently reported receiving dream

Registry for Prophetic Dreams

To cope with the greatest frustration of any investigator of prophetic dreams—that they prove to be so only in retrospect—Robert Nelson established his Central Premonition Registry in 1968. He spread word of its address—Box 482, Times Square Station, New York, New York 10036—in newspaper articles and through television appearances in which he invited anyone who believed that he had had a prophetic dream to send a detailed description to the registry. Nelson promised to catalog and file the dream descriptions he received and to search daily for any correlation linking the dreams with news events.

To date, the registry has received descriptions of about 8,000 dreams, and of these, Nelson has found 48 that bear a recognizable and detailed similarity to events that occurred after a particular dream had been registered with him. One example of such a hit was recorded by an Ohio woman who dreamed of the crash of a light plane at an airport near her home. In her dream the plane appeared to be damaged, possibly from hitting another plane or a pole. It "turned left and crashed into a hill near the river," she reported. About nine days after this dream had been recorded, newspapers carried the story of the death of a local attorney in a very similar crash. A propeller was bent when the plane "began to dip to the left," and "hit the top of a floodwall alongside the airport." The dreamer had envisioned "three like soldiers crawling on the ground." In fact, three of the four people in the plane survived.

Surprisingly, nearly half of the registry's hits have

been dreamed and reported by just six people. Two of these "heavy hitters" have each recorded five dreams that seemed to anticipate events.

To keep track of the descriptions he receives, Nelson records them on cards and then files them, along with the dreamer's original letter, under one of 14 headings. The categories include such listings as politics, natural disasters, prominent persons and crime. Each day Nelson and any volunteers he can find comb newspaper and television reports and compare them with the mass of recorded dream information stored in the registry files.

How is a prophetic dream to be recognized by the dreamer? Some who have experienced them say that they are unmistakable, almost oppressive, in their impact and are likely to recur night after night. According to Nelson's experience, they are characterized by "strong emotional impact" and "vivid technicolor." In addition, he says, the dreamer usually feels as though he is an observer and not an active participant in the story that unfolds in the dream. Because he believes that many people have prophetic dreams and simply fail to recognize this fact or even to remember them, Nelson urges those interested to record their dreams on a daily basis. The best technique, he feels, is to quickly outline the dream upon awakening and then to go back and fill in as many additional details as possible. Within each dream's myriad of detail, Nelson firmly believes, there may well be a segment that will reflect future time and events.

Dreams of disaster seem to overshadow all other precognitive dreams. Shakespeare wrote of the dreams that haunted Richard III (left) on the night before he died in battle and of Calpurnia's dream of the death of her husband, Julius Caesar (right). Hitler (above, left, right-hand figure), while on the front in World War I, is said to have dreamed that his position would be buried and to have moved away in time to escape. The death of Archduke Francis Ferdinand, shown above an hour before his assassination, had been foreshadowed in a dream by his tutor. Abraham Lincoln dreamed of seeing his coffin just days before he died.

messages from sick or dying children. Mrs. Morris Griffith of Bangor, North Wales, told the British Society of Psychical Research about one such dream in 1884. Thirteen years earlier, she said, she awoke with a start from a dream in which her son, then in southern Africa, appeared to be emaciated and gravely ill. Several times she heard him calling out to her.

"I felt greatly depressed all through the next day," she went on, "but I did not mention it to my husband, as he was an invalid, and I feared to disturb him. . . . Strange to say, he also suffered from intense low spirits all day, and we were both unable to take dinner, he rising from the table saying, 'I don't care what it costs, I must have the boy back.'" On the following day they received a letter from their son reporting that he was much improved after a recent bout with fever. Yet two months later came another letter with the sorrowful news that he had died on the same night that his mother had seen him in her dream.

Tales of dream-borne messages have often served to dramatize the turning points of war. Legend tells that Hannibal anticipated a military victory in his dream, but King Richard III of England was plagued by "horrible images" before his defeat and death at Bosworth Field. Napoleon is said to have dreamed of a black cat running from one Army to the other and of the rout of his troops just before the Battle of Waterloo. Some researchers might explain such dreams as projections of the commanders' waking fears in their sleeping minds; the conscious brain, they suggest, might have perceived the clues, but the dreaming mind assimilated them.

Dreams of future assassinations are more difficult to account for. Abraham Lincoln dreamed of his death only a few days before John Wilkes Booth murdered him. As Lincoln described the dream to his wife, he was walking through the White House and heard weeping. When he reached the East Room, he saw a body laid out on a catafalque, surrounded by mourners and a detachment of soldiers. Lincoln asked one of the soldiers who the dead man was. "The President," came the reply. "He was killed by an assassin."

The assassination of Archduke Francis Ferdinand of Austria-Hungary, which began World War I, was foreseen in a similarly prophetic dream. Bishop Joseph Lanyi, the archduke's tutor, dreamed that Francis Ferdinand was shot to death while riding in a car in Sarajevo. The alarmed Lanyi recorded details of the dream and attempted to warn the archduke, but that same day he received a telegram reporting the murder as he had pictured it.

A legend concerning Adolf Hitler tells how, as a young corporal in the front lines of the Bavarian Army, he was awakened by a dream in which he saw himself buried by mounds of earth and molten iron. Hitler moved away from the spot where he had been sleeping and advanced uneasily into the no man's land between the opposing Armies. Suddenly there was a loud explosion several yards away. Scampering back to shelter, Hitler beheld a large crater where he had been asleep. The men who had slept beside him were buried under an avalanche of dirt.

Is it possible that the contents of dreams such as those of Lincoln, Lanyi and Hitler could have come from a source outside their own imaginations? The Egyptians never doubted it. An Egyptian papyrus dream book that was used some 1,350 years before Christ attempted to explain the good and bad messages that dreams could hold. A dream about sawing wood, the papyrus said, foretold an enemy's death, while a vision of one's teeth falling out meant that the dreamer's relatives were plotting to kill him.

The Greeks, too, sought messages in their dreams. An ancient Greek with a physical or spiritual malady was directed to one of the numerous "incubation temples," where he would fast, make offerings and hear the instructions of priests before falling asleep to await the dream that would suggest a remedy. Philosophers such as Heraclitus and Plato even anticipated Viennese psychoanalyst Sigmund Freud by suggesting that a sleeper retreats into a world of his own private creation. As Plato wrote, "There exists in every one of us, even in some reputed most respectable, a terrible, fierce, and lawless brood of desires which it seems are revealed in our sleep."

Nonetheless, the ancients continued to seek in their dreams messages from outside themselves. One of the best and most successful ancient interpreters of these messages was Artemidorus, a Greek soothsayer who plied his trade in the 2nd century A.D. Artemidorus assured loyal readers of his dream books that he was a dedicated student of their reveries. "I have done no other by day and night but meditate and spend my spirit in the judgment and interpretation of dreams," he averred solemnly. Even Freud would eventually concede that Artemidorus was, in fact, a skillful dream analyst. The old soothsayer recognized that dreams were supremely individualistic, varied and complicated, "for our spirits and our nature are fertile, and recreate and sport themselves in variety." To make his interpretations, he studied the dreamer as well as the dream, inquiring in great detail into his condition, occupation and background.

Artemidorus divided dreams into two classes, those that were the product of ordinary workaday life and those that pertained to the future. As an example of the latter, he told of a person who dreamed that he was having his head shaved: "In general a bad dream, because it signifies the same thing that nudity does, and indeed foretells sudden and dire misfortune. To sailors it clearly portends shipwreck, and to the sick a most critical collapse, but not death. . . . In addition, to have one's scalp scratched signifies a cancellation of interest in the case of a debtor, but for others it means a loss through those by whom they have been scratched. . . . For we say that a man has been scalped if he has suffered a loss and been deceived by another person."

In one form or another, Artemidorus' books on dreams were preserved for well over 1,000 years, and they continued to be published and consulted even while rationalists scorned the notion that there could be any meaning in dreams.

From the Renaissance to the 19th century, the elite decried dreams as the province of the incorrigibly

Tradition holds that Buddha was conceived when Queen Maya dreamed of a white elephant descending from Heaven, as portrayed in this 10th-century Chinese painting.

Mohammed, who experienced vivid dreams and visions, is shown in an Iranian work (above, right) ascending to Heaven.

Constantine I is said to have received reassurance from Christ in a dream, as depicted in the Renaissance work at right.

Joseph reveals that the Pharaoh's dreams portend seven fat and seven lean years, in a painting by Raphael (below, right).

In Jacob's dream, as shown in William Blake's painting, Jacob saw angels ascending and descending a ladder to Heaven.

superstitious—"the children of an idle brain," as Shakespeare described them in *Romeo and Juliet,* "begot of nothing but vain fantasy." And like unfashionable beliefs in every age, the idea that dreams carried important messages, from somewhere and to someone, went underground. During the centuries of skepticism, however, believers in country towns and back streets kept Artemidorus in print: his work was published in Greek in 1518, in Latin in 1539, in French in 1546, and finally, in 1644, in the first of 24 English editions to appear during the next 96 years. The penny press responded to the obvious demand with a spate of imitations bearing titles such as *The Old Egyptian Fortune-Teller's Last Legacy* and *Mother Bridget's Dream Book and Oracle of Fate.* But to the degree that dreams were discussed at all in polite society, their origins were dismissed, as the poet John Dryden dismissed them, as all too human:

> All dreams, as in old Galen I have read,
> Are from repletion and complexion bred,
> From rising fumes of indigested food,
> And noxious humors that infect the blood.

When science finally reinvested dream study with legitimacy in the 19th century, the most popular hypothesis was that dreams were triggered by a particular external stimulus—a barking dog, for instance, would generate a dream in which the sleeper was fleeing a pack of rabid hounds, or the smell of cologne, a dream about a perfumery. The French researcher L. F. Alfred Maury believed that he had demonstrated this principle beyond dispute, particularly after a bed board struck him on the neck while he slept, inducing—or so he believed—a dream that he was being rudely guillotined during the revolution.

But with the turn of the century, the systematic and thorough dream analyses made by Freud began to permanently alter the way people thought of their dreams as well as themselves. Drawing on his own dreams and those of his patients, Freud viewed the perplexing visions of the dreamer as "the royal road to the unconscious," a pathway to the world of long-buried impulses and conflicts lurking beneath consciousness. The strange creatures and puzzling events in our dreams, Freud argued, were symbols of desires too frightening for conscious thought; dreams were the mechanisms by which we attempted to fulfill in carefully disguised form the forbidden sexual longings of childhood.

Freud's ideas did much to revive the practice of dream interpretation and gave it scientific respectability. Like the ancients, he believed that dreams carried meaning, but he looked for that meaning in a dialogue between doctor and dream-

Freud's Dream of Irma

Sigmund Freud emphasized the importance of dreams to therapy.

In 1900, Sigmund Freud wrote to an acquaintance that he could imagine that one day the site of his dream about Irma might be marked by a monument that would read, "The Secret of Dreams was revealed to Dr. Sigm. Freud." With that dream, laid out in his monumental work *The Interpretation of Dreams,* Freud suggested to the world how dream analysis might work. The dream itself concerned a close friend and patient who had left Freud's care only partially cured. In Freud's dream he meets his patient in a great hall and tells her that it is her own fault that she is still in pain. She complains to him of her physical suffering, and when he examines her throat, he finds evidence of infection. Finally, he calls in another physician (Dr. M.). The doctors conclude that the infection was caused by a bad injection (of propionic acid), possibly given with a dirty syringe.

Freud noted that much of the dream's imagery had been stimulated by the preceding day's events. But he added, "Nevertheless, no one who . . . had knowledge of the content of the dream could guess what the dream signified. Nor do I myself know. I am puzzled by the morbid symptoms of which Irma complains in the dream, for they are not the symptoms for which I treated her. I smile at the nonsensical idea of an injection of propionic acid, and at Dr. M.'s attempt at consolation. . . . In order to learn the significance of all these details I resolve to undertake an exhaustive analysis." Thus, element by element, Freud pulled the dream apart, examining every image in an effort to discover what other thoughts it evoked. He wondered at Irma's appearance and considered Irma's stance. It reminded him of another woman he had once seen standing in a similar manner, a woman unlikely, because of her reserve, to seek his treatment. A white spot on Irma's throat reminded Freud of diphtheria, then of his anxiety at his own daughter's illness. A scab reminded him of cocaine and of being criticized for having suggested its use to a patient. He next remembered a friend who had died of cocaine abuse. After dwelling, equally thoroughly, on every other image in the dream, Freud finally gathered together its many intertwined threads. Thus he finally faced his anxiety at his failure to cure Irma and his wish to find something or someone else—another doctor, a bad injection or Irma herself—to blame for it. He concluded that "when the work of interpretation has been completed the dream can be recognized as wish fulfillment."

er, in which the dreamer was encouraged to link conscious thoughts about dreams to deeper, hidden impulses and memories. Freud, like the Greeks, thought that dreams had therapeutic value, but while the Greeks saw them as a way to physical healing, Freud used them to treat emotional disorders.

Freud's theory aspired to a comprehensive explanation of dreaming, and, as such, it was obliged to confront the question of the function, or purpose, of dreams. His explanation, of course, was that dreams were the "guardians of sleep," that the workings of the dream permitted fulfillment—in disguise—of thwarted desires, thus allowing the body to rest. Yet when later dream students discovered that dreams are apparently essential to every sleeper every night, the possibility arose that sleep was the guardian of dreams and not vice versa. Another objection to Freud's thesis was that the dreamers he analyzed were his neurotically disturbed patients, not a cross section of the populace. Yet the most persistent criticism of Freud has been directed at his contention that the content of most dreams involved disguised sexual wishes. Carl G. Jung and others, for example, asked how this might relate to an obvious sexual dream. In addition, Jung, Freud's eminent disciple-turned-critic, believed that sexuality was only one of several themes that emerged in most people's dreams, and that dreams served to reveal rather than to disguise the unconscious: "so flowerlike is [the dream] in its candor and veracity," he wrote, "that it makes us blush for the deceitfulness of our lives."

Interestingly enough, neither Freud nor Jung completely ruled out the possibility that at least some dreams might bear messages from the outside. While Freud dismissed precognitive dreams as "quite out of the question," Jung surmised that one might dream of a future event as one of a number of probabilities gleaned from conscious knowledge. Jung also wrote that telepathy "undoubtedly exists." Freud, on the other hand, said that while he had never personally experienced a telepathic dream and had never witnessed one among his patients, it might be possible that sleep created a favorable condition for telepathy and that such messages might conceivably enter a sleeper's mind. Citing the possibility of thought transference in the "communal will" of insect societies, he wondered whether telepathy might have been "the original archaic method by which individuals understood one another."

Scientific investigation of telepathy and other paranormal experiences had begun shortly before Freud started his work, with the creation of the British Society for Psychical Research in 1882. Eventually the society's researchers uncovered 149 instances in which telepathic messages seemed to have been received in dreams; more than half concerned the death of someone known to the dreamer. In order to determine whether coincidence might account for these incidents, the investigators sent out questionnaires, asking more than 5,000 people if, within the last 12 years, they had dreamed of the death of anyone they knew; the replies satisfied the society that something more than chance had been at work.

A similar technique was employed in a recent experiment at a university in Georgia. Polling 433 students, psychologist David Ryback found that 100 reported at least an occasional predictive dream, and an additional 32 reported that "they often had dreams which either corresponded to events occurring at the same time or which predicted events that occurred later." One student dreamed that he was in a bank when two armed men rushed in and robbed it. The next day, he said, he was opening a checking account at an Atlanta bank when the scene he had dreamed unfolded before his eyes.

Many psychologists and psychoanalysts have been startled to discover a striking correspondence between an incident in their lives and an occurrence in a patient's dream, suggesting that the dreamer had telepathically incorporated the analyst's thoughts in his dreams. The English analyst W. H. Gillespie told of departing from his regular route while driving to work one morning, and taking a street called Horseferry Road. On the following day a patient began to recount a dream, saying, "I was on Horseferry Road." Dr. Montague Ullman, a psychiatrist who has conducted numerous experiments in dream telepathy at a Brooklyn hospital, heard a patient describe a dream involving a chromium soap dish on the same day that the analyst had been thinking about a chromium dish sent to him by mistake.

The English dream psychologist and researcher Dr. Ann Faraday experienced a similarly mysterious phenomenon: dreaming concurrently with her husband. Faraday saw herself wandering around their bedroom and looking out a window that had somehow moved to a wall where it did not belong. When she awoke and

told her husband about it, he showed her some notes he had made about an eerily similar dream he had experienced that same night. In the husband's dream he was sleeping on the wrong side of the bed and he noticed that the window was in the wrong wall.

In the early days of dream research, it was virtually impossible to tell whether dream images might have been influenced telepathically. For example, a problem that plagued Viennese psychologist Wilfred Daim when he launched the first scientific series of dream-telepathy experiments in the late 1940s was this: even if telepathy occurred, he could never show conclusively that a dreaming subject had received a message at the moment of its transmission. Furthermore, when dreamers awoke, their memories of their dreams were often so vague as to be virtually useless. Then in 1953 a team of researchers under the direction of Dr. Nathaniel Kleitman at the University of Chicago made a major breakthrough in the study of dreams. In effect, they found that sleep consists of two distinct and alternating phases. During the first phase physical and mental activity subside. In the second phase, however, the sleeper breathes irregularly, his brain hums along as if he were awake, and beneath his closed eyelids his eyes move with extreme rapidity. When a sleeper was awakened during the first phase of sleep, he would ordinarily re-

Jung believed dreams and fantasies revealed inherently recognizable symbols.

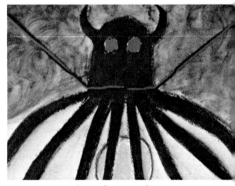

One patient drew her mother as an enormous black widow spider that had been harnessed.

As a part of Jungian therapy, patients have drawn pictures expressing their fantasies. The creator of the picture at far right saw sexual symbols in her drawing and was able to accept it only after a long struggle. The bird shown at right, drawn by another patient, was said to represent a return to the world.

The Dreaming Mind: Target for Telepathy

Is it possible that when we are asleep, when our waking minds no longer filter out disconnected and seemingly extraneous impressions and feelings, we can perceive extrasensory messages? This was a question that had haunted New York psychiatrist Montague Ullman ever since he began his practice in the 1940s. Ullman was struck by how often his patients told him of dreams that appeared to refer to incidents in his own life, incidents about which his patients seemingly could not have known. Could it be, Ullman wondered, that he was subconsciously sending telepathic messages that his patients were receiving while asleep and dreaming?

In 1953, Ullman decided to test his theory. With the help of Laura A. Dale of the American Society for Psychical Research, he embarked upon a two-year experiment in which each tried to dream telepathically of events in the life or dreams of the other. The experiment was loosely structured, yet the results persuaded Ullman that more than coincidence was at work. He strongly believed that serious investigation of dream telepathy was needed.

Fortunately, new means for conducting such investigations were already beginning to come to light. In the same year that Ullman started his first tentative dream experiments, Drs. Nathaniel Kleitman and Eugene Aserinsky of the University of Chicago announced that while monitoring brain waves with an electroencephalograph, they had discovered rapid eye movement (REM), a quick, darting movement of the eyes that pinpoints the exact times when a sleeping person is dreaming. A sleeper awakened during REM sleep will almost always report that he had been dreaming and will be able to describe his dream vividly and accurately before he forgets it.

Armed with this discovery, Ullman was able to devise a new dream-telepathy experiment. The plan was for a volunteer subject, attached by electrodes to an electroencephalograph, to go to sleep in a room in Ullman's laboratory. An observer in another room would wait until the subject showed signs of entering the dreaming state and then telephone a sender located several miles away. The sender would open an envelope and begin to concentrate on the target picture that had been sealed inside. Unfortunately, Ullman's first subject seemed never to enter the dreaming state, although she did report one dream about horses racing up a hill. Two weeks later Ullman learned that one of the target pictures, though never removed from its envelope, had been of a race of horse-drawn chariots.

In a subsequent experiment in which Ullman was acting as the sender, his mind wandered to the book *Spartacus* while he was supposed to be concentrating on a target picture. His subject later reported having dreamed of the movie *Spartacus* during the session. Though unexpected, such results seemed encouraging.

In 1962, Ullman obtained grants that enabled him to set up a full-scale dream laboratory within the Department of Psychiatry at Maimonides Medical Center in Brooklyn. Here in 1965, with the assistance of Dr. Stanley Krippner, he launched his most famous series of experiments. The series was to be judged by three professionals selected for their knowledge of parapsychology and psychology. Target pictures were chosen for "emotional intensity, vividness, color and simplicity," and 10 subjects, all with positive attitudes toward psi research, were recruited. On the nights of the experiments a sender concentrated on a randomly selected

target picture whenever the subject entered REM sleep, and after dreaming and in the morning subjects were asked what associations the dreams evoked. The judges then compared the target pictures with every image in the lengthy transcripts of dream descriptions and associations, ranking each image from 1 for greatest correspondence to 12 for least. Many of the results were inconclusive, and some indicated no trace of telepathy, but there were also some highly suggestive successes and they convinced Ullman of the reality of dream telepathy.

When, for example, a sender had concentrated on a reproduction of Millard Sheets's painting *Mystic Night,* which shows a group of women performing some esoteric nocturnal ritual among bluish-green trees and mountains, the dreamer reported successive dreams of: "being with a group of people, . . . participating in something" (dream one); "a lot of mountains and trees" (dream two); "I kept seeing blue" (dream three); "trees, again, and greenery and the country" (dream four). In the morning she said she had felt "there's some sort of primitive aspect . . . some sort of tribal ritual in the jungle."

When George Bellows's *Dempsey and Firpo,* a painting of a prizefight in New York's Madison Square Garden, was used as a target, the dreamer reported, "There's some kind of a feeling of moving . . . something about Madison Square Garden and a boxing fight." Alex Katz's *Interior of the Synagogue* elicited this

dreamer's description: "Some kind of impression of school . . . something about a synagogue." Marc Chagall's *Green Violinist* brought forth: "something to do with music"; Henri Rousseau's *Repast of the Lion:* "There were two puppies. . . . It seemed like the two of them had been sort of fighting before. You could kind of see their jaws were open and you could see their teeth."

And thus it went: among many misses, some seemingly unexplainable hits. Perhaps not everyone can receive telepathic dream messages; perhaps no one can. But Ullman's research at least created the impression that there are people who may be able to do so very well indeed.

Among Montague Ullman and Stanley Krippner's most significant Maimonides experiments were their attempts to influence dreams telepathically. As the subject slept and his REM, or dream, sleep was monitored, a sender in another room would concentrate on a painting, attempting to transmit its image to the dreamer. Among the paintings used were Sheets's *Mystic Night* (far left), Rousseau's *Repast of the Lion* (below, center) and Bellows's *Dempsey and Firpo* (below). Although the project's statistical findings were inconclusive, a few sleepers reported dreams that bore a startling resemblance to the target paintings.

port that he was not dreaming. If awakened during the rapid-eye-movement (REM) phase, however, he was usually found to have been dreaming. REM, or dream, interludes have since been found to occur about every 90 minutes during the night and to last for up to about one hour. Further experiments have produced evidence of REM sleep in newborn infants as well as in all mammals tested. Scientists also have discovered that when a sleeper is deprived of REM sleep, he spends more time dreaming on the following night, probably to compensate for lost dreams. Thus, for still unexplained reasons, dreaming seems to be as essential a function as eating and drinking.

Most important for dream researchers, however, observers now could tell precisely when a subject was dreaming. Furthermore, if the subject was awakened in the midst of a REM session, his recollection of his dream would be, in the words of pioneer REM researcher William Dement, "vivid, long, real, bizarre, and complicated—not just fragmentary images."

Thus, at a stroke, two of the central problems in dream research were solved, and the way was opened for investigation of the legendary phenomenon of dream telepathy. Quick to seize the thread of inquiry was Dr. Montague Ullman. Ullman had been trying to construct meaningful dream-telepathy experiments since the 1940s, but, as with others in the field, the results of his efforts had been more tantalizing than satisfactory. Now armed with the new knowledge brought to light by the Chicago research team, Ullman was able to embark on a series of experiments far more sophisticated than anything previously attempted.

In essence, the experiments begun in 1965 by Ullman in the dream laboratory of the Maimonides Medical Center in Brooklyn were an effort to transmit specific images telepathically into the minds of sleeping subjects. The subjects' REM sleep and electrical brain activity were monitored, and before the REM phase passed, the subject was awakened and asked to record a description of his dream. In the ter-

Diagnosis by Dream

Vasili Nikolayevich Kasatkin believes that dreams may warn of disease.

A young student was experiencing recurring nightmares that his body was immobilized by a strangling python. Finally, he became ill and sought medical help. Yet the doctor he consulted could find nothing at all wrong. Nonetheless, about a year later the student developed a serious spinal tumor that threatened to leave his body completely paralyzed. In another case, a woman dreamed over and over again of being crushed by earth until she was barely able to breathe. Two months later she was diagnosed as having tuberculosis.

For Soviet scientist and medical doctor Vasili Nikolayevich Kasatkin, these dreams were neither random coincidences nor examples of dream-sleep precognition. Instead, he believed, they were part of a significant cerebral pattern, one demonstrating the brain's ability to sense illness and to provide dream-encoded warnings long before recognizable symptoms appear. Kasatkin theorized that what he called the dream band, the brain's outer layer of active cells, registered "the minutest deviation from normal conditions" in the body. He believed that the cells of this band are acutely sensitive and, especially at night when distractions are at a minimum, might pick up minute physiological changes that would otherwise go unnoticed. It has been Kasatkin's contention that a thor-

ough understanding of and familiarity with such dreams might constitute a potentially valuable tool for diagnosis.

Kasatkin has been a professor of medical sciences for many years; he is also the author of *Theory of Dreams,* a text said to have been used in Soviet medical schools since the 1960s. Yet little is actually known about him in the West. Nonetheless, when Henry Gris and William Dick, U.S. journalists with extensive experience in the Soviet Union, set out to write a series of articles on that country's research into parapsychology, they began hearing tales of a so-called dream collector. The pair decided that such a person might provide interesting information for their study and asked the Soviet press agency to try to arrange an interview.

Gris and Dick finally met Kasatkin in early 1975. They were permitted to conduct several hours of interviews and were quickly impressed with their subject. "It was obvious," they wrote, "that Dr. Kasatkin really believed in all this, with all his heart and mind. He was devoted to his research, convinced he could help people." Kasatkin told the two journalists that he had become deeply interested in dreams when he was a young doctor during the German siege of Leningrad in World War II. People were starving, with hundreds dying each day, yet there was little he could do except listen to their anxious words. Gradually, he noticed that he could determine which of his patients were closest to death by the nature of the dreams they reported to him. "Even though everybody in Leningrad dreams of food—none of us seem to minology of the experimenters, a hit was a dream that closely corresponded to the image they had tried to transmit.

The results of these now-famous experiments are still a subject of controversy. Ullman and his research team felt that the number of hits that occurred could not be ascribed to chance. His critics rejected such an assumption, faulting some of his procedures and controls, and arguing that in many cases Ullman's interpretation of what constituted a hit had been too subjective. In any event, even accepting Ullman's procedures and interpretations, the overall ratio of hits to misses was not overwhelmingly impressive. Yet what was impressive was the uncanny accuracy of some of the hits that Ullman reported. In a few of the cases he presented, dreamers described highly complex target images in such near-perfect detail that the results seemed to defy any explanation but telepathy.

Did Ullman and his colleagues demonstrate that dreams can indeed sometimes represent messages from outside and the corollary—that human beings possess a latent ESP capacity? A majority of the heirs of Artemidorus, Freud and Jung dispute such a conclusion. Yet certainly the scientific skepticism of 50 years ago has been shaken.

And so the mystery of the essential nature of dreams abides. Abides, indeed, even if a dream is merely a message sent from the self to the self, and its subject matter deals solely with the problems and themes that dominate waking life—human relations, sexuality, security, self-esteem, illness and death. Yet if this is so, why are waking dilemmas manifested in such persistently perplexing and bizarre forms? If dreams are merely self-generated messages to ourselves, why should they be in codes that are barely decipherable?

What's in a dream? Are they real or are they fantasy? Perhaps the question should not be confined to dreams alone. As Havelock Ellis once said, "Dreams are real while they last. Can we say more of life?"

dream of anything else—some of my patients do have repeated additional, different dreams," he wrote in his notes. "I make them tell me about them. And they point to symptoms of an illness they don't actually show until a few days later." As a result, Kasatkin vowed that if he escaped the devastating siege, he would continue research into this strange phenomenon.

A nightmare of being trapped by the heat and lava of a volcano might reflect the onset of gastric disorder, says Kasatkin.

had designed had collapsed and buried him. Dreams of bodily wounds, such as repeated stabbings, might be warnings that internal organs were seriously diseased. Sometimes, Kasatkin found, dreams might be disguised; for example, a friend or acquaintance, not the dreamer, might be harmed in the nightmare. And he discovered that dreams were likely to reflect the realities of one's

Kasatkin survived and by 1975 had collected thousands of cases in which, he believed, he could detect certain predictive patterns. Dreams of breathing difficulty, he found, such as that of the woman who dreamed that her rib cage was being crushed, were warnings of lung disease, such as cancer or tuberculosis. Hypertension, in contrast, might be foretold by dreams of anxiety, such as that of an engineer who dreamed repeatedly that a building he

life—a housewife, for instance, might dream of being stabbed by a butcher knife, while a soldier might dream of a sword. Occasional nightmares, Kasatkin believed, should be ignored, but when such nightmares recur, he felt that they ought to be taken as warnings. If doctors were skilled in recognizing and interpreting such dreams, Kasatkin has contended, they might be able to detect serious illnesses at an early and treatable stage.

Kasatkin's diagnostic technique includes sketching his patients' dreams. He believes, for instance, that a dream of feeling weak as a blade slices the neck might indicate mental disorder, while a dream of a wounded torso could suggest kidney disease.

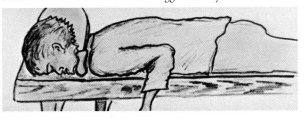

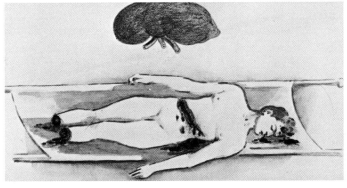

Bizarre Patterns of Coincidence

A motorcycle and an automobile collide in the town of Stourbridge, England. The cyclist is a man by the name of Frederick Chance; the driver of the car is also named Frederick Chance, no relation. Two cars bump on a road near London. Out of the first car steps Ian Purvis. Out of the second car steps another man. He too is called Ian Purvis. A Berkeley, California, woman locks herself out of her house one morning and spends a frustrating 10 minutes trying to get back in. The postman appears with a letter from her brother, who lives in Seattle. Inside the letter is a spare house key that he had borrowed and promised to return.

Coincidences are among the more delightful oddities of daily life, surprising exceptions to the normal order of things that make us wonder about the larger patterns and greater meanings of existence. Yet the standard dictionary definition of *coincidence*—"the occurrence of events that happen at the same time by accident but seem to have some connection"—hardly accounts for the awe and wonder that intricate coincidences seem to trigger. Something more than accident would seem to be operating when two Ian Purvises and two Frederick Chances collide in the same country. Consider the story told by British actor Edward H. Sothern in his book *The Melancholy Tale of "Me."* It seems that the actor's father had been given an engraved gold matchbox by the Prince of Wales but had lost it during a hunt. The elder Sothern had a duplicate made, which he subsequently gave to Edward's brother, Sam. Sam, in turn, eventually gave it to an Australian named Labertouche. One day 20 years later, when Sam was himself hunting, he was approached by an elderly farmer who had heard that Sam's name was Sothern. That same morning, it seems, one of the farmer's hands had discovered the original matchbox while plowing. So struck was Sam by this coincidence that he wrote about it to his brother, Edward, then on tour in the United States. Edward read Sam's letter on a train in which, by chance, he shared a compartment with another actor, Arthur Lawrence. When Edward told Lawrence about his brother's find, the astonished Lawrence produced the duplicate matchbox, which had been given to him several years before by Labertouche.

Perhaps no one was more interested in coincidence than the Swiss psychiatrist Carl G. Jung. Jung was fascinated by nearly every aspect of the paranormal: he studied astrology and the *I Ching,* followed J. B. Rhine's experiments with the keenest interest, and even reported personal encounters with what appeared to be spirits. For much of his life, however, Jung thought that psychic phenomena should be viewed as purely psychological manifestations, "unconscious autonomic complexes that are being projected." Yet by the time he was 72, Jung had ceased to feel that a single cause might account for the variety of apparent paranormal effects. The explanation, he felt, had to lie in something beyond what is normally defined as cause and effect. A key to defining this something, he believed, was to be found in the phenomenon of coincidence.

In 1952, with the help of Nobel Prize–winning physicist Wolfgang Pauli, Jung published a theory suggesting that an unknown principle might be responsible for what he called synchronicity, or the "simultaneous occurrence of a certain psychic state with one or more external events which appear as meaningful parallels to the momentary subjective state." Jung felt that although most people could understand cause and effect only in terms of their day-to-day experiences, it was possible that other different forms of space and time might exist. If so, he reasoned, then apparent coincidences might be related in unknown ways.

As a psychiatrist, Jung was interested in synchronicity primarily as it related to psychic states and events. As an example, he cited the case of a patient who was proving to be "psychologically inaccessible. The difficulty," he wrote, "lay in the fact that she always knew better about everything." The young woman possessed a "highly polished Cartesian rationalism with an impeccably 'geometrical' idea of reality," which kept her from acknowledging the existence of the subconscious. Jung's hope was that "something unexpected and irrational would turn up" to pierce her armor. And it did when his patient reported a dream she had had, in which she had been given a golden scarab.

"While she was still telling me this dream," Jung wrote, "I heard something behind me gently tapping on the window. . . . I turned around and saw that it was a fairly large flying insect that was knocking against the window-pane from outside in the obvious effort to get into the dark room. . . . I opened the window immediately and caught the insect in the air as it flew in. It was a scarabaeid beetle . . . whose gold-green colour most nearly resembles that of a golden scarab. I handed the beetle to my patient with the words, 'Here is your scarab.' This experience punctured the desired hole in her rationalism. . . . The treatment could now be continued with satisfactory results."

One theorist who has pursued Jung's concept of synchronicity is the British writer Arthur Koestler. In such books as *The Roots of Coincidence* and *Janus,*

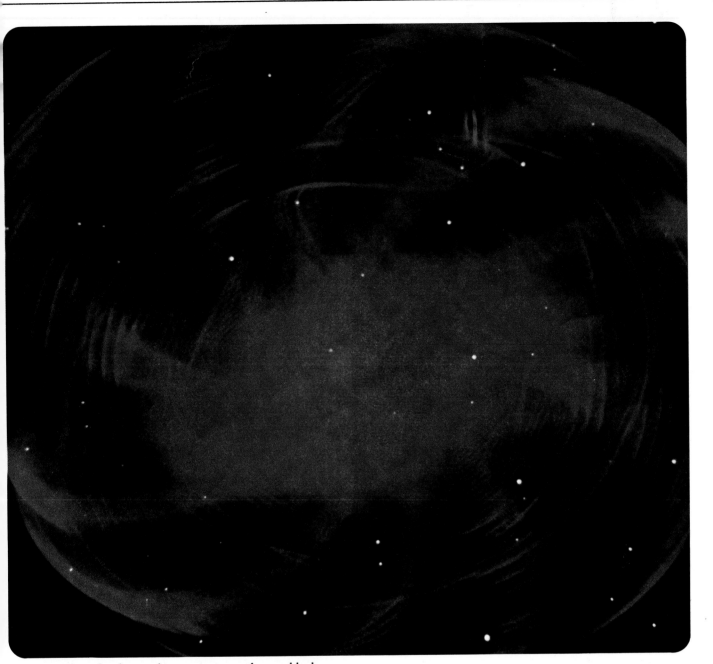

From simple day-to-day occurrences that suddenly seem to be related, to unconnected, distant events that touch as fleetingly as the light forms in the laser image above, coincidences, some theorists have suggested, challenge our most basic concepts of time and space.

Koestler surveyed the frontiers of modern scientific thought and research, and suggested that many commonly held concepts of reality are already obsolete. Time is not uniform or one-directional, he pointed out: in a black hole, for example, it can be suspended and perhaps even reversed. In addition, location, in certain situations, may be an illusion: it is in the very nature of an electron that its position *and* velocity can never be determined at the same time. And predictable effects do exist without precise causes: the laws of prob-

ability, for example, can predict with uncanny accuracy the overall result of a large number of events, each of which is in itself unpredictable.

From evidence such as this, advised Koestler, one has no choice but to infer the existence of other levels of reality. By acknowledging that such principles almost certainly exist, Koestler insisted, "we might become more receptive to phenomena around us which a one-sided emphasis on physical science has made us ignore; might feel the draught that is blowing through the chinks of the causal edifice; pay more attention to confluential events; include the paranormal phenomena in our concept of normality; and realize that we have been living in the 'Country of the Blind.'"

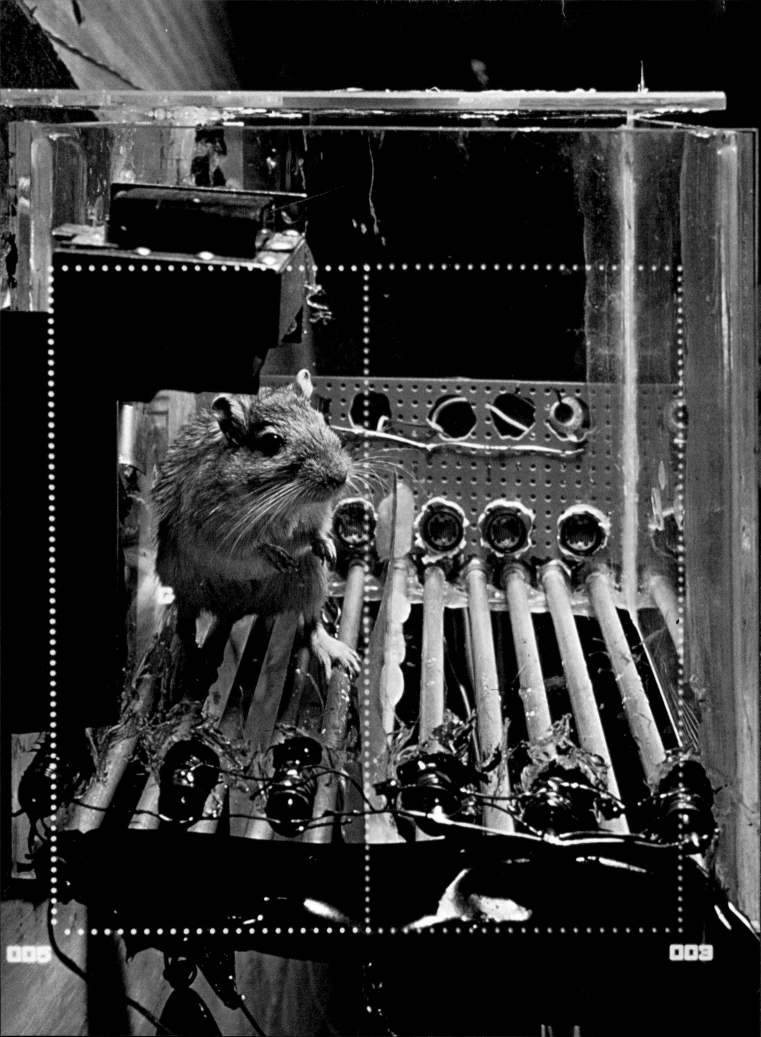

Do animals possess special powers that
enable them to sense danger, communicate telepathically
and track their masters great distances?

ANIMAL PSI

Can animals, such as this dog, said to have returned after death, express unusual powers?

The extraordinary canine journey began in August 1923. Bobbie was then two years old, a large dog, partly English sheepdog, but mostly collie. And in a small Indiana town he had become separated from his owners, who were restaurant operators on vacation from their home in the state of Oregon. At first Bobbie seemed to have difficulty in getting his bearings. He wandered in wide circles, covering perhaps 1,000 miles but progressing only about 200 miles in the direction he desperately needed to travel—to the west toward Oregon and his family. Then, late that fall, Bobbie apparently began to find his way and, incredibly enough, to move along a course that would take him home.

Westward, across Illinois and Iowa, Bobbie traveled, trapping food and cadging shelter whenever and wherever he could. Sometimes he caught and devoured squirrels and ran down rabbits. At other times friendly people took him in for a night or perhaps even longer. Once he shared mulligan stew with the inhabitants of a hobo camp. In Des Moines, Iowa, he spent Thanksgiving and several weeks that followed with a friendly family and then, as he headed west again, barely managed to escape a dogcatcher.

Inexplicable animal behavior led the Parapsychology Laboratory, then at Duke University, to test gerbils (left) and other animals for such things as precognition and clairvoyance.

During those weeks on the road Bobbie became increasingly gaunt. Yet he stopped only long enough to regain his strength before moving on, always westward. He swam rivers, including the mighty, ice-choked Missouri; in midwinter, he managed to cross the cruel and icy Rocky Mountains. Toward the end of his journey, the pads on his paws became so worn that the bones showed through. Then in February, nearly six months after he had begun his remarkable odyssey, Bobbie stumbled into an old farmhouse outside Silverton, Oregon, a house in which he had lived as a puppy with his owners. The next morning, he plodded on into town and entered the restaurant where his family now lived. There, in the family's second-floor living quarters, Bobbie's owner, Frank Brazier, lay sleeping after working the night shift in his restaurant. Bobbie's 3,000-mile journey had finally ended, and summoning a last reserve of strength, he sprang onto the bed and began licking the face of his master.

The chronicle of Bobbie's incredible journey, as impossible as it may seem, was in fact authenticated by the president of the Oregon Humane Society, who was able to reconstruct the dog's route and interview many of the people who had seen or befriended Bobbie along the way. In the end, Bobbie became one of history's most honored canine heroes, the recipient of many medals, ceremonial keys to several cities, even a gold collar. Yet though Bobbie was honored for his remarkable courage, devotion and perseverance, what is perhaps most remarkable is the fundamental question raised by his journey: How did he find his way home? He did not follow his master's east-west routes; the dog's path never approached those taken by Brazier in driving east and then returning home to Oregon. In fact, Bobbie appears to have traveled thousands of miles over terrain that he had never before seen, scented or would otherwise have had any reason to find familiar.

As a result, many of the people who have studied the story of Bobbie believe that the dog found his way home through a power or special sense unlike any of the now-recognized forms of canine perception. This mysterious animal power or sense is sometimes thought to be a type of extrasensory perception (ESP), but more often is simply called psi. Psi, the 23rd letter of the Greek alphabet, has been adopted to designate a wide range of possible paranormal abilities. Thus animal psi—anpsi, in shortened form—refers to any kind of communication between an animal and its environment, a person or another animal that seems to occur through unidentified or unexplained channels.

Stories of puzzling animal behavior that sustain to some degree the possibility of the existence of anpsi have been appearing for centuries. Such stories tell not only of remarkable homing behavior but also of other equally extraordinary feats: pets that find their masters in places where they have never before traveled; animals that predict impending danger, including natural disasters; dogs that seem to sense their own death or that of their masters hundreds of miles away.

Only in recent times, however, have scientists begun to investigate such stories and conduct laboratory experiments to determine if such a thing as anpsi might actually exist. According to an article written by the respected and cautious psychical investigator Dr. Robert L. Morris while at the University of California at Santa Barbara, this new research suggests that "psi may be present throughout much of the animal kingdom."

Some of the impetus for anpsi research stems from the ongoing effort to explore and define the possible existence of psi capacities in human beings. It has been theorized by some researchers, for example, that psi might be easier to detect in animals than in people, because even if it were to exist in humans, it might be largely suppressed by speech. Further encouragement for the exploration of anpsi has come from the discoveries, amassed by conventional science during the past several decades, of remarkable sensory capabilities in animals. Thanks in part to these studies, researchers now know that certain animals make extraordinary use of the five senses known in humans, and that some animals possess senses that humans lack completely. The bat, for example, navigates in the dark by means of echo-location, or sonar; it sends out high-pitched squeaks and listens for the echoes that reverberate from objects that are in its sonar path. Several species of fish, called knife fish, which exist in Africa, Southeast Asia and South America, generate an electric field, enabling them to detect their prey and any other creatures that may encroach upon it. Another strange sense is found in rattlesnakes and other pit vipers, which have special heat detectors situated just behind their nostrils. These detectors are so sensitive that they are capable of registering the minute changes of temperature caused by the approach of other animals. Such unusual abilities, wrote the Dutch etholo-

Sensors located behind the nostrils enable the pit viper to detect minute variations in temperature.

Many animal species depend on special senses that have been discovered only recently. In bats that sense is a form of hearing: a bat sends out sound waves that ricochet off objects and return to the bat, telling it what may lie ahead.

gist Niko Tinbergen in 1965, "are all based on processes which we did not know about—and which were thus 'extra-sensory' in this sense—only 25 years ago." By this definition, he pointed out, "extrasensory perception among living creatures may well occur widely."

The systematic study of anpsi in the United States owes much to the research and determination of the late Joseph Banks Rhine, who pioneered in the search for evidence of extrasensory perception and other psychic capacities in humans. During his tenure at Duke University's Parapsychology Laboratory, Rhine directed many investigations of animal powers and accumulated a file of 500 stories of animal behavior that might suggest the possible existence of anpsi. From his study of the collected stories, which had largely been sent to him unsolicited by people interested in his work, Rhine outlined five basic categories of animal behavior in which psychic capabilities might be considered to be at work. The cases, according to Rhine, seemed to demonstrate that animals could react in advance to a "master's return," could in some unknown way sense "impending danger," and could somehow know of the "death of the master at a distance." Animals like Bobbie, he felt, had also shown dramatic "homing behavior" and an ability to find a missing loved one even if the person was in "wholly unfamiliar territory."

One of Rhine's categories, the ability of many creatures to return home through unfamiliar territory, had long been a well-known and thought-provoking phenomenon. Homing is perhaps most familiar in pigeons that, no matter where they are released, return to their roosts after flights of hundreds and even thousands of miles. Yet Rhine's files abounded with stories of cats and dogs that found their way home without apparent help from identifiable senses.

However revolutionary the idea that such creatures might be guided by some form of ESP, there are cases that support the possibility of psychic communication between owner and animal. A series of experiments conducted in 1965 and 1966 at the Research Institute at the Rockland State Hospital in New York suggests that this possibility may be supportable. For the experiments, Dr. Aristide Esser, a psychiatrist and neurologist at Rockland, had two copper-lined chambers constructed in the hospital, chambers that screened out sound and other vibrations. For one of his most successful tests he placed two hunting dogs, both beagles, in one room; in the other, he enclosed the dogs' master. Pictures of animals were projected on a screen in the man's chamber, and he was instructed to shoot with an air gun at any that he would hunt. Esser reported that as the experiment progressed, whenever the man shot at the slides, his dogs barked and whined as they might have on a real hunt, though they could neither see nor hear their master. As a result, Esser suggested that the beagles might have been in communication with their master, perhaps through telepathy.

Other circumstantial support for the existence of unknown powers of communication in animals has come from several extensive investigations of cases in which a pet that has become separated from its owner at one location has been able to find its way to the owner at a new location. Known as psi-trailing, this is probably the most carefully documented of all anpsi categories. Rhine and his daughter Sara Feather, also a parapsychologist, have evaluated many psi-trailing cases.

When disaster is about to strike, some stories suggest, dogs bay, rats abandon buildings and zoo animals may become unmanageable, as is said to have happened in Skoplje, Yugoslavia (left), before it was leveled by a 1963 earthquake. Such behavior may be due to extraordinary animal sensitivity to natural phenomena.

Fish possess pressure-sensitive cells that enable them to detect slight movements in surrounding waters.

Pikki the Russian Mind Reader

"Suppose we have the following task: to suggest that the dog go to a table and fetch a book lying upon it. I call him and he comes. I take his head between my hands as if I am symbolically inculcating in him the thought that he is entirely in my power. . . .

"I turn the dog toward myself with an imperious gesture and look into his eyes, somewhere into his interior. . . . I mentally put before him the part of the floor leading to the table, then the legs of the table, then the tablecloth, and finally the book. The dog already begins to get nervous . . . tries to get loose. . . . I mentally give him the command, or rather the mental push: 'Go!' He tears himself away like an automaton, approaches the table, seizes the book with his teeth. The task is done."

This remarkable passage is taken from *My Quadruped and Winged Friends* by Russian circus-animal trainer Vladimir Durov, a pioneer in probing the possibility of the existence of extrasensory powers in animals. The early-1900s text is actually a description of a process repeated countless times with one of Durov's most successful pets. This animal, the best known and reportedly the most efficient in carrying out Durov's wordless commands (and later those of other experimenters), was a fox terrier named Pikki. She was characterized by Prof. Vladimir Bechterev, the neurophysiologist to whom Durov brought his dogs for testing just before World War I, as "a very lively and nimble dog." Indeed, Pikki's alleged feats had already achieved considerable notice. But it was on the strength of the dog's demonstrations in front of Bechterev and his colleagues that some Russian scientists began to wonder about a theory that Durov had entertained for years: that wordless, signless communication between humans and animals might be possible.

Seemingly totally obedient to the unspoken mandates of her master and others, including Bechterev, Pikki might deftly fetch a handkerchief from the hands of one onlooker and a glove from the knee of another, scramble up on a table, paw a portrait of an unknown person and take sheet music from a piano. All such tasks were mentally transmitted, according to Russian researchers, with great care taken to avoid any inadvertent cuing by eye movement or facial expression. On one occasion, in fact, Pikki was ordered to attack a toy stuffed wolf propped in a corner of the room; she did, with great ferocity. Later, because it was thought that Durov might have unintentionally prompted the attack by facial expression, the experiment was repeated, with Durov adopting a laughing expression in contrast to his mental command. Nonetheless, the dog attacked as before. Even when the only human in the room with Pikki had no knowledge of the instruction being contemplated, the Russians claimed, the dog still followed directions, successfully picking up paper and then running to a chair—exactly as ordered.

To do so, they used four major criteria: 1) reliability of the source of information; 2) positive identification of the animal through such characteristics as a name tag or unusual scar; 3) consistency and credibility of the details; and 4) adequacy of corroborative evidence such as testimony from additional witnesses. In all, after years of study, Rhine and Feather found no fewer than 54 cases involving dogs, cats and birds that seemed to meet the criteria that they had established.

J. B. Rhine personally investigated one intriguing psi-trailing case in 1952—a journey that would seem to be one of the longest trips on record involving a cat seeking its master. The cat was named Sugar and he had belonged to the family of Stacy Woods, a school principal in Anderson, California. When the family moved to a farm in Gage, Oklahoma, however, they reluctantly left Sugar with a neighbor because the cat became terrified when riding in automobiles. Yet about 14 months later, when Woods and his wife were milking in the barn in Oklahoma, a cat leaped from an open window and landed on Mrs. Woods's shoulder. The feline newcomer looked and acted so much like Sugar that the Woods family joked that their old cat must have made the journey all the way from California. Soon enough, however, the family decided that the cat had to be Sugar, for he had the same unusual bone deformity at his left hip joint. Only later did the Woodses learn that three weeks after they had left Sugar with their neighbors, the cat had disappeared. In the course of his research Rhine noted that the Woodses' cat was strong and vigorous, an able hunter that, according to Mr. Woods, had been known to catch half-grown jack rabbits. "Such a cat," Rhine concluded, "would be able, if any quadruped could, to make its way over the extremely rugged terrain in the fifteen hundred miles between California and Oklahoma, provided he could find the way."

But how could he find the way? And, indeed, how did an animal find the correct route in an even more unusual case, one also evaluated by Rhine and Feather? The principal in this story was a pigeon, a creature noted for its ability to home on a geographical location but not noted for its powers of psi-trailing. The pigeon in this incident did not even have a name, only the number 167 on an identifying band affixed to its leg. A young boy, Hugh Brady Perkins, had discovered the bird in his backyard in Summersville, West Virginia, in 1940 and had subsequently tamed it as a pet. The following winter the boy was driven at night to a hospital some 120 miles away for surgery. The pigeon, of course, stayed behind. Yet one snowy night while Perkins was recuperating, he heard a fluttering at the window. When a nurse opened it to humor the boy, a pigeon came in. The band on the bird's leg confirmed the boy's suspicion—it bore the number 167.

Some investigators have speculated that psi-trailing

Centuries of Clever Horses

For centuries, carnivals, circuses and open-air exhibitions have featured a menagerie of animals that allegedly communicated with people, possessed high intelligence or demonstrated psychic powers. There have been talking dogs, learned pigs, even a mind-reading goose. Yet among the most impressive of these clever animals have been several members of a species not ordinarily renowned for its intelligence—the horse.

John Bank's famous "talking" horse, Morocco, which entertained crowds in France near the end of the 16th century, may even have earned his clever master a charge of witchcraft. For the animal could, by stamping his foot, indicate the totals of a pair of dice hidden from his view—or the amount of money a spectator placed in his master's hand.

Another famous "wonder horse," Lady, performed in a red barn near Richmond, Virginia, for nearly three decades. She spelled out answers by nuzzling levers to raise the letters on a horse-sized keyboard. In the process she gave personal advice and correctly picked Harry Truman over Thomas Dewey in the 1948 Presidential election. In 1927, parapsychologists J. B. and Louisa Rhine pitched a tent next to the red barn and painstakingly studied Lady's remarkable feats. What they suspected was that Lady was telepathic and was thus receiving information and appropriate answers from her owner via extrasensory perception. Yet when the Rhines revisited the horse a few months later, they could not detect with their tests the kind of ESP powers that they had thought Lady possessed.

Did Lady, Morocco and other wonder horses exhibit psychic powers or some form of special intelligence? One answer may be found in the classic case of Clever Hans, probably the most celebrated wonder horse of all. Clever Hans, a Russian stallion, was just plain Hans in 1900 when he was discovered by a retired Berlin schoolmaster named Wilhelm von Osten. In the years that followed, Hans became the old teacher's most remarkable pupil and showed such skill in mathematics and other endeavors that Von Osten added the name *Kluge,* or Clever.

Clever Hans was trained to respond to questions by shaking his head, by nodding and by stomping his right forefoot. The number of stomps provided the answers to basic mathematical problems and even indicated what time it was. And by nuzzling alphabet blocks or by stomping

John Bank might have been labeled a witch because of his horse's uncanny powers.

Lady, the "clairvoyant" horse, tapped out special "messages" on a large keyboard.

numbers coded to letters on a blackboard, Hans was also able to spell in German. He demonstrated a schoolchild's knowledge of national events and could answer questions posed in French. Some educators classified his apparent intelligence at about the fifth-grade level.

By 1904, this odd horse had become something of a celebrity. Curious crowds packed the courtyard of the large apartment house where Von Osten lived to watch Hans's noontime performances. Among the many witnesses were psychologists, circus trainers, philosophers and other scholars. Though skeptics suspected trickery, they could find no evidence of it. In addition, Von Osten derived no financial gain from Hans's seeming genius, and he cooperated fully with a commission assembled to investigate the horse. What's more, the investigators found that Hans was able to answer questions even when his owner was absent.

It was left for Oskar Pfungst, a young psychologist from the University of Berlin, to unravel the mystery concerning Hans's seemingly extraordinary ability. First, Pfungst noted that Hans succeeded in replying to questions only when there was someone present at the demonstration who knew the correct answer.

Then, by restricting the horse's vision, the psychologist managed to show that Hans was in fact receiving information with his eyes—but how? Pfungst began studying Von Osten and others who asked questions of the horse. Gradually, Pfungst realized what was happening: questioners were cuing the horse with changes in body position. After posing a question, they would lean forward anxiously to catch Hans's response; this was the signal for the horse to begin stomping. As soon as Hans reached the correct number of thumps, the questioner would relax, however slightly and unconsciously, perhaps changing the attitude of his head or leaning back slightly. When this occurred, Hans stopped, knowing that he had satisfied his questioners.

To test his theory, Pfungst acted as a stand-in for Hans. The psychologist would ask his subjects to concentrate on a number between 1 and 100. He then slowly began tapping out an answer with his right forefinger, watching intently for changes in body position. Finally, when his questioners relaxed, he—like Hans—knew that he had arrived at the correct answer.

Extraordinary canine sensitivities may have kept Winston (above, left) rooted to the crossroads where he had last seen his master. In Italy, a dog named Fido kept a 13-year vigil for his dead master and was given a gold medal for his steadfastness by the people of his town.

somehow occurs because of bonds of affection that exist between pet and owner. In their book *The Strange World of Animals and Pets,* psi enthusiasts Vincent and Margaret Gaddis made the dramatic assertion that pets follow "a directional beam of love, a magnet of the heart." This sentimental-sounding explanation may, in reality, derive some support from the research laboratory. For example, one of the earliest investigations of psychic communication—conducted at the Parapsychology Laboratory at Duke University by Dr. Karlis Osis in the early 1950s—showed what might be considered a degree of influence engendered by affectional bonds. Osis was working at the time with kittens in a T-shaped maze, attempting to will them to turn right or left according to a random sequence. Ultimately, the researcher reported, the cats made more "correct" choices than could be attributed to chance, and he concluded that telepathy between man and cats might be the best explanation. One of Osis's most interesting findings, however, was that the animals that most often chose the direction that he wished them to take were kittens with which he had established a special rapport, and his star performer was the cat he habitually allowed to jump on his shoulder and ride around the laboratory.

The remaining three categories in Rhine's anpsi speculations involve not just special rapport with a loved one, but an even more difficult-to-imagine power—precognition, the alleged ability to perceive future events. Many pet owners may be familiar with one manifestation of such a phenomenon. Typically, a dog whose master has been away suddenly becomes excited and hurries to the front door or gate; shortly thereafter, the master unexpectedly arrives home. In her book *The Hidden Springs,* Renée Haynes told how a dachshund named Charlotte ensured that her master would have a hot meal waiting for him when he returned without

warning from a trip. The dog triggered such a hospitable welcome precisely four hours before the master's otherwise unexpected arrival: she would trot to the front gate and sit there in such obvious anticipation that the man's Chinese cook would begin preparing food.

Just as extraordinary are stories of animal behavior that appears to foretell danger. Animals have been credited with predicting—through strange and erratic behavior—earthquakes, avalanches, cyclones, even volcanic eruptions. For example, in 1963, hours before an earthquake destroyed much of Skoplje, Yugoslavia, animals at the zoo went wild, roaring, pacing their cages or charging the bars. And in parts of China, animals are considered to be potential earthquake predictors.

Yet the explanation for premonitions of natural disasters may in fact be found in an animal's special sensory apparatus rather than in some form of extrasensory perception. It has been suggested, for example, that animals may perceive the minute vibrations that precede a full-scale earthquake, or that they may detect drops in barometric pressure occurring before a hurricane. Fish, for example, are known to possess a highly delicate pressure-detection system. Known as the lateral line system, it consists of hair-like projections, each encased in a tiny, jelly-like mass. The gel is affected by the slightest vibration in the surrounding water and, in turn, triggers a reaction in the hair-like projections. Thus the fish is warned of nearby movement, including, presumably, the faintest early tremors of an earthquake.

Other instances of apparent animal precognition are perhaps more difficult to explain. During World War II, combatants in Europe sometimes watched dogs, cats and other animals for signs that a bombing raid was about to begin. During the Battle of Britain, it is said, many civilians watched for certain changes in cat behavior. When the hair stood up on a cat's back and the animal scurried for an air-raid shelter, many civilians raced there as well.

An even more bizarre type of animal early-warning system was reported by a leading German parapsychologist, Dr. Hans Bender of the Freiburg Institute of Parapsychology. The institute gathered some 500 reports of animal behavior suggesting the existence of psi activity prior to catastrophes, including one of a duck that began making an uproar in a Freiburg park just before the worst Allied bombing raid in the last days of the war. The bird renewed its alarm every 15 minutes, sending hundreds of people to safety in air-raid shelters. During the raid the duck died, but after the war when Freiburg was rebuilt, the grateful citizenry erected a monument to commemorate the bird.

More often, however, tales of seeming precognition center around a domesticated creature, particularly one with strong attachment to a single human. Author Bill Schul, in *The Psychic Power of Animals,* recalled the time when his horse stopped and refused to budge for nearly a minute just before lightning flashed into the road ahead—"at a spot where we would likely have been had she not paused." In another story, Rags, a stray dog that took up residence at Sing Sing Prison in 1929, stationed himself one night in front of the cell of a prisoner who, despondent over being turned down for a pardon, intended to hang himself with a bed sheet. Because the dog's growling threatened to alert a guard, the prisoner was forced to give up his suicidal plans. In a third case, Abraham Lincoln's dog is said to have begun howling and racing about the White House shortly before the President was assassinated.

Another strange tale of seemingly precognitive behavior reported by Schul comes from the 1940s and involves hordes of mice that inhabited a Manhattan town house. On three different occasions, so the story goes, mice were seen abandoning the town house en masse, much as rats are said to leave a sinking ship. A few days after the first exodus, the socialite who was leasing the building committed suicide. A few days after the second incident, the wealthy playboy who had moved into the house died. And finally, a few days after the third rodent exodus, the prominent businessman who had purchased the building crashed his private plane in the Hudson River and drowned.

Is it really possible that horses, dogs or rats could experience precognition? Interestingly enough, two French biologists may have found some evidence of this

ability in mice in a cleverly designed experiment that was reported in 1968. The principal researchers in the investigation gave their names as Pierre Duval and Evelyn Montredon, pseudonyms for two "university scientists who for professional reasons wished to remain anonymous." Duval and Montredon wanted to determine whether mice could foresee a relatively small impending danger—an electric shock. To do so, the scientists placed mice in a cage divided by a barrier that the animals might easily cross. Then a series of shocks was randomly delivered to one side of the cage or the other. The entire experiment was automated to avoid unintentional influence by the researchers; even the monitoring of the mice's movements was systematized with photoelectric cells, projectors and mirrors.

In their analysis of the mice's behavior, the researchers ignored all cases in which a mouse remained where it was and all those in which it jumped the barrier upon receiving a shock. In the cases that remained, the mice reportedly jumped the barrier before a shock and without other apparent explanation 53 times more than would have been expected by chance, a result deemed statistically significant by the experimenters. These findings, which suggested to the French researchers that experimental animals may possess some form of precognitive powers, have been essentially replicated in laboratory work with, for example, rats, hamsters and gerbils.

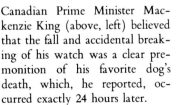

Possibly relying on special sensitivities, the cat at left reportedly tracked its owners some 100 miles. Similar unexplained sensing might have helped the collie at lower left find its owners after two changes of residence. The Labrador retriever at near left is allegedly capable of communicating telepathically with its trainer.

It is claimed that when Lord Carnarvon (below, center), sponsor of the Tut expedition, died in Cairo, his beloved dog in England died as well.

Canadian Prime Minister Mackenzie King (above, left) believed that the fall and accidental breaking of his watch was a clear premonition of his favorite dog's death, which, he reported, occurred exactly 24 hours later.

Sugar, the cat at far left, is said to have followed his owners from California to Oklahoma, while the French cat Tiki (right) is believed to have covered some 300 miles in finding its way back home after being lost.

Robert Morris (above), then at the Psychical Research Foundation, tried to measure what, if any, influence a subject's thoughts might have over a kitten's movements.

Paralleling such laboratory findings are many anecdotes sent to the Parapsychology Laboratory at Duke telling of animals that seemed to be motivated by a foreknowledge of danger to themselves. Dr. Louisa Rhine, J. B. Rhine's wife and herself a parapsychologist, has reported on one such incident, an account involving a beagle named Skippy that loved to go rabbit hunting in Wisconsin with her master, a teen-age boy. On one occasion, however, Skippy seemed to want to stay indoors and finally had to be carried out to the car for the day's hunt. Unfortunately, while dog and master were in the fields, a nearsighted hunter, seeing Skippy move and thinking she was a rabbit, shot and killed the dog.

Death has turned out to be such a common theme in anecdotal accounts of unusual animal behavior that experimenters have tried to find a link between it and precognition in the laboratory. In a study conducted by J. G. Craig and W. C. Treurniet at the University of Waterloo in Ontario, Canada, rats were released at one corner of a reference grid and their activity was monitored and recorded. Later, half of these rats were randomly selected to be killed. An analysis of the movements of the rats who died showed that they had been more active on the reference grid than those who were spared. "The imminence of death," concluded the researchers, "was somehow reflected in their behavior"—just as Skippy's uncharacteristic actions seemed to presage the dog's demise.

Yet the mysterious feeling that something may be about to go wrong can also influence a pet's master. Mackenzie King, who was prime minister of Canada for 22 years, has told of having such a premonition concerning his dog Pat. The prime minister's sense of doom was triggered by the sudden fall of a watch, a fall that left the hands stopped at 4:20. "I am not a psychic," King said later. "But I knew then, as if a voice were speaking to me, that Pat would die before another 24 hours went by." During the following night Pat crawled into his master's bed. He died there—precisely at 4:20.

A final category of behavior suggesting the possible existence of anpsi may be the most provocative of all. These are cases of animals, usually dogs, that are said to have begun to howl and behave strangely at the moment that their distant masters encountered danger or even death. In a case reported by a veterinarian, a dog that had been left with him while its owners drove to Florida howled for a full hour at exactly the time that the family was marooned in a flash flood. In another story, a family dog in New Jersey is said to have burrowed under the house and started whining and crying at precisely the time the family's older son was killed in an automobile accident many miles away. And in England during World War I, Bob, a collie, is said to have sat on his haunches and howled at what was believed to be the exact moment at which his master was killed in France.

A case that particularly baffled investigators had as its central figure an English nobleman, Lord Carnarvon, who sponsored the expedition that discovered the tomb of the ancient Egyptian ruler Tutankhamen in 1922. The workers who unearthed the tomb thought that a curse had been buried with it; and, indeed, four months after the discovery, Lord Carnarvon died in Cairo. At the moment of his death, it is said, all the lights in Cairo blinked out for no known reason. Even more puzzling is the claim that at the same instant, at Highclere, Lord Carnarvon's estate 2,000 miles away in England, his favorite dog cried out and dropped dead.

A hint that appears to bear on such phenomena came out of the work conducted in Dr. Aristide Esser's specially constructed copper-lined chambers at the Research Institute at Rockland State Hospital in New York. In one chamber Esser placed a dog, a woman's pet boxer, and monitored it with an electrocardiograph. In the other chamber he enclosed the boxer's mistress. As part of the experiment, a male co-worker surprised the woman by entering the room where she sat, shouting and making veiled threats of physical attack. The woman was understandably terrified. Infinitely more difficult to understand, however, is why her pet boxer apparently became terrified as well. Though the dog was out of sight and out of earshot of his mistress, his heartbeat shot up violently during the period that his mistress believed herself to be in danger.

Such a suggestion of possible psi communication between dog and mistress was remarkable enough. Yet Esser went on to gather evidence suggestive of psi communication between two dogs when one of the dogs was in danger. In this project a female boxer and her daughter were trained to cower at the sight of a raised, rolled-up newspaper. The two dogs were then separated and placed in the chambers. Moments later, the experimenter entered the mother's chamber and raised a rolled-up newspaper. At the sight the mother cowered—and far away in the other chamber, the daughter cowered as well. For Esser these experiments demonstrated the possibility that some form of telepathic communication might exist among dogs.

In certain extraordinary instances, however, it appears to be the human who perceives that an animal is in peril. Sylvia Fisher, a student of parapsychology in Virginia, described her sensations in such an instance: the "feeling of panic and a choking sensation" she experienced one day at the grocery store. She rushed home, arriving in time to rescue her struggling and choking dog, Ramie, whose collar was caught in a crate.

Sometimes the unaccountable conviction that a pet is in peril may appear in a dream. The English novelist Sir Henry Rider Haggard, author of *King Solomon's Mines,* told of dreaming that he was trapped inside the

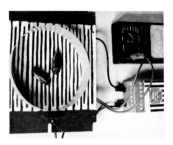

Physicist Helmut Schmidt wanted to know if cockroaches might avoid shocks by using telekinetic powers. When the insects received more than expected, it was suggested that Schmidt's thoughts might have influenced the results.

body of his daughter's black retriever, Bob. "I saw Bob lying on his side among brushwood by water," he reported to the Society for Psychical Research in London in October 1904. "My own personality in some mysterious way seemed to me to be arising from the body of the dog, which I knew quite surely to be Bob and no other, so much so that my head was against its head, which was lifted up at an unnatural angle. In my vision, the dog was trying to speak to me in words, and, failing, transmitted to my mind in an undefined fashion the knowledge that it was dying."

Four days later, Haggard found Bob's body floating in a nearby river. An investigation revealed that the dog had probably been struck by a train on a trestle bridge over the river on the night that Haggard experienced his unusual dream. Did the dog transmit in some unexplained fashion a sense of his death struggle? Did Haggard possess extrasensory powers that enabled him to sense the scene while he was asleep? Or was it all merely macabre coincidence?

Existing scientific techniques, of course, cannot fully answer such questions, raised again and again by reports of spontaneously occurring psi. At best the value of anecdotal evidence is limited. Fraud, for example,

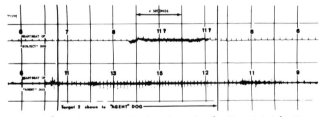

To test for psi communication in animals, Dr. Aristide Esser used the copper-lined rooms in the laboratory diagramed below. In one experiment a female boxer, or agent, was placed in an upstairs shielded chamber while her daughter, the subject, was in a downstairs room. The electrocardiogram above shows that six seconds after the mother dog's heart began racing at the sight of a raised newspaper, her daughter's heart began to pound as well.

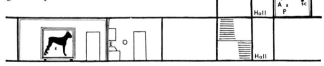

Homing In on the Mysteries of Migration

Of all the aspects of animal behavior that might be interpreted as suggesting the existence of psi, few have been more carefully scrutinized by conventional science than the ability of birds to find their way home. Every year thousands of different species, perhaps 10 billion birds in all, migrate to nesting sites after journeys of hundreds or even thousands of miles. Studies of albatrosses in the Pacific Ocean, for example, have shown that each winter, after a journey of tens of thousands of miles, the birds find their way to familiar locations, often to within a few feet of their nesting sites of the previous year.

The avian sensitivities that make migratory behavior possible, however, are still being identified by scientists. During the 1950s a major piece of the puzzle was found. In an ingenious set of experiments with starlings, the late German ornithologist Gustav Kramer showed that birds use the position of the sun as an aid in their navigations. Kramer noted that starlings in his outside aviary became restless with the onset of the migratory season, fluttering their wings as if actually flying in place on their perches and facing the direction of their normal migratory route. He then shielded the starlings from the sun and, with a mirror, reflected its rays into the cage from various other directions. The birds quickly reoriented their body axes as the reflected image of the sun moved. The experiment also indicated that starlings became confused and disoriented on overcast days. More recent work with indigo buntings has shown that they navigate by using star positions, and pigeons have been found to employ a kind of avian radar to locate the moon even during the day. Polarized and ultraviolet light, barometric pressure, odor and low-frequency sound have all been studied as possible sources of navigational clues for various birds.

Celestial navigation, it is believed, is also partly responsible for the remarkable migration of the salmon, which swims 1,000 miles or more to spawn in the stream in which it was hatched. Yet after the salmon reaches coastal waters, another sensory mechanism appears to take over. Through the sense of smell, some researchers feel, the migratory fish may finally recognize its primal stream.

What intrigues parapsychologists and other scientists, however, is how birds and other creatures determine the particular direction in which to navigate. This question is especially fascinating in relation to the extraordinary feats performed by homing pigeons. In field experiments, pigeons have been chloroformed before being transported to distant locations and have still managed to find their way home. In a few cases pigeons whose wings had been damaged have nonetheless returned home on foot.

Some researchers now believe that special sensitivity to the earth's magnetic field may account in part for the pigeon's remarkable ability to find home. This is because scientists have discovered that pigeons' heads contain magnetite, an iron oxide, which might be useful in detecting minute variations in the magnetic field. Supporting such a conclusion are studies in which the flight patterns of birds

After many years of research, no one can yet fully explain how a homing pigeon finds home. Does a pigeon scout its roost by means of physical clues, or might some form of psi capability be in operation? Tests in which a pigeon loft was moved proved to be inconclusive. The pigeons returned only to the loft's first location.

became disoriented when the birds flew through a distorted magnetic field or were shielded from all magnetic radiation.

In the absence of a complete explanation, a Duke University parapsychologist, the late J. Gaither Pratt, set out some years ago to determine if pigeons' extraordinary homing behavior might result from extrasensory capabilities. Since other theories had assumed that pigeons used their sensory apparatus to home on a fixed geographic location, Pratt decided to determine whether pigeons might home instead on a loft moved randomly to a number of locations.

With financial backing from the Office of Naval Research, Pratt set up a transportable pigeon loft in the woods of North Carolina. He planned to move it back and forth between two locations some 25 miles apart so that the birds would become accustomed to both sites without developing a strong preference for either one. Eventually, he believed, he might set the birds down midway between the two points and move their loft randomly to one or the other. If the pigeons still flew directly to their movable roost, he reasoned, it would suggest that they had located it by ESP. Unfortunately, the plan failed because the pigeons failed to cooperate. They preferred only their first environment and could not be persuaded to remain in the second even if their loft was located there.

can seldom be ruled out entirely, nor can the possibility that the details of a dramatic event may become distorted, misinterpreted or dramatized in the reports of numerous witnesses. Laboratory experiments, though they offer the opportunity for stricter controls, also present problems. Results of many anpsi experiments have been difficult to replicate. Animals, like humans undergoing tests for psi abilities, tend to perform erratically under laboratory conditions. Moreover, as in other branches of science, anpsi research has had its share of inadequately controlled experiments as well as an instance of fraud. In 1974 a researcher resigned from J. B. Rhine's Institute for Parapsychology in North Carolina after admitting to his colleagues that, feeling pressure to produce positive results, he had falsified data in tests for alleged psi capabilities in rats.

Perhaps the greatest difficulty facing anpsi laboratory research is the question of the experimenter's relationship with the animals he tests. When apparent evidence of psi shows up in an experiment, who possesses the presumed psychic power—if it exists—the animal subject or the human researcher? In the early 1970s, for example, Dr. Helmut Schmidt, a physicist and psi researcher, faced this problem while investigating psychokinesis—the alleged ability of humans or animals to affect the environment through non-physical means. Schmidt wanted to see whether cockroaches might, through psychokinesis, reduce the number of electric shocks being delivered automatically to the cage in which they were housed. The results were intriguing. Instead of receiving fewer shocks than would have been generated by the unhampered workings of the laboratory equipment, the cockroaches received significantly more. One interpretation of these results was that Schmidt, who admittedly disliked cockroaches, was affecting the shock rate through the force of his own mind. As Joseph Wylder, an author who firmly believes in anpsi, has pointed out, much laboratory research "ends with unanswered questions."

Many of the enigmas of anpsi research—the unsolved problems, the occasionally impressive but more-often contradictory results, the compelling animal anecdotes—are embodied in the story of a remarkable mongrel dog named Chris. Chris was one of history's so-called clever animals—dogs, horses, pigs and other creatures that have seemed to be endowed with intellectual as well as psychic powers. By pawing at the sleeve of his master, George Wood, a chemical engineer in Rhode Island, Chris seemed to be able to answer nearly every question put to him. The number of times he pawed his questioner's arm indicated his answers to mathematical problems. This technique also served as an alphabet code so that Chris might spell out words and sentences for his audience. It was even said that Chris could successfully predict the winners of horse races. Not surprisingly, Chris became a canine celebrity, the subject of various "interviews" in the newspapers and a popular guest on television programs and the stage.

What made Chris unique, however, was the extent to which he was painstakingly tested by psi researchers. Beginning in 1954, the dog and his master collaborated with Duke University parapsychologists in a series of tests to determine if Chris was clairvoyant—that he could perceive information without the use of the known senses. Wood taught Chris to respond to a standard ESP testing tool—a deck of 25 Zener cards, each bearing one of five symbols, such as a circle, star or cross. Chris was trained to paw once if he "thought" the next card in the deck would be a circle, twice if a cross and so on.

The results were astonishing. In the earliest experiments Chris appeared to guess the correct card nearly 75 percent of the time. And he continued to score significantly above chance even when experimental conditions were tightened, for example, when the Zener cards were placed in opaque envelopes, and when Wood took the cards to a separate room while another person recorded Chris's guesses. In one set of trials, Chris was so successful that the odds against his performance's occurring by chance were estimated at 1,000 million to 1. The only time Chris seemed to falter was when a parapsychologist from Duke, Remi Cadoret, was present as an observer. During those sessions Chris did poorly—so badly, in fact, that the results were significantly below chance. Cadoret suspected that his presence might have created stress for Chris and affected his performance, much as human psi performance appears to be influenced adversely by the pressure to match earlier successful experiments.

Though there was great temptation to conclude that Chris was indeed a clairvoyant dog, Cadoret and other Duke researchers could not be sure. For one thing, they were never able to completely rule out the possibility that George Wood, when present, or friends who worked with Chris were unconsciously communicating the correct answers by means of sensory cues—changes in facial expression, for example, or some slight movement of the hands or eyes. Significantly, however, many of the Zener-card experiments were so carefully planned that Wood and the other humans present did not actually know the order of the cards. Thus, if humans were influencing the answers that Chris gave, it would seem that they themselves must have been clairvoyant.

The truth about Chris—and about the intriguing issue of anpsi—remains a mystery. For in 1959, Chris suffered a heart attack, which curtailed his capacity to undergo ESP testing, and some years later he died. Nonetheless, the scientific examination of anpsi continues. And as the powers of animals, sensory and possibly extrasensory, are better understood, the unexplained powers of humans may be clarified as well.

Fact vs. Phenomenon

Can Humans Communicate With Plants?

Though the Scottish Highlands are filled with sites of stunning natural beauty, Findhorn is not one of them. A drab, wind-swept little town on the North Sea coast about 35 miles east of fabled Loch Ness, Findhorn had as its least attractive feature—until fairly recently—a rubbish-strewn trailer park. Yet it was to settle in precisely this unpromising spot that Peter Caddy came, in late 1962, with his wife, Eileen, three children and a family friend named Dorothy Maclean.

The little group was unlike most mobile-home itinerants. Caddy, an unemployed former hotel manager, was a devout Rosicrucian; his wife claimed to be a clairvoyant and liked to be called by her spiritual name, Elixir; and Maclean was a self-described "sensitive." All three firmly believed that they had been called to the dismal Findhorn Caravan Park for some purpose as yet unrevealed.

The following spring, Caddy, still unemployed, decided to start a garden. This seemed a formidable enterprise because of both Findhorn's chill northern climate and the sandy, apparently unfertile soil around the trailer park; but, buoyed by mystical assurances from Maclean and his wife, Caddy forged ahead. Making ingenious use of soil manipulation, mulch and natural fertilizers, he produced that year a vegetable crop that was a marvel to the locals. The crops he grew in following years astonished all Britain and became famous throughout the world. Agronomists and horticulturalists were at a loss to explain how Caddy could produce relatively enormous yields, including such prizes as 40-pound cabbages, in so bleak an environment. To Caddy the explanation was simple: he was in loving communication with the devas, the elemental spirits of the plants in his garden. "Ultimately," he says, "since it is love that fulfills all laws, it was my love for the garden that put me in tune with it." In return for this love, according to Caddy, the devas have furnished the group with a ceaseless flow of metaphysical truths, useful gardening tips and bumper harvests.

The idea that humans may be able to communicate with plants is an ancient one, extending from prehistoric fertility rituals to the modern day. The early-20th-century Indian scientist Sir Jagadis Chandra Bose believed that plants have sensory systems that are in some ways analogous to the nervous systems found in animals. Luther Burbank, one of the most famous of U.S. horticulturalists, went so far as to state that he could make a plant conform to a pattern by use of loving willpower alone. Prayer seemed the best way to influence plants to the Reverend Franklin Loehr of California, who, in the 1950s, claimed to have shown that praying over plants had increased their growth by as much as 20 percent. Though scientists scoffed, it was later discovered that a high level of carbon dioxide in exhaled breath might have aided the plants. Careful investigation of claims such as Loehr's is, however, a relatively recent phenomenon.

Among the first to attempt to measure plant sensitivity was Dr. Bernard Grad, now at McGill University in Montreal, Canada. In the mid-1960s he tested the effect of the laying on of hands of a professed psychic healer, Oskar Estebany. One test set out to measure Estebany's influence over the growth rate of sprouting barley seeds. Estebany was asked to hold and concentrate on a water-filled flask while another flask was left untouched. Then Grad, who was not told which flask was which, used the two to water two sets of seeds. The seeds were photographed as they grew, and their growth rates were compared. Amazingly enough, according to Grad, the plants that received Estebany's treated water grew at a greater rate than the others.

Polygraph expert Cleve Backster believes that lie-detector tests have indicated that some plants can read his thoughts.

Another who tried to measure plant sensitivity was polygraph expert Cleve Backster, who, in 1968, caused a minor furor when he published the results of his two-year experiment in what amounted to "plant ESP." Initially, Backster's work consisted of wiring a polygraph to the top leaves of a dragon tree, or dracaena, in order to determine whether the machine's galvanometer could measure the rate at which water rose from the plant's roots. A minute after the plant was watered, the polygraph traced a curve that, according to Backster, was "similar to a reaction pattern of a human subject experiencing an emotional stimulation of short duration." Later, when he immersed a leaf of the plant in hot coffee, Backster reported, his polygraph registered no reaction, but when he visualized burning the leaf, the needle on the chart swept upward. "Maybe plants see better *without* eyes," he surmised, "better than humans do *with* them."

Most scientists disagreed with Backster's claims, and the few who tried to replicate his work failed to do so. One who said he succeeded was Marcel Vogel, then with the IBM Advanced Systems Development Division in Los Gatos, California. But Vogel's interpretation of his results differed from Backster's. "My own view," he said, "is that human beings are the causative agency in man-plant communication by sensitizing, or 'charging,' the plant to be receptive of thoughts and emotions." Critics, however, were quick to denounce this thesis.

Not surprisingly, most scientists remain unimpressed. Yet in truth, relatively little is known about what might be called plant sensitivity, except that human concern with it will undoubtedly continue.

The Findhorn community in Scotland attributes its spectacular gardening successes to messages from devas, or plant spirits.

Luther Burbank's remarkable gift for creating new varieties of plants has been ascribed to his special rapport with them.

In psychokinesis research, investigators
are working to determine if thought processes
can influence physical objects and events.

MIND OVER MATTER

Nina Kulagina's brain waves
are monitored as she attempts
to will matches to move.

The Russian woman spreads her fingers and extends them about six inches above the object on the table before her. The object is nothing more than an ordinary box compass, and the woman, to all appearances, is a typical Leningrad housewife—an attractive woman, slightly plump and about 40 years old. Yet she is engaged in a bizarre performance, and as she stares intently at the compass, her muscles begin to tighten and deeply grooved lines of strain etch her face. In a few minutes beads of sweat moisten her brow, and then, as if in response to the woman's fierce intensity, the needle on the compass begins to quiver. The woman's hands, still hovering above the compass, start to move, tracing circular patterns in the air; the needle, in apparent defiance of the force of the earth's magnetic field, seems to respond to the movements of her hands. Soon it is spinning around the face of the compass much as a second hand moves rapidly around a clock.

This extraordinary scene, a scene that seems to defy a number of known physical laws, appears in a 1967 Russian documentary film, one of several films that chronicle the remarkable feats of Nina Serge-

yevna Kulagina. According to testimony given by Soviet scientists and certain Western parapsychologists who have witnessed Kulagina at work, she possesses an extraordinary talent—that of psychokinesis, or the control of external matter with the power of the human mind. Through such unexplained focusing and directing of mental energy, it is reported, Kulagina can perform a variety of seemingly impossible tasks: she can make matches skitter across a table, levitate a Ping-Pong ball, move a piece of bread, dislodge from a shelf a vase weighing half a pound, cause painful burns to appear on human flesh, and even stop the heartbeat of a laboratory frog. Thanks in large part to such displays by Kulagina and a number of other psychic performers, the investigation of psychokinesis has become the fastest-growing and in many ways the most fascinating, exciting, and puzzling branch of parapsychology.

In actuality, *psychokinesis,* or simply PK, is a hybrid word derived from the Greek words representing *mind* and *motion.* Even more than telepathy, clairvoyance and precognition, PK strains credulity, for unlike extrasensory perception (ESP) and its varied receptor states, PK is an outward expression of power by allegedly unexplained and invisible means. And some researchers who may in certain cases accept the possibility of extrasensory perception seem to rebel at the idea that the mind alone may effect physical change. Nonetheless, intuitive belief in some form of PK is manifest-

While magician James Randi (top, left) regularly decries the ease with which psychic effects may be faked, subjects like Ingo Swann (above, center) continue to demonstrate their alleged powers. Research techniques pit human subjects (top, right) against elaborate testing and recording devices (left).

Electric People

In 1846, when Angelique Cottin of La Perriere, France, was 14, practical control of electricity was still some 30 years in the future. Thus the sudden appearance of what seemed to be uncontrolled electrical energy in the girl was both mystifying and terrifying. For 10 weeks in all, Cottin appeared to be "charged": her touch sent heavy furniture flying across the room, those around her could not grasp any object she held, and in her presence, compasses danced madly. Sometimes the young girl's powerful seizures brought her to the edge of convulsion, and she often ran away at the first indication of an attack.

Cottin, whose case was reported by French physicist François Arago, was one of a handful of historical figures known as electric people, victims of something called "high-voltage syndrome," a condition that may be related to the alleged psychokinetic powers of certain subjects now being studied in the United States, the Soviet Union and other countries.

Joni Michell and Robert J. M. Rickard collected a number of such cases for their book *Phenomena*. One concerned Jennie Morgan of Sedalia, Missouri. Sparks allegedly flew from the girl to objects nearby; a handshake with this late-19th-century teen-ager was reportedly enough to cause, in certain cases, unconsciousness. The authors also mentioned the case of Caroline Clare of Canada, reported by the Ontario Medical Association. According to their investigation, her affliction included acute magnetization of her body—knives and forks clung to her skin. Louis Hamburger, whose case was studied by the Maryland College of Pharmacy, suffered similarly from magnetization, while whenever Frank McKinstry of Joplin, Missouri, was so careless as to stop in his tracks while "charged," so the story went, his feet would stick to the earth, and strangers had to pry them loose before he could move again.

It has long been known, of course, that humans do generate electricity. Tiny electrical charges help move signals from one cell to the next in the brain, and the electroencephalograph, which measures electrical impulses, is a common tool for measuring various kinds of activity in the brain. Massive electric shocks to the brain, in the form of electroshock therapy, are still used as treatment in certain cases involving severe mental depression, although the technique is not as yet fully understood. Near-fatal accidental doses of electric shock, as well, have produced some remarkably beneficial effects. In 1906, for example, French astronomer Camille Flammarion reported on a paralyzed man who, after being struck by lightning, "gradually and permanently recovered the use of his limbs. A weakness of the right eye also disappeared, and the invalid could write without spectacles. On the other hand, he became deaf." In another of Flammarion's cases, a woman who had been paralyzed for 38 years "recovered the use of her legs after a stroke of lightning."

ed in myriad ways by people everywhere. The golfer and bowler, for example, twist and contort their torsos after sending the ball on its way in an effort to guide it to the target; the gambler blows on his dice and implores them to fall in beneficial patterns; and the card player talks to his deck of cards. All are attempts, however whimsical, to influence the course of events through the power of the mind.

Yet historically, reports of PK incidents have been much less frequent than tales of telepathic communication and precognitive perception. Some cases of allegedly spontaneous PK have involved objects that inexplicably fell off a shelf at a moment of personal crisis or a clock that, in the words of a song, "stopped short, never to go again, when the old man died." More common occurrences have involved claims of consciously caused PK—rainmakers who asserted that they could control the moisture in the skies; the mediums of the 19th century who, in the séance room, claimed to be able to move tables and provoke various matter-altering feats. Scientists, however, have been quick to challenge such claims. English scientist Michael Faraday conducted experiments in 1853 that indicated that psychic table tipping was the result of human muscle power; the pressure of the medium's finger tips, he suggested, was sufficient to displace the weight of a table. And though Faraday was gracious enough to attribute honorable intent to the spiritualists he examined, a modern parapsychologist, Charles Honorton, has nonetheless admitted, "The history of PK, even more than that of ESP, is tainted with fraud, malobservation, and uncontrolled events occurring in suspicious circumstances."

It was to remove such taint that the 20th-century pioneer of psi research, Joseph Banks Rhine, began in 1934 to study PK under controlled laboratory conditions. The inspiration for his work came from an unlikely source: a professional gambler who, having heard of Rhine's ESP research, walked into his laboratory at Duke University one day and suggested that the scientist examine a phenomenon that the gambler had experienced at the gaming tables. When he was in a "hot" frame of mind, the young man reported, he could quite clearly influence the turn of the dice. Moments later, so the story goes, Rhine and his visitor were crouched in a corner of the laboratory, rolling dice in the name of science.

In the end, Rhine was sufficiently impressed with the stunt's results to launch a series of scientifically controlled dice-rolling experiments. As was true in his ESP experiments with specially marked Zener cards, however, Rhine did not expect to uncover evidence of what he called psychokinesis on every roll of the dice. He depended instead upon statistical evidence: the subject would make a series of 24 throws of a single die or 12 throws of a pair, attempting to turn up either a designated face or a particular combination of faces

Polish medium Stanislawa Tomczyk's apparent psychokinetic abilities were extensively investigated in the early 1900s by the German physician Baron von Schrenck-Notzing.

stance of high motivation occurred after a student at the Duke divinity school suggested a possible parallel between psychokinesis and prayer. Rhine, in turn, challenged him to a strange sort of competition, a dice-rolling contest between a team of four divinity students interested in demonstrating the power of prayer and a team of four young men noted for their success in rolling dice. Interestingly enough, the contest between these two highly motivated, if seemingly antithetical, teams ended in a virtual draw, although Rhine was clearly the experimental winner. The researcher reported that the combined scores of the two teams so exceeded chance that they were likely to occur only once in many billions of tests.

There were, however, significant problems involving these early tests. Many were too loosely controlled to meet scientific standards, sometimes with the experimenter himself serving as a subject. The tests also failed to account for the possible skill of a subject in throwing the dice or for performance anomalies that might have been caused by the dice themselves. The dice, for example, had recessed markers on them, a condition that made the faces bearing higher numbers lighter in weight and thus increased the likelihood that they might turn up with greater frequency. And when Rhine tightened experimental conditions—using precision-made dice, for example, and devising a machine to automatically pitch the dice—results tended to be less spectacular.

In any case, Rhine did not publish his dice-throwing results for nearly a decade after he had launched his PK experiments. In part, the delay was due to the highly sensational nature of psychokinesis. Already deeply engaged in controversy concerning his ESP research, Rhine was reluctant to unleash an even greater storm with his concepts of PK. In addition, Rhine must surely have been disappointed with the uneven results that he had obtained with his unusual experiments.

throughout. The total score was then compared with probability tables, which indicated what might be expected if chance alone were in operation. For example, if a subject were to roll a single die 24 times, the number six would be expected to turn up four times simply by chance. A score significantly above or below such a level might suggest the existence of an unknown factor, possibly the influence of PK.

At first, Rhine's subjects threw dice by hand or from a cup, and the results were spectacular. Scores reported in the first 562 recorded test runs reached staggering odds against chance of 1 in a billion. In addition, the best results seemed to be achieved when subjects were the most highly motivated. A prime in-

In early tests for psychokinesis, subjects tried to mentally influence the fall of dice over a large number of tries; the results were then statistically evaluated to show deviation

from chance. In later experiments, designed to counter criticism that subjects might physically influence the results, J. B. Rhine (at left, above) employed an automatic dice roller.

What finally helped trigger publication of Rhine's results was a highly fortuitous discovery by a research assistant named Betty Humphrey. In reviewing the score sheets of nine years of PK experiments, Humphrey noted an interesting statistical anomaly. Subjects had tended to score significantly better with the dice early in the experimental sequence than they had toward the end. Such a sharp drop in performance, which was similar to a decline effect noted earlier in ESP experiments, presumably reflected a decline in the subject's interest. It also suggested, in reverse fashion, that something *had* been in operation early in the tests, and the researchers felt that that something might be PK. In the PK tests, in fact, the drop-off was calculated as occurring at odds against chance of 100 million to 1.

In all, the decline effect was only one of several similarities noted between ESP findings and PK research. Both seemed subject, for example, to what is known as the sheep-goat effect (subjects, the sheep, who believe in the possibility of psi tend to produce results suggestive of psi, while the goats, who are skeptical, balk and score poorly), and both sometimes appeared to be related to unconscious functions. Certainly, both were subject to

A subject at Duke attempts to influence the fall of objects tossed by a machine.

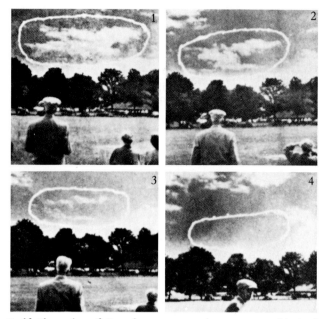

Rolf Alexander of Canada appears to demonstrate a kind of psychokinesis: his alleged ability to disperse a cloud (circled in the numbered sequence above) by concentrating on it.

similar criticisms about experimental procedure, possible recording errors and the difficulty of replication. A notable critic of parapsychology, for example, Martin Gardner, suggested in his book *In the Name of Science* that the decline effect can be explained by analyzing recording errors. He cited an error-detection experiment conducted at Yale University that showed that all recording clerks normally make a few errors but that a bias for or against parapsychology markedly affected the slant of such errors in scoring PK experiments. Gardner suggested that at the beginning of an experiment, when interest and expectations are high, the pro-psi scientist makes recording errors in favor of PK; later, however, he may become bored and make only random mistakes that do not sustain or detract from the final results. Hence, said Gardner, PK scores tend to decline as an experiment wears on.

Such criticism notwithstanding, the decline effect became the linchpin of Rhine's case for PK in the dice-rolling research, experimentation that was widely cited as the most conclusive evidence for the existence of mind over matter. Yet laboratory investigation of PK soon moved in a new direction. And at Duke, researchers began using tests in which subjects attempted to will dice to land in a particular place—at a specified spot within a checkerboard pattern, for example, or on one side or the other of a line dividing the dice table—rather than turn up specific numbers or number com-

Swedish engineer Haakon Forwald tried to prove that a subject's willpower could affect the roll of tumbling cubes.

binations. Using such tests, a Swedish engineer, Haakon Forwald, tried to measure the PK force exerted on dice-like cubes made of wood, metal or other materials. He set up a platform with a chute leading from it to a tabletop at the bottom, and he claimed to have achieved some success in influencing dice rolled down the chute to land on one side rather than the other of a line on the tabletop. In another series of tests he tried to control the movement of only a few of a number of dice rolled at once, and again he reported a degree of success. In spite of Forwald's highly positive results, however, his methods struck many parapsychologists as being fuzzy and inadequate. His results were additionally tainted by the fact that the Swedish researcher often functioned as both experimenter and subject in his work, a situation generally avoided in scientific experimentation.

In the United States, tests of alleged ability to influence movement were designed by a Duke research associate, W. E. Cox, who was a former businessman with a flair for devising experimental gadgetry. Cox came up with a variety of PK experiments, projects that employed metal balls, marbles and even electrical relays as targets for PK. In Cox's most novel experiment, his target was a spray of water. Research subjects attempted to mentally influence the deflection of water droplets from the spray into one of two tubes. According to Cox's account, they succeeded with a frequency considerably above chance expectation.

An even more ingenious experiment was reported by an English parapsychologist, Nigel Richmond, who announced that he was able to influence the movement of paramecia, tiny single-celled organisms that inhabit pond water. In his project, Richmond placed a drop of water on a microscope slide and then put a paramecium in the middle. According to Richmond, the statistical results showed that he was able to will at a substantial degree above chance the direction in which the creature would swim.

By the 1960s a number of parapsychologists felt that the possible existence of psychokinesis had been sufficiently demonstrated in the laboratory. The case for PK was statistical, of course, and the strength of the force the researchers believed they had isolated seemed to be weak and unpredictable, less convincing in fact than that reportedly involved in ESP. In addition, the experimental evidence involved only mental influence over *moving* targets. None of the PK subjects had demonstrated even the slightest statistical ability to influence a static target. J. B. Rhine, with his statistical investigation of dice rolling, had rescued the study of PK from the gloom of the séance room, but increasing-

ly during the 1970s the attention of interested parapsychologists turned from ordinary laboratory subjects to a handful of remarkable people—psychics, mediums, mystics—said to possess the power to influence static objects and materials.

One of the most successful psychics to be tested under laboratory conditions was Ingo Swann, a New York artist. At City College in New York, psychologist Gertrude Schmeidler devised an unusual experiment to test Swann's extraordinary claim that he could mentally alter the surface temperature of nearby objects. In the project, Schmeidler used what are known as thermistors, temperature-sensitive instruments that were linked to a recording device. Some thermistors were exposed; others were sealed in thermos bottles. Swann sat some distance away—anywhere from 4 to 24 feet—and, upon Schmeidler's command of "Make it hotter" or "Make it cooler," attempted to change the temperature of a given thermistor.

The results were not spectacular in layman's terms—the greatest temperature change was about 1 degree—but Schmeidler nonetheless considered them highly significant. Yet in subsequent experiments, using other subjects, no one came close to equaling Swann's performance. Interestingly enough, in several instances during the research, Swann's skin temperature actually fluctuated in correspondence with temperature changes in the target thermistor. Even more surprising was the fact that a minute change in the temperature of one target thermistor was sometimes accompanied by fluctuations in the temperature of other thermistors—in the opposite direction. This finding induced Schmeidler to make the remarkable suggestion that Swann had somehow drawn energy from his surroundings to heat the target thermistor and then had cooled it by returning that energy to its original home. Parapsychologist D.

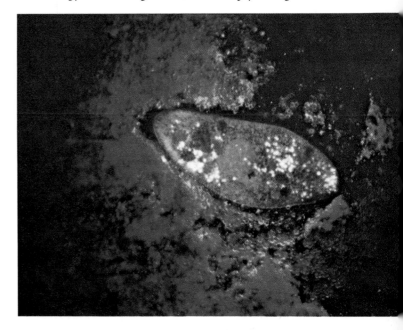

British experiments tried to determine the reaction of a paramecium like the one shown at right to human thoughts.

Scott Rogo described the process as "a sort of psychic version of robbing Peter to pay Paul."

Another psychic who announced that he could influence static materials was Ted Serios, a colorful ex-bellhop from Chicago who had a penchant for dramatics and hard drinking. Serios reported that he could imprint mental images on self-developing Polaroid film, a process that was later labeled thoughtography. Working with an early Polaroid camera, Serios did occasionally seem to succeed in producing images on the film—sometimes in the presence of serious investigators.

Dr. Jule Eisenbud, a Denver psychiatrist, studied Serios for nearly two years and reported that he could find no explanation other than psychokinesis for Serios's remarkable pictures. In a typical test, Eisenbud would select a target subject—vehicles, for example—and then Serios would go to work. While Eisenbud grasped the camera, Serios would stare intently at it, holding against the lens what he called his gizmo—a black paper cylinder about an inch in diameter—a device that Serios said helped focus his mental powers. Most of the time there would appear on the film an indistinct image of something that might resemble the target—a motorcycle, for instance, or an automobile. Eisenbud published his results in 1967 in a book called *The World of Ted Serios,* and parapsychologists at the University of Virginia soon reported a successful replication of the Serios experiments. The editor of *Psychoanalytic Review* was quoted on the dust jacket of Eisenbud's book as saying that the study of Ted Serios "represents the most significant contribution to our knowledge of mental processes since Freud's discovery of psychoanalysis."

The editors of *Popular Photography* magazine, however, were less impressed. When they sent a team of investigators—a professional magician and two photographers who were skilled in magic—to study Serios, he was unable to produce any thoughtographs. The team's suspicions focused on Serios's black gizmo. Though Eisenbud said that he had closely examined the device, the *Popular Photography* team pointed out that a specially rigged cylinder might be substituted for the first one with only a little sleight-of-hand manipulation. This special gizmo, the investigators suggested, might have hidden inside it a tiny lens and a transparency of a desired subject. Through such a lens a thoughtograph might then be projected onto the lens of the Polaroid camera. Not long after the magazine's investigation and the resulting debunking article, Serios was reported to have lost his special powers.

Better known than Serios, and even more controversial, was Uri Geller, the young Israeli showman who caused a sensation during the early 1970s with his television appearances in Europe, the United States and Japan. To the astonishment and delight of television audiences, Geller seemed able to bend or break metal with a few light strokes of his fingers and excessive mental concentration. His television performances unleashed what parapsychologists later labeled "the Geller effect." After such demonstrations television stations and newspapers were besieged by hundreds of letters and calls from viewers reporting that while Geller was bending metal on the screen, an epidemic of psychokinetic aftereffects swept their homes. Among the claims were stories of blades on kitchen knives suddenly curling and broken clocks starting to run. E. Alan Price, a South African parapsychologist who collected such tales, actually tried stroking a heavy steel key while Geller was talking on the radio. Four hours later, Price said, he discovered that the key "had bent nearly double."

Geller, who began his career as a nightclub performer in Israel, turned out to be the source of both delight and frustration for the parapsychologists who tried to investigate his apparent abilities. Good-looking, boyish and charming, he frequently beguiled scientists with impromptu demonstrations. At lunch with Gerald Feinberg, a Columbia University physicist, he casually made a fork bend, apparently using only the force of his mind. At a gathering of physicists in England, he held a Geiger counter in his hand, then appeared to trigger a sudden burst of activity in the device. At a private meeting in his New York apartment with parapsychologist W. E. Cox, Geller managed to start a pocket watch even though Cox had carefully jammed the works beforehand with a strip of aluminum foil so placed that it seemed to be impossible to dislodge. When Cox opened the watch, he found that the strip of foil had been moved. Geller's explanation of his apparent powers was as bizarre as some of the effects he produced. It was the gift, he said, of intelligent beings from "another universe."

In the scientist's laboratory, however, Geller's PK powers proved all but impossible to harness. Temperamental and given to extreme excitability, Geller as a research subject insisted on controlling the conditions of an experiment. In fact, his most notable—some say notorious—laboratory demonstration was not a test of PK at all but of another ability Geller was said to possess—clairvoyance. The experiments were conducted at Stanford Research Institute (SRI) by physicists Russell Targ and Harold Puthoff. The project was arranged in part by the man who had helped finance Geller's trip to the United States, Edgar Mitchell, the former astronaut who now heads his own organization for psi research.

According to Targ and Puthoff, Geller, while isolated in a double-steel-walled room designed to block electromagnetic radiation, succeeded in duplicating several drawings that were randomly selected by a researcher who was hidden from view in a separate room. Geller also was reported to have succeeded in 8 out of 10 attempts to guess the uppermost face of a die that was hidden inside a steel box. He had, however, opted to pass on some of the attempts. When the results of this work were published in the prestigious British science magazine *Nature,* their appearance launched fierce controversy. The magazine, in fact, included an editorial pointing out that there had been flaws in the experiment's design and saying that it had been reluctant to publish the report. Critics said the experiments were laxly controlled and surrounded by "a circus atmosphere." Much was made of the fact that Geller's U.S. sponsor, Dr. Henry Puharich, a physician and parapsychologist, was an expert in medical electronics and, indeed, had patented a radio receiver so small that it might be implanted in a tooth. Such a device, *New Scientist* critic Joseph Hanlon said, could have been used by Geller to communicate with an accomplice who might have been privy to the concealed drawings in one of the clairvoyance tests.

Geller's most outspoken debunkers, however, were U.S. professional magicians, who suggested several ways in which he could produce what seemed to be psychokinetic effects through sleight-of-hand techniques. Some parapsychologists concede that Geller did occasionally resort to trickery but they maintain that this happened only when his genuine powers failed him. In their opinion he is both psychic and showman.

What distinguishes the Russian housewife Nina Kulagina from Geller and other highly publicized psychokinetic performers is the absence of any direct evidence of sleight of hand in her work and her willingness to perform in the scientist's laboratory. Now a grandmother in her early fifties, Kulagina does not accept money for her PK work, nor does she object to being searched or X-rayed or rigged with equipment to monitor her physiological responses. Her only apparent brush

with notoriety was a short-term jail sentence that, according to differing reports, resulted from illegal black-market activity or from failure to pay a debt. Skeptics challenge Kulagina at their peril: she is said to have induced in one doubting witness the symptoms of a heart attack.

Kulagina was discovered during the 1960s by a Soviet scientist who was testing her for another psychic capacity—so-called eyeless sight, the purported ability to sense colors through the finger tips. Since then, she has been tested for PK by Soviet researchers, with her husband, an engineer, included among them, in more than 100 sessions, many of which were conducted under allegedly tightly controlled laboratory conditions. According to various Soviet accounts, she has caused objects to move toward her, away from her and in circular patterns; she has affected plastic, metal and fabric; she has altered the position of objects shielded by Plexiglas and other screening materials (though not objects placed in a vacuum); she has moved objects up to a yard away from her, though seldom in one movement. Sometimes, it has been said, objects have moved even after Kulagina stopped concentrating on them. In addition, it has been reported that the Russian woman has separated egg white from yolk in a saline solution and forced the two to drift apart. In one strange incident her hand, placed upon the arm of British researcher Benson Herbert, reportedly created intense pain and left a burn-like mark that took eight days to heal.

During a PK-testing session, Kulagina appears to work under enormous self-induced stress, an observation borne out by monitoring of her physiological state. At such times her pulse rate sometimes soars over 200 beats

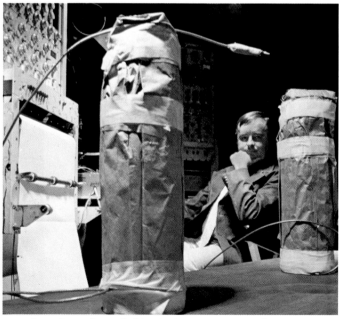

Ingo Swann's psychokinetic powers were tested in an experiment designed to determine if he could influence the temperatures of thermometers sealed inside insulated bottles.

Ted Serios claimed that he could project mental images onto film, but professional photographers pointed out that a simple, hand-held device could produce the very same effect.

per minute; brain activity at the rear of her head increases until it is four times the normal level; and, according to one report, a magnetic field surrounds her body. During a two-hour research session Kulagina may lose up to two pounds and finish exhausted, complaining of aching muscles, dizziness and insomnia.

Western parapsychologists have studied Kulagina at work, although Soviet authorities have prevented them from carrying out full-scale controlled experiments with her. Precisely what it is that may emanate from Kulagina to affect and move external matter still mystifies Westerners as well as Soviet scientists. One Soviet physicist says it is "a new and unknown form of energy." Others call it "bioenergetics" and postulate that it somehow nullifies the force of gravity. Many researchers, both Soviet and U.S., speculate that such strange energy forms, if they exist, could have strategically advantageous military applications.

Of particular interest to U.S. researchers is Kulagina's own story of how she first became aware of her strange abilities. "I was very angry and upset one day," she told two U.S. writers, Sheila Ostrander and Lynn Schroeder. "I was walking toward a cupboard in my apartment when sud-

denly a pitcher in the cupboard moved to the edge of the shelf, fell and smashed to bits." After that, Kulagina said, other objects moved about, doors opened and closed, lights went on and off—all apparently without external influence. The effects as she described them, which did not at first appear to be consciously willed, bear a remarkable resemblance to another PK-related phenomenon that has begun to intrigue psi researchers—so-called poltergeist activity.

The word *poltergeist* comes from German and means "racketing ghost" or "noisy spirit." It describes disturbances that erupt spontaneously in a household—inexplicable rapping noises, pots and pans that fly through the air, pictures that crash to the floor. Through the ages poltergeist activity usually has been attributed to the devil or some other malevolent—and noisy—spirit. Since such eruptions typically center on a single living individual, however, some parapsychologists now believe that poltergeist activity is actually an involuntary, or unconscious, form of psychokinesis.

Though the most common effects attributed to poltergeists are rapping sounds and the flinging about of household objects, other effects have been reported

that are even more bizarre. Water may suddenly and inexplicably erupt from the walls of a house, for example, or showers of stones may bombard a building on the outside and somehow pass through its walls, a highly unlikely phenomenon known as teleportation. In one incident, in a law office in Rosenheim, Germany, a small town near Munich, light bulbs reportedly rotated in their sockets, cabinet drawers opened by themselves and telephones repeatedly dialed certain numbers—without apparent human assistance. In another case, in a farmhouse near Macomb, Illinois, more than 200 fires broke out during a two-week period; after the house burned, two barns, the milk house and chicken house went up in rapid succession, leaving only six outhouses standing.

One of the world's foremost stalkers of poltergeists is William Roll, project director of the Psychical Research Foundation in Durham, North Carolina. Roll first became interested in psi phenomena after personally experiencing a number of strange incidents as a teen-ager. When he was a student at the University of

Uri Geller (left), who claimed to be able to bend metal objects by psychokinesis, demonstrated his alleged powers on television, sometimes with seemingly astonishing results. German housewife Barbara Schied (far left) was one of many viewers who said that household objects had bent mysteriously during the time that Geller's program had been on the air.

In the Soviet Union, Nina Kulagina has allegedly produced highly impressive psychokinetic effects, including the appearance of a burn-like mark on the arm of a British researcher.

California at Berkeley, for example, he awoke from a nap, got up—or thought he got up—to flip on a light and was astonished to perceive that his finger seemed to go right through the switch. Roll's first poltergeist investigation involved the celebrated case of a house in Seaford, New York, in 1958. That case, in which the family complained of strange occurrences, such as popping bottle caps, thumping sounds and flying porcelain figurines, became the basis for a television documentary.

In the Seaford case and in others personally investigated by Roll, the researcher first attempts to rule out obvious explanations. He is constantly on the alert for pets that might move objects, noisy squirrels in the attic, or sudden chimney drafts that might blow things around. Roll also looks for evidence of pranksters or fraud—strings or other mechanical devices that might explain the bizarre happenings.

Roll's investigatory adventures attest that the life of a poltergeist hunter who leaves the security of the laboratory is not an easy one. Although alleged poltergeists seldom cause bodily harm to humans, Roll has had a number of close calls. In an apartment in Newark, New Jersey, a small bottle flew off an end table and struck him on the head. In a house in Olive Hill, Kentucky, he reports, he watched as a kitchen table flew into the air, rotated 45 degrees and landed on two chairs in front of him. In his book *The Poltergeist,* Roll related the story of a strange blow that struck a policeman investigating a poltergeist case in Sicily before the turn of the century. The policeman locked his club in a bureau drawer and dared the noisy spirits to get it. Then, so the story goes, the drawer flew open, and the club began to belabor the policeman about the head.

One of Roll's most bizarre cases started late in 1966 in Miami, Florida, at the warehouse of a business known as Tropication Arts, a wholesale distributor of souvenirs and novelty items. As the sequence began, alligator ashtrays, zombie highball glasses and other wares kept turning up smashed to pieces. Finally the manager called the police and advised them that "a ghost" was wreaking havoc in his warehouse. When police arrived, they were treated to a display of flying glassware and boxes that appeared to tumble off the shelves. Television crews, reporters and insurance investigators followed and so did a professional magician who reported that he was unable to find evidence of wires, strings or other man-made devices that might account for the activities at Tropication Arts.

Roll arrived at the height of the disturbances and soon was joined by J. Gaither Pratt, an experienced Duke University psi researcher. Roll and Pratt did not actually see any objects move, but they were present during no fewer than 78 incidents of breakage. From the beginning, Roll and Pratt focused their interest on one of the warehouse's shipping clerks, Julio Vasquez, a 19-year-old Cuban refugee. The glasses and ashtrays seemed to fly about only when Vasquez was present, even though he was not in a position to manipulate them by normal means.

As a result, Roll and Pratt strongly suspected that Vasquez might be serving unwittingly as the poltergeist, projecting, without knowing it, unconscious psychokinetic energy. Certainly there was adequate evidence that Vasquez was unhappy. He had been separated from his mother and grandmother, who had remained in Cuba; he was having trouble with his stepmother; and he did not like one of his bosses at Tropication Arts. On one occasion he reported to Roll that all the breakage in the warehouse "makes me feel happy; I don't know why."

Later Vasquez agreed to undergo a series of tests at J. B. Rhine's psi laboratory in Durham, North Carolina. In dice-rolling experiments used to test for PK, the young man failed to achieve any results that could be considered statistically significant. Nonetheless, it has been reported that on several occasions the tightly fastened door on the dice-throwing mechanism popped open without apparent cause and a large vase shattered,

Muscle Over Mind

Michel Chevreul probed psychic phenomena for the French Academy of Science.

It is an experiment that anyone can attempt, and it seems at first glance to provide ample proof of the power of the mind over matter: a pendulum is held out at arm's length with arm, hand and fingers kept perfectly still. The holder then imagines a swinging pendulum. Soon enough, the pendulum being held begins to move—swinging in the imagined direction. In fact, this phenomenon is produced by imperceptible, involuntary twitches in the subject's muscles, and it was first discovered as part of an investigation of psychokinetic phenomena in the séance rooms of the 19th century.

The experiment was devised by French chemist Michel Chevreul. As one of the most brilliant scientists of his day—his accomplishments include the introduction of modern analytical techniques to organic chemistry, a remarkable analysis of the visual effects of placing colors side by side, and pioneering studies in psychology—he was invited in 1853 to be chairman of the French Academy of Science's committee to investigate psychic phenomena. It was for this committee that he performed his methodical study of the pendulum and proved that the popular divining tool was controlled not by spirits but by the muscles of the subject who was holding it.

This discovery shed light on a number of other allegedly paranormal activities. The movements of the pointer on a Ouija board, for instance, are certainly influenced by the sitters' own muscle contractions, and so, too, are the dips of the dowsing rod, though dowsing's successes remain controversial and have thus far defied full explanation. Involuntary muscle contractions undoubtedly also play a part in that most characteristic of séance activities, table tipping.

In an ingenious test of this phenomenon, British physicist Michael Faraday used a table whose top was actually composed of two boards separated by glass rollers. At an otherwise normal séance, participants sat with their hands resting on the top board while awaiting communication from the spirit world. Later, having determined that the only board to have shifted position was the top one, Faraday reasoned that the energy to move it must have come from the sitters themselves, even though they were not aware of generating it. Similar findings have been made in the analysis of modern poltergeist cases. In some instances, for example, subjects who have been seen causing poltergeist-like disturbances have, when subjected to polygraph tests, shown no awareness of their physical acts.

also without explanation. The researchers were interested as well in projective psychological tests, which were aimed at probing the subject's unconscious. The tests confirmed that, like many people who seem to be plagued by poltergeist activity, Vasquez was unhappy. A psychologist who tested Vasquez reported "many examples of aggressive feelings and impulses which are disturbing and unacceptable to him."

In fact, Vasquez seemed to fit the classic profile that emerged from Roll's investigations of poltergeist disturbances. In a review of 116 such cases that occurred during the past three centuries all over the world, Roll found that at least 32 cases clearly centered around one person and sometimes two. In the vast majority of cases, the focal person was a teen-ager, frequently one with emotional troubles. "The red thread running through most of the cases I have investigated, or am familiar with," Roll wrote, "is tension in family situations or extensions of them."

Like Julio Vasquez, many of the young people at the center of poltergeist disturbances seem to be seething with internal anger. Roll and other parapsychologists suggest that these angry youngsters, instead of expressing their hostility in conventional ways, vent it through psychokinesis. They postulate that PK acts as a safety valve for pent-up psychic energy and thus provides a means of expressing hostility without guilt or the threat of punishment. In support of their theory, researchers point out that the antics of the poltergeist—pounding on the wall, throwing things—resemble the behavior of an angry child. And on certain occasions, the nature of poltergeist damage seems to point directly at conflict between parent and child. In one home, for example, the wreckage included two broken records, "My Mother" and "At Home With Me," that had belonged to the suspected child's mother.

In addition, periods of poltergeist activity often seem to coincide with visible tensions in a family and particularly with tensions surrounding the sexual transformations associated with puberty. Disturbances seem suddenly to erupt, then typically disappear in a few weeks, perhaps because the stress has been dissipated. One investigator recorded on tape the tapping and scratching noises that occurred in monthly cycles in the home of a 12-year-old girl and reported that the trouble suddenly stopped when the girl reached puberty.

If the seething unconscious is indeed responsible for poltergeist activity, the focal person, or agent, nonetheless appears to remain unaware of it. This may be true even when the agent attempts to help the poltergeist. Roll cited the case of a 13-year-old boy who seemed to be the center of a barrage of flying objects in his apartment in a public housing project in Newark, New Jersey—a case that the newspapers dubbed "the project poltergeist." When the youth was taken to Rhine's laboratory for testing, Roll studied him through

William Roll's investigation of what seemed to be poltergeist activity in Miami, including extensive monitoring of target areas and objects, yielded no evidence of tampering, though breakage (left) continued. When it was theorized that 19-year-old Julio Vasquez was involved in some way, Roll, shown in his office (below), invited Vasquez to Durham for extensive testing (below, left). Included in the examination were physical and psychological evaluations and brain-wave monitoring.

a concealed one-way mirror and saw him throw a number of objects. Yet later lie-detector tests indicated that the boy had no conscious awareness of having caused either the fraudulent events in the laboratory or the earlier disturbances in his apartment. For Roll, however, discovery of fraud in one aspect of a case does not necessarily mean that previous disturbances are also fraudulent. Roll theorizes that if spontaneously occurring PK events reduce tension in an agent—make him "feel happy," as in the case of Julio Vasquez—then the subject may attempt to augment alleged poltergeist activities by consciously imitating them.

In recent years Roll has added another element to poltergeist theory by speculating on the possible existence of a link with epilepsy. Reviewing his examination of 116 cases, he found that a disproportionate number of apparent agents suffered from symptoms similar to those of epileptics. Stress, he pointed out, appears to trigger both phenomena. (The word *epilepsy* comes from Greek and means, appropriately enough, "to be possessed by a spirit.") During an epileptic seizure, massive electrical discharges occur in the brain, and Roll, along with other investigators, theorizes that these may be transformed into another form of energy, one capable of upsetting furniture, propelling objects, setting fires and knocking on walls.

Poltergeist studies, together with research on psychic performers such as Nina Kulagina, are considered by parapsychologists to provide strong support for the existence of psychokinesis. Yet perhaps the most persuasive evidence derives from a remarkable recent development—an atomic-age updating of the PK statistical studies launched by J. B. Rhine nearly a half century ago. The new experimental procedure was devised in the late 1960s by Helmut Schmidt, a German-born physicist, while he was a senior research scientist for Boeing Aircraft. The technique is based on what one researcher has called "nature's own dice"—the random decay of radioactive particles.

Schmidt harnessed this process, which may be one of the most random events to occur in nature, in a device in which he devised a unique type of random-number generator. At the operational core of the device, which is contained in a rectangular metal box not much bigger than an unabridged dictionary, is a small amount of radioactive strontium 90. As the substance decays, subatomic particles are randomly released at the rate of about 10 per second. In Schmidt's original device each freed particle caused a high-frequency oscillating switch, moving back and forth about 1 million times per second, to stop in either of two positions. Schmidt called these two positions +1 and –1, or simply heads and tails—hence his nickname for the gadget, the "electronic coin flipper." Without outside intervention or influence, Schmidt's electronic coin flipper stopped on a purely random basis half of the time in

Psychokinesis: Sleight of Hand or Mind?

Among the most vociferous critics of parapsychology are those performers who make their living by seeming to violate the laws of nature—professional magicians. And one of the most persistent of these debunkers is magician and escape artist James (The Amazing) Randi. In the mid-1970s, Randi set out to expose what he strongly suspected was fraud in the metal-bending feats of self-proclaimed psychic Uri Geller. Randi had heard that Geller had once worked the music halls as a performer in his native Israel; in addition, Geller was reported to have once been found guilty of breach of contract for doing sleight of hand rather than the psychic feats he had promised. "If you want to catch a burglar, you go to a burglar, not to a scientist," said Randi. "If you want to catch a magician, go to a magician."

In his study, Randi videotaped most of Geller's U.S. television performances then replayed them in slow motion. On one tape he believed that he saw Geller bending and breaking a spoon that appeared to have been previously broken and then soldered together. Randi also demonstrated for reporters and television cameras several other techniques with which metal can be bent without benefit of psychokinesis. For example, a magician with strong fingers can surreptitiously bend a key during his performance by pressing it against a hard surface, such as a table or chair leg. He can then keep the curve concealed until he is ready to "will" the key to bend. The opportunity to physically bend a key without being noticed is provided by misdirection—the performer diverts audience attention from the point of action.

Another magician, Milbourne Christopher, has described how even a clever child can generate poltergeist disturbances without psychokinetic powers. In his book *ESP, Seers and Psychics,* Christopher boasted of tricking the parapsychologist and poltergeist sleuth J. Gaither Pratt by making a china figurine seem to leap from a bookcase shelf and crash eight feet away. Though Christopher did not reveal how he had effected the trick, he did point out that a schoolchild, by secretly jerking on a heavy thread or horsehair wrapped around the base of a bottle, can create the illusion of flying objects. The gullibility of witnesses, particularly those who wish to believe, can also greatly enhance the impact of such tactics.

Though common sense might suggest that physicists and other scientists trained in careful observation ought to be highly credible witnesses, magicians insist that exactly the opposite is true. "Any magician will tell you that scientists are the easiest persons in the world to fool," wrote Martin Gardner, a columnist for *Scientific American* and an amateur magician for some 50 years. Gardner is also a leading member of the Committee for the Scientific Investigation of Claims of the Paranormal, a group of skeptical magicians, scientists and writers. In a scientist's laboratory, explained Gardner in an article in *Technology Review,* "there are no hidden mirrors or secret compartments or concealed magnets. . . . The thinking of a scientist is rational, based on a lifetime of experience with a rational world. But the methods of magic are irrational and totally outside a scientist's experience."

As a case in point, Gardner cited the strange odyssey of John Taylor, a mathematical physicist at King's College, University of London. In 1973, after appearing on a television show with Uri Geller, Taylor became an enthusiastic apostle of psychokinesis. In his book *Superminds,* he revealed his conviction that not only Geller but also droves of children possessed psychokinetic abilities. He described, for example, an experiment in which a number of children were asked to use their minds to bend metal strips sealed inside glass tubes. Though none of Taylor's subjects could produce such changes in the laboratory, several succeeded at home. At about the same time, magician James Randi visited Taylor's laboratory incognito and found that the tubes could be easily opened. Nonetheless, Taylor refused to accept the possibility of fraud until, after extensive testing, he failed to find signs of abnormal electromagnetic radiation in a number of subjects. It was this force, he had reported, that might produce psychokinetic effects, a belief that he has since publicly retracted.

In contrast to Taylor's approach was the work of two English researchers at the University of Bath. They tested six children, all of whom claimed to be able to bend metal by mental power. The investigators gave the youngsters metal rods or spoons and sent them into the laboratory with an observer who had been instructed to avert his gaze at regular intervals. Meanwhile, the researchers watched the children through a one-way mirror. When the in-lab observer looked the other way, the children did not bother with sleight of hand at all. They simply went to work physically, using both hands and in one case both feet to bend the bits of metal they had been given.

British researcher John Taylor, investigating psychokinetic ability, tested the hands of this girl for indications of radioactivity.

the heads position and half in the tails position.

Using Schmidt's device, or one of the more complicated ones he has since invented, the subject provides the outside intervention—PK—by attempting to will the machine to register either heads or tails. Most subjects have no idea of what is occurring inside the device. All that they see is a ring of nine light bulbs with one illuminated. When the oscillator stops at heads, the next bulb in a clockwise direction lights up. When it stops at tails, the light moves to the next bulb in the opposite direction. The subject is asked to make the light move in one direction or the other—through the power of mental concentration.

Schmidt's findings with his electronic coin flipper have been so impressive—overall scores at odds against chance of about 1,000 to 1—that he was invited to speak at a meeting of the prestigious American Physical Society in 1979. A psychologist who also was on the program, Ray Hyman of the University of Oregon, later called Schmidt's experiments "the most sophisticated and challenging, in my opinion, that have as yet appeared in parapsychological history."

Hyman's comment was especially significant in view of the fact that he once described himself as an "open-minded skeptic who has never seen a genuine psychic phenomenon." Hyman, however, added the caveat that it was much to soon to assess "the ultimate status" of electronic-coin-flipping procedures. Schmidt's device, by recording automatically and ensuring randomness, has negated many of the criticisms that surrounded Rhine's dice-throwing experiments. But it is not foolproof. Psychology professor C.E.M. Hansel has pointed out that Schmidt's machine has no test to detect any inadvertent bias that might creep into the random series it is supposed to generate. Yet perhaps most damaging to Schmidt's case is the fact that his results have yet to be matched by other experimenters trying to repeat his work—a failure that he interprets in terms of such psychological variables as motivation of the subject and attitude of the experimenter.

As experiments such as Schmidt's provide hints that a mind-directed force might exist, however, parapsychologists will be called upon to develop a theory explaining precisely what psychokinesis might be— whether manifested by Nina Kulagina and the movement of a compass needle or by a subject attempting to influence the decay of subatomic particles on a random-number generator. To do so they must continue to attempt to resolve the many mysteries surrounding their phantom quarry, PK. For example, if subjects are able to achieve above-average scores in influencing 100 separate rolls of one die, should they not also be able to influence the movements of 100 dice rolled at once? Experimental results thus far have been contradictory. And what might happen if subjects were asked to perform two PK tasks at once—for instance, to influence

where a die will fall as well as what face it will show when it does so? Results in one such experiment were intriguing: evidence seemed to indicate that subjects are *more* successful at PK tasks that they consider *less* important. Another unanswered question is whether PK, like ESP, might be at work even when people are not aware of it, perhaps tipping the balance in what are ordinarily considered to be streaks of luck or good fortune. Some oblique support for this possibility has come from a test in which a subject achieved positive results even though he did not know he was in a PK experiment. PK's relationship with time, too, is yet to be explained. Schmidt, for example, has conducted experiments in which, unbeknown to the subjects, the patterns of random decay that they were attempting to influence had been generated by his device on a previous day and recorded on magnetic tape. Strangely enough, Schmidt reported, such subjects did seem to be able to affect the sequence of heads and tails, even though it had been taped 24 hours before. Did this indicate, however tentatively, that the subjects were influencing the tape itself, or did it suggest that psychokinesis was functioning in some strangely retroactive manner? At present, as in so many areas of psi research, difficult questions exist in much more tangible form than meaningful answers.

As psi studies became more sophisticated, researchers began employing random-number generators (inset), which are designed to detect the release of decaying radioactive particles and create random sequences. Helmut Schmidt (below), inventor of such machines, uses one to test for psychokinetic powers.

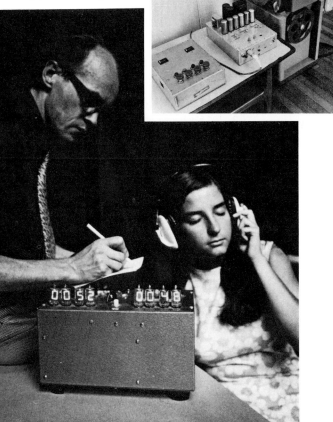

Great Feats: Arcane Art of Fire Walking

On the borderline between the natural and the supernatural there exists a class of phenomena that, for want of a better term, might be called "impossible" physical feats. Many of the people who perform these prodigious acts of endurance, strength or resistance to pain describe their abilities in terms of unique occult or religious powers. In most cases, of course, they possess neither and may be either deluded or dishonest in representing their accomplishments as such. Some are superb athletes; others are illusionists. Yet a few appear capable of effecting seemingly impossible things in ways that are not only unexplained but that appear to defy explanation.

A case in point is this story concerning fire walking, told by Dr. William Tufts Brigham, a well-known ethnologist at Honolulu's Bishop Museum. Brigham had grown up in Hawaii and as a youth had persuaded three friends who were kahunas, or native priests, to teach him the art of fire walking when an opportunity arose. He was therefore understandably excited one day when a fresh lava flow appeared near Kilauea, one that seemed ideal for the long-awaited fire-walking demonstration.

After an arduous three-day climb along the slopes of a still-rumbling volcano, Brigham and his friends came to a gorge enclosing a field of new lava. "When the rocks we threw on the lava surface showed that it had hardened enough to bear our weight," he recalled, "the kahunas arose and clambered down the side of the wall. . . . The lava was blackening on the surface, but all across it ran heat discolorations that came and went as they do on cooling iron before a blacksmith plunges it into his tub. . . . The very thought of running over that flat inferno to the other side made me tremble."

At the edge of the shimmering lava flow, the kahunas stopped and calmly began chanting in archaic Hawaiian while Brigham felt he was being "all but roasted" by the intense heat.

Then, barefoot, and "without a moment of hesitation the oldest man trotted out on that terrifically hot surface." As Brigham watched in awe, he suddenly felt himself being pushed roughly from behind, and a moment later he too was running for his life across the fiery plain of the bed of lava.

Brigham still wore his boots, but after he had taken only a few steps, their seams burned. One sole fell off, the other flapped, and he had to finish his run in his stocking feet. Oddly enough, instead of bursting into flames, his socks seemed to char only where they touched the smoldering uppers of the ruined boots; and, as Brigham told the story, "I had a sensation of intense heat on my face and body, but almost no sensation in my feet." When Brigham at last reached the far side of the lava field, his feet still did not feel warm and, like the feet of the kahunas, showed not a single blister. In fact, the trek back down the volcano's slope was vastly more painful for the bootless Brigham than anything that he had experienced on the lava field. Until the day of his death in 1926, Brigham had but one explanation for his fire walk. "It's magic," he would say, "part of the bulk of magic done by the kahunas and other primitive peoples."

Brigham's experience may have been extraordinary, but it was hardly unique. Ritual fire walking has been performed throughout the world for thousands of years and has been practiced in modern times in such

Billed as the Fire King, Julian Xavier Chabert astounded French audiences in the 19th century with his seeming invincibility in the face of extreme heat and deadly poison. His varied skills included the apparent ability to ingest molten lead as well as boiling oil, to crouch comfortably in ovens heated to 400° F, and to gulp down lethal fluids.

Fire walkers, such as those performing in the Fiji Islands (top), generally take only a few steps in crossing a 12- to 60-foot pit of glowing coals or white-hot stones (above), then emerge, showing no sign of blisters or burns.

varied places as India, Malaysia, Japan, Fiji, Tahiti, Hawaii, the Philippines, New Zealand and the Balkans. Most often, fire walkers cross a layer of burning coals set at the bottom of a shallow trench. Sometimes they walk directly through a log fire or along a path of white-hot stones. They may do such things for any number of reasons: to appease the gods, to attain spiritual purification, to prove guilt or innocence, or simply to fulfill a vow. But although walks of more than 60 feet have been recorded, the walkers in nearly every case have reportedly emerged unscathed.

How is this possible? Aside from religious or occult interpretations, there have been a variety of proposed scientific explanations. It has been argued, for example, that hot coals in a trench may be banked in such a way as to create a path where all oxygen has been burned away and combustion is therefore impossible. Yet this theory has never been satisfactorily demonstrated, and it does not cover other types of fire walking, such as walking on hot lava. It also does not explain immunity to radiant heat. Harry Houdini, the famous magician, suggested that those fire walkers who were not tricksters may have coated the soles of their feet with some sort of fire-resistant ointment. But repeated, careful medical examinations of fire walkers' feet have failed to disclose the presence of any such preparation; many scientists express doubt that such a substance even exists.

Perhaps a more plausible explanation is that provided by a U.S. scholar, Dr. Mayne Reid Coe, Jr., who has walked 30-foot fire pits, licked red-hot iron bars and performed various other incredible feats. Coe once theorized that vaporized moisture from perspiration or saliva forms a kind of minute air cushion that briefly protects flesh from direct contact with a superheated material. Thanks to this protective shield, Coe suggested, if exposure is sufficiently brief, no injury will result. Yet such a theoretical shield, if indeed it might exist, does not appear to work for everyone. In a famous fire-walking experiment conducted by the University of London in 1935, a young Kashmiri named Kuda Bux walked an 11-foot-long fire pit without harm. Yet when two onlookers tried to follow suit, both wound up with blisters and one with bleeding feet after but a few seconds' exposure.

Great Feats of Strength and Endurance

Nor would Coe's theory of moisture-protection explain the reported exploits of other types of fire handlers. A famous example is that of Nathan Coker, an elderly Maryland blacksmith who, in 1871, before a committee of investigators, held a red-hot shovel against the soles of his feet until it had cooled. He then reheated the shovel and licked it until his tongue turned black. Finally Coker poured molten lead into his bare hands, transferred the fiery liquid to his mouth, and held it there until the lead had solidified. According to the New York *Herald,* which reported at length and with great excitement on these proceedings, doctors could find no trace of injury on Coker's hands, feet, mouth or tongue.

To be sure, there is no certain way of verifying such century-old accounts. Even if one accepts the good faith of the reporters, the possibility of fraud remains. Professional magicians such as Houdini have explained in detail how the seemingly undetectable illusions of such feats can be created. Thus it is all but impossible to evaluate the claims of famous "fire kings" of the past. Researchers know, for example, that a 19th-century Frenchman named Julian Xavier Chabert seemed to be able to sit in a heated oven holding a leg of mutton until the meat was thoroughly cooked. There are accounts as well concerning Josephine Girardelli, "The Great Phenomena of Nature" [*sic*], who enchanted English audiences in 1814 when she seemed to wash her hands in boiling lead. And in 1751, England's Royal Society went so far as to award Robert Powell a purse of gold and a large silver medal for his apparent feats of fire eating. (An impressed contemporary wrote of Powell, "Such is his passion for this terrible element, that if he were to come hungry into your kitchen, while a sirloin was roasting, he would eat up the fire and leave the beef.") Although it is difficult to determine which, if any, of these feats might have been genuine, it is worth noting that they were unusual only in that they were voluntary; for most of human history, men have been subjecting one another to grueling ordeals by fire in order to demonstrate fealty, determine guilt or establish the truth under difficult circumstances.

Assuming that some portion of fire walking, fire handling or other superhuman feats is, though scientifically inexplicable, nonetheless possible, there remains a broader psychological problem to confront. What prompts people to attempt feats that appear to defy the laws of nature? Why, for example, should the

Feats such as lying on a bed of jagged spikes (above) are performed by Hindu and Islamic fakirs as a special means of communing with God. Some Western researchers believe that a form of self-induced trance may help explain the seeming invulnerability of such men to pain.

Dutch mystic Mirin Dajo have endured being run through with sword blades more than 500 times? Although Dajo eventually died of complications arising from such wounds, it is incredible that he could have survived even one impalement. And why do Indian fakirs subject themselves to the agonies of lying on beds of nails (one reportedly for a period of 111 days) or yogis to unbelievably long fasts or burial alive?

Certainly intense religious feeling accounts for a large percentage of such heroics, just as it appears to account for many other inexplicable phenomena. Spiritual aspiration, it would seem, is sufficient to motivate the devout to inflict upon themselves all manner of painful treatment, from the wearing of hair shirts to the ritual mortification still performed in public by members of Islamic sects. For all such believers, whether Christian mystics or fakirs within the Islamic or Hindu

A 1920s and 1930s vaudevillian known only as Mortado won renown for a bizarre feat that appeared to send jets of water spouting from various points on his body.

Houdini reportedly developed the trick but it remained for a performer named Moro (above) to bring it to vaudeville. He had himself frozen in ice, then had the block rolled out onto the stage.

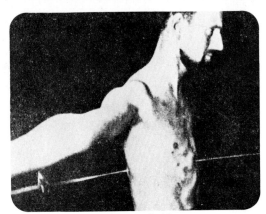

In Mirin Dajo's remarkable demonstration, he allowed an epee to be driven into his back and out his chest. To silence skeptics the Dutch mystic once used a hollow epee and had water pumped through it.

Joseph L. Greenstein ("The Mighty Atom") toured the United States for decades, performing such feats as bending steel bars, driving nails with his fists and biting through chain links.

traditions, the goal of such ordeals is transcendence of the physical plane—considered the most specifically human aspect of our existence—in the hope of achieving true union with God or the universe.

Among non-religious practitioners of feats that seem physically impossible, a similar desire to transcend the recognized limits of the human body is evident, though the goal is expressed differently. A clue to that impulse, or motive, may be found in the words that a famous U.S. strong man, Joseph L. Greenstein ("The Mighty Atom"), used to repeat to himself before performing one of his incredible iron-bending feats. "I am man," Greenstein would intone. "I am possessed of the Power. You are metal . . . without will. My will is superior to you. The Power will overcome you. You will bend . . . you will break."

There are no definitive answers, of course, and yet it may be that the impulse to transcend every limitation imposed by time, space, matter and the senses—to gain command over all things, including ourselves—is part of our human inheritance. And perhaps the people who attempt impossible physical feats—who seek to demonstrate the primacy of mind over matter—are merely partaking of this universal need.

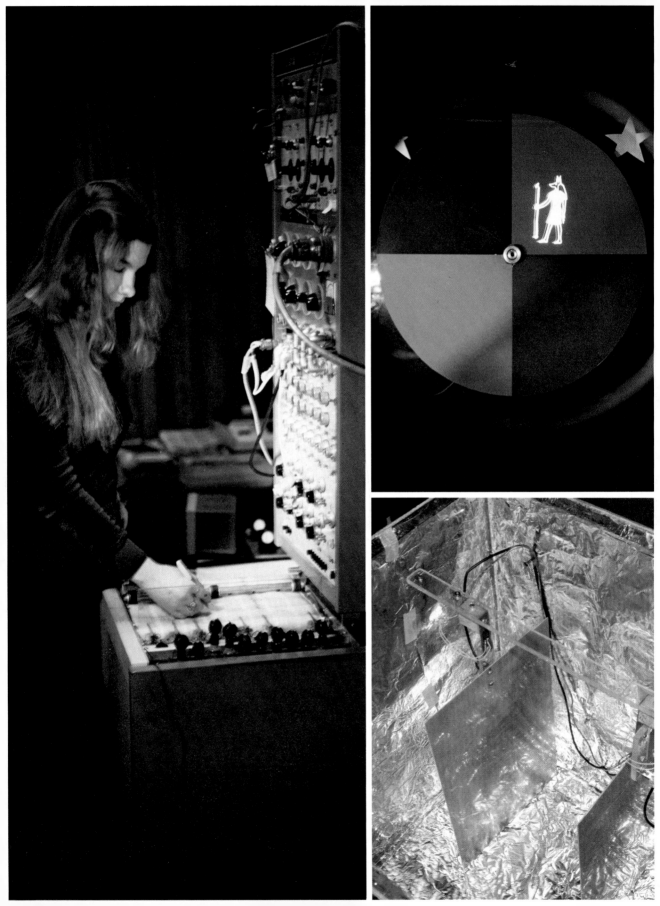

Stories of out-of-body experiences
suggest but hardly prove that some form of the self
may flee the body in times of crisis.

LEAVING THE BODY

Psychic Alex Tanous begins an
out-of-body attempt with the
words: "Mind, go to the box."

Nothing in his life had prepared the
young medic for the extraordinary
sensation of viewing his own body from a
point outside it. So incredible was the
event that even decades later he preferred
to keep his name off the public record,
perhaps for fear of being considered bizarre and unreliable. Yet he knew that he
had not been dreaming or hallucinating.

The most vividly convincing aspect
of the medic's experience was that the
squadron buildings, the hangars and the
medical hut on the hillside were impossible to see from the small airfield situated
in a grassy hollow below. If this had not been the case,
it is conceivable that the young doctor might never
have become consultant physician to the Royal Air
Force, Fellow of the Royal College of Physicians and
Commander of the Order of the British Empire. As it
was, because of the location of the hangars, his com-
manding officer was able to verify his tale.

At the time of the incident—April 1916—the subject was a medical officer attached to the 2nd Brigade
of the Royal Flying Corps in Clairmarais, France. In
response to an emergency casualty report from another

At the American Society for Psychical Research in New
York, delicate sensors are used in out-of-body studies. When
Alex Tanous (above), lying in a distant room, correctly de-
scribed target images (above, left), more activity was detected
in an attached sensing chamber (left) than at other times.
Polygraph (far left) was employed to record such activity.

airfield, he and a pilot had scrambled
aboard an idle plane and had begun to
make a hurried takeoff.

Before the plane had gained adequate height or speed, however, the pilot
made a sharp turn; the craft lost its upward thrust and began hurtling downward. Strangely detached and calm, the
medic found himself wondering which
wing would be the first to strike the
ground. Then: "Suddenly I was looking
down on my body on the ground from
some 200 feet vertically above it."

The medic had been thrown clear
and was lying on his back, apparently unconscious,
though he felt himself to be in a state of pleasant
awareness. He could see the uninjured pilot and two
senior officers run toward his body and bend over it.
"My spirit, or whatever you like to call it, hovering
there, was wondering why they were bothering to pay
any attention to my body, and I distinctly remember
wishing they would leave it alone."

From his viewpoint high above the airfield, the
young doctor saw the ambulance start out of its hangar
and stall; the driver get out, crank the starting handle
and leap back into his seat; the medical orderly rush
out of the field hut and jump into the ambulance as it
started; the ambulance pause while the orderly ran back
to pick up something apparently forgotten; and the orderly jump back into the ambulance, which continued
its disrupted journey.

Having observed all this, the still-unconscious man

felt himself—"and it was most definitely me, and not something else"—traveling away from the airfield at great speed. He had a sense of moving toward a nearby town, then of going far beyond it toward the open sea. Still unconcerned, he wondered why he was making such an incredible journey. Even as he speculated, "a sort of retraction occurred," and he was once more hovering above his body. With an abrupt shift of viewpoint he was aware that the medical orderly was pouring a stimulant down his throat, and he opened his eyes to his accustomed world.

Later, as he lay paralyzed in the hospital, the young medic reflected on his trip. A person might have imagined the lightning-swift passage to the sea, but what about the activities he seemed to have perceived near the hangars? Bewildered yet impressed by the clarity of the recollected scene, he gave his C.O. a complete account of his experience. Eventually the C.O.'s discreet inquiries verified the details of everything that the young medic said he had seen.

A bizarre experience, perhaps, but not unique; not even very unusual. For the most casual survey turns up

Some theorists believe that a special cord binds the astral body to the living body, as shown in this Chinese print. The cord, they suggest, can stretch endlessly during astral flight.

instances of out-of-body experiences among people of all walks of life, ages and states of health. Characteristically in such cases the experiencer believes he has been projected some distance from his physical body and perceives both the body and its environment from that external viewpoint. The subject feels alert and aware, however, and more than usually observant. His perceptions may contain some information that he could not have obtained through ordinary channels. Often he seems to himself to be occupying a second body, either an externalized double of his physical self or some sort of featureless, usually invisible form.

Modern researchers apply the term *ecsomatic state* to out-of-body experiences or employ abbreviations such as OOB's, OOBE's and OBE's. Yet OBE's by whatever name crosscut societies as well as time. During the 1970s Dr. Dean Sheils, then an associate professor of psychology at the University of Wisconsin, analyzed data from some 70 non-Western cultures to explore current beliefs in OBE's. He reported that the OBE belief appears in about 95 percent of the cultures surveyed and that the descriptions of OBE's are strikingly similar. Typically the "something" leaves the body, often during periods of unconsciousness or natural sleep; the occurrence is distinguishable from normal dreams; and the OBE is ordinarily spontaneous, although shamans and psychics are said to project or exteriorize at will.

Similar data have not been lacking in the Western world. In 1952 the late sociologist Hornell Hart asked 155 Duke University students, "Have you ever actually seen your physical body from a viewpoint completely outside that body, like standing beside the bed and looking at yourself lying in the bed, or like floating in the air near your body?" No less than 30 percent said that they had. When psychologist Francis Banks posed a similar question to a group of churchgoers, 45 percent answered yes. English parapsychologist Celia Green, director of the Institute of Psychophysical Research in Oxford, England, began collecting OBE accounts in the 1960s. In 1966 she surveyed a sample of 115 undergraduates at Southampton University; 19 percent answered that they had experienced out-of-body projection. In the following year she put the same question to 350 Oxford students; 34 percent replied affirmatively.

In 1974, Dr. John Palmer and his colleague Michael Dennis, then working at the University of Virginia School of Medicine, conducted a random mail survey of 700 adult residents of Charlottesville, Virginia, and 300 University of Virginia students. Of the 341 townspeople who replied, 14 percent said that they had experienced out-of-body phenomena. Of the 266 students who responded, 25 percent answered in the affirmative. A remarkable 34 percent of the people in both studies who said they had had an OBE reported having "been out" as often as eight times.

Aleksey Tolstoy (above) claimed to have met D. D. Home hours before the famous psychic's arrival in St. Petersburg. Home believed astral projection was involved.

Eerie stories of having met their doubles have been told by (clockwise from left) Guy de Maupassant, Goethe, Dostoyevsky, Edgar Allan Poe and D. H. Lawrence.

Altogether, there are scores of OBE's on record. The anonymous British medic had no reason to be shy about his experience; it was unlike many others only in its verifiable details and drama. A good deal simpler and far more typical, however, is an OBE reported by parapsychologist D. Scott Rogo.

It was a hot August afternoon in 1965 when Rogo, then a student, flopped down on his bed for his usual after-class nap. This time, however, he could not sleep. "I began to feel oddly chilly and started to tremble," he wrote in his 1978 book, *Mind Beyond the Body*. "I flipped over onto my side, realizing at the same moment that my whole body was pulsating and that I was almost paralyzed. . . . An instant later I found myself floating in the air and, in another instant, I was standing at the foot of the bed staring at myself. I made an abrupt about-face . . . and tried to walk toward the door to my room, which led to a hallway. I felt as though I were gliding through jelly as I moved, and I lost balance for a moment and almost fell over. Everything was blurred by a cloudy hue that enveloped a whitish form, which I perceived as my body. A moment later I found myself awakening on my bed. But I also realized that I had never been asleep!"

It may not be surprising that Rogo, as a parapsychologist, was relatively unperturbed by his experience. For a layman to have such a calm reaction, however, might seem surprising. And yet an attitude of emotional detachment from the normal self was common among subjects interviewed by Celia Green. As one reported: "While driving fast along a road the drone of the engine and vibration seemed to lull me into a stupor and I remember I seemed to leave my motorbike like a zoom lens in reverse and was hovering over a hill watching myself and friend tearing along the road below and I seemed to think 'I shouldn't be here, get back on that bike!' and the next instant I was in the saddle again." Another of Green's respondents was performing in a concert when she found herself at the back of the hall listening to her onstage voice and criticizing it. A third, a preacher, became aware of separation from his body while delivering a sermon one evening; from the far end of the church he saw his body in the pulpit and heard his voice drone on unfalteringly.

While OBE's sometimes occur under such pedestrian conditions, they are more likely to happen at times of pain, stress or other intolerable circumstances. Thus the violence of war has on occasion induced the sensation that the self is being catapulted outward from a tormented body. A prototypical case is recorded for August 3, 1944, when an explosive-laden armored tank received a direct hit from a German shell and a British armored-car officer was blown 20 feet over a five-foot hedge.

As he lay on the ground, his battle dress in flames and burning phosphorus searing his flesh, the officer was aware of existing as two persons. One lay in a field, moaning and crying with fear while his limbs waved wildly. "The other 'me' was floating up in the air, about twenty feet from the ground, from which position I could see not only my other self on the ground, but also the hedge, the road, and the car, which was surrounded by smoke and burning fiercely." As the person lying on the ground, the man was quite conscious of making the horrible sounds; as the other

Escape From Pain

Intolerable pain has sometimes precipitated unusually intense out-of-body episodes. Such was the experience reported by Ed Morrell, who was sentenced to a life term in San Quentin at the turn of the century.

After winning a pardon in 1909, Morrell wrote a book, *The Twenty-Fifth Man,* about his ordeals. His most horrifying experiences occurred after he was falsely accused of hiding guns in the prison. To make him reveal the guns' whereabouts, his jailers used the "Bloody Straitjacket," a full-body wrapping so tight it induced a "sense of suffocation similar to the experience of being buried alive." Morrell described the stabbing pains, gradual numbness and bodily excretions that ate into his skin like acid, saying that they made being "squeezed to death by a giant boa constrictor . . . pale before the death terrors of the jacket." The first torture session, Morrell wrote, left him in a state of despair unlike any that he had known in prison.

The next episode in the jacket, however, was different. As he lay in excruciating pain on the floor of his cell, he felt his consciousness slowly leave his physical body and float freely beyond the prison walls. Free of anguish and constraints, he experienced the curious sensation of gliding languidly "into the living, breathing outside world." And every time he "returned" to his cell, he felt rested and refreshed. Astonished by Morrell's failure to break even after repeated tortures in the jacket, the prison warden ordered his guards to redouble their efforts. A second jacket was laced over the first, yet whenever the guards came to release Morrell, they found him in good spirits. In his disassociated state, Morrell enjoyed periods of exquisite escape, journeying where he chose and occasionally observing events that he was later able to corroborate.

Morrell's stoicism—and a change in wardens—finally brought him release, first from his five years in solitary confinement and, four years later, from prison. Not surprisingly, perhaps, he never experienced the sensation of being out of body after his last siege in the jacket. However the skeptical mind may view Morrell's experience, the state he described—of some level of consciousness functioning independently of the physical body—apparently allowed him to survive.

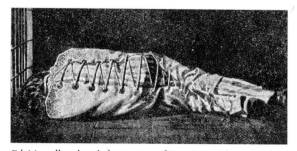

Ed Morrell endured the torture of San Quentin's straitjackets by allegedly leaving his body and gliding freely in space.

in the air, he heard them as coming from another person. "I remember telling myself, 'It's no use gibbering like that—roll over and over to put the flames out!'" Finally, the physical body did what it was told, and the man rolled under the hedge into a ditch that was partially filled with water. The flames went out, panic faded, and the officer "became one person again."

Mathematical formulas helped Arthur Koestler survive wartime terror.

Ernest Hemingway was a youth of 19 serving with an ambulance unit at the Italian front when he had an OBE. In the middle of the night of July 8, 1918, an Austrian mortar shell loaded with bits of scrap metal exploded near the Italian trenches, and Hemingway's legs were savaged by the shell's flying shrapnel.

"I felt my soul or something coming right out of my body," he later told his friend Guy Hickok, European correspondent for the Brooklyn *Daily Eagle,* "like you'd pull a silk handkerchief out of a pocket by one corner. It flew around and then came back and went in again, and I wasn't dead any more." Using this incident 10 years later in *A Farewell to Arms,* Hemingway had his hero Frederick Henry say: "I felt myself rush bodily out of myself and out and out and out and all the time bodily in the wind. I went out swiftly, all of myself, and I knew I was dead and that it had all been a mistake to think you just die. Then I floated, and instead of going on I felt myself slide back. I breathed and I was back."

While a correspondent in the Spanish civil war, author Arthur Koestler was captured by Franco's forces and thrust into solitary confinement under threat of imminent execution. In his isolation he began scratching mathematical formulas on the walls of his cell. Deriving satisfaction from the significance of the symbols, he became so enchanted by what he felt was a perfect mathematical statement about the infinite that the prospect of being shot receded into irrelevancy.

Although there are obviously many varieties of OBE, the combined findings of many researchers make it possible to paint a broad picture of frequently reported characteristics. During an OBE the "I"-consciousness seems to be aware that it is in another vehicle, which may or may not be visible to an onlooker. Some subjects feel the second body to be an exact, if transparent, replica of the physical body; others liken it to a mist, a vapor, a white cloud, an eye, a glowing ball, or something like a magnetic or electric field. Not uncommonly, the out-of-body form is thought to give off its own light, and some subjects report seeing a luminous cord connecting the ecsomatic self with the physical body.

Movement out of the physical body is often accompanied by a clicking sound, an apparent blackout or a journey down a long tunnel, and may seem to be assisted by some other disembodied entity.

The pattern also suggests that the projected form is immune to gravity and may walk, glide, float or fly. It may hover lazily in the vicinity of the physical body, or it may seem to travel great distances beyond the limits of time and space. It may also be able to pass through matter with ease but is very seldom capable of touching or moving objects. The subject usually feels he is traveling in the world of everyday life but sometimes enters regions of otherworldly beauty or depression, and may see other apparitions during his experience. The out-of-body self may even seem to demonstrate some form of extrasensory perception.

Skeptics, who are numerous, explain out-of-body accounts in terms of dreams, hallucinations, wishful self-delusions, ESP, gross misperception of natural events, psychotic episodes or deliberate hoax. No doubt each one of these factors might operate in a given instance, yet the mass of OBE cases is not so easily dealt with. For the sheer volume of anecdotal data does at least suggest that the OBE is a genuine phenomenon; it suggests, indeed, that the consciousness apparently leaving the body may be a real self, one capable of functioning independently of the physical body's mass of bone, tissue and brain cells.

If the case for OBE's is to be proved, however, it will probably have to be done under controlled laboratory conditions using subjects capable of leaving their bodies almost at will. Such an experiment was attempted in 1965 and 1966 by Dr. Charles T. Tart, a pioneer in the field and now a professor of psychology at the University of California at Davis. As an instructor at the University of Virginia School of Medicine, Tart carried out one series of tests with a gifted subject named Robert Monroe, a successful Virginia businessman and electronics engineer who had been experiencing vivid OBE's since 1958 and claimed to be able to induce them. For the tests, Monroe was placed in a makeshift laboratory bedroom where his brain waves, heartbeat and eye movements could be monitored. He was, in theory, to leave his body there and project

Ernest Hemingway felt his soul depart his body after having been badly wounded.

Mutual Out-of-Body Experience

Some out-of-body experiences turn out to be relatively pedestrian adventures involving people who make unexpected trips for more or less specific and practical reasons and, though amazed by them, are not struck by their transcendental implications. Such was the case of Walter McBride, an Indiana farmer, whose alleged journey in 1935 was prosaic in essence and yet contained a number of characteristic out-of-body elements plus an unusual one: mutual recognition between the out-of-body entity and a surprised observer.

As McBride later reported to OBE researcher Sylvan Muldoon, "About eight o'clock on the evening of 23rd December, I went to my bedroom which is on the lower floor of my house. I blew out the lamp and retired, in the usual manner, feeling quite normal in every way. . . . The next thing I knew I was, preposterous as it sounds, floating in the room, but in a lighted atmosphere. I was wide awake at the time. The light was not from a material source because I had blown out the lamp and the room had been dark when I went to bed. The light was whitish and cast no shadows; it was not like the light of the sun."

McBride felt himself floating upward through his house. "The ceiling and upper floor failed to stop me. . . . I passed through them with ease. After reaching a certain height I happened to turn upright, and, looking downward, to my amazement, *I saw my body lying upon the bed.*" With equal amazement he found himself heading in a sort of wave-like motion toward his old home, several miles away. He was aware, without knowing how, that he was going to visit his father, about whose health he had been concerned. He also sensed the presence of some sort of guide who was traveling with him.

Eventually, he entered the master bedroom of his old family house by passing nonchalantly through its walls and stood at the foot of his father's bed. " 'Father,' I said to him, 'Father!' But I did not seem to make him hear my voice. Yet I thought he was watching me, for his eyes were fixed upon me and there seemed to be a look of surprise upon his face."

McBride's return home was uneventful. When he found himself in his bedroom once again, "the first thing I saw was my own body, still lying on the bed where I had left it. . . . I was clearly conscious all the time and . . . on reentering my physical self . . . was instantly alert with no feeling of drowsiness." McBride got up, noted the time of the occurrence and wrote down every detail of his remarkable journey.

On Christmas Day he visited his father in the normal fashion. In the presence of two other visitors, the older man spontaneously verified his son's account. *"He had seen me,"* McBride reported, "just as I had stood at the foot of his bed. Coincidentally, he too had written down the time of his vision, and it tallied with the time as I had written it down."

How-To of Astral Flight

The concept of the astral body—"the starry envelope of the soul"—is one of the oldest and most universal of man's ideas about himself. It is mentioned in ancient Indian, Egyptian and Greek texts, as well as in the Bible, and was a literary staple through the Middle Ages. In certain religious and cultural groups, it remains a powerful belief.

Thought to be a perfect replica of the physical body in which it is housed, the astral body is made of far lighter stuff—luminous, translucent and eminently suited to the out-of-body travel of which it is allegedly capable. In theory, one of the main functions of the astral body is to transport the soul at the moment of death, but those who claim to have experienced astral projection make it seem no more unusual an experience than dreaming.

The primary, if now antiquated, text in such historical speculations is a book called *The Projection of the Astral Body*, first published in London in 1929. The authors were Hereward Carrington, an Englishman, and Sylvan Muldoon, from the United States, who not only claimed to be a habitual astral traveler but was convinced that astral projection was within anyone's capability if only sufficient desire was present.

In his introduction to the book, Carrington offered a "summary of the doctrine and teachings regarding the astral body and its projection." A more succinct description, though one not taken seriously by modern researchers, would be hard to find anywhere.

"The astral body, then," Carrington wrote, "coincides with the physical body during the hours of full, waking consciousness, but in sleep the astral body withdraws to a greater or lesser degree, usually hovering just above it, neither conscious nor controlled. In trance, syncope, while fainting, when under the influence of an anaesthetic, etc., the astral body similarly withdraws from the physical.

Such cases of withdrawal constitute instances of *automatic* or *involuntary projection*.

"As opposed to such cases we place those of *conscious* or *voluntary projection*, in which the subject 'wills' to leave his physical body. . . . He is then fully alert and conscious in his astral body; he can look upon his own physical mechanism, and travel about at will, perhaps viewing scenes and visiting places he has never seen before. . . .

"The astral and physical bodies are . . . connected by means of a . . . cord, . . . along which vital currents pass. Should this cord be severed, death instantly results. . . . [But] This cord—the 'Silver Cord' spoken of in *Ecclesiastes*—is elastic, and capable of great extension. It constitutes the essential link between the two bodies."

With the concept thus authoritatively explained, Carrington and Muldoon proceeded to give the history and "laws of the art" of astral projection. Their description included instructive attention to such subtopics as "phantom velocity" (there are three speeds of astral travel); "cord activity range"; "repercussion of the astral body"; and "symptoms of astral exteriorization."

According to Carrington and Muldoon, the mechanical laws of astral travel are quite strict. In Muldoon's case, the basic procedure was the same from the occasion of his first astonishing and involuntary projection, at the age of 12, through the many hundreds of trips that followed. Whether voluntary or involuntary in character, the process begins, according to Muldoon, with a sensation of bodily rigidity (catalepsy); one then feels one's astral body, still in a horizontal position, slowly begin to move upward out of alignment with one's physical self, until it reaches a height of about six feet. At this point the astral body is rather abruptly uprighted, and from then on, it is free to move as it pleases.

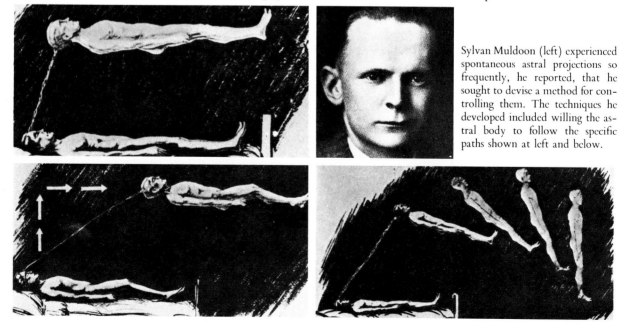

Sylvan Muldoon (left) experienced spontaneous astral projections so frequently, he reported, that he sought to devise a method for controlling them. The techniques he developed included willing the astral body to follow the specific paths shown at left and below.

himself into the adjoining control room. There he would try to read a randomly selected, five-digit number set on a shelf above eye level and observe the actions of the monitoring technician.

Reclining on an army cot with uncomfortable electrodes clamped on his ears, Monroe found it difficult to relax enough to induce separation. He continued to be unsuccessful until the eighth and last session, when, he later reported, he managed two brief OBE's. In the first, he moved from his room "through a darkened area" and came upon two men and a woman engrossed in a conversation. Not "seeing" too well and feeling disoriented, he decided to return to his body and make a fresh start. On his second try, Monroe's non-physical body allegedly rolled off the cot and floated to the floor. He slowly drifted through the doorway into the control room but could not find the lab technician at her usual place. Without noticing the target number, Monroe passed into a brightly lit outer corridor and saw the technician talking to a man he did not recognize.

Excited, but conscious of some discomfort, Monroe returned to his physical body and found that he was suffering from a dry throat and a throbbing ear. Calling to the technician to report his OBE's, he told her that he had spotted her outside the control room with a man he had not seen before. The technician confirmed that she had been standing in the corridor with her husband, who had come to visit her.

Tart's experiments were provocative but inconclusive. The electroencephalograph findings were ambiguous, and altogether, Monroe's evidence of being out of body seemed slight. Tart's own conclusion, however, was that his studies showed that OBE's are not "beyond the pale of scientific investigation."

Meanwhile, the American Society for Psychical Research (ASPR) in New York had for some time been studying death-related phenomena in an effort to determine whether or not some aspect of the self escapes the body at the moment of death. By the time Tart began his investigations, the ASPR had conducted two major surveys of deathbed observations made by physicians and nurses, collecting nearly 1,000 reports relating to visions, apparitions and the emotions of the dying. When funds ran out before the project was completed, the study seemed fated to end. It was later revived, however, by a remarkable circumstance.

In November 1949 an Arizona miner named James Kidd went out prospecting, never to return. Several years later he was declared legally dead, indigent and intestate, but during the mid-1950s, Arizona estate tax commissioner Geraldine C. Swift began turning up various bank accounts, securities and stock certificates in Kidd's name amounting to roughly $175,000—a bonanza for the state if no legitimate claimants appeared.

Arizona was preparing to collect the money when,

What It Is Like to "Be Out"

Celia Green investigated hundreds of out-of-body experiences.

The sensation of seeming to travel out of the body is virtually impossible to explain to those who have not experienced it, believers feel, because it is so unlike normal conscious existence. Nonetheless, a sampling of comments from a few of the respondents in a study conducted by Celia Green, a British parapsychologist, provides some sense of what "being out" has meant to different people:

"I am disembodied, but in a small space which has a definite size and location."

"Reality was my 'floating self' and the objects below seemed as shadows against the reality of my floating self."

"What seemed to have escaped was whatever made the physical body me; i.e. whatever gave me personality or character."

"The part of me that was out of my body was the real me, as I knew it, the part that sees, thinks and feels emotionally."

"I feel in an extraordinarily light colourful body, buoyant, joyful and somehow 4 dimensional, as if I could, if I wanted to see the inside as well as out."

"I have found that the eyesight blacks out, and something else seems to start."

"I 'saw' with whole consciousness."

"I was quite calm and unworried and thought, So that's what I look like. The sensation is nothing like looking in a mirror."

"It wasn't weird or frightening; in fact if there is a reaction, it is one of feeling superior."

"I have never been so wide awake or experienced such a wonderful sense of freedom before."

"I suddenly felt filled with the utmost joy and happiness. I felt such great freedom."

"All movement was instantaneous. To think was to *have* acted."

"And then a feeling . . . of terrible fear came to me. I knew I HAD to return to my body before it was touched. There was a dreadful sense of urgency, or it would be too late."

"The thought came to me—if I drift away from here how am I going to find my way back?"

"The escaped me felt absolutely wonderful, very light and full of the most wonderful vitality, in fact more well than I have ever felt before or since."

"I had no further interest in my physical body, or indeed my physical life. I only wanted to pursue and prolong this happy state of being where everything was more bright, vivid and real than anything I had previously known."

in 1964, James Kidd's handwritten will turned up in a safe-deposit box. It had been scrawled in pencil on a page torn out of a notebook and was datelined Phoenix, Arizona. The document was straightforward: "This is my first and only will and is dated the second day in January 1946. I have no heirs have not been married in my life, after all my funeral expenses have been paid and $100 one hundred dollars to some preacher of the gospel to say fare well at my grave sell all my property which is all in cash and stocks with E. F. Hutton Co Phoenix some in safety box, and have this balance money to go in a research or some scientific proof of a soul of the human body which leaves at death I think in time there can be a Photograph of soul leaving the human at death,   James Kidd."

It took more than eight years and the intervention of the chief justice of the Arizona Supreme Court to resolve the matter of James Kidd's will. Finally, the ASPR was awarded the money—by then amounting to $279,450. It granted one-third to the Psychical Research Foundation in Durham, North Carolina, and used the remainder to set up its own experimental program at its headquarters in a Manhattan brownstone. The project was headed by Dr. Karlis Osis, the ASPR's director of research, and an artist named Ingo Swann became the first test subject.

Born in a small town in the Rocky Mountains, Swann is said to have had his first OBE at the age of three while under an anesthetic. After that, OBE's occurred frequently, and by the time he arrived at the ASPR office, he had trained himself, he claimed, to project his body anywhere at any time.

Research psychologist Janet Mitchell, working with Osis, conducted a series of exploratory sessions with the subject in an effort to determine whether he could, while having an OBE, identify targets beyond his normal range of vision. Swann, sitting in a room illuminated by a soft overhead light, was festooned with cables connecting the electrodes on his scalp to a polygraph in an adjoining room. Set on a platform suspended two feet below the ceiling and about 10 feet off the floor were various target materials (changed from session to session), objects such as an umbrella, an apple, scissors, a cross, a black leather letter-opener case, printed letters and numbers, and colorful geometric designs cut out of construction paper.

Virtually immobilized by wires and constantly monitored by Mitchell for changes in brain-wave tracings, respiration and blood pressure, Swann described the objects he believed he saw from various out-of-body positions and made sketches of them. His reports were impressive. During some tries, Swann was able to sketch almost exactly what was situated on the platform. The only exceptions were objects he said he could not see because of his out-of-body angle of approach or the fall of light and shadow upon the targets. He also had diffi-

culty in identifying numbers or letters as anything other than general shapes. Yet even these apparent failures were heartening, the researchers felt, for they suggested that Swann was indeed "seeing" from an out-of-body perspective rather than employing some form of extra-sensory perception, which, they felt, would not have been affected by visual obstacles.

After a number of tests, eight sets of targets and sketches were shuffled and given to psychologist Boneita Perskari, who knew nothing about the experiments, to sort into matching pairs. Ultimately she correctly matched all the target objects with Swann's sketched responses. Statistically, according to Janet Mitchell, there was but 1 chance in 40,000 of achieving such a perfect score. During the times that Swann reported he was out of body, the instruments attached to Swann's scalp recorded smaller and more rapid brain waves in regions relating to vision.

Meanwhile, the Psychical Research Foundation was studying psychic phenomena that might support belief in the existence of a spirit, or soul. In February 1973, Dr. Robert Morris, research coordinator of the PRF, began a series of out-of-body tests with an undergraduate researcher-subject named Stuart Blue Harary, from nearby Duke University. Harary claimed to have been having OBE's all his life—and feeling alienated from other people because of them.

Wired to a variety of psychophysiological recording devices, Harary attempted to initiate an out-of-body trip. He was asked to project himself out of one PRF building and into an adjacent building where he

Dr. Karlis Osis (below) of the American Society for Psychical Research planned and supervised the first out-of-body experiments underwritten by James Kidd's extraordinary bequest.

would try to discern target drawings and alphabet letters. His efforts were moderately successful; throughout the sequence of tests he managed several accurate or approximate identifications of target images, particularly with regard to color and general shape, but his perception was often distorted. When on one occasion he felt himself touching Joseph Janis, a PRF staff member who was monitoring the target room, he became so excited that he "flew right back to the ol' body."

The experiments then moved into a new phase. Harary attempted to project from one PRF building to another and report on the identities and positions of randomly chosen human detectors stationed in the experimental area. The detectors were told to be alert for a brief out-of-body visit within a given period. Harary was at first remarkably successful at spotting the detectors and reporting their positions, but his accuracy soon tapered off. A number of the detectors performed well

for a time; some reported "seeing sparkling lights or even an apparition" during the period that Harary was supposed to be out of body.

Harary was next directed to try and make his presence known to animals. Selected hamsters and gerbils offered no reaction to his alleged out-of-body visits, but a snake became violently active. Harary then acquired a pair of kittens as pets and chose the more responsive one to work with. Spirit was an affectionate and lively little cat; the question was whether she would detect Harary's out-of-body presence and respond to it.

Morris placed the kitten in a large, deep cage with its floor marked into 24 numbered 10-inch squares so that Spirit's activity could be measured. Harary at the time was in Duke University Hospital, half a mile away, preparing to project his out-of-body self at randomly determined times. As Morris watched, the kitten romped over the squares, making prodigious efforts to escape and meowing constantly. Yet, the investigator later wrote, "it did not show this behavior at all during Blue's OOBE periods. It was as though the cat detected the experience and responded by being calm and contented where it was."

During the summer of the psychic kitten, D. Scott Rogo joined the PRF for several weeks as a consultant and did a pair of target studies with Harary. In the first, the OB-er correctly described and named two out of three objects in a display; the second was less successful but led Rogo to conclude that Harary was perceiving target objects with other-than-normal vision. Perhaps the most tantalizing moment in Rogo's experiments with Harary occurred when Harary's out-of-body presence apparently caused an alteration in the atmosphere, suggesting, however wildly, that he was extracting energy from it in order to manifest his consciousness outside his body.

To discover whether any such physical effects might occur consistently during OBE's an elaborate test was conducted at the headquarters of the ASPR in 1978 and 1979. Dr. Karlis Osis and Donna McCormick used as their subject a college teacher and out-of-body adept from Portland, Maine, named Alex Tanous.

Tanous was stationed in a soundproof room at one end of the third floor in the society's building in Manhattan. The targets he was to identify were located in a room at the opposite side of the building, with five shut doors intervening. The monitoring equipment was housed in a room adjacent to the targets.

Tanous's task was very narrowly defined. The target display was to be a composite of several elements: one of five possible pictures would be projected onto one of four differently colored quadrants on a circular plate. In addition, the plate could be rotated so that each color might appear in any one of the four positions. Line drawing, color and quadrant position would all be randomly selected, and the only position from

Prospector James Kidd's will, which provided funds for OBE research, was discovered by Arizona estate tax commissioner Geraldine Swift (below). Competing claims for the Kidd estate are piled high on the desk of Judge Robert Myers.

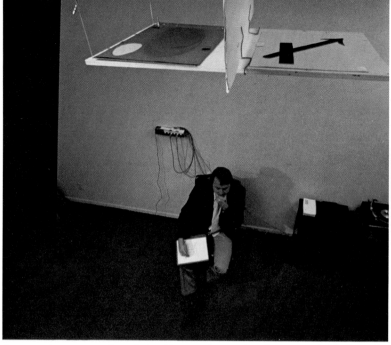

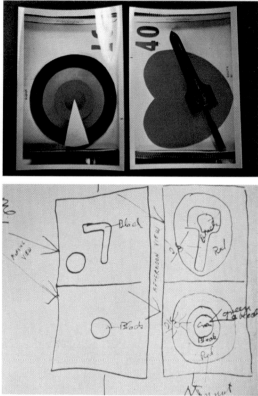

In experiments conducted in New York City, Ingo Swann tried to prove that he could leave his body. By out-of-body projection, researchers felt, Swann might be able to tell them what lay on a shelf above his head. In one test, Swann attempted to sketch two pictures placed on the shelf (above, right). His re-creations are shown at right.

which a correct reading of the display could be made was directly in front of the apparatus. There the researchers had erected a shielded chamber equipped with sensors capable of detecting the slightest vibrations.

The investigators hoped that a direct hit—correct identification of the projected image—would confirm that Tanous had made a successful out-of-body journey to the reading location inside the shielded chamber. But most intriguing to the researchers was the prospect that such direct hits would correspond with any detectable variation in activity inside the chamber as registered by the device's sensors.

The results were provocative: through a total of 197 trials conducted during 20 sessions, Tanous made 114 hits and 83 misses. Consistently through the trials, the sensors recorded a significantly higher level of activity when Tanous hit than when he missed.

Quite independently, a group of Soviet scientists has suggested something that might be related to Tanous's performance: that within the body there is an energy system that forms the separable self. They have variously called that self "the energy" or "the biological plasma body." Western researchers, among them Rogo, are intrigued by this idea. " 'Mind' might be a type of energy," wrote Rogo. "When the mind leaves the body it might be able to mold a vehicle for itself from this energy. Different types of OBE states might have corresponding vehicles."

Despite such experimentation and theorizing, however, researchers have not succeeded in trapping a soul in the laboratory, as James Kidd had hoped. Yet OBE

enthusiasts are anything but pessimistic. Instead, they seem buoyed by the attitude of their subjects. "The effect on a person of having an OOBE is enormous," observed Dr. Charles Tart. "In almost all cases, his reaction is approximately, 'I no longer *believe* in survival after death—I *know* my consciousness will survive death because I have *experienced* my consciousness existing outside of my physical body.' "

Inevitably perhaps, it has been suggested that the OBE is no more than a psychological mechanism to cope with the dread prospect of ceasing to exist. "OOB experiences," wrote New York psychiatrist Dr. Jan Ehrenwald, "are expressions of man's perennial quest for immortality; they are faltering attempts to assert the reality and autonomous existence of the 'soul'—a deliberate challenge to the threat of extinction."

But, as Rogo pointed out, "Just because the OBE may be a method of defying death does not mean that it is a purely symbolic and/or hallucinatory experience. The fact that man has a psychological need to believe in an afterlife does not automatically mean that we do not survive death." In a trio of classic OBE cases, subjects spoke afterward of being happy to accept what seemed to them the otherworldly existence they had encountered. All three showed reluctance to return to normal experience, even though they had entered the out-of-body state altogether unwittingly.

The anonymous World War I medic who "died" in a plane crash provides one of the cases. Concluding his account, he wrote, "One interesting effect this experience had upon me was the great removal of any fear of death, because of the extraordinarily pleasant experience of what one felt and became aware of when one was apparently detached from one's body."

The same sentiments were expressed some 20 years later by Sir Auckland Geddes, an eminent British anatomist, in an address to the Royal Society of Medicine. One night, according to Geddes, he suddenly became violently ill with gastroenteritis. By morning he was so debilitated and in such pain that he could not even telephone for help. He accepted the probability of death and prosaically made a rapid review of his financial situation. As his physical condition grew worse, he felt his consciousness slip out of his body. Looking down, he could see not only his bed with his own body in it but everything in his house and garden; then it seemed to him that he was viewing scenes in London and in Scotland and wherever his attention was directed. "I was free in a time-dimension of space, wherein 'now' was in some way equivalent to 'here' in the ordinary three-dimensional space of everyday life."

Just as Geddes was beginning to recognize people he had known, he saw his daughter come into his bedroom, look at his body and hurry to the phone. "I saw my doctor leave his patients and come very quickly, and heard him say or saw him think, 'He is nearly gone.'" Watching but unable to speak, Geddes saw the doctor injecting his body with something that he learned afterward had been camphor.

"I was drawn back and I was intensely annoyed, because . . . once I was back, all the clarity of vision . . . disappeared, and I was just possessed of a glimmer of consciousness, which was suffused with pain."

Neither case would outwardly appear to support Ehrenwald's theory of the OBE as an expression of the need to deny death. However, Ehrenwald also suggests that the OBE may represent an attempted escape "from a debilitated, mangled perishable body," an act that would, in fact, be *denying* the possibility of death." On the other hand, he says, the OBE could be a rehearsal for death itself. Just how close such an experience may be to death is something that only a physician on the scene could answer.

Dr. George C. Ritchie is currently a psychiatrist and a writer. In 1943, then a private in the Army, he died. Ritchie had just completed basic training in Texas and was about to be shipped to Richmond, Virginia, when he developed what he thought was a chest cold. He checked in at the base hospital and collapsed in the X-ray room. The diagnosis was double lobar pneumonia.

When Ritchie awoke in an unfamiliar hospital room, his first thought, according to his report, was that he had better get started for Richmond. He climbed out of bed, feeling completely recovered, and looked for his uniform. It was nowhere to be seen, but he noticed to his surprise that someone was lying on the bed he had just left. He looked closer and saw that

the man, slack-jawed and gray-faced, was dead. On a finger of the body's left hand was the fraternity ring Ritchie had worn for two years. Astounded and appalled, Ritchie realized that the dead man was himself—yet he felt that a part of him still lived.

Confused beyond reason, but aware that he was supposed to be on his way to Richmond, Ritchie hurried out of the room and passed right through an orderly. Then, Ritchie reported, he found himself outside the hospital, hurtling through the air at tremendous speed. Below him was a town; he swooped down and rested beside a telephone pole, which, since he had lost his "firmness of flesh," he was unable to grasp.

In Ritchie's hospital room, Dr. Donald Francy found no trace of respiration or heartbeat in the body on the bed. At his orders the ward attendant covered the body with a sheet. At about the same time, apparently, Ritchie remembered the body on the bed and decided he had better return to it. Scarcely had he thought this when he found himself back at the hospital, searching through the wards for his physical self. Eventually he entered a small room that he seemed to recognize. His body, with the ring on and its face covered by a sheet, lay in deadly stillness. Ritchie tried to pull the cover back, but his hand seemed to pass through the fabric.

D. Scott Rogo, studying Stuart Blue Harary's OBE capacity, felt Harary was perceiving targets with something other than ESP or normal vision.

Dr. Jan Ehrenwald (below) views out-of-body stories of people reportedly brought back from death, such as George Ritchie (below, right), as part of man's quest for immortality.

An Extraordinary Out-of-Body "Fly-In"

One of the most remarkable projects in the history of out-of-body research began in the early 1970s when the American Society for Psychical Research staged a unique sort of do-it-yourself investigation. Soon dubbed the "fly-in," the project, under the direction of the society's Dr. Karlis Osis, was launched with an appeal for subjects who felt they could project at will from wherever they happened to be. The subjects were asked to beam into a target area, inspect an array of objects and afterward report their experiences in detail.

The fly-in got under way early in January 1973, with more than 100 volunteers selected from the unexpectedly large number of persons who applied. The volunteers were instructed to make an out-of-body journey to Osis's office on the fourth floor of the ASPR building in New York City at a prearranged time and view the target objects from a specific position.

When all the reports were in, it was clear that the experiment had not been a major success. Only 15 percent of the participants were able to provide convincing evidence that they had indeed visited the ASPR office. Yet among the "failures" were some who seemed to have traveled but were led astray: Terry Marmoreo, for example, projecting from Toronto, Canada, reported that she paused on her way to the ASPR office to watch a fire in the next block. Another psychic visitor reportedly dawdled on the first floor of the ASPR building and spent some time watching several persons preparing an art exhibition. Another projector, seemingly uninterested in the inanimate objects in Osis's office, claimed to have glided into an apartment across the street and enjoyed a silent visit with its occupants.

Among the alleged successes, proof of actual visitation seemed impressive. Psychic Alex Tanous, who reported that he launched his consciousness from Portland, Maine, several times during the fly-in, not only correctly identified an assortment of objects on the coffee table—his given task—but observed a researcher's cup of tea on the table. A medium named Elwood Babbitt reported that he flew in from his backwoods home in Wendell, Massachusetts. He scored a hit on his third try when he correctly observed and later sketched a large plant at the right rear of the office, a picture hanging on the wall, and a plasticine figure of a smiling girl on the right-hand side of the target table.

The smiling girl added a special dimension to the experiment. Osis had secretly commissioned an artist to make it a double figure that would appear as one thing when viewed from the front and something quite different when viewed from the back. Thus the artist cut off half of the back of the head of the sculpture, slicing from the top down through the ear. Then she added a sculpture of Archie Bunker's chair, one that filled the space where the neck and the back part of the hair should have been. Osis wanted to find out whether Babbitt would see the figurine from his out-of-body position or get an overall ESP-type

During "fly-in" project in New York, medium Elwood Babbitt (above, right) correctly sketched target objects (above) once in three tries. Another participant reportedly saw Claudette Kiely (right), a fly-in visitor from Massachusetts, at the project's office.

impression from no particular viewpoint. And indeed Babbitt seemed to demonstrate out-of-body sight—he described the face and missed the chair, which was not visible from the doorway where he said he was standing.

Another surprise for Osis came late one evening when he was spending the night in the empty ASPR building. He was aroused from sleep by a series of loud knocks at his locked office door; a search of the building, however, revealed no signs of a break-in. The next morning Osis received a phone call from Marmoreo, the fly-in subject from Toronto, who enjoyed a hearty laugh and asked Osis how he had slept. She had, she said, been snooping around in her out-of-body state in order to familiarize herself with the ASPR building, and thus had discovered the sleeping researcher.

In general, however, Osis was not impressed. "The overall results were not significant," he wrote afterward; "only some of the OB-ers seemed to 'see' things clearly enough for definite identification." Even the most gifted of the subjects, including Babbitt and Tanous, often viewed and described objects in terms of their shapes and colors rather than as specific things with names. One possible implication, some have suggested, may be that other-than-physical eyes have a less-than-physical perspective.

Yet there were some fascinating peripheral reports. One of Osis's colleagues and psychic Christine Whiting, for example, who sat in the target room for some time, both saw "blue mist" before Whiting reportedly perceived Claudette Kiely, an out-of-body visitor from Massachusetts. Whiting also spotted Tanous, a total stranger, bent like a jackknife and hovering over the target display. "Miss Whiting," Tanous wrote later, "not only described my position and my location in space, she also saw me in a shirt with rolled-up sleeves and in corduroy pants. I was wearing a shirt with rolled-up sleeves at the time and . . . pants . . . that even a short distance away look like corduroy." When Whiting met Tanous months later, she recognized him as the man she had seen hovering over the table.

The thought came to him that he would never get back into his body; he was truly dead.

With that, the room suddenly filled with brilliant light, according to Ritchie, and he sensed a compassionate, comforting presence. Instantly he was exuberantly happy. With incredible speed but enormous clarity, every scene of his life passed in review—every event and thought and conversation, flashing by in separate pictures. He sensed the presence gently questioning him about his brief life on earth; and then the hospital walls were gone and he entered another realm. Next, he recalled, "I saw a city—but a city, if such a thing is conceivable, constructed out of light. At that time I had not read the Book of Revelation, nor, incidentally, anything on the subject of life after death. But here was a city in which the walls, houses, streets, seemed to give off light, while moving among them were beings as blindingly bright as the One who stood beside me." An instant later the walls of the hospital closed around him. The dazzling light faded, and he seemed to fall asleep.

Ritchie woke up in his body. He was not happy and yearned to be back where he had been when dead. Yet he was not only alive but unimpaired, in spite of the fact that his medical chart—signed by the attending physician—showed that he had died on December 20, 1943, of double lobar pneumonia. He had been clinically dead for nine minutes when an attendant noticed movement under the sheet that covered him and went racing for the doctor. A shot of adrenalin had jolted Ritchie back to life, free of the brain damage that might have been expected following such a protracted period of oxygen deprivation.

By the mid-1970s, thanks in part to the medical profession's increased concern with the psychology of dying, general interest in near-death OBE's had increased dramatically. Two researchers who stimulated this growth were Dr. Elisabeth Kübler-Ross, a psychiatrist who has worked extensively with dying patients and their families, and philosopher-psychiatrist Dr. Raymond A. Moody, author of the landmark book *Life After Life*. The hundreds of death-experience accounts gathered by Kübler-Ross, Moody and others vary widely, yet they share a key theme, peace.

Kübler-Ross recounted the story told her by a terminally ill patient who had been near death many times. The woman was in a hospital under intensive care when a nurse saw that she was dying and hastily summoned help. "Meanwhile, this woman felt herself float out of her body. In fact, she said she could look down and see how pale her face looked. Yet at the same time she felt absolutely wonderful. She had a great sense of peace and relief."

The patient watched the doctors working on her body. "She heard what they said, which members of the team wanted to give up trying to revive her and which did not. Her recall of details was so acute that

she was even able to repeat a joke an attendant made to relieve the tension. She wanted to tell them to relax, that it was all OK. But her body showed no vital signs—no respiration, no blood pressure, no brain-wave activity. Finally, she was declared dead." Not long afterward, however, according to her story, her out-of-body self returned, and she was resuscitated.

Some who have returned from the brink of death report the sensation of floating down a dark tunnel leading to a beautiful place. One of Moody's informants, having risen out of his body after a cardiac arrest, "seemed to turn over and go up. It was dark—you could call it a hole or a tunnel—and there was this bright light. It got brighter and brighter. And I seemed to go *through* it. All of a sudden I was just somewhere else. There was a gold-looking light, everywhere. Beautiful. I couldn't find a source anywhere. It was just all around, coming from everywhere."

Subjects often report being met and welcomed, either by friends and relatives or by a sort of guiding light. Not infrequently, according to many accounts, a brilliant presence asks the dying person to review his past life. Then, as Private Ritchie found, something like an incredibly fast motion picture flashes before the eyes. One of Moody's informants recalled that "when the light appeared, the first thing he said to me was, 'What do you have to show me that you've done with your life?' And that's when the flashbacks started."

It is possible, of course, that the dying may imagine such heartening, light-filled visions because of religious beliefs or their desire to find Heaven. Yet not everyone who undergoes such an experience feels enveloped in love and light. Many survivors have told of their surprise and bafflement after dissociation: they perceived that they were dead, they say, but death was not what they had expected and they did not know where to go or what to do next. One woman observed, "The strange thing was that I had always been taught that the minute you died you would be right at these beautiful gates, pearly gates. But there I was hovering around my own physical body, and that was it! I was just baffled." A man reported, "I thought I was dead, and I wasn't sorry that I was dead, but I just couldn't figure out where I was supposed to go."

This man's experience may one day be explained in prosaic terms. On the other hand, it may be an indication that the "I"-consciousness is indeed capable of entering other realms and existing beyond the time of bodily death. In his book *Journeys Out of the Body*, Robert Monroe described his own reported projection to "no particular place, just a grayness" during which he was accosted by an angry dead man. The man's voice dripped with sarcasm as he said, "Well, *now* are you ready to learn the secrets of the universe? I hope you're ready, because nobody took the trouble to tell *me* when I was back there."

Strange Aura of Kirlian Photographs

One night in 1970, Dr. Thelma Moss, a psychologist at the University of California's Center for Health Sciences at Los Angeles, settled down to read a new book she had been asked to review. At first she was mildly put off by what she felt was the book's "extravagantly journalistic style," but as she turned the pages, she experienced a sense of excitement. The book was *Psychic Discoveries Behind the Iron Curtain,* by Sheila Ostrander and Lynn Schroeder. One of the best-selling parapsychological works of the decade, the book examined some 30 years of Soviet and East European scientific exploration of paranormal phenomena. One type of research in particular caught Moss's attention: the Kirlian Effect, allegedly a means of capturing on film the glowing emanations of what might be called the life force itself.

Semyon Kirlian, the discoverer of the Kirlian Effect, was an obscure, largely self-educated electrician and part-time inventor who lived with his wife, Valentina, in a modest two-room apartment in the Russian city of Krasnodar. In 1939, using equipment at the local hospital, where he worked as a maintenance man and electrician, he constructed an unusual device for making photographs of any object placed in a high-frequency electrical field. His first subject was his own hand. When Kirlian developed the photographic plate, he was startled to see that a mysterious glow emanated from the finger tips in the dark, silhouette-like image. Fascinated by this unexpected result, he and his wife continued experimenting, gradually perfecting their techniques and equipment and photographing an ever-expanding range of subjects, both live and inanimate.

The results were provocative in the extreme. A fresh-cut leaf, for example, would be surrounded by a bright aura and its surface spangled with myriad points of light. A few days later, the same leaf would have a dimmer aura, and most of the points of light would be gone. An inert object, such as a coin, would show only a faint aura and no points of light at all. A human hand might produce light effects that were blurred and disorganized if its owner was ill or worried but that might be bright and sharp if he seemed in good health.

Psychologist Thelma Moss, one of the first U.S. researchers to test Kirlian photography, believes it involves "bioenergy."

In one experiment (conducted by some of Kirlian's followers), part of a leaf was torn off before the leaf was photographed. The developed image was, the researchers reported, typical of that of a fresh-cut leaf in all but one respect: filling the space left by the missing piece was a "phantom leaf," a faint aural light that exactly duplicated the leaf's original outline.

The Kirlians continued to work during the postwar decades, eventually introducing color photography to their investigative techniques. Not until the 1960s, however, did they obtain a modest government research grant; thereafter official enthusiasm began to grow. Had the Kirlians, with their "bioluminescent" images, discovered evidence of a new form of energy? Had they, in fact, confirmed what psychics had been insisting for 1,000 years—that all living things are surrounded with an invisible aura? Might not the Kirlian Effect be turned to practical uses in such fields as medicine, psychology, agriculture, biology and perhaps even criminology? Such possibilities seemed endless.

They seemed endless, too, to Thelma Moss and a handful of U.S. researchers when they first learned of the Kirlian Effect in the early 1970s. What particularly excited Moss was the effect's promise of repeatability under laboratory conditions—a quality often lacking in other so-called psychic phenomena. Within months of reading about Kirlian photography, Moss was in the Soviet Union, conferring with researchers and acquiring scientific literature. Back in California in early 1971, she and one of her students, Kendall Johnson, set about constructing a Kirlian device of their own. After many trials—and a number of failures—they succeeded.

Other U.S. investigators, such as Dr. Stanley Krippner, and William Tiller of Stanford University's Department of Materials Science, soon followed Moss's lead, and by May 1972, Kirlian research in the United States was sufficiently advanced to sustain what was called the First Western Hemisphere Conference on Kirlian Photography, Acupuncture and the Human Aura. Some conferees reported that they had been able to replicate some of the specific effects claimed by the

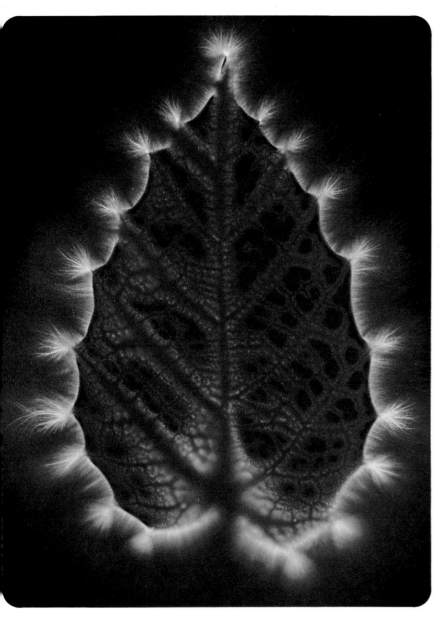

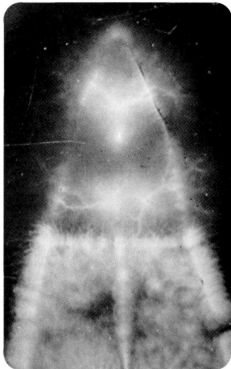

Kirlian photograph of a healthy leaf (left) shows a bright, symmetrical corona. More remarkable is the picture above, also Kirlian, which purportedly demonstrates a phenomenon known as the "phantom leaf" effect. The tip of the ivy leaf, which appears to be slightly fainter than the remainder, had actually been cut off before the picture was made.

Soviets and added a few of their own. E. Douglas Dean, for example, photographed the hands of a psychic healer and reported that the corona of light surrounding her finger tips flared whenever she thought of healing. Moss and Johnson reported on a subject who could "invariably change his blue-white corona to a red blotch by deliberately making himself angry."

But as enthusiasm for Kirlian photography grew, so did skepticism. An October 15, 1976, article in the influential journal *Science* argued that the Kirlian Effect was probably produced solely by the amount of moisture present in the subject. As for repeatability, the authors of the article also noted that at least 25 variables had to be controlled before any Kirlian photograph could be interpreted, thus implying that many famous Kirlian photographs might be useless. Some physicists have speculated that the effect may merely represent

displacement currents that affect photographic emulsions but reveal little about the subject itself.

Meanwhile, research continues. Moss has claimed 100 percent success in using the effect to predict the ability of soybean seeds to germinate. She has also reported making Kirlian videotapes showing plant auras getting brighter at the approach of a human hand. Physicists at Drexel University report correlations between fluctuations in finger-pad coronas and forms of minor pain, mental exertion and hyperventilation.

Yet, while fragments of alleged evidence accumulate, a central problem remains: What actually produces the Kirlian Effect? Is it a new form of energy or merely a new manifestation of a known form? For Thelma Moss, at least, the answer is clear. "I wouldn't see any purpose mucking about in this field," she said, "if I thought it were entirely an electrical phenomenon."

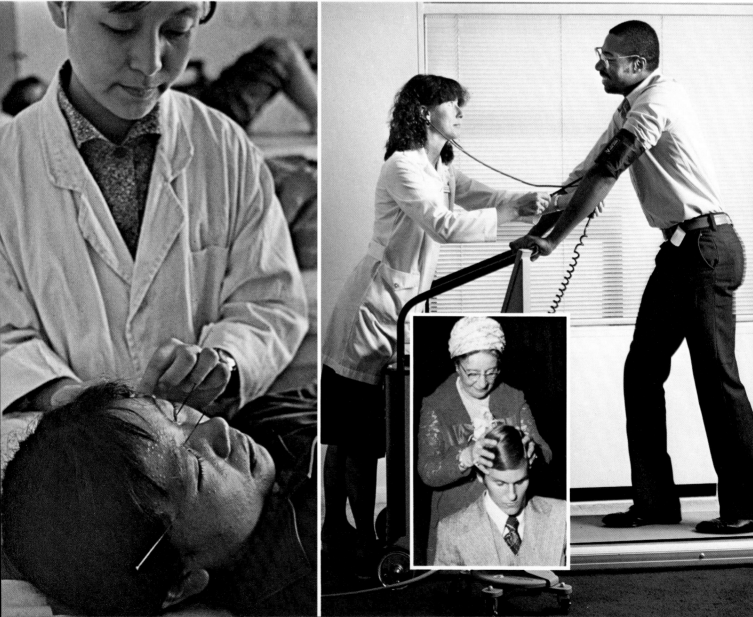

Faith, the laying on of hands and
unexplained powers of the mind and body are all
elements in the fight against disease.

HEALING

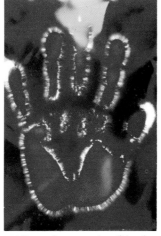

Kirlian photograph of healer
Olga Worrall's hand allegedly reveals "healing energy."

Shortly after the exploratory surgical procedure began, the attending doctors found evidence that confirmed their worst fears. The pain that had brought the patient to their attention was the pain of advanced stomach cancer, and it was clear that there was nothing to do but send the man home to die. In a gesture of hope, however, the doctors suggested to the patient's wife that she bring her husband in for a series of checkups. The appointments were not kept; it was assumed that the man had died. Nine years later the cancer patient was re-admitted to the same hospital with heart problems. In explaining to doctors why her husband had missed the earlier appointments, the patient's wife said that after his "surgery" her husband "had never had a bit of stomach distress."

• Thirteen months after being told that he had a sarcoma of the left pelvis, a young inductee in the Italian Army traveled to Lourdes, the Roman Catholic shrine in southwest France. At the time of Vittorio Micheli's pilgrimage, his left femur had detached from the diseased pelvis, and he could neither stand on nor control his left leg, which was encased from hip to toe in a heavy plaster cast. Arriving in Lourdes, Micheli was

Among the many factors that may influence healing are prayer (top, pilgrims at Lourdes); acupuncture (far left, showing treatment for sinusitis); biofeedback (left, training to reduce hypertension); and the laying on of hands (inset).

immersed in the baths and immediately experienced two remarkable changes in his condition: his appetite, which had steadily declined during his illness, was restored, and the pain, which had steadily increased during the course of the disease, disappeared. He soon had the feeling that his pelvis and femur were reattaching. Believing himself cured, he returned home. Although his skeptical doctors insisted that he continue to wear the cast, Micheli was able to walk within a month. Two months later, X-rays indicated that the sarcoma was indeed receding and that the pelvic bone had begun to regenerate. Medical review of Micheli's case over a period of five years confirmed that the sarcoma had disappeared.

• "I want to see you as soon as possible," the woman had written in desperation to Ethel DeLoach. "I have been going to a gynecologist who told me I have two lumps in my left breast. He wants me . . . to have my breast removed." A few days later, DeLoach, a professional healer who lives in New Jersey, received Mrs. H., a middle-aged woman afflicted with more than lumps in her breast. She was overweight, depressed, suffered from poor vision as a result of an unsuccessful cataract operation, had had a kidney removed, had severely damaged hearing, and was in considerable pain from ulcerations on both legs. In a short while, as the visitor lay on the couch in her living room, DeLoach began her treatment, passing her hands slowly over the woman's sick body. When the procedure was over, Mrs. H.

The history of healing has been largely one of faith: good health was often beyond an individual's control or comprehension, its restoration the preserve of such figures as the traveling medicine men depicted in this 15th-century Turkish miniature.

reported feeling somewhat better. A month later she wrote that the lumps in her breast had softened, her legs no longer hurt and her hearing was improved. She asked for a second treatment. When Mrs. H. arrived a week later, she was 10 pounds lighter and her mood was correspondingly brighter. DeLoach repeated her technique, and three weeks later received another letter from Mrs. H. advising that her doctor had confirmed that the lumps in her breast had shrunk. In subsequent letters Mrs. H. said that her leg ulcers and eyesight had shown even more dramatic improvement.

• The patient, a 61-year-old man with throat cancer, had failed to respond to conventional treatment when he agreed to Dr. O. Carl Simonton's experimental regimen of brief mental exercises repeated three times a day. First, the patient was told to meditate for 2½ minutes, silently repeating the word *relax* with every exhaled breath while concentrating on relaxing the muscles of his throat and jaw and those surrounding the eyes. Next he was told to visualize something extremely pleasurable for 1½ minutes, after which he was to replace that mental picture with one of his tumor as he imagined it to be. With the tumor vividly outlined in his mind, he was instructed to imagine particles of radiation bombarding it and then to picture white blood cells clearing away the cells killed by radiation. For seven weeks the patient followed this daily program, at the end of which time the tumor's growth seemed to have been arrested, and the patient, who had been given no better than a 10 percent chance to live, was pronounced ready for release.

This Egyptian healing statue of basalt is more than 2,000 years old.

Four cures or four miracles? Four instances of spontaneous remission or simply four examples of the body's remarkable and dimly understood powers of recovery and healing?

It is impossible to answer such questions with any certainty today. For despite the extraordinary accomplishments of modern medicine, much of what the body does to keep itself well and to restore itself when diseased remains a mystery to even the most sophisticated of researchers. Yet when a life is saved as if by miracle or pain subsides without explanation, it is difficult to ignore the possible influence of psychic, or paranormal, healing. Whether such healing can be attributed to supranormal forces, or to latent, rarely summoned faculties within the human body, remains a compelling—and controversial—question. Yet evidence is accumulating that suggests that a variety of approaches to healing, from the laying on of hands to biofeedback, hypnosis, and other means of influencing the mind, may have a role to play in unleashing the body's remarkable regenerative forces.

The four cases described above certainly hint at such a possibility. In each case, the medically predicted course of a disease, cancer, appears to have been dramatically reversed. And in each case, the patient had faith that he or she would recover and exhibited as well a strong will to live, two factors that contemporary medicine has come to emphasize more and more. Historically such positive psychological states have often been cited as crucial allies in mobilizing the body's healing mechanism, and a number of recent investigations seem to suggest that they may, in fact, be critical.

Yet while some researchers have pursued such psychological approaches, a few have sought to isolate more exotic factors to explain non-medical healing, some element perhaps that corresponds to the life force revered in many religions and cultures. The ancient Egyptians called it the *ka;* the Hindus, the *prana;* and the Chinese, the *T' chi.* Is it possible that such a life force actually courses through the human body? Might certain people who claim to be gifted healers dispense some measurable form of energy capable of mobilizing that force?

To a degree, the history of healing reflects a continuing struggle between the exotic and the practical. At one extreme stands the tradition of disease as mysterious and amenable to miraculous influence, exemplified by the belief of the ancient Greeks that illness was a manifestation of divine displeasure. Opposed to this tradition is that of the scientist and practical man, the herbalist, the applier of leeches, the instigator of purgatives, the bleeder. The earliest spokesman for the scientific tradition was Hippocrates, who in the 5th century B.C. declared epilepsy to be naturally caused. Men believed it to be of divine origin, he argued, only because they did not understand it. Yet even with such champions as Hippocrates, healing, until modern times, has remained largely a matter of faith, and often of disappointment.

In Europe, for instance, from about the 11th century through the early 19th century, people believed that kings—and queens—had the power to heal disease by the laying on of hands. A disfiguring tubercular inflammation known as scrofula was called the "king's evil" because a royal gesture was thought to cause as well as cure it. The tradition of the king's touch survived in England into the early 18th century, with Queen Anne (who touched Samuel Johnson to no avail) last performing the rite some three months before her death in 1714. The last recorded case of royal laying on of hands in Europe occurred in 1825 when

Faith healing was common among early Christians, as shown in this Florentine fresco of Saint Peter tending to the sick.

the French king Charles X touched about 120 persons brought to him by the doctors Alibert and Dupuytren.

Such early paranormal healing, however, was not confined to royalty. Europe's monarchs had at least one significant rival in Valentine Greatrakes, a commoner known as the Irish Stroker. Born in 1629, Greatrakes became convinced at the age of 33 that he possessed the royal touch. Within a few years he made public his belief and his apparent gift for healing. Though his success inspired unhappiness at court, he was permitted to practice his techniques.

Modern observers have studied Greatrakes's methods, along with those of Franz Anton Mesmer, whose theory of animal magnetism was to electrify Europe a century later. When Mesmer earned his medical degree in Vienna in 1766, he had already begun to formulate his theory of an invisible flow of magnetic current through all objects in the universe, including the human body. Health, Mesmer theorized, was dependent on harmony between the "fluid" within and that outside the body, an alignment, in a sense, of an individual life force with the universal. This indefinable substance, Mesmer argued, might be manipulated by magnets. In time, however, he came to an important realization: his success in healing was due not to the magnets, but to his own powers of mental suggestion. Though he continued to speak in physical terms, claiming that fluid

The Royal Touch

The royal, or king's, touch was the special gift of healing claimed by English and French sovereigns from the Middle Ages to the Victorian Era. Their claim was a relatively modest one, generally confined to the treatment of a tubercular inflammation called scrofula that, while nasty, was not normally fatal. There was no known cure for scrofula, which caused sores and growths about the face and neck, but it had a tendency to clear up spontaneously, making it an ideal disease on which to demonstrate the alleged gift of healing.

The first French account of the practice dates it to King Philip I, who ruled from 1060 to 1108 and is said to have "zealously applied himself to the exercise of this glorious and miraculous power." Shakespeare, however, suggested an earlier date for the English rite in *Macbeth*, when he had the fleeing Malcolm observe the "healing benediction" at the court of Edward the Confessor, who reigned from 1042 to 1066. Whether Edward actually practiced the touch or was merely given credit for doing so at his canonization a century later, the value of the rite was interpreted correctly by the descendants of both its putative fathers. By claiming to heal scrofula, a sovereign made himself a savior to his subjects, thus reinforcing the divine right by which he held the power to rule.

In the early days of the rite, one might arrive at court seeking the touch almost without announcement, but as monarchies grew grander, the rite was usually reserved for great feast days. The number of persons touched by individual rulers varied greatly; in some years only hundreds were blessed, but in 1698, when gout prevented Louis XIV from appearing as planned on Easter Sunday, a crowd of 3,000 turned out at the next opportunity, Pentecost. While it endured, the royal touch was beneficent, but the mutual sympathy it promoted between ruler and ruled was in the end not enough to protect the French crown or sustain the power of the British throne.

Edward the Confessor, England's sainted 11th-century king, is shown above touching to heal scrofula.

coursing through a patient's body was obedient to his directive, he was actually influencing moods and emotions. Thus Mesmer's critics, who charged that his cures existed only in his patients' minds, were probably right. Nevertheless, the afflictions of many of his patients were real, and somehow Mesmer succeeded in guiding some to health.

Mesmer's treatment of Maria Theresa Paradies, a young woman who had suffered from hysterical blindness since the age of three, is in many ways reminiscent of Josef Breuer's case of Anna O., cited by Sigmund Freud as an early instance of classic psychoanalytic treatment. Maria, a moderately celebrated pianist in the Vienna of Gluck and Mozart (both close friends of Mesmer's), had already been subjected to a variety of treatments when her parents brought her, at the age of 18, to Mesmer. She had been bled, purged and blistered, had suffered electric-shock therapy and had been locked into a suffocating helmet-like contraption made of plaster. When she appeared before Mesmer, her eyes bulged grotesquely, swollen and misaligned not because of any true physical ailment, but because of the practices of a succession of doctors.

Mesmer's methods were painless, soothing, and produced almost immediate results. By the fourth day of treatment, Maria's father reported that his child "felt real relief and her eyes returned to their normal position. We could see that the left eye was smaller than the right, but the treatment gradually caused them to become the same size."

To ensure that the girl was not overwhelmed by her cure, Mesmer kept her with her eyes bandaged in a darkened room. She was then exposed gradually to increased doses of light until her eyes were strong enough to perceive colors. From that point her control over the muscles of her eyes increased steadily. In fact, Maria was demonstrably close to being fully cured—as a deputation from the Vienna Faculty of Medicine concluded after a visit to Mesmer's clinic—when she was abruptly withdrawn from Mesmer's care by her parents. It is not known why, although the professional jealousy of an ophthalmologist who had unsuccessfully treated Maria may have caused the man to interfere and persuade the Paradieses to abandon Mesmer. In any event, patient and therapist were forcibly separated, prompting a scandal that ultimately drove Mesmer out of Vienna and on to Paris, a more hospitable climate for the natural healing techniques he espoused. There Mesmer attracted a broad following that served both to make him wealthy and to disseminate the still-inchoate ideas that lay behind his apparently successful techniques. But when the report of a royal commission formed to investigate his theories declared that there was no such thing as the elixir he claimed to realign, Mesmer's reputation was badly damaged. Eventually, he was forced to retire to Switzerland.

Treatment in Franz Anton Mesmer's Parisian salon was an elegant affair. While Mesmer's patients gathered around an oversize oaken tub, called the *Baquet*, which was dotted with "curative" iron rods, Mesmer (right) moved among them discussing cures.

Although the term *mesmerize* has come to mean "to hold sway over another" and is frequently used as a synonym for *hypnotize*, there is no evidence that Mesmer's patients were entranced, and they were certainly not hypnotized. What Mesmer seems to have done, by means of an unparalleled bedside manner, is persuade patients to give up their ailments and thereby cure themselves. The magnets, soft music and stroking Mesmer employed were, to some extent, the 18th-century equivalents of the healing techniques used by some therapists today. And as Mesmer himself recognized but was afraid to advertise, his most effective aid was not magnetic force but the power of suggestion.

Badly understood in its own time, mesmerism, in garbled form, lingered into the 19th century. It was eventually adopted in the United States by an uneducated New England clockmaker named Phineas Parkhurst Quimby, who expanded Mesmer's ideas into a full-blown philosophy of influence and suggestibility.

With a 19-year-old self-proclaimed clairvoyant named Lucius Burkmar serving as guinea pig, test pilot and living laboratory, Quimby confirmed what earlier observation and instinct had told him—that the mind and the body it serves can be manipulated with relative ease. At first Quimby seems to have been more interested in telepathy than healing. In one test, he claimed that he could, by thinking about a wild animal, cause Burkmar to be terrified. A later lesson seems to have anticipated the work of psychologist B. F. Skinner by nearly a century: Quimby supposedly cured Burkmar of his boyhood habit of sucking lemons by making him suck imaginary lemons one after another until he could stand them no longer.

Quimby's understanding of the fact that he could make others respond to his thoughts was pivotal: "At last I found out that mind was something that could be changed. I called it spiritual matter, because I found it could be condensed into a solid and receive a name called 'tumor,' and by the same power under a different direction it might be dissolved and made to disappear."

For the most part, Burkmar's feats do indeed sound amazing. He is said, for example, to have prescribed remedies identical to those suggested by various physicians, but whereas the physicians' treatments had failed, Burkmar's (Quimby's) succeeded. Quimby summarized his observations in a letter to a Portland, Maine, newspaper in February 1862: "I also found that any medicine would cure if he [Lucius] ordered it. This led me to . . . the stand I now take: that the cure is not in the medicine, but in the confidence of the doctor or medium."

Quimby eventually came to realize that his authority alone was sufficient, and by the time he was approached by the long-suffering Mary Patterson, better known today as Mary Baker Eddy, founder of modern Christian Science, he had shed Burkmar as an intermediary and was performing healing rites directly. He had also declared that diseases and their cures were the consequence of suggestion.

Eddy, Quimby's most famous patient, came to him as a 41-year-old woman who had been immobilized by illness most of her life: she was a virtual cripple when she appeared for treatment at his Portland office. Yet she came away cured and converted, and within a few years had created her own highly persuasive philosophy of healing. Whereas Quimby probably had been an agnostic, Eddy incorporated fundamentalist views into her movement and called it Christian Science. The essential dogma was similar, however: illness and health are both illusions; there is no physical world, therefore there is no disease, and no need for medical intervention. The way to achieve health, Eddy believed, was by reordering one's perceptions.

The principles and techniques that Eddy espoused and taught to her students require adherents to reject most generally accepted concepts of medicine, and it is of interest that the rise of Christian Science in the United States occurred virtually simultaneously with two landmark advances in medicine, Louis Pasteur's identification of germs as agents of infection in 1862, and Joseph Lister's discovery in 1865 of antisepsis.

The advances of modern medicine, however, have never fully succeeded in supplanting non-traditional approaches to healing, and the two have now coexisted, though generally at arm's length, for more than a century. There is good reason for this: certain diseases, such as cancer and those affecting the cardiovascular system, have yet to be brought under control, and some patients suffer chronic pain that modern medical techniques cannot fully alleviate. As a result, many sufferers have sought alternative forms of healing. And remark-

Phineas P. Quimby's interpretation of mesmerism inspired his patient Mary Baker Eddy to establish Christian Science. One of her early ads is shown above.

ably enough by the standards of conventional medicine, a small number seem to have been cured.

What might be called the "miracle" cure occupies a unique position in the spectrum of unconventional healing. The word itself is employed frequently and colloquially to describe all kinds of improvements in health, yet miracles as defined by the Catholic Church are rare events indeed. A case in point is Lourdes, the most famous of all Catholic healing shrines. Since 1858 when 14-year-old Bernadette Soubirous experienced a vision of the Blessed Virgin at Lourdes, millions of supplicants have visited the shrine. In that time thousands of cures have been attributed to Lourdes by patients who have lowered themselves into the waters of its grotto. The Church, however, has certified only 64 cases as miracles.

To receive such certification, a cure must pass through four stages of review, three medical and one ecclesiastical, and must satisfy seven criteria established by the Church: the original illness or disability must be beyond doubt and serious; must be either extremely difficult or impossible (by available medical means) to cure; and must have resisted all previous medical treatment (if any was attempted). The cure, in turn, should be sudden or extremely rapid, permanent and perfect. Although the 1962 case of Vittorio Micheli's relief from cancer of the hip would seem to meet all seven criteria, the Church has not yet ruled on it.

Despite the rigorous review system imposed by the Church, the miracles of Lourdes have been subjected to criticism by modern researchers who note that a great many cures appear to involve psychosomatic or hysterical illnesses. The Church, however, which assigns a classification of "remarkable" to hundreds of cures that it fails to certify as true miracles, seems relatively unconcerned about such criticisms, emphasizing that the significance of Lourdes is not as a site for the production of cures but as a source of spiritual renewal.

A quite different approach, but one that nonetheless involves faith and belief in a higher being, is known as absent healing, and one of its most famous practitioners was Edgar Cayce. Absent healing was a way of life for Cayce for 43 years. Until his death in 1945, Cayce claimed to need only a patient's name and address to produce, while in a self-induced trance, a diagnosis and a detailed prescription for treatment. His suggested remedies included changes in diet and the use of herbs, chiropractic manipulation, and modern medicinal compounds that, as a layman with little formal education, he could barely pronounce. Estimates of Cayce's success vary, yet he is thought by some to have been one of the most effective healers of his day.

Another practitioner of absent healing and also of the laying on of hands was Harry Edwards, founder of the National Federation of Spiritual Healers in England,

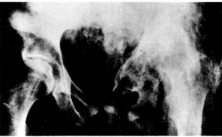

Since Bernadette Soubirous' vision at Lourdes in 1858, thousands have bathed in the shrine's waters. Yet only 64 cases have been certified as miracles by the Church. The X-ray above shows a tumor in the hip of Vittorio Micheli, a Lourdes pilgrim who later claimed to be cured.

a group with hospital privileges throughout the United Kingdom. Like Cayce, Kathryn Kuhlman, Ambrose and Olga Worrall, and many others practicing in the 20th century, Edwards ascribed his abilities to the intervention of God. Yet he objected to the phrase *faith healing* because it implied that faith was essential in the person being cured, something he knew from experience to be untrue: Edwards's second attempt at healing took place at long distance and without his subject's knowledge. As Edwards explained long afterward to Paris Flammonde, author of *The Mystic Healers,* the diseased man "was an adamant atheist and his wife dared not tell him that she'd sought spiritual help for him." Nonetheless, Edwards claimed that his long-distance cure had worked.

Procedures and techniques vary greatly, however, in the field of paranormal healing. Ethel DeLoach, for example, the New Jersey housewife who treated Mrs. H., had never attempted faith healing until her daughter was kicked by a horse and she was forced to help in some manner because no doctor was available. The technique she now uses is similar to the laying on of hands, but instead of actually touching a patient's body, she passes her hands over it. DeLoach reports that during her treatment, a patient may experience a prickling sensation much like that produced by the actual insertion of

Better known as the center of Catholic devotion to the rosary as a means of achieving peace, Fátima, Portugal, where the Virgin supposedly appeared to three children, has reported miraculous cures.

acupuncture needles. Significantly, DeLoach has studied acupuncture, and instead of passing her hands over the point of an illness, she follows the meridian lines of the ancient Oriental science.

Traditional acupuncture itself must be considered, to some degree, part of paranormal healing. For despite its antiquity and its demonstrated effectiveness as an anesthetic, and more erratically as a healing agent, its workings remain inexplicable. However, some scientists engaged in pain research suspect that the insertion of acupuncture needles at critical points may stimulate production of chemicals called endorphins, the body's own opiates. If so, acupuncture may be counted not as a mysterious and isolated practice but as a technique for mobilizing the human body's natural healing capacities.

In search of such benefits, science continues to assay paranormal healing: in the last 10 to 15 years various techniques have been subjected to a variety of laboratory tests, while outside the laboratory, physicians, psychiatrists and nurses have begun to draw on

Lightning Cure

The boldest of psychic healers would avoid making promises in a case like Edwin Robinson's. The long-distance truck driver was 53 when a bad accident on the road left him blind and nearly deaf and, according to his doctors, with no hope of recovery. One rainy day in June 1980, however, Robinson thought to check his pet chicken, Took-Took, which was outside near the garage of his house in Falmouth, Maine. He carried an aluminum cane, as usual, and was wearing his hearing aid. As he passed beneath a poplar tree, bad luck struck again; or so it seemed at first. With no warning, a bolt of lightning knocked Robinson unconscious. Yet 20 minutes later, when the 62-year-old man awoke, he discovered that he could see better than ever before—perfectly, in fact—and that his hearing was fully restored.

"I don't know how to explain it," his ophthalmologist, Dr. Albert Moulton, said when he first learned of Robinson's recovery. Then he grew more definite. "It's a miracle," he said. "I don't know what to expect, but I think the return is permanent. . . . Shocks do strange things."

As for Robinson, who remarked after the event, "I'm all recharged now, literally," life continued to improve. A month after the incident, hair began to sprout on his bald head. "It's coming in thick," he told the *New York Times*. "My wife is all excited about it. I was bald for 35 years. They told me it was hereditary."

Robinson's extraordinary good fortune remains unexplained. Yet for those inclined to dabble in theories of energy, balance, harmony and such, it may be worth noting that there were actually two casualties on the day that the lightning bolt struck: Robinson's hearing device was completely burned out, he reported, and so was the poplar tree.

Retired truck driver Edwin Robinson's sight and hearing were suddenly restored when he was struck by lightning.

the field's strengths and to incorporate seemingly unconventional practices into their professional work.

Virtually any observer of human nature is aware that mind and body share a continuing, reciprocal influence. Thus much of the discussion of psychic healing involves intangibles, such as the will to live, and their capacity to influence the body's natural healing mechanisms. Yet while acknowledging the importance of such factors, some scientists, in common with many adherents of psychic healing, have sought more concrete explanations for unexplained cures. In that search they have tried to measure the influence of healers on such things as mice, plants, enzymes, and even atomic particles.

Olga and Ambrose Worrall, who claim continued success as healers, have both participated in several such experiments. Mrs. Worrall believes that the workings of paranormal healing remain an open question, one that she thinks will be answered only by scientific investigation. "Is it the healer?" she has asked in her writings. "Is it the patient? Is it the environment? Is it medication or manipulation? Or is it none of these or all of these? Perhaps something else is at work." She concludes that "the most any healer can do is to provide conditions that permit healing to take place."

One experiment in which the Worralls took part was conducted by Dr. Robert N. Miller, an industrial research scientist working out of Atlanta. In the experiment, he attempted to test the effect of prayer on the growth of ryegrass seed. According to Miller's description of the project, he planted 10 seeds in good growing soil and watered them daily until their growth rate had been stabilized at 0.006 inch per hour over several days. He then telephoned the Worralls in Baltimore, 600 miles away, and asked them to begin praying. At nine o'clock the next morning they began. Twenty-three hours later, Miller reported, he checked his chart and observed that beginning at precisely nine o'clock the day before, the seeds' growth rate had started to climb. By 8:00 a.m. of the second day, 47 hours after the praying had begun, he said, the growth rate had reached 0.0525 inch per hour, for an increase of 775 percent. In the next two days the growth rate lessened somewhat but never again dropped to what it had been before the Worralls started praying.

In 1974, Miller, in association with Dr. Philip B. Reinhart of the physics department of Agnes Scott College in Georgia, tested Olga Worrall again, this time using a cloud chamber, a device capable of tracking the motions of high-energy atomic particles. Such particles appear as a fixed vapor pattern, and the scientists hoped to discover whether a healer's hands might alter that pattern. When, as a preliminary test, members of the research team placed their hands on the outside of the cloud chamber, no change was observed. Mrs. Worrall then placed her hands on either side of the chamber,

Sleight-of-Hand Surgeons

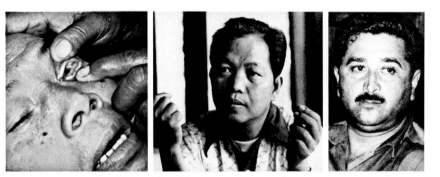

Psychic surgeons who claim to be able to operate on such sensitive organs as the eye—without anesthesia or antiseptics—have flourished in the Philippines. Filipino "surgeon" Tony Agpaoa is shown above, center; the Brazilian Arigó, who died in 1971, is at right.

Medical investigators have had a relatively easy time exposing the phenomenon known as psychic surgery, which annually draws thousands of ill persons to the Philippines on specially arranged package tours that combine sightseeing with a trip to one of the many healers who operate in and around Manila.

The sleight of hand necessary to simulate an incision in a patient's abdomen or to appear to extract a tumor has been observed firsthand and even recorded on film. One film clip showed that when a "surgeon" was supposed to be inserting his fingers into a patient's body, he was actually burrowing into the patient's flesh with his knuckles; his finger tips were clearly visible. In other cases, samples of patients' "blood" and "tissue," when tested, turned out to be of animal origin.

Even the most sophisticated of the Filipino healers, the wealthy Tony Agpaoa, has been caught—and exposed. In 1973 a team of Italian investigators reported that the red liquid that appeared during Agpaoa's operations proved to be neither human nor animal blood and that two "renal stones" taken from a patient were in fact lumps of salt and pumice. Supposedly fresh fragments of bone and tissue, it also turned out, had already begun to decompose.

Less easily explained, however, are the feats of a Brazilian healer named Arigó, who, before his death in a car crash in 1971, practiced a brand of healing that included both impromptu, non-antiseptic surgery, usually with a pocketknife, and the prescription of modern pharmaceutical remedies.

Arigó was born in Minas Gerais, Brazil. He attended school for only four years, was never trained in a profession or trade, and as a young man worked on and off as a laborer or farmhand. When he was 30, he reportedly fell into a severe depression that was accompanied by nightmares, sleepwalking and sleep-talking. When he consulted a local spiritualist, he was told that a spirit was trying to work through him. The symptoms abated, and Arigó began his career as a healer by successfully treating a local politician who had an inoperable lung tumor.

Most of Arigó's 20 years as a healer were spent in a clinic in Belo Horizonte, to which as many as 300 patients a day came seeking help. Those patients he felt could be as easily helped by available conventional means he sent away. The rest he treated surgically or by prescription, to the mystification of the medical experts who flocked to see what was going on. Among them was a doctor and psychic researcher from the United States, Henry Puharich. He first visited Arigó's clinic in 1963 with a cameraman in tow. After watching Arigó operate on a number of patients without anesthesia or antiseptics, Puharich volunteered himself.

While a crowd of nearly 100 looked on, "Arigó with a flourish requested that someone furnish him with a pocket knife. . . . [He] took hold of my right wrist with his left hand and wielded the borrowed pocket knife with his right hand. . . . I turned . . . toward my cameraman and directed [his] work. The next thing I knew was that Arigó had placed a tumor and the knife in my hand. In spite of being perfectly conscious, I had not felt any pain. . . . Yet there was the incision in my arm, which was bleeding, and there was the tumor. . . . the film showed that the entire operation had lasted five seconds. Arigó had made two strokes with the knife. . . . The skin had split wide open and the tumor was clearly visible. Arigó then squeezed the tumor as one might squeeze a boil, and the tumor popped out."

Puharich expected to suffer from a degree of infection afterward, but though he covered the incision with nothing more than a Band-Aid and did not clean it, the wound healed within three days. Puharich was convinced. He made two trips in all to Brazil to observe as Arigó made hundreds of accurate diagnoses, correctly estimated blood pressure without instruments, and called out the complex names of drugs to be written down by an assistant and presented to patients afterward. When Puharich asked Arigó how he arrived at a diagnosis, the healer told him, "I simply listen to a voice in my right ear and I repeat whatever it says. It is always right."

Arigó said that the voice belonged to a long-dead German named Adolphus Fritz, who had attended but never finished medical school. After five years' study, Puharich could not decide whether Arigó actually believed the voice to be real or not. In any case, Puharich was unable to explain in conventional terms what he had observed. As he reported a year after Arigó's death, "Our nice modern equipment proved that genuine healing took place under bizarre conditions and unbelievable circumstances. Clearly, we have a lot of research ahead of us."

and just as she does when attempting to heal human patients, she imagined energy flowing from her hands. As she did so, the researchers reported, they observed a wave pattern emanating on the line between her hands. When she shifted her hands 90 degrees, they said, the pattern shifted 90 degrees as well. In a related experiment, Mrs. Worrall tried to produce the same effect at long distance. Once again, according to the scientists, the vapor pattern was altered.

The strange powers of Oskar Estebany have also been tested repeatedly under strict laboratory conditions. Estebany, a former Hungarian Army officer now living in Montreal, had his first encounter with psychic healing while treating injured cavalry horses. By the time he came to the attention of Dr. Bernard Grad, a biochemist at McGill University in Montreal, he had achieved considerable acclaim as a healer of humans by the laying on of hands. Grad mounted a series of experiments with Estebany, using mice and plant life as subjects. In the first, 48 female mice of the same strain and age were anesthetized and a small piece of skin was removed from their backs. The resulting wounds were traced on paper so that their exact size could be recorded. The mice were divided into three groups, one of which was to be treated by Estebany. With a cage containing mice balanced in his left hand, Estebany held his right hand over the cage for 15 minutes, a

Dr. Dolores Krieger has taught her therapeutic touch at nursing schools.

process that was repeated twice a day, five days a week, with all of his mice. A second group of mice received no treatment at all. A third group received a heat treatment to simulate the heat of Estebany's hands. Two weeks after the experiment began, Grad reported, the wounds on Estebany's mice had healed, while those of the two control groups were still open. Statistical analysis suggested that the probability of such differences occurring by chance was less than 1 in 1,000. Grad concluded that something had in fact emanated from Estebany's hands, that it did accelerate the healing process, but that the active factor was not heat.

Because Estebany seemed especially successful in treating patients with thyroid irregularities, Grad conducted a number of experiments using mice with goiters, a thyroid disorder. In the first, a six-week experiment, Grad found that Estebany's laying on of hands had effectively slowed the development of goiters that were artificially stimulated in the mice. In a second test, Estebany attempted to treat the mice indirectly, using cotton and wool pads that he had held in his hand. The pads were introduced into the rodents' cages for two hours a day, and again, Grad found, the goiters' growth was slowed. In a third experiment, Estebany's techniques were said to greatly accelerate the recovery of mice in which goiters had been artificially induced by a diet low in iodine.

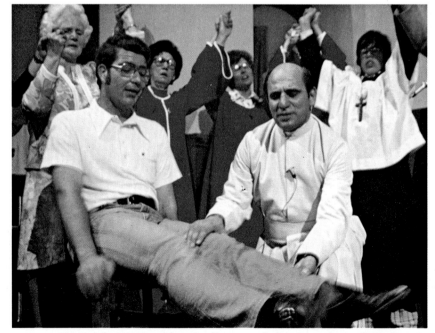

Fr. Ralph DiOrio (above), director of the Apostolate of Healing in Leicester, Massachusetts, says healing is the "force of God working through me as a medium." Roman Catholic nun and biochemist Sister Justa Smith (right) has investigated the capacity of healers to influence enzymes.

Grad's work with Estebany prompted a U.S. biochemist who is also a Franciscan nun, Sister Justa Smith, to test the effect of healing on an even more basic natural process, enzyme activity. At the conclusion of extensive testing, Smith estimated that the effect of Estebany's healing touch on the enzyme selected for the study, trypsin, was equal to the effect produced by a magnetic field of 13,000 gauss. Yet when tests were undertaken to determine whether some form of magnetic field existed between Estebany's hands, the results were negative. Whatever force the healer might have been exerting, it seemed that existing technologies could not measure it.

Another study, one conducted by Dr. Thelma Moss, had as its subject a Los Angeles doctor who had been unobtrusively treating pain and illness through the laying on of hands for more than 30 years, though never in his highly traditional medical practice. Dr. Hans Engel was elected president of the Los Angeles Academy of Family Physicians in 1977. A year later he published a monograph in which he told about his experiences with unusual forms of treatment. As he reported, he first discovered his ability to relieve pain when he was newly married and his wife complained of a headache. Out of sympathy he made a move to place his hand on her forehead and was surprised to find that as his fingers

Tests studied Oskar Estebany's alleged powers to promote healing in mice.

neared the corner of her left eyebrow, he felt as though "I were passing my hand an inch or two above an ice cube." Engel refrained from touching his wife's brow, he said, but kept his hand close to the cold spot, which she then told him was the locus of her pain. He continued to hold his hand over the area until, about a minute later, the sensation of cold subsided. Simultaneously, his wife announced that her headache was gone.

Engel continued his at-home laying on of hands for many years, with his wife as his only subject. And then, in 1962, while attending a medical convention, he underwent a test for glaucoma at one of the demonstration booths and was told that he had the disease, which can lead to blindness if not treated. Engel began the prescribed regimen of daily eyedrops, which he was told he would have to use for the rest of his life. But two years after his glaucoma had been diagnosed, the pressure in his eyeballs inexplicably returned to normal. In 1972, shortly after two highly painful emotional experiences, Engel was diagnosed as having a form of lymphoma related to leukemia. He believed that he had only six months to live, and after a few weeks, he stopped taking anti-cancer drugs. So convinced was Engel of his imminent death that he wrote an article about a dying doctor's feeling toward his patients, one that was published anonymously in a medical journal. As Engel recalled

In a laboratory test of healer Olga Worrall's alleged powers, her prayers—spanning a distance of 600 miles—reportedly stimulated plant growth.

Hilda Charlton (right), who claims to be a "spiritual teacher," applies her healing touch.

Evangelist Kathryn Kuhlman thought of her alleged powers to aid healing as conveying the force of the Holy Spirit.

in his 1978 monograph, "about this time . . . somehow my outlook on life changed and I again considered the possibility of a personal future.

"Some months later, all the [enlarged] lymph nodes began to melt away, and I have been in excellent health since then."

Engel was aware that spontaneous remissions do occur, but believed it extremely unlikely for one person to have had two separate remissions from two different diseases. After seeing Thelma Moss on television talking about healing, he reassessed his experiences. Overcoming his "innate aversion to such 'non-scientific nonsense,'" Engel contacted Moss and continued with what he calls his "strange passes" over patients.

When Engel's monograph on healing was published in 1978, 43 patients had received treatment as part of a long-term formal experiment. In an attempt to gauge the effectiveness of Engel's laying on of hands, patient response was rated on a scale of 0 to 4. Seven patients reported no improvement, 8 showed "minimal response," 11 showed "moderate" response, 13 showed "marked improvement," and 4 reported total relief. Patients treated included a man in great pain from lesions due to Gaucher's disease, a deterioration of the bone (discharged as a 3, signifying marked improvement); two women suffering from tic douloureux (one was discharged as a 0, the other as a 4); a man with osteosclerosis of the shoulder, discharged as a 1; and a woman with a severe case of tennis elbow who had already been treated—unsuccessfully—by conventional medicine, acupuncture and hypnosis; she reported total relief.

The overall results of the experiment were so difficult to define, however, that a statistical analysis of the patients on the basis of selected social, psychological and demographic characteristics was launched. Yet no factors accounting for the differences could be isolated. In fact, the only question that yielded any correlation with success of the treatment was that of prior patient experience with psychic phenomena. Those who claimed prior experience "tended to respond less to energy healing than those who had had no such experience."

Another professional in the world of orthodox medicine who has become interested in the potential of psychic healing is Dr. Dolores Krieger, professor of nursing at New York University and a long-time student of Eastern religion. In 1971 she became intrigued by the apparent similarities between hemoglobin, which carries oxygen to the tissues, and the energy-giving substance Hindus call prana, the vital, moving force that keeps the body alive. "Eastern literature states," Krieger wrote in 1975, "that the healthy person has an overabundance of

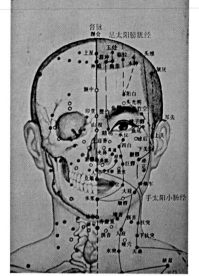

Many of the points at which acupuncture needles are inserted were specified thousands of years ago.

prana and that the ill person has a deficit. Indeed, the deficit is the illness. . . . The literature also states that prana is intrinsic in what we would call the oxygen molecule." Making a theoretical connection between that observation and the work of Sister Justa Smith on the effect of a healer's treatment on the enzyme trypsin, Krieger determined to carry out similar experiments with hemoglobin.

Enlisting the help of Oskar Estebany, Krieger transported a test group of 19 ill people and a control group of 9 healthy people to a farm in Massachusetts. During the six days of the experiment, each sick person was treated by Estebany once or twice a day. Meanwhile, all medication was suspended, and the test and control groups followed the same diet and schedule. Hemoglobin values were taken from all participants at the beginning and at the end of the experiment. The results were unmistakable: significant changes in hemoglobin were observed among those who were ill.

In summarizing her findings, Krieger wrote, "Taken together they indicate impressive evidence that 'something happens' during . . . laying on of hands . . . this 'something' is of a nature that can measurably affect human hemoglobin values and so demands further and intensive study."

Similar conclusions seem to be appropriate to other experiments in psychic healing. It appears that something may happen when healers direct their energy to the sick, but what that energy might be and whether it triggers healing, remain open questions.

In the meantime, an interest in the practical applications of various healing concepts appears to be growing among medical professionals. One example is the practice of therapeutic touch by registered nurses in traditional hospital surroundings, which grew out of Krieger's work with Estebany and Dora Kunz, who also practices laying on of hands. "During these research studies," Krieger wrote in the *American Journal of Nursing,* "I became convinced that healing by the laying on of hands is a natural potential in man, given at least two intervening variables that I think are critical to the process: the intent to help heal another, and a fairly healthy body." Krieger first tried laying on of hands, or, as she called it, therapeutic touch, herself, then expanded her research to include 32 nurses. It was decided that half would incorporate therapeutic touch into their patient care, half would not. She reported that the results were as before, with the treated group recording significant changes in hemoglobin value and the control group showing no change.

In 1972, Krieger began teaching her therapeutic

Enigma of Hypnosis

Hypnosis has for so long been a staple of the sideshow and the stage that its overdue legitimization as a medical, psychiatric and, to a lesser extent, legal tool comes as a surprise to many people. Among the positive aspects of hypnosis that have been obscured until recently are the facts that the hypnotic state can be achieved by about 70 percent of the population and that it primarily involves not the surrender of autonomy but a deepening of consciousness and, through suggestion, increased control over the autonomic functions of the body. It is also characterized less by "lost time" and amnesiac aftermath than by periods of intense lucidity in which the subject may be able to reach back into earliest memory to retrieve information that might otherwise be unrecoverable.

Nonetheless, far more attention has been paid to the potential abuses of hypnosis than to its positive applications. Indeed, so fearful have some members of the medical community and the general public been of this little-understood phenomenon that its use for entertainment purposes has been severely restricted for most of this century, with, for example, the National Association of Broadcasters' television code prohibiting the demonstration of a hypnotic session on camera. To a degree, such caution is reasonable, for the hypnotic trance, though a latent capacity in most of us, is a complex state that may offer uniquely direct access to the subconscious.

Focusing attention helps mute mental activity as a subject is hypnotized.

Although the hypnotic state and various means of achieving it were known to the ancient Egyptians and Greeks, the recorded history of hypnosis is actually very brief. It is often dated, inaccurately, from the mid-18th-century experiments of Franz Anton Mesmer. Yet despite the extraordinary effect Mesmer had on his patients, he did not hypnotize them. The first practitioner of hypnosis in modern times was actually a disciple of Mesmer's, the Marquis de Puységur, who in the 1780s inadvertently induced a deep trance in one of his patients while attempting to bring about the hysterical crisis characteristic of Mesmer's treatments.

Neither Puységur nor any of his contemporary "mesmerizers" ever fully comprehended the phenomenon they employed. Instead they persisted in the belief that they were somehow harnessing the "animal magnetism" first postulated by Mesmer. Thus for several decades hypnotism was employed by both medical practitioners and occult enthusiasts and, in the process, acquired much of its unsavory reputation. One after another, early theorists offered bizarre explanations that owed little to science and much to the imagination or pre-existing biases. Even James Braid, the English doctor who rehabilitated "mesmerism" in the 1840s, renamed it hypnotism (from the

Greek word for *sleep*), and used it to alleviate patients' pain during surgery, essentially misunderstood the process.

Not until the 1930s and the work of psychologist Clark Hull did hypnotism begin to receive the careful experimentation it deserved. As Hull pointed out in *Hypnosis and Suggestibility*, one of the biggest obstacles to scientific assessment of hypnosis had been its practical efficacy. Though its reputation waxed and waned over the years, "the dominant motive throughout the entire history of hypnotism has been clinical, that of curing human ills. A worse method for the establishment of scientific principles . . . could hardly have been devised. . . . The physician's task is to effect a cure in the quickest manner possible using more or less simultaneously any and all means at his disposal."

As hypnotism was supplemented by other methods of treatment, however, more attention was given to the intricacies of its operation. Fifty years of serious experimentation have not solved all its mysteries, but many of the myths and misapprehensions about hypnotism have been dispelled, while new discoveries have markedly enlarged its therapeutic applications.

Though it continues to be compared to the sleeping state, hypnosis is actually an altered state of consciousness into which some people lapse quite naturally without realizing it—while daydreaming, for example. Hypnosis can be induced in a number of ways but is most commonly achieved through a combination of visual and aural stimuli

New York police detective John McGrath demonstrates hypnotic technique.

that produces a high level of relaxation and concentration.

In the hypnotic state a subject is able to block out everyday sights, sounds, memories and information in order to focus on a particular goal with unusual intensity. This filtering process may be especially useful in psychotherapy, allowing a patient to retrieve crucial images from the past, and in police work, where witnesses who cannot consciously recall details may be able to remember them while hypnotized. Through hypnosis, some 15 percent of the population appears to be able to regress into various childhood periods and vividly re-experience events and the emotions that accompanied them.

One widespread practical use of hypnosis is to counteract pain. Terminal cancer patients have used hypnosis to lessen their agonies and reduce anxiety without medication and its side effects. Patients suffering from arthritis or migraine headaches, overeaters, smokers, women giving birth, clinically depressed patients, have all been successfully treated with hypnotherapy. As of 1978, one-third of all medical and dental schools in the United States were offering courses in hypnosis, twice as many as in 1974.

"Touch and Care" Clinic

Dr. Robert L. Swearingen, an orthopedic surgeon who runs an emergency clinic at a ski resort in Colorado, made a remarkable and accidental discovery about pain and healing several years ago. Lying before him on an X-ray table was a patient suffering from a dislocated shoulder. "I called for the nurse to bring medication," Swearingen recalled at a symposium on healing held in California in 1978, but "she was not available—too many other patients. I looked down at my patient and saw in his face a combination of anticipation, trust and fear. I realized my total dependence on anaesthesia or some type of medication. As a physician, with all my training, I felt very weak. I really didn't know what to do. It was somewhat overwhelming."

Then Swearingen remembered something inspiring that he had once read: "If not you, who? If not now, when?" He attempted to apply the message. "I put one hand on the patient's elbow and the other on his shoulder. As I did so, he told me without words, 'Go ahead.' I thought, 'This is nice. I can keep him comfortable until I get the dope.' I kept pulling down, kept talking to him and kept touching the muscles and working with him in a way I really don't recall because it all comes so naturally now. The end of the story is that the shoulder went back in place—no pain medication and no pain."

An even more remarkable conclusion to the story is that Swearingen has made "touch and care" treatment part of the everyday routine at his clinic and has taught his methods to members of the ski patrol, the rescue workers who bring accident victims down from the ski slopes. Members of the rescue teams are now instructed to remove their thick gloves at high altitudes before handling injured skiers, and they are urged to approach their often traumatized subjects in a spirit of hopefulness and "wholeness." Swearingen, who treats from 50 to 80 fractures a year without pain medication, also told the conference that his surgical nurse can "get tight ski pants off a patient with a shattered leg without significant pain. . . . Caring, touching and talking and approaching the total being" are all part of the technique, but Swearingen makes a distinction between what he does and actual healing.

"As we reduce the fracture, as we put the bones back in place, we are totally cognizant that this isn't healing, this is facilitation. The healing is what takes place afterward. In order to facilitate it, we teach the people here how to meditate. We draw little pictures, first of the broken bone, what it looks like. Then we draw a second picture of what it should look like in a week or ten days, with a beneficial blood clot formed around it. The third picture shows a scaffolding type of fibrous tissue forming and the fourth shows calcium being laid down. The only thing is, we cheat! We speed up the process by having them meditate on things happening before they are supposed to!"

touch at nursing schools around the United States and in Canada, and soon afterward organized a national network of nurses trained in the technique. Therapeutic touch is now practiced by nurses in numerous hospitals in the United States. Although the medical community remains unconvinced of the biochemical changes Krieger claims for her method, the improved quality of nursing care that arises from the innovative therapy has been widely endorsed.

Another kind of mind-body health care that has received substantial support in the world of orthodox medicine is biofeedback, a system that trains people to control many bodily functions and processes, such as temperature, blood pressure, muscle contraction and even heartbeat, that were long thought to be involuntary, or autonomic. In biofeedback training a patient is connected to a sensitive monitor that provides a running commentary on the relevant body activity. The patient is instructed to picture what he wants his body to do—lower his blood pressure, for example, or slow his heart rate—then tell his body to do it, and relax. The monitors begin to feed information back to the patient—that his blood pressure has dropped several points or that his heartbeat has begun to slow. The immediate confirmation that change has occurred stimulates in some patients a greater confidence—and greater success—in their capacity to influence their bodies. Biofeedback, says Alyce Green, who with her husband, Dr. Elmer Green, founder of the Biofeedback and Psychophysiology Center at the Menninger Foundation in Kansas, is one of the foremost specialists in the field, "does nothing *to* the person." It is, instead, "a tool for releasing potential."

The extent of that potential is under study in medical centers around the country. At Emory University in Atlanta, biofeedback has been used to rehabilitate damaged muscles. At the Center for Behavioral Psychiatry and Psychology in Birmingham, Michigan, and at the Menninger clinic, it is used to control migraine headaches. In California, at the University of California San Francisco Medical Center, psychologist Bernard Engle has trained people to alter their heartbeat rates.

At Columbia Presbyterian Medical Center in New York, Dr. Kenneth Greenspan, a psychiatrist and the director of Columbia's Laboratory and Center for Stress-Related Disorders, has used biofeedback to treat post-surgical cardiovascular patients. Greenspan achieved remarkable results with a group of 22 such patients over a three-month period. The patients, virtual cripples as a result of circulatory disease, were taught how to raise the temperature in their limbs in order to send more blood to the affected areas and thus make use of functioning blood vessels and bypass blood clots. Stress brought on by pain and fear of cardiac failure was reduced as well. At the end of treatment, which also included meditation and breathing exercises, all the patients had achieved significant improvement in mobility

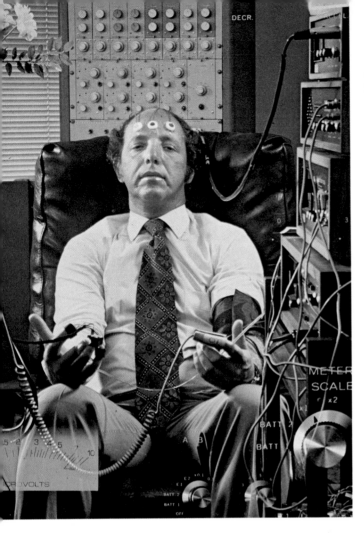

Using sensitive monitoring instruments, Dr. Elmer Green, a biofeedback pioneer with the Menninger Foundation, measures the brain-wave activity of an Indian yogi seated on a bed of nails.

Dr. Kenneth Greenspan of New York is shown attached to a battery of the biofeedback devices he uses to treat patients. Multiple images reveal the meters his patients must monitor to effect changes in normally uncontrollable bodily processes.

and relief from pain. A few had even started jogging. "Patients come to us feeling like victims," Greenspan told one writer, "sick and unsure of what to expect, and we try to help them develop an attitude of mastery. . . . The goal is self-responsibility for the maintenance of one's own health, and to assist the doctor within us."

The abilities that biofeedback seems to unleash in patients—control over the involuntary nervous system—are similar to abilities that have been observed among yogis and others who have never heard of biofeedback. For such people, the something that signals the body to heal or protect itself or shut down channels of pain is always on. In biofeedback, however, the degree of control tends to decline once training ends; without the feedback itself, the self-regulating facility weakens. Still, as research continues into instrument-oriented biofeedback and related techniques such as visualization, the achievement of what Kenneth Greenspan calls "self-responsibility for . . . one's own health" seems more possible than ever before.

One who believes in the efficacy of visualization in the treatment of cancer is Dr. O. Carl Simonton, formerly head of radiation therapy at Travis Air Force Base in California and now director of the Cancer Counseling and Research Center in Fort Worth, Texas. Simonton's first attempt at using biofeedback-style

techniques against that disease had been with the 61-year-old victim of untreatable throat cancer who was released from the hospital after seven weeks of Simonton's regimen. Since that treatment, Simonton has tried to combine visualization with psychotherapy, relaxation exercises and radiation. Although critics point out that only the most highly motivated cancer victims make the trip to Fort Worth and that bedridden patients in the last stages of the disease are not able to do so, there is little question that Simonton has achieved some impressive results. In a 4½-year period, for example, during which 159 "incurable" patients with an average life expectancy of one year were treated by Simonton and his staff, survival time was extended to an average of two years, and even among the 96 who died, survival time had been increased to 20 months.

Despite such achievements, however, many crucial questions remain unanswered. Spontaneous recovery, seemingly miraculous cures, and the mind's conscious and unconscious powers may or may not be harnessed one day for the benefit of mankind. Yet such things certainly hint at the presence of powerful and as-yet-unexplained healing capacities within the human body. The search for appropriate means of locating and tapping such capacities may constitute an important part of future medical care.

Fact vs. Phenomenon

Possession—and Exorcism

Fr. Karl Patzelt performed 14 rites of exorcism in a California home in 1973.

The trouble began in the spring of 1972. Fires broke out throughout the house in which a young Catholic couple lived with their new baby in Daly City, California, a suburb south of San Francisco. A 10-inch crucifix flew off a bedroom wall, landing on a bed 12 feet away. Other objects, including a steak knife, whizzed dangerously through the house. As the couple, whose identity was not made public, later told a reporter from the San Francisco *Examiner*, the house seemed to be occupied by "a whole army of demons." The devil himself, they were convinced, had made his presence known by attacking them directly. "Often, he would knock one of us totally unconscious," they said. "He would choke us, twist our arms behind our backs."

The manifestations continued, with brief respites, for almost two years. In desperation, the couple finally turned for help to the Reverend Karl Patzelt of Our Lady of Fatima Church in San Francisco. After making a study of the case, Patzelt pronounced the frightening incidents to be "disturbances caused by the Evil One," an interpretation falling just short of what the Catholic Church defines as possession—actual control by the devil of a person's body. Instead, Patzelt labeled the bizarre occurrences in Daly City a case of "obsession," by which is meant a lesser diabolical disturbance. In this instance the target appeared to be the entire family, including the baby, and, just as with a case of possession, the rite of exorcism was decided upon. Between August 19 and September 8, 1973, Patzelt performed 14 ceremonies of exorcism, according to the dictates of the *Rituale Romanum*, the rite set down in 1614 under Pope Paul V. Afterward, the San Francisco *Examiner* reported, the Daly City manifestations ceased.

A liturgical book, the *Rituale Romanum* specifically instructs the exorcist in how to determine possession and offers a variety of prayers and scripture readings to be used in the exorcism, including the words, "I cast thee out, Most Unclean Spirit." Those who are conducting the exorcism pay particular attention to phrases that appear to disturb the evil presence and intentionally repeat them a number of times. Similar procedures are used by other Christian churches, among them the Greek Orthodox, the Anglican and Episcopal churches.

Belief in possession and rites of exorcism, which extend back in time at least to the Babylonians and possibly to even earlier peoples, are relatively rare today. Nonetheless, they serve as dramatic reminders of man's continuing efforts to comprehend and control unknown forces in the world in which he lives. Some of the earliest documents recording a belief in spirit possession were found in the palace of Assurbanipal, a ruler of ancient Assyria, at Nineveh. On one clay tablet, perhaps dating to 650 B.C., is inscribed the desperate appeal of a suffering man who asks his gods how he can rid himself of a tyrannical ghost who seems to possess his body and soul.

More familiar to modern readers are the New Testament accounts of Christ's exorcism of the Gadarene and other sufferers. They serve churches around the world today as a basis for the practice of exorcism. The Book of Luke tells that when the possessed man appeared before Jesus on the shores of the Galilee, Jesus addressed him, saying, " 'What is your name?' And he said, 'Legion'; for many demons had entered him. And they begged him not to command them to depart into the abyss. Now a large herd of swine was feeding there on the hillside; and they begged him to let them enter these. So he gave them leave. Then the demons came out of the man and entered the swine, and the herd rushed down the steep bank into the lake and were drowned." In current rites, employed in the Daly City case and made famous in the book and movie *The Exorcist*, the devil or devils are subjected to relatively little direct address. Instead, forbidding commands are repeated over and over until it is felt that the possessing entities have finally departed.

In psychological terms, which is how many modern authorities believe it is best to examine the matter of possession and exorcism, the rite appears to bring about the equivalent of a mental and emotional catharsis. In such a state, some experts suggest, neurotic conflicts, compulsive-obsessive notions, buried memories of

The devil, his many legions and the act of exorcism were all frighteningly real to Christians of the Middle Ages, as depicted in this 15th-century Italian painting.

Saint Benedict appears on an anti-Satan medal.

deeply traumatic events, infantile or adult guilts, may all be subjected to some degree of release. Aware that these interpretations are not without support, ecclesiastical authorities are extremely careful in seeking to rule out all possible psychological and physiological conditions before deciding that possession has occurred.

Nonetheless, considerable physical and psychological risks remain whenever exorcism is permitted. Some psychologists maintain that existing neurotic or psychosomatic tendencies may well be reinforced by the acknowledgment of possession, while the intense relationship that develops between the exorcist, invariably a man in the Christian rite, and the victim, sometimes a woman, can itself be charged with emotional and psychological hazards.

That there are very real physical dangers present in the rigorous rite was made tragically clear on July 1, 1976, in West Germany, when Anneliese Michel, a 23-year-old student of education, died of malnutrition after enduring numerous rites of exorcism over some 10 months. In 1978 a court in the town of Aschaffenburg found the two priests who had participated in the rites and the young woman's parents all guilty of negligent homicide. The four received suspended sentences from the court.

While the Christian concept of possession reflects the presence of evil forces, not every culture shares that view. In certain societies, according to the French church historian Robert Amadou, writing in the magazine *Tomorrow* in 1954, possession is regarded as "an act of inspiration from the gods." Although the patterns of behavior universally recognized as characterizing possession are "sometimes considered as the results of an evil

spell," Amadou wrote, they are more often seen as the "symptom of a happy spiritual experience or of a beneficent spirit incarnation."

The Zar cult of Egypt sustains a possession theory that appears to fall somewhere in between. As described by *New York Times* correspondent Christopher S. Wren in a 1979 report from "the narrow back streets of Old Cairo," the Zar cult, which includes rites of exorcism among its beliefs, is "a meld of group therapy, superstition and entertainment, as well as a confidence game run by a clan of organizers who promise to intercede with the evil spirits that they say wander the city's dense slums."

Participants in the Zar cult, Wren wrote, "believe that an afrit, or genie, can possess a woman out of jealousy, envy or love. Once within her, the devil can never be driven out, only placated in a ritual that will dissuade him from causing harm." To that end, women believing themselves possessed join in wild, convulsive dancing not unlike that of the whirling dervishes, an Islamic sect whose members spin themselves into a cataleptic state.

Such therapeutic uses of possession have long been observed in many different cultures. In *The Devil's Bride, Exorcism: Past and Present,* Martin Ebon suggested that the possession and exorcism rituals of China, the Caribbean and eastern India all fulfill an important community need: in the emotional release brought on by ceremonial exorcism the community's shared sense of purpose is powerfully reinforced.

Thus even today, whether viewed in terms of religion or psychology, belief in possession and exorcism remains undeniably powerful.

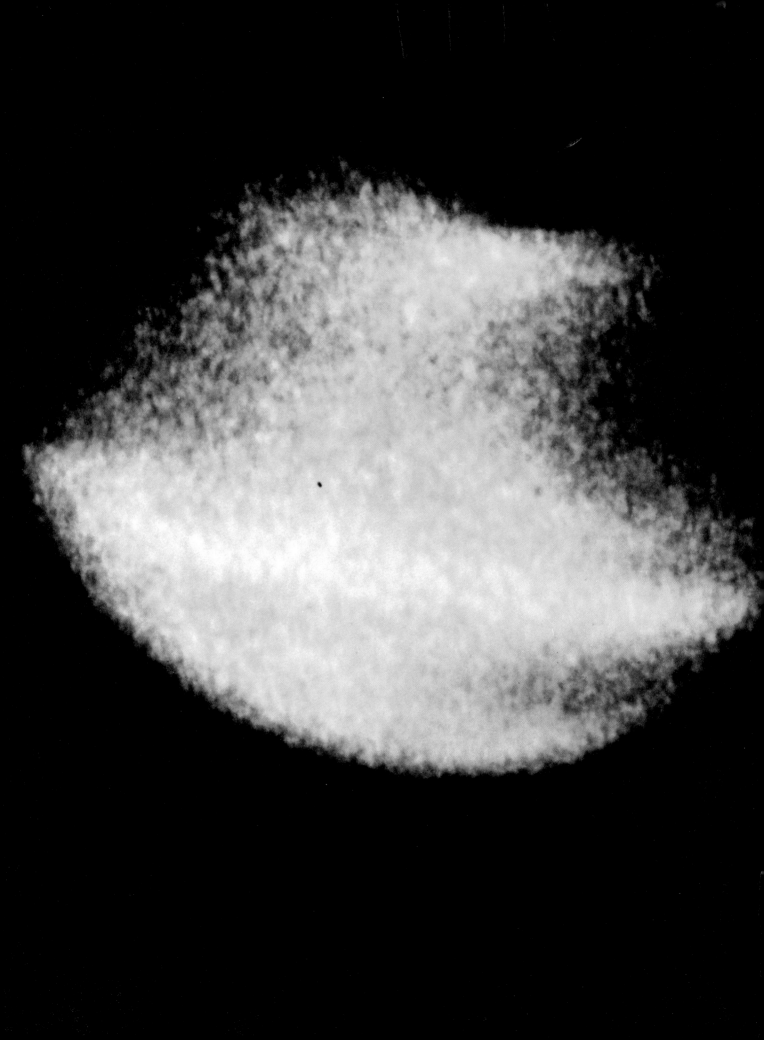

Throughout history man has
witnessed, and struggled to explain, the
presence of bizarre objects in the sky.

ENIGMA OF UFO'S

Computer analysis of the New Zealand picture at left showed differences in light intensities in the UFO.

I't's approaching from due east towards me," the young Australian pilot radioed. "It seems to me that he's flying over me at speeds I can't identify. It is flying past. It is a long shape. It's coming for me right now. It's got a green light."

Thus began the bizarre series of events that occurred in the night skies south of Melbourne late in 1978.

Moments later, the pilot, Frederick Valentich, reported, "The thing is orbiting on top of me." He then radioed that his plane's engine was faltering. "It's hovering and it's not an aircraft," he continued. "It's—"

At this point, the radio transmission was broken off. When nothing further was heard from Valentich, it was assumed that his plane had crashed into the dark waters of the Tasman Sea. Months later no trace of the plane had been found.

Yet in the days immediately following Valentich's disappearance, there were more reports of mysterious glowing objects in the skies over Australia and its eastern neighbor New Zealand. Although none of these reported sightings included such a fateful incident as the young pilot's unexplained encounter and disappearance, one of them had an awesome impact. It began early in the morning of the last day of 1978. Just east

of New Zealand's South Island, a three-member Melbourne television crew was airborne in an Argosy cargo plane, retracing the aerial route between Wellington and Christchurch, a route along which bright, unidentified lights had been spotted by the crews of two aircraft 10 days before.

At just after midnight, the crew spotted strange moving lights.

For the next two hours the plane and the TV crew on board played a curious game of hide-and-seek with the mysterious lights. As the plane flew south to Christchurch, one witness described on tape, "bright, pulsating lights . . . appearing and disappearing." At the same time, unexplained radar images were detected by Wellington radar. One image seemed to pace the plane as witnesses on board watched a flashing light that appeared for a few minutes. During the return flight, a light approached within 10 miles of the cargo plane. This light was described by a TV crewman as having a "brightly lit bottom and transparent sort of sphere on top."

Whatever the nature of the object, it was subjected to remarkably comprehensive human and electronic scrutiny. For it not only was seen by the TV crew and the plane's two pilots but it also was tracked by the plane's airborne radar. Most extraordinary of all, the object's elusive presence was documented on color film.

In all, the TV cameraman shot some 23,000 frames of 16-mm. film, which were later turned over to an optical physicist employed by the U.S. Navy, Dr. Bruce Maccabee, for analysis and computer enhance-

The picture at left was taken from a cargo plane flying over New Zealand. Unidentified object it shows was tracked on both ground and airborne radar systems.

ment. The film revealed an intriguing, if brief, series of images of mysterious flying objects. One sequence showed a bell-shaped form that was bright on the bottom, as described by a cameraman at the time. A single frame of this sequence showed what seems to be the track of the object as it moved in a classic loop, indicating extremely rapid relative motion between the camera and the object. Another sequence showed an object that oscillated at a constant frequency from a large, bright yellowish-white circular shape to a dim yellow and red triangular shape.

From his study of the film, Maccabee estimated that one of the objects, if it was in fact 10 nautical miles away, as indicated on the airplane radar, was between 60 and 100 feet across. His analysis suggested as well that the object was emitting an extremely powerful

Observers in the 18th century were mystified by glowing objects, some natural, some fictitious, in the night sky. The engraving at right shows not only a comet, meteors and stars but a dragon as well.

Some biblical scholars believe Ezekiel's account of God in a UFO-like flying chariot may have been a hallucination. Other investigators speculate that Ezekiel might have seen a parahelion, a halo created by atmospheric ice crystals.

light, equivalent to the candlepower of an enormous incandescent bulb of 100,000 watts. His research (assuming that camera movement or other phenomena were not factors) also produced this startling finding: while flying the figure-eight loop, one of the UFO's might have been traveling at roughly 3,000 miles per hour.

After Maccabee had completed his study, the film and other documentation were submitted to nearly a score of U.S. scientists, experts in optics, biophysics, radar, optical physiology and astronomy. They agreed unanimously that they could not explain any of the events that occurred during the New Zealand sighting. In their judgment, contrary to the publicly stated opinions of other researchers, the unidentified lights were not Venus or other planets, stars, meteors, high-altitude balloons, off-course aircraft, satellites, atmospheric illusions, reflected lights or even a hoax. They were, they concluded, true UFO's, or unidentified flying objects.

The New Zealand sighting marked the first time in history that on-the-spot tape recordings were made while UFO's were observed, filmed and simultaneously tracked on radar. As Maccabee has said, "If there were no UFO's involved, then it was a series of remarkably fortuitous coincidences."

Although it was remarkable, the New Zealand case is unique only in the breadth of its documentation. For in the past three decades, there have been at least 70,000 reports of mysterious objects in the sky and countless more, perhaps 10 times as many, that have gone unreported. The vast majority of these sightings do not qualify as UFO's, of course. Fully 95 percent or more have been explained in terms of identifiable phenomena such as aircraft, weather balloons, lightning, rockets, birds and even insects.

They are thus all too pedestrian IFO's—identified flying objects. The remainder, roughly 5 percent, have not been explained even after investigation by competent observers. And it is this residue of unexplained, perhaps inexplicable, sightings that represents what has come to be called the UFO phenomenon.

This phenomenon has been described by Dr. J. Allen Hynek, an astronomer and one of the world's best-known and respected UFO researchers. He calls it "so strange and foreign to our daily terrestrial mode of thought that it is frequently met by ridicule and derision by persons and organizations unacquainted with the facts. Yet, the phenomenon persists; it has not faded away, as many of us expected it would when, years ago, we regarded it as a passing fad or whimsy. Instead, it has touched on the lives of an increasing number of people around the world."

People practically everywhere have reported seeing UFO's. Reports of UFO's have come from no fewer than 133 countries all over the globe, from such tiny nations as Grenada and Kuwait as well as from such major powers as the United States, Russia, England,

Von Däniken: Ancient Astronauts and Modern Arguments

How could semi-savages in the Fertile Crescent suddenly give life to a culture as advanced as that of the Sumerians with astronomy, mathematics and a written language? In what fashion did the ancient people of the Nile acquire the knowledge to build the colossal pyramid of Cheops? How could they have leveled the rocky terrain beneath it and moved the pyramid's massive blocks when they had no wheels, wood or ropes?

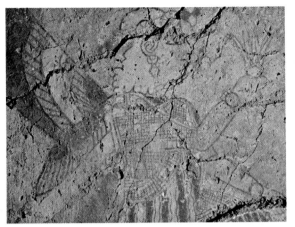

According to the theories of Erich von Däniken, this winged Assyrian god might represent an early space traveler.

For Erich von Däniken such questions raise an intriguing (if fundamentally unlikely) possibility: that the ancients were aided in their labors by "unknown intelligences." Von Däniken's theory, in basic form, suggests that somewhere between 10,000 and 40,000 years ago superintelligent astronauts arrived on earth, mated with early man and produced *Homo sapiens*. Later, Von Däniken goes on, the astronauts returned, perhaps a number of times, to further the course of human existence by revealing the fundamentals of metal making, agriculture and written language.

In support of his speculations, Von Däniken points out that the mythologies of almost every culture include tales of winged gods and flying devices that might represent primitive man's descriptions of Von Däniken's travelers. Strange coincidences in architecture as well, Von Däniken feels, may indicate the presence of ancient visitors. The height of the Cheops pyramid, for instance, Von Däniken suggests, when multiplied by 1,000 million roughly corresponds to the distance to the sun.

The myriad of detail and interpretation amassed by Von Däniken is in a sense unique, if not especially convincing. Unfortunately, it is unique, too, in the controversy that has surrounded it. The popularity of his books—more than 40 million have been sold—has astounded and dismayed archeologists, historians, theologians and other researchers who, like Von Däniken, are exploring the possibility that life may exist beyond Earth.

Two Australian teachers, for example, asked a group of scholars to examine Von Däniken's *Chariots of the Gods* and write down their findings. The result: 17 short papers that point out en masse hundreds of factual errors in the materials Von Däniken presents. A professor of Near Eastern archeology noted that Sumerian culture did not appear suddenly but developed over a period of 6,000 years (from 9000 B.C. to 3000 B.C.) and that the techniques employed in the construction of the pyramids are now well known. Barges, ropes, wood and earthen ramps were all used, and all have been found, either in pictures or in actuality. In addition, the Egyptians probably used their knowledge of irrigation to flood and level pyramid-base areas, drilling holes to a standard depth from the water's surface. As for the height of the Cheops pyramid, when multiplied by 1,000 million, it does not equal the distance to the sun.

While scholars may be annoyed by Von Däniken's "errors, misstatements and untruths," they are truly exasperated by the reasoning—or lack of it—that permits the author to create theories based on "non sequiturs," "shibboleths" and "rhetorical questions." Carl Sagan, one of many scientists interested in the possibility of extraterrestrial life, has criticized Von Däniken for "temporal chauvinism." Of Von Däniken's speculation that miles of ancient straight lines on Peru's Nazca Plain may be an ancient airfield, Sagan says, "The space vehicle sets down on the ground, the great bay opens, and out wheel what? B-24 Liberators, Spitfires? Most remarkable that they need airfields." Von Däniken has been attacked in similar fashion for his interpretation of early drawings and sculpture. Would interstellar space travelers, his detractors ask, really turn out to look like modern astronauts, men who have only just reached the moon? Of Von Däniken's theory as a whole, Ronald Story, author of *The Space-Gods Revealed, A Close Look at the Theories of Erich von Däniken*, has said that any beings with genes that could be crossed with proto-men "would already be of the same or closely related species."

And yet, given their implausibility, why are Von Däniken's theories so popular? Perhaps the fairest answer is that, however porous Von Däniken's arguments, however shaky his facts, he nonetheless considers fundamental issues—the mysteries of human accomplishment, the existence of life in outer space—that *are* of great importance and interest. Unfortunately, his considerations seem more often to impede rather than advance man's eternal quest to explain the unknown.

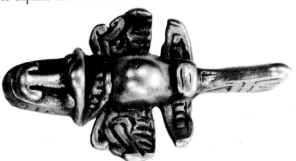

This Colombian figure may depict an ancient airplane, another of the many ideas proposed by Erich von Däniken.

Eye of the Beholder

Mysterious orbs seen in 1566 and shown in this 17th-century Swiss print may have been afterimages in the eye.

The human eye, whether spotting an unidentified flying object in the night sky or examining the crimson filigree of a sunlit rose, is the most compact, portable and flexible optical device in the world. Yet it is hardly perfect, and its pictures may be flawed and distorted not only by quirks and built-in limitations but also by environmental and emotional factors. Tiny objects in the eye's liquid, for example, can appear as darting shapes in a clear daylight sky. "Almost everyone has floaters," says Hershel W. Leibowitz, an expert in the psychology of perception, at Pennsylvania State University, "and most people, at one time or another, will see non-existent lights."

Myopia, or nearsightedness, and hypermetropia, or farsightedness, can also distort visual stimuli. According to one study, myopia is prevalent in about a quarter of certain European populations and in 60 percent of some Japanese groups. Thus, it seems likely that at least some UFO sightings have been made by people whose vision was impaired by myopia.

The human eye also depends heavily on cues—known objects and familiar distances—to help it gauge the unknown. If, for example, a subject is shown a single, immobile point of light in an otherwise darkened room, the light, most often in seconds, will appear to move. For some, such movements may be arc-like, for others they may appear in back-and-forth patterns or in darting fashion. In any event, though the light source is immobile, the movement "seen" by the observer is very real, just as UFO's may be perceived to be real.

Emotional factors can also have a great impact on what the brain "sees." In a case in Illinois in 1978, dozens of people reported sighting the dome top and rotating lights of a gigantic airborne saucer. What they had seen in fact was a panel of message-bearing lights on an advertising plane. Then, through fear and their preconceptions of UFO's, they had created their own close encounter of the imagined kind.

France and China. In Spain, UFO's are known as Objetos Voladores no Identificados; in Germany, they are Fliegende Untertassen; in France, Soucoupes Volantes; in Czechoslovakia, Letajici Talire.

Everywhere, too, by whatever name, UFO's are the subject of endless speculation, emotion, fear and often bitter controversy. Some scientists believe that UFO's are interplanetary space vehicles sent by intelligent beings from another world; others speculate that they might represent some sort of paranormal reality here on earth. The majority of scientists, however, doubt that such paranormal or extraterrestrial UFO's exist. They attribute all reported sightings to either conventional phenomena, psychological delusion, mass hysteria or deliberate hoax. In the words of the late Dr. Edward U. Condon, a physicist, past president of the American Association for the Advancement of Science and head of an Air Force commission created to study UFO's: "Flying saucers and astrology are not the only pseudosciences which have a considerable following among us. . . . In my view, publishers who publish or teachers who teach any of the pseudosciences as established truth should, on being found guilty, be publicly horsewhipped, and forever banned from further activity in the usually honorable professions."

Yet from earliest times, people *have* been seeing things in the skies. These early sightings, depicted in art and writing, most often took the form of gods, dragons, human shapes or wheels of fire. In the biblical Book of Genesis, Jacob dreamed of an angel-lined ladder ascending to Heaven. Thousands of years later, on the eve of his first sighting of the New World, Christopher Columbus espied from the deck of the *Santa Maria* "a light glimmering at a great distance." And just before the turn of the 20th century, there were reports across the U.S. Middle West of giant airships, strange dirigibles rumored to be of unearthly origin.

Perhaps the most vivid description of an early UFO came from the biblical prophet Ezekiel, who said: "As I looked, behold, a stormy wind came out of the north, and a great cloud, with brightness round about it, and fire flashing forth continually, and in the midst of the fire, as it were gleaming bronze. And from the midst of it came the likeness of four living creatures. . . . they had the form of men, but each had four faces, and each of them had four wings. . . . And when they went, I heard the sound of their wings like the sound of many waters."

The visions of Ezekiel and other early chroniclers have been seized upon by some modern theorists as evidence that spaceships visited the earth in ancient times. The foremost proponent of this notion is the Swiss author Erich von Däniken. Beginning with his *Chariots of the Gods*, published in 1968, Von Däniken has boldly suggested that many of man's ancient works, such as the pyramids, could have been produced only

Bizarre circular shapes in the sky often spawn dramatic reports of UFO sightings. The formations above, photographed over Santos, Brazil, are rare cloud configurations often mistaken for UFO's. They are known as lenticular, or lens-shaped, clouds.

Natural "Flying" Objects

For all their vastness, the skies around planet Earth are crammed with natural, identified flying objects—comets, meteors, planets, the moon and stars—that can beguile the most astute and highly trained of observers. Especially when distorted by the ever-changing atmosphere, these heavenly bodies can trick the eye and mind into thinking they are UFO's. Some of the most startlingly UFO-like visions are actually magnified mirages. If, for instance, a layer of cold air is trapped beneath a layer of hot air, light passing between them is refracted. If this occurs near the horizon, a star or planet can suddenly show in the sky, even though it is below the horizon and should not be visible at all. If, in addition, conditions are such that the atmosphere magnifies, the image will appear as a huge glowing ball. Changing air conditions may make the ball flash and alter color, just as air irregularities make distant stars appear to twinkle. Such atmospheric distortions can be especially startling to people in airplanes. Ice crystals, snow, fog and mist can also distort natural sources of light. Masses of airborne ice crystals, for example, can gather light into impressive vertical columns. With the addition of snowflakes, such a column may appear to be crossed by a horizontal band, creating the illusion of a shimmering cross suspended in front of the sun. In the opinion of at least one researcher, it was the sight of such a natural phenomenon that prompted the conversion of Constantine the Great to Christianity in A.D. 312.

Ball lightning, or globe lightning—nearly as mysterious and almost as controversial as UFO's—is another easily misidentified natural atmospheric phenomenon. With no known cause, such glowing red, yellow or orange balls appear, move about and disappear, usually in no more than a few seconds. They have even been known to burn and melt objects with which they come in contact, and occasionally they make hissing sounds.

Friction caused by the movement of great air masses of different temperatures can produce another kind of phenomenon: Saint Elmo's fire. This halo-like electrical discharge sometimes glitters around the conducting surfaces of airplane wings, ships at sea and church steeples during stormy weather.

One of the strangest explanations for UFO sightings involves Saint Elmo's fire and another kind of natural phenomenon: giant swarms of insects. According to two U.S. Department of Agriculture entomologists who devised the theory, stormy weather can produce such strong electrical fields that Saint Elmo's fire may actually flood through a swarm of insects. Such a bizarre combination, they suggest, may have been the cause of a number of sightings reported over Utah in the late 1960s. The speculation they offer is nearly as awesome as the wildest of UFO tales, involving as it does an infestation of electrified moths so enormous that it resembled a "free-floating discothèque in the sky."

with the help of superior beings from other planets. UFO antagonists, on the other hand, often make a different point, emphasizing the close relationship over the centuries between the "look" of existing technology and the ever-changing "look" of UFO's.

The modern history of seeing things in the skies is something else—a voluminous and disturbing record of eyewitness reports, often buttressed with impressive documentation, that have survived the scrutiny of many scientists. As a modern phenomenon, UFO reports, aside from accounts of "foo-fighters"—strange lights and circular craft—turned in by World War II pilots, began with the now-classic 1947 sighting by Kenneth Arnold near Mount Rainier in the state of Washington. An Idaho businessman and veteran pilot, Arnold was flying his own private plane when he saw a series of nine silvery, disc-like objects darting in and around the Cascade Range. The objects were flying in a chain-like formation, Arnold said, at an estimated speed of some 1,200 miles per hour. He told a reporter that the objects swerved erratically, "like pie plates skipping over the water."

The reporter remembered the graphic simile, added his own words, and the next day, the story of Arnold's "flying saucers" exploded in the headlines. The label stuck during the following months as hundreds more sightings of unidentified objects poured in from around the world. It seemed an apt tag, for many of the reports involved objects that literally seemed to be shaped like one inverted plate or saucer atop another.

From the beginning, many people were convinced that the new UFO's were interplanetary space vehicles. Indeed, less than a month after Arnold's sighting came the first report of human-like creatures actually landing. A survey worker in the wilds of Brazil described 7-foot beings wearing transparent, inflated suits. Other people told tales of meeting 3-foot dwarfs, hairy creatures and humanoids of various bizarre permutations.

Soon enough, "contactees"—human intermediaries who claimed the ability to communicate with these alien visitors—began to appear. The most celebrated contactee during those early years was George Adamski, a Polish-born American who had founded a mystical cult in California. Drawn to the desert one day in 1952, when he was 61, Adamski went looking for a visitor from outer space—and found one. The visitor was from Venus, Adamski later wrote, a young man with long hair but otherwise of remarkably Earth-like features. In the company of this Venusian and a couple of other interplanetary visitors, Adamski said, he took a few trips into space, including a voyage to the vicinity of the moon. By Adamski's account, given not many years before U.S. astronauts found the lunar surface to be a barren and inhospitable place, the moon teemed with rivers, towns and people.

Whether a charlatan or honestly deluded, Adamski

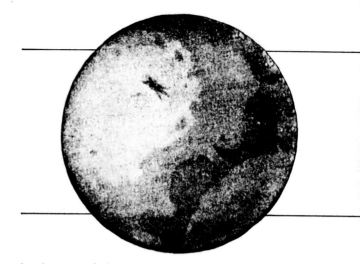

The director of the Zacatecas Observatory in Mexico was studying sunspots when he noticed cricket-like objects flying across the sun. The photograph he made of one such object in 1883 may be among the first ever taken of a UFO.

was neither the first nor the last "believer" to profit from the UFO phenomenon. Cults quickly proliferated, complete with a growing body of myth, legend, tantalizing rumors and newsletters to disseminate them. One of the most persistent rumors, even today, concerns UFO's that are alleged to have crashed in North America, killing their crews. These crewmen, described as about 4 feet tall with silverish complexions, or their ships were supposedly recovered by the U.S. Air Force and spirited to a secret vault somewhere in the United States. Another staple of UFO folklore is the MIB's—men in black. These shadowy figures are variously said to be agents of the U.S. or Soviet governments or perhaps even visitors from outer space. They are reported to have turned up after certain UFO sightings to intimidate witnesses and destroy or steal evidence.

While cults and other dedicated believers manned one frontier in the furor over UFO's in the United States, the federal government moved to occupy the other extreme, the role of official debunker. The sudden flap of public sightings in the late 1940s forced the U.S. Air Force to investigate the new phenomenon. The investigation lasted for more than 20 years under several different code names, including Project Sign, Project Grudge and finally Project Blue Book. Yet with a very small staff that usually numbered no more than three, and very low priority, Blue Book seems to have been largely an exercise in government public relations.

Nonetheless, the Air Force contributed, if inadvertently, to UFO research by hiring, as a part-time consultant, Dr. J. Allen Hynek. Hynek, then an astronomer at Ohio State University and later associate director of the Smithsonian Astrophysical Observatory and chairman of the astronomy department at Northwestern University, recalled that he agreed to serve "almost in a sense of sport." And for many years, as he pursued elusive UFO's, Hynek remained a skeptic. In fact, he won notoriety and scorn among die-hard UFO

George Adamski was one of the first to "report" meeting visitors from outer space. These pictures, taken in the early 1950s, according to Adamski, show six glowing scout ships emerging from the bottom of a larger, cigar-shaped craft.

believers in 1966 when he attributed a wave of dramatic sightings over the state of Michigan to mirages arising from "swamp gas."

By the late 1960s, however, Hynek had become convinced that Blue Book was nothing more than a "public-relations effort designed to debunk the whole thing." He was also now convinced not that UFO's were real, but that they constituted a *real phenomenon,* one warranting serious scientific investigation. To pursue such an investigation, he joined a handful of other scientists in the United States and Europe, a group of scholars who considered themselves a kind of "invisible college," a title used by savants of the Dark Ages who worked secretly to avoid being linked with the devil.

In recent years, this college has become the highly visible Center for UFO Studies, directed by Hynek, at Evanston, Illinois. Hynek and his colleagues there have found a number of patterns in UFO reports. They seem to come in cycles, with major flaps occurring about every five years; they occur more frequently at night than in daylight; and they often take place on isolated roads in rural areas. The objects involved occasionally seem to violate the basic laws of physics and aerodynamics—hovering effortlessly a few feet above the ground, for example, or accelerating with great speed. Moreover, those who report the sightings tend to represent a cross section of ages, occupations and levels of education. They include one U.S. President (Jimmy

The term "saucer" may have been used in 1878 by a Texas farmer to describe a UFO. More than 70 years later this saucer-like craft was built by the U.S. Army and Air Force; it never flew more than a few feet off the ground.

Carter), astronauts, astronomers, pilots, policemen, laborers, housewives. They also include in many countries well-organized citizens' groups whose purpose it is to investigate reported UFO sightings. Most witnesses say that before their sighting they had no interest in UFO's. They tend to be, as a former director of intelligence of the U.S. Air Force once put it, "credible observers of relatively incredible things." In Spain, one study showed that group sightings were most likely to involve friends, family members and work colleagues, unlikely subjects at best for hallucinations and fantastic visions. As Sen. Barry Goldwater has said, "I do not believe that we are the only planet of the billions that exist that has life on it. I've had too many very experienced pilot friends of mine see something they couldn't explain."

These "relatively incredible things" have been systematically classified by Hynek into groups that are generally accepted by UFO researchers around the world. Hynek divides UFO reports into two major categories based upon the distance at which the observation was made. The first category takes in all reports of sightings made at a distance of greater than 500 feet and is subdivided into three classes: nocturnal lights, daylight discs and radar-visual.

Nocturnal lights are by far the most frequently reported type of sighting. These lights—alone or in groups—hover motionless or dart about the skies in trajectories unlike those of known phenomena. Daylight discs cover daytime sightings such as the one by Kenneth Arnold near Mount Rainier in 1947. These disc- or saucer-shaped UFO's often give off a fluorescent glow. Radar-visual sightings cover incidents observed simultaneously by witnesses and radar, as in the case of the sightings over New Zealand in the early morning hours of December 31, 1978.

Though the sheer quantity of reports in this first major category is impressive, critics insist that few sightings are truly unidentified. With sufficient investigation, they say, conventional explanations can be found. They point out, for example, that radar scans are notorious for producing anomalous images called "angels," which can be caused by, among other things, flocks of birds, atmospheric conditions and technical deficiencies in the equipment itself.

Similarly, they find reasons for discounting both nocturnal lights and daylight discs. One possible cause of UFO sightings, of course, is simple misperception. The human visual system has built-in limitations and aberrations that can fool the mind it serves—as when a distant bright object appears to follow a car or airplane, or when the moon rises ponderously at the horizon only to shrink in size as it climbs the night sky. The atmosphere also can distort vision, serving as a kind of invisible lens capable of creating shimmering mirages in the sky or on the earth's surface.

One leading debunker of UFO's, Philip J. Klass, believes that many sightings can be accounted for as simple mistakes in identification. Even trained observers such as pilots and astronomers often misidentify aerial activity, Klass says. He cites the astronomer who was certain he had seen a brilliantly lit UFO blazing over his home near Tucson, Arizona—only to learn that it was a Titan test missile launched from Vandenberg Air Force Base in California. Yet an Air Force hoax study conducted some years ago, in which a number of parachute-borne flares were released over Clearwater, Florida, indicated that most of 80 random observers reported accurately on the floating light patterns and, in general terms, identified their source as well. Nonetheless, Klass, an electrical engineer and an editor of *Aviation Week and Space Technology* magazine, has stated flatly: "In the more than 11 years that I have been investigating major UFO incidents, some dating back 20 years, I have yet to encounter a single case that seems to me to be unexplainable in prosaic, terrestrial terms, that defies our present 'laws of physics.'"

While simple mistakes and other such causes may possibly help account for the first major category of UFO's, nocturnal lights, daylight discs, radar-visual, the second major category, close encounters, poses a different problem. Here, the observer reports encounters so close—500 feet or less—that mistakes in perception or identification would seem far less likely.

Hynek classifies three different types of close encounters, first, second and third kinds, on the basis of variances in the interaction reported between the UFO and the witnesses. In a close encounter of the first kind, for example, the UFO is simply seen near at hand. It does not leave a direct physical trace on the environment, nor are alien beings evident, though the sighting may have enormous impact on observers. People experiencing a CE-I, said one witness, would have it "etched in their memory for all time."

A vivid example of the emotional impact of a CE-I is the case of Dale Spaur, a deputy sheriff in Portage County, Ohio, which was investigated by the U.S. Air Force's Project Blue Book. Early on the morning of April 17, 1966, Spaur and another deputy stopped at the side of the road to investigate an abandoned car. Suddenly, rising above a nearby woods, Spaur recalls, "I saw this thing." By Spaur's account, it was as "big as a house" and bright enough to make "your eyes water." It was topped by a dome and gleaming with an intense purplish-white light. Spaur and his companion radioed their bizarre report to headquarters and were ordered to give chase.

Across northern Ohio and into Pennsylvania, for more than 70 miles, they chased the object at speeds of up to 105 miles per hour. Midway in the chase, they were joined by a second cruiser, manned by a policeman who had monitored the chase on his radio and

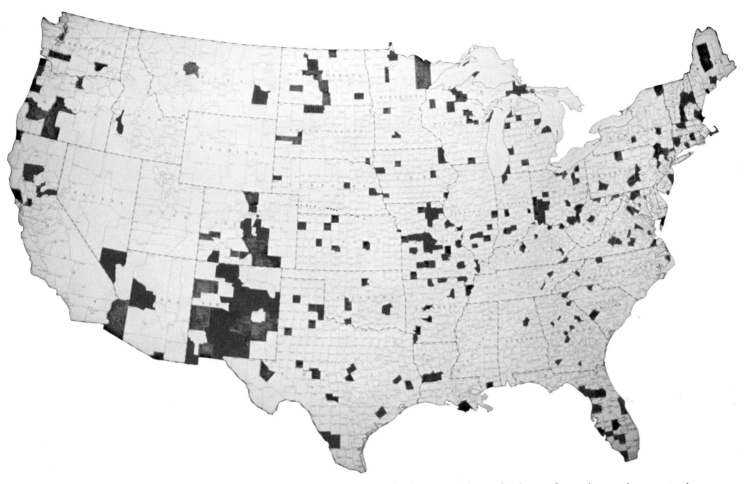

This map, based on computer analysis of more than 18,000 alleged UFO cases, shows counties in the United States where reported sightings have occurred with greater frequency than might be expected on the basis of population density. Red counties are "hot spots" with highest concentrations of reports; blue ones have had an unexpectedly high number of sightings.

then spotted the UFO. The chase ended in Conway, Pennsylvania, where a fourth policeman told the others he had been watching the object for the past 10 minutes. Together, the four watched as whatever it was shot straight up into the air and disappeared.

In contrast to CE-I cases, close encounters of the second kind leave a tangible calling card—a measurable effect on animate or inanimate matter. Consider the following CE-II, one of the strangest on record because of the damage done to man-made structures. The encounter occurred in the small village of Saladare, in Ethiopia, at 11:30 in the morning, on August 7, 1970, and lasted about 10 minutes. During that time, with a roar like that of a low-flying airplane, a red glowing ball swept over the village, destroying houses, knocking down the stone walls of a bridge, uprooting trees, and melting asphalt and cooking utensils but, strangely enough, not starting fires. In Scandinavia, in 1972, several mysterious, CE–II–related radioactive impressions were discovered in Nams Fjord. In the same year, in Rumania, a night watchman reported seeing a strange object descend and later found a perfect circle in a cornfield, one with a hole six inches wide and eight feet deep at its center. And only a few years earlier, in

Valensole, France, a farmer spotted a rugby-ball-like metal object on four legs in a field of lavender. When the UFO zoomed away, it left behind a patch of flattened, scorched vegetation where, the story goes, the farmer was never again able to grow lavender.

Witnesses in CE-II's often report another type of phenomenon—interference with electrical circuitry. In the apparent presence of a UFO, television sets go on the blink, car headlights dim or go out, automobile engines sputter and die. When the UFO disappears, witnesses report, everything works again.

One of the most remarkable instances of apparent electric interference took place on the night of November 2, 1957, around the little town of Levelland, Texas. The policeman on duty that night was Patrolman A. J. Fowler. Within a period of two hours and 15 minutes, Fowler had calls from seven different motorists. Each reported seeing a large glowing object either hovering overhead or stationary on the road. In every case, the callers said, their car headlights blinked out and the engine died. In addition, shortly after the rash of reports, UFO's were seen by five different lawmen—two sheriff's deputies, two policemen and a town constable.

Even more puzzling are the stories of other phys-

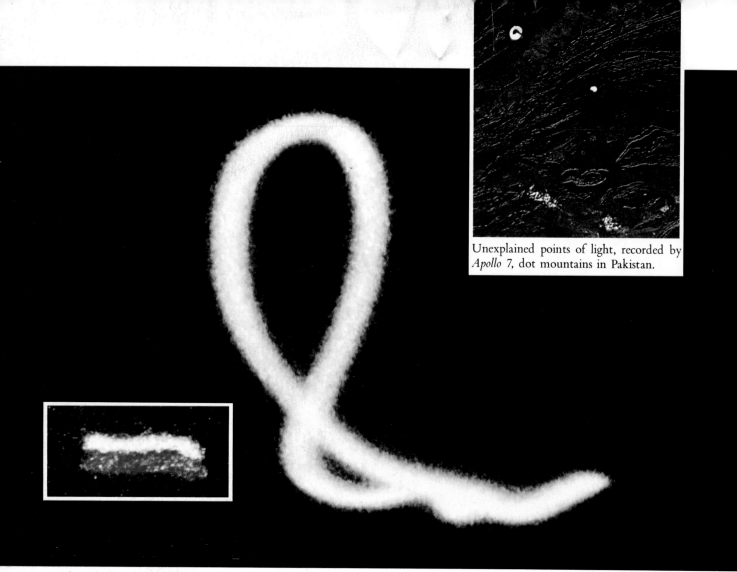

Unexplained points of light, recorded by *Apollo 7,* dot mountains in Pakistan.

Film, dual radar tracking and eyewitnesses make the New Zealand pictures above part of one of the most intriguing UFO incidents to date. One object appeared to change color (inset), while another seemed to trace a figure eight.

Close Look at Airborne Anomalies

Despite the specificity of their images and the vibrancy of their color, photographs of UFO's—like reports of sightings—can neither prove nor disprove the existence of unexplained flying objects. Many UFO photographs, of course, can be identified as fraudulent, and there are basic tests to help detect fakes, intentional or otherwise. For example, analysis of lighting conditions and film imagery can detect lens flares and film defects. Overlapping images can reveal the presence of double exposures; a type of photometric analysis that correlates distance with atmospheric conditions can show if an apparently distant disc is actually close to the camera. Internal inconsistencies in a series of pictures (inexplicable changes in tree and cloud position, for instance, during a reportedly short sequence of UFO pictures) can also help expose "unexplainable"

UFO photographs. In every case the photographer and his story are as essential to analysis as the photograph itself, and every aspect of the personal account must be checked against evidential elements in the photograph.

After careful analysis most UFO photographs are explainable in terms of known phenomena, human deceit or camera and film-processing defects. There remain, however, a few that some experts feel cannot be dismissed. Such investigators believe painstaking examination of these images might supply crucial information about the phenomenon. For example, depending on lighting conditions, the use of sophisticated computer techniques might reveal undetected UFO images on film and provide crucial information on size, color, brightness, speed and even the underlying shape of a UFO.

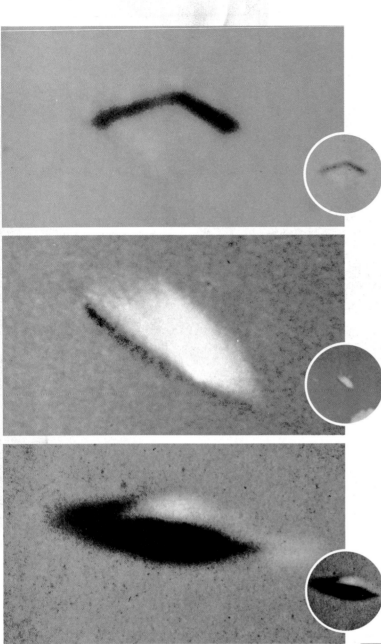

A team of French scientists photographed this strange object from a plane over Chad in 1973. The French team had been on board observing a solar eclipse.

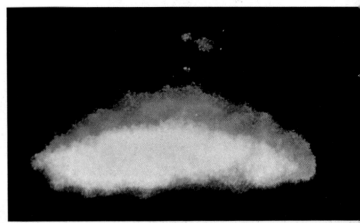

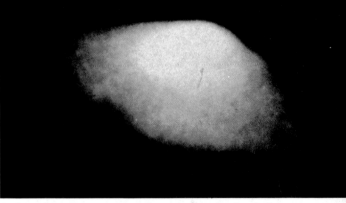

At least five witnesses reported seeing this glowing ball of light over Minnesota in 1965. The incident was investigated by the U.S. Air Force but never explained.

A 14-year-old boy in Tulsa, Oklahoma, took this picture in 1965. His family said they saw the object change colors and heard it whine as it accelerated.

The pictures above (each is an enlargement of the smaller, inset image) have been analyzed but not explained. They were taken by a teacher in Hawaii (top); a German computer programmer vacationing in Austria (center); and a free-lance photographer in Hawaii (bottom). The photographer was actually taking the picture at left and only later discovered the UFO.

At the site of a reported UFO landing in Brazil, three holes were found. Were they made by a UFO's tripod supports?

No explanation has ever been found for the nest-shaped marking that appeared in an Australian field in 1971.

ical effects experienced during CE-II's. A man in Florida said his arms and legs were temporarily paralyzed and his clothes felt very hot. A schoolteacher in Wisconsin, describing the disablement of her car on a lonely road with a UFO overhead, talked of feeling a "scalding dry heat" on her feet.

CE-II's don't always result in reported discomfort, however. In a few cases, witnesses have told of remarkable healing associated with UFO's. The French researcher Aimé Michel has chronicled the extraordinary case of a prominent French physician whose right arm and leg were partially paralyzed after he stepped on a mine during the Algerian War. One night in 1968, the doctor told Michel, he was awakened by the cries of his child. The child was gesturing toward the window. The doctor looked out and saw flashes of light—two identical discs in the sky. The discs suddenly merged into one and headed toward the doctor, beaming a powerful shaft of light. The doctor said he heard an explosion and the disc disappeared. Afterward, he realized that the swelling and pain in one of his legs, which had been injured three days previously in a wood-chopping accident, had vanished. Later, the effects of his war wounds also went away. What's more, about six days after the doctor's incredible encounter, a triangular red mark appeared around his navel. The strange mark, according to the doctor's account, also showed up on the child's stomach and periodically recurred simultaneously on both father and child.

Although the healing and other reported physical effects of CE-II's strain credulity, close encounters of the third kind are clearly the strangest of all. They seem preposterous, the realm of science fiction, for close encounters of the third kind involve human-like creatures and very often the boarding of UFO's themselves. Indeed, this category lent its name to a popular American science-fiction movie about UFO's, a project that Hynek served as technical consultant.

Hynek wryly admits that he, like other scientists, used to joke about "the little green men." He knows

that "our common sense recoils at the very thought of humanoids." Hynek's skepticism about encounters with UFO "occupants" was first shaken in 1964 by a case in Socorro, New Mexico. As in many other close encounters, the witness was a policeman, Lonnie Zamora. Zamora, who had a reputation for being tough on speeders, was giving chase to an earthly miscreant when he "heard a roar and saw a flame in the sky." Zamora broke off his chase of the car in order to investigate further. What he saw 150 yards or so away in a rocky gully, according to his testimony, was "two people in white coveralls" near an oval-shaped craft. When Zamora got out of his police cruiser for a closer look, the craft launched into the air in a roar of blue and orange flames.

Hynek, who investigated the case for the Air Force, wrote later of "my strong desire to find a natural explanation for the sight." But Hynek personally observed physical traces on the ground, including imprints that might have been landing marks, along with charred greasewood bushes. He also concluded that Zamora's "character and record were unimpeachable." The case thus went into the Blue Book files with the intriguing, though inconclusive, label "unidentified."

There exist hundreds of other reports of close encounters with animated creatures. Some of these creatures are said to be human-like in appearance, others huge or hairy or small and elf-like. They have been encountered by clergymen, engineers, farmers, housewives, physicians, policemen—people from virtually all stations of earthly life. Yet no one has come back with any artifacts. As Philip Klass says: "Of all the dozens of people who claim to have been aboard a flying saucer, not one has bothered to pick up the equivalent of a paper clip or an ashtray or a book of matches."

Many of the witnesses say they merely saw these creatures. Others report they were actually abducted by the occupants of the UFO and taken aboard. Sometimes these stories come to light months or years later and occasionally only under what is called regression hypnosis. This technique sometimes enables a subject to regain memories of experiences of which he or she was not previously aware, though it cannot prove that the experiences actually occurred. Such was the case in the most celebrated of the abduction encounters, the story of Barney and Betty Hill, the New Hampshire husband and wife whose fantastic tale has been recounted in detail by John Fuller in *The Interrupted Journey*.

Around the world people involved in CE-III's experience reactions that seem to reflect cultural patterns. In France, where officials tend to take a tolerant view of UFO's, witnesses are curious about their alien visitors, occasionally even attempting to approach them. In the United States, witnesses often react with fear or hostility. During a widely publicized encounter near Hopkinsville, Kentucky, a family of farm folk said they had attempted to ward off the unwelcome visitors (lit-

---

"Traces" of UFO Touchdowns

If reports of UFO sightings, flyovers and touchdowns number in the thousands, why haven't there been more cases in which actual physical evidence has been found and analyzed? In fact, some 1,300 such cases have been reported over the last 20 years, in two dozen countries. They have involved a wide range of residues, from dark, oily substances to gray and silver powders, variegated flakes and crystals, and strangely tinted and occasionally even phosphorescent liquids. Unfortunately, on analysis, none of these "traces" have provided conclusive proof of the existence of UFO's. A substance called angel's hair, a web-like fibrous material, has been turning up for centuries in strange settings in Britain, France, Italy and the United States. Yet three separate laboratory analyses have demonstrated three unrelated "results." In one case the substance was found to be insoluble in sulfuric acid, in another it was reported to resemble the amino-acid composition of spider webbing, and in a third it was determined to be ordinary nylon filament.

Bits or fragments alleged to have come from UFO's are more rarely found and thus provoke greater controversy than purported residues. The most intriguing case involved three tiny chunks of a light metal that splashed into the Atlantic Ocean off Brazil after a reported UFO blowup in 1957. Collected by an unidentified witness and examined in both Brazil and the United States, the metal turned out to be a very pure form of magnesium, one that lacked many elements normally present in earthly magnesium and that contained some, like strontium, not normally present. Of doubtful "earthly origin," UFO supporters announced. All too true, debunkers responded, because the fragments came from a meteor. The U.S. Air Force's Condon committee was even more conservative, reporting that the fragments might have been part of a batch of magnesium prepared by the Dow Chemical Company as early as 1940.

---

tle men, less than 4 feet tall "with long arms and a large, round head") by shooting at them. The rifle and shotgun fire apparently had no effect on the invaders. One of the marksmen said he heard his bullet "hit the critter and ricochet off."

In Latin America, encounters tend to involve extremely close contact. Take the young Brazilian farmer Antonio Villas Boas, who said that in 1957, while working his fields, he was taken aboard a huge egg-shaped craft by three beings. He said he was stripped naked and had a blood sample taken from his chin. Then, according to Villas Boas, a nude woman—4 feet 5 inches tall with large blue slanted eyes—entered the room, embraced him and engaged him in what might be termed the closest encounter of all. Remarkably, a Brazilian doctor is alleged to have found some evidence to support Villas Boas's wild story—scars on his chin and indications that he had been exposed to high amounts of radiation.

Though only one earthly witness, Villas Boas himself, could attest to his experience, fully one-third of CE-III's have involved more than one observer. The multi-witness case that stands out most dramatically in UFO annals occurred in 1959 in Papua New Guinea. The scene was an Anglican mission station, and the principal witness—there were said to be 38 witnesses in all—was Father William Gill, an Australian priest. Though there had been numerous recent reports of sightings over the general area, Father Gill was a skeptic. In fact, a few hours before his close encounter, Gill wrote to another priest, a UFO enthusiast, "My simple mind still requires scientific evidence."

That evening of June 26, Gill and others at the mission found themselves watching "this sparkling object," described as a large, circular-shaped craft with a wide base on four legs. By Gill's account, which was backed by the signatures of 25 of the witnesses, the craft hovered at about 300 to 400 feet. Then, bathed in a blue light that flowed upward, there appeared on top of the craft four human figures. The craft, sometimes accompanied by a pair of smaller objects, was visible off and on for about four hours. The following evening, the UFO reappeared over the mission. Once more, Father Gill and about a dozen onlookers saw the four figures. "Two of the figures seemed to be doing something near the center of the deck," Gill wrote later. "They were occasionally bending over and raising their arms as though adjusting or 'setting up' something not visible. One figure seemed to be standing, looking down at us. . . . I stretched my arm above my head and waved. To our surprise the figure did the same."

Soon, recalled Gill, he and a New Guinean assistant were "waving our arms and all four seemed to wave back. There seemed to be no doubt that our movements were answered. All the mission boys made audible gasps (of either joy or surprise, perhaps both)."

Fact vs. Phenomenon

Sketching the Unknown: Hand Drawings of UFO's

Of the estimated 100,000 people who claim to have seen UFO's, several hundred have been able to draw pictures of what they reportedly saw. Skeptics attribute such vivid depictions of close-range encounters to delusion or deliberate lying. Yet analysis of a large number of cases seems to suggest more complex sources. Close encounters have been reported by a broad cross section of the population, and, according to Jacques Vallée, "most witnesses held steady jobs, often positions of social responsibility" at the time of their sightings.

Investigators of such reports are hampered by the absence of a foolproof means of evaluating them. Unfortunately, neither hypnotism nor a lie-detector test can establish the truth beyond the limits of a subject's belief. Yet hypnotism, which has triggered detailed recollections of bizarre encounters, has now generated fascinating speculation on the nature of UFO sightings and their relationship with the human brain.

Preliminary work has been conducted by a professor in the English department of California State University at Long Beach, Alvin H. Lawson. Lawson compared the under-hypnosis accounts of four persons who had reported being abducted by UFO aliens with those of four student volunteers without UFO experience who imagined abduction through hypnotic suggestion. The accounts of both groups, Lawson found, were substantially the same. What's more, many details, such as musical humming and a sensation of floating, paralleled those reported by people who had undergone drug-induced hallucinations or who had had near-death experiences. These similarities have led Lawson and others to speculate on the existence in the brain of a kind of universal mental response to catastrophic stimuli of various kinds.

Yet several factors divide "real" UFO contactees from Lawson's volunteers. Only actual UFO "witnesses" are totally convinced of the reality of their encounter, and only among this group has a "sighting" or abduction been experienced by more than one person. Furthermore, assuming acceptance of a catastrophic-stimuli hypothesis, a major question remains: What triggers the response in a typical UFO sighting?

Showing remarkable similarity are UFO drawings by (from left) Marius de Wilde, who reported seeing a UFO in Quarouble, France, in 1954; François Panero and a friend, who said they saw strange beings a month later in Toulouse; and Tiago Filho, who announced that the UFO above, right, landed in Brazil in 1969.

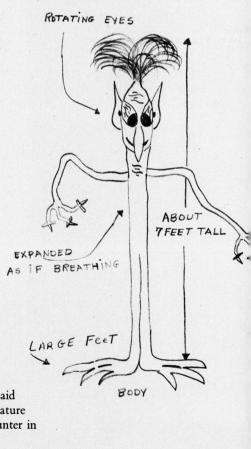

ROTATING EYES

EXPANDED AS IF BREATHING

ABOUT 7 FEET TALL

LARGE FEET

BODY

Jennings Frederick said that he met this creature during a 1968 encounter in West Virginia.

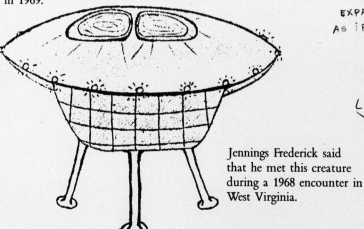

Californian Joe Lugo, his wife, daughter and a niece reported seeing this craft near his home in 1975; they convinced an investigator from Northwestern University's Center for UFO's of their sincerity.

Jennings Frederick, who reported a number of sightings, drew not only the 7-foot-tall spaceman on facing page, but also the three views at left of an enormous space vehicle in which he claimed he encountered another strange creature.

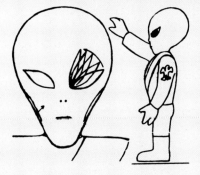

Sheriff's deputy Arthur Strauch drew this picture of the object he photographed in St. George, Minnesota, in 1965. (Strauch's photograph appears on page 315.) The craft was also seen by his wife, his son and two friends.

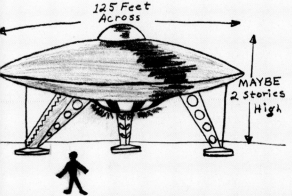

125 Feet Across

MAYBE 2 Stories High

Mother of seven children, Betty Andreasson reported being abducted in Massachusetts by the creature at left. Barney Hill drew the picture below of beings he said kidnapped him and his wife in New Hampshire. Both events were recalled under hypnosis.

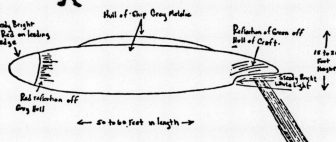

Four Army officers, all with aviation experience, say they nearly collided with this vehicle during a flight near Columbus, Ohio, in 1973. A man on the ground also witnessed the frightening incident.

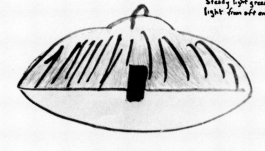

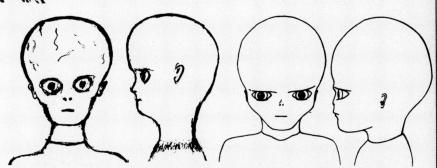

Similarities in victims' descriptions of their alien abductors include small stature, child-like appearance, large eyes, and slit-like mouth, as shown in two drawings made during incidents reported independently.

When a group of 10- and 11-year-old schoolchildren in Wales told their headmaster that they had seen a strange object, he separated them and asked them to draw it. Two representative versions of their drawings are at left.

The Andreasson Case

A UFO investigator records one of many sessions in which Betty Andreasson, under hypnosis, told of her abduction by alien beings and her visit to their planet.

It was while under hypnosis in 1977 that Betty Andreasson first revealed her extraordinary story: she had been taken on board a UFO, then transported to what seemed to be a distant, alien world. For 10 years she had been haunted by memories of that bizarre night when 3- to 4-foot-tall beings with pear-shaped heads invaded her Massachusetts home. The strange encounter was similar to other UFO reports: as it occurred, a stillness came over the house, lights dimmed, and a red glow could be seen outside.

Yet Andreasson could remember little more of the incident. Then in 1975 she read an advertisement prepared by Dr. J. Allen Hynek asking about UFO experiences and, relieved to find that someone was studying the phenomenon, she responded. Hynek gave her name to a UFO investigation team, and the team, along with an independent hypnotherapist, helped Andreasson relive her abduction. In a series of painful and exhausting sessions, she told how the alien beings had drifted effortlessly through a closed kitchen door, while most of her family began to enter a state of suspended animation. Then, she remembered, she had floated in a semi-trance aboard the UFO, where her body was scanned and a needle probe was inserted into her head. After the examination she visited an alien world filled with monkey-like creatures and bright, floating crystals. There, she believes, she was given a special message for mankind.

As a deeply religious person, Betty Andreasson remains convinced that her experience had great significance. An investigation of her background allegedly revealed a reputation for honesty; a psychiatric examination found her free of "symptoms of active thought disorders or psychiatric problems." And yet whether her experience was real or a form of self-hypnosis or hallucination, it remains a haunting example of the closest of UFO encounters.

As darkness fell over the compound, Gill signaled to the craft with a flashlight. "After a minute or two of this, the UFO apparently acknowledged the signal by making wavering motions back and forth (in a side-direction, like a pendulum)."

After this remarkable exchange, although Gill and the others shouted and beckoned, "the figures apparently lost interest in us, for they disappeared below deck." Gill himself went in to dinner, an act that has struck investigators—believers and non-believers alike—as extremely curious. After all, how could he leave the scene at a time like that? Gill explained later that he thought that the craft could be explained in conventional terms. He believed it was a type of hovercraft, perhaps "some new device of the Americans." "It was only in retrospect," he said, "that the whole thing seemed really extraordinary."

A detailed critical analysis of the New Guinea episode was prepared by Dr. Donald Menzel, the late Harvard astronomer and self-styled "archenemy of UFO's." Menzel hypothesized that what Father Gill actually saw was the planet Venus. According to Menzel, Gill probably mistook it for a UFO because he was myopic and not wearing his glasses. As for all those witnesses, said Menzel, the gullible natives were simply going along with the priest, "their great white leader." Gill replied that he did see Venus—and mentioned it in his original report—and that he was most certainly wearing his glasses. As for the natives, said Gill, it was a period of anti-European unrest on New Guinea, and they were not likely to see things in the sky just because the white priest said they were there.

For the most part, skeptics are forced to explain close encounters of the third kind as lies or mental delusions. Many UFO reports have turned out to be hoaxes: college students staging an elaborate prank or someone flipping a frisbee-like object into the air and photographing it as "proof" of a UFO. None of the major encounters considered significant by Hynek and other serious investigators have proved to be a lie or a prank. In most major encounters, the motivation for prevarication or fabrication seems lacking. Though a few self-styled participants in close encounters have parlayed them into best-selling books or other personal gains, the great majority, far from seeking public exposure, have assiduously shunned publicity.

Mental instability as an explanation is even more difficult to establish. A lie-detector test can often reveal hoaxes, but it cannot tell for certain whether the witness actually experienced the events in question—only that he truly believes he did. Certainly, hallucinations or delusions might account for single-witness encounters. But hallucinations seem totally implausible as an explanation in cases of multiple-witness sightings such as the New Guinea episode.

If all UFO's cannot be explained in conventional

terms—if they are not always the result of misperception, natural phenomena, misidentification, fabrication or mental aberration—what might they be? Among those who believe in UFO's—and a Gallup poll taken in 1978 found that 57 percent of U.S. citizens who had heard of them did—the most popular explanation is that they are controlled by some form of extraterrestrial intelligence. This speculation is bolstered, in part at least, by the widely held view among scientists that intelligent life might exist beyond Earth, though most scientists reject the possibility that UFO's are real. In recent years, for example, radio astronomy has proved that the raw materials for life exist elsewhere. More than 100 different complex molecules from which life might be formed have been detected.

Statistically, the probability of the existence of extraterrestrial intelligence is so huge as to boggle the mind. For the universe contains trillions and trillions of stars: the estimated figure is a one followed by at least 20 zeros. Many of these stars resemble our sun and presumably have planetary systems that could give rise to some form of life, intelligence and civilization. Speculative estimates of the number of planets with such civilizations range from 50,000 to 1 billion or more.

One of the most prominent of U.S. exobiologists—scientists who study the possibility of extraterrestrial life—is Cornell University astronomer Carl Sagan. Sagan has estimated that our Milky Way galaxy alone may have some 250 billion stars. About a million of these, he believes, may have planets capable of supporting some form of technical civilization.

So certain are exobiologists of the existence of extraterrestrial intelligence that coded radio messages have been beamed into the vastness of our Milky Way. Moreover, the U.S. space probe *Pioneer 10,* aiming for a rendezvous 2 million years hence with the star Aldebaran, carries an aluminum plaque bearing a coded message from Earth, including drawings of a stylized man and woman. In addition, for more than two decades, giant radio-astronomy telescopes have been sporadically listening for transmissions from other worlds. In 1978 the search for messages from outer space took a fascinating turn: biologists began looking for special meanings in the coded genetic messages contained within certain viruses. The core of this highly speculative and provocative notion—that advanced civilizations may have originally "seeded" life on Earth by launching microorganisms into space—was suggested in 1973 by the British scientist and Nobel Prize laureate Francis Crick. In 1979, Japanese researchers announced that the genetic sequence in one particular virus, found in intestinal bacteria, seemed, in their opinion, suspiciously contrived. Part of the sequence, they felt, might constitute a message created billions of years ago in another world by another intelligence.

Many UFO researchers view the elaborate search for signals from extraterrestrial intelligence with a certain irony. They ask, in effect, what if such messages are being transmitted by UFO's already at hand?

Assume, however wild the speculation may be, that UFO's are indeed interplanetary vehicles. The civilization that sends them presumably has found a way to overcome the immense technical barriers posed by traversing the universe. The greatest of these barriers is distance. For it takes years for light, moving at an astounding 186,000 miles per second, to travel from the nearest stars in our Milky Way. If earthlings could somehow find the means to fly at such speeds, a trip from one end of the Milky Way to the other would require 60,000 years. According to Einstein's special theory of relativity, however, time would pass more slowly for those on board the spacecraft. Watches and heartbeats would slow, and thus such travelers might make the trip in less than a lifetime.

Such speculation, of course, presumes traveling near the speed of light, a capability vastly beyond our present systems of propulsion and virtually beyond human comprehension. Yet it has been suggested that the universe itself may provide an answer to the problem

A network of black holes (small black circles within larger violet circles, connected by violet lines) might permit objects to travel through time and space, some scientists conjecture.

of interplanetary propulsion, perhaps by supplying some seemingly impossible method of transcending known and accepted boundaries of space and time.

Carl Sagan, an exobiologist who is highly skeptical of the existence of UFO's, discusses this in his book *The Cosmic Connection*. Sagan, along with other astronomers, conjectures that the highly speculative concept that postulates the existence of black holes could provide the answer. These strange "holes" in the universe might serve as a kind of intergalactic "rapid-transit system." Black holes, it is now thought, result from the death of stars that are more massive than our own sun. When such a star collapses, the theory suggests, it contracts into an area less than a mile across—a black hole with such an extraordinary gravitational pull that it may even trap particles of light and so exist in perfect darkness. Thus it cannot be seen, but its gravitational pull can be felt.

Though the physics of black holes is poorly understood, Sagan uses them to conjure up vivid images of a fling through space: "An object that plunges down a rotating black hole may re-emerge elsewhere and elsewhen—in another place and another time. Black holes may be apertures to distant galaxies and to remote epochs. They may be shortcuts through space and time." Wondering how the holes might be used, Sagan goes on to imagine, "although it is the sheerest speculation, a federation of societies in the Galaxy that have established a black hole rapid-transit system. A vehicle is rapidly routed through an interlaced network of black holes to the black hole nearest its destination."

Thus, at least in the realm of conjecture, travelers from another world might reach the earth in UFO's by careening along this "black hole rapid-transit system." More prosaically, how valid is a highly speculative, extraterrestrial explanation for today's phenomenon of the UFO? One answer came from a panel of scientists commissioned by the French government in 1978. This group studied 11 UFO sightings in great detail, assigning a four-person team, including a psychologist, to each case. Of the 11 cases, the researchers found that only 1 could be accounted for by conventional phenomena. The panel's originally secret report concluded that something real lay behind the other sightings—a "flying machine . . . whose modes of sustenance and propulsion are beyond our knowledge."

Quite a different answer came from a U.S. panel of scientists that tested the extraterrestrial hypothesis in the late 1960s. The study was commissioned by the U.S. Air Force under a $500,000 contract and carried out by the University of Colorado. Almost from the beginning, the program was plagued by controversy. Its chairman, physicist Dr. Edward U. Condon, was quoted a few months after the study began as saying, "My attitude right now is that there's nothing to it . . . but I'm not supposed to reach a conclusion for another year." Then Condon fired two psychologists who were generally regarded as pro-UFO for allegedly leaking a memo by Condon's second-in-command. The memo strongly implied that the study's conclusions were conceived before the committee ever convened.

In any case, the Condon committee's final report, which was published in 1969, reached the following conclusion: "No direct evidence whatever of a convincing nature now exists for the claim that any UFO's represent spacecraft visiting earth from another civilization." Shortly thereafter, largely upon the recommendation of the Condon committee, the Air Force closed its Project Blue Book, ending a 21-year-long investigation of thousands of UFO sightings.

To many UFO researchers, the Condon committee's report was a "Cosmic Watergate," as ex-nuclear physicist Stanton Friedman puts it. They quibbled less with its negative findings than with its conclusion that "further extensive study of UFO's probably cannot be justified." In fact, Hynek insists the committee tackled the wrong problem. Instead of testing the extraterrestrial hypothesis, it ought to have examined the question

A NASA craft took this picture of Mars in 1976. Such missions have

of whether or not UFO's are a real phenomenon. Nonetheless, Hynek believes the committee inadvertently proved the reality of UFO's: of the 100-odd sightings investigated in detail, nearly one-third eluded plausible explanation and hence remain truly "unidentified" flying objects.

It is possible, of course, that UFO's are real but not extraterrestrial in origin. Interestingly, the creatures reported in close encounters of the third kind typically resemble human beings or some form of elf-like beings that might well have been generated by the human mind. They seem to breathe our air and adjust to our gravity with little difficulty, as if the earth, not a faraway planet, were their home. "They may be visitors from *inner* space, from a parallel reality, or from another dimension," Hynek has suggested.

This view of UFO's as visitors from inner space has intrigued the French researcher Jacques Vallée, a computer specialist with a background in astronomy. In *Passport to Magonia* and other books, Vallée has explored the parallels between close encounters and myths from practically every culture that tell of contact between humans and alien creatures such as elves, trolls, angels, demons and monsters. "In antiquity," he says, "they were visualized as 'gods'; in our time, as interplanetary travelers. . . . It may be that there is inherent in our species, a sort of built-in defense mechanism that reveals itself only in times of extreme social stress, and that one of its manifestations is the phenomenon known as UFO's."

Vallée even postulates what he calls a "control system," which subtly manipulates human consciousness through UFO's. But who or what controls the control system? And how can it impress its images upon human perception while defying our known physical laws? The nature of such a control system, Vallée concedes, remains totally in the realm of the unknown. Such mysteries, of course, are no less elusive than the UFO phenomenon itself. And yet, be they creations of inner space or visitors from distant galaxies, natural manifestations of unknown forces or projections of the human mind, there exist certain unexplained phenomena that we have come to call UFO's, and they will undoubtedly continue to be provocative.

shown that there is no extraterrestrial life in our solar system, yet most researchers agree that it may exist elsewhere in the universe.

Bermuda Triangle: Myth or Reality?

Among the many mysteries that haunt the world's oceans, perhaps none is better known or more poorly understood than that involving a wedge-shaped portion of the western Atlantic: the Bermuda Triangle. According to legend, hundreds of ships and thousands of human beings have vanished in this sinister marine graveyard lying between Florida, Bermuda and Puerto Rico. The number of disappearances, it is said, far exceeds the laws of chance. Yet there seems no reason why the Triangle should be a deathtrap—if it is—and still less why its victims might leave so little evidence of their fate.

Almost every imaginable theory has been put forward to explain the "jinx" of the Triangle. Some people have suggested that it may be an area of such extreme gravitational and magnetic deviation that radios fail and compasses provide wrong readings. Others blame radiations from still-functioning machinery in the lost continent of Atlantis. And several authors have hypothesized that the Triangle may be a hunting ground for predatory visitors from outer space.

What is the truth about the Bermuda Triangle? The pertinent facts are these:

Surprisingly enough, the idea of the Bermuda Triangle is fairly recent. Far from being an immemorial legend, it seems to have originated in an article written by Vincent H. Gaddis for *Argosy* magazine in 1964. Other articles by other writers, most of them rehashing Gaddis's claims, soon followed. Perhaps no one was more taken with the Bermuda Triangle than the late Ivan T. Sanderson, a prolific writer on occult subjects. Sanderson not only accepted Gaddis's claims but suggested that the Bermuda Triangle was one of several mysteriously lethal regions—"vile vortices," Sanderson called them—regularly spaced about the globe.

By 1973 the idea of a Bermuda Triangle had taken such a firm hold on the public imagination that the *Encyclopaedia Britannica* decided to accord it an entry. That same year, the first best seller on the subject was published, Bantam Books' paperback edition of John Wallace Spencer's *Limbo of the Lost*. The following year the biggest best seller of them all appeared, Charles Berlitz's *The Bermuda Triangle*. Then, in 1975, Lawrence D. Kusche published a devastating attack, *The Bermuda Triangle Mystery—Solved*.

As Kusche points out in his book, the first question to ask is also the most fundamental: Is there any mystery at all? Kusche painstakingly analyzed reports of shipping and aircraft losses in the Triangle from about 1800; he found that many of the so-called unexplained disappearances either never occurred or were perfectly explainable. As for the remainder, their number and frequency did not exceed (or, in some cases, even come up to) statistics for similar ocean areas.

Typical of Kusche's reasoning is his analysis of one of the Triangle's most celebrated cases: the Lost Patrol incident. According to the story, five Fort Lauderdale-based Grumman Avenger torpedo bombers, all manned by experienced pilots and crews, disappeared in the Triangle during a routine patrol on December 5, 1945. The flight leader had earlier called the Fort Lauderdale control tower to report that they were lost: "We don't know which way is west. Everything is wrong . . . strange . . . we can't be sure of any direction. Even the ocean doesn't look as it should." At 4:25 p.m. another voice called the tower, "We must be about 225 miles northeast of base. It looks like we are—" Then there was silence. Immediately a 13-man Martin Mariner flying boat was dispatched. After a few routine transmissions, the Mariner too fell silent. No trace of the Avengers or the Mariner was ever found. That the Avengers and the Mariner did disappear cannot be doubted, but Kusche found, on carefully reading the 400-page Navy report, that nearly every other aspect of the popular story was wrong. The Avenger pilots were not experienced airmen: all were students except for Lt. Charles Taylor, the flight leader, and he was new to the area. Neither of the radio transmissions mentioned above appears to have been made. Taylor's actual transmissions indicate that his compass was malfunctioning and that he was thoroughly lost. By about 8:00 p.m., in bad weather and the dark of night, the Avengers ran out of fuel and crashed.

The Mariner flying boat did not take off until after dark—at 7:27 p.m. Some 20 minutes later, observers aboard the steamship *Gaines Mills* reported seeing a midair explosion. Unfortunately, Mariner planes had a history of such accidents; some pilots had taken to calling them "flying gas tanks."

The Lost Patrol incident certainly was bizarre. But if Kusche is correct in his analysis, it was hardly inexplicable. As Kusche says of the Triangle legend, "It began because of careless research and was elaborated upon and perpetuated by writers who either purposely or unknowingly made use of misconceptions, faulty reasoning and sensationalism." The U.S. Coast Guard seconds Kusche's views. In an official handout, a spokesman notes: "The combined forces of nature and the unpredictability of mankind outdo even the most farfetched science fiction many times each year."

Bermuda

Florida

Puerto Rico

While on a U.S.-Russian project, Soviet scientists discovered whirlpools in the Bermuda Triangle but no proof that mysterious forces were at work.

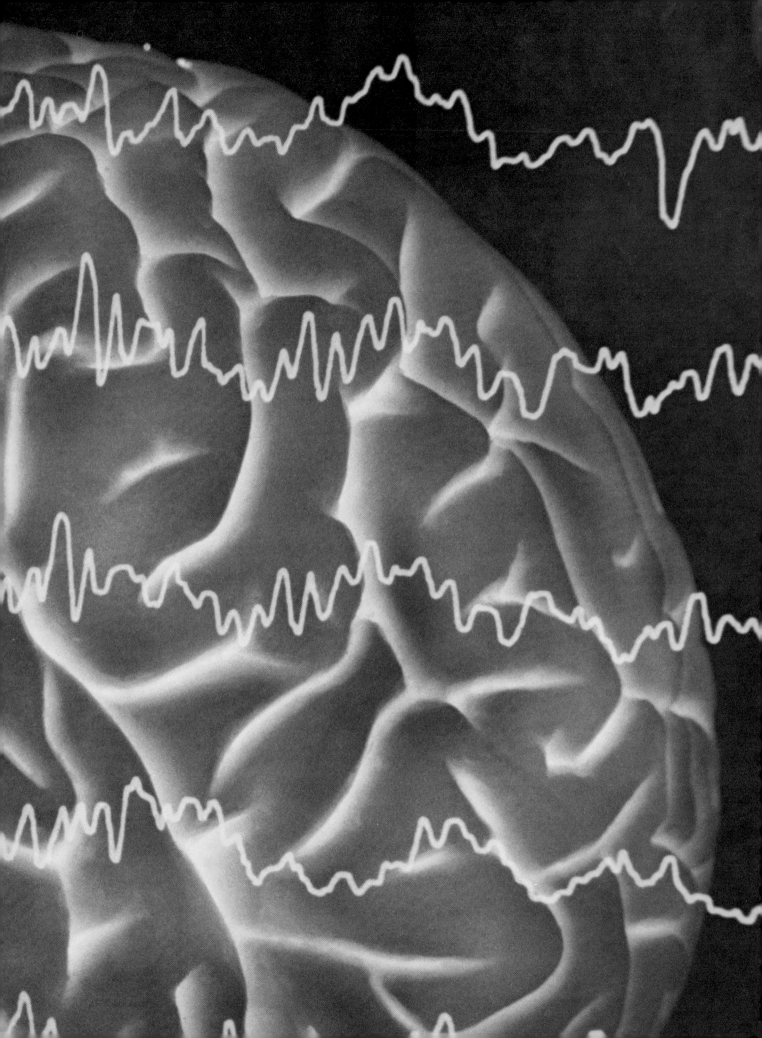

Brain research, biofeedback and even
the bizarre world of particle physics may
one day help explain psi phenomena.

PSI AND THE BRAIN

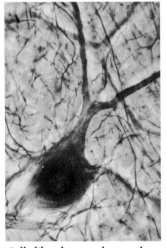

Cells like the one shown above
form incredibly complex net-
works in the human brain.

*The universe is not only queerer than we
think but queerer than we can think.*
— Prof. J.B.S. Haldane

They are to be found in almost every scientific quarter these days, involving everything from warts to subatomic particles, strange and yet very real and scientifically acceptable manifestations of the queerness of a universe that is undergoing constant exploration and reappraisal. Consider the human brain, that three-pound double handful of porridge-like tissue that after 50 years of intensive research still retains most of its fundamental mysteries. It is composed not just of millions of cells but of nearly as many cells as there are stars in the Milky Way: 16 billion, according to one estimate. What is more, according to other calculations, those 16 billion cells are capable of processing more than 10 times their number in bits of information *every second*—possibly 200 billion bits in all. Consider in addition this remarkable brain fact: using biofeedback techniques, a person, often in less than an hour, can learn to control a *single* large motor nerve cell within this same multi-billion-cell system, even as the system takes in information, lays down memories and spins the web of consciousness. Consider as well

The brain and the electric impulses that flow through it (alpha waves are shown at left) have been studied for years. New research, some suggest, may help explain psi phenomena.

a slightly more pedestrian, but nonetheless extraordinary bit of cerebral magic: hypnotic suggestion can actually make clusters of cells, warts, vanish from the outside of the body.

And yet, in comparison to the hocus-pocus occurring in another hard-to-believe universe—the buzzing, blooming world of particle physics, a world in which subatomic energy packets appear to defy time, space and the need to possess mass—the brain's complexities seem relatively down-to-earth. So strange in fact is this world that one physicist has resorted to these happy-go-lucky terms to describe it: "Particles no longer move stiffly and formally, if not majestically, in predetermined paths. Rather it is Marx Brothers hyperkinetic pandemonium, Charlie Chaplin slapstick, Helter Skelter now you see it, now you don't. In fact, it is not even clear what it is that has a path. It's psychedelic confusion—until one sees the subtle order." Note in conclusion one last bit of theoretical queerness: There are particles known as neutrinos that have no observable mass, no electric charge or other physical properties and thus are thought to be capable, traveling at the speed of light, of passing through anything. During the time that your eyes scan these sentences, according to the theories of particle physics, neutrinos by the billions are whizzing through the billions of cells in your head.

The fundamental question in terms of psi raised by these strange circumstances is this: If odd, awesome and anomalistic events happen in other fields—and are accepted by scientists—why should telepathy, clairvoyance, precognition and psychokinesis be so hard to accept? Surely the possibility that two minds might communicate directly without known sensory means is no less staggering than the idea that neutrinos exist or that hypnotic suggestion can whisk warts away. And surely the possibility that a mind might move an object at a distance with no known connection is no harder to accept than that a mind, aided by biofeedback, can learn to pick out and control a single cell in a multi-billion-cell nervous system. The answer to the question, of course, is as basic as it is obvious. It is that the strange doings in particle physics and hypnosis, in brain research and biofeedback, are impressive gleanings from the very frontiers of established science, frontiers that have been constructed on the basis of theoretically convincing and scientifically supportable investigations. In contrast, psi research, to a large degree, has been delinquent or unconvincing in these areas, though, as supporters suggest, this may be as much the result of psi's strange and elusive nature as of faulty or inadequate experimental technique. There is a second answer to the question of psi recognition, however, one that may be less obvious but no less significant in impact. It is that if psi powers are proved to exist—to everybody's satisfaction—established science will face major convulsions in its most basic tenets, and this is a situation that few scientists wish to contribute to or face. The irony of the predicament—the specter that haunts the no man's land between the queerness of accepted science and the queerness of unaccepted psi—is that it is exactly on the scientific frontier that support for psi may be found. And the search, tenuous, controversial, alarming to some scientists though it may be, has been under way for some time.

One of the most interesting, easily understood and psi-attractive discoveries to emerge from modern brain research was the finding that the brain is made up not only of billions of neurons, or brain cells, but that these cells come in two packages, or hemispheres. Early anatomists could see this, of course, but what modern researchers have discovered is quite remarkable: the two brain halves possess and can express different powers and capacities. It is almost as if two people, two bundles of consciousness, were living in the same skull, one dominant, one recessive, but both in constant communication and busily at work at different tasks as they generate the day-to-day miracles of human existence.

How did researchers discover this extraordinary cerebral situation? In the relatively common manner of science—through a combination of luck, imagination and skill. The first step was taken by a surgeon following the suggestion of psychologists. In an attempt to control the spread of life-endangering epilepsy from one hemisphere to the other in a number of patients, the surgeon cut the bundles of fibers that link the brain

In the strange world of particle physics, the dots of light shown above depict the location of atoms in a substance known as iridium. Because of their unusual properties, infinitely smaller particles are sometimes mentioned in psi speculations.

halves. The surgery was successful, the medical crisis alleviated; but, as one scientific observer has noted, the psychological testing that followed was "more successful." For, led by Roger Sperry at the California Institute of Technology, researchers evolved a painstakingly detailed series of test procedures to determine exactly what went on where in the now-isolated brain halves. Normally, due to the crossover wiring pattern of the human nervous system, the left brain hemisphere is in charge in right-handed people, with the right brain taking orders from it. Yet by carefully tinkering with the input of information to the split brain halves, using, for example, just the right hand or just the right or left visual field, Sperry and others began to chart the functions that made the cerebral roommates different. The normally dominant left brain, they found, turned out to be the home of logical, analytical, time-sensing, verbal and mathematical skills, the home, in a sense, of rational man. The right-brain brother, on the other hand, emerged as a beguiling fellow, a kind of space musician, a seer of the wholeness of things, an intuitive, non-verbal bundle of consciousness skilled in spatial relations, in the recognition of faces and images, in dreaming, in creative expression and musical ability.

An extraordinary state of brain affairs, and researchers in several fields soon went to work prospecting for answers to everything from life's great philosophical issues (Who am I? What is reality?) to how best to help learning-disabled children. Not surprisingly, parapsychologists became interested in split brains too, and, tentatively and circumspectly, they began to wonder if that non-verbal, intuitive right-brain half might not be the home of psi powers as well. As psychiatrist Jan Ehrenwald wrote in *The ESP Experience,* "If a skeptic is inclined to dismiss the quest for psi phenomena as a wild goose chase, he is likely to consider the search for the actual habitat of the rare birds as an even more foolhardy undertaking. Yet there can be no doubt that psi phenomena, regardless of their purported nonphysical, extrasensory, paranormal nature, have a foothold somewhere in our neurophysiological organization." Richard Broughton, a British parapsychologist, reached the same theoretical conclusion by pursuing a slightly different course. If paranormal information arrives or exists in the nervous system, he reasoned, it has to pass at some point through the cerebral cortex. If so, he wondered, might it not be found in one hemisphere or the other? And, he continued, because the expression of psi seems so unpredictable and so unstable, and is almost always released through words generated by the left brain, perhaps it passes through but does not actually originate in that brain half. Wrote Broughton in a paper entitled "Psi and the Two Halves of the Brain," "Just for the fun of it, perhaps we should give the so-called minor hemisphere a better chance in the ESP game. Maybe there is something in the left hemisphere which does not like ESP or is incompatible with the kind of information which ESP represents."

Why not? Why couldn't the faculties of extrasensory perception (ESP) and psychokinesis (PK), if they exist, share brain space in the non-verbal, creative side of the brain? Well, they might, and no researcher today can prove that they do not, any more than any researcher can prove that they do. In any case, there is a certain amount of circumstantial evidence that tentatively supports the possibility. In his paper, Broughton makes a number of references to spiritualism. In the *Encyclopedia of Psychic Science,* for example, Broughton found reports that the famous medium Eusapia Palladino changed hand dominance, from right to left, in the course of her trances. The implication: she changed brain dominance as well, shifting control in times of psychic activity to her right brain, the hemisphere in charge of her left hand. Broughton also mentioned a spiritualistic writing device known as the planchette, emphasizing the rough quality of the messages scrawled

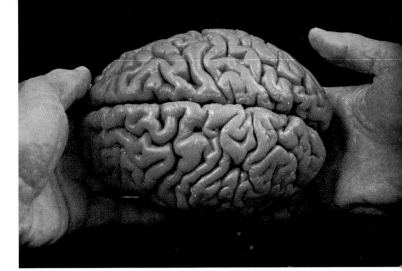

The life-endangering contortions and brain-wave patterns of epileptics during seizures (below) led surgeons to divide the brains of some patients. Such surgery enabled psychologists to study the brain halves and led to speculation that psi powers might exist in the right brain (top in the picture above).

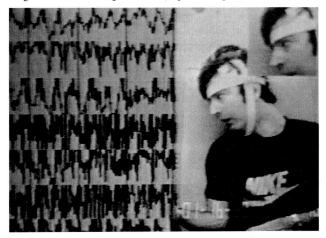

by it. The point that Broughton and other parapsychologists make is that such drawings and the rudimentary bits of speech that occasionally emerge during trances and other psi-conducive states are very like those produced by people who have suffered damage to their normally verbal left-brain halves. Is it not possible, the researchers suggest, that in both cases the right brain was controlling the drawing and speaking, in one instance out of necessity, in the other because right-brain ESP powers were at work?

The powers of PK also might originate in the right brain, Ehrenwald has suggested as well. "Even a high-class PK subject's leverage upon dice thrown from a cup," he wrote, "on a compass needle, or on a match box placed on a tabletop is a fitful, capricious, unpredictable affair. The same is true for a brain-injured patient, suffering from motor apraxia, trying to carry out such simple tasks as lighting a cigarette or tying his shoelaces. We know that here, too, a lesion in certain areas of the left hemisphere is at fault. A PK subject, it could be stated, behaves like a patient who has to make do without the left hemisphere presiding over his motor performance."

Suppose that psi phenomena do exist in some as yet unexplained way in the right brain, normally frustrated by the verbal dominance of the consciousness next door. This possibility raises two more questions: How did psi get into the right brain in the first place and how best might it be gotten out? Broughton, among others, offered an appealing, highly speculative solution to the first problem, one that has about it a kind of pleasing logic, if little or no factual support. "In terms of human evolution," he wrote, "it may be supposed that some type of psi ability existed prior to elaborate linguistic communication. Psi ability could be very helpful in group hunting and just group survival. As linguistic communication developed, psi communication could have waned in importance or perhaps even become socially undesirable so that mechanisms were evolved to suppress it or restrict its appearance in normal social behavior."

Wild evolutionary speculation, of course, as Broughton readily admitted. And yet the idea does provide an explanation of how psi capacities might have developed in the brain. The question that has teased mankind ever since has been how to get them out from behind the scrim of consciousness on some relatively regular, useful and predictable basis. A formidable obstacle to such speculative considerations is the fact that no researcher knows exactly what consciousness is any more than he knows what creates it or what its exact relationship may be with the operations of the brain. Yet most people do realize that consciousness is changeable, that it can be altered by a variety of factors, ranging from sleep to psychedelic drugs, hypno-

sis and even the gossamer reveries of daydreams. As William James wrote nearly 100 years ago after taking laughing gas, "One conclusion was forced upon my mind at that time, and my impression of its truth has ever since remained unshaken. It is that our normal waking consciousness, rational consciousness as we call it, is but one special type of consciousness, whilst all about it, parted from it by the flimsiest of screens there lie potential forms of consciousness entirely different."

Is there then a special kind of psi-consciousness, perhaps related to the trance of the medium or of the frenzied shaman, one that might open a high road to the right brain and the psi powers that may lie within it? There may be, of course, but as yet researchers have not found it. Nonetheless, the hunt goes on. Sleep and dreams, insanity and trances, hypnosis and sensory deprivation and overload, psychedelic states, brain-wave modification and even simple relaxation have all been investigated in the effort, as one researcher described it, "to circumvent the brain's normal defence mechanism if psi is to be given a chance to show itself." Thus far, sleep, most especially during dreams, and the suggestive power of hypnosis seem to have come closest to giving psi a chance to appear. There is some evidence, for example, to indicate that dreaming takes place in the right hemisphere: brain damage to the area can interfere with dreams, and split-brain patients sometimes report that they do not dream at all. And yet, after comprehensive testing, the evidence seems inconclusive and, to most scientists, unconvincing, despite a number of experimental situations in which images appeared to be transmitted to the dreaming mind with extraordinary

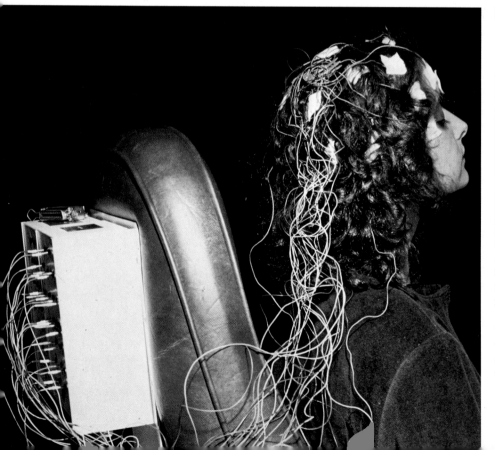

Altered states of consciousness, such as hypnosis and dream sleep (monitoring equipment is shown above), have long intrigued researchers interested in extrasensory powers.

The woman at left is having her brain waves recorded. Biofeedback techniques may one day help control and amplify such waves and possibly enhance psi sensitivity.

accuracy. Hypnosis can produce remarkable physical responses: touch a pencil to a hypnotized subject's skin, suggest it is a hot iron, and the subject's skin may blister. In addition, recent experimental work involving the churning up of powerful emotional states and the recall of non-verbal memories—both functions associated with the right brain—has indicated that hypnosis may be able to temporarily separate the brain halves. And yet studies linking hypnosis and psi phenomena have been at best uneven, some reportedly showing positive results, some negative and a few nothing at all. Even when it is most effective, hypnosis appears to function in a secondary rather than primary manner, inducing subjects to enter an open, relaxed state of mind, one that might contribute to positive psi performance.

Such a relaxed, internally alert state of mind has been linked with psi in a different way—through brain waves, especially those known as alpha waves. It was in 1928 that a psychiatrist, Hans Berger, reported that the tiny amounts of electric current in the human brain flow in rhythms, or wave patterns. In the years since, scientists have isolated four patterns: alpha waves, which run between 8 to 12 cycles per second and are associated with relaxation and meditation; beta waves, which flow at 13 to 23 cycles per second and are apparently related to front-brain operations; delta waves, which are the slowest moving, at less than 4 cycles per second, and are prominent during deep sleep; and theta waves, exhibiting a frequency of 4 to 7 cycles per second, which may be allied with mood changes.

Alpha waves may have ties with reported instances of psi sensing, though the bonds appear to be nearly as transient as the waves themselves. Some work has indicated, for example, that alpha waves may help set the scene for psi receptivity, then increase in frequency as actual testing begins. Another study reported that subjects did especially well at psi tasks when they generated alpha waves *and* noted distinct changes in their internal states. In addition, there is some evidence to suggest that on certain occasions, when one identical twin produces alpha waves, the other, situated in a different room, may also begin producing them. In some ways, however, the best and perhaps simplest advice for those interested in psi contact may be that offered by Mary Craig Sinclair, the wife of Upton Sinclair and a perceptive and active telepathist, more than 50 years ago: "Relax all mental interest in everything in the environment; inhibit all thoughts which try to wander into consciousness. . . . Drop your body, a dead-weight, from your conscious mind. . . . To make the conscious mind a blank it is necessary to 'let go' of . . . consciousness of the body."

A quite different but more basic problem concerning psi phenomena is one that also confronts the world at large today—energy. In terms of psi, however, the question is not one of quantity but of identity: if psi exists, what does it operate on? Generally speaking, there are three plausible energy theories suggesting how telepathy or clairvoyance—if they exist—might work. First, psi powers may require and use some form of energy that we already know about; second, psi phenomena may use some form of energy we do not know about; and, third, telepathy may work because, in the unexplained cosmic order of things, all minds are in some way in communication, or some few connect at certain times, perhaps due to a unique kind of warping of space and time. However grandiose this last idea—the concept of the linking of all living things—it has been around for thousands of years and has found expression in religion, philosophy and science. There is, for example, something called Hegel's axiom of internal relations—its idea being, in the most basic terms, that if you change the position of a lamp on a desk, you may actually be altering the actions of an elephant in Africa.

Known energy, unknown energy or a dip in the cosmic pool—these appear to be the choices if psi phenomena are to operate. Energy, as we perceive it today, involves both gravity and electromagnetism, though particle physicists recognize two other basic kinds, which they refer to as strong and weak interactions. Electromagnetism encompasses many forms of radiant energy, extending from cosmic rays (at 10^{28} cycles per

Although tests of unusual communication between identical twins have been inconclusive, researchers are studying similarities in their perceptions and the "wiring" of their brains.

second) to FM, television and AM radio waves (the latter at 10^6 cycles per second) and on down to VLF (very low frequency) waves at sonic frequencies. Not surprisingly, brain waves, the tiny electrical patterns identified by Berger, have been studied as a possible power source for telepathic transmission, despite the fact that they are extremely weak and that it would take millions of such waves to illuminate a small bulb. Nonetheless, an Italian neurologist, F. Cazzamalli, performed a series of experiments that indicated, he believed, that the human brain, under certain conditions, might generate enough electromagnetic energy to form radio waves. Cazzamalli's speculative assumption was that such waves, traveling from one brain to another, might account for telepathic communication. Yet research conducted by a Soviet physicist, L. L. Vasiliev, made this seem unlikely. Vasiliev attempted to induce hypnosis telepathically in a number of subjects; he was allegedly able to do this even at great distances and even when both sender and receiver were shielded by electromagnetic-wave-blocking metal cabinets. Thus, wrote Vasiliev, "According to our conclusion the Cazzamalli 'brain wireless waves,' if in fact they exist, have no connection whatever with the phenomena of mental suggestion." This does not rule out some wildly unpredictable breakthrough linking psi and the electromagnetic band, but present indications are that if psi uses energy, it must be of an exotic and esoteric kind, perhaps its own special brand of "psychic energy." Nor is such a term and such speculation necessarily as fanciful as they may sound. A number of experienced and successful doctors and scientists, an occasional Nobel Prize winner among them, have speculated at length about the existence and use of unknown and unexplained forms of energy in the brain. As Swedish psychiatrist Nils O. Jacobson wrote in *Life Without Death,* "We could picture the brain as a transformer station, a device which transforms 'low-tension' physical energy to 'high tension' psychic energy, or the reverse." Impossible, of course, and yet a Czech inventor named Robert Pavlita has constructed a number of small devices known as psychotronic, or bioplasmic, generators, which, if various reports are true, are able to gather and store psychic energy, then release it and produce a variety of psi phenomena. According to Pavlita, such energy can be refracted, polarized and combined with other energy forms; it can be conducted by paper, wool and even wood; and it can be used to promote healing as well as to kill flies. The potential for destructive use of such energy, if it exists, is quite real, of course, though the possibility of distortion in reports concerning it is probably just as real. Nonetheless, a Defense Intelligence Agency report referred to the energy this way: "Both Czech and U.S. researchers have described Robert Pavlita's work with psychotronic generators as possibly the most important contemporary development

in the field of parapsychology and as a major contribution to the deeper understanding, mastery and utilization of biological energy for human advantage."

This may be an example of psychic energy in action today—if the reports on Pavlita's work reflect to even a slight degree what is actually occurring in Czechoslovakia. And yet nearly 30 years ago, a Nobel Prize-winning brain scientist, Sir John Eccles, postulated the existence in the brain of an unknown but PK-like force that performed extraordinary services. According to Eccles, a kind of "two way traffic" between mind and matter exists in the brain, traffic that permits the will, the mind or the conscious self, to influence brain-cell circuitry. This was remarkable speculation, and Eccles carried it even further, expressing the belief that both ESP and PK are in fact irregular manifestations of the same unknown force. Eccles, however, was not specific about the nature of his force. More recent theorizers have been more exacting, attempting to explain psi phenomena in terms of particles that seem suspiciously similar to those, such as neutrinos, whizzing around in the queer world of particle physics. V. A. Firsoff, an eminent British astronomer, was one of the first to postulate the existence of psychic energy particles. He called his particles "mindons" and suggested that they might have properties somewhat similar to those exhibited by neutrinos. Sir Cyril Burt, the controversial British psychologist, used the term "psychon" to meld psi phenomena with quantum mechanics. And in 1965 the late British mathematician Adrian Dobbs theorized the existence of what he called "psitrons," infinitely small entities, somewhat resembling neutrinos, that, traveling in swarms and exhibiting only imaginary mass, might account not only for telepathy but precognition as well. In simplest terms, according to Dobbs, telepathy was workable because brain activity at transmission time would churn up a cloud of psitrons, and being invulnerable to loss of energy from friction, such psitrons might go where they pleased, carrying with them a telepathic message, which would enter the brain circuitry of the receiver.

Dobbs also tackled perhaps the most difficult of all psi-related subjects: precognition, knowing that something is going to happen before it does so. His future-time theory was based not only on the existence of clouds of psitrons, emerging from one brain and settling with a message into a second cerebral system, but also on a double-dip concept of time. According to this idea, which did not originate with Dobbs, one time dimension moves forward from present to future in the manner to which we are accustomed, while a second, non-sequential time zone exists as well, containing probable outcomes of future events, or "precasts," as Dobbs called them. Thus in Dobbs's theory, psitrons become the messengers that enter the precast-rich second time zone, scan its contents and report back on the future. The idea is diverting, psitrons are pleasing beasts of psi-phenomena burden, and as Arthur Koestler noted in *The Roots of Coincidence,* "At least these theories, based on assumptions which sound weird but hardly more weird than those of modern physics, go a long way towards removing the aura of superstition from the 'extra' in extra-sensory perception. The odour of the alchemist's kitchen is replaced by the smell of quark in the laboratory."

Koestler is right, in the broadest possible sense, because while what is happening in particle physics in no way proves that similar things are occurring—or even may occur—in the psi-phenomena field, such happenings indicate that queer occurrences are possible *someplace.* There have been speculations, for example, about hypothetical particles known as tachyons, which have imaginary mass and thus can travel faster than the speed of light and can, in theory, arrive before they depart. As one scientist has written, "For example if there was a rifle that shot forth tachyon 'bullets' the target would appear to be impacted *before* the tachyon bullet was propelled from the rifle's barrel." There is another strange sort of occurrence that is often mentioned, one known as the Einstein-Podolsky-Rosen paradox. In experiments, the EPR paradox advises, two particles are generated that, apparently joined by some form of unknown, non-local connection, move apart at the speed of light. The experimenter then takes action to alter the course of one particle, and the second particle changes course as well. The crucial question is: How does particle B know that something has happened to change particle A's course?

Is there then an unknown energy system linking even the tiniest bits of matter? Or are we, as one researcher has theorized, occasionally brought into strange avenues of telepathic communication by a form of "space warp"? Questions are clearly outrunning answers in many scientific quarters these days; yet if comparison between the queer world of particle physics and the queer world of psi phenomena is at present infinitely more esoteric than substantive, it may nonetheless serve a useful purpose. For psi and the brain may have a future together, one whose importance might be expressed by these words: "If there is to be any civilization," U.S. biophysicist R. A. McConnell wrote in 1975, "and any science a decade or two from now, I am confident that physicists, psychologists, and biologists will be putting much of their fundamental research effort into the understanding of psychic energy—its role in the brain and in the world at large."

The picture at right, taken inside a bubble chamber, shows the delicate tracks made by bits of energy following a subatomic collision. Such constant, yet hard-to-imagine, exchanges challenge everyday concepts of time, space and reality.

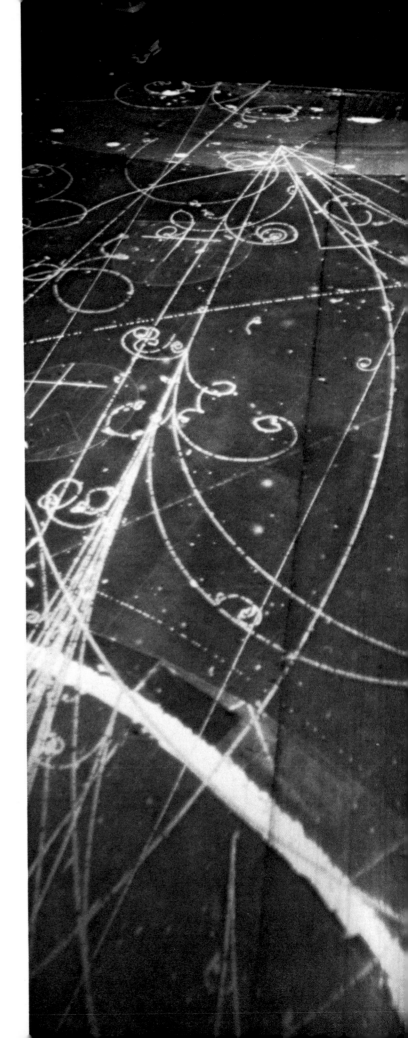

MISCELLANEA OF THE UNKNOWN

An assortment of people, terms and phenomena of recurring interest relating to the mysterious and the unknown

Agharta A mythical underground kingdom, Agharta is the construct of science-fiction writer Robert Ernst Dickhoff, whose book by that name appeared in 1951. Dickhoff's fanciful world extends outward beneath the surface of the earth from Antarctica, connecting the subterranean regions of the United States, Brazil, Tibet, and the Pacific islands, and is inhabited by descendants of the Martians who he claims settled on (or under) the earth 80,000 years ago. Agharta is one of a large number of subterranean empires conjured up by imaginative writers and theorists of the improbable over the years, but while most make Atlantis or Lemuria their starting point, Dickhoff appears to have based his creation upon an ancient Tibetan legend.

Bilocation This term refers to a particular form of out-of-body experience in which an individual's double, or astral body, not only travels some distance from his physical body but is actually observed by someone in the second location. As with other varieties of astral projection, accounts of this phenomenon—while relatively rare—have circulated in various parts of the world for centuries. Christian tradition ascribes such incidents to a number of saints, among them Saint Anthony of Padua, Saint Severus of Ravenna and Saint Ambrose of Milan. Probably the best-known report concerns Saint Alphonsus Liguori, who, during a period of confinement and fasting in a cell in Arezzo, Italy, in 1774, announced on awakening one morning that he had been at the bedside of the dying Pope Clement XIV in Rome, a four-day journey away. This statement was greeted with disbelief, so the story goes, until it was learned that the pope had indeed just died and that Alphonsus Liguori had been seen at his deathbed.

Black box A diagnostic device, the black box was devised early in this century by Dr. Albert Abrams of San Francisco, one of the first theorists of radiesthesia, or dowsing, for medical purposes. Traditionally trained, Abrams was a respected neurologist when he became interested in unconventional medical alternatives. In 1910 he parted company with orthodoxy and wrote a book called *Spondylotherapy*, which espoused a synthesis of osteopathic and chiropractic therapeutics; his ideas were ridiculed by his medical peers but embraced by laymen, and Abrams began a national series of lectures to explain his techniques. In 1914 he published a more sophisticated and extensive work, *New Concepts of Diagnosis and Treatment*, which set forth his position that disease was the result of a "disharmony of electronic oscillation," a modern reiteration of the age-old life-force concept of illness. For the purpose of measuring the extent of and locating the source of this disharmony, Abrams offered the black box, also known as the E.R.A. or the oscilloclast, a sealed box containing a thin rubber sheet stretched over a metal plate, and adorned on the outside with several rheostats. A sample of the patient's blood was placed inside the box, which was attached to a metal plate affixed to the forehead of a healthy person. By tapping the abdomen of the healthy person, the diagnostician was supposedly able to identify "areas of dullness" indicative of disharmony. Although there was some evidence that Abrams occasionally succeeded in accurately diagnosing patients with his black box, the technique produced uneven results with other practitioners. Many believers in the principles of radiesthesia remained, however, and similar devices continue to be manufactured in the United States and Great Britain.

Black Mass A so-called Black Mass is an occult ceremony that reverses or parodies the classical Mass—black vestments instead of white, prayers said backward, blasphemy instead of piety,

Mme. de Montespan, sponsor of a Black Mass

sexuality instead of chastity, and the worship of Satan instead of God. According to Doreen Valiente, author of *An ABC of Witchcraft Past and Present*, "The Black Mass does not belong to genuine witchcraft because the latter has its own traditions and rituals. The real witch is a pagan, and the Old Horned God of the witches is much older than Christianity or the Christian Devil or Satan."

According to Prof. Rossell Hope Robbins, who compiled the much-respected *Encyclopedia of Witchcraft and Demonology*, "No matter how titillating, all accounts of black masses (with one exception) must be dismissed as unfounded speculation. The black mass as something that historically occurred is one of the biggest intellectual frauds ever imposed on the lay public."

The one Exception referred to by Professor Robbins is well documented and took place in France in 1672 during the reign of Louis XIV. Mme. de Montespan, Louis' mistress, instigated a series of Black Masses in the hope of rekindling the king's interest in her and of curing him of wandering into the arms of more seductive women at court. After having seven children by the king and not being at the top of her form (she supposedly weighed 200 pounds at the time), Mme. de Montespan sought the good offices of the notorious abortionist Catherine Deshayes Monvoisin, known as La Voisin. This woman, who was alleged to have dispatched some 2,500 infants, also was a genius with poison. La Voisin worked with several co-conspirators, but her most notable colleague was a 67-year-old priest, the Abbé Guibourg. This ruthless character, the father of several children, created a bizarre program for reuniting the king and his mistress. His Mass included sacrificing a baby while simultaneously uttering incantations to two mythical demons—Astaroth and Asmodeus. The former, a foul-smelling figure, was supposed to have the talent for obtaining favors from rulers; the latter demon was said to be capable of exterminating unwanted people.

Most other accounts of alleged Black Masses are figments of the imaginations of the Inquisitors during the 16th and 17th centuries and of such authors as Frenchman Donatien Alphonse François, the Marquis de Sade, in his books *Justine* and *Juliette*. Another author, Joris-Karl Huysmans, in his book *Là-Bas* (Down There), wrote an account of a Black Mass that respected demonologists consider to be pure fiction.

Blake's The Ancient of Days

Blake, William English poet, painter, engraver, artistic and social visionary, Blake was one of the most expansive, versatile and undervalued artists of the early Romantic age. Born in London in 1757, Blake lived there in relative poverty and obscurity for all but 3 of his 70 years, although his imagination touched the world, the past and the future. He was apprenticed to an engraver as a boy of 14 and remained a printmaker all his life. His own art developed out of the engraving process: he engraved his fantastic drawings on copper plates then watercolored the prints by hand, sometimes redoing a series several times over in deepening colors. In this manner he illustrated and issued all of his poems, which were allegorical, mythological and extraordinarily prescient of 20th-century psychological and social concerns: alienation, suspension of sensibility in favor of rationalism, industrial violence and political repression were all interwoven in his sometimes apocalyptic, sometimes optimistic visions.

Burbank, Luther A U.S. horticulturist (1849-1926) of unconventional methods and unprecedented success, Burbank was a lifelong believer in human ESP and in a reciprocal relationship among plants and humans. Burbank's instinctive, adventurous and high-speed approach to plant breeding infuriated more cautious experimenters. He kept few notes on the thousands of fruit and vegetable experiments he had

going at a given time, although his catalogs, which boasted of stupendous victories in the garden, suggested that someone was keeping scrupulous count of bulbs, seedlings, cuttings, colors and species. The pedigree of each offering was numerically precise: "six new gladioli, the best of a million seedlings"; "the growing of 10,000 hybrid climatis plants for several years to get a final six good ones"; "discarding 18,000 calla lilies to get one plant." The way one visitor to Burbank's vast nursery in Santa Rosa, California, about 50 miles north of San Francisco, described Burbank's methods, it seems likely that the 18,000 discarded calla lilies were yanked out of the ground by Burbank personally on a morning dash through the growing bed. "He seemed to have an instinct that told him if a tiny plant would grow to bear the kind of fruit or flowers he wanted. I couldn't see any difference between them, even if I stooped and looked closely, but Burbank did no more than glance at them."

There was no mystery about it: long before the notion gained popularity among 20th-century home gardeners, Luther Burbank, according to some people, was talking to his plants. While he was conducting his experiments with cactuses, Burbank supposedly once said that he often talked to the plants to create a vibration of love. There is nothing to fear, he would tell them. Defensive thorns are not needed for protection.

In an article Burbank wrote for *Hearst's International* magazine in June 1923, in which he described his mother's brain as "both a transmitting and a receiving radio-telephone instrument," he told of his own frequent telepathic communications with a friend and of a sister who had also inherited the mother's facility. He confessed as well a fact he had kept quiet for many years, his gift for healing. By then, three years before his death, there were few who knew the wizard of horticulture who would have been greatly surprised to learn that he had a healing touch as well as a fertile one. Around Santa Rosa, Burbank's exceptional relationship with nature was old news: though the town received little notice in comparison with the attention given San Francisco, Santa Rosa suffered an equivalent devastation in the 1906 earthquake; the entire business district was leveled, and farmhouses and barns

collapsed throughout the countryside. Burbank was not totally immune: the small house in which he and his aging mother lived broke in two, and the chimney toppled to the ground. But not a pane of glass shattered in the greenhouse, 30 feet away, while in downtown Santa Rosa, the collapse of a building that housed a photographic studio destroyed everything inside except 500 fragile glass negatives on which were recorded some of Burbank's prize horticultural specimens.

Cattle mutilation A widely disputed phenomenon, cattle mutilation has received much attention in the press in the last decade as potential evidence of UFO activity. Beginning in the late 1960s, increasing numbers of ranchers and farmers throughout the United States reported finding cattle that appeared to have been mutilated. As accounts of such incidents accumulated (the numbers vary—one estimate is 8,000 to 10,000 cattle and horses), a tradition developed about the "classic" mutilation: no footprints of predators, human or animal, were visible within a wide circle surrounding the dead animal; the carcasses were bloodless, suggesting that the blood had been drained; specific organs were "uniformly" missing, all seeming to have been "surgically removed"; these organs included the genitals, internal reproductive organs, eyes, tongue, lips, ears and nose. Some theorists suggested that "Satanic cults" were responsible, but the most popular explanation, bolstered by unverified reports of mysterious lights in the sky, among other things, was that the mutilations were the work of extraterrestrial figures that swooped down to earth to perform their purposeful surgery.

So alarmed by these stories did the citizenry of New Mexico become, that a special investigator was assigned to look into the matter, and a federal grant awarded to pay for the investigation. The lengthy and skeptical report that resulted stated in no uncertain terms that no pattern of mutilations could be found (although the report conceded that a small number of such incidents had occurred, possibly prompted by media attention) and that the many reports of such incidents were based on natural predatory practice, with missing flesh, congealed blood and bodily parts consumed by birds, smaller animals and feeding insects.

Collective apparitions Hallucinations of persons living or dead involving more than one percipient, collective apparitions account for approximately 8 percent of all reported hallucinations,

Mass hallucination in 1681 print

according to a survey conducted by the Society of Psychical Research (SPR) shortly after its founding in 1882. Accounts of such apparitions often have a greater impact than do similar stories of individual hallucinations. The report of a lone percipient can be discounted rather easily by the skeptic (as well as by the doubtful percipient), while the presence of a second (or third or fourth) observer tends to confirm the "reality" of the event on some level. At the same time the fact of collective apparitions complicates consideration of the most widely accepted theory proposed to explain the phenomenon generally—that is, that apparitions are telepathically produced. Assuming that the apparitional agent, a friend of the percipient, say, telepathically transmits an image of himself in order to alert the percipient to his (the apparitional figure's) impending death, how then does a bystander, ignorant of the apparitional person's existence, also experience the apparition? And to what purpose? Of more logical appeal is the SPR-documented case of a pair of brothers serving on the same ship who awoke one night in adjacent cots to see their father standing between them. Each brother observed the father, who they later learned had died at about that hour, from a different perspective. Their three-dimensional view of him strongly suggests that the apparition literally occupied the physical space in which he appeared. Both the hypothetical instance and the recorded case repeat circumstances routinely reported in collective hallucinations. Theorists of telepathy as the source of all hallucinations suggest that in such cases the image is transmitted first to the original percipient and then relayed to the second percipient and all others. Proponents of hallucinations as energy "occupations" of space point to collective apparitions as proof of their supposition.

Cryptomnesia An unconscious, or hidden, memory that when recollected is taken for new thought, cryptomnesia also encompasses a variety of apparent mental anomalies concerning actual events, information, ideas and images. Most common are incidents in which a person suddenly evinces fluency in a language never studied; gives false information while in a hypnotic trance; or plagiarizes another's work unintentionally and with no thought to obscuring the fact. An instance of the first is the case of an uneducated young woman who suddenly began declaiming in ancient Greek and Hebrew while in a high fever. It turned out that she had once worked as a maid for a scholar who was accustomed to reciting aloud in those two languages. An example of the second is the famous episode of Bridey Murphy, the Irish alter ego of a U.S. housewife named Virginia Tighe. Under hypnosis, Tighe most convincingly "became" Bridey Murphy and in a heavy brogue described her former life in detail. On investigation, it was learned that as a child, Tighe had known the family of an Irish woman whose maiden name was Bridie Murphy, and the memory had remained intact but unrecognized in Tighe's unconscious until it emerged under hypnosis. Tracing incidents of plagiarism to cryptomnesia is trickier, since the dissociation process that takes place is so effective that it is virtually impossible for the plagiarist to recollect knowledge of his original reading or viewing of the material in question. Many eminent figures have found themselves embarrassed by unintended plagiarism of others' work. Among them was Sigmund Freud, who, on excitedly announcing to his longtime friend Wilhelm Fliess, a Berlin physician, his theory that individuals begin life as bisexual beings, was informed that Fliess had suggested the same idea to Freud two years earlier. The reminder stirred Freud's conscious memory, and he eventually recalled the original conversation in full. He was, however, rudely shaken by the episode.

"It is painful to have to surrender one's originality in this way," he confessed.

Déjà vu French for "already seen," *déjà vu* refers to the common sensation that one has experienced a situation, scene or sequence of events previously. Such sensations are usually accompanied by a greatly heightened consciousness and the conviction that one can actually predict what will happen next. While the experience seems to provoke anxiety in some people, others respond to it with delight, whether the scene involves familiar material and characters or, as is equally common, is in a place or from a time of which the percipient has no knowledge, such as when a first-time traveler in a foreign country unexpectedly comes upon a village that he recognizes in every detail. On his first trip to Africa, Carl G. Jung had such an experience: staring out the window of a train, he spotted a solitary tribesman standing on a cliff. "It was," he wrote, "as if I were this moment returning to the land of my youth, and as if I knew that dark-skinned man ... had been waiting for me for five thousand years." Jung termed his experience "recognition of the immemorially known."

A great many theories have been proposed to explain *déjà vu*, but no single one has gained wide acceptance, and no medical proof has been offered to explain it biologically, although Arthur Wigan suggested in 1884 that the phenomenon could be the result of the fact that one hemisphere of the brain registers data a fraction of a second sooner than the other. A related theory, proposed by Frederic W. H. Myers in 1895, is that the unconscious, or subliminal consciousness, acknowledges events an instant sooner than the conscious brain.

Other possible explanations that have been seriously advanced are that *déjà vu* results from one or another form of ESP—clairvoyance, telepathy, precognition or precognitive dreams; that it is proof of reincarnation, or that it is evidence of pre-natal consciousness, being based on memories of experiences of one's mother and not oneself.

Dematerialization The disappearance of all or part of a medium's physical body, or of other solid physical objects, during a séance, dematerialization is also the reverse of materialization, or the appearance of apports—objects that show up, seemingly out of nowhere, during a séance. Mediumistic literature is filled with accounts of spectacular dematerializations, under which heading are also included such famous "shrinkings," or compactions, of mediums as that of Eusapia Palladino.

A typical account of a dematerialization is that of Dr. P. Bribier, a witness to such an event. "Lucie disappeared by degrees," the doctor wrote, "in two seconds . . . as she had come . . . in front of the curtains beside which I was standing. The curtains did not move. . . . Just as the last white spot was disappearing from the carpet where the figure had been, I stooped down and put my hand upon it, but could feel nothing."

Perhaps the most marvelous dematerialization on record, however, is that experienced by a Mme. d'Esperance, a medium who dematerialized while fully conscious and with corroborating witnesses to confirm the otherwise incredible events. The supposed episode took place in Helsingfors, Finland, on December 11, 1895. For about 15 minutes, Mme. d'Esperance's lower body simply disappeared, her skirt lying flat on the chair as though nothing lay underneath. "I relaxed my muscles and let my hands fall upon my lap," the medium recalled, "and then I found that, instead of resting against my knees, they rested against the chair in which I was sitting. This discovery disturbed me greatly and I wondered if I were dreaming. I patted my skirt carefully, all over, trying to locate my limbs and the lower half of my body. . . . all . . . had entirely disappeared. . . . Nevertheless, I felt just as usual—better than usual, in fact. . . . Leaning forward to see if my feet were in their proper place, I almost lost my balance. This frightened me very much. . . . I reached over and took Prof. Seiling's hand, asking him to tell me if I was really seated in the chair. I awaited his answer in perfect agony of suspense. I felt his hand just as if it touched my knees; but he said: 'There is nothing there but your skirts.'"

Devil's Sea A rumored danger zone off the southeast coast of Japan, the Devil's Sea is the Bermuda Triangle of the Pacific. The term seems to be of somewhat hyperbolic origin, based on the loss of only nine ships over a five-year period in the early 1950s in an area of unspecified size, but extending possibly as far as 750 miles out from land. Eight of the ships were fishing boats, only one of which carried a radio transmitter; the ninth, a ship transporting scientists to the site of an underwater volcanic eruption, sent no SOS, although it is not known whether the vessel was equipped with a radio. Twenty years later a U.S. investigator discovered that the phrase "Devil's Sea" was unfamiliar to Japanese maritime officials, and thus it appears that the "legend" of the Devil's Sea was spun from several easily misinterpreted newspaper accounts.

Dykshoorn, Marinus Bernardus A Dutch-born clairvoyant who claims exceptional success in assisting police in the solving of crimes, particularly murders, Dykshoorn has been "endorsed" as a psychic by the Dutch government and travels on a passport stamped "clairvoyant." Born in July 1920, he says that his abilities confused and troubled him as a child. Purportedly a constant witness to scenes from other people's lives, he had no way of knowing that his experience was not normal until late adolescence. He did not attempt to use his abilities professionally until 1948, at which time he adopted a thin loop of wire as an aid in concentration, using it much as a dowser uses a forked twig in seeking water. He still uses it in his police work, done gratis, and in the lectures and demonstrations he gives to support himself and his family.

When invited to assist in a murder investigation, Dykshoorn, who now lives in New York, asks to be taken to the scene of the crime, where allegedly tunes in on the last five minutes of the victim's life. If the victim was strangled, red blotches are likely to appear around Dykshoorn's neck, or he may gasp and gag or choke; if death was by shooting, red marks will simulate bullet holes on Dykshoorn's body. As he concentrates, his image of the murder grows ever clearer until he can provide details such as where the body was found, what weapon was used, in what direction the murderer fled and, most valuably, what the murderer looked like.

In his lectures, Dykshoorn reportedly indulges in remarkably accurate mind reading and fortunetelling, to the delight of audiences. He told writer Dan Greenburg that although he has the ability, he is reluctant to heal because it may entail the temporary transfer of patients' pain to him and because it is not his field. Besides, he said, although the afflicted promise to pay when in pain, once cured, they rarely do. Annoyed one time by a fellow he had just cured of a slipped disc, Dykshoorn shook the man's hand a second time and gave the pain back.

Enochian language A language of magic, Enochian was recorded by Dr. John Dee, a 16th-century magician. Dee attributed Enochian to the "angels" with whom he "communicated" through his assistant Edward Kelley, and explained that it was transmitted to him in the form of 19 "Keys," or "Calls"—formal incantations or invocations of occult powers. As a language of magic, it has been periodically adopted by occultists ever since. Aleister Crowley revived it for use in his rituals at the beginning of the 20th century, and more recently it has been appropriated by Satanist Anton La Vey.

Amulet to ward off the evil eye

Evil eye Belief in the power of certain individuals to harm others merely by looking at them has probably existed in one form or another since before mankind began to keep records. References to it have been found in the annals of the ancient Sumerians, Egyptians and Babylonians; in Greek and Roman mythology; even in the Bible, which counsels in the Book of Proverbs, in the King James Version, "Eat thou not the bread of *him that hath* an evil eye. . . . The morsel *which* thou hast eaten shalt thou vomit up." Though not as prevalent today as in the past, the belief can still be found in many areas of the world, including parts of Asia, northern Africa, southern Europe and some Mesoamerican Indian cultures.

The use of the evil eye—sometimes called overlooking—is most commonly thought to be motivated by envy. (In societies where the belief is strong, in fact, a compliment or display of admiration, especially from a stranger, may well be taken as a concealed threat.) The supposed effects of the evil eye can assume myriad forms, ranging from financial troubles and romantic disappointments to headaches, sudden fatigue, accidents, illness and even death. To ward them off, a wide variety of invocations, gestures, amulets and other defenses may be employed by potential victims. Two of the best-known gestures, long familiar in Mediterranean countries, are the *mano cornuta* (Italian for "horned hand"), in which a fist is made with the forefinger and pinkie extended, and the *mano in fica* (fig), in which a fist is made with the thumb protruding between the forefinger and middle finger.

Interestingly, overlooking is not always thought to be voluntary or maliciously intended. Indeed, there have been numerous cases over the years of prominent and highly regarded figures—including at least one pope— who were nevertheless reputed to possess and use the power, however involuntarily.

Ganzfeld German for "entire field," ganzfeld is an artificially induced state of sensory stimulation minus actual information. Ganzfeld is intended to promote hallucination, greater receptivity to ESP signals, a meditative state or a trance. It can be achieved visually by affixing translucent Ping-Pong balls to the eyes and projecting light through them, or aurally by playing random noise, or white sound, through earphones.

Graphology The study of handwriting, graphology is used by some as a tool in the interpretation of personality. Although experiments have failed to demonstrate sufficient scientific basis for graphologists' claims, the idea that aspects of character and personality are displayed in the idiosyncratic loops, elisions, spacing and tilts that make up a person's script has a powerful logic for many people, including the managers of many large corporations who use graphologists to advise them on the weaknesses and strengths of prospective employees. Surely, believers feel, if a psychologist can deduce a subject's state of mind from his reaction to a set of images or inkblots, and if a child's sense of self can be determined from the kind

of drawing he produces, then handwriting must be a useful, if not foolproof, guide to character.

One reason it is not is that it is a learned skill and one that is heavily weighted by cultural and national preferences, by continually changing aesthetic values and fashions in writing materials, as well as by the prejudices of the original instructor. Distinguishing what is individually significant, and therefore revealing, from what is simply acquired, habitual or imitative is difficult. Though the sort of correspondences that graphologists deal in—such as that widely spaced letters connote generosity; *t*'s that are only half crossed betray a procrastinator; carefully dotted *i*'s indicate a conservative, precise nature—are amusing, equally general conclusions can be arrived at by observing hairstyles or ways of dressing.

One exception to graphology's limits is in detection of forgeries in signature. However muddled the message of handwriting, a person does develop a truly identifiable signature, and expert opinion on the legitimacy of what is so often an unintelligible scribble across a page is admissible in most courts of law.

Grimoire A grimoire is a book of magic spells, rituals and incantations, usually of elaborate presentation and ostentatious piety. Most grimoires date from the 16th century to the 18th century, although their compilers uniformly claimed that their contents were based on ancient texts, preferably Hebraic or Egyptian.

As how-to manuals, grimoires have seldom been taken seriously by students of the occult, but as historical artifacts, they are fascinating. Most grimoires circulated in manuscript form, although a rare number were printed. So complicated and exaggerated were the preliminaries to magical transactions as outlined in the grimoires that E. M. Butler remarked that they seemed "calculated to deal the death blow to any notions . . . [among practitioners] that magic is a short cut to their desires."

Among the best known of the grimoires are the *Key of Solomon*, which appears to be based largely and loosely on cabalistic and astrological lore, and which includes detailed directions on how to summon both angels and demons; the *Grand Grimoire*, which, while it purports to be a direct transcription of Solomonic writings on the occult, also leans on a

European Gypsy in the 20th century

more recent source, the scholar-magician Agrippa, and includes a Faustian recipe for making a foolproof pact with the devil; the *Grimoire of Honorius the Great,* libelously named for a pope of the 13th century but thought to have been produced in the 16th century. The *Honorius* employs many elements of the Catholic Mass in its instructions for contacting the devil and was understandably thought to be an especially scandalous work.

Gypsies A nomadic people, Gypsies are believed to have left India by way of Persia and Egypt (hence the name Gypsy) sometime before the end of the first millennium A.D. Traveling in large bands into northern Europe and the British Isles, across Africa and into Spain, the Gypsies eventually established themselves throughout the Western world, including the United States, South America and Australia. Although some have been assimilated, the majority remain a people apart, speaking a separate language, Romany, and living Gypsy lives whether in the middle of New York or on the edge of a Hungarian village. As the perennial and ostentatious "other" wherever they happen to be, Gypsies have been persecuted throughout history: in the Middle Ages they were accused of witchcraft; in World War II an estimated 500,000 European Gypsies were murdered by the Nazis. Despite lesser harassment today, some 5 million Gypsies are thought to live in various parts of the world.

Hollow earth According to the hollow-earth theory, a race superior to our own lives somewhere beneath the surface of the earth. Some proponents of this theory base their arguments on the existence of UFO's, which they say are not from outer space but from innermost space, and on some ambiguous comments made by Adm. Richard E. Byrd after he flew over the two poles.

Saint Joan, a 19th-century view

Though no one has ever located them, entrances to this fabulous world are said to exist at both poles.

Joan of Arc The patron saint of France, Joan of Arc was a peasant girl of about 13 when she first heard the voices of Saints Michael, Catherine and Margaret urging her to "go to succor the king of France." Probably the most famous clairaudient in history, she is but one of many whose experiences resulted in accusations of heresy or witchcraft.

France was in the last years of the Hundred Years' War and bitterly divided when Joan was born in the town of Domrémy-la-Pucelle in approximately 1412. The Duke of Burgundy and his English allies controlled most of the north, including Rheims, Rouen and Paris, while the frail dauphin, Charles VII, had retreated to the south; from there he seemed incapable of defending his kingdom or claiming his title.

In the autumn of 1428, about the time the English began their siege of Orléans, the voices speaking to Joan grew more insistent. In February 1429 she finally succeeded in persuading a local military commander to provide her an escort to the dauphin at Chinon, where she was able to convince the dauphin and his advisers that her voices were genuine and of heavenly origin. In May 1429 the young peasant woman led the French Army into battle and lifted the siege of Orléans. A few months later she stood beside the dauphin as he was crowned king at Rheims, but in May 1430 she was captured by the Burgundians at Compiègne and eventually turned over to the English, who tried her as a heretic. One of the main charges against her stemmed from her claim to have followed the will of God as transmitted by the saints. She was convicted and burned at the stake on May 30, 1431.

Clairaudience is a markedly rarer phenomenon than clairvoyance, but accounts of it suggest an equivalent clarity and realism in the experience, which must be distinguished from the "inner voice" of dreams and mediumistic trances.

Leonard, Gladys Osborne One of the best known and most thoroughly investigated of modern mediums, Leonard was born in Lancashire, England, in 1882, and her development as a medium can be considered to some extent as typical of the experience of gifted psychics generally.

At an early age she was traumatized by events surrounding the sudden death of a friend of the family: no one thought to explain the man's abrupt disappearance, and an impatient housemaid told the child only that he was to be buried "under the earth." The child asked, "Where he can't get out?" and was told, "Of course he can't get out." As if to compensate for the terror this explanation set off, Leonard began to have early-morning visions of the "most beautiful places." When she described her thrilling scenes, however, she was reprimanded; she soon learned to keep them to herself, and they eventually disappeared. In adolescence she discovered spiritualism but was told by her mother that such ideas were "vile and wicked." At the age of 24, spending the night in another town, away from her family, she woke to see a vision of her mother surrounded by a bright light and in apparent good health, although she knew her to be quite sick. When she learned afterward that her mother had died at that moment, her belief in her gifts was confirmed. While attempting a séance with some friends, she succeeded in going into a trance, during which Feda, a young Indian girl who had been married to Leonard's great-great-grandfather, made herself known. Leonard's work with Feda as her control was studied for 40 years. She willingly participated in controlled experiments to ascertain whether her gifts were in fact mediumistic or superbly telepathic, submitting to verifications by detectives and repeated tests with written materials over long periods of time. Investigators failed to conclude one way or another, but Leonard's honesty and attunement to a paranormal force of some sort appeared to be strongly documented.

Mother Shipton

Carriages without horses shall go
Around the world thoughts shall fly
In the twinkling of an eye
Iron in water shall float
As easy as a wooden boat
Gold shall be found, and found
In a land that's not now known
A house of glass shall come to pass
In England, but alas!

These prophecies of railroads, the telegraph, iron-clad ships, the California gold rush and the Crystal Palace built in London in 1851 were allegedly made in the 15th century by Mother Shipton and republished in 1641. Those were the dates suggested in an 1862 forgery by Charles Hindley, who attributed these and other predictions to the seer whose prophecies have intrigued English people for generations.

An enterprising writer, Richard Head, who achieved notoriety with a book called *The English Rogue*, had published a batch of Shipton predictions in 1667, complete with a description and biographical sketch of the seer. Since, no matter which version of Mother Shipton's birth date—1448 or 1486—one accepts, this work appeared some 200 years after she was supposedly born, Head's description of what Shipton looked like at birth is a remarkable feat of retrocognition: "With very great goggling, but sharp and fiery eyes; her nose of incredible and unproportionable length, having in it many crooks and turnings, adorned with many strange pimples of divers colors, as red and blue mixed, which, like vapors of brimstone, gave such a lustre to the affrighted spectators in the dead time of the night, that one of them confessed several times that her nurse needed no other light to assist her in the performance of her duty." By 1686 another writer (anonymous) had published a *Strange and Wonderful History of Mother Shipton*, which changed a few dates and gave her the name Ursula.

The authors of the Shipton books were playing it safe with most of her prophecies, quoting them as having been made centuries earlier but publishing their works after the predicted events had already taken place. Thus it was after Sir Walter Raleigh had brought tobacco and the potato from the Americas that Hindley quoted Mother Shipton as having uttered long ago:

Over a wild and stormy sea
Shall a noble sail,

Who to find will not fail
A new and far countree
From whence he shall bring
A herb and a root
That all men shall suit.

Was there really ever a Mother Shipton? Quite possibly not. But if she is nothing more than the invention of a 17th-century hack writer, the fictitious predictions assigned to her have nonetheless managed to survive for several centuries.

Muscle reading A "mind-reading" technique, muscle reading depends on careful attention to involuntary muscle movement. A blindfolded percipient interprets the pressure of a subject's hand on his shoulder as he approaches an object silently thought of in advance by the subject, whereas an unbound percipient watches the subject's face for unintentional signals indicating whether he has made a correct guess. Muscle reading is not considered a psychic ability but a parlor trick that can be picked up with sufficient practice.

Personation The temporary assumption of another's physical characteristics, habits, symptoms of illness or other identifying traits, personation is frequently experienced by participants in séances, with the individuals personated usually being known to them. Mediums often experience personation of subjects not known to them but known to their clients. In one unusual case of hysterical personation a young woman rejected by a lover began to display many of the young man's gestures, to speak in a voice resembling his and to change her handwriting to approximate his. In addition, personation is rather easily achieved in the hypnotic state by suggestion.

Planchette Invented by a French spiritualist in the mid-19th century, a planchette is an instrument used to aid communication with spirits through the phenomenon known as automatic writing. An improvement on the Ouija board, the planchette consists of a thin, heart-shaped piece of wood resting on small wheeled casters, fitted with a pen or pencil pointing downward. The hand of the user—presumably guided by the subconscious mind, if not by the force of a departed spirit—rests on the planchette and moves it to create messages on a sheet of paper below. It has also been popular as a toy.

Retrocognition A vivid, realistic image, or vision, of past events, sometimes perceived by more than one of the senses, retrocognition is one of the rarer manifestations of ESP. It differs from *déjà vu* in two ways: first, the scene is new to the percipient, and second, there is rarely any sense of personal connection with what is seen. In fact, most reports suggest that the percipient has in some way, almost invariably unexpectedly, been treated to a sudden glimpse back through time. The experience of Coleen Buterbaugh is a good modern example of retrocognition. An errand led Buterbaugh to a room on the campus of Nebraska Wesleyan University in which everything seemed "quite normal" at first. Then "about four steps into the room . . . the odor hit me. . . . I felt . . . someone in the room with me. . . . I looked up, and there she was. She had her back to me, . . . She wasn't at all aware of my presence. . . . She was not transparent and yet I knew she wasn't real. . . . [But it was] when I looked out the window behind the desk, that I got frightened. . . . there wasn't one modern thing out there. . . . That was when I realized that these people were not in my time, but that I was back in their time."

Mother Shipton and friend

When she reported her "vision" to others, she learned that what she had seen in the room and out the window was the campus as it had been 50 years earlier. As far as is known, Buterbaugh's experience, which was extensively reviewed by the American Society for Psychical Research, was unprompted by any recent associations or information. Some cases of retrocognition, however, do seem to arise from great concentration or obsessional thinking of some kind. The distinguished English historian Arnold Toynbee reported in the 10th volume of his 12-volume *Study of*

History that he enjoyed a half-dozen episodes of "communion" with the distant past while preparing that work over many years. The experiences occurred under such disparate circumstances as while quietly reading in a room at Oxford of the Italian confederacy (1st century B.C.), while "musing on the summit of the citadel of Mistra," and during a stroll along the Buckingham Palace Road. The last was the most intense and suffused the historian with what must have been the most welcome of feelings, that he was "in communion, not just with this or that episode in History, but all that had been, and was, and was to come."

Somnambulism A half-waking, or trance, state in which consciousness is suspended, yet the subject walks, talks and/or performs other ordinary functions, somnambulism can occur spontaneously during sleep, in the hours approaching a fever's crisis, or in ecstasy. It can also be induced artificially, for example, through hypnosis.

Speaking in tongues Primarily a form of religious expression characterized by an outpouring of nonsense syllables or foreign words unknown to the speaker, speaking in tongues is also a common psychic phenomenon. Glossolalia, as it is also called, has been known since the first days of Christianity: the Apostles of Christ gathered together on Pentecost are said to have burst forth in tongues when the Holy Ghost appeared to them and to have used the gift in their missionary work among non-Hebrew peoples. The phenomenon has had a cyclical popularity and respectability throughout history: outbreaks have included those at Loudun, in France, where a group of Ursuline nuns began speaking in several foreign languages (and were accused of being witches), and among dialect-speaking refugees from the Cévennes, who unaccountably spoke perfect French. The last 20 years have seen a revival of the practice among groups from virtually all the U.S. Christian denominations. Condemned early in the 1960s by church officials, speaking in tongues is now accepted as a legitimate religious phenomenon not only by fundamentalist sects but by the Roman Catholic and Episcopal churches. Glossolalia is less rarely manifested by non-religious persons, but it occurs occasionally among mediums, usually in the form called xenoglossy, or foreign tongues. Particularly adept at xenoglossy was a young medium of the 19th century named Laura Edmonds, who allegedly conducted conversations in Greek, Spanish and Chippewa while in a trance. Psychologists differ in their estimates of the healthiness of glossolalia: some see it as the manifestation of unresolved conflicts, while others regard it as a useful means of venting intense religious feelings.

Steiner, Rudolf Founder of the Anthroposophical Society, Rudolf Steiner espoused a spiritual philosophy that combined occult and Christian principles with a reverence for nature and the environment. Born in Kraljevica, on the Austro-Hungarian border (now Yugoslavia) in 1861, Steiner was a Goethe scholar and an enthusiast of Theosophy. His academic training (he had a doctorate in philosophy) and practical inclinations led him to split with the Theosophists and found his own society in 1912. Though he remained committed to spiritual investigation and mysticism, Steiner turned his attention to a broad range of cultural and educational activities, placing great emphasis on color and bodily rhythm, on the establishment of an architectural style expressive of a spiritual life, and on the development of a number of enlightened educational and farming experiments. Some 70 Anthroposophical schools still operate around the world and are highly regarded as innovative institutions that promote individuality, spontaneity and excellence. Steiner died in 1925.

Teleportation A form of psychokinesis in which objects allegedly can be made to traverse space. It is said that such objects can pass through walls, ceilings and doors, arriving at their destination sometimes hot to the touch but otherwise unscathed.

According to an account in the *Encyclopaedia of the Unexplained,* Mrs. Samuel Guppy, a 19th-century British medium, "produced live lobsters and eels, and fresh flowers, fruit and vegetables apparently out of nowhere at her séances." In the heyday of spiritualism, teleportation under the guidance of a medium included the movement of human beings as well.

Vanishing people Few mysteries are more intriguing than those involving people who have unaccountably disappeared—vanished with no advance warning and scarcely a trace left behind. Among the most puzzling of cases is that of the small Eskimo village of Angikuni, in Canada's Northwest Territories. In November 1930, according to the account in Frank Edwards's popular book *Stranger Than Science,* a trapper named Joe Labelle visited the remote village, whose people he had known for years, and was startled to find no signs of life—no people moving about, no dogs barking, nothing. Labelle searched through the simple huts and found things in order, as if all the inhabitants—about 30 men, women and children—had suddenly departed in the midst of a perfectly normal day. When Canadian authorities examined the site, they concluded that it had been abandoned for about two months, though they were at a loss to explain why. Finding no signs of violence, no tracks leading away—no clues to shed any light on the villagers' fate—they were forced at length to give up their investigation, and the mystery remains unsolved.

Another case of this sort, and perhaps the most celebrated, involves the reputed disappearance in 1880 of David Lang, a Tennessee farmer, in full view of several witnesses. Lang, so the story goes, was walking across the pasture in front of his house; his wife and two young children were just outside the house, and two family friends—a Judge August Peck, from the nearby town of Gallatin, and Peck's brother-in-law—were approaching in a buggy. Lang saw the buggy, returned his friends' wave—then suddenly vanished. A frantic search found no trace of him, and a more extensive manhunt that followed proved equally fruitless. The shock allegedly left Mrs. Lang bedridden for the rest of her life, and Lang's daughter is said to have spent decades trying to make contact with her father through various extrasensory means. Although the David Lang mystery has been recounted in print many times, some critics have questioned its authenticity, noting in particular that no historical documentation—local census records, deeds, newspaper accounts or other contemporary evidence—has been found to confirm that any of the people involved actually existed.

Worth, Patience Credited with producing a large body of literary work through the mediumship of a St. Louis housewife, Mrs. John H. Curran, Patience Worth was the alleged spirit of a 17th-century Englishwoman.

In one of the most famous examples of automatism, or automatic writing, a phenomenon that peaked early in the 20th century, the reported abilities of Patience Worth seemed to far outstrip those of her agent, Mrs. Curran. Curran had left school at the age of 14 and had done very little reading afterward; her ignorance of history was huge, she had traveled very little and had apparently been exposed to no one of erudition either as a child or as an adult. Yet the novels that she "transcribed" beginning in 1913 dealt authentically with historical details from many periods and were furthermore described by contemporary critics as being superior in style, characterization and plot. Among them were *The Sorry Tale,* set in Palestine at the time of Christ; *Telka,* set in medieval England; and *Hope Trueblood,* one of the most highly praised ("a novel of decided promise," declared one reviewer), which takes place in Victorian England, some 200 years after its putative author was killed in an Indian massacre after immigrating to America from a farm in Dorsetshire.

The writings have been endlessly analyzed by literary scholars and linguists, yet no persuasive evidence has been found to pin down the true source of Patience Worth's works. Some theorists believe in a strict spiritualist interpretation—there was a Patience Worth, and she was a gifted and prescient writer—while others suggest that Curran knew far more, and was far more skilled, than her conscious mind could ever acknowledge.

Detail from a 17th-century work on magic

BIBLIOGRAPHY

GENERAL REFERENCE

CHRISTIAN, PAUL, *The History and Practice of Magic,* ed. and rev. Ross Nichols. The Citadel Press, 1963. 2 vols.

CLARIE, THOMAS C., *Occult Bibliography.* The Scarecrow Press, Inc., 1978.

EBERHART, GEORGE M. (comp.), *A Geo-Bibliography of Anomalies.* Greenwood Press, 1980.

HASTINGS, JAMES (ed.), *Encyclopaedia of Religion and Ethics.* Charles Scribner's Sons, 1928. 13 vols.

HITCHING, FRANCIS, *The Mysterious World.* Holt, Rinehart & Winston, 1979.

SHEPARD, LESLIE (ed.), *Encyclopedia of Occultism and Parapsychology.* Gale Research Co., 1978. 2 vols., with supplements.

THORNDIKE, LYNN, *A History of Magic and Experimental Science.* Columbia University Press, 1923. 8 vols.

WEBB, JAMES, *The Occult Underground.* Open Court Publishing Co., 1974.

WOLMAN, BENJAMIN B. (ed.), *Handbook of Parapsychology.* Van Nostrand Reinhold Co., 1977.

ANCIENT UNKNOWNS

BOUISSON, MAURICE, *Magic,* trans. G. Almayrac. E. P. Dutton & Co., Inc., 1961.

BURLAND, C. A., *The Magical Arts.* Arthur Barker Ltd., 1966.

FRAZER, SIR JAMES GEORGE, *The Golden Bough.* Macmillan Publishing Co., Inc., 1922.

LEWINSOHN, RICHARD, *Science, Prophecy and Prediction,* trans. Arnold J. Pomerans. Harper & Brothers, Publishers, 1961.

EARTH SHRINES

BURL, AUBREY, *The Stone Circles of the British Isles.* Yale University Press, 1976.

CORLISS, WILLIAM R. (comp.), *Ancient Man.* The Sourcebook Project, 1978.

KRUPP, E. C. (ed.), *In Search of Ancient Astronomies.* McGraw-Hill Book Co., 1978.

WAUCHOPE, ROBERT, *Lost Tribes and Sunken Continents.* The University of Chicago Press, 1962.

ATLANTIS

BRAMWELL, JAMES, *Lost Atlantis.* Harper & Brothers, Publishers, 1938.

DE CAMP, LYON SPRAGUE, and LEY, WILLY, *Lands Beyond.* Rinehart & Co., Inc., 1952.

DONNELLY, IGNATIUS, *Atlantis,* 18th ed. Harper & Brothers, 1882.

GALANOPOULOS, A. G., and BACON, EDWARD, *Atlantis.* The Bobbs-Merrill Co., 1969.

LUCE, J. V., *Lost Atlantis.* McGraw-Hill Book Co., 1969.

RAMAGE, EDWIN S. (ed.), *Atlantis.* Indiana University Press, 1978.

SPENCE, LEWIS, *The History of Atlantis.* University Books, Inc., 1968.

ART OF MAGIC

BARRETT, FRANCIS, *The Magus.* University Books, Inc., 1967.

BUTLER, E. M., *The Myth of the Magus.* Cambridge University Press, 1948.

CAVENDISH, RICHARD, *The Black Arts.* Capricorn Books, 1967.

LÉVI, ELIPHAS, *The History of Magic,* trans. Arthur Edward Waite. Samuel Weiser Inc., 1973.

SELIGMANN, KURT, *The History of Magic.* Pantheon Books Inc., 1948.

WITCHCRAFT

BAROJA, JULIO CARO, *The World of the Witches,* trans. O.N.V. Glendinning. The University of Chicago Press, 1965.

COHN, NORMAN, *Europe's Inner Demons.* The New American Library Inc., 1977.

KORS, ALAN C., and PETERS, EDWARD (eds.), *Witchcraft in Europe 1100–1700.* University of Pennsylvania Press, 1972.

KRAMER, HEINRICH, and SPRENGER, JAMES, *The Malleus Maleficarum of Heinrich Kramer and James Sprenger,* trans. the Reverend Montague Summers. Dover Publications, Inc., 1971.

ROBBINS, ROSSELL HOPE, *The Encyclopedia of Witchcraft and Demonology.* Crown Publishers, Inc., 1974.

RUSSELL, JEFFREY BURTON, *Witchcraft in the Middle Ages.* Cornell University Press, 1972.

MONSTERS

CARRINGTON, RICHARD, *Mermaids and Mastodons.* Rinehart & Co., Inc., 1957.

HEUVELMANS, BERNARD, *In the Wake of the Sea-Serpents,* trans. Richard Garnett. Hill & Wang, Inc., 1968.

———, *On the Track of Unknown Animals,* trans. Richard Garnett. Hill & Wang, Inc., 1958.

NAPIER, JOHN, *Bigfoot.* E. P. Dutton & Co., Inc., 1973.

SUMMERS, MONTAGUE, *The Vampire.* University Books, Inc., 1960.

THOMPSON, C.J.S., *The Mystery and Lore of Monsters.* Citadel Press Inc., 1970.

WOODWARD, IAN, *The Werewolf Delusion.* Paddington Press, Ltd., 1979.

DIVINATION

DE GIVRY, EMILE GRILLOT, *Picture Museum of Sorcery, Magic and Alchemy,* trans. J. Courtenay Locke. University Books, Inc., 1963.

INGLIS, BRIAN, *Natural and Supernatural.* Hodder & Stoughton, Ltd., 1977.

MIDDLETON, JOHN (ed.), *Magic, Witchcraft, and Curing.* The Natural History Press, 1967.

ASTROLOGY

GAUQUELIN, MICHEL, *The Scientific Basis of Astrology,* trans. James Hughes. Stein & Day, Inc., 1969.

HOWE, ELLIC, *Astrology.* Walker & Co., 1967.

JEROME, LAWRENCE E., *Astrology Disproved.* Prometheus Books, 1977.

MacNEICE, LOUIS, *Astrology.* Doubleday & Co., Inc., 1964.

SMITH, RICHARD FURNALD, *Prelude to Science.* Charles Scribner's Sons, 1975.

REINCARNATION

CURRIE, IAN, *You Cannot Die.* Methuen, Inc., 1978.

HEAD, JOSEPH, and CRANSTON, S. L. (eds.), *Reincarnation.* Crown Publishers, Inc., Julian Press, 1977.

MacGREGOR, GEDDES, *Reincarnation in Christianity.* The Theosophical Publishing House, Quest Books, 1978.

STEVENSON, IAN, *Twenty Cases Suggestive of Reincarnation,* 2nd ed. University Press of Virginia, 1974.

GHOSTS AND SPIRITS

BANNISTER, PAUL, *Strange Happenings.* Grosset & Dunlap, 1978.

CARRINGTON, HEREWARD, and FODOR, NANDOR, *Haunted People.* The New American Library, Inc., Signet Mystic Books, 1968.

HAINING, PETER, *Ghosts.* Macmillan

Publishing Co., Inc., 1975.

MOTLEY, MARY, *Morning Glory.* St. Martin's Press, 1963.

MYERS, FREDERIC W. H., *Human Personality and Its Survival of Bodily Death.* Longmans, Green, & Co., 1903. 2 vols.

NORMAN, DIANA, *Tom Corbett's Stately Ghosts of England.* Taplinger Publishing Co., Inc., 1970.

SHERIDAN, CLARE, *My Crowded Sanctuary,* 2nd ed. Methuen & Co., Ltd., 1946.

SMYTH, FRANK, *Ghosts and Poltergeists.* Doubleday & Co., Inc., 1976.

TYRRELL, G.N.M., *Apparitions,* rev. ed. Gerald Duckworth & Co., Ltd., 1953.

SPIRITUALISM

CHRISTOPHER, MILBOURNE, *ESP, Seers and Psychics.* Thomas Y. Crowell Co., 1970.

———, *Search for the Soul.* Thomas Y. Crowell, Publishers, 1979.

MOORE, R. LAURENCE, *In Search of White Crows.* Oxford University Press, 1977.

PODMORE, FRANK, *Mediums of the 19th Century.* University Books, Inc., 1963.

PRINCE, WALTER FRANKLIN, *The Enchanted Boundary.* Boston Society for Psychic Research, 1930.

SIDGWICK, ELEANOR M., and others, *Phantasms of the Living,* 2 vols. in 1. University Books, Inc., 1962.

PSI AND SCIENCE

EHRENWALD, JAN, *The ESP Experience.* Basic Books, Inc., 1978.

GARDNER, MARTIN, *Fads and Fallacies in the Name of Science.* Dover Publications, Inc., 1957.

HANSEL, C.E.M., *ESP and Parapsychology.* Prometheus Books, 1980.

KRIPPNER, STANLEY (ed.), *Advances in Parapsychological Research, 2. Extrasensory Perception.* Plenum Press, 1978.

RHINE, J. B., *Extra-Sensory Perception.* Bruce Humphries Publishers, 1964.

———, *New Frontiers of the Mind.* Farrar & Rinehart Inc., 1937.

SCHMEIDLER, GERTRUDE RAFFEL, *ESP and Personality Patterns.* Yale University Press, 1958.

POWER OF DREAMS

DEMENT, WILLIAM C., *Some Must Watch While Some Must Sleep.* W. W. Norton & Co., Inc., 1978.

DEVEREUX, GEORGE (ed.), *Psychoanalysis and the Occult.* International Universities Press, Inc., 1953.

FREUD, SIGMUND, *The Interpretation of Dreams,* trans. Dr. A. A. Brill. The Modern Library, 1950.

———, *Introductory Lectures on Psychoanalysis,* ed. and trans. James Strachey. W. W. Norton & Co., Inc., 1966.

LINCOLN, JACKSON STEWARD, *The Dream in Primitive Cultures.* Johnson Reprint Corp., 1970.

MACKENZIE, NORMAN, *Dreams and Dreaming.* The Vanguard Press, Inc., 1965.

ULLMAN, MONTAGUE, and KRIPPNER, STANLEY, with VAUGHAN, ALAN, *Dream Telepathy.* Penguin Books, Inc., 1974.

ANIMAL PSI

BURTON, MAURICE, *The Sixth Sense of Animals.* Taplinger Publishing Co., 1973.

GADDIS, VINCENT, and GADDIS, MARGARET, *The Strange World of Animals and Pets.* Cowles Book Co., Inc., 1970.

LORENZ, KONRAD, *Studies in Animal and Human Behaviour,* trans. Robert Martin. Harvard University Press, 1970–71. 2 vols.

TINBERGEN, NIKO, *Animal Behavior.* Time-Life Books, 1965.

MIND OVER MATTER

GAULD, ALAN, and CORNELL, A. D., *Poltergeists.* Routledge & Kegan Paul, Ltd., 1979.

GOSS, MICHAEL (comp.), *Poltergeists.* The Scarecrow Press, Inc., 1979.

HINTZE, NAOMI A., and PRATT, J. GAITHER, *The Psychic Realm.* Random House, Inc., 1975.

ROGO, D. SCOTT, *Minds and Motion.* Taplinger Publishing Co., Inc., 1978.

ROLL, WILLIAM G., *The Poltergeist.* The Scarecrow Press, Inc., 1976.

WATSON, LYALL, *Supernature.* Bantam Books, Inc., 1974.

WILSON, COLIN, and HOLROYD, STUART, *Great Mysteries.* Aldus Books, 1975.

LEAVING THE BODY

GREEN, CELIA, *Out-of-the-Body Experiences.* Institute of Psychophysical Research, 1968.

GREENHOUSE, HERBERT B., *The Astral Journey.* Avon Books, 1976.

ROGO, D. SCOTT (ed.), *Mind Beyond the Body.* Penguin Books, Inc., 1978.

HEALING

BURANELLI, VINCENT, *The Wizard From Vienna.* Coward, McCann & Geoghegan, Inc., 1975.

FLAMMONDE, PARIS, *The Mystic Healers.* Stein & Day, 1974.

MEEK, GEORGE W. (ed.), *Healers and the Healing Process.* The Theosophical Publishing House, 1977.

WEATHERHEAD, LESLIE D., *Psychology, Religion and Healing.* Abingdon-Cokesbury Press, 1951.

WEST, D. J., *Eleven Lourdes Miracles.* Helix Press, 1957.

ENIGMA OF UFO'S

CATOE, LYNN E., *UFOs and Related Subjects.* Gale Research Co., 1978.

FULLER, CURTIS (ed.), *Proceedings of the First International UFO Congress.* Warner Books, Inc., 1980.

HAINES, RICHARD F. (ed.), *UFO Phenomena and the Behavioral Scientist.* The Scarecrow Press, Inc., 1979.

HENDRY, ALLAN A., *The UFO Handbook.* Doubleday & Co., Inc., 1979.

HYNEK, J. ALLEN, *The UFO Experience.* Ballantine Books, 1974.

KLASS, PHILIP J., *UFOs Explained.* Vintage Books, 1976.

MENZEL, DONALD H., and TAVES, ERNEST H., *The UFO Enigma.* Doubleday & Co., Inc., 1977.

SAGAN, CARL, and PAGE, THORNTON (eds.), *UFO's.* Cornell University Press, 1973.

PSI AND THE BRAIN

CAPRA, FRITJOF, *The Tao of Physics.* Bantam Books, Inc., 1977.

GAZZANIGA, MICHAEL S., *The Bisected Brain.* Meredith Corp., Appleton-Century-Crofts, Educational Division, 1970.

PENFIELD, WILDER, *The Mystery of the Mind.* Princeton University Press, 1975.

RESTAK, RICHARD M., *The Brain.* Doubleday & Co., Inc., 1979.

SHAPIN, BETTY, and COLY, LISETTE (eds.), *Brain/Mind and Parapsychology.* Parapsychology Foundation, Inc., 1979.

TAYLOR, GORDON RATTRAY, *The Natural History of the Mind.* E. P. Dutton & Co., Inc., 1979.

ZUKAV, GARY, *The Dancing Wu Li Masters.* Bantam Books, Inc., 1980.

INDEX

Page numbers in **bold** type refer to illustrations.

Acknowledgments

Special appreciation for valuable help in the text research is extended to these organizations: Library of Congress; The New York Public Library; American Museum of Natural History; The Smithsonian Institution; New York Botanical Garden; New York Zoological Society; The Brooklyn Museum; The Metropolitan Museum of Art; Cornell University, Rare Books Division; National Aeronautics and Space Administration; Mutual U.F.O. Network; National Investigations Committee on Aerial Phenomena; Center for U.F.O. Studies.

Picture Credits

Pictures; *right* UPI. **ASTROLOGY 134** *top left* Reproduced by courtesy of the Trustees of the British Museum; *top right* Biblioteca Apostolica Vaticana (Vat. Greco 1291, f. 9r)/Madeline Grimoldi Archives; *center* Reproduced by permission of the British Library; *bottom left* Bibliothèque Nationale; *bottom right* Museo Nazionale, Naples/Madeline Grimoldi Archives. **135** Reproduced by permission of the British Library. **136** Courtesy of the Pennsylvania Academy of the Fine Arts. **137** *left* Editions Flammarion, Paris; *right* Osterreichische Nationalbibliothek, Vienna. **138** *top* Photo Michael Holford; *bottom* Reproduced by courtesy of the Curators of the Bodleian Library. **139** Chartres Cathedral/Giraudon. **140** *left & right* Reproduced by permission of the British Library. **141** Reproduced by courtesy of the Trustees of the British Museum, Photo © Aldus Books. **142** *upper* George Buctel. **142-143** *bottom* George Buctel; *top* Reprinted from *Astrology* by Louis MacNeice, © 1964 Aldus Books. **144** *left* The Bettmann Archive; *right* Michel Gauquelin. **145** Ric Ergenbright. **146-147** U.S. Naval Observatory Photograph. **148-149** NASA. **REINCARNATION 150** Reproduced by courtesy of the Trustees of the British Museum. **151** TAP Service. **152** Reproduced by courtesy of the Trustees of the British Museum. **153** *left* Robert Harding Picture Library; *right* Axel Poignant. **154** *top* Culver Pictures; *bottom* Courtesy of Dreyers Forlag, Oslo. **155** Scala/Editorial Photocolor Archives. **156** Collection of the Newark Museum. **157** Tom Zimberoff/Sygma. **159** C. M. Dixon Photographic Library. **160** *left & right* Wide World Photos. **161** *left to right:* Margaret Thomas/The Washington Post; Photo Trends; The Granger Collection, New York; *upper right* BBC Hulton Picture Library; *lower right* Wide World Photos. **162** Museum Boymans-van Beuningen, Rotterdam. **163** Photo Researchers. **164** *left* Reproduced by courtesy of the Trustees of the British Museum; *right* BBC Hulton Picture Library. **165** *top left* Aaron Sussman/Fortean Picture Library; *bottom left* Courtesy of the Midnight Globe. **GHOSTS AND SPIRITS 166** *center* Robert Harding Picture Library; *bottom* Marion Bodine. **167** Alain Keler/Sygma. **168** Topkapi Saray Museum. **169** *left & right* New York Public Library, Picture Collection. **170** *upper left* By courtesy of the National Portrait Gallery, London; *bottom left* T. Howarth/Woodfin Camp & Associates; *upper middle* New York Public Library, Art and Architecture Division; *bottom middle* Reprinted by permission of Harold Ober Associates, Inc. © 1961 by Mary Motley; *remainder* Picturepoint, London. **171** The Granger Collection, New York. **173** *upper left* Used by permission of Macmillan Publishing Co., Inc. from *Ghosts: The Illustrated History* by Peter Haining, © 1975 by Peter Haining and Sidgwick and Jackson Ltd.; *upper right* The Bettmann Archive; *bottom* Reprinted from *Haunted New England* by Mary Bolte & Mary Eastman with the permission of The Chatham Press, Old Greenwich, Conn. **174** *left* Raymond Lamont Brown; *middle* Fortean Picture Library; *right* Mary Evans Picture Library/Harry Price College, University of London. **175** *top left* Bill Watkins/Fujifotos; *center* Roy J. Sabine; *bottom left* Syndication International Ltd.; *right* F. S. Blance. **176** *left & right* John Goldblatt/Camera Press/Photo Trends. **177** Paul Bannister/Courtesy of National Enquirer. **178** *top* New York Public Library, Picture Collection; *bottom* Mary Evans Picture Library/Harry Price College, University of London. **179** *left & right* Mary Evans Picture Library/Harry Price College, University of London. **180** *upper & bottom* Wide World Photos. **181** Lochon/Gamma-Liaison. **182 & 183** Courtesy of Iris Owen. **SPIRITUALISM 184** Fortean Picture Library. **185** John H. Cutten Associates, London. **186** Culver Pictures. **187** *top left* The Granger Collection, New York; *bottom* George Adams/Courtesy of Aldus Books; *remainder* The Bettmann Archive. **188** *left & right* John H. Cutten Associates. **189** *left* UPI; *right* The Mansell Collection. **190** Mary Evans Picture Library. **191** *top* Private Collection/Photo Michael Holford; *bottom* Mary Evans Picture Library/Society for Psychical Research. **192** *top left & right* John H. Cutten Associates, London; *bottom* The Mansell Collection. **193** *top* The Illustrated London News Picture Library; *inset* John H. Cutten Associates, London. **194** The Granger Collection, New York. **195** *left & right* Reprinted from *The Lady With the Magic Eyes* by John Symonds, © 1959 Thomas Yoseloff, Publisher. **196** Reprinted by permission of Sterling Publishing Company Inc. from the book *The Original Houdini Scrapbook* by Walter B. Gibson, © 1976 by Sterling Publishing Company, Inc. **197** *upper left* Wide World Photos; *bottom* UPI. **199** Ted Dobson/Photo Trends. **200** Culver Pictures. **201** Culver Pictures. **PSI AND SCIENCE 202** Michal Heron. **203** Wide World Photos. **204** *left* John H. Cutten Associates, London; *right upper & bottom* Wide World Photos. **205** *top left* Mary Evans Picture Library; *top right* Courtesy of the Foundation for Research on the Nature of Man; *lower left* George Buctel/Based on information courtesy of the Foundation for Research on the Nature of Man; *lower right* Pressefoto Leif Geiges. **206** *upper & bottom left* Wide World Photos; *remainder* Stanford Research Institute International. **207** Don Snyder. **209** *left* Henry Groskinsky, Life Magazine, © Time Inc.; *top right* Roger Malloch/Magnum Photos; *bottom right & inset* Michal Heron. **210** Reprinted from a paper by Hiroshi Motoyama from Impact of Science on Society, Vol. XXIV, No. 4, 1974. **211** *top* Reprinted from *Some Must Watch While Some Must Sleep* by William C. Dement, with the permission of W. W. Norton & Company, Inc.; *lower left* Dan McCoy/Black Star; *lower right* John Running/Stock, Boston. **212** William G. Muller. **213** Wide World Photos. **214** *left* Psi Search; *right* Harvey Stein. **215** *top* Bill Eppridge/Time Magazine; *upper left* Courtesy of Dr. Berthold Eric Schwarz; *bottom* UPI. **216 & 217** George Buctel. **218** David Austen/Stock, Boston. **219** Henry Groskinsky, Life Magazine, © Time Inc. **220** Don Snyder. **221** *left* Julian Wasser, Life Magazine, © 1969 Time Inc.; *right* Wide World Photos. **POWER OF DREAMS 222** The Tate Gallery, London. **223** Chris Springmann/Black Star. **224** *left* The Bettmann Archive; *right* Reproduced by courtesy of the Trustees of the British Museum. **225** Schack Galerie/Kunst-Dias Blauel. **227** *top left & center* The Bettmann Archive; *top right* The Granger Collection, New York; *lower left* Culver Pictures. **228** *top & bottom* Reproduced by courtesy of the Trustees of the British Museum. **229** *top* Reproduced by permission of the British Library; *remainder* Scala/Editorial Photocolor Archives. **230** The Bettmann Archive. **231** *upper left* Wide World Photos; *upper right* Courtesy of Dr. Ignaz Reichstein; *remainder* Courtesy of Dr. Helga Mehren. **232** Courtesy of the Art Institute of Chicago. **233** *left* The Metropolitan Museum of Art, Bequest of Samuel A. Lewisohn; *right* National Gallery of Art, Wash-

ington, Gift of Chester Dale. **234 & 235** Henry Gris Collection. **237** Laser Effect by Laserium/Laser Images, Inc. **ANIMAL PSI 238** Henry Groskinsky, Life Magazine, © Time Inc. **239** Syndication International/Photo Trends. **240** *left* C. B. Frith/Bruce Coleman Inc.; *right* Robert W. Mitchell/Animals Animals. **241** *left* Wide World Photos; *right* Breck P. Kent/Animals Animals. **243** *top* Mary Evans Picture Library; *bottom* Hank Walker, Life Magazine, © 1952 Time Inc. **244** *left* Wide World Photos; *right* The Illustrated London News Picture Library. **245** *far upper left* Syndication International/Photo Trends; *bottom left* Courtesy of the Foundation for Research on the Nature of Man; *upper & lower middle left* Wide World Photos; *upper middle right* UPI; *lower middle right* BBC Hulton Picture Library; *far right* Transworld Feature Syndicate, Inc. **246** Don Snyder. **247** *top* Courtesy of Helmut Schmidt and the Foundation for Research on the Nature of Man; *bottom* Courtesy of Dr. Aristide H. Esser. **248** *top & lower* Tracy Mathewson/National Audubon Society/Photo Researchers. **250** Henry Groskinsky, Life Magazine, © Time Inc. **251** *upper* Jerry Howard/Stock, Boston; *bottom* Library of Congress. **MIND OVER MATTER 252** *top left* Henry Groskinsky/Time Magazine; *top right* Henry Groskinsky, Life Magazine, © Time Inc.; *middle right* Don Snyder; *bottom* Michal Heron. **253** Pressefoto Leif Geiges. **255** *top* Roger-Viollet; *left & right* Courtesy of the Foundation for Research on the Nature of Man. **256** *top left* John H. Cutten Associates, London; *bottom* left Courtesy of Kåre Forwald; *remainder* Reprinted from *The Power of the Mind* by Rolf Alexander, © 1956 T. Werner Laurie, Ltd., London. **257** Oxford Scientific Films/Animals Animals. **259** *left* Henry Groskinsky, Life Magazine, © Time Inc.; *right* G. Brimacombe, Life Magazine, © 1967 Time Inc. **260** *left* Paul Bannister/Courtesy of National Enquirer; *right* Don Snyder. **261** Private Collection. **262** The Granger Collection, New York. **263** *top & lower left* Psychical Research Foundation, Inc.; *right* Wide World Photos. **264** The Observer Magazine Ltd. **265** *upper right* Mary Evans Picture Library; *bottom* Psi Search. **266** Mary Evans Picture Library/Harry Price College, University of London. **267** *top* Philip J. Griffiths/Magnum Photos; *bottom* Rene Burri/Magnum Photos. **268** Bruno Barbey/Magnum Photos. **269** *top left & right* The Bettmann Archive; *lower left* Collection of Milbourne Christopher; *bottom* From *The Mighty Atom, The Life & Times of Joseph L. Greenstein, Biography of a Superman* by Ed Spielman. **LEAVING THE BODY 270 & 271** American Society for Psychical Research, Inc. **272** Courtesy of Samuel Weiser, Inc., New York. **273** *lower left* The Bettmann Archive; *top right & lower right* The Granger Collection, New York; *remainder* Culver Pictures. **274** *top* Harry Redl/Photo Trends; *bottom* New York Public Library, Picture Collection. **275** The Bettmann Archive. **276** Reprinted from *Man, Myth & Magic*, © 1970 Marshall Cavendish Corporation, New York. **277** John H. Cutten Associates, London. **278** Bob Wagoner. **279** *upper & bottom* Richard Meek, Life Magazine, © Time Inc. **280** *left* Henry Groskinsky, Life Magazine, © Time Inc.; *remainder* American Society for Psychical Research, Inc. **281** *upper* Psi Search; *bottom left* Courtesy of Dr. Jan Ehrenwald; *bottom right* Courtesy of Dr. George Ritchie. **282** *top right* Jeff Albertson/Stock, Boston; *remainder* American Society for Psychical Research, Inc. **284** Don Snyder. **285** *left* Manfred Kage/Peter Arnold, Inc.; *right* Thelma Moss. **HEALING 286** *bottom right* David Attie; *inset* Courtesy of Dr. Olga N. Worrall; *remainder* Bruno Barbey/Magnum Photos. **287** Thelma Moss. **288** *top* R. & S. Michaud/Woodfin Camp & Associates; *bottom* The Louvre Museum/Giraudon. **289** Scala/Editorial Photocolor Archives. **290** Cambridge University Library. **291** *top* BBC Hulton Picture Library; *lower* Jean-Loup Charmet. **292** *upper* The Granger Collection, New York; *bottom left & right* The Bettmann Archive. **293** *top left to right:* National Catholic News Service; Peter Tynan-O'Mahony/Photo Trends; Courtesy of Dr. Théodore Mangiapan; *bottom* Klaus D. Francke/Peter Arnold, Inc. **294** UPI. **295** *left to right:* John H. Cutten Associates, London; Sarah Barrell/Sygma; Souvenir Press Ltd. **296** *top* Sandor Acs; *bottom left* Jeff Jacobson/Magnum Photos; *bottom right* Don Snyder. **297** *top* Courtesy of Oszkar Estebany; *bottom left to right:* Don Snyder; Peter Simon/Stock, Boston; Sylvia Norris/Photo Trends. **298** Bruno Barbey/Magnum Photos. **299** *left* Mike Maas/The Image Bank; *right* Alain Jullien. **301** *left* David Attie; *right* Elda Hartley/Colorific! **302** UPI. **303** *left & right* Scala/Editorial Photocolor Archives; *top & lower right* Wide World Photos. **ENIGMA OF UFO'S 304 & 305** Global Communications. **306** *upper* By permission of the Houghton Library, Harvard University; *bottom* Jean-Loup Charmet. **307** *top* Musées Nationaux, Paris; *bottom* Courtesy of the Gold Museum, Bogota, Colombia. **308** Aldus Archives. **309** APRO. **310** ICUFON. **311** *top* Reprinted by permission of Neville Spearman Limited, Sudbury, Suffolk, England; *bottom* UPI. **314** *top right* NASA; *remainder* Global Communications. **315** *middle right* APRO; *bottom right* © 1966 by The Oklahoma Journal Publishing Co.; *remainder* ICUFON. **316** *left* Manchete/Pictorial Parade; *right* Wide World Photos. **318** *upper left to right:* UPI; Wide World Photos; Manchete/Pictorial Parade; *far right* Drawing by Jennings H. Frederick, courtesy of Gray Barker's Newsletter; *bottom left* Drawing by Paul Cherny, courtesy of the San Francisco Examiner. **319** *top left (three drawings)* By Jennings H. Frederick, courtesy of Gray Barker's Newsletter; *middle left* Sandler Institutional Films, Inc.; *bottom left (two drawings)* Syndication International/Photo Trends; *right top to bottom:* APRO; Syndication International/Photo Trends; Drawing by Barney Hill from *Creatures From UFO's* by Daniel Cohen, with the permission of Dodd, Mead & Company, New York; *bottom right (four drawings)* National Enquirer. **320** From the book *The Andreasson Affair* by Raymond E. Fowler, © 1979 by Raymond E. Fowler and Betty Andreasson. Published by Prentice-Hall, Inc., Englewood Cliffs, New Jersey. **321** Painting by Jon Lomberg. **322-323** NASA, courtesy of the Goddard Space Flight Center. **325** Douglas W. Young/Photo Researchers; *inset* Wide World Photos. **PSI AND THE BRAIN 326** Eugene Miscenich/Medical World News. **327** Manfred Kage/Peter Arnold, Inc. **328** Courtesy of Dr. Tien T. Tsong, Pennsylvania State University, Department of Physics. **329 & 330** Dan McCoy/Rainbow. **331** Henry Groskinsky, Life Magazine, © Time Inc. **333** Arthur J. Klosky/Jancart Ltd. **MISCELLANEA OF THE UNKNOWN 334** The Granger Collection, New York. **335** The Pierpont Morgan Library. **336** Mary Evans Picture Library, Harry Price College, University of London. **337** From *Encyclopedia of Religion and Ethics*, © 1928 Charles Scribner's Sons. **338** Josef Koudelka/Magnum Photos. **339** The Granger Collection, New York. **340** The Bettmann Archive. **341** Mary Evans Picture Library.